A Folk Divided

Homeland Swedes and Swedish Americans, 1840–1940

H. ARNOLD BARTON

SOUTHERN ILLINOIS UNIVERSITY PRESS
Carbondale and Edwardsville

Publication of this book has been made possible in part by a grant
from the Swedish Council for Research in the
Humanities and Social Sciences, Stockholm.

97 96 95 94   4 3 2 1

Library of Congress Cataloging-in-Publication Data

Barton, H. Arnold (Hildor Arnold), 1929–
    A folk divided : homeland Swedes and Swedish Americans, 1840–1940
/ H. Arnold Barton.
        p.   cm.
    Includes bibliographical references and index.
    1. Swedish Americans—Ethnic identity. 2. Sweden—Emigration and
immigration—History.   I. Title.
E184.S23B27   1994
305.83'97—dc20   93-32345
ISBN 0-8093-1943-8   CIP
ISBN 0-8093-1944-6 pbk.

The paper used in this publication meets the minimum requirements of
American National Standard for Information Sciences—Permanence of
Paper for Printed Library Materials, ANSI Z39.48-1984. ♾

Du är min broder, fastän vidder skilja
oss nu, men handen ändå räckas må.
Jag är din syster, vilken skulle vilja,
att en gång rätt du kunde mig förstå.

Thou art my brother, although distance
separates us now, our hands may yet reach out.
I am thy sister, who would wish that thou
some day couldst rightly understand me.

—Signe Ankarfelt

Contents

Illustrations

Preface

What happens to a people—the product of an ancient culture and way of life—when it becomes divided and separated through a great overseas migration? More specifically, how do the two parts of such a divided people relate to each other? What ideas do they have regarding each other as the process continues and as time and circumstance cause them to develop in separate ways of their own? The purpose of this book is to seek answers to such questions in the case of the Swedes during the period of their great migration, between roughly 1840 and 1940.

Such a study necessarily involves a threefold complex of attitudes: toward America as a country; toward emigration as a phenomenon; and toward the emigrants as people. Much scholarly attention has been given to European views of America, and some to those regarding emigration. Rather surprisingly, almost none has been devoted to ideas in the lands of origin about the emigrants themselves, nor, conversely, to the views of the emigrants regarding their former compatriots.

In Sweden, historians have until recently tended to concentrate upon analysis, mainly statistical, of the emigrating group, whereas American scholars have been primarily interested in the Americanization of the immigrants and their relations with other elements of the American population. It is the transatlantic relationship at the human level that provides the focus of my investigation.

Briefly stated, emigration created a complex love-hate relationship between those who sought new lives in the New World and those who remained in the old homeland. The emigrants generally felt, and indeed lovingly cultivated, nostalgia and pride in the land of their birth. Yet they often keenly resented conditions that had compelled them, in their view, to leave it, and hence those institutions, traditions, and elements of society that they held accountable for such conditions. Their former compatriots, meanwhile, could not but see the emigration as symptomatic of serious problems at home. While some considered these to be the consequence of long-standing social and economic inequities that could only be overcome through far-reaching reforms, others upheld the existing order and instead placed the blame on the emigrants themselves for their naiveté, lack of patriotism, and vain lust for worldly gain.

All Swedish commentary on America, the emigration, and the emigrants during the period of the great migration was also commentary—explicit or implicit—upon Sweden itself. Even when not specifically mentioned, the great land to the West and its open door was a basic underlying premise in Swedish public debate. Similarly, all that Swedish Americans had to say about Sweden and the Swedish emigration was at the same time commentary on America and upon their own situation there.

Meanwhile, views on all the basic questions were divided on both sides of the Atlantic, reflecting social class, cultural and political outlook, and changing circumstances in both Sweden and America throughout the great migration and even beyond. Virtually every idea voiced on one side of the ocean was echoed to some degree—albeit often for different purposes— on the other.

Central to the whole debate was the question of a Swedish-American identity. Swedes who settled abroad naturally came to think and behave in new ways, giving rise to mixed reactions both at home and among themselves. Did the emigrants represent the best or the worst elements of their nation? Did they, upon becoming "Swedish Americans," combine the best or the worst qualities of their old and new homelands? Was it indeed possible in any meaningful sense to be *both* Swedish and American? From the study of immigrant institutions and cultural retention, historians in the United States—and now in Sweden as well—have turned increasingly in recent years to the process of ethnogenesis, the creation of ethnic identities, and the very nature of ethnicity itself. (See "An Essay on Sources," below.) The development of ethnic consciousness and organized activity in America has traditionally been described mainly in terms of defensive reactions by immigrant groups to the exclusive nativism of the older Americans. The case of the Swedish Americans makes it clear that it was at least as much a response to the immigrants' need to justify themselves in the eyes of their former compatriots and, not least, before their own consciences, by asserting their own rightful but unique place in the Swedish national community.

Other or more finely differentiated relationships also play a part in this study: of Swedish immigrants and their descendants to the older Americans; of Swedish Americans to other ethnic groups in America; of earlier to later emigrants from Sweden; of specific groups in Sweden to particular groups of Swedish immigrants in the United States.

The Swedes provide a particularly good subject for a study of this kind. Sweden contributed a sizable group of immigrants, some 1.2 million persons, which made it the first among the Scandinavian and seventh among all countries of origin for European immigrants to the United States. Only Ireland and Norway experienced heavier emigration relative to their total populations. Swedes began arriving on these shores in significant numbers as early as the 1840s, making the history of their migration longer and more varied than those of most other immigrant groups. From the beginning of the era they were a notably literate people, and they had a strong historical sense. Swedes therefore produced a remarkably large, varied, and well-preserved body of documentation. They showed from the start considerable interest in the broader social, political, and religious questions of their time.

The arguments that at times raged so fiercely over the emigration and the emigrants left no final answers. The overwhelming fact remained that between 1840 and 1930, one Swede out of five, on the average, voluntarily left the homeland for America, and that of these at least four-fifths remained there permanently. This is what all parties concerned had to come to terms with as best they could. It was a conflict of views in which all were right in their own ways, and all were wrong.

A few words about sources and translation are in order. As will be seen, the available documentation is immense and varied, especially as the subject touches, in one way or another, upon virtually everything of significance that was taking place in both Sweden and the United States over a century or more. The real problem is where to draw the line. One important source, however, has not *systematically* been mined, nor could it be in a study as broad as this: namely, the periodical press, especially the Swedish and Swedish-American newspapers. With few exceptions, the bibliographical aids do not exist that would allow for a comprehensive survey of their contents except by ploughing through each separate back-file—and for that life is too short! This is, however, less serious than it might appear, since the existing literature does provide references to many, if not most, of the more significant articles, since many contemporary books and pamphlets consist of reprinted newspaper articles, and since beyond a certain point the researcher finds himself or herself encountering again and again the same basic ideas expressed in almost identical words.

It is in the nature of things that writing on such emotionally loaded subjects as emigration and emigrants should be couched in strongly rhetorical terms, making the fullest use of evocative resources unique to the Swedish language. In translation it is impossible always to preserve the rich emotional overtones. I can only hope that I have succeeded in conveying adequately not only the literal meaning but also the flavor and spirit of the passages I have directly quoted.

For basic background I have, along the way, briefly summarized the history of the Swedish emigration and of the Swedes in the United States.

The particular focus of this study meanwhile calls for a more thorough presentation of the ethnic culture of the Swedish Americans than has heretofore been available. Toward the end of his life, Albin Widén, that pioneer Swedish scholar of the migration, told me it had long been his ambition to write Swedish America's cultural history. On long summer evenings at his home in Äppelviken I learned much from him, and in providing such a cultural survey, within a larger framework, I hold him in fond memory.

Many others have directly or indirectly contributed to this work. Franklin D. Scott and the late Sten Carlsson originally encouraged and inspired me to enter the field of Swedish-American studies. Dag Blanck, who shuttles regularly across the Atlantic, has been a steady source of insights and suggestions, and has helped with practical details. Among those who have provided ideas, criticism, information, and research materials, the following deserve special mention: in Sweden, Gunilla Larsson, Lennart Limberg, Harald Runblom, Nils Runeby, Lars-Göran Tedebrand, Eva Tedenmyr, and Jarl Torbacke; in the United States, Henry Hanson, Anne-Charlotte Harvey, Vicky Oliver, Alan Swanson, Mariann Tiblin, and Kermit Westerberg.

I appreciate greatly the help I have received from the Royal Library in Stockholm, Morris Library at Southern Illinois University at Carbondale, the Swenson Swedish Immigration Research Center at Augustana College, Rock Island, Illinois, and the Swedish-American Historical Society at North Park College, Chicago. Southern Illinois University and its history department have given me research and secretarial support, together with sabbatical leave. I am indebted to the University of Minnesota Press for permission to make use of material from my *Letters from the Promised Land: Swedes in America, 1840–1914* (1975) and to the *Swedish-American Historical Quarterly* (before 1982 the *Swedish Pioneer Historical Quarterly*) for the use of certain passages from my articles published there.

Publication of this book has been made possible in part by a generous grant from the Swedish Council for Research in the Humanities and Social Sciences, Stockholm.

To Angela K. Calcaterra go my sincere thanks for word-processing my manuscript with unfailing expertise, patience, and cheerfulness. I likewise appreciate Sally Master's careful editing of this book.

I am, as always, deeply grateful to my wife, Aina—herself a Swedish immigrant—not only for her interest and encouragement but for the constant insights she has given me into the complex relationships within a divided folk.

Finally, Tell G. Dahllöf has played a uniquely valuable part in this project. Beginning in the early 1940s, he assembled in Stockholm the largest private collection anywhere concerning Sweden and America, consisting of some ten thousand titles. From the early 1970s, when I first got to know him, he warmly encouraged me to make use of it, and this possibility was ultimately influential in persuading me to embark upon this study. During 1985 and 1986, he gave me the keys and the free use of his collection, for a total of ten months during three sojourns in Stockholm, until the collection was acquired by the University of Minnesota. Without this resource, and in the absence of comprehensive finding aids, I could not have put together any reasonably complete working bibliography for my topic, at least without years of drudgerous searching; direct and immediate access to numerous rare and little-known items was invaluable to me. For his generosity, as well as his expert knowledge, helpfulness, and constant enthusiasm, I am happy to dedicate this book to Tell Dahllöf.

H.A.B.

PART ONE

This country can be at the same time both a Canaan and a Siberia.

—Peter Cassel, 1846

If you have reached the goal of your desires, without a fatherland—what have you won?

—Ph. v. T., 1854

Yes, the trip was extra hard, but you forget everything when you see all that wheat!

—Ernst Beckman, 1883

It has not been Sweden's, but Swedish America's cause for which I have above all striven.

—Johan A. Enander, 1899

Spring Tide,
to 1902

*S*ince the founding of their own short-lived colony of New Sweden in the mid-seventeenth century, Swedes have shown a particular interest in America, periodically renewed through the eighteenth and early nineteenth centuries by the accounts of Swedish travelers and sojourners.

In part for internal political reasons, the American Revolution aroused widespread enthusiasm in Sweden. Following the French Revolution and the defeat of Napoleon, however, opinion there, as elsewhere during the era of the Holy Alliance, became deeply divided. Those who still held to the faith of the Enlightenment in reasoned progress looked to America as the last, best hope of humanity, while for Romantic conservatives America stood for soulless materialism and the reckless repudiation of traditional values. Not until the conclusion of the Civil War, meanwhile, could either side feel altogether assured of the ultimate survival of the republic and its ideals.

Although individual Swedes had arrived in America since colonial times, the great Swedish emigration began, in a small way, during the early 1840s. With a series of serious crop failures in Sweden during the later 1860s it become a mass movement, reaching its first peak in 1869, when 32,053 persons departed the homeland. Following a lull in the 1870s, it again rose sharply during the 1880s and early 1890s, reaching its all-time high, 46,252 persons, in 1887. Swedish emigration thereafter fell off rapidly following the onset of the American economic crisis of 1893. By the turn of the century it began to appear to many that the "America Fever" had run its course, although such hopes would soon prove premature.

Reactions in Sweden to the emigration passed through various phases. The departure of the first small groups of emigrants in the early 1840s produced an immediate response in the press and public opinion. From the beginning, basic ideas were expressed that would thereafter dominate public debate concerning the great emigration until it finally ended in the 1920s. Conservatives pointed to their own country's great potentialities for development and tended to regard those who abandoned it as either fools or knaves. Liberals meanwhile saw in the emigration alarming signs that all was not well at home and thus appealed for fundamental reforms to outbid the attractions of the New World. To them, the emigrants represented the most capable and enterprising elements of Sweden's population—those the homeland could least afford to lose—who understandably sought abroad for opportunities denied them at home under antiquated conditions.

After preserving the Union in the Civil War, the United States entered upon a sustained period of dynamic economic growth. The same years—between 1865 and around 1890—were marked in Sweden by economic stagnation and political discontent. As emigration reached its highest levels, it was no longer able to arouse the same level of indignation as it had at first and came generally to be accepted with weary resignation. Nevertheless, the first serious attempts were now made to inquire into its causes.

By the 1870s, following the first great wave of arrivals, Swedish immigrants were beginning to come to terms with their new life in America and to evolve distinctive characteristics of their own, supported by a growing network of religious and secular organizations, newspapers, educational institutions, and commercial enterprises. Their emerging sense of identity reveals both the preservation of fundamental homeland values and the rejection of traditions and practices that had alienated them in Sweden, as well as adaptation to the realities of American life.

The evolving Swedish-American community was presented to the Swedish public through the published accounts of a number of perceptive and generally sympathetic Swedish visitors to the United States. At the same time, the reactions of certain Swedish-American travelers to the land they had last seen long years before, as well as the first attempts at self-examination within the Swedish-American community, add perspective to the growing cleavage between those who left the old homeland and those who stayed.

ONE

Prologue:
Before the Great Migration

The Swedish presence in North America is a long one. In 1626 Gustav II Adolf chartered a Swedish West Indian Company to colonize and trade with the New World. Twelve years later, in 1638, this company established a colony on the Delaware River. New Sweden was the last of the European colonial empires to be founded in North America, as well as the smallest, least populous, and shortest-lived. At its height, occupying parts of present-day Delaware, Pennsylvania, and New Jersey, it never counted more than a few hundred Swedish and Finnish settlers—Finland then being part of the Swedish kingdom. It was lost to the Dutch in New Netherland in 1655, who in turn surrendered it to the English in 1664.[1] Yet the descendants of the original colonists preserved their Swedish speech and Lutheran faith within their own congregations, supported by pastors sent out to them by the Swedish state church, until the late eighteenth century.

Perhaps the greatest significance of New Sweden has been the central role it has played in forming the self-image of Swedish—and Finnish—Americans from the late nineteenth century onward. From the beginning, however, it created in Sweden a particularly strong and enduring interest in North America.[2]

The earliest European views of the New World focused largely upon the native Indians. Europeans were repelled by what they perceived to be the Indians' primitive barbarism, yet they were no less inclined to see in the Indians' way of life true happiness, wisdom, and virtue. Thus, from the beginning, images of America as a desolate, uncivilized wilderness combined with those of an unspoiled Eden, offering the hope of fresh beginnings.

During the eighteenth century, as the English colonies on the Atlantic seaboard grew in population, wealth, and culture, European interest turned increasingly to the colonists. In Sweden, influential books by Pastor Israel Acrelius, who had served the Swedish congregations on the Delaware, and by Pehr Kalm, one of Carl Linnaeus's widely traveled disciples, published in the 1750s, played an influential role.[3]

Again, European reactions were mixed. According to a long-standing view, the New World was an inferior environment, with less fertile soil and a more extreme climate than that of the Old World. Far more significant, however, was the concept of America as a new rural paradise, offering unlimited opportunity to poor but enterprising Europeans. Here they would escape the vice and oppression of their old homelands to live in simple virtue as free men. Indeed, the greatest concern of those who idealized America in such fashion was that the sins of the Old World might follow Europeans across the sea to corrupt the new social order.[4]

At the same time, America held out a more awesome prospect than a return to simple innocence. Long before the discovery of the Western Hemisphere, the idea had gained currency that the center of civilization had migrated from east to west: from the Egyptians, Assyrians, Persians, Greeks, Romans, and Arabs, to the modern Europeans. By the seventeenth century this concept was beginning to span the Atlantic.[5] It was stoutly proclaimed among the English separatists and Puritans who escaped what they viewed as a spiritually corrupt Old World to build their Christian commonwealth in the New. They would not be the last to arrive on these shores bearing what they staunchly believed to be the true Ark of the Covenant.

From the refuge of true faith, America came by the eighteenth century to be envisioned as the future center of civilization itself. George Berkeley proclaimed in 1723 that "Westward the course of empire takes it way. . . . Time's noblest offspring is the last." In 1730 an anonymous poem in a Philadelphia almanac made no less bold to prophesy: "'Tis here Apollo does erect his throne"; here the liberal arts would be cultivated to such perfection that "Europe shall mourn her ancient fame declined, and Phila-delphia be the Athens of mankind."[6]

The interest of enlightened Europe was indeed particularly taken with the Quaker commonwealth of Pennsylvania. In his travel account from the mid-1750s, Pehr Kalm praised its religious and economic freedom, which made every inhabitant "a king in his own home." It would be hard, he concluded, to imagine that anyone could wish for any greater freedom.[7]

Increasingly America became a great symbol for the European Enlighten-ment, a development that reached its height with the American Revolution in the 1770s and 1780s. The Americans' struggle for liberty, equality, and justice confirmed in actual practice the ideals of the "Party of Philosophy."[8] In Franklin and Washington classically educated Europeans recognized a new Cato and a new Cincinnatus. Interest in Sweden was heightened both by the participation of numerous Swedish officers as volunteers in the

French and other forces allied against Great Britain and by the beginnings of political unrest at home. It was largely with an eye to his own country that Major Pehr af Lund wrote in his newspaper, *Tryck-Friheten den Wälsignade,* in April 1783 that the knowledge that "there is one place on earth where man can be free from his chains" should "frighten despots and hold them in reign."[9]

The outbreak of the French Revolution by 1789 seemed a triumphant vindication of the principles of the Enlightenment and of the free Americans. In 1790 Carl Fredrik Nordenskiöld, editor of the radical journal *Medborgaren* ("The Citizen"), proclaimed that "America has taught Nations to know their rights. . . . Philosophers, Friends of Mankind, Citizens, what a magnificent prospect for you!"[10]

As the appeal of the French Revolution became increasingly sullied through excesses and atrocities, the defenders of the Enlightenment were consoled by the evident success of their principles in the United States. Axel Gabriel Silfverstolpe wrote in *Stockholms-Posten* in 1793 that the American Revolution had taken place when the Americans themselves were ready for it, thus "Franklin's and Washington's political reforms have led America to all the social felicity human reason has yet been able to envision." Europeans confused freedom with license, whereas every American knew the meaning of "true freedom." "Why should not we also," he concluded, "be able to fill our hearts with a common ideal which combines Equality and Happiness, without need of fear?"[11]

In Sweden, under the Gustavian autocracy, admiration for America was coupled with the identification of American practice and ancient Nordic ideals that were conceived to have been corrupted through harmful alien influences. The idea of recovering the values of a past Swedish "Golden Age" on the free soil of the New World would thereafter remain one of the fundamental themes of Swedish—and eventually Swedish-American—discussion of America. The nature of the good old values would naturally vary with time to encompass the rights of conscience and citizenship, the dignity of honest toil and of the common person, the distribution of land ownership and of the wealth of the nation, and society's responsibility for the well-being of its members. America was not only the cradle of the future; it offered the final refuge for the Old World's traditional ideals.

The first decades of the nineteenth century brought a growing reaction not only against Revolutionary and Napoleonic France but against the Enlightenment itself, which was widely condemned as the root cause of the present unrest. Sweden itself experienced a severe ordeal through its involvement in the Napoleonic wars after 1805.[12]

Following Napoleon's final defeat in 1815, the political conservatism of monarchical Europe in the era of Prince Metternich and the Holy Alliance—including the new Swedish-Norwegian dual monarchy established in

1814—was opposed to all that American republicanism represented: national self-determination, popular sovereignty, democratic franchise, parliamentary rule, the constitutionally guaranteed rights of citizens.

Political conservatism was now reinforced by the Romantic movement, which rebelled against the dry rationalism of the Enlightenment to seek a deeper and truer wisdom through inspiration, the emotions, and each nation's unique heritage from the past. The tide of opinion regarding America, which heretofore had been prevailingly positive, flowed by the 1820s largely in the opposite direction. America was regarded increasingly as the soulless battleground of egotistical private interests, inhabited by what Prince Talleyrand is supposed to have described as "a population, to be sure, but not a people."[13]

The literary critic Vilhelm Fredrik Palmblad expressed the conservative Romantic view in 1821 that liberalism "promises us no fruits but those the North American tree of liberty has already born: commerce, wealth, the highest production of grain, wool, livestock, children, but where feeling is impoverished, genius is tolerated as a luxury or at most is valued for the mercantile value of its products, weighed upon the scale of commerce."[14]

America remained, meanwhile, the guiding star for the growing liberal opposition to Karl XIV Johan's conservative regime. Here, too, the force of Romantic enthusiasm could be aroused, for there were still those who sought their shining vision in the future, rather than in the past. The post-Napoleonic years were a bleak time. The European economy, not least the Scandinavian, was badly depressed, and fears of renewed strife and social dissolution remained widespread. Never did the idea of the westward course of civilization from the Old World to the New hold greater fascination.

"A Letter from a German from and about Philadelphia, in December 1814," published in *Stockholms Posten* in 1816 largely summarizes the liberals' vision of America. Its author rejoiced at finding himself in the land where one enjoys "the greatest possible measure of political freedom and need not give heed to anything but the law" and where one "lives as a free man among free men."

> Nowhere in the world does human activity have such unlimited scope for its development as in America. Industry and determination encounter here none of the obstacles which bar their way in most European countries. . . . Here one finds no titles, no beribboned orders and stars, and yet all goes its glorious way undisturbed, with order and love for mankind. One feels transported back to the days of the republics of antiquity, where individual ambition faded before the common patriotism and respect for the law was the only lever which guided and set in motion the machinery of state.[15]

Emanuel Sundelius praised the Americans in 1821 for "their reasonable view that all occupations must be judged equally honorable and well-regarded which provide income and prosperity in an honest fashion." In his diary, Johan Peter Theorell wrote in 1818, "There is life, activity, and growth; here death and decay." There, he noted the following year, "man is worth what he is capable of being worth." The idea of America as Europe's last, best hope received its classic statement from Esaias Tegnér, Sweden's most celebrated poet of the day, at the three-hundredth anniversary of the Reformation at Lund University in 1817: "If it be true, as many aver, that dusk is descending over old Europe, far to the west, beyond the sea, where the sun sets for us, it rises for a more fortunate world. Thither has Europe already sent many of its fondest hopes, there mankind will save its household gods, as Aeneas rescued his from the fall of Ilium."[16]

It is from around 1820 that Harald Elovson notes the beginning of a consistent, ongoing debate about America and what it stood for in Sweden. Hitherto, statements regarding those matters had generally been sporadic and unconnected. [17] As political conflict intensified through the century, America emerged as an ever more central symbol, around which or against which contending parties rallied.

That the opposing concepts of America could be stated in such dogmatic fashion points up the fact that very few Swedes had yet gained any first hand experience of that part of the world. Following Kalm's and Acrelius's books in the 1750s, virtually no Swedish accounts of America came out in print before the 1820s. Swedish curiosity about the New World had to be largely satisfied by foreign writings, in the original or translation. Indeed, much of the opinion regarding America expressed in Sweden at this time consisted of commentary on English, French, German, or American works.[18]

To be sure a few Swedes visited or even settled in North America during these decades, but observations of American life, contained in the private correspondence of some of these, were not published until a century or more later, if at all.[19] The unpublished letters and accounts written by Pastor Nils Collin in New Jersey and Pennsylvania, mainly to his family, are meanwhile of particular interest for this period. In 1771, a year after his arrival, he found America "polite enough and not as unpleasant as many in Sweden believe." No one was considered better than anyone else, even wealthy landowners ploughed their own fields, and all were called ladies and gentlemen. By late 1775 his view was considerably more jaundiced. Egotism was the ruling passion, corrupting business and personal behavior. Deception and fraud were admired as shrewdness. Manners were simple to the point of crudeness. "The leading trait in the character of an American is an immoderate love of freedom, or rather, license. . . . The reigns of government hang so slack that they are seldom felt, and the hand that guides is never seen. All of this means that the people know nothing, and want to know nothing, of any control, and that each and every one considers himself an independent prince. .... All government action arouses their suspicion."[20]

In 1792 and 1793 Collin warned against both American and European depictions of the new land as an earthly paradise where fortune could be won without effort, and he feared the arrival on American shores of the worst scum from Europe. It is worth dwelling upon his views, as they already include so many of the ideas on American government and society that would be repeatedly expressed in Swedish accounts of the United States throughout the nineteenth and even twentieth centuries.[21]

In 1824 Baron Axel Klinckowström, a young engineer sent over by the Swedish government to study railroad construction in 1818, published his travel letters from the United States. Klinckowström was on the whole enthusiastic about the United States, not least as an engineer, although as a nobleman he was at times bemused by some of the more flagrant manifestations of American egalitarianism. Three more Swedish accounts appeared in 1835: Carl August Gosselman and Carl David Arfwedson were well impressed, particularly with the benefits of American economic freedom, whereas Carl Ulric von Hauswolff ridiculed the crudities of American social life.[22] These writings provoked lively commentary and the press debate in particular which followed Hauswolff's negative account show, according to the historian Nils Runeby, how stereotyped both the americanophile and americanophobe positions had become in Sweden already by the 1830s.[23]

Two firsthand accounts from the earlier nineteenth century that did not come into print also shed light upon Swedish reactions to America in this period. The merchant Olof Wijk declared in 1829 that he would not wish at any price to be an inhabitant of "that republican land," for "I love *law-bound freedom,* not *license.*" The diplomat, Gustaf af Nordin, wrote from Washington that half a year in the United States would suffice to cure the Swedish liberals of their enthusiasm after seeing "their idol in its own temple." Freedom was illusory when everyone was "a slave to the whims and fancies of the masses, against which there is no appeal." Alarmed over the rising liberal opposition at home, Nordin offered—although he did not publish—the apparently most comprehensive Swedish condemnation of America up to that time.[24]

By the 1830s the growing numbers of Europeans, especially British and Germans, embarking for America made emigration an increasingly important factor in European attitudes toward the New World. Before the end of the decade the first sizable groups were departing from Norway, a development followed with keen interest in its sister kingdom, Sweden.

This was a matter that as yet had scarcely affected the Swedes. Since the loss of the New Sweden colony in 1655, only a few individuals from Sweden had found their way to the New World.[25] Swedish discussion of emigration thus remained essentially theoretical. But this did not mean that the question had not already given cause for much concern. During the middle of the eighteenth century there had been alarm over a relatively small drift of Swedish and Finnish peasants into neighboring Denmark, Norway, and the Russian domains. The resulting debate anticipated that which would rage in Sweden a century and a half later, following emigration on a vastly greater scale, with, in effect, conservatives urging restrictions and their rivals arguing for reforms.[26]

In the event, population, which grew rapidly from the end of the eighteenth century, outstripped economic development. Commerce and industry remained relatively stagnant throughout the first half of the nineteenth century. At least three-quarters of Sweden's inhabitants remained on the land in agriculture and related occupations, leading to the division of peasant landholdings into smaller and smaller plots and the steady growth of a rural laboring class without land of its own.

Under the influence of English economists of the Manchester School, the "populationist" faith in the benefits of a large and growing labor force began to give way, in Sweden as elsewhere, to Malthusian fears of overpopulation and mass impoverishment. In a pamphlet on poverty and poor relief in Sweden, Pastor Petrus Læstadius in 1840 depicted in alarming terms his country's growing predicament and found its obvious answer in emigration. Among all forms of restriction, he wrote,

> none surely must be as contrary to nature as forbidding the inhabitants of a land from leaving that land and settling in another. . . . *Sweden suffers from overpopulation,* but emigration is forbidden, and yet there are perhaps few countries in the world that have so great cause, on the contrary, to encourage it. . . . These children, which our poor relief boards must feed, what are they to do here? Indeed, breed new candidates for poor relief. No, let them go to America or wherever they wish, here there will still be folk who can work and who want to eat.

Similar arguments were advanced by Lars Johan Hierta, the editor of the liberal *Aftonbladet,* when he moved in the Riksdag that spring the repeal of existing restrictions against emigration.[27]

In surveying European and Swedish ideas about America and even about emigration down to around 1840, one cannot but be impressed by how many of the basic views on these subjects were already crystalized by that time in forms that would vary surprisingly little down to the present century, on both sides of the ideological divide. Admiration for America was firmly rooted in the liberal camp; repudiation was as clearly associated with conservatism.

There were some who wavered between the two camps. There was, moreover, more common ground than it might first appear. Conservatives could not deny America's prosperity. Nor were better informed liberals able to overlook the rawness of the Americans' manners and their often seemingly anarchic disregard for law and order. It was a question of how little conservatives were prepared to tolerate and how much liberals were able to explain away.

Yet even among America's well-wishers there were differences of opinion from the beginning of American independence as to the extent to which the young republic could serve as a viable model to old Europe. Political radicals, like L. M. Philipson in 1792, might speak polemically of recreating the Old World in the image of the New. But others, already then, were less certain. Pastor Collin in Pennsylvania at that very time condemned as equally foolish those who would "tear down the thrones of kings or urge crowns for the heads of republics." More specifically, he argued, both the United States' and Sweden's forms of government were well suited to the different conditions prevailing in each. The historian Erik Gustaf Geijer expressed this idea best in 1835: "The New World shows, in the North American free states, the model of a great, powerful, and fortunate republic; to be sure under its own conditions, which will not return a second time and which are entirely lacking in the Old World. It is without dangerous, or at least powerful, neighbors, and it casts out into the wilderness the most dangerous enemy of republics, *internal dissention*, which here [at home] only wins new ground."[28]

The question of the applicability of the American model to the Old World lay at the root of the whole ongoing debate in Europe over the mythical land beyond the sea, as well as over immigration to its shores. And so it has remained to the present day.

In 1824 the provincial governor of Dalarna wrote confidently: "A poor peasant in Dalarna could not be persuaded to abandon his ancestors' meager soil, as long as it gave him his daily oaten bread, even if one were to offer him ground to cultivate in a far-away place as fertile as the banks of the Ohio or Mississippi."[29]

By 1840 the time had come in Sweden when peasants, not only from Dalarna but from the entire country, would soon decamp for the Mississippi Valley and emigration would cease to be a matter of only theoretical interest.

TWO

The Flow Begins, 1840–1865

In the spring of 1841, there was considerable excitement in the old university town of Uppsala when Gustaf Unonius, a recent graduate and supernumerary government clerk born in Finland, departed for the United States of America, together with his young wife, their maid, and two university students. By fall they were clearing the wilderness for their own "New Upsala" at Pine Lake, Wisconsin.

Unonius would remain in America for seventeen years, during which he became an Episcopalian missionary among the early Swedish and Norwegian immigrants in the Midwest. With time he became increasingly disillusioned with the rough-and-tumble of American life and returned to Sweden in 1858. He then wrote his reminiscences from America, one of the classics of the Swedish migration, and sought to dissuade his countrymen from leaving their homeland.[1] Far more influential, however, were his enthusiastic letters from Pine Lake, written during his first year there, when he and his companions were still filled with the dream of a life of pastoral simplicity and republican virtue amid a bountiful and unspoiled nature. These letters were published in the liberal *Aftonbladet* in Stockholm and widely read throughout Sweden.

Writing from Milwaukee in October 1841, Unonius cautioned those who might follow against "exaggerated hopes and golden air castles," while praising the soil as "the most fertile and wonderful that can be found." With hard work, he and his friends expected within a few years to enjoy a good livelihood. "We do not regret our undertaking," Unonius assured his readers. "We are living a free and independent life in one of the most beautiful valleys the world can offer." Turning to less tangible benefits, he concluded: "I am partial to a republican form of government, and I have realized my youthful dream of social equality. ... It is no disgrace to work here. Both the gentleman and the day laborer work. No epithets of degradation are applied to men of humble toil; only those whose conduct merits it are looked down upon.... Liberty is still stronger in my affections than the bright silver dollar that bears her image."

Unonius's early descriptions of America were not altogether uncritical, yet where he found fault he also found mitigating circumstances, as in his widely publicized letter of January 1842:

> It is true that the American is a braggart. ... We find him to be a proud egotist, a quarrelsome patriot, and, if I may say so, an intolerable fellow citizen. Instead of the jealousy that prevails among other nationalities, he has these faults, if faults they be. During the struggles which rend and agitate the countries of the Old World he sees in the progress of his peaceful fatherland the results of liberty and equality which he considers impossible to obtain under any other conditions.

After describing his "joy and contentment" in a life of hard work and "simple, wholesome customs" on the American frontier, Unonius wrote, "It seems to me, as Tegnér somewhere says: 'Here the Europeans at last must send their household gods.' ... I willingly admit that there are deplorable shortcomings and much room for improvement; nevertheless I am convinced that America more closely than any other country in the world approaches the ideal which nature seems to have intended for the happiness and comfort of humanity."[2]

Gustaf Unonius liked to call himself Sweden's first emigrant, since he had been the first to emigrate after the ordinance of May 1840 had removed the old requirement for the king's permission in each case, and it has been traditional albeit somewhat arbitrary practice to date the beginning of the great Swedish migration from his departure in 1841. During the next few years a number of other Swedes of upper- or middle-class origins joined the little colony at Pine Lake, either for idealistic reasons or to escape from personal problems at home. In May 1843, *Aftonbladet* was predicting the rise of a "new Svithiod"—an archaic, poetic name for Sweden—across the ocean, "as we are informed that settlers from the Scandinavian peninsula are constantly arriving in that land."[3]

As the first account of America coming from a self-avowed emigrant, Unonius's letters in *Aftonbladet* directly stimulated interest in emigration in a way that earlier travel accounts had not. Moreover, as would-be farmers on the American frontier, the Pine Lake settlers drew the attention of levels of Swedish society far different from their own. The Dream of America was revealed in terms meaningful to the Swedish peasant.

Among those who read Unonius's accounts in *Aftonbladet* was Peter (Pehr) Cassel, a miller and housebuilder near Kisa in Östergötland province, who was also acquainted with the family of one of the Pine Lake settlers nearby. A man active in various progressive causes in his neighborhood, Cassel organized a group of seventeen persons from Kisa parish that, joined by others along the way, emigrated in 1845 to Iowa, where they established their New Sweden settlement in Jefferson County. They were the first sizable group of Swedish peasants to emigrate, and New Sweden, Iowa, would be the first lasting Swedish settlement in the American Midwest.

Peter Cassel's letters from America, printed in *Östgötha Corresponden-ten* in Linköping, aroused even greater interest among the Swedish peasantry than Unonius's, coming as they did from a practical farmer and a man of their own kind. Writing in February 1846, Cassel claimed: "The ease of making a living here and the increasing prosperity of the farmers, year by year and day by day, exceeds anything we anticipated. If only half the work expended on the soil of the fatherland were utilized here, the yield would reach the wildest imagination." The topsoil was rich and deep, and—what was particularly impressive to Swedish peasants—"there is not a single stone on the surface." All crops grew "to an astonishing degree," there was an abundance of game, the climate was mild, and wages for labor were good. In words recalling Unonius and the liberal creed, he went on:

> Freedom and equality are the fundamental principles of the Constitution of the United States. There is no such thing as class distinction here, no counts, barons, lords, or lordly estates. The one is as good as another, and everyone lives in the unrestricted enjoyment of personal liberty. A Swedish *bonde* [peasant], raised under oppression and accustomed to poverty and want, here finds himself elevated to a new world, as it were, where all his former hazy ideas of a society conforming more closely to nature's laws are suddenly made real and he enjoyes a satisfaction in life that he has never before experienced.[4]

The evident results followed promptly. Before the end of 1846, three even larger groups of emigrants were organized in Östergötland and left for America. That same year Peter Cassel's letter, together with other related materials, was printed in booklet form in Västervik.[5]

Peasant discontent was concerned not only with material grievances in this period. There was also growing dissatisfaction with the dry formalism of the state Lutheran church and the general complacency of its clergy, which found expression in widespread pietistic revival movements. While most of the "Readers" (*läsare*), as the pietists were known, sought to purify and rejuvenate the state church itself, some broke out of the Lutheran fold altogether, in violation of existing laws.

The most prominent group of separatists were the group that during the early 1840s formed around the peasant and self-styled prophet, Eric Jansson, mainly in Hälsingland. Jansson proclaimed a doctrine of earthly perfection and he and his followers publicly burned Lutheran devotional books. After repeated brushes with the law and with outraged local opinion, Eric Jansson departed for America in 1846, condemning his homeland to eternal damnation. He was joined, over the next several years, by some 1,500 of his followers.

On the prairie in northwestern Illinois the Janssonists built their new godly community, Bishop Hill, from which numerous reports went back to Sweden concerning God's bounty in the new land. "I now take pen in hand," wrote a Janssonist named A. Andersson to a friend in Västmanland in 1847.

> Moved by the spirit of the Lord, when I consider how God has blessed us here on this new soil by a hundredfold in both spiritual and worldly goods over what we possessed in our fatherland, so that I may say like David: I cannot tell of all Thy goodness, which Thou doest with the sons of man who fear Thee. . . . See now how Jesus' word has been fulfilled in us, namely that we who have forsaken all have already been repaid a hundredfold, and according to His promise our final reward is to be life everlasting. And so I do not ask too much of you when I urge you to forsake everything and come here to us.

Such accounts did not fail to have effect. The Bishop Hill colony was from the beginning far larger than Peter Cassel's settlement in Iowa, and by the later 1840s the arrival of increasing numbers of Swedes in addition to the Janssonist sectaries had firmly established northern Illinois as the center of what was to become Swedish America.[6]

Up to the 1840s America as myth and reality had been the concern of a small, educated elite in Sweden, interested in the broader questions of the day. During that decade the beginning of emigration on a significant scale, involving peasant farmers from an increasing number of provinces, made America an immediate and practical concern to all levels of Swedish society. This interest was fed, among the broader masses, from a variety of sources encouraging emigration and offering concrete information to potential emigrants. By all odds most important in this respect were the "America-letters" sent home by Swedes already in the United States.

Such letters were numerous from the start, for although the Riksdag had passed a law requiring a school in every parish as late as 1842, which could only be fully implemented some decades later, literacy in Sweden was already by then probably more widespread than anywhere else in Europe.[7] The high cost of postage during the earlier emigration nonetheless meant that these letters were usually composed with some care, over days or weeks. Most praised America, often in the most extravagant terms. Upon reaching their destinations in Sweden, the America-letters were avidly read by a wide circle of relatives and friends, borrowed, and often copied. Many were printed, in whole or in part, in newspapers, not least in the affected provinces, in which case choice, editing, and accompanying commentary

Plate 1. S. V. Helander, *The Emigrants.* The sadness of parting portrayed by a nineteenth-century Swedish artist. (Courtesy of Nordiska Museet, Stockholm.)

Plate 2. Gustaf Unonius's home at Pine Lake, Wisconsin, in the early 1840s. The vision of a life of simple contentment and republican virtue amid idyllic surroundings on the American frontier. (From G. Unonius, *Minnen af en sjuttonårig vistelse i Nordvästra Amerika,* Uppsala, 1861–62.)

Plate 3. "God has blessed us here on this new soil by a hundredfold in both spiritual and worldly goods over what we possessed in our fatherland," wrote a Bishop Hill settler in 1847. Olof Krans's *Breaking Prairie* embodies the land-hungry peasant's eternal dream: deep, rich loam as far as the eye can reach and not a stone to be seen anywhere. (Courtesy of the Bishop Hill Historic Site, Illinois Historic Preservation Agency.)

Plate 4. A group of Swedish immigrants passing through Boston on their way west in 1853. The early immigrants were characterized as "Americans" before they ever left home. Once in the United States they eagerly sought to become part of American life. (Courtesy of the Swedish Emigrant Institute, Växjö.)

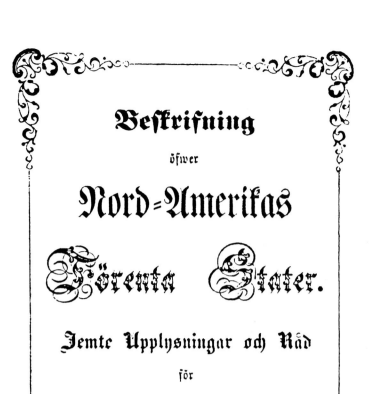

Beskrifning

öfwer

Nord-Amerikas

Förenta Stater.

Jemte Upplysningar och Råd

för

Utwandrare.

Författad af

Johan Bolin,

Comminister i Sjösås pastorat i Werjö stift.

———————————

Wexiö.

Tryckt hos A. G. Deurells Enka.

1853.

Plate 5. Johan Bolin's emigrant guide book, *Beskrifning öfwer Nord-Amerikas För-enta Stater* (Description of North America's United States), was published in Växjö, 1853. One of the most widely read and influential books of its kind, it was written by a rural pastor who in fact never visited America.

Per Svenssons nybygge i Amerika: 1. Sådant han drömde sig det.

Plate 6. Per Svensson in America: As he imagined it (*above*) and how it actually turned out (*next page*). Illustrations to "A. A.'s" cautionary tale from 1869 in *Läsning för folket,* describing "in gripping fashion how it goes for most of those who foolishly emigrate to America," where they "often bitterly regret that they have exchanged a bird in the hand for ten in the bush." (Courtesy of Nordiska Museet, Stockholm.)

Per Svenssons nybygge i Amerika. 2. Sådant det i verkligheten blef.

Plate 7. An immigrant couple's first home in Minnesota, 1872. Swedish settlers on the frontier at first naturally made use of old-country skills. The log cabin is unmistakably Swedish in style and construction. (Courtesy of the Swedish Emigrant Institute, Växjö.)

tended to serve editorial objectives of either condoning or condeming emigration.

Firsthand accounts from persons of their own kind, above all from relatives and friends, gained the confidence of the peasantry in ways that published writings about America by members of the educated classes never could. Thanks to these direct contacts, widespread chain reactions were set in motion, causing over the years ever increasing numbers to leave particular parishes in Sweden to rejoin kinfolk and former neighbors in the American Midwest. Similarly, almost from the beginning, such networks originating across the Atlantic led to what George M. Stephenson called the "swarming of the Swedes," from the soon overcrowded early settlements in Illinois and Iowa, to establish new daughter colonies further north and west.

How could Swedish peasants not have been impressed by Peter Cassel's claim in 1846 that cornfields in America were "more like woods than grainfields" and that American corn yielded as much as seven hundred times the amount of seed planted? Or in a less sensational vein, what of Mary Jonson's letter in 1859 to her parents from New Sweden, Iowa: "Do not worry too much about me. I got along well in Sweden, and this being a better country, I will do even better here. As my plans are now, I have no desire to be in Sweden. I never expect to speak with you again in this life.":[8] Naturally such accounts from America contained in emigrant letters home lost nothing in the retelling.

Already in 1841—the year Gustaf Unonius departed for America—C. A. von Scheele brought out the first Swedish emigrant guidebook on behalf of a short-lived Emigration Society organized in Stockholm the year before, to be followed in time by a long series of such handbooks for prospective emigrants. Between 1849 and 1855, no less than nine were published in Sweden, all of which show notable similarities. Indeed, they were largely cribbed, if not directly plagiarized, from each other and from similar foreign guides. All were written by members of the educated classes and while they naturally depicted America in favorable terms they also warned against its pitfalls. Except for Carl Edvard Swalander, an emigrant agent in Gothenburg, none had any personal stake in emigration, and the author of one of the most widely read guides, Johan Bolin, a rural pastor in Småland, never even visited the land he described.[9]

For the most part the authors of the guidebooks concentrated on practical advice to prospective emigrants, but they could on occasion wax lyrical. Swalander wrote in 1853 that the emigrants should "employ the voyage as a new birth bath," thus to gradually wash away the old world's deeply rooted sins and vices, so that, like souls cleansed of all evil, they would enter into the new and youthful world where only diligence, thrift, and consideration for others is of value.[10]

By the mid-1840s there were already those who were prepared to assist emigrants in securing passage across the Atlantic. The Emigration Society in Stockholm had been organized in 1840 for such a purpose, although it apparently accomplished little. The first local emigrant agent may have been the Kisa apothecary, Carl Gustaf Sundius, who had encouraged the Cassel enterprise in 1845 and thereafter helped others in his area to emigrate.[11] By the early 1850s, others, such as Swalander in Gothenburg, served as emigrant agents. As long as emigrants continued to travel in relatively small groups on sailing vessels filled largely with cargo, their activity remained a sideline. But it laid the groundwork for the well-organized agencies of later decades.

During the 1850s, if not before, successful emigrants on occasion faced the rigors of the ocean crossing to visit the homeland, arousing enormous interest and curiosity in their home parishes and well beyond, and frequently taking back with them to America sizable followings.[12] In 1854 a new type of emigrant recruiter appeared when the Illinois Central Railroad sent Oscar Malmborg, a Swedish-born veteran of the Mexican War, back to his homeland to encourage settlement on its land grant. He would in time be followed by the agents of other American and Canadian railroads.[13]

The early Swedish and Norwegian immigrants were on the whole well-received in the United States. At a time of rising concern over large-scale Catholic immigration from Ireland and parts of Germany, the Scandinavians appeared as welcome reinforcements for the defense of traditional American values. The ground had been prepared by much interest in the United States since the 1830s in the Norse discovery of North America and the appearance during the 1830s and 1840s of the first American writings on Sweden's seventeenth-century colony on the Delaware. "To an American," the traveler Charles Loring Brace wrote enthusiastically, "a visit to the home of the old Northmen is a visit back to his forefather's house. A thousand signs tell him he is at the cradle of the race which leads modern enterprise, and whose Viking power in both hemispheres has not ceased to be felt."[14]

In Sweden, the beginning of emigration on some scale by the mid-1840s added a new dimension to the well-established and doctrinaire debate over America. The exploits in the New World of Gustaf Unonius and his small band of upper-class idealists and adventurers remained a matter of rather abstract interest and curiosity compared with the immediate reactions aroused by Peter Cassel and his peasant following in 1845. "A Traveler in Östergötland" in May that year wrote in *Najaden* (Karlskrona) of having met some of the group. All, he pointed out, were well-to-do farmers respected in their community, and he deplored conditions in Sweden that understandably caused such people to depart. They were, he recognized, "the first emigrant group of any size from our country," and he foresaw that "hundreds" of other Swedes would surely follow them.

C. F. Ridderstad, the editor of *Östgötha Correspondenten* (Linköping), revealed the quandary of moderate and thoughtful observers of this disturbing new phenomenon. "If the political malady in Sweden is the cause of emigration," he wrote, "the government must realize that reforms are necessary." Yet at heart he found emigration deeply repugnant, a "mania" that "ought rather to be stemmed than encouraged," and he concluded with the rhetorical appeal:

> Thus only dost thou leave thy homeland's strand,
> Because gold does not refine itself from rock.
> Alone for *easy* bread, held in a weakling's hand,
> Thou fliest, frivolous, to an unknown strand.
>
> ....
>
> With the *plow* dig bread out of thy frozen land,
> Draw sword against the world for thy free strand![15]

The Cassel party and the controversy surrounding it in the Swedish newspapers in 1845 and 1846 is worth more than passing notice, for it contained already the essential outlines of the whole great conflict over emigration that would rage in the Swedish press and opinion down to the American Civil War and beyond. As for Peter Cassel himself, after three years in Iowa, he wrote his brother in December 1848, showing an indomitable but more chastened enthusiasm for the new land:

> Nobody in Sweden can imagine all the advantages America offers sober, honest, and industrious persons; for them it is a veritable land of Canaan, where the natural resources are literally flowing with milk and honey. But for those who neither can nor will work, who have left Sweden with other plans for making a living, they will without exception find a Siberia, and the sooner they leave, the better, if they want to escape the greatest want and misery. Thus you see that this country can be at the same time both a Canaan and a Siberia. Truly it is a peculiar country.[16]

Opposition to emigration was, deepest down, instinctive and emotional. At the grassroots level it appeared as a vague but disquieting threat to the fundamental bonds of blood and community. Charles J. Hoflund recalled in later years his family's emigration from Småland in 1850.

> As soon as it was known that father had decided to go to America there was an onslaught of relatives and friends, begging and protesting with tears not to go, and picturing all manner of calamities to which we might be exposed. So it required a good deal of courage to give up what was considered a good thing for an uncertainty, to leave a place that had supported us and our forebears for generations, and not a kith or kin had ever left it for unknown or strange pastures.

In his novel, *The Emigrants,* Vilhelm Moberg has described how the determination of his protagonist, Karl Oskar Nilsson, to leave for America in 1850 was "taken as a reproach, an insult even, to the parish as a whole and to each individual: the community and its people were not good enough for him." Eric Norelius, who departed in 1850, would later describe how "Mother went with us as far as the churchyard so that she could say that she had followed us to the grave."[17]

There was bitter reproach, too, in letters to emigrants in America from those they had left behind. Kare Jons Dotter wrote in 1848 from Hälsingland to her daughter in Bishop Hill: "My heart grieves and my eyes flow with tears when I think of your emigrating, and the sorrow and longing you left me with. . . . This was the reward you gave me for all the unstinting efforts I made for your earthly future." In 1852, the daughter, Marta Ersdotter, wrote from Bishop Hill that she was still determined never to look back like "Lot's wife."[18]

The parish clergy tended to regard with profound skepticism the prospect of simple peasants facing the perils of a strange new world and with mounting alarm at the worldly and independent spirit revealed by such ideas. Various reminiscences describe the earnest efforts of local pastors to dissuade would-be emigrants from their undertaking. D. A. Peterson later described how their pastor in Östergötland gravely warned his father in 1849 of the hazards of the ocean crossing, "ferocious beasts," "bloodthirsty Indians," and above all, the Americans themselves, "a people without religion or morality of any kind whatever." By leaving for America, "you do yourself an irreparable injury both for this world and for the next."[19]

In the Swedish press, the opponents of emigration played upon a wide range of themes, philosophical as well as emotional. They refused to believe that Sweden was overpopulated. Already in 1846, the agronomist Johan Teofil Nathorst asked rhetorically whether it was right that Sweden should ship its rural poor to America or Australia "while we have thousands of *tunnland* of uncultivated land in our own country?" *Växjöbladet* in 1856 condemned it as unpatriotic "to deprive society of the labor which it will so badly need for all the great tasks that lie ahead."[20]

Emigration, in the eyes of its opponents, was harmful not only to the fatherland but to the emigrants themselves, in a spiritual if not a material sense. America offered a free field to religious heresies of every sort to ensnare simple, unsuspecting souls. The conservative politician, August von Hartmansdorff, wrote in 1853: "How fortunate are we not, meanwhile, through the existence of our state church to be able to escape all the confusion, covetousness, competition, and disputation, and to be able, each of us, to tend to our affairs peacefully while the leaders of society make provision for the management of church and state."[21]

But beyond concern over the spiritual welfare of the emigrants lay deeper anxieties regarding the new restless and skeptical spirit which emigration embodied. Christianity, the theologian Peter Fjellstedt maintained in 1848, was the basis for the true happiness of peoples: "Away, therefore, with the harmful delusion . . . that all the unfortunate conditions which are complained of among us result from shortcomings to be found in the laws and constitution." "Man is made for *church* and *state,*" wrote Bishop Johan Jakob Hedrén of Linköping in 1853; both emigration and the rising movement for religious freedom in Sweden he regarded as products of the same spirit, "the general dissolution of the bonds of society." The emigrants, he held, were impelled by "hatred for those bonds which are suspected to be the causes of discontent, whereas in reality they have been the right help and protection against it. This vexation will presumably not long prevent the freedom they seek from becoming burdensome and oppressive." *Helsingborgsposten* attacked in 1857 "our so-called liberals; *historic* rights they refuse to recognize, they demand *rational* rights." The same year, Johan Peter Theorell described the emigration in *Vinterbladet* (Stockholm) as part of the "general madness that has seized power throughout Europe."[22]

Some conservatives were aware of a need for greater concern for the poorer classes, in a traditional paternalistic and Christian spirit. Otto von Feilitzen wrote in *Svenska Tidningen* (Stockholm) in 1853 that the working man should be given a home, work, and schooling, which should impart true Christianity and inspire moral behavior. Still, one should not "hold out to the working class the prospect of pleasures which can only belong to the realm of a refined upbringing, or of attaining any other political role in society than that it already has."[23]

Typically, conservatives, who by definition considered the existing society sound and sought to conserve it, tended to blame emigration upon faults of character among the emigrants themselves. Some simply dismissed them as rogues and ne'er-do-wells, whom the country was well rid of. "Wherever an indolent soul is found who quickly descends into the proletariat," *Hudiksvalls Veckoblad* declared in 1850, following the Janssonist exodus, "off to the Promised Land in the West he makes his pilgrimage, there . . . without effort, to drink both milk and honey." Leonard Fredrik Rääf wrote to a friend from Östergötland in 1852 that emigration brought the benefit of "freeing us from a crowd of rabble, idlers, and restless spirits." *Nya Wermlandstidningen* (Karlstad) attributed emigration in 1855 to "a growing lust for adventure, or more correctly, for idle drifting from place to place," and claimed that in general "no workers are more lazy, immoral, and indifferent than those who emigrate to other places."[24]

Nonetheless, compared with the prevailing folklore concerning the emigration, printed condemnations of the emigrants themselves are fewer than one might expect. As the opponents of emigration hoped to appeal to the better sense and higher moral sensibilities of those who might be tempted to depart, it behooved them to avoid too insulting and provocative language. It may be imagined that such ideas were expressed more freely in private conversation in manor houses and parsonages.

A more frequent theme was the delusive and unseemly lust of the emigrants for more worldly goods than their lot in life provided. The religious paper, *Väktaren* (Stockholm), wrote in 1855: "It pains the heart when one sees those who claim to honor Him, who though rich became poor for the sake of His brethren, dissatisfied with their lot and defying God, venture out upon a hazardous journey only in order to win worldly advantages."

Happiness, the governor of Jönköping County (*län*) maintained in a circular in 1852, "is nowhere to be found except in fear of God, virtue, and industry, and for these she opens her arms wherever Providence has given a people a fatherland."[25]

"Thoughtless or ungrateful lust after greater worldly fortune," as the governor expressed it, together with the ignorance and naiveté of those tempted to emigrate, in turn led the search for the true villains of the piece to those "outside agitators" which to the conservative mind must lie behind any unrest within a basically sound society.

In the first instance, this meant the Swedish liberals, who were accused of mindlessly propagating a dangerously overidealized picture of America. In 1847 the conservative *Tiden* (Stockholm) accused *Aftonbladet* of such misrepresentation, thanks to which "flocks of Swedish citizens in recent years have emigrated to the alleged Canaan, to be exposed on the way to hard suffering and after their arrival to need, hardship, hunger, misery, and sickness." *Svenska Tidningen* held that the liberals exploited the Swedes' "creative and dreamy nature," encouraging them to yearn for an "atomic, individual freedom," the "ideal for the fantasies of all dreamers."[26]

The emigrants themselves were meanwhile sending home glowing, and—in the minds of the opponents of emigration—wildly exaggerated, accounts of America. In 1854, Peter Wieselgren held that letters from America boasted of "grass as high as a man and freedom as high as the sky." "But," Wieselgren asked indignantly, "what can come of such representations by the ignorant for the ignorant?"[27]

Already, too, before the American Civil War, the activities of the first emigrant agents aroused the ire and apprehensions of those opposed to emigration. Oscar Malmborg made a second recruiting trip to Sweden for the Illinois Central Railroad in 1861. That fall an anonymous poem appeared in *Barometern* (Kalmar) in response to Malmborg's "invitation to occupy the Promised Land in Illinois," which ended:

> Remain thou in thy fatherland!
> Do always good and right,
> And know—for an industrious hand
> Joyful toil is light.

> Tend the soil that thou hast got,
> Obey the law's command,
> And be contented with thy lot,
> The rest lies in God's hand.[28]

The defenders of emigration had their own battery of arguments. Sweden, it was held, could not presently provide for its growing population, due not only to the limitations of climate and terrain but also to antiquated laws restricting economic activity. Only emigration could remove the threat of progressive impoverishment. In America, *Malmöposten* stated in 1855, one was free from a "mass of prejudices, restrictions, and obselete laws, which oppress people in old Europe and which will never be swept away until there is a world revolution." Love of one's native soil, Christian Berlin declared at the Riksdag of 1856–57, could not restrain one from leaving it if one could not acquire any part of it. Low wages, *Aftonbladet* claimed in 1855, were the real cause of emigration and its cure would be to raise them, thereby placing the blame on the employers rather than on the employees.[29]

America, the same newspaper stated in 1854, was the one country "where revolutionary ideas have no future;" the religious and philanthropic United States thus offered the strongest shield against social upheaval. But early socialists in Sweden had their own vision of the New World. Already in 1850, *Reform* (Stockholm) wrote: *"Labor's* right to the *full* value [of its product] is the concept that will break the old bonds and lead to a new *economic* and a new *legal* doctrine. Perhaps we should learn from America the meaning of *economic* freedom, just as we formerly were able to learn there what *political* freedom means."[30]

While the opponents of emigration painted a dark picture of religious and moral conditions in the United States, its defenders offered similar criticisms of the religious establishment in Sweden itself. In 1846 *Söndagsbladet* (Stockholm) blamed the clergy of the state church for the Janssonist exodus, thanks to its "godless behavior, a Jesuitical attitude, a boundless forgetfulness of duty."

For many, meanwhile, it was America's religious freedom that gave depth and vitality to its spiritual life. In 1840 Pastor Petrus Læstadius believed that there was more true religiosity there than in Sweden, for where conscience is free "there, too, everyone has *some* form of belief," whereas in a land with "the catholicism of a state church commanding the allegiance of all, there are many without any faith or religion." The earliest Swedish Lutheran pastors to minister to their countrymen in America, including Lars Paul Esbjörn, Tufve Nilsson Hasselquist, Erland Carlsson, and others, were associated with the pietistic movement for reform within the Swedish church.[31]

Emigration brought closer contacts with religious denominations of Anglo-American origins, particularly the Methodists, Baptists, and before long, the Mormons. While they were prohibited by law from proselytizing until 1860, Swedish-American missionaries had already begun to make inroads by the early 1850s. For those who thus withdrew from the state church, America was the promised land, either as a refuge for the faith or a model for the good cause at home. The Baptist missionary Anders Wiberg wrote to a friend from America in 1854, "Oh, poor, blind fatherland. ... How dark do you not appear from this land of light, life, and freedom!"[32]

Even those who regarded emigration from a secular viewpoint could conceive of it in providential terms. For *Göteborgs Handels- och Sjöfarts-tidning* in 1852, it was part of the grand design of Providence that the "Caucasian peoples" should spread throughout the world. Through this, the Nordic peoples would ultimately "rise again to a new position of strength at the cost of the older peoples." *Aftonbladet* maintained the same year that the United States "is the land where modern culture will some day reach its fullest flowering, which will some day bring rejuvenation to the Old World."[33]

The moral to be drawn from the emigration was thus, according to its defendants, the long-overdue need to cleanse the Augian stables at home. Current emigration statistics, *Göteborgs Handels- och Sjöfartstidning* declared in 1849, "silence all the tumult and abuse toward the United States, which the lackeys of monarchism in recent years have made all efforts to spread on this side of the ocean." To ignore the emigration, *Norrlandsposten* (Gävle) maintained the same year, would be to disregard evils that have "shaken the structure of society, have crushed thrones, destroyed mighty dynasties, and brought kingdoms to the brink of ruin." Sweden's political, religious, and economic institutions were more backward than those of "almost all of civilized Europe," *Öresundsposten* (Helsingborg) claimed in 1856, adding that the sentence of exile might well be abolished since conditions were such that "the people go voluntarily and in droves into exile."[34]

In no respect were the defenders of emigration at greater variance from their adversaries than in their view of the basic character and motivation of the emigrants. To them, the latter were undeserving victims of outside circumstances that persons of spirit and intelligence could hardly be expected to endure. To the claims that emigration was a "mania," *Göteborgs Handels- och Sjöfartstidning* responded in 1851: "Yes, indeed. The mania of wanting to eat one's fill after one has worked oneself hungry! The craze of wanting to support oneself and one's family in an honest manner!"[35]

Meanwhile, it was not the most impoverished classes, without the necessary means, who were departing. In 1849 *Norrlandsposten* called for essential reforms in Sweden "before it is too late and the indomitable instinct for freedom, more or less developed, drives into unwilling exile the best part of Sweden's splendid peasantry, which seeks freedom in a foreign land." *Budbäraren* (Stockholm) warned in 1852 that emigration was not a cure for overpopulation, "for through emigration it is not the consuming but the producing part of the population who leave the land." It hoped that the emigrants would form large settlements in America, "so that our nationality might blossom anew on the other side of the ocean, in case it should go under here."[36]

Although *Malmöposten* admitted in 1855 that the great wave of emigration naturally included "adventurers, vagabonds, windbags, and all kinds of less apparent swindlers and idlers," it held that it was precisely such types who came to grief in the New World. Soon there would be nothing left in Europe but thrones, bayonets, and pulpits, Magnus Jacob Crusenstolpe—that bellwether of radical causes—wrote in his paper, *Ställningar och förhållanden* in 1853. "Their Majesties will find themselves *without subjects*, but face to face, surrounded by soldiers, clergymen; and police constables!" In short, to their defenders, the emigrants represented the best, rather than the worst, elements of society.[37]

Just as their opponents sought the beam in their eye, so too did those who justified emigration look for the mote in their adversaries'. "The public is now beginning to see that beneath pious and godly phrases and polished language there often lie feelings and thoughts more concerned with personal gain and advantage than with what is just and in the general interest," wrote *Öresundsposten* in 1856. Oscar Malmborg, the Illinois Central's man in Sweden, was more direct when he wrote of the large landowners who sought to oppose his recruitment efforts in 1861 that they wanted not only the peasants' land but their labor as well, "and the more of it the better, because it is cheaper."[38]

The Swedish debate about America and emigration drew sustenance from the published accounts of certain Swedes who traveled in the United States during these years. Of these, the best known were Per Adam Siljeström—who, supported by a government grant, studied the American educational system—and the novelist Fredrika Bremer.

Siljeström was highly enthusiastic over what he encountered. Here he found in practice those ancient Nordic virtues "which our skalds have celebrated in song" and which formed the necessary moral basis for the republican form of government. The Americans gave proof of "morality and religiosity, industry and orderliness, together with a deeply rooted belief in the need for progress." The problems of American life he ascribed to the immigration of many of the dregs of Europe, which had created a stratum of "wretchedness, ignorance, and immorality." His travel account, published in two volumes in 1852 and 1854, thus presented an idealized view of the New World, strongly reminiscent of the eighteenth-century Enlightenment. In it he had virtually nothing to say about Swedish emigrants. Yet in his journal, *Dagens häfder* (Stockholm), he sounded a new note in the current debate on emigration when in 1854 he invoked the need for his countrymen to treat the emigrants with sympathy and consideration. It would not be easy for them to leave the land of their birth. A "loving handclasp in their hour of departure" might therefore "make their separation from home, if possible, less bitter and strengthen the bond that will tie them, once they have left, to their native soil."[39] Decades would pass, during which Swedish emigration would swell to unimagined proportions, before such an idea would greatly affect Swedish opinion.

Far more widely read was Fredrika Bremer's *Homes of the New World*, which appeared in English in London as soon as it came out in Swedish in 1853–54 and remains one of the classic European accounts of mid-nineteenth-century America. Nils Runeby has described Fredrika Bremer as characteristic of a new generation of European liberals who, disillusioned by the failure of the revolutions of 1848–49, put their faith in emigration to still undeveloped parts of the world. Her main purpose in visiting the United States, as she put it, was to see firsthand whether her belief that it provided a model for other lands could withstand a direct confrontation with reality. Although she was aware that the young republic was still in a state of flux as it spread across a vast continent, she gave on the whole a strongly positive view of America, where, as she wrote to her sister in 1851, she found "a warmer heartbeat, a more energetic, strong and youthful life." Like Siljeström, she gave little attention to the still relatively few and scattered Swedish immigrants, although she did visit Gustaf Unonius's little Pine Lake colony in Wisconsin and foretold that Minnesota might one day become a glorious new Scandinavia.[40]

In 1853 Anders Wiberg, a former Lutheran state church pastor who had become a Baptist, brought out in *Aftonbladet* an account of his travels that year in the American Middle West, which is of particular interest since it is the first to devote considerable attention to the Swedes and their earliest settlements in the United States.

Wiberg was highly enthusiastic about America: its majestic landscapes, vast resources, dynamic development, and not least, religious tolerance. Arriving in Chicago, then a metropolis of some 50,000 inhabitants, he discovered "large numbers of Swedes"—some 1,400 he claimed—whose situation, however, he did not find encouraging.

> These, our countrymen, had generally quite a bad reputation, and were considered worse than the otherwise despised Irish. Last summer, a large number of Swedish emigrants died here, and the high mortality rate was attributed to their beastly and immoral way of life. . . . Contributing also in large measure . . . is the fact that in order to stay in the cities they must crowd themselves into the worse hovels, which has been the case with the Swedes both here and in other cities.

A hard judgment, it would seem. Still, the answer, in Wiberg's mind, lay in getting his countrymen out onto the land in the "most fertile areas on the earth," where "everyone, even the poorest, can find a good living, if they can and will work."

This view seemed amply confirmed as Wiberg continued westward to the thriving Swedish pioneer settlements at Andover, Galesburg, Bishop Hill, and Rock Island in Illinois and New Sweden and Burlington in Iowa. "It was a moving sight during our journey [he wrote from Iowa] to see a tall Swede either riding in a wagon or galloping on horseback over the flatlands of western America, and I imagined the time when thousands of their descendants would call this land their fatherland and their home."

Wiberg's description of Bishop Hill includes a lengthy, laudatory account of the colony from the *Weekly Rock Island Republican,* one of the earliest expressions of an Anglo-American tendency to favor the Swedes and other Scandinavians at a time when "Know-Nothing" nativism was aroused against most immigrants in America.[41]

Clas Edvard Habicht, Swedish-Norwegian consul general in New York, was able to report already in 1850: "In general, the Swedish immigrants, as well as the Norwegians, stand higher in the estimation of the Americans than several other nations, for the manliness and honesty that have always distinguished their national character."[42]

Opposition to emigration in Sweden found expression not only in public debate and private discussion among better educated and well-informed circles, but in writings by persons of such background intended to deter the broader masses from the temptation to emigrate.

The earliest publications of this kind were somewhat ambivalent. In 1842 Carl David Arfwedson published, under the pseudonym, "An Impartial Countryman," a slender pamphlet giving advice "to those who next year intend to depart from Sweden and Norway for the United States." He recognized that circumstances could exist "when any change would be better than existing conditions" and therefore advised that those who did depart should travel and settle in organized groups. Yet his basic message was that it was a "perilous thing" to emigrate from one's fatherland. Many, misled by "brilliant hopes," had left what was tried and true at home "to grasp after the golden fruits." But few succeeded, and the only gain for many was an untimely grave in foreign soil. "Stay therefore where you are, if you can. Providence has not without reason placed you in the North. Here you belong, here you shall also, man of the North, die."[43] The correspondence and commentaries surrounding the emigration of Peter Cassel's group which came out in *Östgötha Correspondenten* in 1846, was similarly ambivalent, to a point, as noted.

A far more direct appeal against emigration was written by the landowner and philanthropist Carl Adam von Nolcken and published in his journal *Läsning för Allmogen,* which was aimed at the edification of the peasantry, in 1855. He described how emigration had long taken place from Europe's most populous countries, most recently to "the tempting land of gold," California. Now, however, it was beginning in Sweden as well, which was hardly overpopulated and needed the labor of its sons and daughters to develop its wealth.

> Lust for money and dislike for work are the most common motives [for emigration], and one may well add discontent with what one has, and an unrest that runs through all of our time. It is not discreditable to wish to gain wealth—especially if one is prepared to work hard for it—but it is a matter of what one sacrifices to this desire, and how high a value one places upon money. If one breaks asunder those bonds that tie us here on earth, if one smothers one's nobler feelings out of mere lust for gain, then this striving for greater wealth and better conditions deserves our condemnation and contempt.

The Swedish peasant, however, was ill-suited for life abroad, where unimagined snares and perils lay in wait. And, von Nolcken added pointedly, his womenfolk faced even greater hardship and deprivation. "Happiness," he admonished, "does not depend upon possessing much but rather upon *being contented with your lot.*"[44]

The kind of society that von Nolcken and those of like mind envisioned for Sweden was well described in a book entitled *Familjen* (The Family) in the Swedish translation published in 1856, by the German professor Wilhelm Heinrich Riehl, who presented an idealized picture of peasant life in Lower Saxony, "where brother seeks to enhance the honor of the house in his brother's service, where the wife is enthroned by the hearth in the hall, and the housefolk build their cottages under the patriarchal protection of the farmstead." The same work went on to describe both emigration and women's emancipation as symptoms of social dissolution.[45]

Nolcken's appeal in 1855 set the tone for anti-emigration propaganda essentially down to the end of Sweden's great migration. "If you have reached the goal of your desires, without a fatherland—what have you won?" asked "Ph. v. T." in *Läsning för Folket* the following year.[46] The most fundamental appeal of those who strove to stem the tide of emigration could hardly be more succinctly expressed.

An anonymous "Warning to Emigrants," likewise published in *Läsning för Folket* in 1863 admitted the frustrations that such attempts faced.

> Those, especially of the peasant class, who have *once* made up their minds to leave the fatherland and, as emigrants, to seek their fortunes far beyond its borders, can almost never be persuaded to abandon their plan, premature though it may be. The "Promised Land" with its supposed bliss plays constantly upon their imaginations and they long with feverish unrest for the time when they may begin their adventurous journey. In vain do their wiser relatives and friends seek to warn them against this perilous undertaking, and it is as fruitless to represent to them all the dangers, hardships, and disappointments to which they expose themselves. They do not believe their

admonitions, but only the often false and almost always exaggerated reports of the advantages of the new land that happen to come to their knowledge.

The author nonetheless held that if he saved even one person from emigrating his effort would not have been in vain. To this end he played heavily upon the theme of the emigrant's future repentance when after cutting his ties to the homeland there could be no return to it, unless hearth and home had become so indifferent to him that he "had never deserved to have a fatherland."

Gustaf Unonius, now back in Sweden, also cautioned against accepting misleading or ill-informed reports from America. His warning was, however, sober and restrained, and the following year he wrote to a publisher: "We must be careful not to paint too black a picture [of conditions in America] or to make ourselves guilty of an injustice, which could perhaps serve to encourage the urge to emigrate instead of restraining it."[47]

Many so-called emigrant songs have been preserved. Some of these were undoubtedly of genuine folk origins. Far more commonly, however, they were pieces composed to meet the popular tastes of a generally urban public and were hawked in the streets. To what extent such commercial ballads may have been known in the rural districts from which the great majority of the emigrants themselves came is difficult to imagine. Few of them evidently had any currency among the Swedes settled in America.

Most "emigrant ballads" provide a more accurate portrayal of the ideas and attitudes of those who composed them, or those the latter judged to be most current and fashionable at the time, rather than those of the emigrants whose situation they purported to describe. They thus reflect, on a drastically oversimplified and emotionally gripping level, the more sophisticated public debate over America and emigration. Some songs reproach the homeland, in indignant or pathetic tones, for conditions that drive its sons and daughters from its shores. More frequently, however, they ridicule the emigrants' gullibility and absurdly exaggerated dreams of America, describe their heartrending departure from home and family, or the agonies of homesickness and despair which overcome them in an alien land.[48] In the balance, these songs comprise a strongly sentimental indictment of emigration, in a form that very likely had a more direct emotional impact than the anti-emigration literature of the time. The question remains in both cases whether those most exposed to or most likely to be impressed by such literary products were also those most disposed to emigrate.

In the face of what evidently was the beginning of a major popular movement—in the most literal sense—the government and its officials showed both alarm and perplexity. Older bureaucratic traditions sanctioned direct intervention against activities that might be deemed contrary

to the public interest. At the same time the liberal doctrine of the inviolabil-
ity of individual rights had steadily been gaining ground. There was moreover still no clear consensus whether Sweden's rapidly growing population
was a bane or a blessing.

Still, beginning in Östergötland in 1849, a number of provincial governors (*landshövdingar*) took it upon themselves to issue circulars warning
against the hazards of emigration. The circular emanating from the governor of Jönköping County in 1852 has been cited above. The governors'
five-year reports to the Riksdag show an increasing concern with the problem. The loss of labor and capital, as well as the rising burden of poor
relief, brought about through emigration was discussed at the Riksdag of
1853–54, at which several motions were presented to limit agricultural
laborers' freedom of movement. In the ensuing debates the Peasant Estate
showed itself particularly concerned. The farmer Nils Andersson from
Värmland argued that "every person should, as a member of society, church,
and state, stand under the authority of community, church, and state, and
be bound to them by bonds so strong that they cannot impudently be
thrown off."[49]

Nothing came of these efforts. Similarly, a motion aimed directly at
limiting emigration, obviously to preserve agricultural labor, died in committee at the Riksdag of 1862–63. According to the committee report, "*this
method* of attaching inhabitants to their homeland [can] neither be worthy
of it nor produce the desired result, especially as such a measure would
conflict with the views of recent times, as well as with the freedom which
Swedes have become accustomed to enjoy, while the proposed law in
practice could easily be circumvented by those against whom it were
directed." Official propaganda against emigration was likewise deemed
useless. Thus Sweden drifted into the 1860s with no established policy
toward emigration.[50]

The perplexity created on the local level by emigration and the controversy it aroused is particularly well illustrated by a long letter written by an
assistant pastor (*komminister*), Sven Stenvall in Berga parish in Småland—a
province early affected—to the Swedish-American Lutheran minister Erland Carlsson in Chicago in March 1854.

> People are attacked as if by some epidemic, and to try to dissuade them is
> useless. They shy away and will not let any minister or public official talk
> to them about the matter. They are afraid they might be swerved from their
> decision and get mad if one refers to the subject. The other Sunday, ... [I
> pointed out] what a precious gift an earthly fatherland is, including house
> and home, etc., and that without a call from God or being in peril of one's
> soul no one ought to desert his native country ... and that those who
> thoughtlessly can exchange all these advantages for something uncertain are
> ungrateful and act foolishly. This caused bitterness in some, so that on their

way home they said, "Now the preachers are getting worked up; they are getting anxious about their privileges, and fear a shortage of servants," etc.

Stenvall wondered, indeed, "whether a great deal of imperfection does not adhere to our native land after all—the laboring classes are driven to their wits' end to keep alive." America surely offered great advantages, "especially material ones, and those are, sad to say, the things that people mostly strive for in our day." To be sure, America was filled with competing religious sects, but Stenvall could not but wonder whether many of their adherents were not at heart better Christians than many Lutherans. "Most of the emigrants," he reported, "also write that you have a better brand of Christianity over there than we have here, and that there is no swearing, no drinking, etc." According to one letter from Illinois, there was "four times as decent conduct as in Sweden." Stenvall filled his letter with examples of the extravagant praise of American conditions that had found its way to his parish. He implored Pastor Carlsson for a true account, to lead him, and thus his flock, out of his confusion. "God help us in these troublous times," he ended his letter, "lest lukewarmness or coldness get the upper hand in the things that are most precious and important to us mortals."[51]

The American Civil War, beginning in 1861, temporarily slowed the stream of Swedish emigration. The conflict meanwhile brought to its culmination the whole controversy in Sweden over the American republic and its historical significance in the world since at least the time of the American Revolution. Conservatives had repeatedly asserted that it could never stand the strain of a serious crisis. For liberals, the survival of the Union meant, in effect, the vindication of their most cherished political ideals.

Both the initial setbacks to the Union forces and the failure of the Washington government to make its moral position clear by promptly abolishing slavery tried the faith of many Swedish liberals. The Confederacy meanwhile impressed many in Sweden, as elsewhere in Europe, with its gallant struggle against superior odds, which in turn recalled various national independence movements in Europe itself at the time enjoying widespread sympathy. Emancipation, when it finally came in January 1863, seemed something of an anticlimax to idealistic liberals, tainted by suspicions of mundane economic and political interests.

The turning of the tide with the Union victories at Vicksburg and Gettysburg, however, no less than the freeing of the slaves, rallied the hopes of the beleaguered Swedish liberals, reinforced by the Homestead Act of 1862, which held out to poor emigrants the prospect of free land on America's expanding frontier.[52]

Not only did the Civil War revindicate the cherished ideals of America's friends and admirers in Sweden, it also played a highly symbolic role in emotionally identifying Swedish immigrants with the new homeland of their choice. Almost all were settled in the Northern states and, as they were later proud to recall, in proportion to their numbers they volunteered for service in the Union army at a higher rate than the native Americans.[53] Swedish blood shed on the field of battle confirmed the Swedes' indisputable place in America, and thereafter the veterans of the Grand Army of the Republic held a particularly revered place within the Swedish-American community. From their midst, too, would emerge some of its leading figures in decades to come. Similarly, the Republican party—the "Party of Lincoln"—would long remain almost sacrosanct among Swedish Americans.

We have considered attitudes in Sweden toward America, toward emigration, and toward those who emigrated, down to the mid-1860s. What, meanwhile, did the emigrants think of themselves and the situation they faced?

Traveling to New York as ship's physician aboard the *Ernst Merck* in 1864, Måns Hultin noted in his conversations with emigrants aboard:

> They seldom speak of America and never of Sweden. It appears as though they lived only to eat, drink, dance, sleep, and gape at passing ships, but I have spoken more closely with one or another about their prospects in the new land and I have found them all full of hope and faith. Their conceptions of the land and fate they are going to are naturally highly obscure, and they are most obscure regarding themselves, but the goal which basically, it seems to me, they are expecting and hoping for is not any fresh and newly formed object, unlike all that the past has offered them, but rather is simply the old and well loved in a new and improved edition. It is old Sweden idealized, it is the past, sometimes regretted and deplored yet always inescapable, which now no longer will be painted over and gilded as best one can, but will be rebuilt from the ground up and will be the first step toward a promising future. And it is clear that it could not be otherwise, for what is to be expected no one can judge except from what he had seen.[54]

Hultin was a perceptive observer. These people would not have left their homeland had they not firmly believed they could find something better across the sea. Yet what they envisioned was the peasant's age-old dream of land of his own, economic independence, the chance to put his feet under his own table, as the saying went, free from the impositions and controls of landlords and bureaucrats, both temporal and spiritual.

Yet Hultin was surely mistaken if he imagined that these emigrants dreamed of transplanting to America the whole elaborate peasant culture from which they came. By the middle of the nineteenth century a far-reaching cultural transformation had begun in the Swedish countryside as the more successful and ambitious farmers and their families increasingly abandoned the old ways as a culture of social inferiority and instead adopted the genteel usages of the town middle classes. Where the more prominent families led, others tended to follow. This rejection of the old folkways was strongly reinforced by the pietistic Awakening of the period, which generally condemned as heathen and ungodly many of the more exuberant manifestations of the traditional peasant culture. To those anxious to better their circumstances, socially as well as materially, America offered an escape and a new beginning, the chance to attain an essentially middle-class respectability based on cosmopolitan, rather than purely national or local norms. Once in America, moreover, the strongly nativist Know-Nothing movement of the 1850s discouraged any prideful display of non-American ways.

The early Swedish immigrants thus showed what may appear in retrospect a surprising lack of sentimentality toward the traditional culture they had left and a notable eagerness to adapt to their new habitat and Americanize as quickly as possible. Early letters from Peter Cassel and from the Bishop Hill colonists show great pride over how quickly the settlers and their children were learning English. The founding fathers of Swedish-American Lutheranism, beginning with Lars Paul Esbjörn in 1849, and thereafter including Tufve Nilsson Hasselquist, Erland Carlsson, and Eric Norelius, all envisioned the rapid and easy Americanization of their immigrant countrymen. Hasselquist warned against the exclusiveness of the German Americans. "We are not, and will never be, shut up in our own nationality," Norelius wrote—in English—in *The Missionary* in 1860; "We will be more and more Americanized every day."[55]

This impression is heightened by examinations of the material culture of the early Swedish immigrants. Because of the expense they could bring few possessions with them from the old country. But they were also repeatedly admonished by Swedes already in America to resist the temptation to bring more than the most basic necessities, since goods of better quality could be obtained at reasonable cost in America. If, once there, immigrant settlers on the frontier continued for a time to make use of old craft skills from home, they seem to have done so more out of immediate necessity than by preference.[56]

The early immigrants conceived of their identity in essentially religious terms. The historical or cultural nationalism of the upper and middle classes in Sweden meant little to most Swedish peasants, who identified the state with the bureaucracy and the burdens it imposed. The significance of religion in their thinking can meanwhile scarcely be overestimated, and it goes far toward explaining why peasant emigration could be psychologically conceivable.

Traditional Christianity, including the Lutheran state church of Sweden, taught humble acceptance of one's lot and obedience to duly appointed and ordained spiritual authority in this earthly life, which served only as a trial and preparation for the eternal life to come. Those who were prepared to face the uncertainties and hardships of emigration and separation from those they loved were strengthened by their belief in the true homeland beyond their earthly abode, where souls separated here below would be eternally reunited. And, as P. A. Siljeström put it in 1854, "the simplest peasant common sense easily concludes that it is no further to heaven from America than from Sweden." At the same time, the pietistic movements of the time—both within and outside of the state church—stressed the individual's own responsibility to find the true path to salvation, which led many of the early Swedish immigrants in America to embrace more evangelical and individualistic creeds, such as the Methodist or Baptist.

Such an independent approach to religion naturally fostered a similar attitude toward worldly matters: if through one's own efforts one could assure one's salvation, making use of one's God-given faculties, one could also change one's circumstances in this life through deliberate action. Here pietist individualism joined hands with the central message of the rationalistic eighteenth-century Enlightenment, its belief in secular progress, which now at last had spread from the classes to the masses, to form a potent impulse for change. Characteristically, the new pietism recognized no contradiction between purity of faith and worldly success.[57]

Under such circumstances, the most immediate cultural concern of most early Swedish immigrants in America was to provide for their spiritual needs. Congregations of varying denominations were quickly organized, frequently by lay preachers. Lars Paul Esbjörn's emigration, on his own initiative, to Andover, Illinois, in 1849 began a sustained and growing effort to retain the Swedish immigrants within the Lutheran fold. As the Scandinavians were still few and scattered in the United States, in 1860 a modest group of Swedish and Norwegian Lutheran congregations in the Midwest formed the Augustana Lutheran Synod. The same year it established in Chicago its own Augustana Seminary, to which a preparatory academy and college were soon added, under Esbjörn's leadership until he returned to Sweden in 1863. That same year the seminary and college moved, under Hasselquist, to Paxton, Illinois.[58]

The early tendency to create common Scandinavian institutions reflected not only the relatively small size of all the Scandinavian groups in America in the pioneer period, but also the idealistic Pan-Scandinavianism that flourished among the educated classes in their homelands during the middle decades of the century. The first Scandinavian-American newspaper, *Skandinaven,* published in New York by the Swede Gustaf Öbom from 1851 to 1853, was likewise such a common effort, carrying contributions in both Swedish and Dano-Norwegian.

In 1855 Pastor Hasselquist, then in Galesburg, Illinois, established the first purely Swedish newspaper, *Hemlandet, det Gamla och det Nya* (Homeland, the Old and the New), in order, as he wrote Pastor Carlsson two years earlier, "to free our people from immoral and unchurchly papers."[59] Other, short-lived Swedish newspapers appeared during the later 1850s and early 1860s in Galva and Galesburg, Illinois, and in Red Wing, Minnesota. Although Swedish in language, they expressed strong identification with and pride in the United States, and fulfilled an invaluable role in converting Swedish peasants into informed and committed American citizens.

By the end of the Civil War, when perhaps some twenty-five thousand Swedish-born persons were living in the United States, there were as yet few signs of any distinctive Swedish-American identity or portents that such an identity would ever evolve.

The number of Swedes in America by 1865 was still small, both in absolute terms and in proportion to Sweden's total population. They were far outnumbered by immigrants from the United Kingdom (including Ireland), Germany, and at this point even Norway. But numbers were not really the crux of the matter down to the middle 1860s. Far more significantly, emigration on a substantial scale from the broader masses gave irrefutable proof that something was seriously wrong with Sweden. On this basic proposition, almost all parties were, perforce, in agreement by mid-century. Where they differed—giving rise to widespread and heated debate both in public and in private—was in their diagnosis of the ills that beset Swedish society and the best means, if any, to overcome them.

As emigration became a factor of ever-increasing importance in Swedish attitudes toward the United States, the generally doctrinaire identification of anti-American views with political conservatism and pro-American sympathies with liberalism became in some ways less self-evident. While some opinionmakers in Sweden sought to justify emigration and defend the emigrants, few, if any, of them were happy about it. Those who justified emigration saw it as a regrettable necessity under existing conditions, or at best as a drastic but needful spur to internal reforms.

Positions regarding emigration in this period reveal some apparent logical inconsistencies. If, generally speaking, conservatives sought to conserve a traditional social order based on hierarchy, authority, and respect, it was they who also argued that Sweden was not overpopulated in relation to its undeveloped resources. But the reclamation and cultivation of the large areas of potentially arable land they constantly spoke of would be dependant, in a still preindustrial economy, upon menial, pick-and-shovel labor on a vast scale, which could only be profitable if the labor supply was large and therefore cheap. Under such circumstances Sweden *could* support an even larger population than it already possessed—providing that it preserved the existing social structure with its marked differences in status and wealth. The opponents of emigration could thus largely be described as conservative in a social sense but progressive in an economic sense. In their scale of priorities, the national interest must take precedence over those of its individual subjects.

It was precisely in this latter respect that liberals differed most decisively from conservatives. It was their basic tenet that the state existed to uphold and protect the rights and welfare of its citizens (not subjects), and that if unable to do so it should not hinder them from seeking their legitimate self-interests elsewhere. Rather than witness what they regarded as the exploitation of the poorer classes for the sake of economic development under forms incompatible with individual freedom and dignity, they were logically compelled to consider Sweden overpopulated and hence to con-done emigration, albeit with regret. They tended, in effect, to be liberal in a social, while conservative in an economic sense.

The view of America expressed by the defenders of emigration in this period reflects this combination of social and economic attitudes. America since its discovery had represented many things in the minds of Europeans: the virgin wilderness and the noble savage, religious and political freedom, social equality. During the first half of the nineteenth century it had pro-vided an impressive picture of scientific and technological progress. With the emigration of growing numbers of Swedish peasants to the agricultural frontier in the mid-Mississippi valley, not only the common folk of the Swedish countryside but the articulate supporters of emigration in public debate as well envisioned America as above all a rural Arcadia, offering land, independence, and rude plenty to all who were prepared for honest toil.[60] This meant a return to one of the oldest and most basic dreams of the New World and, at the same time, to the most deep-seated longing of a traditional peasant society.

Finally, it is notable that virtually all the essential themes in the long debate over emigration in Sweden, until it subsided together with the great migration itself in the 1920s, were already set forth during its earliest phase, between 1840 and 1865. The main positions were established. While some condemned the emigration as the result of outside contagion and as harmful both to the fatherland and to the emigrants themselves, others considered it an act of Providence beyond human understanding or control, or conversely as the symptom of serious economic or social maladies that only determined, even drastic, measures could heal.[61] Characteristically, as heirs of the Enlightenment, the defenders of emigration appealed to rational principles and concrete facts, while their adversaries, in the Roman-tic tradition, tended to invoke the intangible and emotional ties of family, native place, fatherland, mother tongue, and ancestral faith. Those who, despite all, were prepared to break such bonds, the conservatives were inclined to regard as rogues, or more likely, fools, deserving either condem-nation or pity. To those who upheld the right to leave the land, the emigrants represented Sweden's best blood.

THREE

A New Sweden Across the Sea

*D*uring the decade and a half following the Civil War, European, including Swedish, emigration reached unprecedented levels. As the numbers of Swedes in the United States rapidly increased many times over, they began to take on a distinctive group identity in the eyes of their former and present countrymen, and—not least—in their own estimation as well. In the face of these developments, as well as of difficult problems at home, Swedish thought regarding America, emigration, and the emigrants provided the basis for much painful reappraisal of Swedish society itself, reinforced by the criticisms, both implicit and explicit, of those who had sought new homes in the New World.

In 1865 there can hardly have been more than 25,000 Swedes in the United States. This figure would soon be surpassed by the *annual* immigration from Sweden. By 1890 the United States census showed a Swedish-American population of 776,093.

This massive increase was the result of both "push" factors exerting pressures to leave the old country and "pull" factors providing inducements to do so. In Sweden the first really heavy migration was triggered by disastrous crop failures in 1867 and 1868, which caused widespread misery and ruined large numbers of smallholders and tenant farmers. Swedish emigration increased from 5,893 in 1867 to 21,472 in 1868 and to 32,035 in 1869. Thereafter it declined to relatively modest levels during the good crop years of the 1870s, but again rose steeply in 1879, when it reached 12,761. It remained high thoughout the 1880s, ranging between 17,664 in 1884 and 46,252 persons—the peak year for the entire Swedish emigration—in 1887.

The mass migration of the 1880s was no longer the result of specific crop failures, like that of the later 1860s, but rather of a serious structural crisis facing European agriculture as a whole, due to the development of a worldwide transportation network and the increasing competition of cheap foreign grain on the European market. This came mainly from the American Midwest, where a growing proportion of it was being produced by Swedish immigrant farmers, whose numbers, through the 1880s were steadily increased by shrinking markets and declining prices at home.

The pull from across the Atlantic meanwhile became ever stronger, above all due to the availability in America of free or cheap land through the Homestead Law of 1862 and the railroad land grants; to improved transportation, with steam vessels dominating the Atlantic traffic and with expanding rail networks; to public and commercial promotional activity; and to the growing numbers of Swedes already in America.[1]

The increasing Swedish population in the United States exercised an ever-growing attraction for their relatives and friends in the homeland. Their letters constantly extolled the advantages of the new land, and many emigrants left disintegrating communities at home to join reintegrating communities, consisting largely of relatives and former neighbors, across the sea. During this period, too, the rapid growth of the Swedish-American population led to its spread into new areas of settlement: into the northern Great Lakes states, the Plains region, the East and West Coasts, and even Texas.

Changing conditions led to the emigration of new social strata. The cost of transportation declined, evidently by over one-half, between 1865 and 1890, while wages for agricultural workers rose on the average by about one-third during the same period. Large numbers were now able to travel to America with money or prepaid tickets advanced by relatives or friends already there. Thus progressively poorer elements of Swedish society contributed a growing share of the emigration. Increasingly, too, the emigration consisted of younger, unmarried persons.

The America-letters of this period characteristically reveal a greater prior familiarity with the new land, thus a more level-headed attitude and realistic expectations. This is shown, for instance, by prompter, more calculating responses to changing economic circumstances on both sides of the ocean, as reflected in fluctuating statistics for both emigration and remigration.[2]

Significant changes were taking place in Sweden during this period. It was, in retrospect, an important preparatory phase in Sweden's industrialization, as improved technology made possible the exploitation of great untapped resources.

As yet, however, industrial development could not yet keep pace with population. Close to three-quarters of Sweden's inhabitants remained on the land and largely underemployed in agriculture and related occupations. Working conditions in the new industries were hard and wages often failed to match living costs, leading to incidents of labor unrest, most notably the sawmill strike in Sundsvall, in which several strikers were killed in

1879 when troops were called in to restore order. During the 1880s, both
the trade union movement and the Social Democratic party, representing
the interests of the working classes, had their first beginnings.

The time had not yet come, however, when socialism had any chance
of playing a role in parliamentary politics. In 1866 the ancient Swedish
Riksdag, following a long campaign by the liberals, at last reorganized itself
according to what was now the established European pattern. The four
medieval Estates of the Nobility, Clergy, Burghers, and landowning Peasants
were replaced by a bicameral legislature, elected under a restricted franchise based on income and property.

The same period witnessed even greater changes in the United States.
Responding to military needs during the Civil War and to the vast program
of railroad construction that followed it, America entered into a period of
dynamic industrial development, fueled by European capital and labor.
The transformations wrought by war and industrialization meanwhile exacted their high price: the ordeal of the Deep South during Reconstruction,
the growing concentration of economic power by great moneyed interests
at the expense of smaller producers, the widening gap between wealth
and poverty, the often ruthless exploitation of a largely immigrant labor
force, corrupt politics, and growing slums, to say nothing of the devastating
ugliness of much of America's urban and industrial landscape. The acute
economic crisis of 1873 gave rise to widespread distress. In places there
were symptoms of discontent, including strikes and the beginnings of labor
unions and socialist political parties. The time was approaching when the
discrepancies between traditional American ideals, as understood both in
the United States and abroad, and American realities would become painfully evident.

Yet the years between 1866 and 1888 were, on the whole, prosperous
and expansive ones. Few Swedes had any direct contact with the Deep
South, lived in Eastern cities, or labored in Eastern mines or factories. For
most of them, America still meant the Midwestern farmers' frontier, and
among them the old vision of economic independence and modest well-
being on land of their own still burned bright, even if it could not always
be realized as quickly as before.

As newcomers, Swedes and other Scandinavians were not invariably
well received at first by the established Americans in the places where
they settled. Even as late as 1887 a history of Warren County, Pennsylvania,
in describing how many Scandinavians, especially Swedes, had arrived
there following the Civil War, states:

> Of some of the later immigrants of these nationalities little in praise can be
> said. Coming as common day laborers, with no apparent ambition, they
> have brought their skepticism and drinking habits with them and are not
> infrequently found in the criminal courts. Indeed the personal appearance

of numbers of them is such stunted, bowlegged, flat featured, and eyes without expression [*sic*] that it would seem to be necessary for several generations of them to come and go, ere they will be able to take on the look and action of the typical native American.[3]

Meanwhile, as immigration from southern and eastern Europe dramatically increased during the 1880s, Swedes and other Nordic immigrants tended to look ever better in Anglo-Saxon eyes. The Scandinavians, the Congregational missionary M. W. Montgomery declared already in 1885, following a visit to their native countries, were *"among the best foreigners who come to American shores."*

> For a republic where there is civil and religious liberty ... that foreign element is most desirable which most readily swings into the current of American life, and becomes inspired with the genius of American institutions. They who love liberty *and* religion will make the best citizens for this republic. Just such are the Scandinavians. They are almost universally Protestants; comparatively few of them are skeptics. ... They ardently love the principles upon which our republic rests, and hence are intensely loyal. In politics they are generally Republican.

In "marked contrast with some foreign elements among us," the Reverend Mr. Montgomery noted that the Scandinavians were

> not peddlers, nor organ grinders, nor beggars; they do not sell ready-made clothing nor keep pawn shops; their religion is not hostile to free institutions; they do not ... live a foreign life; ... they do not seek to break down (what is left of) the American Sabbath; they do not make the United States the plotting-ground against the Government of their native land; they do not seek the shelter of the American flag merely to introduce and foster among us ... socialism, nihilism, communism ... *they are more nearly like Americans than are any other foreign peoples.*

In *The Chautauquan* for December 1887, Albert Shaw praised the Scandinavians as "Aryans," Protestants, and "almost ideal pioneer farmers." "They come," he wrote, "from the early home of the English-speaking races, to freshen and re-inforce the American stock. They are a wholesome, virile race ... the Scandinavian element is invaluable." He particularly appreciated that of all non-English-speaking immigrants, they "become the most rapidly Americanized."[4] In actuality, however, it was precisely during this period that Swedish Americans developed their own distinctive cultural profile.

The changing nature of Swedish emigration from the later 1860s on had far-reaching effects upon the cultural patterns of the Swedes in America.

The increasing shift from family to individual migration promoted a more rapid and complete Americanization than before. Young single immigrants without funds from home had to take such work as they could find, wherever they could find it. This tended to bring them into more immediate contact with the older Anglo-American population and its ways than the earlier immigrants, who had generally come over with their families and formed largely isolated rural settlements of their own. Many of the newer immigrants lived and worked in urban environments, at least until they could afford to marry and buy farms of their own. A growing proportion remained city-dwellers.

Of particular importance to this process of cultural adaptation were the women immigrants. Literature and tradition have preserved the often tragic image of the pioneer immigrant wife and mother bearing her burden of hardship, deprivation, and longing on the untamed frontier, surrounded by an alien culture with which she had little contact.

More characteristic among the newer arrivals, however, was the young, unmarried woman, whose case was altogether different. With a still preponderantly male emigration, marriage prospects declined at home, in some places drastically, while a growing oversupply of female labor held wages down to a minimum. In America, meanwhile, families in comfortable circumstances had live-in housemaids and Scandinavian girls were considered particularly desirable for such employment. As domestic servants in America, they were delighted to find, they were not required to do heavy outdoor work, they had rooms of their own, had regular days off, and were paid weekly. They could dress as fashionably as their mistresses, were treated as members of the families they worked for and like "ladies" by American men, who showed them a courtesy and consideration to which they were quite unaccustomed at home. If dissatisfied, they could quit at any time and seldom had any difficulty in finding new positions. The young women immigrants thus tended to adopt American speech and customs more quickly and easily than their male counterparts, who often labored in work gangs made up largely of their own countrymen. The men often envied the relative ease with which the women could find employment and grumbled over their pretentious American airs.

By the time they were married—usually to Swedish men—the younger women had become enthusiastic apostles of American middle-class gentility, which to them represented a distinct rise in their social and cultural status over their peasant origins. It was above all through their determined influence that Swedish-American homes, family life, and social behavior soon came to bear an unmistakably American stamp.[5]

At the same time there were aspects of the newer immigration that powerfully reinforced the preservation of Swedish cultural traditions in America. First and foremost, the vastly increased numbers of Swedes arriving in the United States now provided the critical mass needed to create and sustain a well-developed network of institutions, both religious and secular, necessary for flourishing, organized ethnic life.

Paradoxical as it may seem, increasing individual immigration, while it facilitated the transition into American life, also played an important part in the retention of Swedish culture. Individual immigrants, separated from family and friends at home, felt a greater psychological need for organizations composed of their own countrymen, which could provide a new sense of community in place of that which had been lost. It came, for instance, to be regarded almost as axiomatic that unmarried Swedish house-maids and their generous contributions to the collection plate were the mainstays of Swedish-American urban congregations and of their associated social and benevolent societies.

Improved and cheaper transportation made the Atlantic crossing far less of a barrier, both practical and psychological, than formerly. Single immigrants still had families and close friends in the homeland. Emigration now no longer demanded an almost irrevocable commitment for the future and the newer immigrants did not burn their bridges behind them. It was now easy enough to return home to visit—or to stay. There was ever more movement in both directions across the ocean. These factors, too, made the newer immigrants more inclined than their pioneer predecessors to maintain contact with their homeland and its culture.

The rapid development of Swedish-American institutions to meet the needs of a dramatically expanding immigrant community in turn created its own dynamic. All competed vigorously for recognition, membership, and support, and therefore sought by all available means both to arouse pride in Swedish origins and to evoke that pride as the basis for a sacred obligation to preserve the ancestral heritage.

The period, 1866 to 1889, saw the rapid expansion of the Augustana Lutheran Church, and to a lesser degree of the Swedish-American free churches, such as the Methodists and Baptists. In 1884 those associated with the more pietistic "Mission Friends" (*Missionsvänner*) in Sweden broke out of the Augustana Synod to establish their own variant of Lutheran-ism, the Evangelical Mission Covenant.

Numerous newspapers, both religious and secular, were established wherever Swedes were settled in America. From their presses various periodicals—mainly for religious denominations or social organizations—and books appeared. Indeed, the books were frequently offered as bonuses to the newspapers' subscribers. A milestone in Swedish-American book publishing was reached in 1884 with the establishment of the Augustana Book Concern in Rock Island, Illinois, which was followed by other Swedish publishing houses. The fare they offered consisted mainly of devotional works, together with reprints of books from Sweden and translations from English. The first works of original Swedish-American literature in both verse and prose, were meanwhile usually carried in the newspapers, privately published by their authors, or frequently both.

During the same period, Swedish, or in some cases, Scandinavian secular societies were organized in many American cities. Most frequently they combined mutual benevolence toward members in need with social and, to a degree, cultural activities. Characteristically, like other Swedish-American institutions at this time, they tended to be American in form and procedure but essentially Swedish in content.

It was from this new network of immigrant institutions that what by the end of the century came to be called "Swedish-America" began to take shape, and with it a distinctive Swedish-American identity, which can scarcely be said to have existed before.[6]

FOUR

A Group Portrait
for Those at Home

*I*n Sweden, there had been much interest, since the seventeenth century, in America as a land and in what it was understood to represent. Beginning in the 1840s, emigration and the emigrants themselves became a matter of growing concern. Now, in the decades following the end of the American Civil War and the onset of mass migration from Sweden, a new focus of interest became apparent in the Swedish Americans—those countrymen who were making new lives for themselves in the United States.

More Swedish observers than ever before visited America for longer or shorter periods and published accounts of their travels and experiences. Characteristically, during this period and thereafter, most of them were journalists, or at least functioned as such during their American sojourns. They catered to an obviously broadening interest in America at a time when newspapers were beginning to reach out, for the first time, to a mass market. While most of the Swedish accounts were concerned with America as a whole, all showed considerable interest in the Swedish immigrants; some, indeed, were concerned primarily with them. The most notable of these visitors—with the years of their visits—were Mauritz Rubenson (1867), P. J. Bladh (1871), Hugo Nisbeth (1872–76), Carl Johan Nyvall (1875), Ernst Beckman (1875, 1882), Carl Gestrin (c. 1870–80), Jonas Jonsson Stadling (1880), Isador Kjellberg (1869–72), and Axel E. Lindvall (1888). Since they show on the whole such a marked similarity of views, they are perhaps best dealt with topically and comparatively.

What is most striking about all these accounts is their good will toward and frank admiration of the United States. In praising American conditions, including those prevailing among their emigrated countrymen, their authors explicitly or implicitly justified emigration and thus criticized existing conditions in Sweden, even though they were not blind to America's problems. The exception was P. J. Bladh, who set out determinedly to destroy "the nimbus of humbug which in so many cases surrounds the 'Promised Land' and the conditions prevailing there, which it is in the interests of so many to preserve undisturbed."[1]

The positive consensus during this period can surely be explained in large part by a certain built-in bias. It was only natural that persons sympathetic toward America and anxious to learn useful lessons there should be those most inclined to visit and write about it and that liberal, pro-American newspapers should be interested in sponsoring them. Indeed, since the appearance of C. A. von Hauswolff's lampoon on American social behavior in 1835, no markedly negative Swedish travel account from America had been published. Still, considering the numerous and often acerbic exposés of American conditions by Swedish visitors from the 1890s onward, the favorable view presented by the Swedish travel accounts during this period demands some further explanation.

The 1850s had been, generally speaking, a good time for Sweden. The country enjoyed a wave of agricultural prosperity, and on the political scene there were high hopes for progressive, modern improvements that ultimately culminated with the Riksdag reform passed at the end of 1865. Yet by then the picture had already begun to change. By the later 1850s grain prices declined and indebted farmers faced hard times.

The Riksdag reform, which took effect in 1866, soon gave rise to much disillusionment. Only 5 percent of the population was eligible to vote in Riksdag elections. This contrasted all too unfavorably with the more liberal provisions in Sweden's sister kingdom, Norway, in Great Britain, France, and even Germany after 1871, but above all in the United States, where every adult male citizen was entitled to vote and hold public office.[2] It appeared as though the old aristocracy of birth was being replaced by a new aristocracy of wealth.

Sweden's evident inability to cope effectively with the disastrous crop failures and resulting famine of 1867–69, and thereafter the long agricultural depression of the 1880s, added further to the atmosphere of gloom, discouragement, and frustration that marked the following two decades in Sweden—a time of general prosperity, rapid growth, and high optimism in the United States. Politically as well as economically, developments in Sweden seemed all too often a matter of too little, too late.

The Swedish travel accounts from America, as well as the published debate over emigration during these years, reflect this painful contrast. The appearance in 1879 of August Strindberg's *Röda rummet* (The Red Room), an angry satire on Swedish life and institutions, shattered the placid surface of Swedish late Romantic idealism, clearing the way for the socially critical Realism of the literary "Generation of the 1880s."[3] Jonas Stadling wrote in 1883, "To visit America, and to have felt the strong heartbeat of the great republic and witnessed its intense and healthy economic, intellectual, moral, and religious life is to be strengthened in one's belief in the triumph of good and humanity's continued development and perfectibility. . . . Pessimism does not thrive under America's high, clear sky and in its free and fertile soil. Here youthful vigor and joy prevail everywhere and in all things."[4]

It was only natural that the literary Realists of the 1880s should be fascinated with America. Furthermore, it comes as no surprise that Isador Kjellberg, the most radical of the Swedish visitors to the United States during this period, belonged to the inner circle around Strindberg in the 1880s.[5]

From the Swedish travelers' accounts of the United States during this period there emerge the main outlines of a composite portrait of the Swedish Americans, beginning with their departure from their native shore. Speaking of the various emigrant nationalities aboard the *Austria* en route from Liverpool in 1867, Mauritz Rubenson waxed enthusiastic.

> Among all whom we see, I believe you would agree with me that those emigrants who come from Sweden seem best-off and are most proper in their appearance. Let us, for example, observe that group sitting on their chest painted with flowers. Look at the man, a farmer from the Växjö region, how he, clad in his gray jacket and blue, broad-billed cap, sits and teaches his three small children, girls with blond hair, between ten and six years old, to read God's word, while their mother busies herself with washing clothes and seeing to the household effects they have brought with them.[6]

It was an idyllic picture to counterbalance those presented by conservative opponents of emigration of a traditional way of life threatened by insidious new ideas.

Writing of arriving immigrants at New York's Castle Garden in 1882, Ernst Beckman described a motley crowd of swarthy Italians, quarrelsome Irish, ragged Russian Jews, arrogant English, and loud-mouthed Germans. But at last, "here come, slowly and quietly—it is no shame to admit that you feel your heart beat more warmly at their appearance—here come the quiet, modest group of Swedes, true-hearted tillers of the soil, in coats that bear the mark of the parish tailor, and demure women with flaxen hair and light blue eyes." To Beckman, they were the bearers of a great historic destiny. The immigrants' arrival was recorded in Castle Garden's great record books, "a kind of chronicle of a peaceful conquest, carried out not by warlike rulers but by peaceful cultivators, whose greatest ambition is to plow the earth in the sweat of their brow out on the endless prairie."[7]

Like the America-letters written during this period by the immigrants themselves, the accounts of the Swedish travelers are filled with reports of individual success and of prosperous Swedish-American communities that had developed from humble beginnings within recent years. Looking out over the surrounding countryside from the steeple of the Lutheran church in Center City, Minnesota, in 1888, Axel Lindvall wrote: "A strange feeling came over me at the thought that as far as the eye could reach over that beautiful tract, it is inhabited and owned by *Swedes,* most of whom came here with nothing but hope and confidence that through their own labors they could make a future for themselves here in the remote wilderness."[8]

Similarly, it pleased the travelers to note repeatedly the good reputation their countrymen and other Scandinavians enjoyed in the New World. Already in 1867, Rubenson, for instance, found that his homeland was well known to the more genteel passengers aboard the *Austria,* not only for John Ericsson, Jenny Lind, and Christina Nilsson, but also for "our emigrants," who were regarded as the "best and strongest" of all.[9]

The commentators were in agreement with the earlier emigrant guidebooks that only those accustomed to or at least prepared for hard physical labor—and not too proud to accept whatever they could get—had realistic chances of success in America. On occasion they took note of failures and ne'er-do-wells who proved the point. Beckman spoke in 1877 of "decayed countrymen" of genteel origins in ragged attire who "fearful of the light slink along the house walls" in the larger cities. Bladh—as might be expected—took grim satisfaction in attributing to Chicago the "dubious honor of having received the lion's share of the big and petty swindlers from Sweden who in recent times have preferred exile to prison."

Gestrin meanwhile recounted how a Swedish-American pastor in New York advised him upon arriving to spend what money he had left as soon as possible so that he would be forced to learn the real meaning of honest labor. "The most notable difference," Gestrin continued, "between the Old and the New World is that honest work *of whatever kind it may be* is respected in the New World. That is the most basic principle of American society. Without it, *freedom* and *equality* are empty words. . . . Only after the immigrant has gone through the preparatory school of humiliation and poverty is he ready to learn the first lesson of the republican catechism."[10]

Not all of the immigrants were of peasant or working-class origins. Beckman, for instance, estimated that between 120 and 130 members of Swedish noble families were in America in 1882 and added pointedly that many of them had done well.[11] Characteristically, however, the Swedish American of whatever background took pride in identifying with the man of toil.

The Swedish visitors found their countrymen in America, with few exceptions, well contented with their lot, despite the hardships they had faced. Rubenson in 1867 asked a number of Swedish immigrants in Chicago whether they wished to return to Sweden but always received the same answer: "Sure, if we could do so as wealthy men or for a visit, but as workers, never." From the Red River Valley in Minnesota Ernst Beckman recounted how an immigrant, "alone, exhausted, close to tears after the trials of the long journey," exclaimed upon arrival: "Yes, the trip was extra hard, but you forget everything when you see all that wheat!"[12]

In Goodhue Country, Minnesota, an old farmer from Småland told Axel Lindvall in 1888 how he had lost a farm when cinch bugs had destroyed his grain, but he added: "In spite of all the setbacks I have had to fight against ... I prefer this country. I came over poor, have been rich, and have lost *everything* several times. But it is easier to start over again here than it is in Sweden." Similarly, a Danish settler in Minnesota told Lindvall, when the latter asked whether he might not like to sell his farm and return to his homeland, "This land is too good to leave,"[13]

The Swedish observers were at the same time well aware of the hardships and deprivations that the immigrants had to face. Hugo Nisbeth left a moving account of his meeting with a woman living in a primitive dugout in western Minnesota in the early 1870s. He asked if she were happy there. "Oh, yes, that of course," she replied, "we can't complain, but however that may be you can never really feel at home here," and "the young woman's eyes scanned, as she said that, sorrowfully across the endless prairie."[14]

Ernst Beckman was especially sensitive to the high personal cost of emigration. He noted on occasion how Swedish Americans seemed more worn and bent from heavy labor than persons of the same ages at home. It was generally believed, Beckman wrote elsewhere, that the Homestead Law of 1862 allowed the settler to acquire land for nothing. "For nothing?" Beckman asked. "Yes, if the sad departure from home and fatherland, the dark misgivings over the future, the oppressive deprivation, the wearisome labor of many years count for nothing." Yet he recognized that if starting out in America was harder than elsewhere, once a good beginning was made "prosperity grows almost by itself." Swedish settlers on the Great Plains, he noted, quickly adopted the old American adage that "if you can't have what you want, you had better like what you have." Such words would be cold comfort where work brought no hope, "but they have a different ring when the vision of a little home, surrounded by fields, breaks like a sunbeam through the clouds of present deprivation."[15]

Beckman wrote of the view, often expressed in Swedish poetry and commentary on the emigration, that the Swedes in America were afflicted with homesickness.

This is, however, usually the case with only two kinds of persons: those who have recently come over and those who have had poor luck. ... Otherwise the Swede, especially if he has emigrated in recent years, does not greatly long to return to Sweden. To one's sorrow one even hears Sweden spoken of with scorn. Farmers who are proud of having been poor and of having now become rich speak of their Swedish fatherland as if it had robbed them of their best strength in unrewarding toil. ... And still, I am convinced, if any outsider should make such an accusation against Old Sweden, they would rise up in fury. Deep down they love her. Is it not possible that their bitterness is often an expression of sorrow that the home the farmer has now made for himself, the field he has plowed, does not lie amid firs sighing in the wind and rustling, white-trunked birches across the sea? As for his son, he is completely American.[16]

The Swedish visitors were ever on the watch for signs of attachment to the Old Country and of the preservation of its traditions on American soil. Attending a church service in a rural Minnesota community, Beckman observed:

The church was a real Swedish country church, built both outside and inside in the Swedish peasant fashion and planned by a Swedish master builder. Whitewashed inside. ... The congregation, as far as the menfolk were concerned, could just as well have come in from, for example, a northern Swedish sawmill community. They looked so thoroughly Swedish, honest and orderly. Their backs were perhaps a bit more bent than would be the case with farmers at home, their faces sharper and more furrowed, their hair earlier streaked with gray. Their clothing was about what you would find among our peasantry living near cities. The women were more modern [in appearance].[17]

Hugo Nisbeth described a Swedish Midsummer picnic near Red Wing, Minnesota. "Here were sung the old, patriotic songs, to be sure not always by 'picked men's voices,' but with all the more force and enthusiasm. Here speeches were held for the fatherland. ... It was not hard to find here, too, how deeply and strongly the emigrated Swede is attached to his old homeland. All the deprivations he endured at home are forgotten. In the midst of his prosperity out here he recalls his humble Swedish home."[18]

Yet if the visitors were more eager to find similarities, what often impressed them most were differences in the conditions and customs of the Swedish Americans from those of the homeland. Most striking were contrasts in the physical environment, which became ever greater as the settlers advanced out onto the Great Plains. Describing a visit to the home of Pastor Erland Carlsson in Andover, Illinois, which seemed to him a typical Swedish parsonage as well as a stronghold of Swedish culture, Ernst Beckman was struck by the contrast with its altogether un-Swedish surroundings. The landscape seemed to him like a frozen sea with its rolling waves of rustling pale yellow corn, where buffalo had grazed not many years before. And the scattered farmsteads on the open prairie were like verdant islands on a gently rolling sea.[19]

Reaching the plains in the Red River Valley on his second visit, Beckman was repelled by the desolation of the landscape, especially after spending a night in a flea-ridden sod hut. Yet he was prepared to admit that "fresh winds blow across the plains. The air is filled with a seething lust to work, with youthful courage which day after day wins new victories for cultivation. And when you see the dense prairie grass or the golden wheat bend before the wind, when occasional clouds sailing across the sky break the grass-green monotony with their shadows—the landscape itself has a certain attraction: it reveals something of the freedom of the boundless sea."[20]

While the Swedish observers on the whole stressed the success and prosperity of their countrymen in America and considered their prospects better on the land than in the cities, they noted variations, especially between older and more recent areas of settlement. Pastor Nyvall, visiting Kansas and Nebraska, painted a particularly depressing picture: "When one gets to know through firsthand contacts what pioneer life in America is like, one wonders how people can endure it. It seemed to me, however, as if some have become so accustomed to living in these hovels that they are not very eager to improve their circumstances."[21]

The implication here was that either the harsh conditions of pioneer life or unfortunate influences from the older Americans accounted for such low standards. Yet other Swedish observers were inclined to place the blame upon the Swedish immigrants themselves. Jonas Stadling, for instance, "saw more than one Swedish family living together with chickens and pigs in a dugout or shanty in which the stench was unbearable, where I heard the same raw oaths as in Sweden, and saw no reading matter other than the Swedish hymnal and the Long Catechism. Among families which had lived longer in the country, there were sometimes also English newspapers and books. Much better behavior was noted among the children who had been brought up in America."

Still, Stadling considered his countrymen soberer and better-behaved in America than in Sweden, and their homes cleaner, neater, and more pleasant. Isador Kjellberg held that "the *Swedish* homes in America, as far as cleanliness and simple good taste are concerned, can hardly be compared with the American ones." The American example could, meanwhile, work wonders. Freed from the "deplorable class barriers" of the Old World, and through "daily contact with enlightened and decent people in different walks of life," Kjellberg had been gratified to see how "young, skilled, and respectable workingmen" from Sweden were so transformed for the better that they were "almost unrecognizable to one who had observed them under other, less favorable circumstances in their old homeland."[22]

Of the Swedish Americans in Chicago, Ernst Beckman noted in 1875 that while their hospitality was "genuinely Swedish," their "way of life and of thinking [is] otherwise, as far as I have been able to determine, quite

American."[23] In no respect did this seem more evident than in the case of the women, to whom the Swedish travelers gave much attention.

The most symbolic and hence the most striking manifestation of their new self-image was their dress. "In vain," Hugo Nisbeth wrote following a church service in Wasa, Minnesota,

> I here expected to see something of Swedish peasant dress, but of it there was no trace. The men were dressed in decent, American suits, but to judge by the women's apparel one would have been more inclined to believe oneself to be at a spectacle in Stockholm rather than in a Swedish farmers' church located in the extreme west of the cultivated part of America. . . . Not only here, but everywhere else where I have been in America, I have found that no one is as quick and willing as the Swede to accept the true American's weakness for dressing his womenfolk well.[24]

Swedish visitors were particularly impressed with the special role given to the hat as the insignia, par excellence, of feminine respectability. In Sweden, ladies wore hats whereas peasant women wore shawls or kerchiefs. By 1882 Ernst Beckman noted that some women emigrants acquired hats before leaving Gothenburg. At a Minnesota church service he recalled seeing ladies' hats "of every conceivable type."[25]

The Swedish maids in New York gave remarkable proof of "the fair sex's wonderful ability to adapt to circumstances," Carl Gestrin observed. "The six months it has taken to reduce the 'gentleman' emigrant to a mere shadow of his former self have changed his mother's servant girl into a *lady*—or something close to it."

> What a change! Regard one of these girls. . . . Civilization's blessings have rained down upon her. . . . Some months ago [when she was] a newly arrived immigrant, a bundle of clothes and a good conscience were all she possessed. She was soon separated from the former, for it contained only old-fashioned things. Might she also have been separated as quickly from the innocence of her heart? Most probably not, for good clothing improves not only the appearance, but also serves to raise self-esteem. Give a poor girl the chance to acquire, through honest work, good clothes and she will think more highly of herself and in like measure make herself respected by others.

"New strength has come to the surface," Gestrin reflected. "Society recruits constantly from its lowest strata, as the trees of the forest draw nurture from roots which lie hidden in the earth."[26]

More, indeed, was involved than outward finery, as Gestrin recognized. August Andrén, a farmer in Halland who cut railroad ties in Nebraska in 1867, gave a colorful account of the social activities of the Scandia Society in Omaha, in which the Swedish girls involved imposed, deftly but firmly, strict American standards of etiquette upon their escorts.[27]

The Swedish visitors—like European observers generally in this period—were much impressed by the independence, directness of manner, and interest in public affairs of American woman, whom they considered intellectually and culturally superior to the more practical-minded American men.[28] Swedish-American girls born or at least raised in the United States showed the same characteristics. Ernst Beckman was much taken in 1882 with a "Miss Janson," a young woman with no recollection of the Old Country, who received him as hostess at her father's prosperous farm in Minnesota. She spoke "like a book" in good, pure Swedish, although naturally with her parents' rustic pronunciation, and eagerly discussed Scandinavian politics, which had been debated by her young people's literary society. Here she and her friends sought as best they could to "slake a thirst for knowledge which in America is in the air. A farm girl who goes in for politics and literary exercises—is that not indeed rather American? That designation may seem either good or bad, as one will."[29]

Children in America had a different upbringing, and to European visitors they seemed willful, undisciplined, and often disrespectful toward their elders. Always eager to find a mitigating explanation, Beckman pointed out how ideas on child-raising differed significantly from European ones: "Blind obedience and physical chastisement they avoid like the plague. . . . One must deal carefully with a free citizen in a free country. One allows him to use his own judgment, appeals to his sense of honor, and in nine cases out of ten he obeys cheerfully, willingly, and with his head held high. . . . Here they seek above all to encourage independence."[30]

Relations between immigrant parents and their children were intimately connected to the language question. Beckman was given to understand in 1882 that Swedes in America were now more attached to their native tongue than they had been a decade or so earlier, when it had at times encountered downright ill will. There were still some parents who did not want their children to hear any Swedish at all. But in most families children were taught both Swedish and English. Among themselves, the children generally seemed to prefer to speak English; "Swedish seems difficult and awkward to them." There was, moreover, an important, additional consideration that would generally be overlooked in the voluminous discussion of the language issue in the time to come: "In English they speak as properly as anyone else; when they open their mouths to speak Swedish, what comes out is a peasant dialect, which they are ashamed of." Clergymen complained that young people were often impatient at having to listen to sermons in Swedish. Beckman concluded that the Swedish language had a future in America only as long as the immigration continued.

Like so many other Swedish commentators after him, Beckman was wistfully bemused by his emigrated countrymen's pragmatic and unsentimental mixing of liberal doses of half-digested English into their Swedish vernacular, with results that in cultivated Swedish ears could only sound comical or grotesque. In one respect, meanwhile, Swedish-American usage revealed an underlying transformation in social relationships. Swedish Americans, Beckman noted, liked to be addressed as "Mr.," "Mrs.," or "Miss," but with visitors from Sweden they pointedly used the informal pronoun, *du,* without the traditional formality of "laying aside titles." In this there was often "a blunt little barb of pridefulness," he observed. "But is it not right that they, who for centuries have condescendingly been addressed as *du* by any dandy in gentleman's clothing, should repay in kind and say *du* in return? Of course, let us gladly admit."[31]

There were meanwhile two institutions that above all served to keep alive Swedish language and culture in America: the pulpit and the press. Toward the Swedish-American churches—and especially toward the largest and most influential of them, the Augustana Lutheran Synod—the Swedish visitors had mixed and largely negative views. Almost all were critical of the Augustana Synod to a greater or lesser extent, despite its manifest commitment to preserving the Swedish heritage. Such hostility primarily reflects the backgrounds of those who naturally felt most drawn to visit the United States. As liberal-minded admirers of American principles, they were strong proponents of religious freedom and tolerance and reacted against anything that smacked of dogmatic orthodoxy or narrow exclusivity. Nyvall was moreover a Mission Friend and Stadling a Baptist.

The Americans took their religion seriously, as Jonas Stadling found upon his arrival in 1880. He was astonished to hear religious questions widely discussed in public, whereas "in Sweden one is almost considered a fanatic if one begins to talk about religion on a journey or in general conversation." The flight of the persecuted Eric Janssonists from Sweden in the 1840s—like that of the seventeenth-century Puritans from England—had given, Ernst Beckman maintained, "an aura of godliness—if not martyr-dom—to the earliest emigration." "Presumably," he added, "the historical background of this emigration has contributed in no small measure to the fact that the Swedes in the United States have made religion as vital a concern as it has always been among America's own children."[32]

In Sweden the Lutheran state church was by its very nature broad enough to shelter various theological tendencies and open to all who belonged to it by right of birth. In America Augustana Lutheranism was free of such constraints, and with their greater autonomy many of its congregations, like those of the Swedish-American "free churches," imposed their own standards of piety and Christian morality.[33] The opposite side of the coin was that so intense a commitment to church and creed led all too often to stolid dogmatism and acrimonious doctrinal strife, which educated and broad-minded visitors from Sweden found particularly distasteful, not least among the representatives of Swedish Lutheranism in America.

Of the four Swedish churches then in Chicago—the others being Methodist, Baptist, and Episcopalian—Mauritz Rubenson in 1867 found the Lutheran church the least impressive, located behind a tailor shop and the office of the newspaper *Hemlandet* housed in the same building. Here he found the parish school,

> one of the sorriest sights I have been witness to . . . a narrow and unhealthy room, where several children of different ages sat drooping over the catechism. It was also evident from the children's faces that they suffered under the burden placed upon them. I asked the teacher—a man who, parenthetically, looked as though he had gone through the Catholic seminary in Quebec—what the children were actually studying, and received the reply that they were to learn the Swedish language and religion, to which he added that the more enterprising also receive *some* instruction in English. These children are being brought up to be citizens of one of the freest of countries, where upon maturity they enjoy the same rights and privileges as the native-born. What use have they for the exclusive study of the Swedish language? How are they benefitted by spending years of their time in memorizing the catechism?[34]

With certain exceptions, the Swedish-American clergy did not create a favorable impression. At the celebration of Reformation Day in Chicago in 1867, Mauritz Rubenson found the the assembled Lutheran divines and seminarians a sorry lot. Similarly Robert Nisbeth commented: "One can hardly expect better results, when it is born in mind that the university students [at Augustana College and Seminary in Paxton] consist for the most part of young peasant lads who, without having the slightest educational background, for three years cram in a mass of undigestible stuff, on the basis of which they are then to go out to edify the world. Anything more revolting can hardly be imagined than to listen to their illogical mish-mash from the pulpit."[35]

Not only did the Augustana clergy seem ignorant to visitors from a land with strong traditions of a learned pastorate, their motives could appear suspect, even sinister. When Mauritz Rubenson asked "various persons" in Chicago about the Lutheran parish school, he received the reply: "If the children do not study Swedish and the catechism, the Lutheran pastors will in the future lose their church as well as their congregation." C. J. Nyvall and Jonas Stadling meanwhile deplored the Augustana Synod's dogmatic refusal to cooperate in any way with other denominations.[36]

The ever fair-minded Ernst Beckman was saddened by the spectacle of sectarian strife among his countrymen in America and recognized that the Augustana Synod suffered from "deplorable faults . . . which are all the more serious as the denomination itself regards them as shining virtues." "These faults derive principally from one and the same source: high ecclesiastical intolerance. It is really true that in the midst of the land of religious tolerance, Augustana, together with one or two sister churches, stands enclosed within the gray walls of religious bigotry." These were hard words indeed from the son of a bishop in the Swedish Lutheran state church.[37]

The radical Isador Kjellberg and the anti-American, conservative P. J. Bladh were also bitter and direct in their accusations. The Augustana church, Kjellberg held, was the conspiracy of a coterie out to gain a fat living for itself. To assure their wealth and power they strove to "keep the immigrated Swedes apart from the Americans, ignorant of the institutions and people of the land and of its language, and so forth, all the while talking about Swedish nationality, of the blessing of being able to hear 'the sacred Word in the beloved Swedish mother tongue,' etc., as though there were any question about preserving Swedish nationality and Swedish language in America! As though it were not best for every Swedish immigrant to become Americanized as soon as possible!" His advice to prospective emigrants ended with the admonition to "avoid and oppose, to your own and others' advantage, Swedish clergymen and Swedish denominations." America, Bladh maintained, would be a better place with far fewer rascals if all the pietist preachers were drowned in the depths of the sea.[38]

Considering the currents of opinion they represented in Sweden, the reactions of these Swedish observers to religious life among their compatriots in America are understandable. They were not unwilling to give credit where credit was due. Both C. J. Nyvall and Ernst Beckman were present at the dedication in 1875 of the new Augustana College and Seminary building in Rock Island, and were impressed by the commitment to learning and to Swedish culture it represented. Even the anticlerical Kjellberg admitted that there were at least some "good people" in the Augustana Synod.[39]

While C. J. Nyvall expressed sympathy over the hardships his clerical brethren faced on the Midwestern frontier, none of the Swedish visitors seem truly to have understood the full range of problems confronting the Swedish-American churches at this time.[40] The earliest Swedish Lutheran clergymen in America were men of peasant background, who had sacrificed much to attain ordination, rather than representatives of the old established clerical families at home. During the early years of their struggle to build a Lutheran church among their countrymen in the new land they faced the chagrin of seeing the Lutheran state church in Sweden favor the Episcopalian Gustaf Unonius and the hierarchical church he represented as the preferred affiliation for arriving Swedish immigrants. No wonder the Augustana Synod, from its beginning in 1860, showed a decided siege mentality, with regard both to competing denominations in America and to the established Church of Sweden.

The one clear advantage of Lutheranism in the battle for Swedish souls in America was its unquestionable appeal as the traditional folk religion with which the great majority of Swedes automatically identified. As the migration reached mass proportions, the Augustana Synod increasingly arrogated to itself the role not only of the true "Swedish" church but also that of the stronghold of the Swedish heritage in America. It is moreover true that the synod—like other Swedish-American church groups—in its genuine concern for both the spiritual and the temporal well-being of its flock, did encourage and promote compact rural colonization by its members, if possible led by their pastors, in preference to more scattered or especially to urban settlement, as shown by the founding of a number of organized colonies in the Midwestern states during this period. An early step in this direction was the removal of Augustana College and Seminary from Chicago to rural Paxton already in 1863, three years after their establishment.

The synod was only beginning, after heroic efforts, to get its house in order when it was almost overwhelmed by the mass immigration of the later 1860s, followed not long after by that of the 1880s. Despite the commitment of T. N. Hasselquist and the synod leadership to the ideal of a learned clergy, this goal became practically impossible to uphold when faced with the urgent need for new congregations and for pastors to serve them. America now appeared more than ever the golden opportunity for numerous ambitious peasant lads in Sweden who lacked background and prospects for clerical careers at home.[41]

Aside from the churches, the most effective cultural force among the Swedes in America was the periodical press. Considering that almost all the Swedish commentators on the United States in this period were journalists of some kind it seems somewhat surprising that they did not write more on this subject. However, Mauritz Rubenson was particularly critical of the Lutheran *Hemlandet* in Chicago, which to him represented the narrow intolerance of the Augustana Synod and which engaged in an acrimonious running battle with the "liberal" or secular Swedish-American papers.[42]

Ernst Beckman presented a fuller picture from 1882. He found it remarkable that "these papers, which are published in a far-away land in the Swedish language are, both figuratively and literally, so many-sided" and that they commanded so much talent. They were not notable for their literary style, but in them one found

> so much the more of an ability, not easily mastered by us Swedes from home with our more round-about ways of expressing ourselves, to get right to the point, to adapt their language to their readership, and to avoid the usual confusion between a newspaper article and an editorial—this last may result from the fact that even the most educated among the Swedish-American newspaperman have learned more from life than out of books. ... The strength of the Swedish-American press lies, meanwhile ... in its spreading of general enlightenment. The Swede usually knows no English when he first comes over. He has very few books. His newspaper provides practically his only reading. Thus, for the immigrant, the Swedish-American newspaper

becomes in a very special sense a bridge between past and present, a cultural bond between the old homeland and the new.[43]

Yet in the polemic exchanges between the leading Swedish-American newspapers Beckman perceived an essential cleavage over what the nature and function of this "bridge" ought to be, behind which lay the basic paradox of Swedish-American life. The Lutheran *Hemlandet,* above all others, sought in every way to strengthen "those bonds woven of love for the cherished sounds of the mother tongue and reverence for the old homeland with its memories." As Beckman described it, "The Swedish heritage is, according to *Hemlandet,* a valuable contribution to the life of America. It is a precious inheritance which it is the Swede's responsibility carefully to preserve. It must not suffocate, not be washed away, not even pushed out by the new language and new ways of thinking."

Svenska Tribunen, the next largest of the Swedish-American newspapers, which represented a secular, liberal view, had the opposite orientation:

> Giving all due recognition to the Swedish heritage as such, [Beckman wrote,] it maintains that anyone who has chosen to cast his lot in America should give highest priority to the English language and American values. Does not the new homeland have the *right* to demand such a sacrifice? . . . In America Swedish is only a transitional language. . . . Let us hope—*Tribunen* says straight out—that Swedish will not be our children's language. At least may they understand that it should be regarded more as an ornament, a noble but not indispensable pleasure. From *Tribunen*'s viewpoint it naturally follows that even *newspapers* in the Swedish language belong only to a transitional phase.[44]

The Swedish visitors were well impressed with the Swedish clubs and societies they encountered. August Andrén described the social events put on by the Scandia Society in Omaha, which was open to all Scandinavians, in 1867. He also recalled its debates on current questions, its men's chorus, its sick benefits and assistance to needy countrymen, and not least its elaborate American rules of order. The same year Mauritz Rubenson, visiting the Svea Society in Chicago, was greatly impressed with how ordinary immigrant workingmen had mastered parliamentary procedure and proper decorum. According to one of its leading personalities, Anders Larson, in 1876, the Svea Society had lost a library of over two thousand books in the Chicago fire of 1871, but had since acquired nearly eight hundred new ones.[45]

In contrast to other nationalities in America, the Swedes were not greatly involved with politics initially. "As for their general political position," Ernst Beckman observed in 1882, "the Swedes are warmly attached to the republican form of government. Without having ever really thought deeply about different types of government, they are convinced of the superiority of the republic."[46] He might have added that they were also mainly loyal supporters of the Republican party, the party of Lincoln, of free men—and of free land.

Factious as the Swedish Americans could often be among themselves, they were largely united in the feeling that they were misrepresented and misunderstood in their old homeland. Swedish visitors met with suspicion when it became evident that they were journalists. "Now you'll go home and run down America," a Swedish farmer in Minnesota told Hugo Nisbeth. When the latter denied the charge and asked why this should be, the farmer replied: " Lord, as if you didn't know, who are a scribbler of that sort! You see, it's the big landowners who don't want to lose their cotters and hired folk, whom they pay low wages to and work hard from morning to evening, who get the newspapers to write that way. You know yourself how they lie and how little they know."[47]

Ernst Beckman met with similar accusations, and like Nisbeth had to admit that the Swedish press was all too often clearly biased against America. But to try in this way to discourage prospective emigrants was, as Beckman explained in 1877, worse than useless, "in our day, when a letter from America costs only five cents and when the Swedish Americans are reckoned in the hundreds of thousands, the truth will always find ways to come to the knowledge of those most interested." The result was, he wrote in 1883, that "when it comes to America, our people obviously put no faith in the Swedish newspapers. . . . Meanwhile, it is very hard to open the common man's eyes also to the bad sides of America." "Everywhere I am overwhelmed with questions about America," wrote Gustaf Peters, an Augustana Lutheran pastor on a visit to Sweden in 1867. "The upper classes and the ministers think it is entirely bad; the peasants think it is wholly good. The truth lies midway between the two extremes."[48]

The only way, according to both Nisbeth and Beckman, that the Swedish press could be useful in regard to emigration—since it could not hope to stop it—would be to pursue a policy of balanced objectivity so that it could restore its credibility and allow individuals to make sober and informed decisions.[49]

In fairness it must be recognized that Swedish Americans often had as exaggerated ideas about opinion in Sweden as Swedish critics had about America. Far from all that came out in Sweden during these years was hostile toward America and its Swedish inhabitants. Indeed, the newspaper articles of Nisbeth, Beckman, Stadling, Kjellberg, and the other Swedish visitors to the United States at this time, and the books which reprinted them, are the clearest proof that Swedish-American fears and suspicions could be greatly overdrawn.[50]

The Creation of a
Swedish-American Identity

From at least the later 1860s there was a small but growing traffic in the opposite direction, of Swedish Americans traveling to the Old Country. Although none of them published books entirely devoted to their visits home in this period, their commentaries and accounts cast light not only on existing differences between the old and new homelands but also upon the Swedish Americans' own developing self-image.

To a friend in Sweden, Anders Larson wrote in 1874 that he would like to revisit the land he had left nearly thirty years before but imagined he would now find himself "a stranger amid a new generation." Younger immigrants felt less hesitant, and Larson noted several times in the mid-1870s how many Chicago Swedes traveled to Sweden with the intention of remaining there, but that most soon returned. Speaking of a group that had departed in 1876, Larson noted the following spring that all were back in Chicago, claiming they did not feel comfortable in Sweden thanks to the social snobbery, the luxury and ostentation among the wealthy, widespread drunkenness, and superficiality in religious life. Isador Kjellberg likewise observed that few old Swedish Americans felt at home in Sweden.[1]

The most notable Swedish-American visitor to the old homeland in this period was Hans Mattson, whose life was truly an American success story. An emigrant from Skåne in 1851, he had been one of the first Swedish settlers in Minnesota, had served with distinction as a colonel in the Union army during the Civil War, and thereafter as Minnesota's secretary of state. During 1868–69 he was in Sweden for the Minnesota Immigration Board to recruit settlers. He was back again between 1871 and 1876 on extended visits as the Northern Pacific Railroad's chief emigrant agent. These visits are described in his well-known *Reminiscences,* which came out in both English and Swedish in 1891, two years before his death.

Colonel Mattson was doubtless the most celebrated Swedish American of his time, the most prominent living symbol of his nationality's success in and patriotic devotion to its new homeland. He was thus able to speak with a certain authority as a spokesman for the Swedish element in America. Throughout, his reminiscences express his unwavering attachment to the democratic ideals of the American republic, together with his pride in his Swedish origins.[2]

Hans Mattson's presence in Sweden created quite a stir. Of his first visit in 1868–69 he recalled: "At that time only a few Swedish emigrants had returned from America, and to see a man who had been eighteen years in America, and had been a colonel in the American army must have been a great curiosity, especially to the country people; for wherever it was known that I would pass, people flocked from their houses to the roads and streets in order to catch a glimpse of the returned traveler."[3]

There followed a season of visits and entertainments in the neighborhood.

> I was received with cordiality everywhere among the common people and the middle classes, while the aristocratic classes looked on with distant coldness, as they always do when a man of the people has succeeded in getting beyond what they would call his legitimate station, and is what we would call, in other words, a self-made man. My plain name and humble ancestry were in their eyes a fault that never could be forgiven. This did not trouble me, however, for I sought no favors, or even recognition from the great, but found plenty of delight in the cordial welcome of the middle classes.

It nonetheless gave him no small satisfaction when he, who had long been a Freemason in America, was received by the Kristianstad lodge, where he marched in procession between two barons, "wearing their gorgeous uniforms, while I was dressed only in a plain black dress suit." "Here is the key to the greatness of this country [America]," Mattson reflected, "Labor is respected, while in most other countries it is looked down upon with slight."[4]

Already on his first day in Sweden in 1868, Mattson was stirred to indignation by an unpleasant little incident of class snobbery involving a poor woman in the Malmö railway station.

> To me [Mattson wrote,] it was a striking example of the difference between Swedish and American ways and courtesy. I venture to say that in no railway station or other public place in the whole United States ... would a poor woman in her circumstances be left one minute without a friend and protector. Men of all classes,—from the millionaire to the day-laborer, or even the street loafer,—would have vied with each other trying to be the first to render her assistance.[5]

Mattson, the plain man and simple citizen of the American republic, showed little sympathy and at best ironic amusement at the institutions and traditions of the Swedish monarchy while stoutly defending the American system of elected public officials. He watched a military review in Kristianstad in which "a large number of finely-uniformed officers, many of them grey with age and service, their breasts covered with decorations and crosses ... reviewed a couple of dozen soldiers with an air of solemn dignity, which might have done honor to a Grant, a Sherman, or a Sheridan, while reviewing our hundreds and thousands of veterans of a hundred battlefields." Moreover, the Union colonel observed, military command, especially in peacetime, required less ability than almost any branch of business.[6]

The ancient and traditional pageantry of monarchy left Mattson unmoved. Describing the ceremonial opening of the Riksdag in 1872, he wrote:

> With all respects for old Swedish customs and manners, I cannot but compare this pageant to a great American circus—minus the menagerie, of course. I would like to describe this serio-comical demonstration for the benefit of my American readers; but I am sorry to say that I can no longer remember the titles of the different officers, heralds, guards, lackeys, pages, etc.,—all of them dressed in the most gorgeous costumes, some of them preceding, others following the king and the royal princes, who were adorned with all the medieval clap-trap insignia of royalty, and wrapped in huge mantles of gay colors, and with long trains borne by courtiers or pages. We can comprehend the importance of a display of this kind a couple of centuries ago, but it seems to me that the common sense of our times demands its abolishment.

Visiting Drottningholm Palace that summer, Mattson and other Americans present agreed it would be an appropriate location for "some charitable institution." When shortly after he traveled on the Göta Canal, he took pride in the peaceful but largely unsung accomplishments of the Swedish people, whose history was still mainly taught as "warfare and the exploits of kings." In fairness it should be mentioned that he was nonetheless very favorably impressed by the personal qualities of the young Oscar II.[7]

Mattson recruited emigrants with great success. During the winter of 1868 he found himself "besieged by people who wished to accompany me back to America in the spring." This unquestionably affected the attitudes he encountered:

> On the whole the first visit to Sweden was exceedingly pleasant, although there would occasionally come up disagreeable incidents whenever America was the subject of discussion. The laboring and middle classes already at that time had a pretty correct idea of America, and the fate that awaited emigrants there; but the ignorance, prejudice and hatred toward America

and everything pertaining to it among the aristocracy, and especially the office holders, was as unpardonable as it was ridiculous. It was claimed by them that all was humbug in America, that it was the paradise of scoundrels, cheats and rascals, and that nothing good could possibly come out of it. They looked upon emigrants almost as criminals, and to contradict them was a sure means of incurring their personal enmity and even insult.[8]

A very different kind of visitor to Sweden was Ernst Teofil Skarstedt, the son of an eminent theologian in Lund, who had emigrated in 1879 and after various misadventures had become a journalist in Chicago's secular Swedish-American press. Early in 1885, he sought to realize his dream of a simple life in the wilderness—like Gustaf Unonius and Henry David Thoreau before him—by moving with his family out to the Washington Territory. After some months he decided to travel with the family back to Sweden to obtain a loan from his father to buy a farm on the slopes of Mount Bell. The story of their visit is recounted in Skarstedt's memoirs, published in 1914.[9]

Skarstedt realized that he had badly offended both his father and his socially pretentious stepmother by giving up his university studies, marrying beneath his own social class, and going off to America, but he longed both for reconciliation and for the freedom to live his own life that a loan would give him. Still, he felt disquieting misgivings:

Our friends in America claimed to know in advance that we would be disappointed with Sweden. . . . Dr. John Rundström consoled me with the thought that the journey need not necessarily be in vain. "It will be a lesson for the future," he explained. "You will, when you return to America, find yourself happy in being able to consider yourself the citizen of a land which, with its magnanimous people, its free institutions, and its rich, indeed inexhaustible resources stands first among all the countries of the world." Magnus Elmblad spoke in a similar tone. "I have long suspected," he wrote, "that you, like myself, would sooner or later run your head against that stone-hard mass of arrogance and vanity, stupidity and disguised humbug which like a monstrous nightmare hangs heavy upon Sweden's so-called educated classes."[10]

Upon arriving in the land of his birth, Skarstedt found himself strangely unmoved. The family was hospitably received by relatives and friends in and around Gothenburg, but they also encountered "unpleasant signs of Swedish snobbery . . . in curt replies from maids, concierges, and headwaiters, and in the haughty and self-important manner of officials and others, all things which an American citizen never can accustom himself to."[11]

Skarstedt, who wished to be "as free and independent in my dress, habits, and behavior as I had been in America," soon found that he had to make galling concessions. Not only was he constrained to wear a collar and tie, he also had to have his two children baptized before his father would receive them in Lund. "In my aroused state of mind," he recalled, "I thought I found humbug in every possible thing. I saw so much hypocrisy, obsequiousness, timidity, sanctimoniousness, and self-importance around me that I was outraged to the core." Lost and disconsolate, he regularly visited Lund's botanical gardens, where "a few languishing specimens of Douglas fir from the Oregon and Washington Territories and of California's mammoth [redwood] trees made me dream of the peaceful primeval forest on the shores of the Pacific Ocean and of a home of one's own under their sheltering branches."[12]

The root of the evils Skarstedt saw around him was quite evidently an antiquated class system, demeaning both to the upper and lower levels of society. He complained of the raw, uncouth behavior of the common third-class passengers on the trains, who drank heavily, swore loudly, and told indecent stories in the presence of women and children. "We understood, naturally, that such scenes could not take place except in the third-class compartments, and wondered whether it were not the absence of this class division on the trains in America that made everyone there try to behave decently, or whether it were a lack of self-control in the Swedish character which made the class division in Sweden necessary." He found "arrogance on the one side and obsequiousness on the other, a manifest scorn for menial labor, a desire to appear to be more than one was."[13]

Like other Swedish Americans, Skarstedt was particularly touchy over Swedish prejudices toward the land of his choice. "At all events, America seemed to us to stand in most respects so far ahead of Sweden, and therefore nothing irritated me so much as when I heard persons who did not know the least thing about America pass self-confident judgment upon its civilization and conditions in general, commiserate with the emigrants, and depreciate or dismiss the advantages which the latter had gained. If I, in all modesty, told something about America, it could happen that in reply I was informed that this could not possibly be so or that the matter was better understood in Sweden."[14]

It was on the whole a sad and unprofitable visit to the old homeland and Skarstedt and his family returned to the American Northwest in early 1886 with no more than a mere pittance from his father.

Together, the authors of the two principal Swedish-American travel accounts from these decades make an oddly assorted pair. Yet both reveal the same unwaivering commitment to the American ideals of freedom and equality in public and in private life, of the dignity of honest labor, and of republican plainness and simplicity—the very values that the liberal-minded Swedish visitors to the United States also prized most highly during this same period.

To describe the Swedish Americans simply in terms of their attitudes toward American and Swedish values is not sufficient in itself. They needed in addition a more positive, ideal image of themselves, a basic Swedish-American ideology. This was provided during these very years by Johan Alfred Enander.

If Hans Mattson was the most outwardly prominent Swedish American of his time, Johan Enander was unquestionably the most influential Swedish-American opinionmaker. Born of peasant background in Västergötland, he had acquired some experience in journalism before emigrating in 1869 to the United States. He there entered the Augustana Seminary to prepare for the ministry, but its rector, T. N. Hasselquist, found a more suitable outlet for young Enander's talents when he was the same year appointed editor of the Augustana Synod's newspaper *Hemlandet* in Chicago. It was an inspired choice. Enander remained *Hemlandet*'s editor throughout most of his career, except for a few years in the 1890s when he served as professor of Swedish language and literature at Augustana College. In 1889 he was appointed United States minister to Denmark, but personal circumstances compelled him to decline. He was meanwhile involved in the publication of various other periodicals.[15]

From the beginning of his editorship, Enander made *Hemlandet* the leading organ for instilling pride in the Swedish heritage and for promoting its preservation in America. He was himself an outstanding representative of a long tradition glorifying the past greatness of the Swedish race, extending back at least to the fifteenth century and best exemplified by Olof Rudbeck (1630–1702), who identified Sweden with the lost Atlantis, the cradle of civilization itself. The Rudbeckian heritage in Sweden was strongly reinforced by the nineteenth-century Romantic movement, which sought ideals for the present in the mists of Nordic antiquity. By the 1860s and 1870s, Swedish cultural life was thoroughly pervaded by the imagery and rhetoric of the Old Norse heritage.

Enander was meanwhile very much a man of his time and culture in envisioning the editorship of a leading newspaper as a position of high moral responsibility and leadership. Increasingly he came to be regarded—and regarded himself—as the tribune of his people, their natural "chieftain," or *hövding*, in the old Nordic tradition.[16]

Already in 1874, five years after arriving in America, Enander commenced publication of a five-part history of the United States in Swedish, completed in 1880. Offered as a bonus to *Hemlandet*'s subscribers, later reprinted in numerous editions, even translated into Norwegian and in part into English, it probably received a wider distribution than any other Swedish-American book publication ever. Its purpose, Enander proclaimed in his forward, was to "arouse, nourish, and increase my compatriots' love for our [American] homeland, its freedom and independence"; at the same time he strove to reveal the outstanding role the Swedish nationality had played in America's history since its earliest beginnings, "so that the piety of our fathers and their love of freedom and country may stand as an inspiration for those generations that now live in this land. ... May these memories from our nationality's heroic past never fade, and may the civic virtues, which were our fathers' proudest trait, never be found wanting in the future among the descendants of the Scandinavian North, who live upon American soil."[17]

In the stout volumes of his history, Enander gave extensive treatment to the Scandinavians' Viking ancestors, the real discoverers of America. The other central episode in Enander's treatment was the story of Sweden's seventeenth-century colony on the Delaware and the later fortunes of the colonists and their descendants. Evidently for practical reasons, Enander dealt in only brief and summary fashion with the then ongoing nineteenth-century Swedish immigration to the United States, but his loving treatment of these earlier themes gave him ample scope to develop and expound his vision of a proud and unique Swedish-American identity. His views were further reinforced, in even more rhetorical fashion, by a number of public speeches which Enander, a stirring orator, gave during this period and later published in 1892.[18]

Of prime importance to the image Enander strove to create was the antiquity of the Nordic, including the Swedish, presence in North America, and thus his people's birthright in the New World, which long predated the founding of the United States. Building upon an already well-established tradition in America, Enander declared the Scandinavian Northmen to have been the first European discoverers and colonizers of North America around 1000 A.D. and maintained that Columbus only undertook his Atlantic voyage in 1492 after having heard stories of the great continent to the west during a visit to Iceland in 1477. In a speech entitled "A Dream," given in Chicago in 1890, Enander pictured a thriving and long-lived Norse colony in Vinland, which, he conjectured, had only finally succumbed to the Black Death in the mid-fourteenth century.[19] Here Enander tread on uncertain ground, for he had not only to confront the Italians and the traditional idealization of Columbus but also his fellow Scandinavians, the Norwegians, who understandably regarded Leif Ericson and his companions as uniquely their own. To Enander, they were "Northmen" from Greenland, "descended from Sweden, Norway, and Denmark."[20]

It was meanwhile indisputable that Sweden had been one of the three European powers to colonize, during the seventeenth century, territory that would comprise the original thirteen United States. Its New Sweden colony on the Delaware River was founded in 1638, within a generation or so of Jamestown, Plymouth, or New Netherland. Descendants of the Swedish settlers later fought valiantly for American freedom and were among the founders of the new republic, in particular John Morton, a signer of the Declaration of Independence, and John Hanson, the first president of the Continental Congress. As Enander never tired of pointing out, the Swedes belonged to the select circle of true plankholders in the United States and had played their vital part in its creation.

The success of the Swedes in America since colonial times derived above all from the basic values they held in common with the closely kindred Anglo-Saxons, above all their love of liberty and equality, respect for the law, courage, and magnanimity. He traced, moreover, the nobler qualities of the English race back to Scandinavian origins. In a speech held in Philadelphia in connection with the centennial of American independence in 1876, Enander declared that "the seeds of that freedom and independence which ripened under the sun of America by the 4th of July 1776 . . . had, centuries earlier . . . been planted in a land beneath the North Star, poor in silver and gold but rich in honor and faith." From "freedom's home on earth"—as Sweden was traditionally described—some Northmen had gone to England, bringing with them the ideal of liberty. In time, some Englishmen, seeking greater freedom, had moved to America. But those who had declared their independence in 1776 were not only of English origin; the descendants of the Delaware Swedes had made their own outstanding contributions. "Whenever the freedom of the American people," Enander declared in 1887, "which traces its earliest roots to the freeborn peoples of the Scandinavian North, has been seriously threatened, Swedish steel has always flashed in the thick of battle in its defense."[21]

But Enander went even further, for he held that the Swedes in America lived up to essential American ideals more fully than the Anglo-Americans themselves. He prepared the ground with his glowing description of the virtues of the ancient Scandinavians: "our forefathers' self-control, contempt for death, independence of spirit, and sense of dignity, which was each day confirmed by fresh deeds of valor and steadfastness." The colonists sent out to New Sweden in the seventeenth century represented, he claimed, the flower of their nation. Only "men and women of good reputation" were allowed to go there. Among them one would seek in vain for "distinguished idlers, derelict drinkers, undisciplined youths, fugitives from the law, and bigoted fantasts." Rather, they were "industrious, sober, respectable farmers and craftsmen," whose ancient rights and freedom were then threatened by a "rich and powerful nobility. . . . From this sturdy stock many of the most distinguished English-speaking families of our adopted homeland are today proud to claim descent."[22]

Enander declared that "No slave groaned under the lash of a Swedish slavedriver," and "no 'heretic' languished within Swedish prison walls on American soil." It had been Gustav II Adolf's noble dream to establish a free asylum in the New World for persecuted Christians of all faiths, although he had been killed on the field of Lützen in 1632, defending Protestantism and freedom of conscience, before this plan could be realized. The Swedes had fairly purchased their territory from the native Indians, treated them with consideration and respect, and enjoyed their fast friendship. In all these respects the Swedes offered a shining contrast to the more cynical, ruthless, and exploitive behavior of the English and Dutch.[23] In effect, Enander maintained that the Swedes were by nature better Americans than the "Americans" themselves, that it was their historic destiny to lead their new homeland to ever higher levels of idealism, in pursuit of all that was "great, noble, and beautiful."[24]

To fulfill this lofty role, it was essential that the Swedish Americans of the present live up to the high examples of their forebears. They were indeed of the same blood and bone. In his 1890 speech, "A Dream," he described the arrival in New York harbor of innumerable ships.

> Among these vessels are many filled, like the dragon ships of yore, with men and weapons from the Northland. The men are Swedish farmers, craftsmen, and laborers, the weapons are those of peace rather than war, of intelligence rather than raw force. To be sure, many of these newcomers lack earthly possessions other than a Bible under their arm and the wanderer's staff in their hand, but they are rich, so far as piety, love of freedom, resourcefulness, honesty and faith, the will and strength to work, sobriety, and industry hold any value on earth. And these riches make it possible for them to gain, through work and prayer, earthly rewards as well and gradually to regain that part of Vinland the Good that was once their fathers' "possession."

Enander's descriptions of the virtues of the ancient Northmen and the New Sweden colonists were clear admonitions to his Swedish American compatriots. "Vain lust for glory, unquenchable thirst for gain, hard-hearted selfishness, consuming envy, and puffed-up pride—the most common vices of our time," he wrote, had no place in New Sweden. The colonists "all belonged to the evangelical Lutheran religion," which they held in simple, joyful faith, free from sanctimonious gloom, bigotry, and hypocrisy. They held together, even under Dutch and later English rule, to maintain their Swedish language, religion, and customs against corrupting alien influences. By remaining true to themselves and their own proud heritage, they were valuable and valued members of the wider society around them.[25]

It is evident from the above that Enander regarded the Swedish Americans as a "nationality" of their own, as distinguished both from the Swedes of the homeland and from the other nationalities that made up the American population. In 1893 he dedicated his volume of selected works to the "Swedish-American nationality."[26] Implicit in this concept was the Swedish American's full right to pass independent judgment upon conditions in the former homeland, including its failings, as would become increasingly evident in Enander's later speeches and writings.

Hans Mattson reflected essentially the same views in concluding his reminiscences of 1891 by pointing out how mightily the Swedes and other Scandinavians had contributed to America since 1638.

> Though proud of their Scandinavian ancestry, they love America and American institutions as deeply and as truly as do the descendants of the Pilgrims. Therefore the Scandinavian-American feels a certain sense of ownership in the glorious heritage of American soil, with its rivers, lakes, mountains, valleys, woods and prairies, and in all its noble institutions; and he feels that the blessings which he enjoys are not his by favor or sufferance, but by right; by moral as well as civil right. For he took possession of the wilderness, endured the hardships of the pioneer, contributed his full share toward the grand results accomplished, and is in mind and heart a true and loyal American citizen.[27]

Even the Augustana Lutheran Synod, the recognized bastion of Swedish heritage in the New World, while striving to rally Swedish immigrants to their ancestral faith, not only accepted but welcomed its position as a free church in a society unencumbered by an official state religion. At a meeting in Stockholm of the Evangelical Patriotic Society (*Evangeliska Fosterlands-stiftelsen*) in 1870, the Synod's president, Reverend T. N. Hasselquist, then on a visit to Sweden, declared:

> For my part, I cannot love the institution of a state church, which is certainly an abuse in accordance both with God's word and with all experience. . . . In a free church the congregation's true purposes must always come first. . . . In a state church the outward is always mixed with the inward, the worldly with the spiritual together, through which the inward, the spiritual—that is, what is most vital—must suffer. This confusion undeniably occurs in the Swedish church, and to the highest degree.

Pastor Eric Norelius expressed the same view to Hugo Nisbeth in Wasa, Minnesota. The Augustana Synod consisted of essentially self-governing congregations, which drafted their own constitutions and by-laws, and elected (and at times dismissed) their own pastors, a point that duly impressed Ernst Beckman. It proudly rejected any insinuation that it had any formal link with the Swedish state church, that it was in any sense a subordinate "daughter church," or that it should adopt the latter's hierarchical form of organization. It was, in sum, a Swedish-American church, rather than a Swedish church in America, no less than the various non-Lutheran Swedish-American denominations.[28]

The new "Swedish America"—as it would soon be called—may be said to have come of age with the impressive celebration of the 250th anniversary of the founding of the Swedish Delaware colony, held in Minneapolis on 14 September 1888, the first of those great commemorative events that have played so vital a role in the formation of Swedish-American ethnic awareness. Organized by a committee that included clergymen of various denominations, newspaper editors of differing viewpoint, professional men, and public officials and chaired by Hans Mattson, it manifestly sought to inspire respect among other Americans and pride among Swedish Americans, as well as to promote unity and a common sense of purpose among contending factions.[29]

Heavy rain forestalled the initial parade on the day itself, but the Exhibition Building in Minneapolis was packed with an estimated 15,000 spectators, many of whom had to stand throughout the three-hour event. The stage, bedecked with the banners of numerous Swedish-American organizations, was crowded with dignitaries, including prominent Danish and Norwegian Americans. There was, meanwhile, no official participation by representatives of the Swedish government nor by visiting notables from Sweden.[30]

Following the invocation by Pastor T. N. Hasselquist, the featured "oration" was held in English by the Honorable William Widgery Thomas, Jr., former United States minister to Stockholm and founder in 1870 of the New Sweden settlement in his native Maine. Thomas, an enthusiastic admirer of Sweden and the Swedes, spiced his presentation with enough Swedish quotations to reveal his proficiency in the language. He recounted the proud exploits of the Swedish people in war and peace, from Nordic antiquity to the singer Jenny Lind and the inventor John Ericsson, whose ironclad *Monitor* had carried the day at the crucial battle of Hampton Roads in 1862. "Surely," he held, "love of freedom and patriotism, and state-craft and valor came over to America, not only in the *Mayflower,* but also in that Swedish ship the *Kalmar Nyckel.*" Throughout America the Swedes were noted for their "honesty and industry, their economy and thrift." What meanwhile may have most gratified the assembled Swedish Americans was to hear this Yankee from Maine declare his belief that "no immigrants of to-day, in both faith and works, so closely resemble the sturdy pilgrim fathers of New England as the Swedes."[31]

It was a message that could have been, and very likely was, directly inspired by Johan Enander, who thereupon followed with a "historical address" in Swedish, summarizing in stirring fashion his filiopietistic vision of New Sweden on the Delaware and ending with the admonition to his fellow Swedish Americans.

Compared with us, the colonists were only a handful of people, but they were a united nationality. . . . Whatever might benefit the entire people and win honor and recognition among other nationalities was the concern of all, for which every heart beat and all hands worked. . . . In the future, as in the past, we wish to fulfill our duty as befits American citizens, but also to demand our right, as such, unto the last sheaf, upholding in every sphere the honor and reputation of the Swedish-American name, until that name becomes a name of honor from sea to sea, comprising within it all that is great, noble, just, and true.[32]

The 7th New York Regimental Band played, Swedish poems in honor of the day were recited, Captain O. G. Lange (reputedly the oldest living Swedish immigrant) was honored. It was a grand occasion, not only for those present but for their compatriots throughout the country who read of it.

The following year, in 1889, a Swedish-American Historical Society was chartered in Illinois. It seems safe to assume that the guiding spirit behind this initiative was Johan Enander and that it was inspired by existing Scotch-Irish and German-American historical societies. But the time was evidently not yet ripe for such an undertaking. Except for a pioneering volume on the Swedes in Illinois by the journalists C. F. Peterson and Eric Johnson— the latter the son of Eric Jansson, the prophet of Bishop Hill—published in 1880, the history of the nineteenth-century Swedish settlement in America still remained virtually untouched. Nothing further is recorded about the newly chartered historical society. Eighteen years would pass before another, more successful effort in this direction would be made.[33]

SIX

What Was Sweden to Do?

*I*n Sweden, the sheer volume of emigration during this period gave rise to much perplexed deliberation over the causes and necessity of the exodus, its consequences for Sweden and for the emigrants themselves, the character of the latter, and what would, could and should be done to stem the tide.

There was a general consensus that the root causes of the emigration were economic, although social considerations were also important. According to Ernst Beckman in 1883, "stomach and kin are the best emigrant recruiters. The advantages which they hold in prospect are mainly two: a larger loaf and a more respected social standing for the man with calloused hands."[1]

Agreement, however, broke down over the question of what the common man ought rightly to expect from life. The traditional conservative view, already well developed during the 1840s and 1850s, is notably represented by a cautionary tale by "A. A.," published in 1869 in *Läsning för folket,* the organ of the Society for the Propagation of Useful Knowledge *(Sällskapet för Nyttiga Kunskapers spridande).* It told how "Per Swensson," a "respected farmer," cultivated his ancestral farm in peace and contentment until his head was turned by the local sexton, who was also an emigrant agent on the side. The latter gave Per to understand that the pastor, "'like all other gentlemen,' was an enemy of enlightenment and freedom" and he praised "glorious America, where 'one man was as good as another.'" When the newspapers warned against emigration, the sexton claimed that they spread lies because they sought for all time to keep "the Swedish people enslaved." Per decided to leave "poor Sweden, which was so far behind the times," and immigrate to America, despite his more level-headed wife's pleas that he content himself with the earthly home and station in life that God had given him. Thus misled by Per's foolish pride and vanity, the family experienced a horrendous ocean crossing. When last heard from, they were living in misery in America, from whence the deeply repentant Per sought to warn credulous countrymen at home against giving ear to the sexton and his ilk. This tale was followed by a poem presumably by the same author, recapitulating it in even more pathetic tones.[2]

The poem was followed by a concluding commentary, "Our Emigrants," most likely that of the editor of *Läsning för folket*. The commentator held that the preceding story was "an undeniably true and striking picture of a large part of our emigrants, of their ideas and motives," but that there could admittedly be other, more valid reasons for emigration. Many European countries faced overpopulation, and in such cases it was natural that people should prefer to depart rather than reduce their demands for life's necessities. Emigration could improve conditions for those who remained at home until a "balance" was restored which would naturally bring it to an end. The question was whether Sweden, with its still undeveloped resources, really was overpopulated, and he urged prospective emigrants seriously to ask themselves whether they could depart in good conscience. Sweden's "strength and well-being" depended upon "the strength and well-being of all its sons."

Those who left for America would not return. "Their children and grandchildren will become as genuinely American as all others in that land. . . . That is simply the fate of migrating peoples. They are swallowed up by their *new* fatherland—for every person must have *some* fatherland." "What is worse," the commentator added, "those who are leaving are by no means those we would most like to be rid of."[3] It was the commentator to the tale of Per Swensson, rather than its author, who better reflected both the frustration and the indecisiveness of those who regarded emigration as both a national and a personal misfortune during these years.

To Swedish liberals, there was nothing morally reprehensible about the desire of individuals to improve their positions in life. "Gold!" exclaimed Ernst Beckman in 1883, "To be sure everyone naturally seeks for it in the New World—just as they do in the Old. But there are, fortunately, only a few who are infected with 'Gold Fever' in the literal sense." That same year, Isador Kjellberg lashed out bitterly at those who accused the emigrants of lack of patriotism:

> *Patriotism*? Let us not misuse so fine a word! Does patriotism consist of withholding the truth from the workingman by claiming, when he asks, against one's better knowledge, that "things are bad in America?" I want nothing to do with such patriotism! If patriotism consists of seeking, through lies, to persuade the poorest classes to remain under the yoke, like mindless beasts, so that we others should be so much better off, then I am lacking

in patriotism. I love my country, as such, but even more I love and sympathize with the human being, the worker. ... Among those who most sternly condemn emigration are those who least value the human and civic value of the workingman. ... They demand that he remain here. What are they prepared to give him to compensate the deprivations this requires?

Kjellberg then contemptuously dismissed the idea that it was "cowardice for a workingman to leave his country for America. ... It is only cowardly, unmanly, heartless, to let oneself become a slave under deplorable circumstances which one *can* overcome."[4]

If an outright prohibition of emigration was incompatible with the personal liberties now considered basic under a constitutional regime, it was nonetheless natural that proposals should be raised in the Riksdag to control or at least direct the flow. Several such measures were proposed and defeated in 1869. The most notable of these was Albert Lindhagen's motion that the government engage agents in North America to report on actual conditions and to counsel arriving emigrants. Together with colleagues from the other Nordic countries, they would channel Scandinavian immigrants into that region best suited for them and where they were already most concentrated—Wisconsin, Minnesota, Dakota Territory, and thence out onto the virgin Canadian prairie. For climatic reasons, Lindhagen envisioned this vast area as virtually their exclusive preserve, in which they could maintain their kindred languages and culture.

But why should the preservation of Swedish nationality be important to Sweden? In answering this question, Lindhagen introduced a new idea that would become prominent in debate over emigration after the turn of the century. As the exodus could not, under existing conditions, be prevented, what ought to be done to turn it "to the benefit of the fatherland"? The numerical strength of a nationality, both within and outside of its original homeland, determined its international standing. "We are too small to be big," Lindhagen declared, "but we are also too big to resign ourselves to never being anything but small."

What would we gain by having a people on the other side of the Atlantic Ocean with the same language and same culture as ourselves? To this, I reply that this gain would be of a purely moral nature, but incalculably great. For the cultural work which we as a nation carry out for our own and all mankind's development, we would be reinforced by a large, numerous people. Our words would be listened to and what we write would be read and reflected upon, not only here at home in our remote part of the world but by a nationality that would now be great enough to make its mark among the other nationalities and place itself on the same level with them. ... Herein would lie strength, and from this would come a self-confidence which we need but which we now by necessity lack.

Even if in time Swedish immigrants in the envisioned cultural colony did not preserve their language and nationality, the population that inhabited a considerable part of the world would bear "our own characteristics."

Lindhagen's proposal aroused little enthusiasm or even discussion in the Riksdag, where it failed to pass, in part because of the obvious practical problems that an effort to direct developments outside the kingdom would involve and in part due to the widespread view that it was to the immigrants' own greatest benefit to assimilate to their new homeland.[5] In 1883, the Stockholm police summarily prohibited emigrant agents from spreading information about American conditions within the city.[6] But such efforts proved worse than useless and simply drew the fire of those who maintained that emigration was both justified and necessary.

In a pamphlet published in 1870, Johan Andersson condemned Lindhagen's Riksdag motion—and by implication any attempt to restrict or regulate emigration—as "childish nonsense." He likewise rejected indignantly claims that emigration was due to a thoughtless lust for adventure in the old Viking spirit. To Andersson, it was a matter of grim necessity, despite Sweden's great potential resources. The real problem was not overpopulation but misgovernment. Here he gave vent to the full range of radical discontents with the new oligarchy that had emerged following the Riksdag reform of 1866, offering a kind of preview to August Strindberg's *Röda rummet* (The Red Room) nearly a decade later. The only element Sweden could well do without was "all those superfluous bureaucrats, who suck its blood and marrow." Andersson hinted darkly that if abuses were not reformed, revolution threatened in the background. Addressing the departing emigrants, he declaimed, "We bid you farewell, you countrymen who go out into the world to seek what here you sought in vain: human rights and human dignity."[7]

The same basic message was delivered the following year by Alex. Nilsson, who contrasted conditions at home with those in the young republic. The United States, he held, was favored by the absence of those necessary pillars of monarchy by God's grace: a nobility, standing army, and state church. The cure for Swedish emigration would require such far-reaching changes as to make Sweden a "free country." In 1872 Nilsson reiterated these ideas even more forcefully in his emigrant guidebook. "In Europe," he wrote, "the wastrel is called a gentleman and the workers rabble," whereas in America manual labor was respected and the surest way to prosperity and respect. The example of America could not fail to exercise its powerful influence upon the Old World, for which it was deeply feared by the European ruling classes. "No one can thus doubt in our times that emigration advances Europe's civilization." To it was due such improvements in working-class conditions as had thus far come about at home.[8]

A more cautious note was sounded in two articles in *Samtiden* by its editor, C. F. Bergstedt, in 1873 and 1874. Bergstedt accepted that emigration was natural, inevitable, and under the right circumstances beneficial to both the fatherland and the emigrants themselves, but he insisted that prospective emigrants should be well informed of the hardships and pitfalls that could await them.[9]

The travelers to America in this period added their own criticisms of Swedish conditions—explicitly or implicitly—in their discussions of the reasons for the emigration. Hugo Nisbeth placed particular emphasis in 1874 upon the drawing power of friends and relatives already in America. He also anticipated a lively debate a few years later when he denied that the emigration resulted in a financial loss to Sweden, in view of the small sums the emigrants took out and the large remittances they sent home. No one who had not experienced real distress, Ernst Beckman wrote in 1877, could blame the emigrants for leaving their homeland. After "two years having mixed their bread dough half-and-half with bark," it should not be surprising if the third year they should be attracted by the thought of "corn cakes and wheat bread in the Mississippi Valley." Jonas Stadling in 1883 stressed humanity's innate instinct for freedom over purely material considerations, important as these were. If Swedes enjoyed the same freedom at home, they would no longer leave. If only all who wished to depart had the necessary means, Isador Kjellberg held in 1883, "We would see, to our dismay, a folk migration of the most frightening dimensions. . . . Probably the Swedish kingdom and Swedish people would cease to exist."[10]

Central to the whole discussion of emigration was the perplexing question of overpopulation, which now began to attract scholarly attention. In a treatise published in 1875, the Uppsala political economist, Professor Wilhelm Erik Svedelius, urged a philosophical acceptance of migration, through which, since the dawn of history, civilization had spread throughout the world. The earliest forefathers of the Swedish race itself were not born in Sweden, he reminded his readers. The European settlement of the New World now further strengthened "Mankind's cultural forces." "Europe gave life to America, now America acts in turn upon Europe," Svedelius wrote. Swedes should take pride in their contribution to this "world-historical" civilizing mission, rather than complain of its cost to the fatherland.

But how great was this cost? Did the emigration really represent a loss to Sweden? Svedelius was doubtful:

> Should it be the case that those who leave should not have been able, had they remained, to obtain enlightenment and bread, but rather that their numbers would simply have increased the burden of poor relief and the mass of proletarians, one certainly cannot deplore their departure. . . . When one considers the crowd of young persons who throng all walks of life, these constantly increasing flocks of children, who overfill every schoolhouse,

one finds it hard to avoid a nagging fear, for one knows not how to answer the question: where are they all to find their bread?

If Sweden was presently losing "a not insignificant mass of labor," this did not mean that the country "is losing what it needs, but rather that Sweden is sharing with other lands a supply which it presently can do without." As economic conditions improved, emigration would automatically decline.[11]

With this largely providential view Ernst Beckman was essentially in agreement in 1877, when he wrote that "the emigration is a fact deriving in part from laws unknown to us. It will presumably continue as long as there is still room on the American continent."[12]

In 1882 the economist Knut Wicksell made his weighty contribution to the debate. He agreed with Svedelius that supply and demand for labor would eventually balance out but held that the labor Sweden lost was not a free resource due to the expense of bringing up and educating young persons who emigrated before working off their debt to society. The heaviest burden fell upon the poorest elements of the population, holding back their material progress. "They are proletarians," Wicksell wrote, "they remain proletarians, and they work themselves to the bone to bring up new proletarians, or—at best—emigrants."

Wicksell meanwhile agreed with Svedelius that Sweden was presently overpopulated. Still, if emigration provided a way out, it was not a permanent or satisfactory solution. The only real answer would be to limit families to two or three children. "We must stop breeding emigrants," Wicksell declared, and he assumed that "practically no educated person" could be altogether unaware of how this should be accomplished. He realized that such ideas faced strong prejudices, but only their success would make it possible for the Swedish people to determine its own future.[13]

The ideas of both Svedelius and Beckman, with a strong religious overlay, reappear in 1882 in a guide for emigrants by O. Bergström, who claimed he had crossed the Atlantic eight times. Bergström stressed that God's first commandment, given to Noah, was "Be fruitful and multiply, and replenish the earth." The migration of peoples was a law of nature and the Nordic peoples had since antiquity contributed mightily to its fulfillment. Bergström denied that emigration had caused Sweden serious losses of labor or capital, as was generally maintained. In most parts of Sweden he found that workers were still earning an average daily wage of only 90 öre. "When Sweden begins to suffer from a lack of workers and wages have risen by at least 100%, there will then be reason to complain of the nation's loss of labor." Furthermore, Bergström responded to the concern over what would become of "these hordes of 'rabble,' as European snobs would call them, upon arrival at Castle Garden in New York," by exclaiming, "My readers! The emigrants have never been otherwise ... it is this 'rabble' from Europe which has made America great, and it is its sons who today form the bone and marrow of the nation. America shows the emigrant's worth."[14]

In 1884 and 1885, a study by an upcoming young statistician, Gustav Sundbärg—following some two hundred pages of tables and graphs—concluded that his "brief survey" suggested "the emigration under present conditions is a necessity deriving from economic life and the organism of the population itself, that the healthy influences of the emigration have already made themselves felt in several respects, and that the fears that have sometimes been aroused regarding its disturbing effects upon the population structure are at least exaggerated."[15]

If there were differences between the scholars there was even greater lack of agreement among those most responsible for implementing government policy on the local level, the provincial governors or *landshövdingar*. This lack of agreement can be seen in their regular five-year reports and especially by a special questionnaire on emigration from their respective counties (*län*) in 1882. The results of the latter inquiry were notably mixed. Some responses considered emigration beneficial to the emigrants themselves or even to the country, while others considered it harmful to either or both. There was similar disagreement as to the causes of emigration, ranging from real material need and the influence of emigrated relatives and friends to such motives as the desire for luxury, a lack of patriotism, or the old "Viking" spirit. Ann-Sofie Kälvemark, who has studied the inquiry of 1882, considers that the governors were sincerely trying to come to grips with a bewilderingly complex problem, and that in only a few cases were they dogmatically for or against emigration.[16]

Both public officials and others tended to look primarily for agrarian answers, from both the technical agricultural and socio–political viewpoints. A good example of the former approach is given by Axel Lindberg, an agronomist, who considered it axiomatic that Sweden was and would remain a basically agricultural country. Thus only determined and concerted efforts to increase agricultural productivity could bring about the economic development needed to provide a decent living standard for all. This would require the fullest possible labor force but would in turn overcome the essentially economic causes of emigration. The panacea, in Lindberg's view, was a massive, government-sponsored project for land reclamation.[17]

In effect, Lindberg and others like him were thinking in the 1880s in terms of the lean years of the later 1860s, when the situation was, in fact, altogether different. Looking back, it is hard to envision how any increase in agricultural production conceivable in Sweden could have overcome the overwhelming competition from cheaper grain from overseas, above all from America. Ultimately, the dynamic developments that would bring the great migration to a close would necessarily take place in other sectors of the Swedish economy.

Lindberg was meanwhile aware that the question of greater production was not entirely a technical one. It would be essential, he wrote, to foster a new spirit of industriousness, rationality, and patriotism in the countryside, to induce more ambitious and enterprising persons to remain.

This social side of the problem was the concern of an article on the Swedish agricultural laborer by the economist J. A. Leffler in 1887, according to whom the real explanation for America's enormous low-cost production of grain was the high effectivity of its relatively small agricultural labor force, which in turn derived from the high motivation of American farm workers, based on good earnings. Swedish agriculture, meanwhile, was caught in a vicious circle: the quality of labor was poor because the laborer was poorly rewarded, while the workers were poorly paid because of the poor quality of their work. Thus farm labor was in fact expensive in relation to its product. "The agricultural laborers ... [tend to] do nothing at all when they are not under direct supervision. Especially in those parts of our country where cultivation is still mainly done with oxen, there is all too often a striking similarity between those in front of and those behind the plow." *Employers* ought, much more than heretofore, to enter into a "friendly, personal relationship with their workers." Ultimately, however, the inculcation of a new spirit depended, Leffler saw, upon a more just system of distribution, "giving the worker a proportionate share of the profits of agriculture."[18]

Here agronomists and economists joined hands with liberally minded visitors to the United States and critical Swedish-American commentators. Already in 1868, Mauritz Rubenson expressed the hope that "the day might soon come when old Sweden could offer all her children the same advantages that the land of the Star-Spangled Banner now does." It was evidently the politically conservative governor, Count Erik Sparre, who in his report for 1879–80 on Älvsborg County put this idea into a form that would thereafter remain the rallying cry of all who sought to end the emigration through fundamental—if need be radical—reform. "The only effective means of combating emigration," he wrote, "is to move America over here—its national economy and everything that makes its greatness."[19]

Meanwhile, a more emotional, visceral reaction to the emigration was provided by many of the Swedish poets of the day, expressed in tones of moralistic indignation or deep pathos. A good example of the former genre is provided by Karl Ludvig Östergren ("Fjalar"), who addressed the prospective emigrant:

> Thou hesitatest yet, ungrateful one?
> So be it then, for once thy goal is reached,
> Then shalt thou long in vain
> For the home from whence thou didst depart.
> Hearest thou? The Northland's rage doth thunder forth.

With contempt each wave pushes farther
From the shores of the Fatherland
Its faithless son, forgetful of all duty.

A more tragic note pervades Carl Snoilsky's well-known poem, "Emigrationen" ("The Emigration"), which compared Sweden's losses in past battles, which had brought the nation glory, with "our own heart's blood that is now gushing/From open wounds toward the West." Once in America, the constant stream was swallowed up, as if by the "broad Mississippi's current." Snoilsky ended, like so many others, by appealing for a Sweden that would be a true home to all its children.[20]

Finally, a very different perspective was offered by Sidney W. Cooper, United States consul in Gothenburg, who in 1884 published a charming account of Swedish life and manners. While mainly concerned with the picturesque aspects of social and cultural life, he was gratified to see sturdy Scandinavians depart for America, "where the qualities which distinguish them are so much needed," in contrast to emigrants from other parts of Europe, including "the troublesome Emerald Isle."

Cooper reported that the slogan, "America in Sweden," had already been heard in the Riksdag itself. "So long as Sweden, foolishly proud and laughably conceited, closes her ears to voices over the sea ... just so long will her pleasant Anderssons and Johanssons, her Nilssons and her Erikssons, shake the dust of their native soil from the wooden shoes which are sounding the death rattle of their country on the cobbles of every quay in Europe." "Bring America to Sweden, by all means," he reiterated, "for then the voice of the emigrant runner will be heard no more in all the land, your farms will not go untilled, your mines will yield their exhaustless treasures, your boundless forests will burden the sea with their precious woods."[21]

It sounded simple: to "bring America to Sweden." This, in effect, is what critical voices had been saying throughout these years. But was the massive transformation of basic conditions that this would imply in all areas of life a real possibility in the Sweden of that era? And, in the minds of many, were it not a Pyrrhic victory indeed if Sweden were to end the emigration at the cost of selling its national birthright for a mess of undigestible American pottage?

SEVEN

Changing Signals

*F*ollowing its all-time peak in 1887, emigration from Sweden remained high until 1894, when it suddenly fell off to a low level that lasted through the end of the decade. In 1898 it was down to 8,535 emigrants, the smallest number in twenty years. Remigration from abroad was meanwhile on the rise, amounting in 1894 to 86 percent of emigration.

Changing circumstances in both Sweden and the United States lay behind the declining net emigration of the later 1890s. Following a gradual and fitful start since the mid-nineteenth century, the new technologies of steam and electricity, mining, forestry, and agriculture combined to produce the rapid breakthrough of industrialization in Sweden during the 1890s, under the cover of protective tariffs first enacted in 1888 against foreign competition. Sizable fortunes were made in iron mining, forest products, manufacturing, and finance, while wages for labor in both industry and agriculture likewise rose. Sweden's new-found pride and confidence in its economic future were made manifest in its participation in the World's Columbian Exposition of 1893 in Chicago and in particular by its own impressive Stockholm Exposition in 1897. In 1889, moreover, the Riksdag passed its first law for the protection of workers against industrial hazards, the beginning of what in time would become an increasingly comprehensive program of social welfare.

During the same decade the lure of America declined dramatically. In 1890 the United States Bureau of the Census announced that the frontier of settlement had ceased to exist. The best farmland was taken and ever more expensive to buy. The growing problems of the Gilded Age were meanwhile coming home to roost, above all the growth of monopoly capitalism in the form of trusts and cartels, at the expense of the farmer, small businessman, and industrial worker. Labor unrest gave rise to union organization, blacklisting, lockouts, and strikes, culminating with the bloody Haymarket Riot in Chicago in 1892 and the Homestead Strike in 1894, both of which cost several lives. Rural America was aroused by the monopolistic practices of the railroads and commodities exchanges, which held down earnings and forced farmers into debt. On top of all this came the disastrous financial "Panic of 1893" and the lean years that followed.

The response to these deteriorating conditions was the Populist movement, which began in 1892 and reached its height in William Jennings Bryan's presidential election campaign in 1896. While directed primarily against the trusts and monopolies, Populism also showed a certain hostility toward immigration, especially that of poverty-ridden Southern and Eastern Europeans prepared to work for starvation wages and thus depress wage levels generally, to the profit of the big capitalists.[1]

American literature and social thought were pervaded by indignation, self-doubt, and pessimism to a degree heretofore unknown in the young republic, as reflected in the writings of such diverse figures as Henry Adams, Edward Bellamy, Henry George, Frank Norris, and the Norwegian-American Thorstein Veblen. The mounting critique of American society as a whole could not but find its way into both the immigrant and the foreign press, including the Swedish-American and the Swedish.

The upsurge of economic development in Sweden during the 1890s, together with undoubted relief over declining emigration, focused attention there increasingly upon internal concerns. This is shown in part by a marked decline in publications dealing with America and the emigration question.[2]

Fewer emigrant guides were published, compared with the numbers in preceding decades, while those that did were more cautious in tone. G. Svensson, in his *Amerika-Boken* (America Book) could still recommend in 1892 that Swedish cotters and smallholders might consider carefully whether they might not do better in America's northwestern states than at home in Sweden, especially if they had "a few thousand crowns" in savings, but warned against the snares and delusions of the larger American cities. By 1902 *Emigrantens vän* (The Emigrant's Friend) edited by P. W. Wilander and containing contributions by forty Swedish Americans in various parts of the United States, was even more reserved. The published letters were sober and matter-of-fact, and while most were positive several were not.[3]

Meanwhile, as Sweden's prospects brightened and America's appeared to wain, there took place in Sweden a manifest recovery of national nerve and will, following the atmosphere of disillusion and pessimism that had prevailed during the past two decades. The new mood found expression in the luxuriant Neo-Romanticism in literature and the arts, which around 1890 rapidly gained ground at the expense of the critical and cosmopolitan Realism of the 1880s. The strongly patriotic National Romanticism of the

1890s and following decades inspired one of the most creative and original epochs of the nation's cultural heritage, which has largely defined a Swedish self-image that has endured with remarkable consistency, at home and abroad, down to the present. In a burst of literary vitality, Verner von Heidenstam, Gustaf Fröding, Erik Axel Karlfeldt, Selma Lagerlöf, and others extolled in prose and verse great deeds of yore, the beauties of their native land, and the cherished folkways of home provinces. The same spirit is expressed in the paintings of Carl Larsson, Anders Zorn, Richard Bergh, Karl Nordström, or Nils Kreuger, and is heard in the compositions of Wilhelm Peterson-Berger, Wilhelm Stenhammar, or Hugo Alfvén, with their loving allusions to Swedish folk music.

In Stockholm, Artur Hazelius founded Skansen, the national outdoor museum for traditional folk arts and architecture from all parts of the land, in 1891 and the grandiose Nordic Museum (*Nordiska museet*) devoted to the nation's history, begun in 1892. The Swedish Tourist Society (*Svenska turistföreningen*), founded in 1886 as a mainly academic organization, in 1891 proclaimed as its goal "to spread knowledge of the land and folk." Throughout Sweden local cultural-historical societies (*hembygdsföreningar*) formed and established their own folklife museums, most often in venerable old farm buildings. Half-forgotten crafts, costumes, dances, games, and songs were enthusiastically collected, preserved, and revived in educated and fashionable circles. Both public buildings and private residences were built in styles inspired by the Viking era, Sweden's seventeenth-century "Age of Greatness," and regional peasant building traditions.[4]

While there was much in National Romanticism that looked backward with nostalgia and regret to an old, rural Sweden already then largely beyond recall, such sentiments were balanced by a reviving determination to solve the problems of the present. Among the most pressing was that of national security in the face of growing international tensions throughout Europe. In particular, Sweden confronted increasing conflict with Norway, its partner under the dynastic union of 1814, which in certain nationalistic circles appeared to call for greater military force. From 1899, moreover, Tsar Nicholas II's government commenced a policy of enforced Russification in the autonomous Grand Duchy of Finland, which aroused Sweden's worst fears regarding its ancient enemy to the east. In response, the period of training for military conscripts was increased from forty-two to ninety days in 1892, then from eight to twelve months in 1901.

With the recovery of optimism and national will, opposition to emigration stiffened to a degree scarcely glimpsed since the prosperous and self-confident 1850s. To a nation in evident need of labor and military resources, emigration again appeared as a betrayal of the bonds of blood, community, and homeland, while America's material advantages seemed increasingly illusory. European Neo-Romanticism during the 1890s upheld the rich traditions of the Old World and bitterly attacked the gross materialism and cultural desolation of American life, seeing in it the advancing threat of a new barbarism. The devastating critique in this spirit delivered by the Norwegian Knut Hamsun in 1888, following his brief experience as an immigrant, was particularly influential throughout Scandinavia.[5]

Polemical attacks on America and emigration took on a renewed stridency. The most characteristic work in this genre during the 1890s was surely a hefty pamphlet by "C.J.U.," the pseudonym for C. J. Malmquist, which posed the question, "Which land's people are really the most fortunate?" This pamphlet appeared in four successively revised editions between 1892 and 1894, and the cover of the last offered discounts on batches of from fifty to one thousand copies, suggesting a wide distribution by interested organizations or individuals. The answer was, of course, that Sweden's population was far better off than those of the other countries discussed, including Britain, France, Denmark, Germany, Russia, and—most pointedly—America. The author described with warm feeling Sweden's healthful climate, beauteous landscape, rich resources, honest and efficient administration, freedom under law, and cozy homes.

America had, to be sure, served Europe well, especially some decades back, by standing open to "all kinds of ne'er-do-wells and scoundrels" who there were forced to work hard and behave themselves to avoid "a noose around the neck or a bullet in the breast," for the spirit there was "not especially compassionate or humane." Immigrant workers meanwhile faced an unbearable burden of labor, while most were "little prepared for the mighty struggle for existence which in America one encounters at every step, or for the violence and cunning to which one is daily exposed." Money was valued more highly than human life, and those who no longer could "work like beasts of burden" faced imminent ruin, especially the foreign-born.

> If we could really learn of all the deprivation, anxiety, poverty, and misery which the great majority of our emigrants find their lot in the great land of America, we would be astonished and not then abandon old, free Sweden as frivolously as often happens now, for the difficulties one leaves behind here one rediscovers there in far greater degree ... and once one is there, there is no escape. ... For when one has turned his back on his home and shut the door behind him, it is not so easy later to open that closed door again. After a few years one is a stranger in his own homeland, indeed, in his fathers' house.

Sweden, meanwhile, offered glorious prospects, blessed as it was with good land and bountiful resources. Its industry employed a multitude of "well-off and satisfied workers." The country was rich, "and richer it shall be, to the extent that it has more good, sober, and industrious members of society." Nowhere did working people live as decently as in Sweden, even those—the author pointedly observed—who did not own their own homes and lived in housing provided by industrialists or estate-owners. Nowhere in the "civilized world" was it easier for them to acquire a "bit of land" of their own. It was heartening to see how well the "skilled and sober workingman" was now treated in his homeland. C.J.U.'s booklet ends by revealing his deepest concern: Sweden's defense against the Russian colossus, which called for patriotism and a solid front against the liberal "mud-slingers" who opposed military demands while condoning emigration.[6]

The problem was that those in Swedish society most inclined to emigrate were those least likely to be affected by the new spirit. The rising industrial working class was by no means convinced that conditions were ideal, as evidenced by the constant growth of labor unions and the fledgling Social Democratic movement. Prices, under tariff protection, were high for consumer goods, while wages fluctuated. Workers' housing in cities and company towns was crowded and generally primitive. And even if it might be possible for a farm laborer to obtain a "bit of land"—as C.J.U. claimed—how large might it be, of what quality, and how much of a livelihood might it alone provide? In his emigrant guidebook of 1902, P. W. Wilander held that those who departed still came primarily from that large part of Sweden's rural population "which never sees any opportunity to become the master of land of its own but must always work for others to exist." As later studies would prove, this was still all too true.[7]

For the educated and well-to-do, National Romantic nostalgia for a society of humane landowners and respectful retainers, of simple contentment with frugal conditions, of religious faith and loyalty to ancient customs, untainted by outside, worldly influences, held a deep emotional appeal. For the working classes of town and countryside, it had little to offer.

By the 1890s the Swedish element in the United States had attained the critical mass needed to sustain an active and varied cultural life of its own. A large and growing proportion consisted of persons long settled in America, well adapted to life there, and their children, born or brought up in the new land. Many old immigrants now lived in comfort or even prosperity, and could give attention and financial support to social and cultural institutions. Low immigration and sizable remigration during the later 1890s kept down the number of raw greenhorns and removed many of those who found it most difficult to adapt to American conditions.

The religious pattern was set in what would henceforth remain its characteristic form. Among the Swedish-American denominations, the Augustana Lutheran church had by far the largest membership, followed by the Mission Covenant, its recent offshoot, and the Swedish Methodists and Baptists. During the 1890s Swedish branches of the Seventh-Day Adventists and the Salvation Army were organized, and there remained since Gustaf Unonius's day a few Swedish Episcopalian congregations. The majority of Swedish Americans, however, did not now formally belong to any Swedish-American church, even though many occasionally attended their services. Others, especially those outside Swedish-American communities, were associated with other Scandinavian or mainline American churches. Some, particularly in the cities, proudly disassociated themselves from any religious affiliation.

New educational institutions continued to appear, most notably the Lutherans' Upsala College in East Orange, New Jersey, in 1893 and the Mission Covenant's North Park College in Chicago in 1894. A number of shorter-lived Swedish colleges and preparatory academies were established in other localities, while most congregations provided for the instruction of children in the ancestral language, usually through "Swede schools" held during the summer vacation.[8]

In an increasingly worldly environment, there was a rapid proliferation of Swedish-American secular organizations. Since many were mutual benefit societies that required large memberships to function most effectively, formerly exclusive clubs opened their doors to a widening clientele, who thereby acquired greater social and cultural polish. The same impulses led to the formation of larger regional federations of lodges, beginning with the Order of Svithiod in 1880, followed by the Viking Order in 1890, both in the Chicago area. In 1896 the first lodge of the Vasa Order of America was organized in New Haven, Connecticut, the beginning of a nationwide federation that eventually would spread to Canada and to Sweden itself.

The enormous increase in all the Scandinavian groups in America since the later 1860s led to the breakup of most of the earlier Scandinavian-American organizations into purely national groupings by the 1890s. Even Swedish-speaking emigrants from Finland now tended to form their own societies. The rapid growth of secular organizations meanwhile created deep cleavages within the Swedish-American community itself, since the churches, especially the Augustana Synod, stoutly opposed any form of "secret society" that might appear to compete with religious ritual and doctrine and reinforced their own networks of clubs, societies, and publications.

The secular societies reflected the rising social and cultural aspirations of their members. Typically the culture they idealized and sought to promote was that of the more prosperous and educated classes in the homeland, rather than the local peasant culture in which most of them had been raised. New impulses came from Swedish National Romanticism, such as its veneration of the Viking past—resulting in parades and historical enactments replete with horned helmets and rude weapons—or the cult of Gustav Adolf, the savior of Protestantism. The often elaborate rituals of the new lodges faithfully reflected the genteel conventions of the Swedish upper classes. Tailcoats, medals, and ribbons were *de rigeur*.[9]

A particularly good example of these trends is the Swedish singing societies. The tradition of male choral singing reached Sweden from Germany with the establishment of Scandinavia's first male chorus at Uppsala University in 1827. The institution has traditionally remained associated with university students and the educated classes generally, and those choruses later formed outside these circles have carefully emulated their practices and repertory. In America the first male choral societies were Scandinavian in membership, beginning with the Freja Society in Chicago in 1869. The Scandinavian Singers Union was established on the East Coast in 1886, mustering nine hundred voices at its national meet in Minneapolis in 1891. But the following year intergroup rivalry broke up this Scandinavian union and the American Union of Swedish Singers, still in existence today, was organized in Chicago, where it was able to assemble five hundred voices at the World's Columbian Exposition in 1893.

The Swedish-American singers turned out in evening dress and white visored caps of the type traditionally worn by graduates of the highly selective Swedish *gymnasium* or higher secondary school—the recognized symbol, that is, of elite social and cultural status. Banquets, balls, and ceremonies played a prominent part in the activities of the singing societies, placing a premium upon dignified and genteel behavior among the brethren and their ladies. The repertory required familiarity with literary Swedish and proper pronunciation of both Swedish and English, while inculcating the deep-lying cultural values it embodied. Altogether, the singing societies exercised an incalculable influence in raising the cultural level of Swedish America, as seemed strikingly demonstrated when a select chorus drawn from the American Union of Swedish Singers toured Sweden in 1897.[10]

The tour provided a particularly welcome chance to demonstrate to the Old Country that its emigrated sons held faithfully to their cultural heritage. "Mistrust and contempt back home toward everything Swedish-American was deeply ingrown and hardened," wrote Hjalmar Nilsson, one of its members, "but here came Sweden's own sons back from the republic far to the west, to show in song that the inborn musical gift, admiration for the heritage which Mother Svea has given all her sons in saga and song, has not been smothered out there in the prosaic land of dollars." It seemed the good will thus created would "melt the frost of indifference in Swedish hearts" and "cast a new light upon the Swedish Americans and their striving to do honor to the Swedish name out here."[11]

The Swedish-American singers attracted much attention, and their tour in 1897 may be regarded as the first of a long series of semiofficial manifestations of Swedish-American friendship in the Old Country. In their speeches of welcome, both Henrik Hedlund, editor of *Göteborgs Handels- och sjö-farts Tidning* in Gothenburg, and King Oscar II himself, at Stockholm's royal palace, expressed what would long thereafter remain the prevailing sentiments on such occasions: regret that Mother Svea had lost so many of her children, combined with pride at their success abroad.[12]

The growth of Swedish national culture evident in the clubs and societies is no less apparent in the Swedish-American colleges during this period, above all at Augustana College in Rock Island, Illinois. In the first years after its founding in Chicago in 1860, Augustana had concentrated primarily upon the education of Lutheran clergymen and showed little concern for Swedish secular culture or the preservation of the Swedish language for its own sake. The great increase in America's Swedish population beginning in the later 1860s reversed this situation and made the colleges progressively more "Swedish" in their cultural orientation. Their student bodies grew in size and variety, leading to the establishment of new, nontheological lines of study, such as music, teacher training, or commerce. In 1885 Augustana College admitted its first women. Faculties were meanwhile augmented with well-qualified teachers from Sweden.

Under such circumstances it would appear that the upsurge of Swedish pride and sentiment at the Swedish-American colleges emanated as much from the students themselves as from inspiring teachers during these years. Pastor Carl Aaron Swensson, one of Swedish America's foremost champions by the 1890s, recalled how in his childhood "many considered it fine to have forgotten Swedish, and sometimes even before they had learned English." At Augustana College in the 1870s he encountered a very different spirit. "I recall," he wrote, "how we were consumed, almost beyond measure, by our Swedish patriotism." In a college debating society, Swensson defended the proposition that "Little Sweden is the world's greatest country."[13] A new generation of students, born or raised in America, and often embarrassed by the vestiges of peasant attitudes and customs that had represented the Old Country culture in their homes, came enthusiastically to embrace by the 1890s the vision of an ideal Sweden as embodied in a heroic past and higher national literary culture.[14]

It was a vision powerfully reinforced by much of Swedish America's own literature, particularly in the lyric vein, which cultivated a longing nostalgia for the idyllic Swedish landscape. In his tribute to "the Swedish Muse in America," Carl G. Norman gave characteristic expression to this mood.

> No matter how rich Nature here may seem to us,
> no matter how fragrant the meadow may be,
> no matter how the flower smiles at us,
> and stars send their bright rays
> down from a sky that is high and wonderful,

the Swedish Muse will turn towards home,
like the dove of the Ark she will not find
rest, until across a bewildering sea she returns
to the childhood home where our dear ones dwell.

Or to quote another verse, by Lars Lundell:

I have been happy, but not here.
This soil is not my homeland dear;
My home is by Lake Siljan.[15]

In sum, Swedish-American culture had become more—rather than less—Swedish with the passing decades. But it had done so in a selective fashion, in response to its own circumstances and needs. It glorified past traditions of national greatness that it could rightly share with the homeland. It idealized Sweden's natural beauty and the steadfast character of its people. It meanwhile attached great importance to moral earnestness and thus tended to condemn the idleness, prodigality, and pleasure-seeking it identified with Sweden's upper classes.

Few Swedish Americans could feel any sympathy toward the elegant loungers or refined Epicurians of the Swedish capital or university towns. Swedish America thus reflected little of that winsome and aristocratic grace that so captivated cultivated foreign travelers in Sweden itself. Only in the larger Swedish-American urban centers can we detect some glimmer of that carefree and urbane tradition, above all in Chicago's little journalistic Bohemia and its American Society of Swedish Engineers, bastion of a unique group of academically trained knights-errant, most of whom eventually returned to the homeland.[16]

If the Swedish part of the evolving Swedish-American identity was essentially cultural, the American part was primarily civic and political. This meant attachment to the republic and to its institutions, which was largely regarded as tantamount to loyalty to the Republican party. By the 1890s, however, this traditional allegiance led to a growing crisis of conscience among many Swedish, as well as other Americans. Originally the "party of free men and free land," the Republican party had progressively come to represent the interests of Big Business, with which various of its leading politicians were involved in scandalous collusion. Midwestern farmers—still including most Swedish Americans—the original backbone of the party, felt increasingly betrayed and restive.

Yet few Swedish Americans defected to the Democratic party, which they tended to associate with the South and the big cities, "Demon Rum" and the Catholic church, the Irish and various newer immigrant nationalities whom they were inclined to consider less truly "American" than themselves. Their natural tendency to identify closely with the older American stock and distance themselves from other, non-Scandinavian immigrant groups is highlighted during these years by the strong support of much of the Swedish-American press, both denominational and secular, for the chauvinist, anti-Catholic American Protective Association, even though certain papers, such as *Svenska Kuriren* and *Svenska Amerikanaren* in Chicago early recognized in its bigotry disquieting signs of a revived "Know-Nothingism" aimed at all immigrants. On the whole, meanwhile, Scandinavian Americans enjoyed favored treatment in the mainstream American press.[17]

A revolt against the Republican allegiance could thus only succeed among the Swedish Americans if carried out under Anglo-American, Protestant, and rural auspices. Such an opportunity was provided by the Populist party organized in 1892, which in 1896 supported William Jennings Bryan in his bid for the presidency. Bryan lost the election to his Republican opponent, William McKinley, but the bastion of Swedish-American Republicanism had been breached.

EIGHT

Visitations and Counter-Visitations

*B*etween 1889 and 1903 a number of Swedish observers visited the United States. In a time of changing signals, their reactions varied widely, from the traditional liberal to sharply critical from both ends of the social and political spectrum. This variety of views contrasted with the high degree of liberal and pro-American consensus among Swedish visitors during the preceding decades, especially since the American Civil War. It would therefore seem most illuminating to consider these visitors and their views one at a time. Even avowedly sympathetic observers from Sweden were now more reserved in their praise. As for the critics, it becomes ever more apparent that their negative reactions to America increasingly derived from mounting fears of the rise throughout the Western World of commercialization and mass culture.[1]

The new critical viewpoint is first and best exemplified by Paul Peter Waldenström, lector at the Gävle *Gymnasium,* member of the Riksdag, theologian, and acknowledged leader of the pietistic Mission Friends movement in Sweden. Both as a moderate liberal politician and a religious publicist, Waldenström was one of Sweden's most influential opinion-makers when he visited the United States in 1889, and his travel account, *Genom Norra Amerikas Förenta Stater* (Through North America's United States), brought out in serial form and then as a stout volume both in Stockholm and Chicago in 1890, was apparently far more widely read than any such previous Swedish work.

A determined controversialist with strong convictions and at times a cuttingly sarcastic wit, Waldenström had a penchant for making enemies; of him Karl Olsson has written that "more dangerous heretics ... have been better liked." During the early 1860s, he had been tempted to serve as a Lutheran pastor among his countrymen in America. In 1889 he crossed the Atlantic in a distinctly skeptical frame of mind. "For my part," he stated at the outset in his account, "I must confess in advance that I am by no means filled with any great admiration for America and American conditions. . . . If anything has served to make me *really Swedish,* it has been my foreign travels, and these include my visit to America." It might be added that he did not speak English.[2] America, he wrote, "seems to me like a young, rich, nervous woman with plumes, rings, brooches, clad in silk and satin, bustle, and shoes with high heels, which make her seem taller than she really is. Old Sweden is more like a shy and unassuming mother in a shawl and cotton apron. There is more gold on the outside of the young woman, but there dwells more gold in the heart of the older."[3]

Waldenström recognized that although many left Sweden for "frivolous" reasons, others had valid enough reasons for doing so. Yet it grieved him that this should be so, and he sympathized deeply with many of the emigrant families aboard his ship. "Oh, back home in Sweden, there is home for me," he wrote from Providence, Rhode Island. "Wherever I see something that resembles Sweden, I feel what the ancient Hebrews must have experienced when on foreign soil they saw something that resembled Jerusalem. Oh, how can it be that patriotic sentiment has been extinguished among so many whose cradles stood in Sweden, who have grown up and long dwelt, indeed who still live, in Sweden itself!"[4]

Waldenström recognized and was gratified that the Swedes he encountered across the entire continent had done well and were well regarded. Yet he had his reservations. A Swedish farmer in Wisconsin told him he had emigrated to improve his lot in life, "and now," he added, "I am as well off as in Sweden." To this, Waldenström responded: "Surely many Swedes would speak in exactly the same way if they were prepared to speak as the heart dictates. But I fear that thousands of Swedes in America would be ashamed to admit that they are not better off there than they were at home." He could not but reflect upon "what significance it would have had for the development of our own country if these people had stayed there."[5]

Waldenström was repelled by much he saw and heard about in the United States. He reflected well-established European prejudices when he declared that in America: "A 'smart' man means a shrewd businessman, and with the question how much he is worth one always means how much money he has. If one looks at things in that way, it is clear that no country on earth can compare with America. But not everyone can look at them that way."

He declaimed against a political corruption that in Europe could only be compared with Russia's and against a system of justice that favored the rich and powerful, while turning a blind eye toward popular violence. America's vaunted freedom, he was given to believe, was hedged around by the arbitrary authority of local officials and gravely compromised by discrimination against those of African and Asian origins. American railroads were so poorly staffed that fatal accidents occurred almost daily and their stations in smaller communities looked like "woodsheds" compared with "our attractive little stations at home." Storm clouds could meanwhile be descried on America's horizon as big business was crowding out small producers and Western farmers.[6]

At a Fourth of July celebration in Chicago Waldenström could not but regret "how little we in Sweden actually do to arouse and strengthen true national feeling."[7] He was particularly dismayed and indignant over Swedish Americans who boasted immoderately about America at Sweden's expense. It deeply irked him that simple folk who at home had seen no more than "Putte village in Skutte parish" should claim to be knowledgeable about Sweden and he shook his head in dismay at naive comparisons between present conditions in America and those prevailing in Sweden twenty-five or thirty years earlier. Nor could most Swedish Americans, despite their assurances, really claim to know much about America as a whole. Such an attitude was scarcely calculated to endear him with the Swedish-American press, with which he engaged in a heated but not unwelcome feud.[8] "When the Swedes speak about the difficulties they had to face in Sweden," he wrote, "they often do so with great contempt. But when they speak of their difficulties in America ... they do so with the greatest delight. Indeed, they are quite carried away and become poetic in describing it all." In a moment of calmer reflection he added:

> That the Swedes love their new fatherland no one can find fault with. On the contrary, they *ought* to do so. But this need not at all mean that kind of attitude toward Old Sweden. Just as one has only *one* mother, one does not have more than one mother country. One may be compelled by circumstances of various kinds to leave one's homeland and seek one's livelihood in another, just as one may be compelled to leave one's parents and their home to make a living in another locality. But it is and remains a trait that is anything but admirable when one thinks and speaks with contempt of the old, maybe humble, parental home with its hard bread, when one has gained a better economic situation elsewhere. This is what I wanted to say on this subject.[9]

As a religious leader, Waldenström was much concerned with spiritual conditions in America, especially among the Swedish Americans. He was everywhere heartily received by Mission Covenant congregations, but since that group had recently seceded from the Swedish Lutheran church in America—unlike in Sweden—this created a strained relationship for him with the Augustana Synod. He did not visit Augustana College, due, he alleged, to the bitter hostility of its venerable president, T. N. Hasselquist, toward the Covenant. Still, he was on friendly terms with a number of Augustana Lutheran pastors and hoped for the day when their synod might recognize it as the Lord's will, that "the believers should, *as believers be united among themselves.*"[10]

Waldenström admitted that the Old World had much to learn from the New. America provided edifying examples of skill, industriousness, perseverance, patriotism, charity, and concern for education. On reading his *Genom Norra Amerikas Förenta Stater* a century later, one may find its critical tone and observations surprisingly tame in relation to the storm of indignation it provoked among Swedish Americans. But its accusations of lack of love for and pride in Sweden hit them precisely where they were bound to feel most vulnerable. The logic of their situation—their having left Sweden by their own choice—placed upon them the heavy burden of proving otherwise. "We Swedish Americans," Andrew A. Stomberg would write in 1928, "well remember with what quiet anxiety we heard, twenty-five or thirty years ago, that yet another Swedish expert was now coming out to 'study' us. It was naturally with a certain nervosity, mixed with curiosity, that we awaited their final judgment, for it has indeed been one of the Swedish Americans' weaknesses that they have been a bit sensitive toward criticism."[11]

If P. P. Waldenström exemplified a new critical view toward America, Isador Kjellberg had in 1883 published the most unqualified defense of America and of the Swedish emigration to appear in nineteenth-century Sweden. In 1890 he revisited the United States, the result of which was his *Amerika-Boken* (America-Book) in 1893.[12]

Kjellberg's description of his departure from Gothenburg on an emigrant ship stands in striking contrast to Waldenström's. The atmosphere was joyful and boisterous, and few tears were to be seen. A great crowd cheered the departing emigrants.

> In this general leave-taking there is, for those who remained behind, surely an expression of the dreams of most of them, sooner or later to be able to come over to America. It means: *"Fortunate are ye! God grant that we soon may follow after!"* ... If all who wished to suddenly got the chance to go to America and received as well assurance of a first, modest employment there, Sweden would at once become a desert, where everything stopped and fell into dissolution through lack of workers. One may say what one will about this, that it would be the height of ingratitude toward a fortunate, beloved fatherland, that is how things nonetheless stand. ... Poor Mother Svea! Something is the matter with Thee, when Thy sons and daughters— Thy stepchildren—can *so* easily leave Thee.[13]

America still offered sober and industrious immigrants far better prospects for success than did the Old Country, as Kjellberg illustrated by describing visits to numerous comfortably situated Swedish Americans in their tidy neighborhoods throughout the East and Midwest. He praised American communal self-government through locally elected officials, including Swedish immigrants who could never have attained such positions of responsibility at home, and maintained that the state church in Sweden produced more religious hypocrites than American religious freedom produced atheists.[14]

As in 1883 Kjellberg emphasized the civilizing effects of freedom and individual responsibility upon those unaccustomed to them in the Old Country. "It is altogether believable," he reflected, "that the majority of the Swedes in Sweden could develop into a truly great, virile, and handsome people under a free, republican constitution. Monarchy is not in general suited to produce comely faces or a true manly bearing."[15]

Not surprisingly, Kjellberg could not resist a thrust at P. P. Waldenström, who had visited America the year before:

> There we have new proof that no "green" gentleman with a one-sided upbringing and a viewpoint that is misdirected from the outset can avoid serious mistakes when he in all haste and on the basis of only a few weeks' observation, expresses himself regarding situations and conditions in the New World, whose free and democratic spirit he cannot abide. Herr Waldenström's customary cocksureness is least of all appropriate in this instance.

He concluded his account with the invocation: "America! Thou are still Mankind's guiding star. May—despite certain threatening developments, above all the *capitalist* and *Jesuit* threats—the American nation never cease to serve all other peoples as their noblest vision, for which so many victims of oppression in this world sigh!"[16]

Isador Kjellberg died before his time in 1895. Yet the nineteenth-century individualistic liberalism he so steadfastly championed was by then on the wane. The Jeffersonian ideal of a society of free and independent farmers, artisans, tradesmen, and entrepreneurs was giving way to the control of capital, to political and administrative power by trusts and cartels, federated labor unions, mass political parties, and the regulatory state. The age of individualism was drawing to a close, it has been said; that of collectivism was beginning.[17]

In 1888, shortly before Waldenström and Kjellberg visited America, Hjalmar Cassel, a twenty-year-old fledgling journalist, returned to Sweden after a year spent editing the newspaper *Svenska Dagbladet* in St. Paul, Minnesota. Having come of age under the influence of the literary Realism of the 1880s, he came out in 1894 with a semi-fictional book based on his American experiences, which recalls Strindberg's *Red Room* of 1879 in iconoclasm and burlesque wit. How much of Cassel's book was fictional is difficult to judge, but it contains some shrewd and hard-hitting commentary on America and its Swedish inhabitants.[18]

The story centers on the struggle between the upright Charles Newstrom, who has just started the "independent" Swedish-American newspaper for which the narrator, Mr. Cassel, works, and the wealthy and corrupt saloonkeeper, B. Johnson, for election to the St. Paul city council. It is replete with adventure, romance, and skullduggery, the latter provided by the despicable Johnson and his following. Cassel was prepared to accept America on its own terms. That, for instance, there was much political corruption he recognized as a matter of course and indeed believed that it probably appeared worse than it actually was. His real criticisms were leveled against his own countrymen in America. It is indicative that his hero was an independent-minded Democrat born in America, while his villain was a Swedish-born ward boss with the Republican party machine behind him.

America, Cassel wrote, was "the land of unhappy Swedes." Many grieved over their ruined lives and cursed America, while even those who had not emigrated to expiate their sins but simply to find a better future "bear within them a disharmonious world-view, created by the contradictions between the land they left and that which has become their new home. They can never cease to feel like Swedes and still they are forced by circumstances to be Americans. . . . and this conflict continues as long as they live."[19]

Cassel was distressed by the low cultural level he found among his immigrated countrymen. At a performance of F. A. Dahlgren's well-worn popular melodrama "Vermländingarne" from 1846, the only Swedish theater piece he had the chance to see in St. Paul, "there was so much stamping and whistling that it was hard to hear what was being said, and one was disturbed during the most moving scenes by salvos of raucous laughter." He concluded that "The Swedish American as a type is anything but aesthetically inclined. In this, as in many other respects, the Yankee spirit has had a deleterious effect upon the Swedish character. Here at home we find a significant interest in the arts even among the working class. In the West this soon disappears under the depraving influence of corrupted American taste and the all-consuming pursuit of the dollar."[20] The Americans, Cassel held, still had the same mentality as when they "lived in log cabins and fought with Indians." "After I had come to the conclusion that it would probably take a couple of hundred years before a person of culture could in good conscience settle down in the United States, I went to bed and slept soundly."[21]

The environment, moreover, if anything exacerbated the fatal Swedish inclination toward jealousy and dissention, which in this story led to the ultimate defeat of both Swedish-American candidates for the St. Paul council seat by an Irishman, which thus denied their group the representation it needed and deserved. Social equality, even among Swedish immigrants, was more illusion than reality. Unlike other Swedish observers, he even accused the younger, unmarried Swedes—at least in the Twin Cities—of distressingly lax morals, once released from the customary constraints of their old home communities.[22]

With their natural reserve, the Swedes were a people little inclined toward politics, while most immigrants of simple background could have little understanding for the Byzantine intricacies of the American system. They thus tended to run with the herd, in their case the Republican party, whose program they still conceived in terms of values and outworn slogans from Civil War days.[23]

Cassel was naturally concerned with the Swedish-American press, and here he had serious charges to make. It had above all two basic purposes in his view: to preach the Republican message and "in every possible way to praise the Swedes [in America] both as a nationality and individually." In the latter respect: "This constant praise has created among the Swedes a spiritual pride that assumes the most absurd forms. . . . Be it noted, meanwhile, that these exaggerated ideas about Swedish qualities by no means extend to old Sweden. No, about it, at least in a political sense, there is nothing good to say. It is only the Swedes in America who are remarkable and only their accomplishments that are to be praised—at the motherland's expense, if so be."

To present its own group in the most favorable light, the Swedish-American press systematically denigrated the "unfortunate Irish," thereby fostering an "artificial enmity." In truth, "if their faults are greater than the Swedes', in many cases their merits are also greater."[24]

The World's Columbian Exposition in 1893 brought to Chicago a number of Swedish journalists, two of whom at least, K. J. Bohlin and Gustaf Gullberg, wrote accounts stereotypical of the European cultural critique of America during the 1890s. Bohlin, who claimed to have lived there some years earlier, wrote, "In America there are freedom and bread, gold and honorary titles, but there are also greater slavery, poverty, and humbug than in any other land under the sun. . . . And who knows if America is still not the land of the future?" For Gullberg, Chicago was America—a "barbaric land"—in microcosm, where "everything is expensive, extravagant, ostentatious, but tasteless, clumsy, and ugly." Neither had much to say specifically about Swedish immigrants, although Bohlin expressed sympathy for those aboard his ship whose "cloud castles" would soon be dispelled by the grim realities of life in the new land, and Gullberg was convinced that despite all their "empty boastfulness," the Swedish immigrants would gladly return home if Sweden could provide them with a better and more secure livelihood.[25]

In 1893, at the request of the Augustana Synod, the Swedish state church sent over one of its bishops to take part in the synod's three-hundredth anniversary celebration of the Swedish church's adoption of the Augsburg Confession. The prelate chosen, K. H. G. von Schéele of the Visby diocese, admitted to some initial reservations, which quickly vanished once he reached America. He traveled from coast to coast, participating in services and commemorative events.

Few are likely to have read Bishop von Schéele's *Hemlandstoner* (Homeland Tones), which came out in 1894–95, either at the time or since; it is heavy going, consists mainly of sermons and religious reflections, and tells little of the author's actual experiences in America. But its positive tone, both toward America and especially the Swedish Americans, is unmistakable. Schéele deplored the prejudices in Sweden regarding the emigrants' alleged lack of attachment to homeland, language, culture, and faith, and the resentments these had aroused among the Swedes in America, in view of the devoted sacrifices they made to preserve their heritage. The latter gave, Schéele wrote, "innumerable, irrefutable proofs that love for old Sweden still lives on in Swedish breasts, increased rather than diminished through separation." Here was a direct denial of P. Waldenström's hurtful accusations, albeit unfortunately in a far less readable presentation. More significant, meanwhile, than what the bishop wrote was the very fact of his visit, through which the Swedish state church, long indifferent or suspicious toward its wayward offshoot in the New World, officially manifested a new spirit of good will and conciliation.[26]

An observer of a new and different type was August Palm, who visited America in 1900. A master tailor from Stockholm, Palm had worked as a journeyman in Germany, where he had been converted to Marxian socialism. In 1881 he initiated a socialist movement in Sweden, despite harassment by the police, and in 1885 became editor of its newspaper, *Social-Demokraten*. He now visited the United States at the invitation of the Scandinavian section of the Socialist Labor party and lectured to Scandinavian socialist gatherings in the East and Middle West.

Although in his account, published in 1901, Palm was mainly concerned with relating the incidents of his journey to his accustomed readership, his ideas about America emerge clearly and show a curious ambivalence. When discussing America in the abstract, he is dogmatically and didactically Marxian, describing the arrogant power of Capital and the "devilish slavery to which the great masses are subjected."[27]

Karl Marx regarded religion as the "opiate of the masses" and August Palm attacked the churches in America, especially among his immigrated countrymen, with particular vehemence. America, he held, was still "the land of humbug *par préférence*," and nowhere did this flourish more profusely than among the proclaimers of the Word, who found the great republic a veritable "El Dorado" for profitable "business" of all kinds. The real harm was done by the ignorant, fanatical, or hypocritical evangelists, real wolves in clerical collars, who exploited their immigrant brothers— and especially sisters.[28] The power of the clergy was largely born up by the Swedish-language press in America, which Palm exaggeratedly considered to be almost entirely under its domination—hence, in his view, the hostile campaign he found directed against himself in the Swedish-language papers.[29]

Still, as a person Palm was too honest and forthright to see America simply in stereotypes. He was fascinated by his direct experience of the country—as opposed to his strictly theoretical viewpoint—and he found much he frankly admired. He admitted that most of the workingmen he actually met and whose homes he visited were in comfortable circumstances and, what particularly impressed him, were well housed. Some, whom he had earlier known in Sweden, were now much better off than they had been there, and Palm pointed out that if conditions were hard for laborers in America they were scarcely better in Sweden. He was impressed by the independence and prosperity attained by Swedish farmers in Minnesota. In that state, too, he praised the impartial exercise of public authority, on occasion against the excesses of big business.[30]

It was naturally discouraging to Palm that American workingmen seemed so little interested in socialism. This was even true, Palm had to admit, among the Swedes and other Scandinavians there. Nevertheless, he could understand there were practical explanations for this situation, above all the sheer size of the country, its still-vast resources, and the wide dispersion, mobility, and ethnic diversity of its working class. Most immigrants had to devote themselves too entirely to making a living and adapting to new conditions to be able to support political causes. These same circumstances made it possible for American politics to be so corrupt.[31] Palm was nonetheless by now a revisionist Marxist who looked to a peaceful and orderly restructuring of society through the political process, rather than through violent revolution. What despite all made him optimistic regarding America was its universal manhood suffrage—a crucial difference from Sweden and most European countries where this still remained an unachieved goal.[32]

Upon leaving America, Palm held that the country had made "an indelible impression for the rest of my life." He regretted that his ignorance of English had kept him from even closer contact and concluded: "For my own part, I must frankly confess that if I had now been only 32 rather than 52 years old, I would surely have gone over and sought my livelihood there, for it is a land with resources, a great land, where there are possibilities and where no one with energy and perseverence need go under."[33]

August Palm's ambivalence toward America was more than personal. In the past the United States had traditionally been seen as the land of promise for the European workingman who sought through honest toil to win economic independence and decent prosperity. Earlier forms of socialism and idealistic communalism had placed high hopes in the young republic. By the later nineteenth century, however, European socialism was beginning to perceive a very different America: the Western World's most flagrant example of the evils of unrestrained capitalism, the "proletarian Hell."[34] August Palm's American journey occurred close to the parting of the ways and he was still able to look in both directions.

In 1890, upon his return to Sweden, Paul Peter Waldenström had written that he would not for anything have missed the experience of visiting America but that it would take a great deal ever to induce him to repeat it.[35] He nonetheless returned to the United States in 1901 and the following year published an account of this journey nearly as fat and probably almost as widely read as his earlier book on America.

Waldenström's second account reveals a notably more sympathetic attitude toward America. In particular he repeatedly praised the energy, enterprise, and productivity of American economic life, making pointed comparisons with Sweden. In Massachusetts he was greatly impressed by the comfortable circumstances of Swedish immigrant industrial workers, who received, by Swedish standards, remarkably high wages. "But," he added, "they also have to work."

> It will not do to stand around and ponder and chat and take a pinch of snuff and go off and drink coffee or a half liter of beer during working hours. No, things have to move along quickly. For that reason an employer can pay his workers twice as much as in Sweden and still—despite tariffs and transportation costs—sell the product of their labor at a price with which the Swedish producer finds it hard to compete. The secret is that the worker in America does more work for his wage than the Swedish worker does in relation to his.[36]

Waldenström often heard Swedes in America boast that they had to work three times as hard there as in Sweden. Many told him that upon revisiting Sweden they had longed to return to America, "as they had become 'really sick' when they saw the lackadaisical way they worked back home. The heart of the American method of working is above all to work, work, work."[37]

At the same time, Waldenström, who now visited the United States at the invitation of Yale University, was appreciative of the spiritual dimension. "One may speak of materialism in America as much as one wishes, but it is meanwhile certain that respect for religion and for a God-fearing way of life is greater there than in perhaps any other land." His positive reaction to the American religious scene at this time was surely affected by the much more amicable relations he now enjoyed with the Augustana Lutheran Synod and its leaders, with the exception of Carl Aaron Swensson, an exception explained further below.[38]

As before, Waldenström was gratified to see how well his countrymen had done for themselves in America and how favorably they were regarded there. More than that, he was deeply moved to discover there the sturdy survival of human types and values from an older and truer Sweden. "Oh, what a picture of the old Sweden," he wrote of the Red Oak area in Iowa. Around Randolph, Kansas, he met "a collection of real Swedish peasants, with great beards and faces that reflected calm determination. Here were handclasps that spoke of mighty labors. ... Oh, what a true picture of Sweden, the mother of us all!" In Boone, Iowa, he admired the "natural nobility" of the pure Swedish peasant types he met. At the same time he recognized that the Swedish-American farmer combined in remarkable degree natural abilities from home with wide and varied experience in the New World.[39]

Many of his earlier readers, Waldenström wrote, would surely remember his sharp criticism of the Swedish Americans for the lack of respect they had shown toward the Old Country. Now, however, he found "a not insignificant change." If before they had, in their ignorance, made disparaging comments about Sweden, they now spoke of it with love and sympathy. This was only right. "Sweden is, in any event, the land which the Swedish Americans have to thank for the upbringing that has enabled them in the new land to become what they have become." The principal reason for this change in attitude he found in the "lively interchange between Sweden and America which has taken place in recent years," especially the growing numbers of Swedish Americans who now visited the old homeland each year, through which they got to know it better than they ever could have before. He nonetheless recognized the natural drift of the immigrants' children toward the English language and the vital role of ongoing immigration for the survival of Swedish in America.[40]

A great deal had happened in Sweden during the past dozen years that would largely explain Waldenström's more positive view of America by 1901. On his first visit he had been an individualist liberal of the older type, but since then his outlook had become progressively more conservative. In particular he was aroused by the seeming threat to Sweden's economic future and religious values posed by labor unionization and the socialist movement headed by August Palm and his friends. Among the present causes of continued emigration, he placed particular emphasis upon "the Social Democratic Reign of Terror," which prevented capable and ambitious workingmen from working as hard as they wished, forced them to go on strike whether they wanted to or not, and exacted a heavy tribute in union dues.[41]

"Work well and earn well" was the American slogan, whereas the "Social Democratic method" consisted of "preventing the capable and energetic worker from doing any more than the lazy incompetent." Good, affordable homes for the working class Waldenström saw as a further bulwark of individual freedom in America, and he could not but marvel at how there "they build a complete house during the time it takes in Sweden to take a pinch of snuff and think about the matter." The Swedish socialists he accused of opposing the spread of privately owned workers' homes, since "the homeless masses have always provided the best material for agitators."

Contemplating the Statue of Liberty as his ship left New York, Waldenström reflected on how "liberty, enjoyed in the light of true understanding, is the foremost requirement for a people's successful development. Therefore freedom is the very heart of American life, and the effort to spread understanding in all areas is surely greater there than in any other country. ... Farewell, Thou great land, which art still small in comparison with what Thou someday shalt be. If only we could take home with us from there something of the industry, strength, persistence, hardiness which are the trademarks of work in America! If we cannot acquire more of these things for our own land, we face a sorrowful fate."[42]

At the very time when August Palm and his associates in the closely interrelated Swedish socialist and labor movements were beginning to develop a new skepticism toward the United States, P. P. Waldenström and a growing segment of the right wing in the Swedish political spectrum conceived a new respect for the dynamic new nation across the ocean and—to a degree—for those of their compatriots who had showed themselves enterprising enough to seek and find their fortunes there.[43] Thus began a striking reversal of views that would last, with some twists and turns along the way, down to the present.

By the 1890s increasing numbers of Swedish Americans visited their old homeland, as P. P. Waldenström had noted with satisfaction. The resulting confrontations between emigrants and the land and people they had left to make a new life could lead to culture shock in varying degree. To return to the scenes of childhood and youth, to family and old friends, could be, and usually was, a deeply moving emotional experience. Yet it could also lead to misunderstanding, embarrassment, wounded sensibilities, and disenchantment on either side.

The contrasts between old and new, Swedish and American, were heightened by the returning emigrants' natural urge to justify themselves to their home communities through a conspicuous display of their success in the New World by dressing elegantly, spending freely, and telling tall tales about the Great Land to the West. In this manner a rich folklore concerning Swedish Americans in the Old Country developed on both sides of the Atlantic, which would provide welcome material for cartoons, popular songs, and the comic stage, as well as more serious forms of literature.

Even those who could not themselves make the sentimental journey home had increasing opportunities to do so vicariously, for a growing number of accounts of visits to Sweden were published during the 1890s and beyond, either in Swedish-American newspapers, in book form, or frequently in both. This was a subject that obviously held great fascination for Swedish-American readers, and it was presented in a variety of ways.

A common approach to the subject and the awkward, embarrassing, or irritating situations it frequently produced was through humor, most commonly in the form of burlesque exaggeration. In a short story from 1900, the Swedish-American journalist and author, Ninian Wærner, described, for instance, the visit home of a former farm girl.

> She was dressed in swishy silk, gloves, and parasol, as well as a hat with a whole bird in it, flapping its wings amid masses of garish artificial flowers and waving grasses. . . . And she chewed "gum" so that her jaw, like a *perpetuum mobile,* was like a cow chewing her cud. And she smelled of "ourangoutang" [the mispronounced name of some presumably cheap perfume] from far away, and she was no longer called Albertina Larsdotter, as she was when she left. No, could anyone believe the like! Tiny Burlington was now the girl's name, to her glory and no one's shame. And when the pastor took his former confirmand by the hand and asked how things went for her in America, she answered, with a shrill laugh and so loudly that all the church folk . . . heard to their wonderment, *"Putti hoäll, sörr!"* ["Pretty well, sir"].[44]

The Swedish-American humorous classic on this subject is surely *Mister Colesons Sverigeresa* (Mr. Coleson's Trip to Sweden), published by the journalist Frithiof Colling, under the pseudonym Gabriel Carlson, in 1896. In this sprightly picaresque novel, Colling, who himself visited Sweden repeatedly between 1885 and 1897, describes the odyssey of "Mister Coleson"—originally Carlsson, of course—back to the land of his origins, in a manner reminiscent both of contemporary Swedish humorous tales about the country bumpkin's visit to the Big City and of Mark Twain's *Innocents Abroad.*

Decked out in his American finery, Mr. Coleson arrives in Gothenburg, where he sees the sights in style, together with his equally well turned-out Swedish-American fellow passenger, "Miss Peterson." There follows the predictable scene in which his family fails to recognize the elegant American gentleman when he appears unannounced at their door. The high point comes when Mr. Coleson, surrounded by his jubilant family, attends the local parish church the following Sunday, where all, naturally, are overwhelmed by his fine apparel and especially by his gold watch.

He soon finds himself the subject of flattering attentions from the finer folk of the neighborhood, at least until he cannily refuses to make the "loans" they all, sooner or later, ask him for, after which they mutter remarks about the impudent upstart. In the meantime he becomes engaged to a local shopkeeper's fair but empty-headed daughter.

All this changes after an escapade-filled visit to Stockholm, where Mr. Coleson loses both his pocketbook and his watch. At once he loses all credit in the old parish, his betrothed breaks off their engagement, and he becomes a local laughing-stock. That is, until his landlady in Stockholm finds the missing valuables and returns them. This leads to Coleson's engagement to her daughter, who proves to be both a snob and a schemer, and who takes this chance to make her way to the land of opportunity to the west while insisting that no place on earth can match Stockholm. On the return voyage, Mr. Coleson again meets the lovely Miss Peterson, and after an amicable and businesslike settlement with his Stockholm fiancee, they become engaged, realizing that, as the Swedish saying goes, "children of the same kind play best together": that only Swedish Americans can really understand each other.[45]

More significant, however, in forming the attitudes of Swedish Americans toward the Old Country—and hence toward themselves—were more straightforward and factual accounts by Swedish-American travelers. Among such observers, none had so great an influence as Carl Aaron Swensson, the Augustana Lutheran pastor, founder and president of Bethany College in Lindsborg, Kansas, and member of his state legislature, who traveled in Sweden during the summer of 1890. His account was serialized in many Swedish-, as well as some English-language newspapers, and when it came out in Stockholm as a stout volume entitled *I Sverige* (In Sweden) the following year, Swensson considered it already to have been read by a million people in America.[46] It was, indeed, the first Swedish-American account of travel in Sweden to appear in book form and was without question the most widely read.

Unlike others who wrote of visits to their old homeland at this time, Swensson was born in America. In an introductory chapter he meanwhile explained at length how thoroughly Swedish he was by background and upbringing. The son of a Swedish pastor who had only reluctantly accepted a call from America, Swensson had grown up in a home permeated with Swedish values.[47]

The reason for providing this background seems evident. P. P. Waldenström had recently encountered strong criticism for writing so extensively and authoritatively on America after only a brief visit and without knowledge of English.[48] Swensson was well advised to establish more solid credentials. The fact that he knew Swedish perfectly and, almost uniquely among his American-raised contemporaries, was a consummate stylist in writing it gave him a strong advantage.

Swensson stated that his account was intended to encourage a love for Sweden among the younger, American-born generation of Swedish Americans.[49] As the book version of his account was published in Swedish in Stockholm, he was meanwhile as anxious to reach a Swedish public. More specifically, C. A. Swensson obviously conceived of *I Sverige* as Swedish America's response to P. P. Waldenström's *Genom Norra Amerika* of the year before. There could be no mistaking whom Swensson was referring to when he wrote in his introductory chapter:

> The trouble with some "Swedish Swedes" is that despite their learning and many-sided knowledge they still seem to accept the principle that a Swede

who dares to believe that any part of the globe outside Sweden is a reality is and should be regarded as a traitor. It is truly a sad and, in my view, unprovoked slander when, like the author in question, one holds that the Swedes in America have forgotten the land in the high North. This is, it seems to me, a distortion of the facts which calls for the most serious vindication.[50]

The ground was cleared for a battle between giants. Both Waldenström and Swensson were highly public figures who accepted as a matter of course the role of tribune for their respective followings. Both were religious leaders, politicians, and practical men of affairs. If Waldenström exercised a powerful influence in Sweden, Swensson can only be compared with J. A. Enander as an opinionmaker among the Swedes in America; while Enander dwelt upon the great deeds of the Swedish race in days of yore, in both the Old and New Worlds, Swensson concentrated upon contemporary Sweden and the Swedish Americans' relationship to it.

Yet for all apparent similarities, deep differences separated Swensson from Waldenström. Thorny points of doctrine stood between the Lutheran and the Mission Friend, or on another level, the champion of the broad folk church and that of the closed sect of true believers. Swensson had moreover become a wholehearted defender of American civic ideals. Finally, it is hard to avoid the conclusion that the conflict between them, which reached an open break by 1902, after Waldenström's second visit to America, was in large part a matter of personality. Waldenström, especially in his first book on America, comes across as pedantic and pedagogic, straight-laced, coolly ironical, and querulous. Swensson in his account of Sweden seems just the opposite: sanguine, open, broad-minded, indeed expansively "American" in what he himself would have considered the best meaning of the term.[51]

Written in installments, Swensson's *I Sverige* consists of a series of *causeries,* in which commentary is intermixed with narrative, often in the form of passing asides. Taken together they show their author's earnest effort to be "really truthful, really just, to be *Swedish-American*" in his reporting on the Old Country, and to reconcile the two branches of a divided people.[52]

The book is dedicated to "Sweden, homeland of my longing." Swensson was filled with enthusiasm over Sweden's idyllic beauty when, as a mature man, he first encountered it. He repeatedly expressed his delight over both the natural and the human landscape. In Norrland, for instance, he reflected:

Yes, Old Sweden, Thou art the land of dreams and ideals for the Swedish American, who has read and admired Thy history, listened to sagas and legends, and sung Thy marvelously beautiful songs and melodies. In Rock Island, St. Peter, and Lindsborg [i.e., Augustana, Gustavus Adolphus, and

Bethany Colleges] there is during the winters a crowd of youths who love not only our wonderful America, rich in future promise, but also the land in the North, where the sighing of the wind in the pine forest sings a somber but heavenly beautiful duet with the rushing waterfall or the playful waves of the lake.

He was deeply stirred by Sweden's heroic past and respectful toward its venerable institutions. Approaching Stockholm for the first time aboard a steamer on Lake Mälaren, he mused: "Certainly I am a republican, but when my mind scans the long series of Swedish hero-kings, whose names shine with clear luster on the firmament of history, the confession always comes to my lips: happy the land that possesses so inspiring a history as Sweden's."[53]

Swensson was both amused and touched by the many signs he saw in Stockholm's parks, admonishing proper behavior: "They bore the stamp of the Swedish sense of orderliness and propriety. . . . There is something so naive and childlike about all the Swedish park regulations. It is as if one had entered into an innocent little world, where everything is arranged and managed according to patriarchal principles. I thought it was all quite delightful."[54]

The movement for a stronger defense in Sweden expressed a heightened national feeling that he found encouraging. "Away with all that miserable idolizing of everything foreign! Let Sweden become Swedish again, let it know and feel that for every Swede it is the world's greatest land."[55]

He was meanwhile deeply impressed with the refined and cultivated life he encountered among people of his own kind in Sweden, compared with the mindless rush and bustle of America. "We Swedish Americans must truly be on our guard lest our entire existence become an unbroken chain of hard work, with Washington's Birthday and the Fourth of July, together with Thanksgiving's fat turkey, thrown in as a kind of diversion. Why should we not, especially in our proud, prosperous America, try to make our earthly existence as pleasant as possible?"[56]

Still, to observe Sweden as a Swedish American did not mean for Swensson uncritical acceptance of everything he found. Like Hans Mattson before him, he was often indignant over the callous treatment of women. Gentlemen of the wealthier classes publicly allowed themselves liberties with waitresses, which in America would have brought them a prompt and resounding box on the ear. He was astonished at the heavy labor women often had to perform. "Women are not valued so highly back there as they are here in the New World. . . . Out in the country I was given cause by what I saw to wonder whether the farmer was not much more concerned with his horse than with his wife."[57]

Swensson was put off by the drunkenness and loud swearing he encountered. Much of the rural youth he found to be "extremely raw and uncouth," certainly as bad or worse than in America, which he attributed largely to the great distances between country churches.[58] At the same time the American college president was apprehensive that far too many young men were receiving a secondary education, often at great sacrifice to their families. "Old Sweden is swarming with 'white-caps,'" he observed, but they received an altogether impractical classical education.[59]

As a clergyman, Swensson was of course interested in Swedish religious life. He was impressed by the clerical colleagues he met, and of a bishop's dinner in Härnösand he wrote for the benefit of his Swedish-American readers that although toasts were drunk, he found wine-drinking among the Swedish clergy to be "so rare and so unexpectedly moderate and orderly that I was understandably surprised thereby, when I thought of all the stories they tell about this in America." Lutheran church attendance he meanwhile found disappointingly low. He found many of the newer religious songs "watery," compared with the sturdy old hymns still sung in Swedish America. Ultimately he held that the Lutheran church in Sweden must separate itself from the state, as in America, to attain a spiritual vigor equal to that of his beloved Augustana Lutheran Synod.[60]

Naturally Swensson was offended by much ignorance of and bias against the United States, which he saw it as his mission to combat as best he could. "I imagine," he wrote, "that many of Sweden's ladies and gentlemen ... would rather travel to Africa than to 'barbaric America.' Oh, how I sometimes laughed, and at times became angry, when they asked in Sweden about American conditions." For this the Swedish press was largely to blame, as it dwelt by preference upon the wild and sensational.

> That this is done in a patriotic spirit, [Swensson reflected] I doubt not, but the effects are the opposite of those intended, for there lies in the Swedish character an irresistible urge for adventure. If the Swedish newspapers described general conditions in our country, the emigration would end all the sooner. But as it is, hearty Swedish youths feel compelled to come over here to see all the frightful things they have read about. ... So we Americans smile up our sleeves when during the summers we read daily in the Stockholm newspapers of sunstrokes, railroad accidents, and cyclones in our "dreadful America," for we know that all of this only brings us more Swedes in the New World, and that is truly a happy thought, since our countrymen are recognized as the best foreigners who come over to us poor devils, who live here so miserably among Indians, buffalos, and train robbers.[61]

In Stockholm, Swensson walked the streets with P. P. Waldenström, who "made petty remarks in his curious way against us Swedes in America for not being, in his opinion, patriotic enough toward old Sweden." "Oh, no," Swensson addressed his readers, "we Swedes in America love Sweden much more than Sweden loves us."[62]

At the end of his account, Swensson held that Swedish Americans were often misled in their ideas about Sweden through their exaggerated reactions against chauvinistic anti-American criticism in Sweden, which could in turn produce the opposite extreme of hyper-Americanism, "both of which arouse the disgust of the objective listener and observer." "But it is becoming better. With each passing year we in America have better opportunities to learn to know our fathers' land and its people and circumstances."[63]

If Swensson was offended by ignorance and ill will toward America in Sweden, he was no less indignant over loutish visitors from America whom he occasionally encountered. While touring Stockholm's royal palace, "our enjoyment was disturbed for a time by a Swedish American from California, whom we purely by chance had in our party. He was one of those tragicomic asses who help give the Swedes a poor opinion of their countrymen in the New World. He expressed himself freely and contemptuously about almost everything in Sweden."[64]

Most seriously, Swensson could not help but notice lingering signs of excessive wealth, poverty, and social cleavage. Like Hans Mattson before him he felt that most of the royal palaces would be better employed as charitable institutions.[65] As much as he admired the gracious way of life of the comfortably situated in Sweden, he could not help noticing in places the pale faces of undernourished children, and he declared, in what he clearly intended as an apologia for the emigration aimed at his Swedish readers, that he would certainly not want to be a cotter (*torpare*) in the land of his fathers:

> You see, first and foremost I like to be able to eat my fill a couple or three times a day, and secondly, I want my children to be able to do the same; but that is not always such an easy matter for many cotters back home in Sweden. Then it is nice to be able to live in a comfortable house and stand up straight in its doorway, and that is not at all possible in many of the cotters' small, joyless dwellings, such as those I saw in Småland and Västergötland. Next, I care about my value as a human being and am not content with being recorded in the church registry as a baptized Christian but then being treated simply like a durable work machine without a will of its own. No sir! I am naturally glad to lift my hat to anyone whomsoever, but I certainly do not want to go and carry it in my hand throughout my life. Work I both can and want to do, but honest work is worth a good and decent wage.

He hastened to add that his readers should not conclude that most inhabitants of the Swedish countryside lived on "herring heads and potato peels," and that, in fact, he found much prosperity there. Only the very poor, he felt, should now consider emigrating. But the fact remained that some Swedes were still very poor.[66]

As the summer wore on, Swensson felt himself ever more confirmed in his American and, most specifically, his Swedish-American identity. The dead weight of the past in the Old World oppressed him. The unhurried pace of life and travel at times called forth his American restlessness: "That we Americans are in many ways more superficial than the Swedes is frankly admitted, but our powers of observation are greater, our thought processes more rapid, we are able, more quickly and calmly, to adapt to new circumstances." Swedish Americans he considered to be basically more religious than the Swedes in the Old Country, and in Strängnäs he met a returned Swedish-American pastor and his wife who longed to go back to Kansas and the Augustana Synod.[67]

> We naturally read with great interest all the news from America [he wrote from Småland]. Lector Waldenström became Swedish in America, he says . . . and we Americans feel, at the same time that we learn to love Sweden all the more, in an unexpected and curious way during a sojourn abroad the strong and tender bonds which attach us to the great, glorious land across the ocean. There is only one America, there is only one land more fortunate than all others, and that country is our new homeland . . . a new world in itself, the link connecting the old, outworn, iron-bound development with . . . the new golden age. For better times are coming, even if the way passes through clouds and storms.[68]

Swensson realized well enough that all was not as it should be in the United States. "As a democracy," he declared, "we are still only in our childhood." America, like other lands, was not free from an "aristocracy," albeit a new kind based on wealth, which threatened the masses with poverty, as he openly stated at a conference of state church clergy in Stockholm. "But in America this cannot take place unchallenged, count on that."[69]

At the end of his account, Swensson weighed the Old Country against the New in an appeal for greater understanding and respect on both sides:

> I have always believed and said that the Swedes are a splendid people. This conviction is all the stronger since I have had the pleasure of seeing them in their homeland. . . . It certainly will not harm us in the least if we, in this great, fortunate, but terribly prosaic land now and then remember the land where our parents' cradles stood and where one, more than we do, *lives life* and thanks God for a true and rightful joy in living. But when, on the other hand, it becomes a question of work and activity, of future and progress, America stands in the front rank. There is surely no country that offers such great hope in coming days for the poor and the young.[70]

C. A. Swensson returned to Sweden for a second visit during the summer of 1897, the result of which was a sizable travel account, again serialized in Swedish- and English-language newspapers in America and published the following year in both languages in Chicago.[71] The immediate occasion for this trip was the Stockholm Exposition of 1897, as well as the celebration of the twenty-five-year jubilee of King Oscar II's reign. Compared with his *I Sverige* from 1891, Swensson's *Åter i Sverige* or *Again in Sweden* from 1898 is something of an anticlimax. It consists largely of excerpts drawn from other sources, describing, for instance, the Exposition or the Swedish tour of the elite chorus of the American Union of Swedish Singers, and it provides extensive information on Sweden's government, public institutions, economy, and resources, drawn from official sources. This difference may be partly due to the fact that Swensson was here writing for an almost entirely American—including non-Swedish-American—public, for which such factual information was useful and welcome, although one may also suspect that his legendary energy was already beginning to flag under the constant overload of work that he took upon himself.

Still, as before, Swensson offers some revealing insights along the way. On the whole these accord well with the views he had expressed seven years earlier. Again, he could be Swedish or American according to mood or circumstance. Yet in the balance, his essentially American identity is more clearly profiled than before.

As ever, Sweden's natural beauty deeply moved him. At the same time, he was gratified to note obvious signs of rapid material progress, which, of course, suggested a somber comparison with the United States at the time. He was greatly impressed by the Stockholm Exposition, the showplace for Sweden's recent development and rising national spirit, and he greatly admired King Oscar, who received him cordially in Marstrand.[72]

Still, as a Swedish American he found himself impatient with the way in which the exposition was promoted. Why, for instance, had not the steamship lines offered special reduced fares to Americans? An estimated twenty thousand Swedish Americans visited the Exposition, but Swensson was sure at least twice as many would have come with such an inducement. The Exposition had not been widely publicized abroad. "But it is always so," he commented. "Sweden and the Swedes are too modest, have not a sufficiency of self-consciousness, and so very often are unable to make free use of their advantages and rights."[73]

As before, he found the amenities of Swedish home and social life deeply appealing. Yet he could not avoid other reflections: "Just think how lovely and attractive, how simple, natural and true is the social life among the cultured Swedes. Happy people, they! And nevertheless we prosaic Americans very often make our way through life easier than these refined and happy Swedes at home. Such is life, such the play of fate. But if they come to America and allow themselves to become fully naturalized they will soon make their mark." In Värmland he observed: "Look there! The harvesters are at work in the field with their old-fashioned scythes. True, it looked poetical, but I admit that the American self-binding reaper is immensely more practical. I need not inform you that the latter machine has found its way to Sweden."[74]

Swensson was, moreover, critical of what seemed to him the happy-go-lucky ways of the Swedish working class:

> I have more respect for the Swedish laborer in America than in Sweden, as a class. Thousands of laborers in Sweden earn a good day's wages which far exceeds the pay that, for example many clergymen must be satisfied with. But how many save a portion of their earnings? I saw sad sights with respect to this matter in Sweden. When the laborer gets his pay he drinks, dances and uses it for sinful pleasures, instead of setting aside useful and necessary savings for the future.[75]

On a train, Swensson fell in with a returned emigrant, which caused him to reflect: "It is a strange, or perhaps I should say, quite a natural thing that all these Swedish-Americans in Sweden long to get back to America. . . . It is a pleasure to revisit Sweden at any time and ever so often, but one who is used to American life, is reluctant to settle down in Sweden when he eventually returns thither."[76]

"Our Swedish Americans become dearer and dearer to me," Swensson wrote, "and I feel also more proud of them since I, through these two journeys, have had opportunities to see something of the popular life in Sweden. Our Christian Swedish-American colleges, our church-life, with people and pastor so closely connected, our good newspaper press, the improved economical conditions, travels and association with people of other nationalities—all this has had a wonderful effect on our people; in this free land in the west." "A cheer for our mother, old Sweden," Swensson concluded his account; "Three cheers for our bride, the young America!"[77]

In 1897 the Chicago Swedish journalist Frans Albin Lindstrand, best known to his readers as "Uncle Ola," traveled widely in the Middle East and Europe, as recounted in 1899. His lengthy account of Sweden consists mainly of enthusiastic descriptions of scenic and historic places, but it offers at times some deeper insights.

Lindstrand was greatly impressed by notable changes to the landscape in his native Västergötland since he had departed forty years earlier. He meanwhile observed a marked shortage of young adult farm labor in the area due to the emigration. His feelings were here divided between "the joy of seeing old friends again" and "sadness at the thought that their lot, often enough, is poverty and dependence." Yet he was glad that conditions seemed gradually to be improving.

There were other changes as well. Lindstrand attended a large Midsummer celebration in Tranås.

But—what a contrast between the folk life now and then! Nowadays a kind of somber shadow lies over the faces of all. Of the old innocently joyous smile which so openly brightened the youth in Sweden during my childhood, there seemed . . . to remain no trace. . . . The people, radiating good health, went about as though in mourning at this celebration, in a glorious natural setting and an invigorating climate. They had everything—except spring's unbridled upsurge of exuberant, healthy joy of life.

Lindstrand was told that the "religious spirit" was placing its "serious stamp" upon society. "Is youth better now than before?" he mused. "That question remains very much on my mind." A "folk festival" in Vadstena Lindstrand also found disappointing. "If the good people of Vadstena had the chance to see our folk fests here in America," he reflected, ". . . they would witness a *Swedish folk fest!*" Ironically, he could only rediscover something of the old spirit in Stockholm, at the recently opened outdoor folklife museum at Skansen, which strove to preserve and revive the old customs that "without doubt" were "of greater value than the new."[78]

Oscar W. Anderson visited Sweden, especially his native Småland, during the summer of 1898, and left an account published in installments in the newspaper *Vårt land* in Jamestown, New York. Anderson, who was of humble origins and had only minimal schooling, had emigrated to America in 1881, and after working in various menial occupations had gone into journalism. His account, "En sommar i Småland" (A Summer in Småland) is marked by a sensitive and poignant lyricism, for Anderson, a man of rare intelligence, self-acquired learning, and philosophical cast of mind, was by then mortally ill with the tuberculosis that would end his life at the age of 37 two years later.[79]

"It is one's childhood memories that stir in the depths of the soul, indelible, unforgettable," Anderson wrote, "It is these that yearly drive more and more Swedish Americans to visit their native villages." Yet he was from the beginning conscious of the distance created by time and space. "In the middle of the morning of May 11, I got off at Mörlunda, where nearly 17 years ago I began my journey to the new world. How like and yet how very unlike. The natural surroundings have probably not changed so much, but it is I who have changed."[80]

Like Lindstrand the year before, Anderson observed the disappearance of old familiar customs with a certain wistfulness. He had idyllic memories of past Midsummer celebrations at Tulunda, but there the young girls now decorated the traditional maypole largely with garlands of paper and even eggshells, rather than of wildflowers. "The whole pastime, at least the time I was there, seemed to me to resemble the artificial wreaths; there was little life in it and just as little in the occasion as a whole."[81] Anderson's own reactions to the change were meanwhile ambivalent. In his childhood

Midsummer had always been a lively time—"too lively perhaps." The young people he now encountered seemed to Anderson to be "a different breed." "Social life is distinguished by a higher tone here, and the ideals are higher." He wished "the same happy conditions" might prevail in the backwoods, "but here one has a completely different story to tell."[82]

Anderson was gratified to observe less drunkenness, profanity, and overeating than formerly. Agricultural practices were beginning to become more rational, employment opportunities were more numerous, and wages were better. Public education, not least in practical subjects, was greatly improved, and a new sense of national pride was evident. Anderson was especially pleased to observe how progressive American influences were beginning to make themselves felt. A former Jamestown resident had opened an American-style meat market in Vimmerby, where customers who had been used to shopping on the town square were now coming in growing numbers. "So American business methods creep in and turn upside down what people were accustomed to before."[83]

At Ingatorp, the local farmers had formed their own trading cooperative. "To get peasants to be partners in a community business in the country is something new here, and the idea comes of course from America. . . . A transformation in the way of life has begun, and the phlegmatic Swede begins little by little to waken out of his thousand-year sleep."

Anderson found the Old World in many ways alien and unsympathetic. Already in Liverpool, on the way over, he declared that Americans would consider it impossible to build such a city, which he regarded as typically English and European.

> Narrow streets, tall iron fences, and reinforced doors in front of both public and private places, parks and residences, testify to the inherited conception on which the community order of the old world is in good part based— that the people must be kept in check by authorities, police power and barriers, their freedom (such as it is) limited by fences and guardianship of one kind or another from beginning to end. And under such conditions it obviously takes much more time to foster in the people a worthwhile use of that freedom which increasing popular enlightenment will eventually demand as their rightful possession.

Discussing the cramped quarters in his Gothenburg hotel, Anderson added, "We began to remember how it had become more crowded the further east we had gone."[84]

"In the beginning it seems amusing to look around in this class-conscious country," he wrote. "Everywhere are signs that indicate humankind must be divided into 'better' and 'inferior' people." "To bring such people to understand the desirability of getting rid of the whole class system is of course unthinkable," he commented. All passengers, the ailing Anderson added, "will also with the same speed probably reach that great central station where all class differences vanish, I expect."[85]

He noted, already in Gothenburg, "that almost everyone who has a chance wants to fleece the Swedish Americans. ... In general they are fairly well supplied with money and they are not stingy—which is common knowledge." They were shamelessly overcharged by waiters and railway porters. "Such business methods, God be praised, we have at least grown away from in America."[86]

Worse yet was widespread hostility toward America, exacerbated by the Spanish-American War, which had broken out in April and which brought to the surface traditional conservative European resentments toward the young republic across the sea. Anderson found the average Swede to have little understanding of the conflict since the newspapers were generally pro-Spanish in bias, and "found it hard to believe that causes other than self-seeking and conquest could have pulled the Americans into the war." In Vimmerby, he visited the local newspaper editor, "a Spanish-oriented soul who combined absolute disregard for the truth with an intense antipathy to everything American."[87]

While many Swedish Americans had returned to Sweden during the recent hard times in the United States, many found Sweden "too circumscribed and life here in general too cramped after having breathed American air for a shorter or longer period," and soon recrossed the ocean. Americans, including those originally from Sweden, were different. "It is no secret that many Swedes are slow-witted and intellectually helplessly sleepy. Their mental abilities lie dormant, I don't know why."[88]

Taken together the accounts both of Swedish travelers in the United States and of Swedish-American visitors to the land of their origins go far toward defining the growing separation between those who had departed and those who had remained at home.

NINE

Swedish America
Self-Appraised

Despite their differences, Swedish and Swedish-American travelers were in essential agreement that Swedish Americans were not simply Swedes who happened to live in America. Nor were they Americans whose origins happened to be in Sweden. They were a distinctive group, for better or worse, with their own characteristics.

Circumstances during the 1890s put Swedish America's intellectual leadership under increasing pressure to examine, explain, and justify their own community, in the face both of harder conditions in the United States, including a rise in anti-immigration sentiment, and of an increasingly militant opposition to emigration and criticism of the Swedish Americans in Sweden. The period was one of intense introspection and of self-vindication, in forms ranging from burlesque humor to high-flown oratory to sober self-examination.

The humorous approach is perhaps best represented by Gustaf Sjöström, alias "Jan Olson from Kil," in the *causeries* he wrote for the newspaper *Hemlandet* in Chicago in 1891 and 1892 and published in book form in 1892. The book contains a spontaneous mixture of plausible experiences, shrewd observations, and pure fantasy, as for instance when Jan Olson tells of his fabulous adventures among the Sioux Indians in the West like a kind of Swedish-American Münchhausen. All of this is presented in a burlesque mixture of the Värmland dialect and English words and expressions.

Jan Olson showed, on the whole, an exuberant enthusiasm for America, the land of opportunity and adventure, although he had his nostalgic moments. Swedish Americans, he reflected at Christmastime 1891, lived better than they had in the Old Country and were "more or less Americanized" in their way of life, to which no one could rightly object. "Times change, and we change with them." Nonetheless,

I believe that however much better their living conditions may be here, all of them still think with love and longing back to their old homes. And surely more than one sensitive soul yearns for the true-heartedness, frankness, and friendship which there amid the simple conditions of the Swedish countryside were far more in evidence than in this land of business. . . . America is good because it feeds us better than Sweden. But man is fortunately not only stomach, but also heart. America is good for the stomach, but Sweden is good for the heart.[1]

Jan Olson nevertheless subscribed to the Swedish-American article of faith that American conditions allowed for the fullest self-realization of Swedes whose humble origins had held them back in the Old Country. He was particularly taken with the young Swedish American girls. "I don't understand how they can look so ladylike. They have more bearing and more dignity in their manner than in the Old Country. . . . In this country they are all 'misses,' every one of them. I am especially glad for the girls, for they certainly did not have an easy time of it in Sweden."[2]

At a parade of Swedish singing societies in Chicago, Jan Olson marveled at how raw Swedish peasant lads could metamorphose into polished choral singers. It could not be denied that "Swedish workingmen somehow become more civilized and refined in this country." He likewise observed, "Peasant lads and lasses have become real fine Americans. . . . They even look rather more intelligent than they did in Sweden."[3]

Like a good many others, Jan Olson tried to return to Sweden with the idea of staying. At first he rejoiced at once again finding himself amid Värmland's hills and dales. But it was hard to settle down.

My thoughts went hither and yon. Sweden or America—that was the question. To tell the truth, it was dreadfully dull in the Old Country. Lively as I am by nature and accustomed as I was to the rush and bustle of America, I felt ill at ease with the quiet, listless life back home. There was no energy, no "go," in the people. I don't want to say that is a fault in them. Perhaps, on the contrary, it is a fault of the Americans that they are too much on the go. But restless as I am, America suits me better. Suddenly I had "America Fever." My decision was quickly made.[4]

Throughout the 1890s, J. A. Enander and his vision of an ideal Swedish America continued to exercise a profound influence. At every opportunity Enander stressed his countrymen's special destiny as the "faithful knights of American freedom" and preached unity within their divided community. He took the lead in the drive to raise a statue of the great Swedish naturalist, Carl Linnaeus, in Chicago's Lincoln Park in 1891, which at its dedication he pronounced to be Swedish America's "national altar to *Concordia*." In 1893 he reminded his Swedish-American compatriots at the time of the

World's Columbian Exposition in Chicago that Columbus had not in fact been America's true discoverer.

At a banquet celebrating his thirty years' activity in America, given in Chicago in 1899, Enander gave the fullest statement of his Swedish-American idealism.

> To arouse to life Swedish national feeling from its deathlike slumber, to kindle in hitherto lukewarm or cold hearts an ardent love for the common language, shared memories of the past, the common treasury of song, and of our culture in general, and to combine this heritage into a harmonious whole with all that is beautiful, noble, and true which the new homeland offers with so bounteous a hand to the immigrant, so that our nationality might be not only a receiving but in equal measure a contributing people— this has been the preeminent goal, not only of my wishes but of the often misunderstood, often misinterpreted striving of my entire life. . . . It has not been Sweden's, but rather Swedish America's cause for which I have above all striven.[5]

A number of Swedish-American publicists served, in effect, as Enander's "apostles to the gentiles" during this period, writing in English to pay tribute to Sweden in general and to its immigrated sons and daughters in America in particular. Their message was aimed both at younger Swedish Americans born or raised in the United States and at the wider American public.

By the 1890s the writing of Swedish- and other Scandinavian-American history began in earnest, following some earlier sporadic efforts. A significant landmark in this process was the publication of *History of the Scandinavians and Successful Scandinavians in the United States* in two volumes in 1893–97, edited and largely written by the Swedish American, O. N. Nelson. The tone was strongly filiopietistic on the part of all the Scandinavian-American contributors, and the emphasis upon "successful" members of their respective groups and their contributions to their new homeland was reinforced by numerous biographical sketches, handsomely illustrated with steelcut engravings. A very different kind of history was meanwhile provided with the appearance in 1890 of the first volume of Pastor Eric Norelius's monumental and painstaking account, in Swedish, of the earliest Swedish settlements in the Midwest and especially of their Lutheran congregations, the cornerstone of a long tradition of Swedish-American local history lasting down to the present day.[6]

As part of a series on "Nations of the World," Victor Nilsson, doctor of philosophy and Old Norse scholar, contributed in 1899 a volume on Sweden. Nilsson held to the widespread view of the time that Scandinavia was the original homeland of the Aryans, that the Swedes were "the oldest and most unmixed race in Europe," and that as such they possessed a distinct national character combining "active heroism," "unusual inventive power," "extraordinary endurance," "moral courage," "self-restraint," and "dignity." The great emigration, "one of the most astounding phenomena of the century," he claimed, had "given America at least 1,200,000 inhabitants."[7]

The influence of J. A. Enander is clearly evident in Lars P. Nelson's pamphlet, *What Has Sweden Done for the United States?*, published in 1903 and expressly intended for "the growing generation of my countrymen, born in America," whose "false pride" in being native Americans should not blind them to the glories of their ancestral heritage. The Swedes, Nelson wrote, had shown a unique adaptability as settlers on foreign shores since Viking times. "For more than forty generations the Swedes have behind them the lives of their ancestors saturated with hard work, thrift and economy, and an independence that never became the slave of priest, landlord or king. Is it any wonder then when such a race is transplanted into a richer soil and a more genial climate that they flourish and make for the good of the state in which they have taken up the white man's burden?" In all aspects of life, Nelson held, the Swedes "associate themselves with the best elements of the native Americans." They were law-abiding, peaceful, productive, and God-fearing folk. Their communities were "uniformly prosperous." They conscientiously fulfilled their obligations as American citizens.[8]

A paean of another kind was the massive *Sweden and the Swedes* published in 1892 by William Widgery Thomas, Jr., now the American minister to Stockholm. An enthusiastic Suecophile ever since he had served as United States consul in Gothenburg during the Civil War, he had in 1870 founded a Swedish settlement in his native Maine, had a Swedish wife, and was fluent in Swedish. His account of Sweden, which first appeared in Swedish, is filled with exhuberant enthusiasm for the Northland and its sturdy inhabitants. "The Lofty North!—Its songs and sagas, its fjelds and fjords, its midnight days and sun-bright nights! What a halo of glory and romance, like its own Northern Lights, illumines this majestic 'Brow of the Universe!'" After discussing the exploits of the wild but glorious Northmen, Thomas adds:

> But these gallant sailors of the far Northland did more than conquer and destroy, they sailed boldly out upon the broad Atlantic. ... Their storm-tossed ships first sailed our western seas; their feet, first of white men, trod the shores of America. ... Scandinavia!—Land of rock and ice; "birthplace of chivalry;" home of heroes!—What glorious memories cluster around thee, as sunset clouds about thy mountain-tops. People with calm exterior of snow, but warmth of geysers in your blood!

To be sure, Thomas had little to say about Swedish emigration as such. But he unquestionably raised Sweden's credit—and by implication that of the Swedish Americans—in the United States.[9]

Certain commemorative events and celebrations meanwhile helped to consolidate the rituals of the Swedish-American creed. The raising of the Linnaeus statue in Chicago in 1891 has been noted. An impressive array of Swedish-American secular societies took part in the World's Columbian Exposition in Chicago in 1893, reinforcing Sweden's own official participation. In 1897 Swedish-American groups throughout the United States celebrated the twenty-fifth jubilee of Oscar II's reign as a welcome opportunity to manifest their warm attachment to their old homeland.[10]

Among the more sober and penetrating analysts of the Swedish-American condition was Colonel Hans Mattson, whose widely read *Reminiscences* came out in 1891, two years before his death. In his concluding chapter Mattson paid tribute to his compatriots in America. But staunch as he had always been in upholding America's ideals and institutions, he here spoke out against the faults and shortcomings that caused growing concern during the 1890s, not least from the immigrants' viewpoint.

The older Americans liked to regard themselves as tolerant, but they were in many respects prejudiced, largely due to their ignorance of other nations. Although the immigrant, especially from northern Europe, was generally well received, he was expected to content himself with menial occupations. "But when he begins to compete with the native American for honor and emolument in the higher walks of life, he is often met with coldness, mingled, perhaps, with a little envy." It would take, Mattson believed, two generations before the children of non-English-speaking immigrants would no longer be affected by such prejudices. Still, he added, people in Sweden were no less misinformed and biased toward Americans, thanks to the stress on the darker sides of American life in the Swedish newspapers.[11]

The comments of Swedish-American travelers in Sweden often touched on what they perceived to be characteristic differences between their people in the old and new homelands. In this respect, none was more deeply concerned with this question throughout his life than C. A. Swensson, for which reason certain of his comments from his second Swedish journey in 1897 deserve special attention here. At a luncheon with Swedish journalists in Stockholm, Swensson became aroused when one of them expressed the commonly held idea that the Swedish immigrants in America were simply menial laborers.

These Swedes although originally belonging to what they please to call "the laboring classes" over there, had by their contact with American life become polished and refined, the peers of anyone, and their native intelligence and nobility now developed and trained, had already given them a proud place among their fellow-citizens in the broad and happy domain of Uncle Sam. ... Yes, even after a summer in Sweden, I am greatly impressed with the proud thought: What a splendid, polished and refined people the Swedes in America are as a class! They are better than their brethren over there. This is my decided conviction.

If he had one main criticism, it was that the Swedish Americans had hitherto tended to be too modest and undemanding in their new homeland. "But the second generation is growing up, and in this one thing at least the sons are unlike their fathers and will demand the recognition so well deserved. A change is already going on; in America the Swedes are becoming Americans, not so polite, not so unassuming, but with more of the 'getting-there' quality in them than their brothers in the fatherland."

It was, meanwhile, the Swedish Americans' solemn duty—toward themselves, their heritage, and America—to preserve their Swedish language and culture, as well as their Lutheran faith. "The United States is the gainer," he declared, "by every nationality preserving and perpetuating whatever good it has inherited and taken with it to these shores."[12]

The ideal of cultural pluralism was perhaps best expressed in Swedish-American circles during this period by David Nyvall, a leading figure in the Evangelical Mission Covenant Church and son of C. J. Nyvall, one of the Swedish travelers we have noted in America during the 1870s, in a speech given in Minneapolis in 1892. Swedes had come to America, Nyvall stated, to find homes of their own, "man's highest earthly goal," which they had been unable to do in the Old Country. A true homeland was indeed a "collection of homes . . . which are the only essential condition, the only sure foundation, for political and civic rights." They had not come in search of freedom, for this they were already accustomed to. "So much the less can it be desirable," Nyvall continued, "for us to forget and despise our old homeland, since it is from there we have brought the tradition of being a free people, which best fits us to make use of freedom in a sober and sensible fashion. This country does not demand this of us. The sum of what I have to say is that he who was a good patriot in the old country in general becomes a good patriot here. . . . For a Swede to despise the Swedish heritage means to despise *himself,* to make himself contemptible to others and to deserve their contempt."[13]

The question of maintaining the Swedish heritage in America was by now increasingly tied to the problem of keeping up the Swedish language among the growing younger generation, and Nyvall naturally devoted much of his attention to this matter. Since American public schools, even in heavily Swedish districts, did not offer formal instruction in Swedish, it was essential that Swedish Americans fill this need themselves. This called for private supplementary classes and, at a higher level, Swedish-American colleges—such as North Park College in Chicago, whose president Nyvall would become in 1894. But above all, it required active commitment on the part of Swedish-born parents. Nyvall meanwhile warned that to present Swedish as a kind of sacred liturgical language or to seek to warn against English as "something tempting and sinful in itself" would be the surest ways to kill the younger generation's interest in the ancestral tongue. Instead, parents should use Swedish in the home. More than that: "We should make an exchange. We should learn English from our children and let them learn Swedish from us."[14]

Preservation of the language both required and made possible a richer cultural life. It called for more and better reading material, which in turn, opened wider perspectives. To know Swedish well by no means precluded a full mastery of English; indeed those most competent in a language were those familiar with more than one. Similarly, Nyvall concluded: "It is precisely this which is remarkable about this country, that many nations here live a common national life ... no one seriously believes that the different nationalities here should make war upon each other, any kind of war other than peaceful competition."[15]

The most objective and penetrating discussion of the Swedish Americans offered by one of their number during the crucial decade of the 1890s was Carl Fredrik Peterson's compendious survey, *Sverige i Amerika* (Sweden in America), published in 1898. Its author had come to America to fight for the Union and the freeing of the slaves, evidently in 1861, although he had been rejected for military service for health reasons. He had thereafter remained a stalwart champion of America's liberal civic ideals, as he saw them, while upholding his Swedish-American compatriots' attachment to their own cultural heritage. Following the usual vicissitudes, he had become a journalist in Chicago and was by 1898 a contributor to several Swedish-language newspapers and the author of a number of books.[16]

In his introduction, Peterson observed that various works had come out during the past decade on the history of the Swedes in America, each "an account of the struggle for existence in the usual sense, which thus made no effort to examine in greater depth the new life which is gradually being created by Swedish and American forces among those multitudes which Sweden has sent here over the past half century." Thus Peterson undertook this "cultural-historical task" of seeking "to show what the Swede has gradually become as a social and political being in this country."[17] To this end Peterson discussed the main aspects of Swedish-American life and the accomplishments of leading Swedish Americans.

His compatriots in America now constituted an impressively large group, around a million persons by Peterson's estimate. The great majority came from Sweden's "most vigorous social classes," the peasantry and the "so-called working class." Although they were in the forefront of that "great effort of cultivation through which state after state has been added," some critics in Sweden had claimed that they had contributed little to America since they did not cultivate any art or science. This was true enough,

Peterson was prepared to admit, but this was no true measure of a folk element's importance. The Swedes had accomplished something still more essential at this stage of America's development by helping to build a "deep, broad, and solid foundation for a great nation, whose soul is the law-bound freedom of the people." The Swedish Americans' great task had thus far been the taming of the continent.[18]

That the Swedish Americans had succeeded, during the half century since the beginning of their large-scale immigration, in preserving their own identity Peterson attributed above all to their churches, particularly the Augustana Lutheran Synod. He was, however, somewhat critical of Augustana Lutheranism, especially in its strongly pietistic early phase. Yet he recognized that only men of unwaivering and literalistic faith could have provided the determined leadership a pioneer church and its frontier parishes at first required. "They were more men of feeling than men of thought," but they were the "stoutest souls," and thus the obvious leaders, whose warm-hearted "practical piety" transcended the narrow confines of dogma. Clerical discipline was always strong in America, where it provided a "necessary counterweight to the theoretically attractive but all too often misused freedom and equality"—ideals which could easily turn the heads of newly arrived immigrants. Nonetheless, the Augustana Synod was a kind of "Jeffersonian" democracy, hence a useful school in the American way. It was therefore mistaken to describe as a "clerical regime" what was really a "regime of deacons or laymen." The congregations themselves elected the pastors who suited them, traditionally conservative as they often might be. Peterson was meanwhile gratified to see that a younger, better educated and more liberal younger generation of Augustana pastors was prepared to recognize the onward march of progress, for "not to keep up with one's times in America means to go under quickly."[19]

"For learning in a general sense, for science and philosophy and art and intellectual striving for purely worldly purposes" the Swedish Americans had long shown little interest. That this was changing was due mainly to the colleges established by the Swedish-American denominations, in particular Augustana College, which in Peterson's view creatively combined progressive American with traditional Swedish values.[20] The press and the secular societies likewise played a vital part both in preserving Swedish language and culture and in familiarizing Swedish immigrants with American ideals and conditions.

While Peterson held that his countrymen's accomplishments in America had thus far been mostly of a practical and material nature, he was nonetheless at pains to show that their cultural attainments were by no means negligible. In so doing he illuminated certain aspects of their mentality.

He showed a particular solicitude for Swedish-American literature, with the useful reminder that the newspaper press carried a far greater proportion of Swedish America's total literary production than ever appeared in book form. The newspapers, moreover, through their sheer numbers and by opening their pages to contributions of all kinds from their readers, stimulated a remarkable amount of literary activity at the grass-roots level.[21]

Peterson observed that the genres in which the Swedish Americans most characteristically expressed themselves were the spiritual and the poetic, perhaps due to the essentially "contemplative" nature of the Swedes, which was stirred to expression by feelings of rootlessness in a new land. It seemed paradoxical that in this age of realism—"and America is assuredly realistic"—Swedish-American literature was "distinctly idealistic" in tone. "This seems all the more inexplicable," he continued, "when one recalls that the trend in literature has been realistic in Sweden for twenty years, during which America's Sweden has sought to create a little Parnassus of its own." In part, this represented a defense of the Swede's basic disposition in a prosaic environment that discouraged idealism. In Sweden, meanwhile, realism in expression was based upon direct contact with living nature, whereas upon moving to America the strings of this "realistic lyre" were broken and the immigrant tended increasingly to idealize in retrospect the old home and its natural setting. If the Swedish-American writer ultimately overcame his nostalgia and acculturated to America, his Muse led him characteristically more toward broadly cosmopolitan than purely indigenous American views. Among the other arts, the Swedish Americans distinguished themselves most particularly in music, especially the vocal and choral forms so closely associated with idealistic poetic expression.[22]

America provided the most powerful stimuli to self-development. "No thinkers?" he replied to European skeptics, "Indeed there are more per square mile than in Sweden, for American life awakens one's slumbering thoughts with the hammer-blows of hard necessity." This included the need to learn the language of the land, which the Swedes, together with the Norwegians, did better and more quickly than any other immigrant groups. Unfortunately this often meant a corresponding neglect of the mother tongue.

> The idea sometimes encountered in Sweden that the Swede in America loses his inborn refinement is far from the mark, for here, on the contrary, he acquires this in far greater measure. It is in this regard as in all others, that America with redoubled pressure accelerates the development of everything that is already there. . . . The seeds which Mother Nature planted within [his] being might perhaps never have reached the light of day under Sweden's social sun, but they sprout quickly here, where no conventional constraints keep them under the ground.[23]

Female immigrants, too, developed under American conditions, although Peterson emphasized that Swedish women in America were still fortunately distinguished by their "true femininity" and thus seldom tempted to follow the excesses of their native-born sisters, including the rising radical movement for women's rights in America.[24]

The Swedish Americans, Peterson maintained, were a preeminently "home-building" people, and visitors from Sweden were constantly impressed by the comfort and good taste of their homes, their refuge from the outside pressures of work and business. Devoted as they were to family life the Swedish Americans enjoyed, however, little of the wider social intercourse within their homes so characteristic of the more leisurely and gracious way of life in Sweden. In the more individualistic Anglo-Saxon tradition, the Swedish American's home was his castle.[25]

Instead, Swedish Americans tended to find an outlet for their natural sociability in their churches or in "those small republics," the numerous secular societies that thrived above all in the cities. Meanwhile: "These purely Swedish organizations become excellent American schools. And at the same time it may be said that they make better Swedes of their members. Back home in Sweden they were more or less provincial. One was in a sense an *Östgöte, Västgöte, Smålänning,* or *Skåning* first, then a Swede. But here one becomes first of all a Swede, and the other comes second."[26]

Peterson devoted much attention to the relationships between the Swedish Americans and both their old and new countrymen. Unlike some of Swedish America's more extreme spokesmen, then and later, he denied that the emigration had taken "the best elements, in all respects, of Sweden's population," although the emigrants possessed, perhaps, "more of the adventurous Viking spirit . . . combined with a certain admirable degree of enterprise in areas of practical activity." In Sweden they had represented an underemployed labor force, and the recent rise in wages there could be largely attributed to the emigrants' departure.[27]

Outwardly Swedish immigrants acclimatized quickly to American life, but in a deeper sense the process was "by no means easy," and they always felt divided in their loyalties between their old and new homelands, "a mixture of both types of love." Still, more than any other Europeans, they proudly identified with the country's older Anglo-American element, which in turn tended to regard them as exemplary citizens. They got along well with other northern European immigrant groups, except for the Irish, but had little contact with the southern Europeans. "What is best in the Swedish character" Peterson maintained, "finds very good resonance in American life." [28]

Repeatedly Peterson described the Norwegian Americans along with, and in the same terms as, the Swedish, but there are evidences of mounting friction, at least on the level of the leadership of the two immigrant communities, reflecting the growing crisis within the Swedish-Norwegian dual monarchy. The Norwegian Americans, he held, were less idealistic and more self-assertive than the Swedish. Peterson, who died in 1901, would have held with P. P. Waldenström's disgruntled comment the following year that in America "the Norwegians are more Norwegian than the Swedes are Swedish."[29]

Many Swedish Americans dreamed of returning to spend their later years in their old homeland, but even if they succeeded in accumulating the necessary means, Peterson warned, they should consider the matter soberly. Usually "they have forgotten one thing, that during the time it has taken to build their little fortunes they have become so Americanized that they can never again become the same Swedes they were before they came here." In America they have been part of a wider world. Moreover, "It is by now all too well known that the Swedish American who returns to Sweden is there regarded with unfriendly eyes unless he has returned as a repentant son, prepared to expiate his 'sin' (emigration) by remaining at home and speaking ill of the country which for a time provided his field of activity."[30]

Still, Peterson distinguished between the anti-Americanism of much of Sweden's elite and the strong sympathies toward the United States among its broader masses, which "stand with one foot in America." Through them the Swedish Americans would ultimately make their greatest contribution to their old homeland. Their letters to Sweden, describing how the workingman's vote weighed as heavily as the millionaire's, "have planted an idea among those who stayed home which in time will make its mark in the Riksdag and bear fruit in new, liberal institutions." Swedish-American newspapers sent back to families in Sweden encouraged people who had no thought of emigrating "to contemplate the good aspects of the American nation and at the same time to think over possibilities for bringing over at least some small part of America to Sweden."[31]

The Swedish Americans likewise had their historic destiny to fulfill in their new homeland. Here conditions were deteriorating from what they once had been. The Swedish Americans had heretofore been the staunchest of Republicans, "the Spartan band, prepared to stand and fall at any Thermopylae ... loyal as honor itself and faithful as young love." They did not adopt new political ideas hastily, and for the most part to abandon Republicanism seemed like "treason against the Republic itself."[32]

It was, however, the inborn idealism of the Swedish character that had led them to fight for the Union in the Civil War, "that great political baptism of fire," and to support the party of Lincoln when it stood for high moral principles. Since then the principles had disappeared, but the Swedes stayed on. The strongest trait in their Swedish heritage was nonetheless their unwavering love of freedom. In the impending struggle between "oppressed labor" and "soulless capital," the Swedish Americans could be counted upon to join with the "best Americans" and the other northern European immigrants to form a "compact phalanx" in defense of America's true ideals.

If this should cease to be, America would no longer be what it was always meant to be: "a people's nation, a nation of working people." This the Swede understood even better than the older American. Although they shared the same basic values, the Swede's

> spiritual depth is far greater than the American's. He does not content himself with the superficial attitude which is characteristic of the native-born. He is above all more moral and he penetrates with his gaze further into the nature of life's questions. If he does not grasp their significance through reasoned thought, he does so instinctively. And once convinced of right and wrong in a cause, no human power can persuade him to act contrary to this conviction, which, on the other hand, is easy for the Yankee, if circumstances otherwise offer tempting opportunities.[33]

The Swedes thus formed, in Peterson's view, a "moral lifeguard for the Republic and for the fair ideals it represents." They were—although he did not use the term—naturally Populists. Their descendants would meanwhile play their vital part in the evolution of American society. Among them, he foretold, "American initiative, which is superior to Swedish, will come to the fore, doubtless combined with the element of humanity, which is greater among the Swedes, and which is not strong among the Anglo-Saxons."

Their influence upon the America of tomorrow, Peterson was convinced, would be all out of proportion to their numbers. Although they would be less identifiably Swedish, they would maintain "those Swedish characteristics which remain sound currency from land to land, from age to age."[34]

Thus could C. F. Peterson, like other idealists of an earlier America who passed from the scene around the turn of the century—such as Hans Mattson or C. A. Swensson—console himself in a dark time and look with hope to the future of his own Swedish America. His penetrating analysis of the Swedish-American condition at the turn of the century deserves the extended treatment given it here, for it would leave its profound imprint on all subsequent speculation on the subject.

How the rank and file of Swedish Americans related to the two homelands is frequently reflected in letters to the editors of Swedish-language newspapers. A revealing example of this was the nearly two hundred responses in 1901 and 1902 to the question posed by *Svenska Amerikanaren* in Chicago: "If Russia decided to annex Sweden, how should we Swedish Americans then conduct ourselves?"

The question was ever an emotional one, for Russia had for centuries been regarded as Sweden's traditional enemy. "Jan Olson" (Gustaf Sjöström) had, for instance, written high-spiritedly in 1892 that in the event of war with Russia, Sweden could count on ten thousand volunteers from Chicago alone, "and we would be good soldiers, for here in this country we have had the chance to become a bit more daring and energetic than they are back home in Sweden." By the turn of the century the matter seemed a good deal more serious as the Tsarist government had implemented its policy of Russification across the Gulf of Bothnia in Finland, while Sweden's security appeared compromised by the growing crisis within the union with Norway. The following year the Swedish-American poet "Ludvig" (Ludvig Holmes) declaimed in *Ungdomsvännen:*

> And if, then, for Sweden that day should dawn
> When the Colossus in the East should rise up
> And eagerly arm for a murderous blow,
> The thousands of voices will echo here,
>
> ....
>
> *To arms for the fatherland in the North!*[35]

The responses to *Svenska Amerikanaren* are meanwhile illuminating. A surprising number were opposed to any involvement on grounds revealing the underlying grievances of many emigrants against the Old Country. Some were simply fatalistic and felt that aid from the Swedish Americans could make little difference against such odds. But "G. A. W." in Chicago doubted that Swedish troops would have the necessary morale to stand up against the Russians, since they had only duties and no rights, "so if Russia annexes Sweden then those in power have only themselves to blame." "Bolivar," a Civil War veteran in Swedesburg, Iowa, pointed out that Swedish Americans had fought bravely in the Civil and Spanish-American Wars for the land that "gave them work and bread" and the vote but that they would have little reason to fight for Sweden. "Let therefore aristocratic gentlemen and conceited patroons defend their lands as best they can." Sweden had a glorious past with its "victories bought with the heart-blood of our people," wrote "Gustavus" from Kenton, Michigan.

> But if we look at the present, what do we see but a land ruled by liquor patroons and other potentates, a land groaning under military burdens and heavy taxes, a land where a price is put on a free citizen's vote, and where success for the individual depends on his birth and not his ability! For that reason we left Sweden to seek a better living and a new homeland; therefore we should, now that we have found these advantages, give our arms in defense of this land which gives us our bread, our freedom and our independence, and not the land we left.

Not surprisingly, meanwhile, nine out of ten respondents urged support for Sweden in men, material, and money. They tended to express themselves in such fervently emotional terms that it is understandable why their opponents generally concealed themselves under pseudonyms. Lasse Olsson in Englevale, North Dakota, considered the Russians unworthy to tread the sacred soil of Sweden and held that the Swedes, like the doughty

Boers of the Transvaal, would show that they could hold their own against all comers in defending "their flag, their people, and their freedom." Any Swedish American who refused to fulfill his moral duty to the motherland in its hour of need, he added, did not deserve to be called a Swede. To come to Sweden's support, A. T. J. Edlund of South Manchester, Connecticut, declared, was "your duty as a civilized man," adding, "Think of Finland, and you will know well enough what to do."

In the light of the limited aid, particularly military volunteers, actually given by immigrant groups in America to their threatened homelands during the twentieth century, one may wonder what the actual response might have been if Swedish America had been put to the test. Nonetheless, behind the letters in *Svenska Amerikanaren* lay many sorely troubled consciences anxious to unburden and justify themselves, within their own community and—to the extent possible—before Mother Svea herself.[36]

As the nineteenth century drew to its close, it appeared that the emigration problem in Sweden was well on its way to a natural solution, and that Swedish America had evolved its own mature identity. The two branches of a divided folk might be expected to continue along set and separate courses. Yet it would very soon become all too evident that the great migration was by no means over and that the question of what it meant to be a Swede in America still faced many vicissitudes.

P A R T T W O

There is scarcely any question, be it political, social,
or economic, in our land that is not directly or
indirectly affected by the emigration.
—Gustav Sundbärg, 1906

To be Swedish is to *be a part of Sweden.* Sweden is the
Swedish people's home.
—Adrian Molin, 1909

The Sweden the Swedish American loves so deeply he bears
within him. Its geographical location lies within his
heart.
—Johan Person, 1912

Hear us, Svea, mother of us all!
—Song for men's chorus

High Tide,
1903–1917

*B*y 1900 emigration from Sweden again began to increase, in what seemed a most alarming manner, from 16,209 persons that year to a new peak of 35,439 in 1903. It thereafter remained at relatively high levels until the beginning of World War I in 1914. What had appeared during the confident later 1890s to be a problem on its way to solving itself arose again with new virulence to confront Swedish society after the turn of the century.

This evoked particularly strong reactions in a time of growing national sentiment. It was perplexing that emigration should again be on the rise when times were generally good in Sweden. But there were deeper causes of concern. The nation's security seemed increasingly threatened in a period of markedly mounting belligerency throughout the Western World. The rapid advance in Sweden, as elsewhere, of socialism and labor unionism meanwhile appeared, in traditionally patriotic eyes, to add the menace of internal dissolution. *Landsorganisationen,* the National Council of Trade Unions, was established in 1898, and in response *Svenska arbetsgivareför-eningen,* the Swedish Employers' Association, in 1902. Society was becoming increasingly polarized.

With the electoral reform of 1907, which established universal manhood suffrage, the Social Democratic party made its real breakthrough into the political arena and grew rapidly in the years that followed. Although under the leadership of Hjalmar Branting the Swedish Social Democrats on the whole embraced a peaceful, revisionist form of Marxism, a vocal minority of "Young Socialists" still looked to revolution to overturn the bourgeois state. The appeal to direct action was reinforced by the labor movement as economic fluctuations resulted in numerous strikes and lockouts, culminating with the General Strike of 1909 and sporadic episodes of violence.

In theory and rhetoric the socialist and labor movements proclaimed class conflict and proletarian solidarity across international boundaries. This seemed to challenge the very concept of the nation-state and the shared values of culture and tradition upon which it was based. Such fears added to the powerful reactions against the new wave of emigration, which likewise seemed a threat to national solidarity and sense of community. The anxieties aroused by the emigration question are reflected by the sheer quantity of the published debate and commentary on the subject that came out between 1903 and America's entry into World War I in 1917, which far surpasses all that had come before. On both sides of the Atlantic, discussion concerning America, the emigration, and the emigrants reached its high-water mark.

In Sweden reactions to the emigration now crystallized into three distinctive forms. There were efforts, as earlier, to analyze the problem objectively and find practical answers to it. At the same time the emotional attacks upon emigration on patriotic grounds that had revived during the 1890s attained their highest pitch of intensity. Finally, a note was sounded that was essentially new in Sweden—although not in Swedish America— that America's sizable and well-established Swedish element represented an important asset to the homeland, deserving of both recognition and moral support. All three types of reaction assumed organized form by 1907 and 1908 and thus exercised widespread influence in both the public and private sectors.

In the United States the Swedish Americans followed the Swedish debate closely, reacting variously to its different manifestations, while continuing to seek an identity that was both Swedish and American, acceptable to both the old and new homelands and, not least, to themselves.

TEN

The Homeland Faces Its Emigration Crisis

The rising optimism of the 1890s had encouraged determined attacks on emigration in Sweden, but no serious attempts to investigate its causes. Such efforts, reminiscent of the 1880s, resumed as emigration again increased after 1900. The first serious contribution in this regard, after nearly a decade and a half, was an article in 1903 by Pontus Fahlbeck, professor of political science at Lund University and conservative member of the Riksdag's First Chamber. A pioneer in statistical method, Fahlbeck recognized the primacy of economic factors in Sweden's earlier emigration but questioned why it should continue when times were good at home. He was thus inclined to look largely to nonmaterial factors.

Fahlbeck identified three basic causes: "1) the strong upward current within Swedish society and the difficulty for large numbers to follow this current as they would wish; 2) the burden of debt on the land; 3) the pull from countrymen living in America."[1] He distinguished between the ascent of individuals from lower to higher status groups and the constant striving of the propertyless to acquire property of their own. Sweden's free and well-developed public education led to hard competition over the higher positions in state and society, thus to failures and frustrations. "It is real misfortune for a society," he wrote, "when in this manner its superstructure threatens to become too great." The other form of mobility, "which consists of transforming the propertyless into property-holders and thus in bringing about movement out of the laboring and serving classes into the capitalist and landowning [elements]" was meanwhile a social restructuring of which "nothing but good could be said." It would "stop one of the worst holes for the stream of emigrants." Sweden had plenty of land for small family farms and through land reforms could create a prosperous smallholder class as in Denmark, provided that improved methods for intensive agriculture were applied.[2]

Regarding rural indebtedness and the drawing power of the Swedes in America, Fahlbeck had less to say. The government should, in his view, impose limits on the size of mortgages, but smaller holdings and increased productivity should in themselves largely solve the problem of debt. He also urged that the activities of emigration agents be restricted and—like most opponents of emigration—he called for publicizing conditions in America "as they really are," to counteract the widespread, established belief that "things are in a bad way in Sweden compared with . . . America." In this regard he had mixed feelings about recent efforts to encourage closer contacts between the Swedish Americans and their homeland, which was a "double-edged sword".[3]

In his emphasis upon a primarily agrarian solution, Fahlbeck revealed his conservative social orientation while recalling such commentators on the problem from the 1880s as J. A. Leffler and Axel Lindberg.[4] The idea of increasing small property-holding as the means to stabilize society had since then been gaining ground. Beginning in 1889, the conservative estate-owner E. G. H. Åkerlund introduced in the Riksdag a series of motions for the government to assist poor persons to acquire small freeholds. His main motive was to counteract the growing socialist movement and he indeed accepted emigration as a welcome escape valve for agitators and dissatisfied workers. Åkerlund's proposal failed to pass the Riksdag, but the first private associations were founded in the 1890s to promote rural smallholding. After the turn of the century such a policy seemed increasingly urgent, to combat not only socialism but emigration, as Fahlbeck's article reveals. In 1904 the Riksdag at last passed legislation establishing a loan fund to expedite this process, setting in motion a sustained *Egna hem* or "Own-Home" movement that would remain a major *Leitmotiv* in Swedish social thought and policy for decades to come.[5]

Finally, Fahlbeck appealed strongly in his article for a full inquest into the causes of the emigration under the auspices of the government's Central Statistical Bureau and considered it strange that this had not been done long since.[6] Already the following year, as will be seen, the Riksdag approved such an investigation and it soon became evident that a key role in it would be played by Gustav Sundbärg of the Statistical Central Bureau, one of Sweden's most eminent statisticians.

Already in 1884, it may be recalled, Sundbärg had investigated in detail the emigration and its impact upon Swedish society, concluding that it was at that time a necessity, that it brought various benefits, and that then prevalent fears as to its harmful effects upon Swedish society were exaggerated. By 1903 Sundbärg had changed his view. In an interview with *Svenska dagbladet* he found it encouraging that the public was beginning to become seriously concerned over emigration, which was "felt now more than at earlier times."[7]

Indeed, Ann-Sofie Kälvemark's study of this period bears out that a scarcity of manpower available for labor on larger estates and for military conscription was in places acute enough to cause understandable apprehensions. During 1903, a national meeting of provincial economic societies, the so-called *Lantbruksriksdag* or Agricultural Parliament in Stockholm, expressed its grave concern over the loss of rural labor; a petition signed by 113 prominent persons in Gothenburg was presented to King Oscar II describing emigration as a danger to the fatherland of "nationally ruinous proportions"; and a motion, ultimately unsuccessful, was made in the Riksdag to restrict the departure of men of military age.[8] Clearly the year 1903 marked a significant turning point.

In anticipation of *Emigrationsutredningen,* the government's official inquest into the emigration, which began its work in early 1907, Gustav Sundbärg set forth his preliminary reflections on the subject in two lectures given in Uppsala in 1906. In the first of these he stated that to discuss the emigration meant nothing less than to discuss Sweden in its entirety, "for there is scarcely any question, be it political, social, or economic, in our land that is not directly or indirectly affected by the emigration."[9] This broad and thorough approach would characterize his work on the inquest commission during the years to come.

Like Pontus Fahlbeck, Sundbärg discussed the various waves of heavy emigration. Down to 1885—around the time he had published his first study of emigration—Sundbärg was able to find specific demographic and economic circumstances to explain them. He placed particular importance upon the high nativity during the period between 1815 and 1830, which not only swelled emigration over two generations but compelled the solution of a series of national economic and social problems through timely legislation, beginning with school reform and ending with care of the poor and elderly.[10] Through emigration the surplus population was cancelled out.

After 1885, however, Sundbärg could no longer ascribe the emigration to specific causes. There was no longer any lack of work or too many young people—rather the reverse. It was thus necessary to look to general, long-term causes. Aristocracy, bureaucracy, and plutocracy still wielded great power and influence in Sweden, creating social discontents that provided a "very fertile soil for emigration." Universal suffrage (enacted the following year for males) would do much to create a healthier situation, as the spirit of the times called for democracy.[11]

At a deeper level, Sundbärg pointed to Sweden's combination of a low mortality rate with Europe's lowest incidence of marriage outside of Ireland.

> If our low mortality thus bears witness to our high level of culture, our low rate of marriage confirms that in our economic world all is not as it ought to be and as we ourselves demand that it should be. This low marriage rate

and the great emigration amount, strictly speaking, to the same thing, seen from different sides. When in a land where there are not normal opportunities to establish homes and families, the land is abandoned by its youth, which seeks to reach that goal elsewhere.

Sweden did not meet "the demands the people itself places upon its economy."[12]

The only real answer to this dilemma would be economic development on a hitherto unprecedented scale, "to make use of what we have and turn this to the benefit of our people—for what we have is not little. ... Our land is great and rich, but we are a small and poor people. Therein lies the disproportion." Although this posed certain practical problems at Sweden's high latitude, the greatest obstacles confronting its economic life lay in the Swedish folk character itself. These Sundbärg identified as the Swede's natural "fantasy," which inspired dreams of grandeur and an often uncritical fascination with all that was foreign and exotic, together with his inbred envy toward those of his own countrymen who succeeded in rising above the common level. Clearly these traits were a powerful force behind the emigration. At home they resulted in a certain carefree inability to make use of limited resources in a calmly rational manner, leading to repeated business failures. Sundbärg meanwhile contrasted the Swede's strong feeling for nature, thus his natural aptitude for the sciences and technology, with his lack of interest and perceptiveness in human affairs. Throughout Sweden's long history, what had been won with the sword had often been lost at "the diplomats' green table." Similarly, the profits of Swedish technology were all too often drained away by foreigners who were better psychologists and therefore more astute businessmen than the unworldly Swedes. According to Sundbärg, the Danes stood in striking contrast to the Swedes in this respect.[13]

Characteristically, there was much talk about what Sweden should do to "become once again a great power." If only the Swedes could stop thinking in such vague and grandiose terms much would be won, Sundbärg concluded, for it was essential that we "learn to see the great in the small, to learn—we also—to value that which lies nearest at hand and not only that which appears like a distant mirage in our fantasy."[14]

In his second Uppsala lecture, a few months later, Sunbärg amplified upon certain of these themes. As contrasted again with the Danes, he held that the Swedes were notably lacking in national, as opposed to local patriotism, which hindered the formation of a national economic policy. In particular he condemned his countrymen's lack of economic realism, their naive belief that they could somehow reap the rewards of the Industrial Revolution without having to face its problems. "No one admires more than the Swede that which is *great*—but then it must be in some other land. Here at home in Sweden we do not look kindly either at great names, great enterprises, great fortunes, or great ideas. We prefer to work for *smallholdings, own-homes,* and the like, through which everyone gets so little that he can never give offense in the eyes of others."[15]

Sundbärg was especially skeptical toward the new *Egna hem* or "Own-Home" policy which sought to combine mutually contradictory goals: to provide genuinely self-sustaining small family farms or simply permanent residences for a settled class of agricultural laborers, needed by the larger landowners and at no cost to them. The latter viewpoint seemed presently to dominate. In addition, there were efforts to assist urban workers to purchase lots and build their own homes.[16] But it was not through such palliatives that the problem of emigration was to be met. There could be no escaping the fact that real economic advance, capable of providing a better life for all, could only come from large-scale industry and economic concentration.[17]

Since it would be he who would direct the government's investigation and in no small measure put his personal stamp upon its findings and recommendations, it is thus of no small interest to see how largely Gustav Sundbärg's conclusions in 1913 were foreshadowed in his lectures in 1906, as will become apparent.

The reasoned analyses and sober prescriptions of scholars like Fahlbeck and Sundbärg, while not lacking in controlled passion and rhetoric, reached only a small, albeit influential readership. Meanwhile a far broader public was exposed to strongly emotional and polemical attacks on emigration and, by implication, the emigrants.

Probably the most widely read of these was a sixteen-page pamphlet by F. A. Wingborg, published in 1903 and reissued in augmented form in 1907 and thereafter in several printings, which combined both emotional and practical appeals, supported by material excerpted from newspapers and other sources. It contained what by the 1890s had become the standard arguments: that emigration violated the sacred bonds of family, native place, and fatherland; that exaggerated, unrealistic hopes in America stood in glaring contrast to actual conditions and risks there; that America no longer offered the opportunities it once had, whereas Sweden held out great prospects, indeed better ones than America now did; that Sweden needed its young people who were fit to work and defend the country; and that once having emigrated, the emigrant would find it hard ever again to fit into Swedish society.

To those who contemplated emigrating, Wingborg admonished:

Remember that the land you are thinking of leaving is *your fatherland* and that here, after all, is where you belong with your memories and all. You have been born and raised here. Surely you have many precious memories from your childhood. Mother and Father have lived here and all our forefathers for thousands of years back. Holiday and workday, sunshine and shadow have come and gone for them as for us. But foremost, under all conditions, the efforts of all these generations have been aimed at preserving their part of a fatherland. It is your fatherland, which you want to cast aside, it is this soil, which you now want to leave, where so many of your forefathers sleep their final sleep.

Turning to would-be female emigrants, Wingborg warned that opportunities for them in America were no longer what they had been, and urged:

Our honest and capable Swedish girls ought therefore to stay home, where they have at least a secure livelihood. It was, besides, never as much fun in America as in Sweden. How peaceful is not the Nordic summer, when there is dancing on the blossoming meadow, and how rich in delights is not the winter with its healthy life and its Christmas games! Maiden! In America your lovely features will soon wither from ceaseless drudgery and your cheeks will pale.

Although Wingborg did not allude to it, accounts in the press of the "white slave trade" in America gave rise at that time to growing concern and to the establishment in 1904 of an information office in Stockholm.[18]

In contrast to the risks and hardships of the New World, Wingborg presented in effect—if not under that name—the "Own-Home" ideal. In Sweden, he declared, it was not difficult to acquire a smallholding capable of providing a decent living. "On ten, or even on five *tunnland* [about 12 or 6 acres, respectively] it is possible for a family not only to live but to live well. The future belongs to the intensive cultivation of smallholdings. On the side, one can profitably raise pigs and chickens. On such cheap and secure terms you cannot become your own master in America." Similarly, industrial workers should seek to build homes of their own near their employment:

One learns to save when one thinks about building. Build modestly. You can add on later. If you get a little land around your house, make it attractive so that you will feel at home. You can always raise vegetables for the household. Maybe you can even keep a few chickens. That always cuts down on expenses. And how secure it then feels to know a bit of land is your own, a house is your own, and to know that your family will not be out on the street if you should pass on.[19]

Wingborg's appeal was sober and restrained compared to an anonymous twenty-page pamphlet that came out in Gothenburg the same year, 1903, and dispensed almost entirely with arguments of a practical nature. It was couched in stern moralistic and religious terms and its author wrote the first sixteen pages with only a single paragraph break as though in an inspired passion.

If you have no other, higher, and nobler motive for leaving your dear fatherland than that you wish to earn a great deal of money, here is my advise: stay at home, for there is hardly anything so miserable and despicable as greed, covetousness, lust for gain, love of this world. And if, under the best of circumstances you succeed in gaining riches, what have you not meanwhile lost? Have you not heard of love of fatherland, love of native place, love of parents, brothers and sisters, kinfolk and friends?[20]

The real question was not whether it was *wise* to emigrate, but whether it was *right,* All citizens owed a debt to their families and to society for their upbringing and education. But what could never be reconciled with worldly gain was disobedience to God's will.

If you leave against your parents' wishes, you trample God's Fourth Commandment underfoot. If you rise against your teachers' warnings and counsel, you defy God in his Fourth Commandment. If you rebel against the wishes of the temporal authority, you set yourself against the will of God as expressed in the Fourth Commandment. You violate God's Fourth Commandment when you leave your fatherland, which it is your duty to uphold, not only with money but with work and defense in time of need. Do you believe that it is a matter of accident or chance that we human beings have been allotted different parts of our world and that you have been given your home here in the North? Oh, no! This is the wise dispensation of God, Who knows best what is to the greatest benefit of each and every one. . . . Long not for a position where God has not placed thee.[21]

In times of dangerous epidemics, the most drastic measures are required, yet "what raging fever carries away as many as does the emigration?" And what was being done to counteract this national catastrophe? The author ended with a fervent appeal that all true patriots join together as one man to combat "the greatest peril and loss that in recent times has threatened our dear fatherland."[22]

In 1905 the young conservative social critic Adrian Molin made his appearance on the scene with his *Svenska spörsmål och kraf* (Swedish Questions and Needs), a collection of essays attacking what he saw as the evils of the day. Among these emigration received a high priority. Behind the present existence of a "Sweden in America," he declared,

lies a half century of the weakness and degradation of our people. . . . It is perhaps the darkest page in Sweden's history, an inescapable testimony of the national ignominy in which our people have lived through decades of their lives. A testimony of disunion and blindness, of inaction, self-betrayal, and decadence. A people without courage and resolution, a distorted image of what it once had been, under life sentence.

No wonder that those still capable of thought and feeling longed to leave for a land that seemed to offer a real future. Now, however, the Swedish people were beginning at last to "awaken to new life." "We condemn those who have abandoned Sweden's cause, who fled from hunger and social injustices instead of fighting for bread and justice, we *must* condemn them as the nation's deserters—but we cannot feel hardness in our hearts toward them when we understand what forces drove them away."

Economic conditions in particular had improved greatly, but still not enough, in Sweden during recent years. Emigration had thus become a kind of endemic disease perpetuated by the deeply rooted myth of America's superiority, against which the Swedes, with their characteristic impatient discontent, fascination for things foreign, and weak national sentiment, were little immune. The only cure, Molin held, would be to make Sweden's own appeal to its people stronger than America's by raising the level of its material and cultural life. "If we work for a moral, religious, and patriotic renaissance among our people ... we then work to restrain emigration and for Sweden's future greatness."[23]

Such condemnations and admonitions, reminiscent of the 1840s and 1850s pointed the way toward the founding of the National Society Against Emigration four years later, in 1907, with Adrian Molin as its leading figure.

While the basic ideas of the scholars and the anti-emigration publicists of this period represented no great departure from earlier discussion, the publication in 1904 of Carl Sundbeck's *Svensk-amerikanerna* (The Swedish Americans) and *Svensk-Amerika lefve!* (Long Life Swedish America!) sounded a new note—indeed a veritable trumpet blast—in the Swedish debate on the causes and consequences of the great migration. In sum, he proclaimed that in the history of the Swedish *people,* the emigration was a noble and heroic episode. As Albert Lindhagen had done over thirty years earlier, he considered it an incalculable gain and indeed the great hope for the future of the Swedish nation—a source of pride and optimism rather than shame and despair.

Carl Sundbeck was probably the most colorful of all of Sweden's many commentators on America and its Swedish population. His fervent nationalism and romantic conservatism made no concessions to the opponents of emigration. At Uppsala he had been one of the founders of *Fosterländska Studentförbundet,* the Student Patriotic Society. Traveling in the Russian Empire, he had there acquainted himself with the ancient fragments of the Swedish folk east of the Baltic: in Finland, Estonia, and even the long-forgotten village of Gammalsvenskby near the Black Sea, settled by Swedes from Estonia in Catherine II's day. Sundbeck had been deeply moved by the unshakable loyalty through the centuries of this ethnic minority, surrounded by alien peoples, to their ancestral language, religion, and culture. To him it seemed natural that the same sentiments must prevail among the far larger Swedish element across the Atlantic, especially if nurtured by understanding and encouragement from the old homeland.[24]

After visiting America in 1902, Sundbeck readily acknowledged that many of his ideas concerning the Swedish Americans and their relationship to the Swedish people as a whole had been inspired by their cultural leaders.[25] Yet their views harmonized closely with those he had already begun to arrive at himself. The venerable Gothicist tradition that had so manifestly inspired J. A. Enander and others in their vision of a "Swedish-American nation" had become combined, by the turn of the century, with newer racial theories, identifying Sweden as the original home of the Aryan race, which in attenuated form provided the creative leadership during historic times throughout Europe and much of Asia, and as the lasting abode of its purest remnant. This complex of ideas gave powerful support to the concept that the Swedish people had a world-historical role to play, transcending that of the Swedish state. If the latter was presently a minor power in the world arena, the former remained the bearer of a great providential destiny in the onward march of mankind.[26]

Some of Sundbeck's basic ideas appear already, in embryonic form, in his *Svenskarne i Amerika,* a kind of guidebook on America, its various regions, the Swedish Americans, and their institutions. It was published in Stockholm in 1900, two years before he first visited the United States and Canada and was based upon available published materials. The tone was set in his introduction, where he proclaimed:

> As will become apparent from what follows, Swedish America is the greatest conquest the Swedish *people* has ever made. America will, in the foreseeable future, include a Swedish population as large and *larger* than that of the old mother country, a population rich in inherited virtues, self-acquired prosperity, and the freely given respect of all other nations. For Sweden this population will forever remain as dear as its own children and its success a source of joy.[27]

It was Sundbeck's hope—reminiscent of Albert Lindhagen's—that the emigrants might be steered to regions in North America where large concentrations of Scandinavians were settled already, thus creating a greater Sweden on both sides of the Atlantic. At that time he was still able to think in Great-Scandinavian, as well as Great-Swedish terms, before the Swedish-Norwegian union reached its final crisis, and he dared to envision an ultimate fusion of the Swedes and Norwegians in the New World into *"one people, one nation,"* thereby leading the way for their brethren in Scandinavia itself.[28]

> That part of Sweden's folk [Sundbeck concluded,] that has provided the rank and file of the emigration has been the very best: farm workers and craftsmen. ... And if, some day, an enemy should sound the trumpets of war against the land of Sweden, shall this not resound powerfully in the hearts of thousands of Swedes who though born west of the ocean have retained the

valiant spirit of their fathers? We love to think so. . . . And if they grasp each
others' hands, the Swedes in old Sweden and the Swedes in the new, American Sweden, there is scarcely a people anywhere that can overpower them.[29]

In 1902 Carl Sundbeck traveled widely in the United States and Canada
to study conditions among the Swedish element there, on a stipendium
from the Swedish government. The result was his *Svensk-amerikanarna,*
which remains an indispensable source of factual information for the
period around the turn of the century.

At the same time, however, he took the opportunity to develop the
ideas anticipated in his *Svenskarne i Amerika.* Sundbeck's stipendium had
aroused considerable controversy in Sweden and at the conclusion of his
new book he expressed doubt that any Swedish publisher would dare to
make public his "findings and experiences."[30] *Svensk-amerikanerna* was
indeed published in the United States, by the Augustana Book Concern,
in 1904. It quickly became a bestseller, at least by the modest criteria of
the Swedish-American book market, and its author was enthusiastically
hailed as the first visitor from the old country to express unreserved
appreciation for the Swedes and their accomplishments in the New World.
To reach a wider public in Sweden, Sundbeck meanwhile published that
same year in Stockholm the numerous speeches he had given to Swedish-
American audiences, which contained in yet more rhetorical form the
essential message of his study.[31]

Again, in these writings, Sundbeck declared America to be the greatest
and most significant conquest his people had ever made. "We are," he told
the assembled Odin Club of Minneapolis in July 1902,

> links in a chain that goes back thousands upon thousands of years into
> Sweden's dim past, back to heathen times, back to shining Valhalla, to the
> abode of Odin, and from him and the mighty Asa folk we have inherited
> qualities which no other people possesses, which may slumber among us,
> but awaken powerfully when opportunity calls. To these belong, first and
> foremost the lust for mighty deeds, the yearning for what is gigantic, great,
> and dangerous.[32]

He fondly imagined what might have been during Sweden's "Age of
Greatness" (1609–1718) if Sweden's colony on the Delaware, first envisioned by the great Gustav II Adolf, had survived and spread across the
North American continent and if Karl XII had defeated Peter the Great at
Poltava in 1709, extending Sweden's dominion across Eurasia, closing the
circle of a world imperium! Now Swedish trailblazers from the west had
reached Bering Straits. What Sweden's two greatest kings had attempted
in vain—to span the world with their power—their people were in the
process of carrying out in peaceful fashion. This they did "not only as
Swedes but as Swedish Americans," having appropriated to themselves the

better parts of the Anglo-Saxon heritage, which itself derived largely from Scandinavia. A "Swedish-American nationality" had evolved, "containing within itself the best of both the old and the new homelands." As Swedish pioneers advanced across the American plains, "their horses trampled the grass here, not as in an enemy land, nonetheless as in a conquered land."[33]

In America the Swedes showed what they were truly worth. "What they were unable to do in the homeland they can do in America; strength and endurance that could only slumber at home are aroused there from their lethargy by the relentless law of necessity and competition and are driven to [achieve] the almost unbelievable."

Sundbeck described to Chicago's Västergötland Society in April 1902 how that city repeatedly witnessed "the onward march of conquering hosts."

> The flood of immigrants surged on in mighty waves. . . . It was a time of adventure, of storm, like the pageantry of a saga. On the crests of this turbulent human sea we descry how the leading figures stand out, sometimes against the stormy night, sometimes against the glow of prairie fires. They stand, like the sea-kings of the Viking age, tall at the prows of their dragon ships, born leaders, taking command by natural right through the historic phases of a mighty folk migration.

Among those Sundbeck particularly singled out as the veritable chieftains of Swedish America were T. N. Hasselquist, Eric Norelius, Carl A. Swensson, and—not least considering their kindred views—J. A. Enander. In their presence Sundbeck became ever more aware of "the new Kingdom, of which we here at home have only the vaguest idea, the kingdom our people out there have created."[34]

During his second visit to the United States in 1901, P. P. Waldenström was deeply moved to find in the rural Midwest countrymen who preserved on American soil the old-fashioned values and virtues of a peasant world now dissolving in Sweden. This became one of the central themes in Sundbeck's treatment of Swedish America. Here he found valor, hope, ambition, steadfast faith, and undying love for the land of their fathers. All of this had, meanwhile, a sharp polemical edge. Swedish America's leaders, he declared, were *"men* in the true meaning of the word, no question of that! No snobbery, no obsequiousness, no official self-importance, no Stockholm frivolity. Men they all were, typical of our countrymen out there."[35]

Swedish America thus became the criterion against which Sundbeck measured the homeland itself—and found it wanting. After the defeat at Poltava the Swedes' sense of mastery and self-assurance had sadly declined for nearly two hundred years, particularly among the upper classes, who increasingly had turned away from the national cultural heritage to "imitate the customs, usages, and tongues of other lands." At last, out of this "slough of weakness and indolence," folk of sturdy Swedish peasant stock had, on their own, performed great deeds across the sea showing the same qualities as their ancestors in Viking times and the Age of Greatness.[36]

Nowhere was the contrast more glaring than in the cultural sphere. While Swedish-American culture was, to be sure, still in its infancy, it showed its truly Swedish colors. "It is hardly to be deplored," Sundbeck wrote,

> that during the most recent decades interchange between Swedish and Swedish-American literature has not been so lively. Our literature in Sweden during this period has largely shown too weak, sickly, and pessimistic, and often too anti-Swedish characteristics for it to have succeeded—even if the book trade between the two countries were satisfactorily arranged—for it to have gained ground among a people as optimistic and also as deeply respectful toward both its religious and its national heritage as the Swedish Americans.

Everywhere the Swedish-American theater upheld the memory of the beloved homeland through plays "in which the feats of our forefathers are presented, as well as depicting folk life here at home, against the background of our landscapes and to the accompaniment of our folksongs." Those dramatists who seek to show "the ugliest sides" of Swedish life and to "belittle the persons and deeds of our forefathers" would receive short shrift in America, for "abroad one wants to see the homeland idealized and not caricatured." The later nineteenth century was a "time of betrayal" in Swedish culture, but "the memories of the great hero-kings, thinkers, skalds, warriors will live on long after recollection of today's dwarfs and wretches has sunk into the sea of forgetfulness."[37]

The surest guarantee of not only Sweden's future security but of its continued greatness therefore lay in America, the bulwark of Western values and culture against the threat from the East. "Sweden!" Sundbeck proclaimed, "Thy name stands no more among the small nations. As of yore Thy name means greatness and power, for as of yore Thy sons have marched out to victory and conquest."[38] More than that, Swedish America was the refuge of true Swedish values and traditions, from which they could reconquer the degenerate homeland. The real leaders of the Swedish people were to be found in America, "Ye chieftains who have returned our folk to itself!"[39]

Sundbeck described his guiding vision as a modern type of imperialism, "to be sure not directly of a political nature, yet containing within itself all the postulates of political significance," based upon "the idea of the union of all Swedes throughout the world." In America, which consisted of an "entire continent," the bands of kinship and national origins fulfilled

biskop Erik. Gud välsigne biskop Torlak i Skalholt, som
styrkt honom till denna färd."

Amerikas förste vigde biskop stiger i land. Utdelande väl-
signelsen åt höger och venster tågar den vördige prelaten upp
i byn. Sedan han här styrkt sig med flera rätter mat, öl och
vin, skrider han, följd af sin
blifvande hjord till en nära
byn liggande slätt. Här
stannar han och yttrar:
"Till Guds och jungfru Ma-
rias ära vilja vi här bygga
en ny kyrka, i hvilken

Biskop Eriks ankomst till Vinland.

Islands, Grönlands och Nordlandens (Skandinaviens) ätt-
lingar kunna lofva och prisa Gud och helgonen för allt det
goda de i detta land rönt och röna; och vilja vi ställa detta
tempel under den helige Olofs synnerliga vård och hägn samt

Plate 8. Bishop Erik's arrival in Vinland. The bishop of Greenland and papal legate
Erik's legendary visit to Vinland around 1120, as proudly imagined by Johan A.
Enander. (From *Valda skrifter af Joh. A. Enander,* I, Chicago, 1892.)

En svensk bondgård i Delaware.

Plate 9. A home in colonial New Sweden. Sweden's seventeenth-century North American colony as fondly envisioned by Johan A. Enander. (From *Valda skrifter af Joh. A. Enander,* I, Chicago, 1892.)

Plate 10. Threshing with a steam-driven threshing machine near Hallock, Minnesota, 1882. America as the land of progress and machine power. (Courtesy of Nordiska Museet, Stockholm.)

Plate 11. In the clover! In America, one man was as good as another, as this picture is intended to show the folks at home. (Courtesy of Swedish Emigrant Institute, Växjö.)

Plate 12. "Everyone wanted to know how much my gold watch was worth." "Mr. Coleson" from America revisits his native "Skryteby" parish. (From Gabriel Carlson, *Mr. Colesons Sverigeresa,* Minneapolis, 1896.)

Plate 13. "A childhood acquaintance, greatly changed!" The transformation of young immigrant women from Sweden never ceased to amaze. (From Gustaf Sjöström, *Jan Olsons äfventyr,* Chicago, 1892.)

En barndomsbekant, mycket förändrad.

Plate 14. Swedish housemaids in America. (Courtesy of Nordiska Museet, Stockholm.) "Not least of all," a Swedish rural pastor wrote, "the imagination of the emigrating girls is captivated by the seductive hat, which is regarded as the symbol of everything having to do with good breeding, elegance, and distinction, but which peasant girls here can hardly wear without being suspected of vanity." (J. Rosengren, et al., *Ny Smålands Beskrifning,* 4 vols., Växjö, 1909, IV:128.)

Plate 15. A peasant interior at Linnabacken, 1904. The poor man's dream of America is evident from the poster on the wall for an Atlantic steamship line, advertising passage to New York. (Courtesy of Nordiska Museet, Stockholm.)

Plate 16. A Swedish school at Chisago Lake Lutheran Church, Center City, Minnesota, summer 1910. Summer schools, provided by congregations, taught Swedish-American children proper Swedish and religion. (Courtesy of Mrs. Emeroy Johnson, St. Peter, Minnesota.)

Plate 17. Old Main, North Park College, Chicago, around 1898. This college, belonging to the Evangelical Mission Covenant, was one of a number of Swedish-American institutions of higher learning established by Swedish-American denominations from 1860 on. (Courtesy of the Covenant Archives and Historical Library, Chicago.)

Plate 18. A Swedish-American male chorus at the Linnaeus statue, 1893. The statue of Sweden's famous eighteenth-century botanist, dedicated with great ceremony in Chicago's Lincoln Park in 1893, was envisioned as a symbol of concord within an often factious Swedish America. As always on such solemn occasions, choral societies played a prominent role. (From *Valkyrian,* New York, 1898.)

Plate 19. The Swedish Ladies' Quartette, in Chicago, 1893. This group (not to be confused with an earlier one with the same name) was one of several in Swedish America which at that time served to keep alive traditional folk culture in the spirit of turn-of-the-century Swedish National Romanticism. In the middle back is the author's great-aunt, Vilhelmina Norelius. (From the author's collection.)

a natural human need for primary loyalties and mutual support. The Swedes scattered across the length and breadth of North America thus formed a vast but durable network.[40]

Essential to this ideal was the same unwavering loyalty in America to language, faith, and customs as among the brother Swedes east of the Baltic. The Swedish heritage faced serious challenges, among which Sundbeck singled out two in particular. The first was the American public school, "which in America uproots and kills all nationality but the English and every language but English." The other, more insidious threat, brought by the Swedes themselves from home, was a schoolmasterish bias against the age-old regional dialects. As a passionate National Romanticist, Sundbeck venerated local culture in all its rich variety. Embarrassment over dialect, he indignantly complained, caused many immigrants to go over to English. "The provincial dialects are far older and more Swedish," he declared, "than 'High Swedish.' They are the language of mothers, they are the most intimate and dearest [form] of our mother tongue. May no one persuade someone who speaks dialect that he therefore does not speak Swedish!"[41]

In maintaining their culture, the Swedish Americans had to rely upon their own resources, without public or outside support. In this regard they had achieved great things, and Sundbeck was repeatedly assured that the Swedish heritage was now more vigorous than ever in America. For this he gave particular credit to the Swedish-American churches and their educational institutions. President Gustaf Andreen of Augustana College and Seminary he saw as an unofficial "president" of Swedish America as a whole. "For a nation which like the Swedish-American does not comprise a political and territorial state but rather a religious, linguistic, and cultural state, the leader of the institutions which first and foremost preserve these cultural treasures corresponds to the head of a state in the usual sense."[42]

Still, for an agrarian romantic like Sundbeck, the churches and colleges also posed problems beyond their linguistic pedantry. The churches in their puritanism discouraged the traditional games and dances that had given warmth and joy to country life at home. The colleges were the standard-bearers of Sweden's higher culture in the New World, yet they lured rural youths away from the strongly Swedish rural settlements—the heartland of Swedish America—onto the shifting sands of cosmopolitan urban America. In Chisago County, Minnesota, he purported to find his ideal Swedish America, "a part of the new homeland, in unusually high degree a copy of the old, of the best we have on this side of the ocean: a steadfast, independent yeomanry on their own soil, rallied around their religious faith, contented in their law-bound freedom, and at home in beautiful natural surroundings." He thus looked above all to the churches' Swedish summer schools, which he urged should also instill pride in Sweden's peasant heritage, to preserve the Swedish presence in the new land. One might imagine Sundbeck would have wished for something like the rural Danish Folk High Schools (*Folkehøjskoler*) which at that time were being replicated in Sweden and were even brought to America by Danish immigrants.[43]

Sundbeck's special solicitude for the Swedish-American farmer meanwhile reflected his own conservative, agrarian political orientation in Sweden. Again he envisioned the New World redressing the balance of the Old as Swedish-American farmers joined Swedish peasants in their common struggle against the menaces of bureaucratic tyranny, big business, and socialism.[44]

Ever mindful of the security of the homeland, Sundbeck held that old Sweden must look to the new Sweden across the Atlantic and that ultimately the strength of the bonds that joined them would depend upon the degree to which the old homeland proved itself worthy of the loyalty of the American Swedes.

> The Swedish identity [*svenskhet*] of Swedish America depends upon us in old Sweden. If we so behave that it is an honor to be called a Swede, the Swedish presence out there will live on for all time, but if the "cowardly, lukewarm, and halfhearted" gain the upper hand here at home, then that will be the end out there! Indeed, should we perish here at home, if only we do so with honor, Sweden will be saved in America, but if we live with shame here no Sweden will arise there.[45]

"No one," Ulf Beijbom has written of Carl Sundbeck, "has with such unbridled fantasy made of the emigrants—naturally without asking them—front-line soldiers in a general offensive against a dechristianizing, liberal, and pacifistic Sweden."[46]

By remaining true to themselves, the Swedes in America would, in Sundbeck's view, likewise be most valuable to and respected in their new homeland. It was easy for them to acquire the outward attributes of the Anglo-Saxon, although the latter could "never attain the Swede's inner nobility in depth of soul and sensitivity." While other nationalities in America "scuffled in the dust" for their share of the spoils, the Swedes, as natural aristocrats, serenely went their way in the new land. "We Old Swedes" might hope, Sundbeck wrote, that "our daughter nation" might in time become the "leading and dominating class" in American society, "as their kin for a thousand years have been masters in England."[47]

E L E V E N

*The Search
for Answers*

For Swedish America's cultural leaders, the apparently studied indifference of official Sweden toward their community was deeply mortifying. In 1900, Ernst Skarstedt complained that the Swedish Americans had been "consigned to oblivion" in the homeland "since we did not stay and rust into immovable, archaic viewpoints in a monarchical land, but were instead presumptuous enough to seek to blaze new trails under a republican flag and, what is all the more unforgivable, have succeeded in our efforts."[1] In 1902 the Riksdag did grant a stipend to Carl Sundbeck, albeit only after much opposition, while the latter's ideas upon his return led, no doubt, to a great deal of consternation. But the time was approaching when the Riksdag would be prepared to devote major attention to the Swedes in America.

On 15 January 1904, C. J. Jakobson, a conservative farmer from Östergötland, arose in the Riksdag's Second Chamber and moved the appointment of a government commission to make a detailed inquiry into the emigration problem. Each year, he stated, thousands of persons in their best years left the fatherland to seek a livelihood which "with industry and economy" could as well be found at home, whereas abroad they faced "untold hardships." There had been a time, "fortunately very long past," when difficult conditions in Sweden had made emigration unavoidable, but now the country could amply provide for "all its sons and daughters."

Jakobson gave his prescriptions for combatting the evil. America undoubtedly offered greater opportunities to acquire one's own home, for which reason this should be made easier in Sweden "on our reclaimable bogs, stretching over hundreds of miles, on our numerous, large crown domains, and indeed almost everywhere where private enterprise can be supported." Above all, the government must take action against "emigrant agitators." "It is the agents and their behavior that constitute the core of the emigration question ... the simplest and most proper way [of dealing with it] would be to prohibit altogether the recruitment of emigrants and all that is connected with it." A government information agency should meanwhile publicize the true state of affairs in America.

Sweden would profit by encouraging as many emigrants as possible to return from America. Most, Jakobson was convinced, quickly came to regret the mistake they had made but lacked the means to return to the homeland. A way should thus be found to help them to come home "just at the moment when they have come to recognize their mistake," which would greatly reduce Sweden's net loss. He proposed sending a naval vessel to the United States several times a year to bring back at no cost those who wished to return, subject to controls to prevent abuse by mere vacation travelers who would soon depart again. At the forthcoming St. Louis World's Fair, which would be visited by "hundreds of thousands" of Swedish Americans, there should be a Swedish exhibit highlighting Sweden's recent economic progress and the easiest ways to return to the homeland.[2]

A supporting motion was made in the Second Chamber on 25 February by Ernst Beckman, the author, it will be recalled, of two perceptive accounts of America and its Swedish element published in 1877 and 1883. He had at that time accepted emigration as a practical necessity—if not indeed as a providential dispensation—and had treated the emigrants with both sympathy and admiration.[3] Like C. J. Jakobson, he now recognized that emigration had become harmful to Sweden, by depriving it of labor necessary for its economic development and by weakening its defense. However: "More serious still is perhaps the *loss of intellectual strength*. It should surely be the common experience that it is primarily among the energetic, intelligent young people that the emigrant host is recruited. It is above all the enterprising who in such great degree seek to make their way in the New World—the slow-witted and unenterprising usually stay home."

Something clearly must be done, and the first step must be a full investigation. Meanwhile,

> I need hardly remind you in advance that all forceful measures, such as the prohibition of emigration and the like must be considered from the start out of the question. Against them our ancient, inherited love of freedom must be irresistably aroused. Likewise it should scarcely be necessary to recall the *self-evident* fact that all such reforms as can cause our Swedish people to feel at home and masters within their own house or bring contentment and new opportunities for work and easier livelihood unquestionably contribute to controlling or reducing emigration.

Needful reforms would, for instance, include universal suffrage, a broadened popular education, more equitable taxation, increased home-ownership, and general economic advance. America's useful example should be followed where applicable, so as to "'bring America over to Sweden' and thus persuade our youth to see their own country as 'the land of the future.'" In particular the American system of education based upon the common public school for all up to the age of fourteen to sixteen offered the means to overcome the "class and caste differences" which so burdened Swedish society and so greatly encouraged emigration. Useful remigration might be promoted by a government employment agency, including a representative in the United States.[4]

On 13 May the Riksdag mandated the establishment of an Emigration Commission (*Emigrationsutredning*), thereby showing broad national consensus. The two motions meanwhile revealed diametrically opposed approaches to the problem: Jakobson's conservative emphasis upon prohibitions reinforced by propaganda as contrasted with Beckman's liberal program of fundamental economic and social reforms.

Already in March 1904, an *ad hoc* committee of the Second Chamber expressed reservations regarding the conservative approach. A government information agency, to be effective, would have to be objective and give favorable as well as unfavorable reports from America; besides, most people were more impressed by letters and remittances from friends and relatives over there. The latter circumstance would also render largely superfluous any attempt to restrict the activities of emigration agents, who in any case could doubtless circumvent any possible legislation. The committee was doubtful that any scheme of assisted remigration would be likely to bring the most enterprising and successful emigrants back to Sweden. It meanwhile favored Beckman's idea of studying those conditions in America most worthy of emulation in Sweden, referring to Japan's success in profiting from foreign experience. Finally, it stated that useful reforms to improve the national economy should not wait for the results of lengthy investigations. Implementation moved forward with due deliberation. In November 1906, the Royal Council at last approved the Emigration Inquest and appointed Gustav Sundbärg as its director on 30 January 1907.[5]

Two days later the newly constituted commission commenced its investigation, which with characteristic Swedish thoroughness it pursued over the following six years, until 1913. Its concept of the task before it was manifestly that stated by its director, Gustav Sundbärg, in 1906, when he said that to discuss the emigration meant to discuss Sweden in its entirety.[6]

The commission's publications came ultimately to include its *Betänkande* or report, an 890-page volume authored by Sundbärg, which came out in 1913, and 20 *Bilagor* or supplementary volumes, published between 1908 and 1913, containing exhaustive statistical and descriptive information on such diverse topics as emigration and agrarian legislation in various European countries, the small farm movement in certain other lands, Mormon proselytizing in Sweden, American working methods, and in particular data on Sweden's population, economy, and living standards.

Agrarian conditions received particular emphasis. Most of this material, invaluable as it is for understanding general conditions in Sweden around the turn of the century, is not of immediate concern to the present study.[7] Parts of the final report and the supplementary volumes of the *Emigrationsutredning*, however, provide welcome insights into the attitudes toward America, the emigration, and the emigrants then prevalent among Swedes in both the Old and New Worlds.

The inquest's final report contains numerous statements concerning the causes, nature, and consequences of emigration in various parts of Sweden solicited from local clergymen and officials, which together provide a digest of the views then held at the grass-roots level of Swedish officialdom. In line with the strong agrarian emphasis of the inquest, they deal almost entirely with rural districts. From these statements, certain basic themes emerge.

The commentators were in essential agreement that neither resources nor employment were lacking in Sweden to provide for the needs of its population. Land was available in sufficient quantities to support far greater numbers of independent family farms. The basic problem was accessibility. As a pastor in Blekinge put it, "Even if a farmer is compelled by lack of labor to leave a part of his land uncultivated, he will not willingly part with any of it for a reasonable price."[8]

There was general agreement not only that the dividing of larger landholdings could produce a far greater number of economically viable, smaller farms, but that indeed the small, family-operated, intensively cultivated farm held the greatest promise for the future development of agriculture. A pastor in Älvsborg County summarized this idea well in stating, "Farmers with grown children also have better prospects than any others for profitably cultivating the soil in our day, since labor has become altogether too expensive for agriculture in general." But, as a pastor in Skaraborg County wrote, this called for "fully suitable dwellings on well-located land" and a "notable heightening of [the cultivators'] level of knowledge and degree of receptivity" to improve farming methods.[9]

Related to the problem of available farmland were deep-rooted traditional peasant values. An official in Jönköping County explained that the custom in his locality of not dividing up farms upon the death of the owner resulted in a surplus population that largely went to America. A farmer's son might go into trade or enter state service, "but to hire out to another farmer or become an industrial laborer will not do at all, just as a farmer's son cannot buy and cultivate a mere croft or small lot or a farmer's daughter marry a laborer, cotter, or petty lot-holder." In Älvsborg County, an official held that while the children of the disappearing landless classes of the countryside now generally moved to the towns and industrial employments, farmers' children went to America, "as it is still so contrary to the peasant aristocracy's ideals and dignity to join, at least here at home, the great crowds of workers with their socialistic tendencies."[10]

In districts with old traditions of emigration, this seemed to continue largely through its own inertia. According to an official in Halland, "Farmers' children have early had their goal staked out for them by their parents and relatives, that is, as soon as they grow up they will leave for America. They have heard nothing else discussed." Naturally people in such regions had many friends and relatives in America who did their best to encourage their emigration.[11]

Much interest attached to the physical and mental quality of those who emigrated, as compared with those who stayed at home. "Unfortunately it is precisely the healthy and strong who emigrate," a district physician in Kalmar County opined. A colleague in Norrbotten concurred, adding that the poorest part of the population was also the most deficient in physical and mental health, "but one seldom sees such persons emigrate." On the other hand, one respondent claimed that those Swedish Americans who eventually returned home were often in broken health.[12]

The impact of America upon the emigrants' home districts also received comment. A district physician in Kristianstad County observed, on the basis of fifteen years' experience, that the relative prosperity of his area was largely due to the earnings of sons and daughters in America. Many, an official in Värmland declared, who had twenty years earlier been burdened with debt, were now free and clear, while many prosperous local farmers had been able to purchase their farms thanks to savings from across the sea. Male returned emigrants, a district physician on the island of Öland stated, often brought with them useful experience. But, he added, "the same cannot be said of the women, who usually have simply conceived exaggerated demands on life and who likewise as a rule soon return to America."[13]

In addition to these general observations, the respondents provided some rare insights into the more purely personal dilemmas that often lay behind emigration. A physician in Älvsborg County wrote: "The situation of grown children living at home in the rural areas can easily drive the children out of the home. No little corner of their own, where they can be themselves; no really independent position; nothing they can call their own, no well-earned pay. . . . To become independent the son or daughter must get away."[14]

Certain of the local pastors and officials evoked old, familiar themes by speaking of inborn lust for adventure or for quick riches in their districts, and an official in Älvsborg County spoke in sententious tones reminiscent of the 1850s when he complained that the emigration arose out of "indolence and disaffection, caused by the evil spirit of the times, [which] is the greatest and only problem."[15]

A counterpart to the statements of local officials in Sweden was the testimony the commission solicited from departing emigrants and established Swedish Americans. Two male investigators, traveling on emigrant ships to Hull, England, questioned male emigrants about their conditions and experiences at home and reasons for leaving, while a female colleague spent some months in Liverpool, interviewing Swedish female emigrants.[16] A selection of brief case histories, as summarized by the investigators, was published in *Supplement* (*Bilaga*) VII to the commission's report in 1908, providing a characteristic profile of the emigration at that time.[17]

Of greater human interest and relevance for present purposes, are the responses in their own words by Swedes in the United States and Canada to the commission's solicitation through Swedish-American newspapers in May 1907, of which 289 were published in the same volume.[18] The respondents were identified only by initials, but their state or province of residence, Swedish county of origin, and year of emigration were given. How closely the views they expressed may have reflected those of the Swedish Americans as a whole must remain a matter of conjecture, although they match well those found in other, contemporary Swedish-American sources. One may naturally suspect that a kind of natural selection resulted in persons with particularly strong views voluntarily responding to the commission's appeal. Under cover of anonymity many of them did not mince their words.

A few of the letters received, notably from recent emigrants, painted America in somber colors. One "N. L." in Minnesota, who had come over in 1902, complained that the Swedish American was generally "still too ignorant to find out the dark sides of America. He does not see the hypocrisy, corruption, the rotten political ethics, and he does not see the hidden feet of clay upon which the colossus rests."[19]

The great majority, however, were outspokenly enthusiastic over their new homeland and correspondingly critical of the conditions in Sweden to which they attributed their departure, as well as those elements of Swedish society they held responsible. As might be expected, they mentioned particularly the grim poverty at home, the situation of too many children and not enough land, the relentless drudgery for pitiful wages, and the discouraging prospects for the future. "M. M.," a woman from Värmland, now in North Dakota, told for instance, of how she had to go out and earn her own bread from the age of eight in peasant households, where she had to get up at 4:00 in the morning and eat "rotten herring and potatoes, served out in small amounts so that I would not eat myself sick." Five years after her communion she could still see "no hope of saving anything in case of illness, but rather I could see the poorhouse waiting for me in the distance." When she was seventeen, "the hour of freedom struck" when her emigrated brothers sent her a prepaid ticket to America.[20]

But nonmaterial considerations were also well to the fore in the letters from America. Sweden's restrictive franchise (prior to 1907) drew fire. "As far as my memories go back," a man from Stockholm who had emigrated in 1887 asked, "what part did a poor workingman have in politics?"[21]

A good deal more indignation, meanwhile, focused upon class snobbery in Sweden. "L. J. S.," who had come from Östergötland in 1871 wrote from Nebraska of a haughty aristocrat in charge of parish poor relief whose disparaging comments "gave rise to great bitterness and a large number, among them myself, emigrated to America, which I have never regretted. Here you are treated like a human being, wherever you are." Once in America, "F. S." in Minnesota, who had arrived in 1902, "came to a Swedish boss with my hat in my hands and my knees shaking, but quickly learned that even a millionaire need not be addressed in any other way than you yourself are addressed." "Here we have rich men," a man who had emigrated in 1868 wrote, "here we have learned men, here we have smart men, here we have bosses who sometimes work us like dogs—but masters we have none!" That class animosities of another kind could also contribute to emigration was shown by an emigrant who feared the rise of socialism at home.[22]

Those who had done well in America were naturally inclined to feel that Sweden's class-bound society held back deserving persons of humble origins. This view was expressed at length by "L. F. L." in Minnesota, who had arrived from Norrbotten in 1891 and who concluded, "Both Swedes and Swedish Americans have greater demands on life than the ruling class in Sweden is willing to fulfill."

"L. F. L." voiced another rankling grievance when he complained: "Mother Svea does not receive with much love her children who return from 'the great outwandering.' . . . The working class is jealous of him and the upper classes make fun of him because his manners are somewhat different from those of the Swedish nobility. They idolize foreigners but despise their own countrymen who have been away for a time, especially if they have been successful."[23]

That hostile accounts of America had little deterrent effect upon the common man in Sweden is attested to, again by the articulate "L. F. L.," who in 1890 had bought a book whose title he remembered as *Sanningen om Amerika* (The Truth about America) by an author whose name he had forgotten:

This book contained a mass of the most ridiculous lies about America, of the same kind as the stories one reads from time to time in our conservative newspapers back home, with which they think they can frighten small children with the bogeyman. They forget that the average Swede knows just as much about American conditions as authors and journalists. . . . This caused me and others who read the book to reflect over what motives could lie behind such a book, and we came to the conclusion that it must be above all to frighten people out of emigrating, and secondly to make the little man satisfied with conditions in Sweden. How successful this was is shown by the fact that all the farm boys in the village to whom I lent the book kept me company over to America the following spring. . . . The economic situation was the least important reason, for all of those who went from my home village that spring were from well-to-do-farm families.[24]

That old emigrants might derive no small satisfaction from the opportunity afforded to speak their mind in anonymity to representatives of their former government is illustrated by "J. M. B." in Connecticut, who had emigrated from Stockholm in 1887. "No one should think that I wish to make offensive or harmful remarks about old Sweden. No, certainly not! I understand very well that a people is formed according to its laws, and if the law had been relatively similar to the American from one hundred years back to the present, the ways of thinking of the Swedes in Sweden would have been different. In sum: *You can not blame a man for what he don't know.*"[25]

The Emigration Commission meanwhile conducted detailed investigations in selected areas of Sweden with particularly high rates of emigration. Among their reports, G. Gerhard Magnusson's from the Jösse district (*härad*) in Värmland, published *Supplement* VIII in 1908, is a minor classic.

If you go into a home to see how a peasant lives and to find out his opinion on the emigration question, you should not be surprised to hear that he has some or all of his children in America. On the contrary, you soon find that it is hardly worth the trouble to try to find any farm where none of the immediate family are in America. On the bureaus you find the American portraits of those who left most recently; on the walls hang American group portraits of perhaps fifteen or twenty relatives, all of whom are in the U.S.A. You can go from cottage to cottage and constantly find these American portraits and all kinds of American knickknacks. . . . The little boy or girl grows up in this American milieu. The only pretty things they see and know about are American knickknacks and American pictures; the only news they hear from out in the world comes to them through the letters which father or mother reads aloud when mail has arrived from older brothers or sisters in Illinois or Massachusetts. . . . And if anyone ever comes to visit, it is an elegant lady or an equally elegant gentleman from America, who used to work out in the fields here at home and was called by some ordinary name, but who now lives on money and has a much prettier and finer name. So it appears to the children in the home. They grow up and are raised to emigrate. . . . Since all the relatives furthermore are already in America they consider it much more secure to be able to go there than to go to Stockholm or Gothenburg.[26]

In their Riksdag motions calling for a government inquest into the emigration in 1904, both C. J. Jakobson and Ernst Beckman had urged that measures be taken to encourage the remigration of Swedes from America. This idea became central to the thinking of the opponents of emigration. In his *Svenska spörsmål och kraf,* Adrian Molin gave particular attention to it in 1905, in so doing revealing the ambiguity in the views of America prevalent in their circles.

While a "Sweden in America" was an unfortunate fact, Molin wrote, it should be turned to account by creating an "America in Sweden," through encouraging as many Swedish Americans as possible to return. American influences should, however, be carefully screened.

> What we have thus far gotten from the life out there is essentially some feeling of all the unsound tendencies that grow from the rich American soil, from a folk soul born out of the witches' cauldron of the mixing of peoples, a whiff of modern Americanism with its raw materialism under the pretense of religion and culture, with its contempt for all of life's ideal values as long as they cannot be used as pious dissimulation to mask egotism, as varnish to cover barbarity and vice. . . . That is not what we need and against all that we wish to rally all the good, healthy forces in the folk soul in overwhelming reaction. Modern Americanism must be resisted, whether it reveals itself in King Dollar's form or in the sickly Jesus cult of the prayer meetings. What we need is something of the strongly pulsating life, enterprise, and effectivity, something of all the good and robust [forces] that uphold the mighty outward strength out there—above all else love of work.

The Swedes, he held, were talented in many ways. "They have created a culture incomparably superior to that which our countrymen find in the great republic and equal to any culture whatsoever in Europe." But they also had their weaknesses: a lack of practical skills, a sluggish pace of work, poor business sense, and a tendency to live beyond their means. Located on the periphery of Europe, they had preserved a remarkable racial purity, but this served to accentuate their weaknesses as well as their strengths. They thus needed an infusion of new blood that would not meanwhile dilute the Swedish stock. "This would occur if we could gain back, on a large scale, those of our sons who have worked out there in the great land of the future, who have accustomed themselves to conditions there, [have] gotten the strong, intensive vitality out there into their blood."[27]

Early in 1907 Pastor Per Pehrsson from Gothenburg moved in the Riksdag the establishment of a state agency for the employment of overseas Swedes in Sweden.[28] The proposal won widespread support, even within the royal family itself. A key role in the scheme was allotted to the industrialist Herman Lagercrantz, who in May 1907 arrived in Washington as the new Swedish minister to the United States. He soon embarked on a speaking tour of Swedish America through which he extolled the bright future of the new dynamic Sweden. Private funds were raised in Sweden to support the cause and plans were laid for Crown Prince Gustav and a select group of Swedish scholars to visit and lecture in America. But his ambitious enterprise soon came to nought. The crown prince became King Gustav V in August, upon the death of Oscar II. The new Monarch's second son, Prince Wilhelm, a naval lieutenant, visited the American East Coast with the battle cruiser *Fylgia* in 1908, and was received with due ceremony by American officials, from the president down, as well as with boundless enthusiasm by eager crowds of Swedish Americans, whose self-esteem was greatly raised. Still, Swedish-American opinion remained cool toward any official Swedish efforts to promote return migration. It became clear to Minister Lagercrantz that influential circles in Theodore Roosevelt's America did not look kindly upon efforts by a foreign government to encourage the departure of useful and productive elements of the population.[29]

Supplement XX to the Emigration Commission's report carries Lagercrantz's disillusioned commentary on the situation from December 1908. Great hopes could not be placed in the return of any great number of Swedish Americans. Pride kept the best emigrants from returning and thereby admitting failure, while the "weak-willed, who lack pride and ambition" could easily enough be persuaded to come home if offered assisted passage. To be sure, many who had long been in America spoke of a desire to return to the homeland. "I meanwhile have reason to believe that this desire represents for them in most cases a dream for the future, which they cherish as such but which they in actuality scarcely wish to make come true. If they do occasionally bring themselves to the decision to return home on a visit with the idea of remaining and actually do so, it most often happens . . . that they come back here, at times with crushed illusions."

Conditions were unquestionably favorable for the working class in America. Neither those who married non-Swedes nor families whose children had reached school age could normally be expected to leave. Swedish Americans formed new friendships that served as "a substitute for their old homeland."

It was, besides, not easy to judge the value to Sweden of prospective returnees. Persons with substantial savings would doubtless be desirable in Sweden. But those who after several years in America only managed to accumulate smaller sums would not, for experience showed that the latter tended soon to return to America and by thus demonstrating their disillusionment encouraged others to emigrate.[30]

The Emigration Commission concurred. G. Gerhard Magnusson was likewise apprehensive that assisted remigration would bring back to Sweden primarily those unable to succeed in America, while if it should attract superior workers this would lead in turn to the emigration of those who lost out in the competition for jobs or who felt foreign experience was needed to get ahead at home. Moreover, to offer any special advantages to returned Swedish Americans would unfailingly create strong resentments leading to increased emigration. The commission did, however, recommend changes to specific laws concerning military service, the right to own property and conduct business, marriage abroad, and reacquisition of citizenship that hindered the return of overseas Swedes.[31]

Although sanguine hopes of a sizable return migration thus met with discouragement, they are highly revealing of the thinking of those who cherished them. All belonged to conservative or moderate liberal circles and were as much concerned over the rising socialist and labor movements as they were over emigration. They held forth their own ideal of a "national awakening," based upon the patriotic rallying of all elements of society around the "blue-gold banner." Both emigration and socialism threatened this vision of the future, but return migration from America seemed to offer the intriguing possibility of using the one evil to combat the other. When Herman Lagercrantz received his appointment to Washington, his friend, the industrialist Karl af Ekström, wrote to him in March 1907, stressing the need for labor in Sweden, "but workers . . . who can give the spoiled workers here a taste for greater intensity and devotion to duty in their work. . . . To get them here would be the greatest service anyone *can* render to old Sweden. . . . Bring home apostles for us, Herr Envoyé, nothing is more vital."[32]

Summarizing the findings of the Emigration Commission in its final report in 1913, Gustav Sundbärg naturally had much to say about Sweden's economy. Although he put his greatest hopes in large scale industrialization, he justified the strong emphasis of the inquest upon agriculture since this was the most depressed sector of the Swedish economy, in which conditions "actually account at present for emigration from our land."[33]

The situation was more hopeful in other parts of the economy, but in discussing them Sundbärg turned to arguments of a noneconomic nature in seeking to explain why they had not developed still more vigorously. The Swedes lacked, he complained, "that *joy in economic creativity,* which is such a remarkably characteristic trait among the Americans, as well as among the English and the present-day Germans." Conditions in Sweden hardly encouraged such a spirit, for if an entrepreneur failed he was dismissed as a "swindler and fraud," whereas if he succeeded he was branded as a "bloodsucker and bandit." Like the Germanic race as a whole, the Swedes were a highly creative and enterprising people, but they were sadly deficient in economic interest and business sense.[34]

Sundbärg considered various social conditions that had bearing on the emigration. Housing for both rural and urban workers he considered perhaps the darkest side of the picture. The growing socialist movement, meanwhile, tended at present to work against emigration to build its strength at home. Still, the "tyranny of the labor unions" did contribute to the departure of a certain number of ambitious workers. "Neo-Malthusian-ism," or the movement for birth control, Sundbärg mistrusted as a decep-tively false solution to emigration, for a declining population would slow economic growth. Sweden had much to learn from America's more open and democratic form of education, as well as its praiseworthy emphasis on the nation's history and geography.[35]

Here Sundbärg returned to one of his central themes: the average Swede's lukewarm sense of patriotism. Military service was generally un-popular, largely because of the widespread, fatalistic view that Sweden could not defend itself while its foreign policy, over a lifetime, showed "practically nothing but failures."[36]

There could be no denying that on the whole life had gone well for the Swedes in America. Although some had "gone under," the inquest showed that these were fewer than commonly believed. Moreover, how many of these would not have come to grief even if they had stayed at home? How many who had succeeded in America might not have failed in Sweden? It was frequently claimed that if the emigrant had worked as hard in Sweden as he did in America, he would have become prosperous at home. "This is," Sundbärg declared, "if regarded as a general rule, quite simply untrue, and whoever speaks in this way *knows* that it is untrue, if only he will fully inform himself of the situation." The drawing power of the Swedes already in America was meanwhile enormous.[37]

This notwithstanding, the Swedish Americans should at least recognize that they owed to the homeland the very qualities that had enabled them to succeed so well in America. "The Swedish Americans owe a far greater debt of gratitude to Sweden than we owe them," he declared ruefully. Only when they fully recognized this could "we deal with each other."[38]

Gradually the emigration problem seemed to be approaching a natural solution. America no longer offered the vast material advantages of the past. Meanwhile, the old Anglo-Saxon, German, Dutch, and Scandinavian stock, which once had provided "phenomenal energy and skill," was being submerged by floods of Southern and Eastern European immigrants. The overall quality of the American population was unquestionably in decline, at the very time that its natural resources were diminishing. In time this deterioration of American conditions must have its effect. Meanwhile Swe-den had the necessary prerequisites for great economic development, if properly utilized.[39]

Sundbärg concluded his and his colleagues' six years of labor on a subdued and almost fatalistic note. When the commission had begun its work many believed it would find some definitive way to end the emigra-tion. Such persons would be disappointed by the final results, for "there is assuredly no royal road to the suppression of emigration—no miracle cures and no universal means." What was needed was a general economic advance. "The most important cure for emigration is simply that in the future we do not *fall behind,* with respect either to economic enterprise or social reform." Sweden, it could be said, had waited twenty years too long for its first railways and thirty years too long for universal (male) suffrage. "But 'to fall behind,' that lies so deep in our phlegmatic Swedish nature that we must constantly strive to overcome that danger."[40]

Gustav Sundbärg's conclusions to the report of the Emigration Commission again make clear, as had his lectures in 1906, that while he attributed the emigration essentially to Sweden's slow economic development, behind this he perceived an even more fundamental cause: the Swedish national character. So central was this factor to his thinking that he authored a supplementary volume to the report devoted entirely to it in 1911, also published commercially the same year, entitled *Det svenska folklynnet* (The Swedish Folk Character).[41] To forearm himself against criticism for stepping outside the bounds of statistical evidence, he prudently added the subtitle, "Aphorisms."

Although Sundbärg also reached a wide public by separately publishing an abridged version of his final report in 1913, no part of the inquest had a more powerful impact upon the Swedish popular consciousness than his slender volume on the national character. This went through at least a half dozen printings in its first year and long continued to be a bestseller. It remains the classic Swedish work of self-characterization, both reflecting and creating a remarkable durable national image. Even today one frequently hears ideas expressed by persons who have surely never heard of Sundbärg, which obviously trace back to his aphorisms. That most of the ideas Sundbärg here expressed had received literary expression in the past and were more or less common currency at the time made the public all the more receptive to his brief and elegantly ironical compendium.[42]

Det svenska folklynnet also reveals, more clearly than Sundbärg's more scholarly contributions to the commission's report, its author's growing pessimism and ire toward the end of his life. In it he essentially reiterated national traits he had first expounded upon in the popularly written *Sveriges land och folk* in 1901, when he had presented them essentially as virtues and sources of moral strength. (Interestingly, these observations were previewed in the Swedish-American yearbook *Ungdomsvännen* in 1900). Already in the first of his Uppsala lectures in 1906, however, he began to see certain of these traits as virtues carried to harmful extremes, and this same viewpoint is conveyed in *Det svenska folklynnet* in 1911 with a passion arising from the tension between wistful admiration and exasperation.[43]

As before, Sundbärg stressed the Swede's "fantasy," uncritical admiration for what was foreign and exotic, lack of national sentiment, envy toward his own countrymen, and feeling for nature rather than for people. By "fantasy" he meant "the Swede's marked desire to be involved in great undertakings," but this also cast its fascination over "all that is *far away*," while "that which lies right in front of him he does not *see*."[44]

Two factors were of particular significance at present, Sundbärg declared. "One is that we Swedes love and are interested in nature, but not in people. The other is that we lack national feeling."[45] The Swede's love for nature was an old and well-established idea, but Sundbärg's assertion that he was lacking in psychological interest or insight was his most original and influential contribution to the ongoing discussion of the national character.[46] This trait he considered to have fateful implications. The Swede inclined toward the natural sciences and practical technology. Typically, the Swedish worker knew all about the machine he tended but had little idea about what kind of person his boss was. The Swede was inept in dealing with other people. His lack of psychological insight left him defenseless against insolence from others, and any unusual or unforeseen personal situation was likely to confuse him, making him the easy prey of more egotistical and less scrupulous types. The Swedes were therefore seldom good diplomats or—more to the point in Sundbärg's view—good businessmen. Thus others profited from what Swedish ingenuity created.[47]

No less harmful was the "remarkable stiffness and hardness" in normal personal relations deriving from the Swede's lack of interest in people. "The arrogance in Swedish social life is astonishing ... *Gemütlichkeit* is what the Swedes lack more than any other nation." This formality prevented easy and natural communication between social classes, creating the dissatisfaction that contributed to emigration. The contrast with the free and easy customs in America was painfully evident.[48]

Sundbärg's most eloquent pages, however, were devoted to his countrymen's lack of national sentiment. Various historic epochs, he claimed, had been dominated by a single great idea. In the sixteenth and seventeenth centuries this had been religion; in the nineteenth it had been nationalism, which since the end of the Napoleonic wars had aroused the peoples of Europe to "the need to give expression to their innermost nature in every aspect of life." Just as Italy had been left aside by the Reformation, so too Sweden had remained outside the stream of nineteenth-century nationalism, since it had not been compelled to fight for either independence or constitutional freedom. It thus failed to undergo the "rebirth" experienced by other nations. Traditional patriotism remained the preserve of conservatism, rather than liberalism.[49]

The Swede's warmest emotional attachment was to his native place, rather than to the nation as a whole; his idealism, meanwhile, tended more toward cosmopolitanism. He was capable of boundless sympathy and admiration for other peoples. "In Sweden," Sundbärg wrote indignantly, "one need be no more of an idealist than to become a *vegetarian—*

to promptly forget that one has a fatherland." Lacking a strong commitment to national solidarity and purpose, the Swede was meanwhile all too inclined to envy his own compatriots.[50] Sundbärg made frequent comparisons with the neighboring Danes and Norwegians, revealing a curious ambivalence. He indignantly condemned what he considered their greater self-centeredness and shrewd opportunism, yet for him they possessed a healthy nationalism, sense of common purpose, and ability to turn their own resources to account which the Swedes sadly lacked.[51]

There is a tone of weary disillusionment in his comments on the Swedish Americans.

> What the Swedish American longs for is surely not Sweden. It is his *home parish*, or perhaps more correctly, a certain cottage by a little lake in the home parish. He also longs for his relatives and friends and acquaintances. All this is very human and beautiful, but it is not actually—patriotism. It is the consciousness of being *Swedish* that is lacking. ... Sweden must as a rule get along without the sympathy and love it *ought* to be able to count on, not only from the Swedes in Sweden but also from the Swedes in America.

He was greatly sobered by the hostility toward the old country expressed by the letters from emigrants contained in *Supplement* VII to the commission's report and indignant over the Swedish Americans' unwillingness to understand the heavy sacrifices Sweden had to make for its defense and that "a people with a thousand-year-old culture *cannot* in an instant carry out such a democratization of its institutions as seems so natural to a people which began its existence yesterday." They should at least "speak of Sweden's shortcomings *in an entirely different tone* than they now do." Their vocal, disdainful criticism had done incalculable damage to what little patriotism remained among broad strata of Sweden's population—even though in America they might flatter themselves by believing they were good, patriotic Swedes. Sweden might not demand love of homeland from the Swedish Americans, but it need not regard them as friends if they did not show it.[52]

Still, despite all, Sundbärg concluded his essay on the national character by recognizing signs, at last, of a national awakening in Sweden, bringing to a close "the era which we have slept through."[53]

Gustav Sundbärg was only incidentally interested in the Swedes already in America. His main concern was the reasons they went there and what could be done about it. He himself never crossed the Atlantic. Certain of his younger colleagues on the commission meanwhile had firsthand experience of America and showed a much livelier interest in the Swedish Americans as a result.

This was particularly striking in the case of the journalist P. G. Norberg, author of a vivid, impressionistic description of "The America of the Swedes and the Swedes of America" in *Supplement* XX, published in 1911. Norberg, who had visited the United States in 1904 and 1908, had come out with a book on the subject in 1910, under the pseudonym "Peter Norden." His contribution to the Emigration Commission's inquest borrowed freely from his book, which will be considered together with other Swedish travel accounts from America in this period, but some of his views may be introduced here.[54]

> When we ask what the Swedish American is like, we find him to be sober and well-dressed, decently behaved and hard-working. The time is surely past when one could seriously look for the explanation for this metamorphosis—with which we have not been able to keep pace here at home—in the humbug that was held to be typical of everything American. We must assume that the fruit has compelled us to recognize the tree.[55]

As a thought experiment he asked how favorably a control group of "a couple of million Swedes in the homeland, drawn entirely from the lower strata of society," would compare in accomplishment and prosperity with the Swedish Americans. "It might almost be claimed that what before emigration was a purely horizontal section of the Swedish nation has been turned into a vertical section in America. For we find Swedish Americans not only among farm and industrial workers but at all levels of society." In place of the sullen Swedish motto, "One man is as good as another," he proposed the optimistic American attitude, "Any man can *become* as good as anyone whosoever."[56]

G. H. von Koch, who contributed a section on social problems among the Swedes in the United States to *Supplement* XX, had been associated with Gustav Sundbärg in liberal circles in Uppsala and was already well known for his work in poor relief, adult education, and the cooperative movement when he visited America in 1908. The resulting book had, like Norberg's, come out in 1910 and will likewise be discussed in due course. In *Supplement* XX he provided much information on particular social problems faced by the Swedes in America and on their own benevolent institutions that dealt with them.[57]

While conditions were harder in America than formerly, von Koch recognized that it still offered many opportunities. The Swedes had done well there, and they were highly regarded. If their charitable organizations were few in proportion to their numbers, this was because few were needed. The number of derelicts among them was "relatively insignificant," and "the greatest number of those who become hopelessly destitute consist of those who are inclined anywhere to become a burden upon society."[58]

In view of Sweden's own brightening economic prospects, von Koch was inclined to stress the immaterial benefits that continued to attract Swedes to America. He had been deeply impressed by the Swedish American's "surprising love for their homeland, usually in the form of an ineradicable feeling for nature and native place." "The social and psychological side of the emigration problem," he wrote, "is indeed of unquestionably as great weight as the economic."[59]

In America von Koch became aware of a growing generational gap between older and more recent emigrants. He found the view widespread among the former that the newer arrivals were of "poorer quality than before." There were complaints of their disinclination for hard work, their "socialistic and anarchistic tendencies," their heavy drinking. It was claimed that only 20 percent of the recent Swedish immigrants could be compared with the "strong, industrious, and law-abiding stock of past times." This impression had been reinforced by Swedish Americans who upon revisiting the homeland were dismayed by slack working habits, radical labor agitation, public drunkenness, and unrestrained swearing. Such ideas von Koch found most widespread among rural Swedish Americans in the "West."[60]

E. H. Thörnberg, a self-educated social thinker of awesome erudition, on his way to becoming a legend in his later years, had served as one of the Emigration Commission's interviewers of departing emigrants in 1907. He, too, had visited America, leading in 1912 to the appearance of a volume of his previously published essays. Interestingly, he traced in the first of these the ebb and flow of the Swedish emigration in relation to shifting economic conditions in both Sweden and the United States in a manner clearly anticipating the theory of "push" and "pull" factors associated with the British historian Brinley Thomas, which since 1960 has so greatly influenced migration research, not least in Sweden.

The ultimate result of this process, according to Thörnberg, was a rapid narrowing of the gap separating European (including Swedish) conditions from American. America was still a rich land, but how great a difference there now was compared with sixty or seventy years earlier. While individuals might still accumulate great wealth, there was a growing mass of poverty and insecurity. The proud tradition of political and social equality was in reality eroding away. "Uncle Sam is marching steadily toward Europe. Gradually he will adopt social attitudes and values which only three or four decades ago were considered to be as foreign to his traditions and nature as East from West."[61]

In 1913 Thörnberg came out with an article on the Swedish Americans and Sweden. Here he stressed the powerful pressures upon immigrants in the United States to learn the English language and adopt American ways, which those from Sweden readily did. While America was still widely believed to be the world's freest and most individualistic nation, "in no other land is the power of the masses over the individual so great." The result was a crushing conformism. The republic, "to which our old Swedish liberal democrats sang songs of praise," had a remarkable capacity to make conservatives of its immigrants, which rendered some of the more progressive political currents in contemporary Sweden suspect in their eyes. Such prejudices were frequently reinforced by the Swedish-American press. Few emigrants who tried to resettle at home long remained there.

Still, despite all, Thörnberg was impressed and moved by the extent to which Swedish language and culture lived on among those Swedes who had become Americans and were gaining the interest of a surprising number of their children. It should thus be a matter of high priority in Sweden to maintain close and cordial cultural ties with the brethren across the sea.[62]

The official purpose of the Emigration Inquest was to analyze existing conditions in Sweden and the ways in which they contributed to the emigration. To this end, the commission assembled an impressive array of statistical and descriptive data that has proved of incomparable value to historians of the period. It documented in great detail Gustav Sundbärg's original contention in 1906 that the Swedes demanded more from life than their society was able to provide or, as "L. F. L." in Minnesota claimed in 1907, than their ruling class was willing to allow.[63]

The inquest was also intended to propose measures to reduce the emigration. Although Gustav Sundbärg tended increasingly to see the problem fatalistically in terms of the Swedish folk character and its faults, he maintained to the end his insistence that large-scale industrialization could alone provide the ultimate answer. Among his younger colleagues there were those, like G. H. von Koch and E. H. Thörnberg, who held a brighter, more optimistic view of Sweden's future and for whom economic development was above all a means to support far-reaching social reforms.[64]

The Emigration Inquest was the most ambitious effort undertaken by the Swedish government to deal with emigration. But what effect may it have had upon the solution of the problem within little more than a decade? Franklin D. Scott has maintained that it had very little. A year after the commission completed its task in 1913, World War I broke out, which quickly reduced emigration to a mere trickle. Although there was a brief upswing following the war, the new American quota laws rapidly reduced the flow from 1924 on.[65]

It is evident, however, that Swedish emigration did not fall off so drastically after 1914 due to outside causes alone. Already by the later 1920s, Swedes were no longer quite filling their much reduced immigration quota in the United States. Clearly Sweden did undergo an impressive transformation, including both the rapid industrialization Gustav Sundbärg had consistently called for and the ambitious program of social benefits von Koch, Thörnberg, and others had seen as the ultimate goal. In part, these developments had been hastened by the pressures of the wartime emergency, even though Sweden had remained neutral. But the Emigration

Inquest and its findings must have had a powerful cumulative effect upon Sweden's leadership and broader public opinion. By the 1920s its youth were beginning to see their own land, rather than America, as "the land of the future," as Ernst Beckman had hoped in his motion calling for the inquest in 1904. As for Ernst Beckman himself, in 1918 he and his American wife retired to Santa Barbara, California, where he died in 1924.[66]

TWELVE

The Anti-Emigration Movement

$\mathscr{A}$ few months after the Emigration Commission began its work in February 1907, a private organization was established in Stockholm in May 1907 to confront the emigration problem. Named *Nationalföreningen mot emigrationen*—the National Society Against Emigration—it embodied the widely felt need to transcend partisan barriers and mobilize patriotic sentiment in all strata of society to take, without delay, whatever measures might be feasible while the government's commission carried out what promised to be a lengthy investigation. A powerful sense of urgency brought together a heterogeneous group of landowners, businessmen, military leaders, and intellectuals, of whom a number were members of the Riksdag. Prince Carl soon became the society's honorary chairman and its board included a symbolic workingman. Sizable private donations were received, as well as grants from the Riksdag and local authorities.

Although some prominent liberals, such as Ernst Beckman and Gustav Sundbärg, were involved, the real leadership in the National Society was markedly conservative and became increasingly so with time. Members of the landed nobility played an active role. The principle movers, however, were a group of academics and businessmen in Gothenburg calling themselves the "Young Right" (*Unghögern*), to stress their nationalism and advocacy of long-overdue reforms as the necessary means of preserving and fortifying traditional social and cultural values—in contrast to the smug complacency of those they considered the "Old Right." This also threw down the gauntlet to their diametrical opposites, the "Young Socialists." They found much to admire in imperial Germany, with its close alliance between crown, rural landlord, and urban industrialist; its strong public authority; and paternalistic system of social welfare. Most would be fervently pro-German during World War I. The youngest of the inner group was the then twenty-seven-year-old Adrian Molin, whose impassioned dedication, energy, and polemical skills quickly made him the director and leading spokesman of the National Society.[1]

Molin's views, already previewed in his *Svenska spörsmål och kraf* in 1905, as seen, are further illuminated by a collection of articles and speeches written between 1907 and 1911, published in the latter year under the title *Vanhäfd* (Neglect), signifying Sweden's shameful failure to mobilize both its material and human resources, which underlay the ruinous emigration. "Only a strong Sweden," he wrote, "or a Sweden determined to become strong, can hold its children. . . . It is a burden to belong to an insignificant people; it is a curse to belong to a people that wants to be insignificant. . . . The solution to the emigration question is above all a matter of the will of the people. Does the Swedish people aspire to life and greatness? The answer to that question provides the answer to the question of emigration."[2] Traditional conservatives were fearful that things might change too rapidly, but of this there was little danger as long as "the old, who are well off, rule and the young, who want to be well off, emigrate. . . . What we need is an effective *popular* policy of reform, carried out in a sober, businesslike fashion and with a *conservative* respect for those values that deserve to be preserved."[3]

Molin recognized that the emigration problem was complex, but that it offered the surest guide to needful reforms. He ironically dismissed those who believed they could end emigration by preaching "contentedness" in a little cottage on a hillside, while extolling Sweden's "excellence" in all things. Nor could it be "talked away" by simply pointing to worsening conditions in America. "The solution of our emigration question lies here at home in Sweden—in our own hands." Sweden should meanwhile be prepared to learn whatever useful lessons America might teach.[4]

Like Carl Sundbeck a few years earlier, but even more forcefully, Molin blamed Sweden's shortcomings—and thus the emigration—upon the lack of firm and imaginative leadership. Again and again he returned to this essential point. "Both the working-class movement and the emigration," he maintained, "are expressions of the lower classes' revolt against the rule of the upper classes and above all against their leadership in the productive work of the nation."[5]

Sweden during its seventeenth-century Age of Greatness had been a militaristic state demanding heavy personal sacrifices of its subjects, but these had been counterbalanced by a proud sense of national greatness, religious pathos, and common destiny. During the eighteenth and nine-teenth centuries, Molin—again like Sundbeck—considered Sweden to have degenerated into a bureaucratic state that existed only to uphold "proper order" and to exploit the people as the "milch cow" of the bureau-cracy itself. The upper classes still made heavy demands, but offered no justification other than the merits of their forefathers. Since they had given their people the pure Evangelical faith during the Reformation, Sweden's ruling classes had provided no "ideals to live, work, and fight for." Thus "the people has gone its own way, seeking ideals where it could find them: in American nationalism and in the working-class movement's religion of solidarity."[6]

In the area of specific reform, Molin's principal demand was for the establishment of new small family farms. "The heart of our land question is simply this," he wrote, "that our land should be cultivated by those who know how to cultivate the land, *and that those who know how to cultivate the land also get land to cultivate.*" This, to Molin, represented the "royal road" to solving the emigration problem. Such a policy could only succeed, however, provided the new farms were large and productive enough to be genuinely self-sustaining.[7]

It was meanwhile essential to encourage a new spirit of hope and dedication. Nothing was more important in this respect than a more patrioti-cally oriented education of the young.

> We should teach them to love Swedish nature and Swedish work—be it an ingenious machine, a well-tilled field, or a handsome ship—love it and be proud of it because it is great and good, but above all because it is *Swedish,* it is ours, we all share it and the honor that it has come about. We thus awaken a sense of solidarity between the young and Sweden. . . . The school must become in the deepest and broadest sense *national,* [its nature must] be determined not by theoretical and universal cultural, but rather by national viewpoints and needs.[8]

By this means the lure of America's "skyscrapers and dollar millionaires" should be countered with Sweden's ancient culture, law-bound society, and real material potentialities. The young must be brought to realize that they all were needed in their homeland, that he who left the land placed his rightful burden on the shoulders of others and weakened the effort necessary to overcome "lassitude and the rule of old men." Given the existing emigration, meanwhile, Molin urged that efforts be made to keep alive the emigrants' concern for their old homeland, to "bind them to Sweden. For this purpose he encouraged the establishment of the Swedish-America Steamship Line, which began its operations out of Gothenburg in 1915.[9]

A comparison between Adrian Molin and Gustav Sundbärg is instructive. The two had much in common: their strong patriotism, their recognition of the complexities of the emigration problem and of the need for reform, their fascination with the Swedish folk character, their style and verve in presentation. Yet there were significant differences. The youth and opti-mism of the young Molin stand in contrast to the disenchantment of Sund-bärg's later years. While Sundbärg, the nineteenth-century liberal, argued for all-out industrialization, Molin, a conservative neo-romantic of a characteristically early twentieth-century type, saw Sweden's salvation in the re-generation of its rural freeholder class through a vigorous "own-home" movement. Although a disillusioned democrat at times, Sundbärg maintained his belief in democracy. Molin sought reform on behalf of the people but mistrusted the people's own judgment. Leadership, in his view, could only come from a dedicated and capable elite. Already within the first few years after its establishment in 1907, the National Society revealed an increasingly conservative and rural-romantic orientation.[10]

The central office of the National Society Against Emigration opened in Stockholm in the fall of 1907, to be followed over the next decade by twenty branch offices throughout Sweden. Its membership grew rapidly, reaching nearly 16,000 by 1917. Its major focus remained throughout its land and informational programs. Concerned above all with the rural youth who provided the rank and file of the emigration, the society aimed at "getting land for them and inducing them to stay at home," as Franklin D. Scott has put it.[11]

Since 1904 the quasi-official Provincial Economic Societies (*Landhushållningssällskap*) administered a loan fund, provided by the government, for the purchase of small properties. After 1907 the National Society established or took part in the establishment of local "own-home" corporations—eleven in all by 1917—subscribing a substantial part of their working capital. Numerous individual loans were likewise provided by members. Such loans were made only to sober and industrious persons who earned their livings through menial labor, and only for small farms and rural homes. The society meanwhile sought to persuade larger landowners to part with surplus land on reasonable terms as a patriotic duty. In some places the purchase and division of larger properties created veritable colonies of new smallholdings. The society took particular pride in the rural resettlement of displaced urban, industrial workers, following the General Strike of 1909. It was also vitally interested in settlement on the extensive crown lands in Sweden's far North.[12]

The society's main and branch offices meanwhile served as information centers, answering practical economic and legal questions for those contemplating emigration or returning home from abroad, to dissuade the former and encourage the latter. The society also sponsored the scholarly investigation of various social and economic problems in Sweden, publishing between 1908 and 1924 nine research reports—three of them by Molin—augmenting in selected areas the work of the government's Emigration Inquiry.[13]

From the beginning, the National Society carried on a vigorous propaganda campaign against emigration, which at first comprised its principal activity. In 1915 it reported having sponsored some eight hundred lectures throughout Sweden, "illuminating American conditions" for an estimated

150,000 listeners. Youth and school organizations were involved in the anti-emigration campaign. The society's magazine, *Hem i Sverige*, carried articles on the problems confronting emigrants in America, on Sweden's economic progress, and the "own-home" movement.[14]

The society published announcements in newspapers and fliers distributed in tens of thousands of copies, imploring those who might consider emigrating to visit its offices to obtain reliable information. "Many succeed in America, and about them you hear, but *remember that many, many, go under, but nobody talks about them and their fate*," warned the most widely distributed of these. "Sweden now has plenty of room for all its sons and daughters," and anyone prepared to work could attain wealth and comfort at home, together with greater security than America could provide.[15]

The society also brought out several brochures or booklets. T. W. Schönberg's *Sanningen om Amerika* (The Truth about America) from 1909 gives their general tone. "It is a known and confirmed fact," it states, "that the Swedish American can only in very exceptional cases bring himself to tell 'the truth about America.'" The Swedes had a weakness for boastfulness, which flourished luxuriantly in America. The legend of easy success there created by the early emigrants lived on, even though conditions in America had become progressively worse. Rather than admit to failure, the emigrant felt compelled to pretend he was successful even when he was not. Any attempt to reveal the "dark sides of life in America" would, moreover, face the determined resistance of the Swedish-American press, whose survival depended upon an uninterrupted stream of new arrivals from Sweden. For those not bound by such selfish considerations, however, it became an ever more obvious duty to break through the barrier of false illusions that kept people at home from "seeing conditions out there as they are."[16]

Among the most widely read of the society's tracts were two cautionary tales in a light, folksy tone. W. Swanston Howard's *När Maja Lisa kom hem från Amerika* (When Maja Lisa Came Home from America) from 1908 tells of the vain and foolish Maja Lisa from Värmland who is lured to America by letters from her friend Maja Stina. No sooner arrived in America, where of course she finds only poorly paid domestic work, Maja Lisa sets about preparing her wardrobe for her triumphal return to her native village with single-minded determination, avoiding any distractions or amusements with her new acquaintances that would cost her money. Within the year she sets off on a third-class ticket for Sweden, "dressed in a cheap but ostentatious American traveling dress and a provocative hat." Arriving home, with her nose in the air and speaking "broken Swedish," Maja Lisa naturally "strikes the natives with astonishment." Although some of the older and wiser laugh behind her back at her gaudy pretentiousness, many of her own age are stricken with "America Fever" and soon depart for the new land. After two months Maja Lisa returns to America, broke but "beaming in triumph and filled with pride over the devastation she had wrought." She was last seen on her hands and knees, scrubbing floors. If the Maja Lisas and Maja Stinas could be made to tell the truth, the author moralizes, the Huldas, Gretas, and Brittas would realize what a good land Sweden really was, provided they took advantage of its opportunities.[17]

Ernst Lindblom's *Per Jansons Amerika-resa* (Per Janson's Trip to America), which came out in 1909, tells of the misadventures of a twenty-year-old youth from a good home, who travels to America, where his naive expectations are quickly disillusioned. He finds that the much-vaunted American freedom and equality are simply humbug and that the Swedes— himself included—are both exploited and looked down upon by the hard-headed Yankees because of their honesty, industry, and respect for the law. In the end Per is happy to escape back to his fatherland.[18]

It was, however, not enough simply to warn of the present risks and hardships of life in America or to preach platitudes about contentment at home. The National Society concentrated not only on making land available for small family farms but upon presenting an idealized view of the way of life such small farms would make possible and on practical ways for individual families to bring this about. This was done in part through the magazine *Hem i Sverige,* but above all in the book, *Svenska allmogehem* (Swedish Country Homes), ostensibly edited by Gustaf Carlsson (in reality primarily by Adrian Molin), and containing contributions by numerous artists, architects, and other experts.

Molin's introduction to *Svenska allmogehem* is a ringing manifesto of his own and his society's basic philosophy.

> Sweden—this is our broad and magnificent land, it is our people's history, our memories, our work, and our struggles at present, and above all it is our hope for the future. To be Swedish is to *be a part of Sweden.* Sweden is the Swedish people's home. . . . We Swedes, all of us, have our roots in the soil of Sweden. And these roots cannot be cut without doing damage to our soul. . . . Only he is Swedish in his heart who knows that when he works, he works for his country, who rejoices and suffers with Sweden, whose heart aches when things go badly for Sweden.

To be sure, all was not yet as it should be at home. Development was needed in industry, but above all in agriculture, which was a "foundation for Sweden's economy and for the health of our people."

> Ever stronger goes forth the appeal: back to the land! It is a matter of showing that just as in our fathers' times the soil of our country can provide both a secure and a good livelihood to its cultivators and that it can sustain good and happy homes. . . . Small family farming is the way of the future for our agriculture. Through small-scale farming we should be able to save thousands of young people each year for Sweden. They will start new families, more

every year. And in the new homes will grow up hosts of children who shall go forth in new campaigns of conquest within our great but sparsely peopled land.[19]

The book provided architectural plans for what Molin described as "simple, sound, inexpensive, and well-disposed dwellings of *a Swedish character*. No cheap imitations of foreign upper-class villas but Swedish homes like those our fathers built. For behind them lay *Swedish thoughts,* and it is Swedish thoughts we ought to be thinking."[20] The accompanying sketches and plans showed attractive rural homes based upon traditional regional types. Much practical advice, moreover, was provided on gardening, the care of fruit trees and berry bushes, the raising of cows, chickens, and pigs, food preservation, improved farm implements, and outbuildings.

In all, *Svenska allmogehem* reveals in fascinating detail the National-Romantic vision of an idyllic rural Sweden in an imagined future. According to the preface to the third printing, which came out already in 1910 in an inexpensive "folk edition," the first edition had comprised 65,000 copies— a remarkably large number for Sweden—of which 60,000 had been given free to schools and other institutions, and this had been followed by a second printing of 10,000 copies, which was already sold out.[21]

It is difficult to evaluate the impact of the National Society Against Emigration. While it focused its main practical efforts upon promoting small-scale rural property-ownership it accounted for only a limited part of the total "own-home" movement in Sweden, which would continue for decades to come, even though the Society doubtless played an important role in giving it impetus and direction. But this in turn raises the broader question of the effectiveness of the "own-home" movement as a whole in Sweden.

Confidence ran high at the beginning of the century in the economic feasibility of the small family farm. In time tens of thousands of new small farms and rural homes were established, but in the long run they did not prove a lasting answer in economic or social terms. The movement was generally dominated during its earlier years by the old Provincial Economic Societies, which tended to favor homes for agricultural laborers, rather than economically independent smallholdings. Although the latter concept gained ground in the 1920s, by then the growing mechanization of agriculture again turned the scales in favor of the larger acreages, which now required more capital but less labor. The same decade saw an increasing drift away from the countryside and a decrease in the numbers of both small farmers and farm workers that has continued down to the present. Many of those, moreover, who acquired rural homes under this program were, or became, only part-time farmers, whose main employments were nonagricultural. By the 1920s, too, the movement concentrated increasingly on promoting "own homes" for industrial workers in new working-class suburbs.[22]

Such developments were not generally foreseen amid the widespread enthusiasm that enveloped the "own-home" movement in its earlier years. As an antidote for emigration it may nevertheless have been more successful than is generally imagined, by keeping in Sweden a sizable number of prospective emigrants at least long enough for Sweden's appeal to catch up with and surpass the lure of America. More important still, it provided Sweden with a sizable stock of good rural housing, thereby promoting a largely decentralized pattern of industrial development in smaller communities, with obvious benefits to the overall quality of life.

As for the National Society's informational and propagandistic activities, this was an area of activity that could only legitimately be exploited by an organized private interest group. The society utilized this opportunity to the full, on a scale far surpassing anything that had previously been seen in Sweden. The sheer number of its lectures and the press runs of its publications of all kinds is highly impressive. Although at times it could arouse stubbornly contrary reactions in Sweden, as well as great indignation in Swedish America, its overall effect—both in criticizing America and the emigration, and in holding out the vision of a better alternative at home— must have been considerable. Many of its clichés still seem well established today in the Swedish popular mind.

It may nonetheless be asked whether the National Society conducted its campaign altogether as effectively as it might have done. This question was raised, for instance, in 1913 by the journalist M. V. Wester, who was sympathetic with its goals, but who regarded its leaders as lacking in practical agricultural knowledge, compared with the more successful Provincial Economic Societies. Thus its own-home agencies had encouraged the establishment of many new smallholdings or entire smallholders' colonies that were poorly located, underfunded, too small, or otherwise infeasible, which indeed encouraged further emigration. Wester urged that the National Society concentrate its efforts upon its publicistic and ideological campaign. Through its involvement in land transactions, its "idealism suffers seriously and the [own-home] movement becomes somehow artificial."[23]

The establishment of the National Society Against Emigration in 1907— together with the beginning of the Emigration Inquest the same year— gave strong encouragement to other, independent efforts to propagandize against emigration in Sweden.

An organization with an already manifest concern with the problem was *Sällskapet för Nykterhet och Folkuppfostran*—The Society for Temperance and Public Enlightenment, the two ideals being considered inseparable in Sweden as elsewhere. In 1904 its pamphlet series included a tract, *Älskar du ditt fosterland?* (Do You Love Your Fatherland?) by Cecilia Milow. In tones reminiscent of Carl Sundbeck, its author described the Swedish Americans' undying love for the land of their birth and contrasted their sturdy virtues with widespread lassitude, lukewarm patriotism, and moral laxity at home, including of course addiction to Drink. The lesson she derived from this was the need for a moral renewal to strengthen Sweden against both its external and its internal enemies. "Never dream of serving other colors! Whoever may tempt you, whoever may flatter you, whoever tries to persuade you to desert your flag—remember that behind it stands all that is near and dear."[24]

In 1907 the same organization brought out a forty-four-page booklet, *Hvad Anders lärde i Amerika* (What Anders Learned in America) by "M." One of the more artfully written works in its genre, it tells the story of a kind of latter-day Swedish "Candide," reminiscent of Voltaire's. Young Anders, dissatisfied with his life as a farm laborer, decides to leave for America. His older and wiser friend Per seeks to dissuade him: "I don't know what you could gain out there that you could not gain here, if you set your mind on it. ... That land is not for us." Per then describes how through patient toil he was able to acquire his own smallholding and the deep satisfaction, worth more than gold, of seeing grain, fruit, and flowers grow on his previously unbroken soil. "A Swede is born and brought up for Sweden," he admonishes. "What business does he have in America?"[25]

But headstrong Anders is not to be deterred. Off he goes to America, which he quickly enough has good reason to repent. A broken-down Swede urges Anders to return home while he can, not because Sweden cannot do without him but because he cannot do without the land that has made him what he is, unless he is prepared to be "pulled down into the mud and become a beggar and thief like I am." In America, he says, "I have lost myself." To add point to this, he disappears with Anders' savings at the first chance. A wealthy Swedish-American businessman points out how hollow his own and other Swedish Americans' material gains have been in America when they no longer have a fatherland.[26]

After seven lean years, Anders is fortunate enough to come home, marry his faithful Lisa, acquire two hectars of land on an overgrown hillside, and build his little cottage with his own hands. Here they work hard but with growing contentment for themselves and their little family. When he comes home from work in the neighborhood, Anders sings with joy and gratitude as he opens his gate and steps into his own little garden.[27]

Throughout this tale, "M." finds numerous opportunities to develop his conservative, National-Romantic views by preaching contentment with modest circumstances and condemning labor unionism as fatal to individual initiative and hard work. In describing both Per's and Anders' "own-homes" he also works in specific, practical information about how such smallholdings may be acquired and developed. Both Per and Anders, be it noted, become homeowning laborers, not self-sufficient farmers. "M." concludes by urging others to add to Sweden's "inner strength" by following their example.[28]

The same basic message—for a juvenile readership—likewise runs through both the schoolbooks and the children's magazines of the period, which stressed devotion to God and fatherland, contentment, and social stability. In the 1910 and later editions of his *Sveriges historia för folkskolan* (Sweden's History for the Primary School), O. Rosenborg, for instance admonished: "Young generation, Sweden's children, grow up in the fear of God and in virtue, in devoted industriousness, cherish the memory of our fathers and learn from them. . . . Do not abandon your native soil! See to it . . . that Sweden may grow great, rich, and joyful through the care of its sons and daughters under the protection of the Almighty." In the magazines various stories express condemnation for young protagonists who foolishly long to emigrate or commiseration for those taken to America against their wishes, while holding up as examples those who courageously refuse to leave their homeland.[29]

A hefty pamphlet by C. Thorborg, published in Karlstad in 1906, reveals the impatience among the more emotional opponents of emigration with the government's commission to study the phenomenon, even before it commenced its work. Emigration posed an immediate threat to the nation's very existence, Thorborg declared. The commission would assemble statistics that would be duly filed in the archives. "It is just as though they thought the emigration would stop because it was decided by the highest authority to seek out its causes. . . . But knowing the Royal Swedish Slowness, it should not be too much to maintain that hundreds of thousands of Sweden's sons and daughters will still leave the fatherland before anything is done officially to cure the emigration epidemic."[30]

The villains of the piece were all those who spread favorable—and thus false—reports about America, including visiting Swedish journalists who never laid aside their "fine cigars and kid gloves" to experience America as workingmen. "In that case they would not be so full of praise for America." Not surprisingly, Thorborg's pamphlet conveys more heat than light, for he could only offer platitudes to deal with the problem. The Swedes should unite, overcome their petty differences, make common sacrifices for the fatherland, stop hankering for foreign temptations.[31] Such exhortations were obviously directed toward the Swedish worker, rather than his employer.

An attack of a different kind upon America and the emigration was delivered by G. Thyreen in his book, *Skall jag resa till Amerika?* (Shall I Go to America?) published in 1911. The author established his credentials by pointing out that he had spent the years 1905 through 1908 in America. The greater part of the book consists of a general discussion of American conditions, emphasizing the alarming decline of the economy and the rising tide of intractable social problems. These findings are reinforced with a plethora of statistics and specific case examples, extracted mainly from American census reports and other public sources, thereby apparently adding substance to the similar but less documented claims of other opponents of emigration.[32]

After laying what might seem a sober and objective groundwork, Thyreen soared off into the blue in the second and most remarkable section of his book, in which he expostulated an entire philosophy of history, society, and culture. Race, in his view, was the essential basis of all societies and nations, and the Germanic race surpassed all others in creativity, idealism, courage, venturesomeness, strength of will, self-reliance, and physical stamina. Indeed, a sweeping survey of the past showed that whereas the Germanic race was numerically preponderant only in northern Europe, it had since the dawn of history provided the small creative elites of most of Eurasia.[33] It was precisely these racial qualities that attracted the great flow of Germanic emigrants to America and gave the new nation its original character. Here, as in the Old World, the Germanic element— and it alone—had been the "bearer of culture and progress." But while the great influx of Germanic blood into America had accounted for its dynamic development, its loss had led to stagnation in Europe.[34]

Thus far Thyreen added little to what by the turn of the century was a widespread, if not generally accepted, theoretical racialism in Swedish intellectual circles.[35] Thyreen went much further, however, in the inferences he drew from this viewpoint. He held that each race had its natural habitat in the world to which it was uniquely adapted and outside of which it could not in the long run survive. "Only in Northern Europe," he declared, "do those of Germanic race preserve all of their health and vigor." There alone did they find "such conditions as they need to thrive and develop, to be themselves. . . . But for those of Germanic race America means death, whereas mankind cannot afford to bury Civilization's foremost champions in the Pale-Faces' great family tomb on the other side of the Atlantic. America must not be allowed to become a direct obstacle to progress."[36]

Two factors above all threatened the white race and especially its Germanic element in America: climate and miscegenation. The former had inexorably brought about a physical degeneration which by now was most advanced among the older Anglo-American stock, whose nativity, moreover, was in constant decline. Even though the Swedes had settled mainly in the northern states, "they nonetheless appear . . . gradually to undergo the same changes in physical appearance and build as the other Europeans. The complexion becomes pallid, the expression and facial features become sharper, the build thinner and at least to all appearances weaker: our countrymen give the impression of being more like Indians than Nordics."[37]

Although the existence of innate racial characteristics was considered almost axiomatic in Sweden, as elsewhere, there was less consensus regarding the effects of racial mixing. Many Swedish families, not least among the nobility and upper middle classes, were proud of some degree of foreign extraction and felt that this conferred unusual and valuable qualities. Thyreen and others like him upheld the ideal of pure and unsullied race. "It is Nature's immutable law," he states, "that through the crossbreeding of the different races of mankind the good qualities of none of them are passed on to the offspring."[38] Thus with a degenerating population and with overexploited material resources approaching exhaustion, America was headed toward its irreversable decline and fall.

All of this led naturally to Thyreen's prescriptions for the homeland, which proved a strange mélange of the extremes of conservatism and radicalism. He inveighed against the dead hand of bureaucracy and the overregulation of Swedish life. Labor unionism he considered incompatible with the Germanic spirit. He called for the abolition of the monarchy and the state church as expressions of foreign traditions of despotism and of the nobility for being largely foreign in both blood and values.[39]

In contrast to this apparent libertarianism he prescribed a series of authoritarian structural reforms in the national economy and called for making Stockholm the sole center for all aspects of national life. Education was to be purged of the "remnants of Antiquity." "We must deal cautiously with books and have them serve us, not gain mastery over us," he warned. "The book is the enemy of life. Nothing suffocates like book dust." Most important were physical training and hygiene. Further, all aspects of the national culture should be cleansed of foreign, non-Germanic influences.[40] Finally, Thyreen recognized the existence of an alien, "Celto-Slavic" strain within the Swedish population itself and called for measures to prevent its intermarriage with those of pure Germanic blood. Nature's course must be accelerated through a vigorous program of public enlightenment to discourage interbreeding of the fair and blue-eyed with the dark and brown-eyed.[41]

G. Thyreen is a striking example of an extreme reaction to the emigration problem. His thought shows also how a protofascist ideology based on *Blut und Boden* was well on its way to development in Sweden—as elsewhere in Europe—during the years before World War I.

In 1916 Carl Bruhn, who identified himself as head of the International Press Association in New York, published a lengthy anti-emigration tract entitled *Stanna hemma!* (Stay Home!) to present the "unvarnished truth" about America. This comprised a particularly hair-raising picture of political corruption, reckless squandering of natural resources, and a faltering economy accompanied by widespread poverty and unemployment.[42]

America, in Bruhn's view, was dominated by an arrogant clique of established Anglo-Americans, whom he particularly resented for their strong anti-German bias in the then ongoing European war. This he considered a crying injustice to the "splendid" Germanic peoples—the Germans and Scandinavians—"which more than any other nationality have established civilization in the United States and thereby made the land what it is. It is not the so-called Americans—the descendants of the Pilgrims and the Dutch—who have forced out the Indians, cut down the forests, broken the ground, and made the land habitable and prosperous. While this 'flower of the land' established commercial centers, the despised immigrants moved west, struggled with nature—and let themselves be exploited by the hymn-singing merchants in the cities."

Meanwhile, both the Anglo-Americans and the older North European immigrants were now being overwhelmed by the recent flood of "raw manpower" from southern and eastern Europe, lured across the Atlantic by ruthless industrialists to drive down wages.[43]

As a self-avowed Swedish American, Bruhn sought to give a fair and balanced picture of his countrymen in the New World.[44] It was by revealing the increasingly hopeless future they faced in America, despite their best efforts, that Bruhn sought to stem the tide. He foresaw a grave economic crisis in the United States following the current European war, when fresh waves of southern and eastern Europeans inundate America's shores. Thus Bruhn's admonition: "Stay home and use your strength in your fatherland. Sweden needs your arms and brain and will know how to reward you, if only you employ the same energy which over here is needed to maintain a meager existence." It was meanwhile the hope that many Swedish Americans with valuable experience might return to the homeland and he was particularly taken with a recent proposal for the establishment there of Swedish-American "colonies" providing an environment congenial enough to keep them in Sweden.[45]

Looking back, it would appear that Carl Bruhn's *Stanna hemma!* in 1916 was the last significant contribution to the long series of Swedish anti-emigration tracts extending back to the 1840s. Since the outbreak of World War I two years earlier, Swedish emigration had fallen off to a mere trickle, and except briefly in 1923, it would never again reach disquieting proportions.

THIRTEEN

Transatlantic Visions and Images

*I*n January 1907 a meeting was held at the Grand Hôtel in Stockholm "to consider what measures might be taken for the support of Swedish culture and Swedish language abroad," resulting in the formation of a committee that became the nucleus of a new, nationwide organization, *Riksföreningen för svenskhetens bevarande i utlandet* (RFSBU) or, in the official English translation, the Society for the Preservation of Swedish Culture in Foreign Lands, with headquarters in Gothenburg, founded in December 1908.[1]

The moving force behind this development was Vilhelm Lundström, an eminent philologist and former editor of *Göteborgs Aftonblad,* who in 1907 became professor of classical languages at Gothenburg University and who would serve between 1912 and 1914 as a conservative member of the Riksdag's Second Chamber. Lundström had been one of four persons who had issued the call to the Stockholm meeting in 1907. He served as secretary on the original committee and, from its establishment, as director of the RFSBU, as well as editor, in name or fact, of its publications.

In Stockholm Lundström, set forth his central idea in January 1907: language and national culture transcended political boundaries and compatriots outside Sweden were of vital importance to the homeland. "Awakening Sweden," he declared, needed all its sons and daughters, wherever they might be. They must be preserved for Swedish language and culture, keeping open the possibility that they might someday return. As he expressed it some thirty years later, in 1938, he had become possessed by "an overpowering sense of obligation to preserve nationally what could be preserved, to seek to turn to account all of that precious Swedish material which, even if no longer to be found at home in the fatherland, still belonged to the Swedish heritage through blood and race, language and inheritance."[2] The constitution of the RFSBU reflected this concept.

The ideas underlying what Vilhelm Lundström called the "All-Swedish Movement" are set forth in his *Allsvenska linjer,* published by the society in 1930. This was a collection of essays that had appeared in various newspapers over a quarter of a century. The original publications and dates are not identified, but the first several clearly derive from the period around the founding of the society.

Lundström had been deeply disturbed by the emigration. In 1938 he recalled the profoundly depressing spectacle of the constant stream of emigrants passing through Gothenburg on their way to America. "The generation that is now young or middle-aged and which did not experience or no longer can remember what it then saw and experienced can scarcely comprehend the impression this outflowing bloodstream made upon a nationally aroused mind."[3]

Such reflections had raised the question in Lundström's mind: "Shall all these Swedish resources in people and energy really be irretrievably lost and can nothing, at least nationally and culturally, be saved for that which is Swedish?"[4] The answer is the Greater-Swedish ideal set forth in the opening essay of his *Allsvenska linjer.* In actuality, he here stated, we have two fatherlands, "the kingdom to which we belong politically" and "our *nationality*" in the ethnographic sense. "Simply expressed, our other fatherland consists of all Swedes throughout the world, *the Swedish stock,* or from the purely linguistic viewpoint, our language area." Language was the central point, "the expression of that which lies deepest within our nature, the binding tie between past and coming generations, our nationality's coat of arms. . . . [W]ithout the preservation of the mother tongue one cannot belong entirely to the Swedish nationality; race and blood, pure as they may be, do not suffice in themselves."[5]

This "other, greater fatherland" was much more extensive than people at home were inclined to realize. "The Swedes in the world amount to nearly nine million, but three of these nine [million] live outside Sweden's political boundaries."

> Within this other fatherland lies our greatest national task at present—the task of culturally, linguistically, and, as far as possible, economically bringing together the entire Swedish stock. This is the task which we call the *Rallying of All Swedes* [*Allsvensk samling*]. . . . It is a fanfare for struggle and conquest. For the rallying in spirit of the greater Swedish fatherland once again is a conquest, surely the last Old Sweden can make. But also the greatest it has ever made.[6]

Lundström took his compatriots in Sweden to task for their "Small-Swedish" (*småsvensk*) indifference to and negligence of those of their own blood and bone abroad, for whom he urged vigorous support and encouragement. At the same time he stressed the importance of national pride and a vigorous, creative national life in the old heartland. To what degree, he wrote, "the other part of the Swedish, people . . . may be entirely or partially preserved or regained for Swedish culture naturally depends upon the survival of feeling for the Swedish race and heritage [in Sweden]. But ultimately it depends upon the *value* that maintaining Swedish culture may in the long run have for the overseas Swede."[7]

Vilhelm Lundström's basic ideas are clearly reminiscent of those so eloquently presented by Carl Sundbeck in 1900 and especially in 1904, and before Sundbeck—in essence—by the Swedish-American patriarch, J. A. Enander, and his following. Sundbeck—if not Albert Lindhagen before him—ought surely to be recognized as at least the spiritual godfather of the All-Swedish movement. Sundbeck does not, however, appear to have played an active role in the Gothenburg-based society. He became as intensely engaged in various causes of a right-wing, patriotic, and Germanophile nature as he once had been by the vision of the Swedes' peaceful conquest of the world beyond.[8]

For practical reasons the RFSBU at first limited its efforts to Swedes living in Western Europe, largely professionals, businessmen, skilled craftsmen, and their families, concentrated mainly in larger cities. These mainly involved promoting Swedish lectures for the adults and Swedish schools for their children.[9]

But this was only the beginning. In an article entitled "When the All-Swedish Idea Was Born," Vilhelm Lundström described how he—like Carl Sundbeck about the same time—had visited the former Swedish lands, Finland and Estonia, with their deeply rooted Swedish ethnic minority, in 1891 and 1892. He had been seized by the pathos of an ancient people, steadfast in its inherited Swedish language, customs, and religion, and its love for the old "homeland," which scarcely gave a thought to its existence. Indeed, Lundström distinguished between two branches of the Swedish people: those inhabiting the "immemorial region of Swedish settlement in Sweden, Finland, and Estonia" and those who from there had spread out to other parts of the world. The preservation and development of the first was essential for the continued existence of the second. In time the East Baltic Swedes would receive the society's most substantial encouragement and support.[10]

By far the greatest number of Swedes outside of Sweden were meanwhile to be found in the United States, and this circumstance Lundström and his associates regarded ambivalently as both Sweden's tragedy and its great historic opportunity. The All-Swedish movement naturally attached high hopes to work in the American field as soon as its means would allow.

A promising opportunity to initiate activity across the Atlantic arose when the Augustana Lutheran Synod, together with Augustana College and Seminary, celebrated its fiftieth anniversary in Rock Island, Illinois, in 1910.

Per Pehrsson, a prominent Gothenburg pastor and conservative member of the Riksdag, who served on the executive board of the RFSBU, traveled to America to attend the ceremonies. On behalf of his society, he presented an ornately decorated proclamation congratulating the college on its half century as a center of Swedish language and culture in America. "May the day never come," it proclaimed, "when the Swedish tongue falls silent within its walls or the Swedish spirit dies within the hearts of its teachers or students. Hail to the fifty-year-old bastion of Swedish culture in the mighty land between the great oceans."[11]

Pehrsson was meanwhile instrumental in organizing *Föreningen for svenskhetens bevarande i Amerika*—the Society for the Preservation of Swedish Culture in America—in Rock Island. It did not, however, have time to proceed very far before World War I created an antiforeign reaction in America which temporarily suspended its operations. It is meanwhile revealing of Swedish-American sensitivity that it was designated a fully independent "sister organization" to the Swedish society, rather than as a subordinate branch.[12]

Two years later, Pastor Pehrsson came out with a brief guide for emigrants that bore little resemblance to such publications from earlier days. While Pehrsson disavowed the intention of discouraging the departure of those whose minds presumably were already made up, he urged them to preserve their language and culture and ultimately to return to the homeland. To this end he provided practical information on Swedish laws concerning citizenship, marriage, and other matters of concern, as well as the addresses of selected Swedish and Swedish-American Lutheran churches abroad.[13]

It has been seen that the powerful reaction in Sweden to the emigration, following its ominous revival from the turn of the century, assumed three distinctive forms, all of which found institutional expression: the government's Emigration Inquest, the National Society Against Emigration, and the Society for the Preservation of Swedish Culture in Foreign Lands. All three were initiated in the first half of that pivotal year, 1907. All three, moreover, reflected the dedication, energy, skills, and guiding ideas of their dominating figures: Gustav Sundbärg, Adrian Molin, and Vilhelm Lundström—true "chieftains" in the tradition of Swedish organizational life. All appealed widely to public opinion and to the Swedish national conscience.

The three organized responses had much in common. All deplored the emigration, and there was in principle no logical contradiction between seeking to end it and attempting to utilize that which had already taken place. Nonetheless, significant differences emerge. Gustav Sundbärg's political and economic liberalism, along with his insistence upon Sweden's industrial modernization, stands in clear contrast to Adrian Molin's backward-looking agrarian National Romanticism. The sober statistical approach of the Emigration Inquest (aside from Sundbärg's speculations over the Swedish national character) contrasts with the emotional propaganda of the National Society Against Emigration and of kindred souls. Sundbärg's indignation toward the Swedish Americans for alleged ingratitude toward their mother country and Molin's skepticism regarding their ultimate attachment to their cultural heritage contrast with Lundström's sanguine belief that with encouragement and support from the ancient homeland a proud and durable Swedish presence might flourish across the Atlantic, as it did across the Baltic.

Swedish imaginative literature scarcely concerned itself with America before the last decade of the nineteenth century. "The American" made his—or rather, *her*—first notable appearance as the wealthy Philistine abroad in Werner von Heidenstam's novel *Endymion* in 1889, where Nelly Harden stands as the antithesis of the traditional cultural values of the Old World but comes at last to recognize the drabness of existence in the great republic and—by implication—in the Western World of the future.[14]

Much the same kind of cultural criticism—albeit at a more modest social level and in a humorous vein—is conveyed by Gustaf Fröding's popular poem "Farväll" from 1891, in which the Swedish-American "Mister Johansson" in quaint American-Swedish dialect ruefully reproaches the girl who had refused to follow him across the sea, ending with the still oft-quoted lines:

> I get three dollars every day
> And am a gentleman by law.
> You could be your own mistress now,
> But missed your chance you did, you know.
>
> You could have gone in hat and gloves,
> Among genteel American ladies
> And lived on goose and good spare-ribs,
> But farewell to you, farewell to you![15]

Per Hallström brought the theme of the immigrant in America into prose fiction, in some of the short stories in his *Vilsna fåglar* (Birds Gone Astray) from 1894, written following a two-year stay in Philadelphia, although his immigrant characters are Germans, rather than Swedes. Typically for much that would follow, Hallström's "stray birds" are sensitive young men of genteel background baffled and defeated in the struggle for existence in a hard environment they can neither comprehend nor master. His tone is one of wistful irony.[16]

It thus remained for the now largely forgotten Hilma Angered-Strandberg to introduce the Swedish immigrant in America into Swedish litera-

ture, through her novels *Den nya världen* (The New World) and *På prärien*
(On the Prairie) in 1898, as well as her collection of short stories *Från
det nya och gamla landet* (From the New Land and the Old) in 1899. She
herself had lived in the United States from 1888 to 1894.[17]

Angered-Strandberg, held steadfastly to the clear-eyed realism of the
1880s as well as to its individualistic liberalism. She shows little of the
high-flown pathos and rhetoric of the Neo-Romanticism of the 1890s, as
exemplified by Heidenstam and his friends. Her novels portray essentially
individual destinies, in which innate traits of character, rather than outside
circumstances, are the determinant factors.

Although well aware of its failings, Angered-Strandberg found America,
in all its variety, an exilarating milieu. *Den nya världen* introduces what
would thereafter remain a prominent theme in Swedish fictional accounts:
the American big city, with its noise, dirt, and confusion, but also its
restless dynamism, as exemplified by New York and Chicago. In *På prärien,*
meanwhile, she deftly satirizes the stultifying atmosphere of a small, nar-
rowly pietistic, conservative Swedish-American Lutheran college, as well
as life among its "professors," and especially their wives, all persons strong
in faith and self-righteousness but woefully lacking in personal culture.
Yet in dealing with these and other Swedish-American types her tone is
generally good-natured and indulgent. Her cutting edge is directed mainly
toward the ignorance and prejudices of the homeland toward America
and its Swedish inhabitants. A recurring theme in these writings is the
confrontation of Swede and Swedish American, in which the latter consistently comes out ahead. In both novels, Swedish Americans return from
visits to the homeland with depressing accounts of the closed-minded
hostility and immobility they have found there. Similarly, Angered-Strandberg's main criticism of the little Swedish-American college community in
På prärien is that it too is largely closed to and prejudiced against the
America it is a part of.[18]

Where the American big city provided an exotic backdrop for episodes
in Hilma Angered-Strandberg's writings, it became a force in its own right
in Henning Berger's better-known short stories from Chicago, brought out
after he had lived there for some years during the 1890s. Berger presents,
in highly stylized Neo-Romantic imagery, the megalopolis as America in
all its most sinister aspects and in glaring contrast to the Old World, the
metaphor for all that is most alien yet also fascinating, to the refined
European sensibility in America.

Berger's underlying theme is that America either defeats the sensitive
stranger coming to its shores or, if he adapts to it well enough to succeed,
alienates him from himself—an idea well-established in the anti-emigration
propaganda of the time.[19] The theme of alienation is all-pervasive. From this
there follows Berger's skepticism over the existence of any real "Swedish
America." In his novel, *Bendel & Co.,* published in 1910, a disillusioned

Swedish immigrant in Chicago says: "You never become an American, and you don't belong to your countrymen here either. For that matter, what is a 'Swedish-American'? To my ears it sounds hermaphroditic."[20]

A far more sensational exposé of America is provided by Henry von Kræmer's long-forgotten novel, *Ur frihetslandets järnkäftar* (From the Iron Jaws of the Land of Freedom), whose title well reflects its message. It traces the bitter experiences of its protagonist, "Erik," a young man of cultivated background, as he toils his way through America at drudgerous, menial jobs, from a radical socialist perspective. Since it is simply a lightly fictionalized account of von Kræmer's own American sojourn around 1913 and since it came out concurrently with the author's published travel letters in 1914, which closely parallel the novel, both will be considered together in connection with the Swedish travel accounts of America from this period.[21]

The reinvigorated anti-emigration movement after the turn of the century sought to heighten awareness not only of Sweden's glorious past and its bountiful natural resources that gave promise of a new age of greatness, but also of the tragedies the emigration left in its wake, a theme deeply appealing to the National-Romantic mood. It found its place in 1906–7 in *Nils Holgerssons underbara resa genom Sverige* (Nils Holgersson's Wonderful Journey Through Sweden) by Selma Lagerlöf, Sweden's most widely read novelist in her time, who received the Nobel Prize for Literature in 1909. This book was commissioned by the Swedish Primary School Board as an attractive means of teaching children their nation's geography. Its unstated but more significant purpose was to instill love of fatherland and optimism in its future. Over the years it has unquestionably reached a greater readership in Sweden than any of Selma Lagerlöf's other, immensely popular works.

In this story, little Nils, who travels the length and breadth of Sweden on the back of a wild goose from Lapland, lands at a run-down, abandoned farm in northern Småland and learns the heart-breaking tale of its recently deceased mistress, an old peasant woman who had once worked joyously for her children's future but who pined away after they all left for America.

In the old woman's house Nils found many of "the kind of things that people with relatives in America have," including the portraits of those who had left. "There were big, strong men and women with serious expressions. There were brides in long veils and gentlemen in fine clothes, and there were children who had curly hair and pretty white dresses. And he thought that they all stared blindly out into the air and wanted to see nothing." This led to more serious reflections and the moral of the tale: "Imagine that parents can long so much for their children! He had never realized this. To think that it can be as if life were over for them when their children are gone!"[22]

In verse, concern with America was most notably reflected in the first years of this century by Karl Gustaf Ossian-Nilsson, whose Swedish patriotic pathos coexisted with a Nietzschian fascination with will and power. Thus in the first part of his collected verse, published in 1907, his "Sverge" lamented:

> Thousands, thousands, upon thousands . . .!
> Who shall light the cottage lights?
> Empty cottages stand in the night—
> All your life blood drains away, Sweden,
> Life drips from your open wound.

The same volume meanwhile brims with righteous indignation over the sluggishness and senile complacency of contemporary Swedish society. In his "John Ericsson," Ossian-Nilsson praises the inventor who made a "world of his own" in "a land where genius is no crime." The twelfth part of the same collection, which likewise came out in 1907, is entitled *Amerikaner* (Americans) and comprises a paean to the youth, vigor, and determination of the New World in contrast to the Old.[23]

Below the level of serious literature in Sweden there flourished an increasingly dense undergrowth of popular novelists—including such generally forgotten names as Sigge Strömberg, Axel Kerfve, Nils Hydén, Karl Williams, and Gustaf Janson—producing for the pulp trade a variety of adventure stories with settings in big American cities or the Wild West, with plucky and resourceful young Swedish protagonists.[24]

If Per Hallström was not the first Swedish author to write about Swedish immigrants in America, he is significant as perhaps the first to present a Swedish-American character on the stage. Not surprisingly, "Mr. Ottenbury" (formerly Österberg) in his drawing-room comedy *Erotikon* from 1908 turns out to be a petty confidence man. Thereafter, in Swedish melodramas and burlesque comedies, visiting Swedish Americans generally appear as either perpetrators or in some cases victims of various kinds of skullduggery. The same may generally be said of a new medium, the cinema, through the 1950s, although certain of the earliest films, beginning in 1910, reflect contemporary anti-emigration propaganda in dramatizing the hardships and disappointments facing the emigrant in an alien land.[25]

Not surprisingly, the first American writers to gain a wide popular following in Sweden at this very time were Upton Sinclair, with his sensational exposés of the darker sides of American urban life, and in particular Jack London, with his tales of adventure in the great wilderness.[26]

The America of Swedish public discussion was always as much edifying myth as it was concrete reality. And nowhere were its mythic qualities more manifest than in Sweden's vital and creative literary life around the turn of the century.

FOURTEEN

Visitors to Alien Shores

$\mathscr{I}$n retrospect, Carl Sundbeck's *Svensk-amerikanerna* from 1904 seems the last of the classic Swedish travel accounts from America concentrating largely or primarily upon its Swedish population. There were, however, a number of significant works by Swedish visitors to the United States between 1904 and America's entry into World War I in 1917. Compared with Sundbeck's, these accounts are shorter, less detailed, and in some cases devoted mainly to general American conditions. With few exceptions, they show a notable similarity in the attitudes and values they express, revealing, it would seem, the emergence of a new broad-based consensus in Sweden regarding America, the emigration, and the emigrants, during this period of national revival.

The visitors are well aware of America's problems and shortcomings. Yet their prevalent tone is one of respect for the United States, appreciation for its dynamism, and a desire to learn rather than condemn. They seek to understand the Swedish Americans in their own terms and to dispel old prejudices that obstruct cordial relations between them and their former homeland. Their appreciation for the positive sides of American life and for the Swedes in the New World is motivated by the desire to spur the pace of the reforms needed at home to bring mass emigration to an end.

The high degree of consensus meanwhile reflects the shift in the political basis of pro-Americanism in Sweden, as in Europe generally, around the turn of the century from the radical to the conservative camp, exemplified in the accounts of August Palm and P. P. Waldenström in 1901 and 1902.[1] Hence there was the apparent paradox of Swedish neoconservatives, who stood in the forefront of the anti-emigration movement, roundly praising America despite its faults. With few exceptions, all the more notable writers of Swedish travel accounts from America between 1904 and 1917 were either neoconservatives or traditional liberals, the latter perpetuating a heritage of pro-Americanism stretching far back into the past century. Several were prominent in organized efforts against emigration. Significantly, those who showed a clearly critical attitude toward America were the socialists Henry von Kræmer and Ture Nerman.

Because of the general similarity between the travelers—persons who, with the exceptions noted, stood between the political extremes of reaction and radicalism—and their viewpoints, values, and aspirations, it seems justified here to consider the views they express topically and comparatively, after first introducing the visitors themselves.

During 1910 and 1911, four significant travel accounts came out, all by persons associated with the three major organized responses to the emigration. The journalist P. G. Norberg visited the United States in 1904 and at greater length in 1908. The result was his *En brygga öfver hafvet* (A Bridge over the Ocean) in 1910, written under the pseudonym "P. Norden." Norberg presents a vivid and enthusiastic tribute to America and its Swedish inhabitants that at the same time delivers a stinging attack against alleged complacency and inertia in Sweden. Norberg is reminiscent of the liberal America enthusiasts of the 1870s and 1880s. His contribution to *Supplement* XX of the Emigration Inquest in 1911 on the Swedish Americans, which drew freely upon his book, has already been noted.[2]

G. H. von Koch, that central figure in the development of Swedish social policy, had long been concerned with the emigration problem, which he had called a "question of life and death for the Swedish people" in 1903. In a speech that year he too appealed that "America should be brought over to Sweden." An extensive visit to America led to the publication of his *Emigranternas land* (The Land of the Emigrants) in 1910, as well as his lengthy section in *Supplement* XX of the Emigration Inquest. His book is a valuable outsider's appraisal of America and its travails at a difficult stage of its development. Yet he remained on the whole optimistic about America's capacity to face and overcome its problems. Von Koch concludes his volume with a seventy-five-page section on the Swedes in America.[3]

Adrian Molin, the dominating figure in the National Society Against Emigration, visited the United States and Canada in 1910, giving rise to several essays under the heading "The Swedes in America" in his *Vanhäfd*, published in 1911. While there was obviously much in American life that was repugnant to his agrarian vision of Sweden's future, he concentrated his attention upon those aspects that in his view could be useful and constructive for the homeland.[4]

The Gothenburg pastor and member of the Riksdag, Per Pehrsson, was on the board of the Society for the Preservation of Swedish Culture in Foreign Lands, on behalf of which he traveled to the United States in 1910, to present formal congratulations to Augustana College and Seminary on their fiftieth anniversary. Following his return, he brought out a forty-page article in the society's yearbook for 1910, also published as a separate booklet. His visit was too short to allow him to offer more than a few glimpses from his travels, but he did give his impressions of the Swedish Americans and urge greater efforts to maintain close ties with them.[5]

In addition to those visitors associated with the organized responses to the emigration in Sweden, there were several others worth noting. Ida Gawell-Blumenthal, the beloved Delsbostintan—"The Girl from Delsbo"— known throughout Sweden for her singing of folk songs and telling of folk tales in the dialect and costume of her Hälsingland parish, toured Swedish America in 1908, as described in her *Stintans Amerikafärd* ("Stinta's" Trip to America) that year. Although unpretentious and anecdotal, it is interesting for its view of Swedish America from the stage, as perceived by a number of folk artists who visited the United States during these years for the express purpose of arousing fond nostalgia for homeland and native place.[6]

Olof Olofsson, a Mission Friend minister from Värmland visited the American East Coast and Middle West, in particular Mission Covenant congregations, and described his experiences in a slender volume in 1912. The author is modest and unassuming, while the views he expresses are generally stereotypical for the time, and would thus seem closer to the grassroots level in provincial Sweden than those of the better-known opinionmakers who dominate the travel literature about America.[7]

C. P. Carlsson, a Methodist minister likewise from Värmland, spent a year in the United States in 1910–11, resulting in his *I palmernas skugga* (In the Shade of the Palms) in 1913. His overriding concern was the decline of true Christian piety and as a particularly alarming symptom, the rise of godless socialism and labor unionism at home. He thus warmly admired America as, in his view, a still basically religious society which made short shrift of radical troublemakers, although he was apprehensive of the rising tide of Catholicism there.[8]

John Wahlborg was a free-church (evidently Baptist) clergyman from Västmanland who visited the United States, including the San Francisco Exposition, in 1915. His account is one of the most humanly appealing of the Swedish travel accounts from America, in all its simplicity. Wahlborg, alias the lightly fictionalized "Pastor Vikman," encounters on his modest Odyssey the salient features of the emigration and of Swedish-American life with gentle humor and warm sympathy.[9]

The notable exception to the generally positive attitudes toward America were the radical socialists Henry von Kræmer and Ture Nerman. Von Kræmer's aristocratic name and lineage concealed the fact that he was the stepson of the Social Democratic leader Hjalmar Branting. Evidently around 1913, he was in Mexico and the United States, following which he brought out in 1914 both his travel letters, under the title *Mexiko-Amerika,* and his aforementioned novel, *Ur frihetslandets järnkäftar,* which largely parallels his letters from the United States. Among the Swedish observers of this period, von Kræmer was unique in having worked at menial jobs, mainly in East Coast factories, and he admitted that his observations of Swedish Americans were based upon recently arrived urban industrial workers in that region. With his educated background, he suffered a double alienation as an outsider both in their midst and in the new land. His fictionalized version in particular is a horror story about living and working conditions for a predominantly immigrant working class. In 1909 von Kræmer had written an anti-emigration pamphlet for the National Society Against Emigration, and in 1914 he again declared a desire to contribute to curing that evil.[10]

Ture Nerman, a doctrinaire radical socialist of genteel background, brought out his impressions from a visit to the United States in 1915 in a book published twenty years later. While much of it is anecdotal, there are chapters illustrating the seamier sides of American life. The final section examines aspects of America from a socialist perspective. He nevertheless does not condemn America out of hand and at times shows greater appreciation and understanding of what he actually saw and experienced than his political ideology would suggest.[11]

Gunnar Cederschiöld, scion of an old aristocratic family, spent half a year in New York, the basis for his account from 1916, written in a light and entertaining style and illustrated with the author's stylized pen drawings. While most of the book deals with life in New York society, the final chapters, more serious in tone, concern the Swedish Americans.[12]

Published Swedish travel accounts from America during this period are too numerous to consider them all. A number of them are simply intended for the armchair tourist and therefore need not detain us. But at least a couple of others deserve passing mention for the occasional glimpses they offer of the Swedish Americans. In 1904 the Lund University male chorus was featured at the St. Louis World's Fair and toured parts of the East and Midwest, the first Swedish choral group to visit the United States. (It may be recalled that a picked Swedish-American male chorus had toured Sweden in 1897.) The Lund singers' experiences were recorded in 1904 by Knut Barr and in 1908 by Professor Rudolf Kjellén, one of the stalwarts of the "Young Right" in Sweden, whose scattered observations reveal much skepticism toward American, including Swedish-American, society. In 1915 and 1916, Ingeborg Lundström, an experienced journalist, concealed her identity to work as a housemaid in wealthy New York homes, an experience she described in 1917 under the pseudonym "Inge Lund," offering some glimpses into the lives of her fellow Swedish female domestics.[13]

The Swedish visitors show above all a common concern with four basic questions affecting their countrymen in the United States: their reasons for leaving the old homeland and their lot in the new; the impact of the

American environment upon the Swedish character; the state of Swedish culture among the immigrants and their descendants; and the maintenance of good relations between Sweden and America, especially its Swedish element.

None of the travelers' accounts express any resentment or indignation over the Swedish Americans' motives for emigrating, while several sought to justify them. Sweden hardly needed the Emigration Inquiry to determine that the main factors were economic, P. G. Norberg declared. Swedish Americans thus thrived in America since it allowed them a decent material existence. Only thereafter, he wrote, did they come to understand all the other things they did not like about Sweden, above all the arrogance of both the employers and the labor movement.[14]

Their encounter with their emigrated countrymen across the Atlantic aroused among the visitors mingled feelings of sadness and pride. On the whole, the Swedish Americans were found to have done well for themselves, especially farmers and those in skilled trades. Even the socialist, Ture Nerman, recognized the favorable conditions for qualified workers, which in his view made it regrettably difficult for socialism to gain a footing in the United States.

There were, however, problems. Molin held that the conditions of wage labor had become harder over the past fifteen to twenty years, since prices had risen faster than wages, which he attributed principally to the heavy immigration from southern and eastern Europe. Unskilled laborers had a hard time staying afloat. Nerman held that the worker received a smaller share of the gross national product in America than in many other countries.[15]

Nothing impressed the Swedish visitors more than the good quality of the housing occupied by Swedish-American urban workingmen and their families and the high degree of individual homeownership among them. "The 'own-home' question," Norberg found, "was solved out here before anyone conceived the 'own-home' idea in Sweden." "From the *social* viewpoint, the matter is quite simple. The basic condition for a decent person is a decent home, and one of the most important conditions for a decent home is a decent dwelling," wrote Adrian Molin, who considered housing to be the strongest motivation behind Swedish urban emigration.[16]

The success of Swedish-American farmers, especially in more fertile and earlier-settled parts of the Midwest, was impressive. "I have never seen so vast and uninterrupted a panorama of Swedish prosperity," Norberg wrote of the countryside around St. Peter, Minnesota. Molin appreciated in particular the American farmer's direct involvement in all aspects of managing and working his farm, in contrast to the Swedish estate-owner of the old school, who considered it beneath his dignity to concern himself with either and devoted himself to the "Swedish gentleman's often expensive habits." But, the eager exponent of the Swedish smallholders' movement hoped, the latter were on their way to well-deserved extinction.[17]

The visitors were meanwhile well aware of the high price of success in America. Rural immigrants had indeed found what they had sought, farms of their own and economic independence, which in many cases seemed almost incredible, considering their start in life, von Koch wrote. But he knew, too, of the "unheard-of hardships" this had cost them. America, according to von Kræmer, gave the worker the means to live more intensively because it wore him out more rapidly.[18]

There were also those who did not succeed, and the presence of Swedish-American derelicts was noted, especially in larger American cities. G. H. von Koch, however, was convinced that such cases were relatively few and was glad to report that the Swedish Americans' own charitable institutions seemed adequate to deal with them, since in America it was wisest "not to place too great hopes in the intervention of the state or community to relieve distress or support the unemployed."[19]

Despite the often hard struggle Swedish Americans had faced, they showed deep pride in the social standing they had attained. G. H. von Koch attributed particular importance to the nonmaterial values that gave the workingman a stronger sense of his dignity and worth in America than in Sweden. Even Henry von Kræmer recognized that

> The American knew nothing of the social pressures that embittered the Swede's life at home. He behaved like a free man, he nodded to folk without distinction and *would* not recognize any social classes—other than the economic. He lived next door to his foreman, or perhaps even his factory boss, but on Sundays he stood in his shirtsleeves with his hands in his pants pockets, smoked a cigar and chatted with his neighbor. Could a Swedish worker ever do that? Would it ever be tolerated at home for a woman factory worker to dress like an upper-class lady? ... Was this the secret why the Swede repudiated his old fatherland and the Swedish maid did not speak Swedish on the streetcar?[20]

There was meanwhile general agreement that, as Pastor Pehrsson put it, "America is no longer an El Dorado, where one can, as before, gain land and farm without any capital except a good back and hard fists." Still, despite his reservations regarding America's future, Adrian Molin admired the Americans' bold optimism, compared with his own countrymen's habitual caution. "Here [in Sweden] the demand for investigations and fear of mistakes are the bulwark of the indifferent and incorrigible," whereas if the Americans made a mistake "they have time to repair it, in the light of experience gained, before we have had time to begin an investigation. It is in that spirit that they work out there."[21]

The travelers were meanwhile essentially agreed that Sweden must not expect America's problems to solve its own. Norberg expressed this idea most clearly. Without expecting miracles, he stated, Sweden must bend every effort toward its own development.

It will not be by slandering America, but rather by *convincing the people* that things will constantly get better here at home that we should be able to keep them here. Not better than in America, but *better than they have been before at home*. As soon as we have reached a reasonable level, equal to that of other nations, there can at last be an end to these eternal comparisons with how things are elsewhere. And in this way the emigration will cease by itself.

In an article published shortly after his return from America, von Koch stated what Sweden needed in terms with which surely all his fellow visitors to America could concur in their own ways: "What is required is to allow the entire people to share in the nation's gains, to spread a sense of common interest, at the same time to demolish obsolete and dangerous class barriers, thus creating, in far greater measure than at present, a chance in life for every citizen."[22] In case any complacency still remained that America's problems would end the emigration, some of the visitors recalled to their readers that Canada now offered much the same enticements that the United States had in the past. And Canada, Norberg declared, "will suffice for the next hundred years."[23]

The visitors showed a particular interest in the effects of life in America upon the Swedish psyche, which they found on the whole to be positive. Norberg—from 1910 the husband of an American wife—took issue with the racial purists of the day when he called the Swedish American a crossbreed born of two very different "parents," and "as is usual with the mixing of two races the parents' *better* qualities come to distinguish the offspring."[24]

"What further cannot be denied," Molin states, "is that America in higher degree than Sweden makes way for personality, or rather gives elbow-room to personality. . . . And it cannot be denied that in general, work and competence are to a much greater extent the criteria for success in America than here at home. . . . No wonder it attracts so many of our best young people."[25]

Norberg enthusiastically described what Americanization in the best sense meant.

> It is adaptation to a faster tempo on the whole, the acceptance of a spirit of greater intensity in work and of the greater joy in work that follows from this. It is a new faith, a new hopefulness at the prospect that neither the laws of [social] caste nor of nature place any insurmountable obstacles in the path of one's success in life, that it is no longer a question of "thus far and no farther," but rather of "go ahead." It gives direction to all those vital energies which before were consumed by brooding and frustration, toward something new to accomplish instead of something old that must be patched up. It is an understanding of and respect for all the human rights of others, to the same degree that one is aware of what one is oneself entitled to in that regard.[26]

This "metamorphosis" was not brought about by magic. It was, as Norberg later put it, "in a word, the emergence of all one's natural good potential through the outward compulsion of new circumstances." "What immense possibilities for development our people possess," Pehrsson declared, "when they have really good soil to grow in—and when they have the whip at their backs!"[27]

The basic differences between Swede and Swedish American were personified in striking fashion in Norberg's comparison between the American farmer and the Swedish peasant.

> Farmer does not really mean the same thing as peasant. A peasant in Sweden one conceives as excellent timber that has never been hewn into shape. A nature, as craggy and inaccessible as the soil from which he forces a living. A thick-skinned type, insensitive to heat or cold, unsusceptible to reason or argument, defiant, dour, undependable, and stubborn. From father to son, father to son, life drags on at the same drudgerous pace, and if it does not rain on the field when it ought to, it is the Lord's fault. ... A farmer is something different. He is a man who works as hard as the Swedish peasant, but methodically and quickly besides. Ever watchful, always interested in new machinery and new methods, and always on his guard against sudden attack from the Master of Wind and Weather. He lives under far less predictable climatic conditions but manages far better, since he relies on himself and not upon chance. He has a wider horizon, richer experience, a better home, and a more sensible diet. He performs his devotions driving his self-binding reaper, if circumstances require, while his Swedish counterpart drowses in a church pew. He is the friend and confidant of the soil, not its slave, bound to it by gratitude, not by chains, and thereby escapes from being rustic and bestial. His home is comfortable and attractive, he has demands on life, newspapers, and a telephone.[28]

P. G. Norberg in particular emphasized not only the acquisition by Swedish immigrants of the more positive American traits but also their steadfast preservation of what was best in their native Swedish character, to a degree that often put the inhabitants of the old homeland to shame. This was an idea by now well established by the Swedish Americans themselves, with J. A. Enander as their standard-bearer, as well as, more recently, by P. P. Waldenström (after his second American journey) and most conspicuously by Carl Sundbeck. "Is it not remarkable," Norberg exclaimed, "that one should have to travel to the New World to find the old Sweden?" "As we have gradually become more closely acquainted with our Swedish-American friend we have had cause for surprise over how different the Swede *in* him is from the Swede at home. We find him sober and hardworking, contented with his lot, full of touching patriotism, and in his old-fashioned naiveté unaffected by the evils of our day."[29]

Henry von Kræmer took exception to this hopeful view. Much of his fictionalized account dwells upon what he saw as the transformation of emigrants into immigrants in Capitalism's Promised Land. Already aboard the Atlantic liner his "Erik" compares the Swedes fresh from the homeland—healthy, natural, hopeful human beings—with the returning Swedish Americans, who had a cold, sharp, arrogant, almost malicious manner about them. The Swedish Americans had, he wrote in *Mexiko-Amerika*— with Eastern industrial workers in mind—become "sluggish, petty bourgeois, and trivial."[30]

For Swedish visitors of conservative views, meanwhile, the old Swedish spirit, as nurtured in the New World, was incompatible with socialism and labor unions. "I have been frequently asked," Pastor Carlsson declared, "what kind of a generation we are nurturing and raising back home in Sweden, since those who are now coming here are so angry and bitter against both God and mankind? The older Swedish Americans are ashamed to be related to such so-called countrymen." If the "Young Socialists" should try their agitation in America, Pastor Pehrsson maintained, "they would learn the hard way that in the golden land of freedom one must be careful not to abuse freedom. 'Uncle Sam' has hard fists and skin on his nose!"[31]

While the Swedish Americans had generally done well for themselves, it was hard for patriotic Swedish visitors concerned with the emigration problem to believe that their former countrymen could ever really feel at home in America. "We can more quickly than other peoples adapt ourselves to the customs and viewpoints of a foreign land, but we can never seriously put down roots there," Cederschiöld declared. "That is surely the reason why the great majority of Swedish Americans I have met strike me as being basically unhappy persons."[32]

G. H. von Koch had much the same view. The Swedish immigrant who arrives in his mature years, he wrote,

> seldom really takes root in the new soil, which causes friction and disharmony, especially in his relations with his children. The Swedish American born in Sweden remains, in other words, neither entirely Swedish nor American, and a more or less constant conflict between the two nationalities takes place within him. . . . Again and again I was struck by the rootlessness of this existence. . . . America will not satisfy unless one allows oneself to become Americanized, and as far as the homeland is concerned, his longing is condemned to a consuming, even if unconscious hunger.[33]

The Swedish Americans were found to be warmly attached to their old homeland. "I consider it the greatest satisfaction of my journey," Pastor Pehrsson wrote, "that I was able to see and experience that deep love for the fatherland that shone from eyes filled with tears." Ida Gawell-Blumenthal—"Delsbostintan"—whose performances brought her into contact with Swedish Americans at their most sentimental, sought eagerly for signs of nostalgia. In Sweden, Norberg asserted, there was much rhetoric about great historic memories of the Vikings or of Karl XII, which often had a hollow ring. "It is altogether different when the Swedish American stands up and bears witness to his Swedish heritage, his faithful love for Mother Svea. As soon as we have accustomed our ear to listening to him, we comprehend what an almost religious inwardness underlies his words. For us these words have become stereotyped and cheapened. When the Swedish American makes use of them, he gives them the best he has."[34]

A related but nonetheless separate question was the extent to which Swedish Americans might actually be prepared to return to Sweden. Several of the visitors, especially Molin and Cederschiöld, placed a high priority upon public efforts in Sweden to encourage such a development. "Nothing," Molin declared, "can more powerfully counteract the exaggerated disbelief here at home in our own country's potentialities than a remigration." Norberg hoped for the establishment of compact Swedish-American colonies at home. Others, however, expressed a greater awareness of the psychological problems involved. Even if adult immigrants could never feel entirely at home in America, Pehrsson realized that "they could not thrive in Sweden either. Both we and they understand this." Von Koch in particular was aware that the Sweden most of the emigrants had left was ever more distant from Sweden as it had now become.[35]

Regarding culture among the Swedish Americans, opinion among the visitors was more divided than in most other respects. The sympathetic von Koch noted how plainly and frugally even well-to-do Swedish-American farm families lived and how work so dominated their lives that there was little chance for "intellectual development." "Whoever expects a class of Swedish farmers in America worthy of the Swedish yeoman farmer's political traditions or which in awareness and interest can compete with the Danish smallholder class, will thus be greatly disappointed." He noted, too, that those farmers' sons who acquired an education tended to leave the land. Molin had strong reservations about Swedish-American culture.

Rudolf Kjellén—the father of "Geopolitics"—upon visiting Augustana College with the Lund University male chorus in 1904, declared in a speech there that the organic bond between land and folk had been broken by emigration. "From Swedish soil we have come, like you, but to Swedish soil we shall return. We have our hopes in the same place as our memories, our future where our past has been." Swedish-America was built not upon bedrock but upon a "stream" flowing between its Swedish source and the sea of American life, even though during this respite it might make valuable, lasting contributions to the new society. From the opposite side of the ideological spectrum, von Kræmer declared that "the life of the Swedes in America is more superficial, mediocre, and trivial than back home, for America is still a pioneer land, a feverish, rampaging gold-digger's land, where the ideal is called dollars." Swedish Americans, in his view, could be considered neither Swedes nor Americans.[36]

Pastor Pehrsson, meanwhile, was highly impressed with what the Swedish immigrants had managed to create for themselves in the cultural sphere, within so short a time and entirely from their own modest resources. He looked forward to the day when Swedish America would take its rightful place as a new "Finland," that is, as a worthy satellite of the Swedish mother-culture.[37]

Norberg warmly defended Swedish-American culture against its detractors. It was ridiculous, he held, to find fault with emigrants from the most deprived backgrounds for lacking the cultural refinement of the educated and cultivated classes in Sweden. It had not been easy for them to preserve their heritage, having arrived in the new land with "only such mementos as they could bring with them from home in the bottom of a trunk. ... Therefore every crumb is precious. For that reason we have every reason to lower our voices and bare our heads before their altars, rather than ridiculing their poor and antiquated rituals." Swedish Americans were Americans, and had to be, in their daily working lives: "They have been active as Swedes *after* their day's work, and if we recall this, it is remarkable what they have accomplished."

Swedish-American culture, Norberg maintained, enshrined Swedish cultural values of an earlier day, which impressed the latter-day Swedish visitor with a "highly old-fashioned atmosphere." "Upon these precious traditions," he wrote, "the entire Swedish-American culture of today is built. The more restlessly the new homeland has moved forward, the more eagerly they themselves as *Americans* have been to take part in this imposing advance, so much the more have they held sacred and venerated the heritage of their fathers in their hearts."[38]

Von Koch was repeatedly impressed with how the passing of time and generations caused the Swede in America to lose contact with the living reality of the homeland. "Just as his language is not the Swedish of 1910 so too the emigrated Swede is not the Swede of today, not the citizen who is in constant contact with the cultural development of an entire people, but rather the Swede of a time gone by, living on fading, fragmentary memories, and lacking the background to understand the new Swedish spirit."

For the younger generation, born or raised in America, the Old Country had only sentimental interest as the land of their parents' birth. This impressed von Koch especially at a "Swedish" young people's evening in Lindsborg, Kansas, the home of Bethany College. "What I found ... was not Swedish youth. The language was there, although spoken with a certain effort, but that was perhaps the only thing that betrayed Swedish origins. The well-dressed young ladies—always in the majority in American social or cultural circles—and the young men descended to be sure from Sweden in the second generation, but in their views and dreams they were American."[39]

Molin wrote, "The more significant and characteristic expressions of Swedish-American cultural life—to the extent one may speak of such, which is possible only in a very modest sense—are connected with the activities of the *societies*, the Swedish-language *press*, and above all the *religious denominations*."[40] There was general agreement regarding the cultural significance of these institutions, including the preeminent role of the churches. Pastors Pehrsson, Olofsson, Carlsson, and Wahlborg were gratified to find the Swedish Americans on the whole a religious people, even though Olofsson had some fears of American spiritual superficiality. The Lutheran Pehrsson naturally upheld the unique position of the Augustana Synod and its educational institutions.[41]

The secular observers meanwhile suggested certain qualifications. Swedish-American religiosity had its own, largely American character. An American would surely be offended by the average Sunday sermon in a state church in Sweden, von Koch maintained. "All he has learned to value: self-reliance, joy in work, belief in human potentialities, is clubbed down mercilessly under the gloomy gospel of contrition. He learns also to understand that the country-dweller who for his spiritual sustenance is given this doctrine, destructive of individuality, must feel as though released from a prison when he breaths the air of America, where personality is respected." Norberg stressed in particular the social activities of the churches, which in America had basement floors "*intended for the living and not for the dead.*" "It is upon this basement that the Lutheran church in America rests; it has its practical activity to thank for its being so immeasurably more vital than the Swedish mother church." Molin saw much truth in the claim that the Augustana Synod was the "bulwark" of the Swedish heritage "out there," but found it salutary to recall that it was "in the first instance a religious institution, in the second place an American, and only in the third place a Swedish one." It would remain Swedish, in his view, only as long as the immigration continued.[42]

The secular societies, too, received credit for maintaining a Swedish presence in America, although they generally received less comment. Norberg was in any event of the opinion that "more important than all that is printed in Swedish out there is what is said and sung in church and organizational activities, what is eaten and drunk together."[43]

The Swedish-American newspapers came under sharp attack from Molin for being "business enterprises, and little else." Any traces of a more idealistic nature he dismissed as "mainly window-dressing." Advertising, he claimed, took precedence over editorial content. What particularly incensed him was their scanty coverage of news from Sweden, except for trivial items from the provinces, and in certain cases their manifest hostility toward the Old Country. Molin noted that their bitterest attacks were aimed at the anti-emigration movement in Sweden, which to him was the key to their truculence since their very existence depended upon a constant flow of new emigrants from the homeland. Pehrsson, meanwhile, was greatly impressed by both the numbers and reported circulation of the Swedish-American periodicals and alone among the visitors took note of both a budding literature and a growing interest in their own history among the Swedish Americans.[44]

"At the heart of the preservation of the Swedish heritage," wrote Pastor Pehrsson, "lies the preservation of the Swedish language." On this point all the visitors were in essential agreement, and they gave much attention to it. There was naturally commentary on what, to Swedish ears, seemed the ludicrous mixing of tongues. Swedish survived in purer form in the countryside than in the cities, according to von Koch, "but it usually consists of a combination of broad dialect and convoluted book language. And it cannot be denied that this mixture seems curiously old-fashioned, if not lifeless. One misses the nuances which life, day by day and year by year, add to a language and which make it the most precise gauge of national and individual culture." Pehrsson noted how those who had learned proper Swedish in the new land tended to speak it in a stiff, overly grammatical fashion, "as though from a book," showing how much they had acquired through the eye, rather than the ear. Nerman claimed that the use of Swedish declined as one preceded westward across the continent.[45]

The preservation of the language was intimately tied to the generational problem. Visiting in New Jersey a workingman he had once known in Sweden, Wahlborg's "Pastor Viklef" observed that his friend's self-willed children insisted on speaking English. "The thing is," the man explained, "we are Swedes and can never become anything else, and our children are Americans in their whole way of thinking and can hereafter hardly be anything else."

The differences between Swede and Swedish-American could best be seen within the immigrant family itself, von Koch wrote, and the frequent refusal of the children to use the old language, even at home, showed poignantly how "not only a generation but an ocean lie between the emigrants and their children." Still, "Not infrequently the English-speaking children grow up to become Swedish-speaking men and women." Both Olofsson and Pehrsson noted wide variations in the use of Swedish among the younger generations, for whom, the latter believed, Swedish expressed the "innermost life," whereas English served everyday needs.[46]

What prospects might there be in the long run for the survival of Swedish language and culture in America? Molin had a decidedly skeptical view. The average Swedish American had left Sweden with little education or knowledge of the homeland. "In all significant respects he is American," Molin declared, "and his children become Americans lock, stock, and barrel."[47]

Von Koch had a more finely shaded grasp of the situation. Reflecting on Lindsborg, Kansas, a traditional Swedish stronghold in America, he realized that it too must sooner or later be assimilated into the American mainstream, just as Sweden's seventeenth-century colony on the Delaware had been.

> To raise [the children] as "Swedes" [he continued,] is quite meaningless. To teach them Swedish is appropriate and should not be neglected, but to start them out in life with principally Swedish interests or, rather, without a sufficient fund of American interests, is to restrict their sphere of activity to the relatively limited radius which the Swedes represent. It is, at the same time, to reduce their possibilities, together with the future prestige of the Swedish name, in this arena of competition among all nationalities.

While some in Sweden might protest that this was an "unpatriotic" attitude, von Koch insisted that Swedish interests would best be served if the Swedish Americans were given the greatest possibilities to make good. And, he added, "Perhaps one may even venture to make the paradoxical assertion that only after an Americanization in the best sense can the uncultivated Swedish emigrant be expected to identify with his little, historic motherland, with interest and pride."[48]

Pastor Pehrsson expressed the greatest optimism among the visitors for an ongoing Swedish presence in America. In their competition with other nationalities Swedish Americans had learned the practical value of organization and solidarity. The Swedish Americans were now "singularly moved by that wave of national sentiment that is sweeping the world and from which a powerful wake has washed up upon our shores." Self-assertion combined, in his view, with abiding love for fatherland.[49]

On the subject of relations between the homeland and its emigrants, several of the visitors were outspoken in their criticism of European—and most specifically Swedish—ignorance of and prejudices against America and the Swedish Americans. Norberg described with biting irony the common stereotype of the Swedish American in the homeland, where he was both suspected of having left because of some kind of skullduggery at home and pitied for having to work like a dog or a Negro in the heartless New World. If he came home with dollars in his pocket all were happy to eat and drink at his expense, but sneered at him behind his back. Norberg pictured the smug self-righteousness of a boardinghouse mistress, in, say, Västerås, who worked her "Amanda" from sunup until late at night, upon reading pitiful tales of poor Swedish working girls who had come to grief in America. At the same time, Norberg wrote,

> We have the most ridiculous and exaggerated ideas about our prestige, our unique prestige, abroad. The day after we have read about some poor devil

who—naturally!—went under overseas, instead of staying home and being well-off, we encounter the well-known headline, "Again a Swede Who Has Succeeded Abroad." ... On the one hand, somber descriptions, veiled in mourning, of the consequences of letting down Mother Svea, on the other, fanfares of toy trumpets over the successes of individuals, which are immediately accepted as universal and beyond criticism.[50]

Meanwhile, Norberg asserted, those to whom anti-emigration propaganda was directed in Sweden paid little head to it. They quietly made their own decisions and departed. "*They* know better," he wrote, "Indeed, they are the only ones who have had reasonable expectations of America. They have never contradicted us, they simply have not believed us. ... The one group talked, the other acted. That was the whole difference."[51]

> If literature ever had use for a Swedish-American type, [Norberg went on,] it settled by preference for one who had failed, who had been broken by an inhuman burden. Or possibly someone who had succeeded but had succumbed to delusions of grandeur in the process. The whole picture was cheap, stereotyped. Humbug, revolvers, oppression, greed, and hardheartedness were the main ingredients. ... We have had enough misunderstanding, enough arrogance.[52]

But, as Pastor Pehrsson noted, "if *we* are to give up our prejudices against our relatives, they also must learn to get rid of *their* prejudices against us." Most still envisioned the homeland as it had been thirty or forty years earlier. Many, Cederschiöld commented, had never seen anything of the homeland but a "poor parish in Småland," from which they generalized about Sweden, while Olofsson added that many felt they knew "America" on the basis of similarly limited experience. In Molin's view the Swedish-American press was especially at fault for presenting an incomplete and distorted picture of the Old Country.[53]

Still, some of the travelers were prepared to admit that various of the Swedish Americans' criticisms of Sweden were well justified. In an article posing the question, "Is Sweden's future threatened?" published in the Swedish-American magazine *Valkyrian* in 1909, von Koch stated candidly that it was quite understandable that many Swedish Americans should feel serious apprehensions that their old homeland was going "to the dogs." Those who returned to visit were rightly indignant over the heavy drinking and boorish behavior they often encountered there, the class conflict, sluggish work tempo, scandals in business life, religious hair-splitting, slander in the press, endless conflicts between capital and labor, and lack of public spirit and of practical optimism—that preeminent American quality. In general the praise the visitors accorded the positive sides of American life bore its own testimony of support of Swedish-American complaints against the land of their birth.[54]

There was general concurrence among the visitors that Sweden should do what it could to maintain good relations with Swedish America. Contact with the Swedish Americans convinced Pehrsson that "the emigration is not simply a loss," and that it was indeed a great asset for Sweden to be so strongly represented in the United States. The effectiveness of Sweden's diplomats there weighed little in comparison with a "Swedish stock of perhaps a couple of million competent, reliable, and intelligent citizens in the United States, who at the same time retain a strong love for their old fatherland." "We cannot afford to lose these bearers of Swedish language and culture," he added, "for as long as the Swedish tongue lives on among them they still belong to us and carry forward and enrich the Swedish heritage."[55]

Close relations with the Swedes in America could be made to profit Swedish trade and shipping. Sizable sums of American money were sent to families at home, were deposited in Swedish banks, and spent by visiting Swedish Americans. There were assurances that the home country could count on substantial help in both men and funds in case of war. The Swedish Americans upheld awareness of and respect for Sweden in the great republic. Meanwhile, anything that raised Sweden's prestige in the world improved their own standing in America. Possessing two cultures gave an "inner strength," according to Pehrsson. "The advantages in upholding Swedish culture, it seems to me, are well balanced on both sides of the Atlantic."[56]

Molin, too, favored efforts to encourage a distinctive Swedish identity in America, but from a narrower and more utilitarian perspective. They should, he wrote, be oriented toward Sweden's own national objectives. The Swedish Americans' interest ought to be to "maintain contact with an old, high culture, far superior to what America has to offer in that respect." For Sweden, the essential motive should be to keep open the possibility of return migration. This in turn would depend upon Sweden's own economic development.

> Here we reach the heart of the matter. The only possibility for the Swedish heritage to be preserved in America is for Sweden, through national strength, economic progress, and hope for the future, to make itself attractive to its children out there. Swedish culture can never be upheld out there by having the emigrants' children learn, for sentimental reasons, laboriously to mangle the language of their fathers and read the catechism in Swedish.[57]

These differing viewpoints are reflected in the visitors' prescriptions for improved relations. If effective cooperation were to be established, von Koch wrote,

> we must also be very careful to avoid giving it a condescending, patronizing appearance from Sweden's side, like that of the motherland toward one

of its provinces. Sensitive toward any air of superiority and imbued with democratic independence as our countrymen become out there, this would shut the door that now stands open. Neither should cooperation consist of one-sided giving on Sweden's part—Swedish America already now has much to offer in return. And finally, no effort should be made from the Swedish side to propagandize for a future return migration.

Sweden should seek to publicize present developments at home, not only among Swedish Americans but among the broader American population as well. He called for an increasing exchange of lecturers, musical ensembles, art exhibits, academic faculty, and interns in practical fields—precisely the kind of exchange the American-Scandinavian Foundation, founded in New York in 1910, the same year von Koch's book came out, undertook to promote. There was also a need for better and more responsible reporting, not only in the Swedish and Swedish-American press, but also in the mainline American press.[58]

Molin meanwhile held that if Sweden showed due appreciation toward the Swedish Americans, it should insist on the same from them. Otherwise, "we must take them to task, for that, I believe, they will respect. In any case that is the only way for us to put our relationship with them onto an even keel."[59]

Swedish Americans revisited their old homeland in growing numbers during the decade and a half before the outbreak of World War I, although few wrote accounts that found their way into print. For the varying reactions of less articulate visitors, we are largely dependent upon the testimony of others. On his return to Sweden, Gunnar Cederschiöld was impressed by the quiet, reverent sense of expectancy among the Swedish Americans aboard his ship. An old immigrant later recalled his visit to the Old Country to the Swedish pastor Lewi Pethrus. "It can't be described. I learned then what it means to feel at home. Everything in Sweden seemed to be my personal possession. ... The Swede who has never been separated from his fatherland has never tasted the sweetness of that feeling of home."[60]

For others, meanwhile, a return to the old home could be a sobering reminder of conditions they had once lived under and of their new demands on life. To educated Swedish observers these expectations might seem banal enough, as they did to the journalist Ingeborg Lundström (pseud. Inge Lund), who worked as a housemaid in New York. When a fellow domestic described how she was saving up for a little home of her own, this evoked for Lundström a dismal picture of Swedish-American everyday life. But, as Sara explained,

You see, when I came here I only remembered what was good back home. But when I then went home and saw how crowded and poor everything

was and how badly working people had to live, I prayed to God to save me
from Sweden. No, give me America! You have to work, for sure, but you
have something to work for, and you live like folk should. But if I had money!
Well, that would be another story. If I was rich I would live in Sweden, of
course.

"Sara had taken me with her into a world of unrelieved monotony and
gray emptiness and struggle and drudgery," Lundström realized, "where
only life's most basic requirement—a hygienic dwelling—provided a ray
of hope." In this last regard, Lundström noted the particular shock experienced by the typical Swedish maid upon being reminded that her old
home had no bathroom![61]

Gunnar Cederschiöld recognized that the visiting Swedish American
was often boastful and extravagant, although he sympathized with the
inner need for self-justification that this expressed. Unfortunately, such
behavior—or even the suspicion of it—could all too often give rise to
painful situations, as in the case of "Linnea," a Chicago maid, later recalled
by the Swedish-American Methodist minister John P. Miller. After years of
saving up, she allowed herself a trip home to Sweden.

> Now she wanted to show what she could afford, so she outfitted herself as
> elegantly as she could for the trip home. Back home at the croft and in the
> neighborhood she attracted attention, to be sure, but it was not flattering
> attention. She herself thought that her sisters were a little old-fashioned and
> backward. For their part, they thought their sister was a real stuck-up snob.
> On one occasion Linnea made a depreciating remark and received a response
> in kind. "What an arrogant hussy you are," they said, "Nothing is good enough
> for you! We are ashamed for you and laugh at your peacock feathers!" And
> so Linnea Jonsson went back to Chicago, bitter against her relatives and
> thereafter always ready to say disparaging things about Sweden. I believe
> Linnea's case was rather typical. She meant no harm and still her visit to
> Sweden was a great disappointment, both to her and to her relatives.[62]

Among those Swedish-American visitors who published accounts of
their experiences, none had a circulation or influence in any way approaching that of C. A. Swensson's substantial and widely read books from
the 1890s. Yet the few published Swedish-American travel accounts of this
period offer their own useful insights. Like Swensson's, they are affectionate
and conciliatory in their attitudes toward the Old Country—as compared,
for instance, with the proud defiance of Hans Mattson or Ernst Skarstedt
in the 1870s and 1880s—yet they too show Swedish-American pride and
independent judgment.

In 1906 a young scholar, Amandus Johnson, visited Sweden. Although
born in Småland, he had been brought to Minnesota at the age of two and
thus saw the ancestral land with fresh eyes. He later recalled:

I had expected that everything in Sweden would be large and magnificent, in accordance with Grandfather's descriptions. This turned out not to be so. The little red cottages along the road were picturesque but not imposing. The trees were small in comparison with the giant trees I had seen in various parts of America, the locomotives were much smaller than our American engines, the same with the streetcars. But everything was clean and proper and there were flower beds around the railroad stations. A little railroad station in America in those days looked like a junk heap in comparison with a Swedish one.[63]

How many others have reacted in much the same way upon their first encounter with Sweden!

The patriarch, J. A. Enander, at last revisited his native land the same year, in 1906.[64] The occasion was the "Swedish America Day" held in Norrköping, at which Enander was the featured speaker, the first of many such celebrations held in Sweden since then. A large crowd was on hand for the festivities, "and never has a mother welcomed her children, who have long been away, with more heart-felt words than the city's newspapers of all shades of opinion welcomed in verse and prose the visiting Swedish Americans." The press showed an appreciation that had been rare in the past.

As the crowd awaited the opening parade in the rain, Enander observed:

That a large percentage of those who stood there waiting consisted of Swedish Americans was easy to see, not only from the miniature American flags carried by men and women, nor simply from their clothing, but from their facial features and bearing, in which there appeared something more determined, energetic, and tough, as well as a greater self-confidence, than among most Swedes.

The parade included seventeenth-century Swedish soldiers from New Sweden on the Delaware, "Columbia" and her maiden attendants, goldminers, cowboys, pioneers, and costumed representatives of Swedish provinces, together with an array of dignitaries who conveyed King Oscar II's greetings and stressed the bonds between the Swedish Americans and the Old Country. In his speech, Enander eloquently presented, directly to his old homeland, the basic ideas and ideals to which he had devoted his long career.[65]

The same ceremonious atmosphere surrounded the Swedish tour of the elite chorus of the American Union of Swedish Singers in 1910, as described by its chronicler and principle spokesman, Victor Nilsson, Ph.D. In the introduction to his account, on "Sweden, land of yore, land of the future," Nilsson enthusiastically described how following their long slumber the "Hyperborean" Swedes were developing modern industry "to become, once again, one of the world's mightiest peoples."[66]

He meanwhile expatiated upon the undying love of the Swedish Americans for their native land and the essential role of song in the preservation of their ancient heritage. "The singers," Nilsson proclaimed, "regard themselves as a life guard of oath-bound warriors with the same motherland to love, the same mother-song to cultivate."[67]

Nilsson recounts above all a long series of festivities and solemnities, and one marvels at the apparent cast-iron constitutions of the Swedish-American stalwarts through their constant round of formal dinners, luncheons, "herring breakfasts," and coffee receptions. These events provided occasions for the expression of the warm sentiments that joined the two parts of the divided people.[68]

The fullest and most insightful picture of Sweden at the height of its national awakening as seen through Swedish-American eyes is that provided by Alex. Olsson, editor of the newspaper *Vestkusten* in San Francisco, who revisited the old homeland in the summer of 1908. It was a fond homecoming. Olsson was deeply moved by the natural beauty of his native land. He came over a hill in Halland, "and down there to the left, shaded by the majestic birches, lies the little home, just as before. How many storms have not shaken its roof tiles and the crowns of the birches since the day I left, how many lovely days of sunshine and moonlit nights have not cast their radiance over it, while I, out there on that distant coast, sought my fortune and only now and then had time, as though in passing, to give a thought to that fair place!"[69]

Olsson was happy to see everywhere signs of rising prosperity, and he was impressed with a new spirit of optimism and enterprise that gave hope for Sweden's future, deriving in large part from the National-Romantic revival of Sweden's ancient folk culture, then at its height.[70]

A high point in his visit was a great traditional Midsummer festival at Delsbo, attended by a large gathering from throughout Sweden, which Olsson described in glowing detail. In the spirit of the time, the conservative premier, Arvid Lindman, took this occasion to deliver a rousing patriotic speech, calling for greater common dedication to the building of a better future for the fatherland. Thereupon schoolteacher G. Karlström spoke "on the significance and value of the dance-games. . . . He pointed out that youth needed to enjoy itself and that games and singing had a precious place in the hearts of the Swedish people." It nonetheless seems revealing that the "serious young people from these parts" did not seem to join in wholeheartedly but tended rather to stand back and watch the games and ring-dances that followed. "Meanwhile the games continued until late at night and happy university and *gymnasium* students, city girls, and a few of the peasantry enjoyed themselves as best they could through the lovely summer evening. . . . Quite a number of both older and younger women came in Delsbo costume, but of men in that costume I saw only three or four."[71]

The contrast between educated city people and plain country folk, between sophisticated nostalgia and the realities of rural life as they had now become, between the new vision of a regenerated and bountiful Sweden combining traditional with contemporary values and the down-to-earth concerns of everyday existence are strikingly revealed. Those who watched from the sidelines on that Midsummer Eve still represented those most likely to dream of America.

Olsson was aware that Sweden faced difficult problems in its economic modernization. Powerful tensions had built up by 1908 between employers and the labor unions, which a year later would reach the breaking point with the great General Strike. Class conflict was the "phantom" haunting all of Europe, Olsson wrote, but he believed it to be particularly intense in Sweden since industrialization was still so recent there. The Swedish labor movement was socialistic, even anarchistic on its extreme left wing. In an epilogue to his book, written after the Swedish General Strike in 1909, Olsson feared that disunity and class conflict had now become more bitter in the old homeland than ever before. Still, in the balance, Olsson's visit left him with a chastened optimism regarding Sweden's future.[72]

The Lutheran pastor Alfred Bergin from Lindsborg, Kansas, traveled in Europe during the summer of 1914, mainly in the homeland he had last seen in 1883. A man of humble origins, he had spent his "dog years" at various menial jobs before attending Augustana College, receiving ordination, and gaining prominence as a contributor to the synod's periodicals. For him, return to the old home was less idyllic than it had been for Alex Olsson. "There is the gate I used to go through when I went home as a child. And there is the dear little house where I first saw mother and life. ... No! What do I see? Nothing! Nothing! The hill is bare. ... I was back home, but had no home. ... At home, but yet a stranger. How many Swedish Americans have not gone through what I now experienced!" Nearby was a farm he remembered well, for when he had worked there as a boy the farmer had brutally beaten him in a fit of rage. Now the man greeted him cheerfully in church, but Bergin reflected ruefully, "Pity him who was poor in Sweden and had such masters!"[73]

His visit was clearly a mixed experience. He admitted that after over thirty years' absence his eager expectations regarding his former countrymen had been "somewhat cooled," yet he loved Sweden, "for no one surely can deny that Swedish America is what it is thanks more to what we brought with us from our homeland in the Far North than to what we have acquired in our new homeland." He was, however, disturbed by the growing secularization of Swedish life, by what impressed him as a morally decadent literature and art, and by the Swedes' evident lack of true patriotism.[74]

A similar ambiguity is apparent in Bergin's attitudes toward the emigration question and the survival of Swedish culture in the New World. He recognized that emigration had "left both the land and people anemic and [that] a great weariness is apparent." He sympathized with the anti-emigration movement and repeatedly claimed that he himself advised against leaving, yet he wondered what Sweden could do with the Swedish Americans if they all were to return. He realized that the Swedish cultural heritage in America was already weakening and would do so all the more to the extent that immigration dried up. Yet he had reservations regarding the efforts of Vilhelm Lundström, Per Pehrsson, and the Society for the Preservation of Swedish Culture in Foreign Lands. He admired their ideals, yet he could not avoid a certain irony:

> Pastor Pehrsson reminds one very much of Alexander the Great in his views. ... Nevertheless he is unselfish enough to wish once again to visit Swedish America. If he could persuade us to come home and take most of America with us, that would be what he would prefer, but if this is not possible, he would like us to give strong support to the Swedish-America Line, donate some armored war-ships to the fatherland, and in every way encourage Professor Vilhelm Lundström in his noble efforts to preserve Swedish culture abroad and at home. ... If I am able to judge my countrymen correctly, love of the fatherland is weaker among those at home than among those who have emigrated.[75]

Bergin had long dreamed that a parish in his native Västergötland would provide an ideal existence, but now he had to confess that if the bishop of Skara were to offer him such a position, he would decline it in favor of Cambridge, Minnesota, or Lindsborg, Kansas.

The outbreak of World War I detained him in Sweden—together with some 10,000 other visitors from America, by his estimate—and it was only through his determined efforts that a group of stranded Scandinavian Americans were able to return home via Kristiania aboard a specially chartered Danish ship.[76]

What is most striking about both Swedish and Swedish-American travel accounts, during the decade and a half before the United States entered World War I, is the contrast they offer to the emotional and often bitter polemics over America, the emigration, and the emigrants of that same period. Compared with the Swedish anti-emigration propaganda and the indignation it could arouse in Swedish America, the travel literature—including that written by persons themselves active in the anti-emigration campaign—is notably calm, objective, sympathetic, appreciative, and conciliatory. It reveals the closeness that still existed, despite all, between Sweden and the United States, including its Swedish element.

During his visit to America in 1915, John Wahlborg's "Pastor Viklef" met a Swedish American who he felt was "certainly a bit hard-handed" in his criticisms of "Old Svea," but whom he was prepared to forgive because "when you speak of Sweden you say 'back home'. ... You cannot imagine how the feelings of us who are still tied to the Old Country are warmed by this. And as long as Mother Svea still holds this place in your hearts we can gladly overlook your little Swedish-American weaknesses."[77] If Swedish Americans could feel that they also had their rightful and respected place in the common heritage, they too could put up with their former compatriots' little Swedish failings. *"Hör oss Svea, moder åt oss alla!"*—"Hear us, Svea, mother of us all!" P. G. Norberg reflected, "Does not that song seem doubly moving when we hear it from across the ocean?"[78]

FIFTEEN

The Heyday of Swedish America

*D*uring the decade and a half preceding America's entry into World War I in 1917, Swedish America was at its zenith. Following the large influx after the turn of the century, the country's Swedish-born population peaked at around 665,000, according to the census of 1910, which together with nearly 700,000 of their American-born children comprised a total Swedish stock of 1,363,554, or 1.48 percent of the population of the United States. Since 1900, meanwhile, the Swedish proportion of America's foreign-born had declined from its high point of 5.6 percent to 5 percent, and whereas the total Swedish stock—the first and second generations together—would continue to increase until 1930 to over one and a half million, the percentage of the Swedish-born fell off after 1910.[1]

Other changes, too, affected the demography of Swedish America. Through both internal migration and direct immigration, a growing proportion of the Swedish stock settled on both the East and West Coasts, particularly in New England and the Pacific Northwest. From the older heartland of Swedish settlement, the upper Middle West, there was a continual drift to the Pacific Coast, as well as to the rapidly developing Canadian Prairie Provinces. Furthermore, the Yukon and Alaska gold rushes around the turn of the century attracted a sizable Swedish participation.[2]

A growing proportion of the newer immigrants—the majority before the end of this period—left urban and industrial employment at home and found similar kinds of work in America. At the same time, hard conditions for American agriculture drove increasing numbers of Swedish-American young people off the farms in search of other opportunities. Whereas in 1890, only about one-third of America's Swedish-born population was urban, by 1910 about three-fifths had become so.[3]

Such figures must nonetheless be taken with a certain reserve. A large part of the second, American-born generation remained on farms their parents had pioneered, while the parents, following a common American practice, moved into town after retiring. Many of the newer immigrants were originally of rural origins. A large floating population of male transient laborers, while nominally residing in towns or cities, was mainly employed outside of them, in harvesting, logging, and railroad-construction. Many urban immigrants, after earning the necessary means, acquired land where this was still possible—on the Dakota plains, for instance, or the Pacific Coast, or in western Canada—and went into farming. The Swedish-American press of the period is filled with land advertisements. The continual countercurrent back to the land was a significant—although frequently overlooked—aspect of the Swedish-American scene.[4]

It was against this background that Swedish America reached its fullest cultural development. In significant ways its culture continued to become ever more consciously and deliberately Swedish. Earlier internal conflicts between denominations or between the religious and secular camps now gave way to a growing sense of common identity and pride in a shared Swedish heritage.[5] The more recent immigrants generally had more formal schooling than their predecessors. Many, too, had been involved in various of the widespread folk movements (*folkrörelser*) in Sweden, which by the end of the nineteenth century were mobilizing a population by now largely uprooted from traditional rural society, such as the dissenting "free" churches or perhaps especially the temperance movement with its crusading zeal for adult education and self-improvement. They were thus, by the National-Romantic era, far more integrated into Sweden's national culture and traditions than earlier generations of immigrants with more provincial cultural horizons. Swedish America's cultural leadership came increasingly to consist of persons with experience in the Swedish folk movements, who like their comrades at home strove to propagate a kind of Swedish national folk culture, including costumes, dances, songs, games, and holiday customs with which many (if not most) older immigrants were unfamiliar from their particular home localities. The Lucia fest, the celebration of Midsummer, costumed folk dancers, and *smörgåsbord* became established rituals of Swedish America.[6]

The Swedish-American churches continued to grow in membership throughout the period. In 1910 the Augustana Synod celebrated its fiftieth anniversary in Rock Island with impressive solemnities, at which visiting Swedish dignitaries gratifyingly emphasized its close religious and cultural ties to the old homeland. The multifarious secular societies and organizations likewise flourished. This was true most notably of the newer, large regional and national federations, such as Svithiod, the Vikings, and especially the Vasa Order of America. The influence of the Swedish folk movements is manifest in the continued enthusiasm for choral singing, as well as the organization of numerous sports clubs. Theatrical societies, some of at least semi-professional status, flourished in larger cities, particularly

Chicago. National Romanticism was reflected in the appearance at this time of provincial societies (*hembygdsföreningar*) dedicated to the enjoyment of local dialects and delicacies.[7]

The Swedish-American press was never more active. In 1910 it reached its high point when no less than 130 periodical publications of all types came out. In 1915 a record number of newspapers, 72 in all, reached a reported circulation of 651,430. This total was surpassed during this period in America's foreign-language press only by the German Americans, while the press runs of the largest Swedish-American papers were greater than all but the largest newspapers in Sweden. Book publishing flourished. During the years 1891 through 1895, the Augustana Book Concern alone printed a total of 310,000 books in Swedish and 3,000 in English; between 1906 and 1910 it published 750,000 books under 151 Swedish titles, as well as 82,000 under 31 English titles. Swedish-American publishing houses meanwhile imported and marketed large quantities of books printed in Sweden.[8]

Continuing the trend away from their original focus upon preparing young men for their respective theological seminaries, the Swedish-American colleges conceived their role increasingly in terms of preserving Sweden's cultural heritage among future generations. The college communities were thus among the more active centers for the Society for the Preservation of Swedish Culture in America. That Swedish America had truly come of age was meanwhile reflected by the founding in 1905 of the Swedish Historical Society of America, its first viable and long-lived organization of that nature. Meanwhile, increasing numbers of Swedish Americans of both the first and second generations were gaining prominence in American life: in business and politics, the professions, scholarship, music, and the fine arts.[9]

This intense ethnic life naturally sustained—and was sustained by—much commercial enterprise, as is immediately evident from even the most cursory glance at the advertising sections in Swedish-American periodicals. Doctors, lawyers, land agents, building contractors, farm-machinery salesmen, and undertakers appealed to the group loyalty of their countrymen. Swedish banks, home-loan associations, and insurance companies were established. Steamship agencies handled a lively traffic in both directions across the Atlantic and usually took care of currency exchange and remittances to Sweden. Newspaper offices in larger communities often doubled as Swedish bookstores, which might also carry gift items from home. At the grassroots level, corner groceries, bakeries, butcher shops, fish markets, and small-town general stores offered a heartwarming array of traditional Swedish foods.

A fascinating picture of the wares and services available to the Swedish-American community, directly in a large urban center as well as indirectly by mail order throughout the country, is offered by the catalog issued in

1913 by the Carl Dahlen Company of 629 Third Avenue in New York. "Harken willingly to the Swedish appeal," its proprietor proclaimed. "Buy Swedish goods, support Swedish industry! I am fully convinced that this appeal will not sound in vain here in America, among our Swedish folk!" The catalog's illustrated pages are replete with a wide variety of decorative household and holiday items, displaying sentimental or patriotic Swedish motifs. There are Swedish embroidery kits and toiletries, as well as satchels and steamer trunks.

A large section is devoted to books and sheet music, giving interesting insights into what might be deemed commercially most promising among a Swedish-American clientele; most of these publications were imported from Sweden, including works by classic nineteenth-century authors and light entertainment, but there are also books dealing with the emigration by Carl Sundbeck, Adrian Molin, E. H. von Koch, and P. G. Norberg ("Peter Norden"), along with Swedish-American works by J. A. Enander, G. N. Malm, Jakob Bonggren, Johan Person, and others. A sizable selection of scripts for popular Swedish stage comedies is offered. There are books on Swedish folk costumes and dances and music for light theatrical, patriotic, and National-Romantic songs. In addition to retail goods, Dahlen operated a steamship agency, currency exchange, drayage service, and storage warehouse for the convenience of countrymen in transit.[10]

At its height, Swedish America nonetheless faced incipient threats, both external and internal. In Sweden the growing anti-emigration movement strove to cut off its flow of new blood from the homeland. In the United States growing reactions against the rising flood of European immigration, while not directed primarily against the Germanic element, threatened the same result. The Swedish-American community itself remained largely fragmented, to the frustration of its would-be leaders. Although to a lesser degree than previously, cleavages could still exist between churches and secular societies.

From the 1890s a new source of inner conflict arose with the arrival of committed socialists and labor union activists from Sweden, often following episodes of labor unrest, especially the General Strike of 1909. Swedish sections were organized within both the Socialist Party of America and the more doctrinaire Socialist Labor party. Swedes were active in local labor unions and played a role in the International Workers of the World (IWW), notably in the person of the songwriter and publicist Joe Hill, born Joel Hägglund in Gävle. The political and labor radicals nonetheless accounted for only a small fraction of the Swedish element in America, regarded with distaste and suspicion by the majority. "There are many Swedes in this city," an activist wrote from Ceder Rapids, Iowa, in 1905, "who do not know what a strike is or what the [Swedish labor] organization means and they do not want to have it explained to them either." Swedish radicals in America were naturally indignant that most of the brethren, however committed they might have been to the cause in the Old Country, soon lost their ardor in the scramble for individual advancement in the new land. The Swedish-American majority meanwhile found a congenial political climate in Theodore Roosevelt's progressive Republicanism.[11]

A far greater threat to ethnic solidarity came meanwhile from the steadily rising proportion of the American-born or American-raised element, in relation to those born and raised in Sweden, and the resulting problems of preserving the old language and culture, exacerbated by natural generational conflicts. Eloquent voices were raised in the defense of heritage. But most Swedish Americans, like most people everywhere, lived their lives according to what in their circumstances seemed most practical and expedient.

Faced with mounting challenges in both Sweden and the United States to the validity or legitimacy of a distinctive Swedish-American identity, as well as with the disintegrative tendencies apparent within their own community, Swedish America's cultural leaders and opinionmakers felt called upon, as never before, to rally, justify, and define their group, both to themselves and to their present and former compatriots. Their search for a unique identity assumed an ever greater urgency.

This search continued to focus upon fundamental questions familiar from the past. How long could, and should, Swedish culture endure in America? What aspects of it were most important to perpetuate, and why? How was the Swedish language to be passed on to coming generations, and how central was its role in the preservation of Swedish culture, values, and identity? In what ways might the Swedish heritage best contribute to the forming of the American nation of the future? What, meanwhile, was the proper relationship of Swedish Americans to their old and new homelands?

A fitting point of departure would be the April day in 1903 when Augustana College celebrated its first Founders' Day in Rock Island. Its president, Gustav Andreen, made what for him was a characteristically conciliatory speech on the Swedish cultural heritage upon which the college was built. "That people which has come to America over these fifty years is the fruit of Sweden's history, culture, and development over the millennia. We Swedish Americans therefore cannot understand ourselves unless we get to know Sweden, its language, its culture."[12]

That same year at the Mission Covenant's North Park College in Chicago, President David Nyvall, wrote an insightful essay on the Swedish national character and its Americanization. Like others, Nyvall stressed the Swede's "lust for great deeds," courage, insistence on lawful rights, and loyalty to his leaders. He also pointed out a greater propensity to conquer than to hold, a tendency toward empty boastfulness in easy times, an abstract and diffuse concept of "right," as opposed to specific rights, and an inclination toward blind "hero worship," which he saw as the corresponding vices born of virtues, against which Swedes must guard themselves in the American environment.

Nyvall meanwhile identified a fifth basic characteristic, which served as a deft thrust at the Swedish critics of emigration. The Swede, he declared:

> is *by nature an emigrant*. It is possible that therein lies a fault, namely the instability and volatility of mind that characterizes the adventurer. So be it then. But an emigrant the Swede has always been and always will be. He loves his fatherland and has given proof of this. But this sentiment is not bound, like serfdom, to the soil alone. He loves his native place, but with a free longing to return there because he is able and free to leave it. It may be that the Swede's urge to emigrate is connected with his taste for what is foreign. But if this is a weakness, it is likewise a strength. Much that is good has in this way become Swedish in language and custom, in land and thought.

The associated danger was that the emigrated Swede might "forget, more quickly than he should, his Swedish heritage and lose his identity," thereby committing "cultural suicide." "Our Swedish culture," he proclaimed, "must meanwhile be planted and cultivated here. It must neither be buried alive nor be conserved as a museum piece." In this way the Swede's idealism and virtues could adapt and live on in the new land, reinforced by the more admirable American qualities.[13]

In 1903 the Augustana Lutheran Pastor Lars Gustaf Abrahamson of Chicago wrote an article hailing Carl Sundbeck in *Prärieblomman,* in which he stated some home truths aimed in principle as much at Sweden as at Swedish America. The Old World, including the Old Country, refused in its blind prejudice to recognize anything of cultural value in America. In reply Abrahamson painted an idealized picture of its Swedish community.

> There exists in this country a new Sweden. Here there are up to two million citizens who proudly trace their origins back to Sweden, who speak their forefathers' language, read their literature, and cherish their history. This people, by turning to account its inherited cultural treasures, has through honesty, industry, and Nordic strength made an important contribution to the cultural activity of this land. It has won for itself a respect which should give joy to Mother Svea.

He meanwhile attacked the lukewarm patriotism of the Old Country. It was difficult to understand widespread opposition to needful military reforms and pessimism over the country's capacity to defend itself, a university student body lacking in patriotic ardor, a working class that preferred to follow the red flag rather than the national banner. The "uncorrupted peasant class" alone still stood fast. Americans, meanwhile, for all their differences, well knew the meaning of true patriotism.[14] As Abrahamson well understood, the patriotic theme was a particularly sensitive one within those conservative circles in Sweden most intransigently opposed to emigration.

As much as L. G. Abrahamson might have wished to address his remarks to a Swedish public, his forum was necessarily a Swedish-American yearbook, which in effect limited him to preaching to the converted. It was reserved for the aging patriarch, J. A. Enander, to speak directly to his former compatriots, when thirty-seven years after leaving Sweden he was the featured speaker at the Swedish-American Day held in Norrköping in 1906. Some of his observations on this occasion have been discussed above.[15] In his oration, Enander presented much the same view as Abrahamson—a Swedish-American ideology which, however, more than anyone, he himself had developed since the 1870s.

"Svea," he proclaimed, "is mother to us all," and the Swedish Americans would have much to tell of their great but so often misrepresented new homeland and their contributions to its development. Today they had little in common either with the "poor emigrants who a generation back left their old fatherland with grief in their hearts and tears in their eyes" or with the proverbial scapegraces Sweden had been glad to get rid of.

> The Swedish Americans are a patriotic people, who have sunk neither into materialism nor weak cosmopolitan indifferentism. . . . Upon four solid cornerstones—home, church, school, and press—the Swedish Americans have built and are building the edifice of the future. In four great virtues—industriousness, sobriety, economy, and forethought—they have found the keys to the future in town and countryside. They are a courageous people, undeterred by any danger and never in the rear echelons. . . . This people, which is proud to trace its origins to "freedom's home on earth," is not only our own and our country's pride, but its hope for the future.

From the Swedish Americans, Enander turned to the old homeland.

> Here in Sweden they have regarded emigration with disapproval. . . . They complain still . . . that its fertilizing stream does not flood over Sweden's domains but rather flows away to America. But do not complain over the stream; complain rather over the bureaucratic barriers that hinder it from watering the old fatherland like a fructifying Nile. . . . complain that political infighting paralyzes efforts in a patriotic spirit to "bring America over the Sweden," the only means by which emigration from the latter can effectively be ended.

Undergoing the trial by fire in America, Enander declared, his countrymen had shown what "good Swedish steel" was worth when cleansed of rust and dirt. He would thus wish, not that Sweden be spared "hard, chastening trials for the awakening of patriotism, will, effectivity, strong national sentiment, and moral greatness," but that this should lead to the same good results in Sweden, "which we Swedish Americans love, as long as it makes itself worthy of our own and our children's love and admiration." On such grounds he dreamed of a "new union between two brother peoples in Sweden and America," based on a common cultural heritage, joining "the best, the noblest our people possesses on both sides of the Atlantic."

Albeit from a proudly Swedish-American viewpoint, Enander was delivering much the same message as Sweden's own apostles of National Awakening in the same period, and he noted with satisfaction that his speech was repeatedly interrupted by loud applause, which at his conclusion was so stormy that the musical fanfare could hardly be heard.[16]

That a sense of Swedish-American distinctiveness could rest upon acute resentments against conditions in the Old Country is well documented in homey, down-to-earth fashion by many of the letters conscientiously published by the Swedish Emigration Inquest in 1908. A more eloquently ironic statement of such grievances is provided in 1909 and 1910 by the memoirs of Theodore A. Hessell, alias "Uncle Slokum," who had arrived in America in 1869.

Speaking of his childhood home, Hessell wrote: "O, smiling, refreshing oasis of my long life's wandering, how often have not I, in my wakeful dreaming, returned to Thee. . . . For Sweden as a whole, I have seldom if ever longed." To come of age in Sweden had meant to remain "absolutely dependent, weak-willed, an automaton, a machine," while a heartless bureaucratism served as a "crowbar" that steadily broke countless Swedes loose from their original naive loyalty to their fatherland. There, poverty was "a crime, which was punished arbitrarily, with contempt and lack of rights." "There is only one civilization," he declared: "Justice, freedom from oppression, for all. Where that civilization has developed the furthest, there is my fatherland."

Still, recalling his departure from Sweden, he reflected on the bitterness of leavetaking and the high price America exacted from those who sought its blessings. Arriving in New York, he found himself "at once where I wanted, and did not want, to be."[17]

There was much in the polemics of Abrahamson, Enander, Hassell, and others that tended to define Swedish America in negative terms of reaction against the Old Country and its society, characteristically in contrast to an idealized picture of the Swedish Americans themselves. There remained, meanwhile, the more positive task of defining what a cultural Swedish America ought to be and how this might best be realized.

In 1903 Pastor Abrahamson had sanguinely described a Swedish-American community some two million strong, who "speak their forefathers' language, read their literature, and cherish their history." For David Nyvall, this remained more an ideal for the future than a present reality, as shown by an essay he wrote in 1907. As president of North Park College on

Chicago's northern outskirts until 1905 (and again after 1912), he was well aware of the possibilities for many-sided ethnic cultural development in large metropolitan areas, yet fearful of the dissolute influences of the big city upon both morality and culture.

The ideal of the rural community as the true bastion of higher values remained strong in early twentieth-century America, and not least in Swedish America, which since the great influx of the 1860s had witnessed repeated efforts, generally under church auspices, to get Swedish immigrants out of the cities into new, compact farming communities in the West and North. Indeed, there was a renewed wave of such activity after the turn of the century. In 1903, Nyvall's own denomination, the Mission Covenant, successfully promoted rural settlement around Turlock in California's San Joaquin Valley, attracting many Swedish Covenanters from Eastern and Midwestern industrial and mining towns. That same year, Pastor Carl A. Swensson in Lindsborg, Kansas, appealed in articles widely published in the Swedish-American press for his countrymen in America to move west and there form new rural colonies where their economic independence, language, culture, and faith might be kept free from corrupting forces.[18]

Nyvall's essay in 1907 was an ardent appeal to create a vital and attractive social and cultural life in rural Swedish-America. The first generation of pioneers had, through heroic effort and self-denial, acquired veritable "land baronies," but their austere way of life not surprisingly held little attraction for their children, who took hard-earned prosperity for granted. Nyvall pitied both those who fled to the seductive distractions of the city and those whose lack of ambition and imagination held them in drudgery on isolated farms. Youth had its right to wholesome and innocent pleasures, and here Nyvall's thoughts were naturally drawn to a romantic idealization of the old Swedish village community, or *byalag,* in which all shared in work, worship, and recreation.

He described "a true home in the country, with the neighbors a bit closer and the pigsty a bit farther away," commodious and comfortable, tastefully furnished, with well-tended lawn and sanded paths, an alley of trees leading up to the house, and vegetable and flower gardens. "Who would not wish to live in such a home in the country? . . . As long as we live in the belief that all community life is town life, the countryside will remain uncultivated, no matter how well tilled it may be."

May the young people be preserved from the cities. . . . Keep them in the country. Create a home life, create a community [*byalag*]. Our rural life still lacks a historic, a truly humane existence. . . . What should the old do for the young? Build roads. Read newspapers. Gather in a fuller life rather than let it drain away. Do not simply accumulate acres of land and corncribs full of corn and herds of livestock. Gather memories around the hearth and gather together the children. Bring in story and fable. Fill the home with song and music. Welcome guests, not just eaters. . . . Make the old home life's center. . . . Let be the empty, miserable tumult of the city. Create a full and independent country way of life in your own home, in a joyous and neighborly community.[19]

It was a moving vision when the century was young, and one which could draw sustenance both from the revived idealism of the American Progressive Era and the rural idyll of Swedish National Romanticism.

In 1913 an Augustana Synod Colonization Society was organized "to gather and keep our people in larger communities and colonies, and thereby to seek to prevent their dispersal." A central office in Minneapolis was to serve as a clearing house for the sale and purchase of properties in Swedish-American settlements, to keep them in Swedish hands, while investigating possibilities for new colonization. Despite initial enthusiasm, this effort came late in the day, and little, if anything, seems to have come from it.[20]

The same ideal inspired Pastor Alfred Bergin of Lindsborg, Kansas, to appeal to the children of Swedish immigrant farmers in 1915 to remain on the land. "Life in the country," he wrote, "is in every way richer and healthier than city life." Here, too, considerations of cultural preservation are manifest. Bergin deplored the fact that so many Swedish properties, especially farms, were now owned by people "who are neither of our stock nor concern themselves with our church." "The Swedish influence upon society is weakened and as a people we become swallowed up by our surroundings. . . . An important condition for our success and our significance here in this country is that the children keep the homes their parents have built. In particular it is important that the landholdings be preserved. These farms have been won by the sweat and labor of our fathers."[21]

No specific matter was discussed more intensely in Swedish America during these years than the language question, the main outlines of which should now be familiar. A new aspect was raised around the turn of the century with the first serious studies of the Swedish language as it evolved on American soil, by President Gustav Andreen of Augustana College, Pastor E. A. Zetterstrand, and the Uppsala scholar Ruben G:son Berg. Far greater concern was meanwhile attached to the language's future in the New World. This, as the journalist Vilhelm Berger (writing under the pseudonym "Felix Vivo") put it in 1903, posed two basic questions: should Swedish Americans, having learned English, sacrifice their Swedish, and if not, how could they avoid doing so?

Responses in the press to the first question were virtually unanimous and characteristically couched in warmly emotional terms. Swedish should be preserved for its antiquity, beauty, and expressiveness. "Where is a language to be found," asked "R. D. H." in 1911, "that grips more deeply the strings of the heart?" The language, its defenders held, was the truest reflection of the Swedish folk soul and the natural beauty of the homeland. It was the vehicle of a cultural heritage far older and richer than that of the New World, which in turn it could and should enrich. Memories of past generations and their great deeds made the safeguarding of the ancestral tongue a sacred duty.

Above all, upon the continued use of Swedish depended the survival of tradition, identity, and solidarity within the Swedish-American community: in J. A. Enander's oft-quoted verse, "the spirit of the Northman, upright and true/never can die in the tongue of our fathers." The language, *Missionsförbundets ungdomstidning* editorialized on 22 April 1913, "is the nationality's very source of life and the strongest bond holding us together," the "key to the national strongbox." "For Swedish America the entire Swedish culture will become only a fairy-tale if the language is lost." Without it, Amandus Johnson warned, his countrymen would be "ground to pieces, reshaped, and then, like a mass without will or character, be mixed together with other nations without leaving behind us any trace of our activity, without setting the mark of our genius upon the civilization of the New World."

Despite the underlying anxieties thus revealed, the situation was by no means yet acute, and it could indeed appear increasingly hopeful. Neither the learned discussion of American Swedish in 1904 nor a lively debate in *Ungdomsvännen* over the future of Swedish-American literature in 1905 betray any fears that the language might die out in the foreseeable future. While Vilhelm Berger recognized that Swedish immigration should diminish as conditions improved at home, he was confident that family ties would long keep it at levels sufficient for Swedish to remain a living tongue in America. To his mind—and most readily agreed—the real answer to his second question in 1903, as to how Swedish could be preserved, lay in the will of the Swedish Americans themselves, as demonstrated by other linguistic groups in both the United States and Europe, not least the East Baltic Swedes. Swedish-American commentators pointed with pride to their community's churches, educational institutions, secular societies, and press as strongholds of the mother tongue.

Gustav Andreen estimated in 1900 that at least a million and a half persons in the United States had some knowledge of Swedish, while only about 5 percent of the Swedish element there did not know the language. "Our fathers at first believed that Swedish would be dead within twenty, then thirty, surely within fifty years. Now fifty years have passed and during that time it has only gained ground, so that now Swedish is spoken and read by more people than ever before. ... A language does not die so easily." Andreen prophesied that Swedish would live on in America at least through the twentieth century and at this time of writing there seems every indication that he was right.[22]

Both the circulation of Swedish-American newspapers and the titles and numbers of Swedish-language books printed in America continued to increase up to 1915. The census of 1910 showed that nearly 700,000 persons in the United States claimed Swedish as their mother tongue. A survey carried out in 1917–18, revealed that only 33 percent of Swedish-born parents of school children in Minneapolis-St. Paul used English in the home, as opposed, for instance, to 61.2 percent among the Germans, 41.3 percent among the Danes, 32.3 percent among the Norwegians, as well as 8.1 percent among the Italians, and only 1.1 percent among the Slovaks. But signs of strain were not lacking. The Swedish-American press—whose very existence depended upon its survival—was sharply critical of those who claimed to forget the old language, even sometimes before learning the new.

As early as 1880 the Augustana Synod had been concerned with the problem of losing young people to other denominations because of a preference for English. Some congregations felt compelled to alternate English- with Swedish-language services. In 1908 some fifteen churches and missions within the Augustana Synod organized an Association of English Churches, joined by a growing number in following years, on the principle of preserving "the faith of the fathers in the language of the children." For the time being, the non-Lutheran Swedish denominations held more closely to the old language.[23]

An address given in 1915 by C. A. Lindvall, president of the Swedish Historical Society of America, summarizes the concern over the language question by the end of this period. The steadfast descendants of the seventeenth-century New Sweden settlers on the Delaware, few in numbers and without supporting institutions, had preserved their mother tongue for two hundred years, he stated. Swedish could survive far into the future—indeed indefinitely—provided the Swedish Americans possessed determination and energy enough to preserve it.[24]

At the annual meeting of the Swedish Historical Society of America in November 1916, Lindvall spoke in more somber tones. He recognized Swedish-American culture as ultimately a "transitional phenomenon, a stage in the great process of fermentation of which the new American nation will in time emerge as pure and clear as any fully mature nation in the Old World." Nonetheless, he concluded,

we believe that the longer we can preserve Swedish speech and Swedish customs, the greater respect we can win for the Swedish name, the brighter and more vital we can make the Swedish strain, the more pure gold of old-fashioned Swedish steadfastness and honor we can bring to it, the greater the Swedish element will be some day in the great American race that will inhabit this continent when all the different peoples here have been melted down into the alloy of a single nation.[25]

Another persistent concern within Swedish America was its lack of universally recognized leaders who might rise above petty factionalism. This was the theme of an article by S. M. Hill in the Historical Society's yearbook for 1915. The "Royal Swedish Envy," so frequently alluded to, kept any Swedish American from achieving a position of undisputed eminence among his own people. Outstanding talents were not lacking, but those who gained real prominence did so within American society at large. Thus, "we had a John Ericsson, but no Carl Schurtz."

Hill, a faculty member at Luther Academy in Wahoo, Nebraska, could nonetheless view the situation with scholarly objectivity.

> The emigrants lived in Sweden under a system of social oppression necessary for the maintenance of good order and proper behavior back home. Rank and caste had firmly established boundaries. ... Even ill will against the clergy had its origins in this caste system, for Sweden's clergy were to keep watch over the sheep and keep them still while they were shorn. The rise of lay preaching was a revolt against this use of the clerical calling, and most of the emigrants had come under the influence of the lay preachers. They wanted nothing to do with the pastor, for he followed the bidding of the masters and not of the Lord. They followed the lay preacher, for he belonged to the people, he spoke like the people, and he shared the people's feelings and views. And for that reason the people felt he spoke for the Lord. All of this has made leadership difficult among us. ... But perhaps this lack is fully compensated by the sense of freedom this allows, so that we would not thrive so well if we had great leaders and more power. Every land and people has the kind of government it deserves.[26]

In retrospect, one wonders whether the situation really was so different among other ethnic groups in America?

The articles discussed above all dealt with selected questions. In 1912, meanwhile, Johan Person came out with his *Svensk-amerikanska studier* (Swedish-American Studies). Born in 1868, Person had come to America in 1887 and worked in the Swedish-American press in various parts of the country. His earlier volume of short stories, *I Svensk-Amerika,* in 1900 had established his literary reputation and is credited with having coined the term "Swedish America."[27] *Svensk-amerikanska studier* is a collection of short essays—only 172 pages in all—on different aspects of the Swedish-American condition, most of which had appeared earlier in Swedish-language newspapers. They reveal Person's broad experience and keen insight, and are written with elegance and economy of style. Together they provide the most balanced and perceptive insider's analysis of Swedish

America at its apex. While certain of his basic ideas are recognizable from earlier commentators, such as C. F. Peterson, J. A. Enander, or Carl A. Swensson, Person provides valuable, new insights from the perspective of his own, later generation.

Like Enander, Person saw his countrymen in America as a people in its own right, even if not in a political sense, sharing common origins, culture, traditions, and memories. "As long as the Swedish language lives on in America, even if not in daily use, as long as a culture of a Swedish character is found here, as long as memories of Sweden are preserved within this atmosphere, as long as something remains by which those of Swedish origins may be recognized and distinguished from other immigrants, there will be a Swedish-American people."[28] This people was greatly misunderstood. In Sweden, where prejudices remained strong, it was widely believed that once in America the emigrant underwent so profound a "metamorphosis" as to become unrecognizable as a Swede. The older Americans remained smugly ignorant of all nationalities but their own, even though they might be more favorably disposed toward the Swedes than toward other immigrants.

Prejudices on both sides were reinforced by the fact that the emigrants were most visible and created the most unfavorable impression at the time they left the old homeland and entered the new. In Sweden they were widely regarded as shiftless and improvident. The majority, nonetheless, "are not of the type who have made themselves impossible in Sweden, but rather those for whom Sweden was impossible—people who wished to raise themselves out of the pariah class, but considered it useless to try in Sweden." Had the old homeland only realized what the children of the "lower classes" were capable of accomplishing, what a "social revolution" might have resulted, to Sweden's gain![29]

This, the Swedish immigrants demonstrated in America, after running the gauntlet (*ekluten*), which to Person constituted the immigrant's central, formative experience. The lonely struggle to adapt to frighteningly different language, conditions, and pace of life in the new land tested character and resulted in the survival of the fittest. "Proportionately more ne'er-do-wells go under here than in Sweden and the survivors are, taken as a whole, physically, psychologically, and morally better here than they are there. . . . The morally weak in most cases go under." In America the immigrant generally had to make his own way, with little of the support from family and friends that was customarily expected at home and which there helped to keep the incompetent afloat. Earlier immigrants in America, well-meaning in their own way, realized they did the new arrivals no favor by shielding them from the hard realities of their new life, a theme Person had dwelt upon in his short stories. The Swedish-American community consisted of "*proven* men and women."[30]

The initial trial nonetheless varied greatly in severity. Those who passed through it most easily were those who had worked hard in Sweden without success. "What seems an inferno to the weakling is for them almost a paradise." Those who suffered the most were immigrants with some education and cultural background. For them the ordeal was doubly difficult, since they tended to be regarded with suspicion, if not ill will, by the majority of their fellow immigrants, who generally believed that people of their kind did not emigrate except for discreditable reasons. The ideals inculcated by the traditional Swedish educational establishment Person felt inhibited an easy adjustment to American values. Lacking such inhibitions, immigrants of more humble backgrounds were at an advantage, and the so-called outstanding Swedish Americans most visible in their own community tended to be self-made men of this type. The more educated minority, if they made good, did so most often within the American mainstream, outside their own ethnic community.[31]

It was thus the immigrants of humble origins who were the most unreservedly satisfied with America, while the educated few were distressed by the crying discrepancies they found between, on one hand, crass materialism, raw social behavior, and political corruption, and on the other, the proud ideals of America's Founding Fathers. Such people, Person wrote, "often express, in words and behavior, a protest against that sort of Americanism—and that is perhaps fortunate for America." They were valuable precisely because of their un-American qualities. Nevertheless, with few exceptions, the Swedish Americans were as loyal to the United States as the country's native-born, and often more so since they were Americans by choice, not by chance. "Sweden is for them a memory—a beautiful memory—but America is their homeland, where they live their present lives and place their future hopes."[32]

Paradoxically, immigrants from Sweden nonetheless became more fully "Swedish" in culture and sentiment in the new land, as C. F. Peterson had earlier observed. The Sweden they left was historically, and still remained, divided into small provincial "kingdoms," with little contact between them on the local level. Emigrants from all parts of the land were meanwhile brought together. "During eight days on the Atlantic the groundwork was laid for that which makes the Swedish Americans one people, thus distinguishing them from the Swedes in Sweden, who consist of at least twenty-four."[33]

There were frequent complaints within Swedish America of a lack of unity, but these Person did not regard with any great alarm.

One does well in such cases to examine more closely the motives behind these songs of woe. It will then be discovered that they arise in most cases from the fact that the Swedish-American people will not rally as a whole behind some individual undertaking to the benefit only of its instigators, nor will it follow an ambitious, self-appointed leader like a herd of sheep after a bellwether. It has been shown that when it is a question of something that deserves common concern, unity is not lacking.[34]

One thing above all was capable of overcoming petty jealousies and drawing the Swedish Americans together: their avid concern with anything that might reflect upon the honor and reputation of the Swedish name among outsiders. For the great majority it was a matter of noblesse oblige to be Swedish. Hence their outrage over the misbehavior of any of their compatriots and their elation over the recognition any of them achieved in American society at large—even if, like John Ericsson, the prime example, such persons had little contact with the Swedish-American community.

Moreover, Person found that whereas recently arrived immigrants—especially the younger women—for understandable reasons sought to become as "American" as possible as quickly as they could, when they married and settled down, they found it natural to revert to their Swedish language and traditions. The immigrant, after becoming acclimatized to American life became "idealistically more Swedish than the Swedes in the land of his childhood and in a practical sense more American than ever before." Meanwhile, "The remarkable nature of [his] love for the land of childhood excludes the thought of ever returning there to stay. Childhood memories and young love never die in this life, but they are never transformed into reality. The Sweden the Swedish American loves so deeply he bears within him. Its geographical location lies in his heart."[35]

Those who did try to go back permanently all too often found themselves homesick for America. They were never free from longing—on either side of the ocean. "That is the fatal thing about having two homelands." It likewise expressed the inborn tension within the Swedish character between love of home and the "Viking spirit," which longed for new horizons.[36]

The immigrants' most immediate priority was to establish homes of their own, an urge reinforced by living in an alien environment. In the short run, this limited their cultural interests and activities, but it formed the essential basis for a more developed culture. This culture was not always fully appreciated by Swedish observers because of its American aspects, such as the main focus of social and cultural life being outside the home, in churches and organizations.[37]

America demanded relentless toil as the price of success, for which reason the Pilgrim Fathers had done well for themselves; that their descendants were now becoming sybarites gave hope, meanwhile, to later immigrants who were prepared to work. But the grim search for profit left little room for the carefree pleasures so warmly cherished in Sweden. "The American," Person claimed, "is unable to enjoy himself. The Swede, on the other hand, is richly endowed in that regard. If the Swedish American can work like an American and enjoy himself like a Swede, he will surpass them both." His inherent seriousness and tendency to make hard work even of his pleasures, Person nonetheless suggested, could benefit from a healthy dose of American humor.[38]

What meanwhile of the future? Again Person was ambivalent. He noted a greater tenacity among the more recent Swedish immigrants on the East Coast in preserving their language and culture than was evident in the Midwest or West. In particular he saw characteristic differences between the more diffident and careful Swedish-born parents and their more self-confident and enterprising children, which he attributed to the American educational system and its values. "At times," he observed, "the difference between them is so great that they seem hardly related to each other."

> The immigrated Swedish Americans [Person wrote] are like a people of their own, separated from their fathers, separated from their children, and not so little misunderstood and rejected by both—a transitional people, who come into conflict, now with the one side, now with the other, and not too seldom with itself—a people which forms a bridge between the old and the new, and which is therefore so much tramped upon.

In general, the children, like their parents, were largely ignorant of Sweden's cultural heritage, while the Old Country as often described by their elders—"a poor land with a class of haughty folks who despise all working people"—was hardly inspiring. Too few, in Person's estimation, learned proper Swedish or showed much desire to use it.[39]

Pessimism alternated with a certain dogged optimism in Johan Person's essays, doubtless shifting with the passing moods of the times when he wrote them, amid his ceaseless editorial cares. He did not give up hope that a truly Swedish-American culture might survive and even flourish. The Swedish Americans had, as a people, passed through the chastening fire, built homes, and established social and cultural institutions which were now thriving as never before. He waxed particularly enthusiastic in describing their musical and literary activities. "It was not the flower of Swedish culture that was transplanted in America," he wrote. "But this is not to say that this culture might not put down roots here and even develop in new directions." Like C. F. Peterson, he discovered a marked poetic vein in his people, deeper even than in the Old Country, for in America the "hectic, arid everyday life demands compensation as diametrically opposed to it as possible." Against this prosaic background, Person could dream of a Swedish-American poetry "able to stand beside the Swedish, or perhaps even by itself." Fresh blood still continued to arrive from Sweden and with greater education the American-born generation might still reclaim its ancient birthright. Swedish America need not—inevitably—vanish into the melting pot, and by living on could make its valuable contributions to an emerging American national identity, whose very strength derived from its unique cosmopolitanism. Johan Person dared to hope against hope.[40]

Four years after the appearance of Person's *Svensk-amerikanska studier,* Vilhelm Berger, editor of *Nordstjernan* in New York, came out with a similar collection of essays, all previously printed in the Swedish-American press, entitled *Svensk-amerikanska meditationer* (Swedish-American Meditations). Even smaller than Person's slim volume, Berger's book is a similarly thoughtful and informed analysis of Swedish-American life at its height. Since he covers most of the same ground as Person, however, as well as other predecessors and contemporaries in both Sweden and Swedish America, and since he later developed on various of his themes in numerous writings during the 1920s and 1930s, his "meditations" from 1916 may be dealt with rather briefly here.

Many of the ideas Berger expressed in these eighteen essays were familiar enough by this time, but they show certain traits of their own. They reveal an author of more robust constitution in both body and spirit than Johan Person, with a greater consistency of outlook and an attitude toward life at once more sanguine and more calmly realistic. He showed a greater concern for historical background and gave more detailed attention to the institutional framework of Swedish America: churches, organization, the press. He was more generous than Person in his appraisal of the role of the churches, especially the Augustana Synod, in preserving the Swedish heritage. Like Person, he was much concerned with the problematic relationship between the Swedish-American culture of a predominantly lower-class, uneducated immigrant community and Sweden's national cultural heritage. Unlike Person, however, Berger did not limit himself to anxious speculation over the survival of a Swedish identity in America, but offered specific, practical suggestions to support it.

In his introductory essay, first printed in 1908, Berger traced the Swedish emigration through its various historic stages, showing an overall shift in basic motivation from predominantly economic to essentially social factors. He meanwhile addressed the perennial question of the ill will among the educated classes in Sweden toward the emigrants and America. Berger recognized there were understandable reasons for such an attitude. Sweden had received a number of "sickly outgrowths" from America, no small amount of "humbug and chicanery," while "none of the enterprise, energy, and respect for work, the good qualities that sustain the American people, have found their way there." The Swedish press did nothing to improve understanding. And still emigration to America continued and could be ended only by well-planned efforts to make Sweden's own attractions surpass America's.[41]

Mutual misunderstanding between Sweden and Swedish America is again considered in Berger's chapter 16, in which he proposed various means to foster cultural cooperation.

The average educated Swede's conception of America is limited mainly to a few vague and contradictory ideas about a land where working people are well off, but where a worker's life is considered worth no more than a fly's; a land where every man or woman who treads the solid ground of honest labor is respected for it, but where at the same time everyone tries to earn money without working for it. He has the idea that the Swedish Americans are a great crowd of savages, interesting to study, easy to make money from if you play upon patriotic themes, and last but not least, well supplied with money. It seems to me as though in Sweden they overestimate the Swedish Americans, regarding their numbers, wealth, love for Sweden—and stupidity. The Swedish Americans, for their part, have the idea that the Swedes are a backward people. Sweden is for them the primeval home of the eternal struggle between upper and lower class, the land of poverty and impossibilities. ... They therefore are not in the least interested in the remarkable development in all areas that in recent years has been taking place in Sweden and has made it a land of progress. They believe it is the same Sweden they left 20 or 30 years ago.

The strengthening of ties across the sea, Berger maintained, must not only aim at reinforcing the Swedish Americans' identification with the culture of the old homeland but also at making Sweden aware of "what it means to have a people of Swedish origin, which through intelligence and civil virtues has won a good name for itself, in one of the great powers of the world." Moreover, any Swedish efforts at conciliation must avoid "any suggestion of a condescending or protective attitude."[42]

The suggestions Berger offered for closer and mutually beneficial cultural exchanges between Sweden and America (not only *Swedish* America) were indeed practicable and pointed toward ways that have been followed since that time in keeping Swedish—and Scandinavian—culture in America, and American culture in the Nordic lands, alive and active. In 1908, Berger could welcome the establishment of an American-Scandinavian Society, forerunner of the American-Scandinavian Foundation organized two years later in New York, which up to the present has given impressive support to cultural exchange in both directions. The year 1910 also witnessed the establishment of the interdisciplinary academic Society for the Advancement of Scandinavian Study, which today flourishes as never before. Both bore witness to a growing appreciation for the culture of the Scandinavian lands among educated American opinion at large.[43]

In 1912 A. A. Stomberg, professor of Scandinavian Languages at the University of Minnesota, saw this appreciation in the light of America's growing immigration crisis:

There are also in our time special reasons why the Anglo-Americans have become more favorably disposed toward Germans and Scandinavians, and show themselves more receptive to the impressions their culture can give.

The great flood of immigrants that has begun to inundate the land, deriving from southern Europe, threatens to sweep away or bury many of the finest fruits of our culture. Those peoples who are now immigrating have been fostered in another school than Americans, Germans, and Scandinavians, and their ideals differ greatly from ours. As in Europe, where the Pan-Germanic movement has been set in motion by the same menacing force that faces us in our own land, we have begun to see in America as well the need to combine our forces for the "struggle that lies ahead."[44]

A vital component in the forging of an identity was the mobilization of the Swedish Americans' own usable past. In this respect the period contains a number of significant landmarks. Most notable was undoubtedly the establishment in Chicago of the Swedish Historical Society of America in 1905. Its first president was naturally the venerable J. A. Enander, and although he died in 1910, his stoutly filiopietistic spirit continued to inspire the society, at least until the later 1920s. Its *Yearbook*, which appeared irregularly, remains a valuable resource for research, thanks above all to the wealth of primary documents it brought out, usually both in the original Swedish and in English translation. From an early date the society also began collecting both manuscript and printed sources.[45]

Amandus Johnson, who had arrived in America in early childhood, was the first academically trained historian of the Swedes in America, even though his doctorate from the University of Pennsylvania in 1908 was in Germanic Languages. Following intensive research in Sweden in 1906, he published his massive, two-volume work, *The Swedish Settlements on the Delaware* in 1911. Although originally inspired by J. A. Enander, Johnson's great study is sober in its presentation, based, he claimed, upon "every document on the subject known to exist." Its imposing bulk and sheer mass of documented detail in themselves impressed and reassured the Swedish-American community of Sweden's presence among North America's earliest colonizers.[46]

History of a different genre is represented by the publication in 1916 of part two of Pastor Eric Norelius' work on the Swedish Lutheran congregations and Swedish settlements in America, detailing the organizational history of the Augustana Synod, its regional conferences, educational and charitable institutions, and missionary activity (which by that time extended to both China and India).[47]

In 1917, following his second visit to the homeland, the veteran Swedish-American journalist Ernst Skarstedt brought out a broad survey of Swedish America through a Stockholm publisher, the first such work by a Swedish-American author to be published in Sweden. In a lengthy introduction Skarstedt spiritedly defended his Swedish-American compatriots before the Swedish public in terms by now familiar. In separate chapters he described in detail the various areas of Swedish-American activity, quoting in extenso from unpublished accounts and correspondence in his own collection. These features alone make this work a reference of lasting value, but its earlier chapters in particular give it the added distinction of providing the first overall survey of Swedish-American history, from the Delaware colony down nearly—as it would turn out—to the end of the great migration. Though research has added much additional detail since 1917, the main outlines of Skarstedt's account have well withstood the test of time.

Skarstedt's *Svensk-amerikanska folket* is not an easy work to categorize. A lengthy chapter is devoted to "Swedish-American types, characters, and originals," in which the author forthrightly takes exception to the main current of thinking among his contemporaries regarding his compatriots in America. "A truly distinctive Swedish-American type does not exist," he maintained. "It has not had time to develop and it is uncertain whether it ever will develop. By the time this might seem to become possible, the Swedish American will have turned into a full-feathered American."

This was not simply a case of the iconoclasm for which Skarstedt was known; he was prepared to defend his Swedish-American countrymen vigorously before Swedish opinion—but only as he knew them, without pretense or self-deception. In what followed, he gave examples of the self-satisfied narrow-mindedness, materialism, and philistinism often encountered in Swedish America. But he more than counterbalanced this with stories and anecdotes about a variety of highly independent and original characters he had known, mainly among the earlier immigrants. For Skarstedt, it was precisely the refusal to conform to type, in either the old or the new land, that redeemed his Swedish-American people, despite all their human failings. He was skeptical of any organized attempts from the old homeland to rally his countrymen in America under the "All-Swedish" banner.[48]

Swedish Americans were meanwhile not alone in exploring their past, for history was evoked in the rising debate over the whole question of immigration in the United States. Anglo-American opinion was ever more inclined to welcome Scandinavians as reinforcements against the rising tide of southern and eastern European immigration. The most notable proponent of this view within the American historical establishment was Kendric Charles Babcock of the University of Illinois, who, after several articles on the subject since the early 1890s, brought out *The Scandinavian Element in the United States* in 1914.

"As related to the progress of civilization in America," Babcock wrote, "all immigrants fall into three classes: those who powerfully re-enforce the strength and virtue of the nation, those who supplement its defects with desirable elements, and those who lower its standards and retard its advancement." Thus the Chinese in California, the "Hungarians in the mines," or the "Hebrews in the sweatshops" augured "nought but evil from foreign immigration."[49]

When they migrated to the American West, the hardy Scandinavians "start out in the new life with decided temperamental advantages over most other immigrants, and even over most native-born Americans." They learned English well, held education in respect, and stoutly opposed the "saloon and liquor traffic." They were moreover distinguished by their "intense Protestantism." "Everywhere and always they are uncompromising enemies of the Roman Catholic church."

> In temperament, early training, and ideals, the Scandinavians more nearly approach the American type than any other class of immigrants, except those from Great Britain. . . . Theirs has been a determined purpose and a serious resolve to "arrive" somewhere in America, and, finding their places, to fill them with honorable endeavor and steady ambition. They have come as families, or with a wholesome desire to establish families for themselves. . . . The immigrants from the North are decently educated, able-bodied, law-abiding men and women, not illiterates, paupers, or criminals. . . . They have no secret societies ramifying through their settlements, no Mafias, "Molly Maguires," anarchist lodges, or other badges of ancient servitude or foreign hates. They will be builders, not destroyers; their greatest service will be as a mighty, silent, steadying influence, re-enforcing those high qualities which are sometimes called Puritan, sometimes American, but which in any case make for local and national peace, progress, and righteousness.[50]

By the early twentieth century, Swedish-American literary production had become quite prolific. The principal outlet for such creativity remained the periodicals—newspapers, monthly magazines, and yearbooks of various kinds—which naturally favored the more compact genres: poetry and the short story. Not infrequently, however, their authors, most often journalists by trade, reprinted their verse or prose in book form, often on their own or through newspaper presses. Most of this literature was intended as nothing more than light entertainment for unsophisticated readers. Swedish-American writers commonly set their stories in the Swedish countryside and gave dialogue in broad local dialect. This popular literature was essentially similar to that which by then was being produced in Sweden itself, also largely through the periodical press, for a growing mass public, likewise largely of more or less recent rural background. Much of the poetry and fiction published in Swedish America consisted moreover of direct imports of this nature from Sweden.

A significant number of poems and stories were nonetheless specifically Swedish-American in theme and setting. Many of these were basically similar in plot and sentiment to those with Swedish backgrounds. Of greatest interest, however, are those directly dealing with situations in which immigrants found themselves in the new land. This literature con-

tains its hidden gems—unpolished as they may often seem—reflecting the
realities of life and underlying concerns of the Swedish Americans in its
own unique ways, as a few examples will show.[51]

Certain basic situations recur in the Swedish-American short story, such
as the tragicomic blunders of the "greenhorn," the unexpected reunion
with an old friend or sweetheart from home under strikingly changed
circumstances, or the visit of the prodigal son or daughter to the old home
in Sweden. A particularly prominent place during the early years of this
century is meanwhile held by what may be called the "conversion experience," in which a young male protagonist with some cultural pretensions
from Sweden eventually overcomes his prejudices to become an enthusiastic Swedish American, while typically losing his heart to the American-
born daughter of earlier Swedish immigrants. This theme was clearly a
literary response to the mounting criticism of the emigration and emigrants
in Sweden.

It seems to have made its first appearance in a short story by Johan
Person from 1903. In it, Göte Borgman, a "young, modern, and somewhat
aesthetically inclined person of culture ... rich in sentiment but rather
poor in feeling," well practiced in conventional patriotism through propos-
ing toasts and singing second tenor, comes to America intending only to
visit and observe.

In Minnesota he finds friends who, having dropped out of school at
home, had done more with their lives than he, at which he "felt his
superiority dwindle almost to humility." In spite of himself, he is drawn
to Minnesota's Nordic landscape and largely Nordic inhabitants. At this
point he meets the fair Winona, a typical "blond, blue-eyed, purely Nordic
beauty."

> It was the first time in his life that Borgman had actually met a woman,
> young or old, on a basis of complete equality. It had never before occurred
> to him that men and women belonged to the same species. His female
> acquaintances in Sweden, girls of good family as well as tavern waitresses, had
> given an altogether different impression. They had either been mysterious,
> enigmatic creatures, whom no one got to know, even through marriage, or
> else pretty playthings—under no circumstances man's equal and comrade.

A true respect for womanhood, convinced him, more than anything else,
that "all was not humbug in America." Borgman was now seized with the
desire to work, and work hard: "Here in America, that part of the world
where the Creator had made his works especially awe-inspiring, it was as
though people more than anywhere else were endowed with the divine
creative power. Borgman felt this. In the past he had always imagined life's
joy was to be a *flaneur* and dreamer, whose every need was satisfied
without work. Now idleness began to feel like a burden of shame." He

understood, too, that only through honest work could he gain Winnie's favor against his rivals.

He meanwhile told Winnie and her father, Mr. Peterson, about Sweden. The latter listened eagerly to Borgman's tales of the "old kings and great deeds of yore" from the land of his birth. In turn the old man told of the adventures and hardships through which the Minnesota frontier had been tamed back in the sailing-ship era and of his love for the soil he had made his own.

In the end, Borgman marries Winnie and settles down to stay in his new homeland. Soon after the wedding he writes home to a friend in Sweden:

> Considering myself and those I associated with back home, I can say that one ought to come to America and get to know one's countrymen here to learn love of country—both of Sweden and America. . . . As for myself, I consider it nobler to love a people than to love a land, and now I can truly say that with all my heart I love my people, wherever they may live. In view of what I have recently experienced, I should perhaps confess that the balance weighs in favor of our countrymen on this side of the Atlantic.[52]

Variants of the conversion theme appear in the short stories written for *Ungdomsvännen* by the Augustana Lutheran minister Carl W. Andeer. One from 1903 tells of a young scholar from Uppsala University who takes a Swedish-American bride home to Sweden. There his marriage is at first regarded as mesalliance, but soon the "lovable young Swedish American . . . won all hearts that were worth winning with her free, forthright manner." The Swedish American's return to and confrontation with his former compatriots is a recurrent motif in Andeer's stories. In a story from 1904, a gathering of upper-class Swedes are shown up in their ignorance and prejudice by the simple dignity and true erudition of a visiting Swedish-American college professor, who likewise succeeds in winning the heart of his host's daughter. Another, published in 1915, after Andeer himself returned permanently to Sweden, stresses the vitalizing influences upon Swedish life of remigrated Swedish Americans.[53]

In 1905 Frithiof Colling, already encountered as the author of the humorous *Mister Colesons Sverigeresa* in 1896 (under the pseudonym "Gabriel Carlson") returned permanently to Sweden. In 1906 he published there a collection of short stories, some on Swedish-American themes. Of the latter, two are of particular interest in reflecting the divided loyalties of a thoughtful returned emigrant.

In one an immigrant known for constantly extolling Sweden at America's expense decides at last to return home. In making his final preparations for departure, however, he is constantly reminded of how easy-going, friendly, and helpful local officials and business people in his small American town and how easy it is to accomplish things. Recalling Sweden's stiff and restrictive bureaucratic regulations, he reflects:

> Was this perhaps because people back home had never learned to take personal responsibility or to make the best of any circumstances that so much control was needed? Or was it because so much supervision, so many rules and regulations, such long scholarly studies, delays, and inquests existed that people back home had lost self-confidence and seldom accomplished anything, at least in the past? ... Perhaps it was not such a bad thing to have fewer detailed regulations and greater demands to look out for oneself.

In the end he decides to remain in America "for the time being."[54]

Another story meanwhile seems to reflect Colling's reconversion from skeptical Swedish American to reborn Swede during the height of Sweden's National Awakening. A nameless Swedish American, returning to the homeland, seeks in "the seaport city" (doubtless Gothenburg) for signs of the American influences he understands to be now manifest in Sweden. He finds an "American bar," but it lacks the true American atmosphere in which people from all walks of life could meet and mingle. He finds a club composed of former Swedish Americans, but it is similarly exclusive: "manual labor was not represented, and of the Jeffersonian simplicity, which they nonetheless sought to praise, there was little trace."

In the countryside, however, the visitor finds many returned Swedish Americans who have used their savings to establish themselves in economic independence, like their countrymen in America. "This was a glimpse of the better America in Sweden." But even among those who had not crossed the ocean he discovers a new lust to work hard to achieve a better life through Sweden's own resources. The old, stubborn adherence to traditional ways and outmoded social cleavages was now in retreat. He begins to find that "life pulsed as strongly in Sweden, perhaps even more strongly than over there in the free West." Indeed, he wonders whether conditions in America, increasingly burdened under the "yoke of Big Capital," are any longer as promising as they once were. "Snobbery seemed on the rise in America while it was on the decline in Sweden." At a great folk fest in Västergötland on a glorious summer day, surrounded by enthusiastic youth, he realizes it is his proper task to join in the building of the new Sweden.[55]

The Swedish American's contributions to Sweden's development is also the theme of a story by the journalist Axel Lundeberg in 1907. Its moral is that "If Sweden has much to learn from America, the latter has much to gain from Sweden, and it is we Swedish Americans who comprise the 'missing link' between the two peoples, and if we strive to fulfill this great task rightly, it will be seen ... this is what Providence intended with the so often and so long misunderstood emigration."[56]

A literary work of quite a different nature was a speech printed as a pamphlet in 1908 by John S. Carlson, professor of history at Gustavus Adolphus College, who claimed to have delivered it hundreds of times before Swedish-American audiences. It consists of a passionate polemic in defense of Swedish language, culture, and Lutheran faith in America, against seductive and treacherous forces that surrounded them.

This is oratory in the grand manner, employing a flowery rhetorical style, in the exalted, archaizing language of Swedish National Romanticism. Carlson's righteous indignation wells up as he recalls America's first discovery by the Northmen. "Mark well, thou haughty Briton, thou proud son of England, thou who hast never been the first in anything, if not in seizing that which others have discovered or acquired. The first-born right to America's discovery is not thine."

"There was a time," Carlson laments, "when the Swedish name was known and honored in America, when the Swedish tongue was heard even here, and Swedish faith and honor were not unknown here. O, fortunate time! Why didst thou not tarry longer?" The answer, in Carlson's mind, was to be found in a nefarious conspiracy by the Anglo- and Irish-American Establishment, to keep the Swedes—and other nationalities—in subjugation by depriving them of their distinctive cultural traits.[57] The underlying, at times even paranoic, fears of an aging Swedish-born generation, now increasingly outnumbered by its American-born descendants, here receive pathetic expression.

Another ever-present, although seldom directly articulated thought on both sides of the Atlantic was what the Swedish Americans would do if their old homeland should be attacked—by the old Russian enemy. This was the subject of a short story, by Carl Atterling, a one-time journalist in Rockford, Illinois, in 1912. Sweden is attacked by an unnamed foe but the situation is saved by the gallant "Swedish-American Volunteer Brigade," filled with "genuine American 'fighting spirit,' self-reliance, and confidence." Many of the volunteers fall "for the fatherland, that had so badly rewarded them, but which despite all retained their deep love."[58] The story was a fantasy, yet also a challenge at a time of growing belligerence in Europe.

At the opposite extreme from such flights of rhetoric lie the lightly fictionalized recollections of pioneer days in Lindsborg, Kansas, as seen through the eyes of a young child and recounted in a child's American Swedish by Anna Olsson, daughter of the settlement's first Lutheran pastor, in her *En prärieunges funderingar* (The Thoughts of a Prairie Child), published in 1917. She describes the dangers, so frightening to a child, of the still untamed prairie. She recalls the doings of the grown-ups, such as genteel coffee parties or the visits of stern-faced men in stovepipe hats and whiskers who argued, sometimes in loud and angry voices, with her father over something mysterious and ominous called "Doctrine."

Most interesting for present purposes is Anna Olsson's depiction of a small child's vision of the old homeland, based on what she heard around her, particularly about Värmland province, which she imagined to lie somewhere way out beyond the "Company House." There was where Grandmother lived and the stars were so bright and the Christmas trees grew so tall and there were so many beautiful flowers—but no rattlesnakes, Texas cows, grasshoppers, tornadoes, or Indians! And she noticed, too, how Mamma often wept for Sweden, but Pappa, who had no time, never did.[59]

In view of its general dependence upon the periodical press, it is not surprising that Swedish-American literature included few novels. (Why, under essentially similar conditions, Norwegian-American authors were notably more prolific in this genre would be a subject worthy of closer inquiry.)

The classic Swedish-American novel is meanwhile unquestionably G. N. Malm's *Charli Johnson, svensk-amerikan,* (Charli Johnson, Swedish American) published in 1909. It too centers on the "conversion" theme, in this case the transformation of Karl Johansson, a young man of some education and culture from Sweden, into "Charli Johnson," a true Swedish American and farmer in Nebraska. A subsidiary theme—one which lay close to the hearts of the kind of people who wrote in Swedish America— was the question of how to broaden the cultural horizons of an immigrant people of predominantly humble rural origins. Malm's novel is also noteworthy for his keen ear for the mixed language of the immigrants, which he skillfully employed in dialogue, both for humorous effect and the delineation of character.[60]

The cultural potentialities of rural Swedish America under the right circumstances come as a revelation to Charli when he visits Lindsborg, Kansas, for the annual spring Messiah Festival. Here Malm gives a glowing account of the little community, centered on its Bethany College, which Ernst Skarstedt in 1911 would describe as a kind of Swedish-American Athens.[61]

In euphoria over what he had experienced, Charli overhears a conversation on a train between a derelict Swede of genteel origins and a visitor from Sweden who is traveling the United States to study Swedish-American conditions, scorning the pretentiousness of the Messiah Festival as simply what might be expected of uneducated "parvenus" in a "wild land without culture." Indignantly Charli confronts the two—the latter of whom was surely modeled after the celebrated P. P. Waldenström—sharply recalling to them that only a few decades ago Indians and buffalo roamed this prairie, now covered by the prosperous farms, churches, and schools of hard-working Swedish immigrants.

Now hear me out! [he continues.] I myself have gone through a struggle, and I have won. That these people have felt a need for something other than the purely material, there can be no doubt, and that they have succeeded in the most appealing way in satisfying this need you should have seen and heard, had not your ingrained prejudices and poisoned, false ideas, inculcated since childhood, blinded your eyes and stopped your ears.

Charli realizes that his conversion is now complete, and he looks forward confidently to taking up his leadership role in his own community. He marries his Swedish-American Annie (Änni) and no longer feels any desire to return to Sweden for good.[62]

Swedish America during the first decade and a half of this century was a lively and many-sided community. In it, more generations of immigrants and their descendants mingled than at any other time. There were still those living who had been among the earliest Swedish pioneers in the 1840s and 1850s, those who had just gotten off the boat, and those who had arrived at every stage in between. With continued immigration, Swedish America remained a relatively young community with the vitality and hopefulness of youth. It encompassed farming settlements in the Midwest and West, small towns, and ethnic neighborhoods in cities like Chicago, Minneapolis, or Worcester, Massachusetts. It was borne up by its far-flung network of churches, organizations, colleges, and publications.

Just as the immigrants fondly recalled the land of their birth, so too both they and their American-born offspring would in later years look back with loving nostalgia to Swedish America in its golden years. Of it, the Augustana College historian, O. Fritiof Ander, himself an immigrant, recalled:

> Political campaigns may have added to the excitement of life in the immigrant community, but they did little to disturb the idyll. And it was an idyll despite the many minor human ills. It was a world of laughter. In it a man felt at home and secure. It was a life of good things to eat and drink, of folk music and dance, and of good stories told in broad dialects. In it a man had learned to laugh at himself and listen to both the tragic and the comic role of the immigrant. The immigrant community had become part of America.[63]

Still, signs were not lacking by 1917 that the end of this idyll lay close at hand.

PART THREE

And so during this time we have grown apart from them
back home. . . . We are no longer the same as we were.
—G. N. Malm, 1919

Why not let the language question solve itself in a
natural way? That of which the heart is full, the mouth
will speak.
—Vilhelm Berger, 1933

If I died in Sweden, no one would come to my funeral
without an invitation. If I die in California, I know all
my friends will come.
—Carl Mangård, 1938

Ebb Tide, 1917–1940

*T*he outbreak of World War I in Europe in August 1914 foreshadowed the end of the great transatlantic migration to the United States. Immigration from Sweden, which in 1913 had totaled 16,329 persons, declined to 9,589 in 1914, and was down to 4,538 by 1915, even though Sweden preserved its neutrality. By 1918, after America's entry into the war, it came to a mere 1,416, the lowest figure since the Civil War. America's participation in the conflict meanwhile unleashed powerful antiforeign sentiments that had long been brewing, which imposed severe trials upon the country's immigrant communities, not least upon the Swedes and other Scandinavians.

Growing nativism, exacerbated by the war, led Congress to set restrictive immigration quotas for each nationality in 1921, 1924, and 1927. Although the first of these did not prevent Swedish immigration from reaching its sudden, final peak in 1923, when no less than 24,948 Swedes came to the United States, it fell off to a yearly average of slightly under 8,400 between 1924 and 1929. During the following decade—the years of the Great Depression—Swedish immigration averaged less than 900 persons a year, well under quota and far below return migration to Sweden. The great migration from Europe was over and beyond recall by the mid-1920s.

Following the wartime ordeal of ethnic America, Swedish-American cultural life revived to a notable degree. Membership in Swedish-American churches and societies grew through the 1920s, until the onset of the Depression. Swedish-language publications and literary culture, however, failed to regain the vitality of the prewar years. With immigration from the Old Country drastically reduced and with the steadily declining ratio of the Swedish-born within the Swedish element, Swedish America's cultural leadership, as well as concerned elements in Sweden, faced a growing dilemma through the 1920s and 1930s over how to preserve what could be preserved of Swedish identity and heritage. With the passing of an era, there was, too, a growing inclination to look back, record, and commemorate the great deeds of the past, most of which still lay within living memory.

Numerous visitors from Sweden continued to write of their experiences and observations in the United States, but with the passing of the emigration problem at home, their interest focused increasingly upon mainstream American life. Their more cursory and occasional treatment of the Swedish Americans lost its polemic edge as the latter came to be regarded—whether sympathetically or unsympathetically—as historical curiosities with ever less relevance to contemporary Sweden. Some Swedish Americans, too, wrote about visits to the old homeland. The travelers' accounts from both sides chronicle an ever widening gap between directions of development in the Old Country and the New.

Despite its neutrality, Sweden was hard-pressed by the economic dislocations of the war and the years immediately following. Still, these same years witnessed developments of decisive significance for the future. In 1917 the growing Social Democratic party for the first time took part in a coalition government. In 1920 it was able to form the first ministry of its own under Hjalmar Branting. The vote in national elections was extended to women in 1921. Although their first ministry lasted only a few months, the Social Democrats would return to power in 1921–23 and in 1924–26; from 1932 until 1976 they would dominate the political scene. Meanwhile, backed by a broad political consensus, the Riksdag commenced the enactment of a wide range of legislation in support of economic development and better living conditions, reinforced by the labor and cooperative movements, laying the basis for the modern Swedish welfare state. Increasingly, working-class Swedes came to envision their future in their own country, rather than across the water.

Under such conditions, the Swedish anti-emigration movement and the passions attached to it rapidly dwindled. Attitudes toward America and its role in the world were meanwhile mixed, showing a new respect for America's strength, as revealed in the war, and at least fleetingly for Wilsonian idealism; yet in like measure there was mistrust and fear of the wave of American material values and popular culture that flooded into the Old World. Both reactions are strongly mirrored in the Swedish literature of the interwar decades.

With its passing, the great migration quickly receded, in Sweden as in

America, into the realm of myth. For a small but vocal group of dedicated leftists, the emigration became a kind of modern morality play: the collective tragedy of the hapless masses who escaped capitalist oppression in their native land only to be swallowed up by the insatiable American Moloch. For most, however, it became transmuted into a saga of bright dreams, stout hearts, and great deeds in the vast land beyond the sunset, bringing a nostalgic whiff of excitement and high adventure into an increasingly well-ordered, secure, and stable society.

SIXTEEN

Swedish America
at the Divide

Following the outbreak of the war in Europe in August 1914 it became evident that while hoping for the continued neutrality of both its old and new homelands, the Swedish-American community, with few exceptions, strongly sympathized with the Central Powers. This was hardly surprising. Germany had exercised powerful cultural influences throughout Scandinavia since the Middle Ages, especially since German unification in 1870–71. Swedes were accustomed to regard the Germans as a closely kindred people and Germany as the home of Martin Luther and the true Evangelical faith, of poets and philosophers, musicians and scientists. Army officers and engineers, scholars and artists, industrialists and labor union leaders could all find inspiration in Germany. All could agree, moreover, that a strong Germany was Europe's bastion against Sweden's ancient enemy, the empire of the Russian tsars, oppressor of Sweden's former domains in the Baltic Provinces and Finland. In Swedish eyes, the war appeared—initially at least—above all as the crusade of Europe's civilized heartland against the forces of Eastern barbarism.

Various Swedish-American newspapers and magazines declared their pro-German sympathies. Already on 6 August 1914, *Hemlandet* in Chicago expressed the hope that a "higher power" would assist Germany and its Kaiser, "for in this war they battle for everything that a civilized people holds sacred," and that if Sweden should be forced to abandon its neutrality it should join the Central Powers. *Svenska Amerikanaren* in Chicago made bold to assert, on 31 December 1914, that the Swedish Americans were the most pro-German of all the nationalities in the United States. Fervently germanophile appeals by Swedish notables appeared in Swedish-American periodicals. As late as February 1916 the Swedish-American authoress Signe Ankarfelt rapturously proclaimed in *Ungdomsvännen*:

It is precisely for the Germanic concepts of society and morality that a struggle perhaps decisive for a long time to come is being waged in these times. The question is that of the "to be or not to be" of the Germanic peoples as the torchbearers for all human striving toward freedom and perfection, not only within state, society, or community, but within each individual, as well as for the realization of the ideal of the Kingdom of Heaven on earth.[1]

Such attitudes were not, however, unanimous, and some newspapers were critical of Prussian militarism. The sinking in May 1915 of the British oceanliner *Lusitania* with the loss of nearly 1,200 lives, including many Americans, cooled Swedish-American enthusiasm for Germany, but also heightened fears of American involvement in the war. Thereafter, the Swedish-American community showed its increasing concern with preserving America's neutrality. Both the Augustana Lutheran Synod and the Mission Covenant petitioned the government against exporting armaments to belligerent powers.[2]

With war seeming ever more imminent, the Mission Covenant's *Missionsvännen,* on 20 March 1917, carried an impassioned attack on those who profited from war. "Why should our boys . . . be sent out to battlefields for the sake of European intrigues and for the protection of greedy militarists' interests? Why cannot the United States on this side of the globe maintain its neutrality when little Sweden can do it even when the fires of war surround it close to its borders?"[3] Meanwhile, threatening fissures appeared within the Swedish-American community. The outspokenly pro-German Dr. Johannes Hoving in New York recalled how by 1916 some were prepared to denounce old acquaintances as German spies. "Ugly traits of character" came to the fore.[4]

When the final crisis came, the Swedish American Ernest Lundeen, Republican congressman from Wisconsin, resolutely opposed the war, with "neither apology nor excuse," together with two congressmen and a senator of Norwegian background. Outside Congress, Charles A. Lindbergh, Sr., of Minnesota, whose term as a Republican congressman had expired in 1916, courageously attacked the "dollar plutocracy" he considered responsible for America's involvement, especially in his book, *Why Is Your Country at War?*, which came out in July 1917. Among the Swedish-American congressmen in 1917, only Irvine Lenroot of Wisconsin strongly supported the government's actions.[5]

America's entry into the war quickly silenced any signs of overt opposition in the Swedish-American press, which hastened to express loyal support for the war effort, with the exception of *Svenska Socialisten* in Chicago, the organ of the Scandinavian Socialist Union. As time passed and growing numbers of Swedish-American men served in the armed forces, opinion became ever more committed. In October 1918, for instance, *Ungdomsvän-*

nen expressed indignation toward Swedish immigrants who while eligible had not become American citizens. "They are not Americans," it declared. "They are scarcely Swedes either, for then they ought to stay where they belong." Such persons ought to be given the choice of "willing citizenship or deportation to the land where they are entitled to live, for here they are not." Underlying fears for the good reputation of the Swedish element in America are thereupon revealed in an attack upon those who allegedly believed that their people were "overseas Swedes" and that "our world is that of the Swedes abroad." Such persons might speak of the heroic traditions and great achievements of the Swedes but lacked true sympathy and understanding for America. "Be Americans!," *Ungdomsvännen* admonished. "Love our homeland! Be a truly reliable support for its government in these trying and demanding times."[6]

The United States government backed by the semi-official American Protective League, effectively stifled any criticism of American foreign policy, while the National Council of Defense ferreted out suspect aliens. Articles on the war in the foreign-language press had to be submitted in translation to local postmasters for prior approval. The Committee on Public Information organized various demonstrations of loyalty among immigrant nationalities and pressed for citizenship and the use of English. Several states passed legislation limiting the teaching of foreign languages in the schools, and in some cases their use in public. Iowa went so far as to ban foreign languages even in church services.[7]

The latter prohibition caused much distress. A Covenant pastor in Iowa wrote to his denomination's headquarters in Chicago, "People weep because the Word of God has been taken from them and we are not able to communicate the Gospel in English." One of his colleagues reported that he had tried his best to preach in English, but "if there is no change, I and several of the older preachers will not be able to keep it up for any length of time." One minister of the Covenant wrote that the governor of Iowa would presumably not arrest anyone for disobedience of the prohibition, "but the people around us, even some of our own members, are ready to brand the minister as pro-German, and threaten to paint our churches yellow or to burn them, even to gather a mob and force the pastor out of the community."[8]

Various prominent Swedish Americans distinguished themselves by their "100% Americanism," among them Governor J. A. A. Burnquist of Minnesota, the former governor of the same state, John Lind, and the ambitious journalist, Edwin Bjorkman, who headed the Scandinavian Section of the Committee on Public Information, working largely through a John Ericsson League of Patriotic Service, organized in March 1918 to coordinate Swedish-American wartime efforts.[9]

Under such conditions, not only did the Swedish-American press and churches react strongly to any outside insinuations against their loyalty, but the press not infrequently echoed with accusations and counteraccusations. When a pacifistic poem by C. A. Lönnquist in *Ungdomsvännen* in July 1917 provoked numerous protests, its editor, Ernst W. Olson warned that the immigrants were being caught in a web of suspicions woven by "too many persons who think they have a patent on patriotism," but who doubtless preferred to "stay home and slay imaginary Philistines" rather than face the enemy overseas. "Nobody but a patent office patriot or a national hysteric will appoint himself censor, detective, prosecutor and judge of his fellow citizens."[10]

Because of their widespread pro-German sentiments at the beginning of the European conflict and outspoken support for American neutrality up to April 1917, the Swedes and other Scandinavians in the United States faced a highly uncomfortable situation, causing many to overreact—or to keep quiet. On occasion individuals found themselves subjected to unjust official or popular persecution, often by fellow Swedish Americans. Passions ran high. The ordeal of Swedish America during 1917 and 1918 was an ignominious and humiliating one.

There were also underlying anxieties that the old homeland might enter the war on the enemy side. It was known that such a course was favored by conservative "activist" circles at home. An alarming diplomatic crisis arose over the Luxburg Affair in September 1917, when it was revealed that the German minister in Argentina had been sending secret military intelligence to Berlin via Swedish diplomatic channels, in violation of Sweden's neutrality. In response, Edwin Bjorkman of the Committee on Public Information urged Swedish-American newspapers to carry articles that would make clear to the Swedish government that it could not count on Swedish-American sympathy or support if it were to follow pro-German policies. Fortunately no other such incidents occurred.[11]

The Swedish Americans meanwhile did their bit for the war effort. Various committees promoted Liberty Bond drives, exhorting those who subscribed to identify themselves as Swedes. Almost 100,000 Swedish citizens registered for the draft, of whom half had obtained their first citizenship papers, as well as larger numbers of American citizens of Swedish birth or descent. Many immigrants found themselves on the front in France not long after leaving Sweden—and frequently escaping military service there. Few sought to evade induction, the most notable exception being 138 members of the Swedish Socialist Club in Rockford, Illinois, who refused to register, to the anxious indignation of the Swedish-American press.[12]

It is, of course, impossible to know how great enthusiasm for the war actually became among the Swedish Americans, or to what extent it was prompted by a sense of duty, as well as an instinct for self-preservation under threatening circumstances. That many, if not most, kept their heads throughout the wartime hysteria is at least suggested by Charles A. Lindbergh, Sr.'s surprisingly narrow loss of the Republican nomination for governor of Minnesota in 1918 to the super-patriotic Governor Burnquist— despite bitter attacks against him for his defense of neutrality.[13]

Belief in America's cause in the war was greatly reinforced by President Wilson's Fourteen Points for a just peace in Europe. Swedish-American newspapers, following the armistice in November 1918, opposed a vengeful policy toward Germany and appealed for a fair and lasting peace settlement. So much the greater was their disillusionment with the Peace of Versailles in June 1919.[14]

A major consequence of World War I was the breakdown of the tsarist regime and the Russian Revolution in 1917, leading to the establishment of the Soviet Union and the Communist International. In the United States a widespread red scare followed—and largely evolved out of—wartime chauvinism. Socialism in any form was viewed as foreign by the great majority of Americans, including Swedish Americans, and the foreign-born indeed played a prominent role in America's small socialist parties, as well as in the new American Communist party organized in 1920. Led by Attorney General Mitchell Palmer, a veritable witchhunt of known or suspected leftists ensued, culminating with the highly-publicized Sacco-Vanzetti trial in Boston in 1920–21. In the process, the fragile structure of organized Swedish-American political and labor radicalism was largely swept away.[15]

A glimpse into that largely forgotten world is provided by a now almost totally unknown novel by Sophia I. Wakkure (actually Carlson), published presumably in the early 1920s by an organization called the Scandinavian Workers' Educational Society in Chicago. It is evidently a fictionalized account of the experiences of its author, a Swedish-speaking working-class immigrant from Finland. Its Swedish heroine, slaving at menial jobs through the war and immediate postwar years, is converted from gradualist social-ism to militant communism by the blatant evils of American capitalism. Wakkure recalls the radicalism of Henry von Kræmer a few years earlier, although she was a true proletarian who remained in America and an outspoken feminist. But as a committed propagandist for the cause, she acknowledged no redeeming features in American society.[16]

Since the 1890s organized efforts had been made, especially in the urban areas of the industrialized Eastern states in response to heavy Southern and Eastern European immigration, to ease the assimilation of the newcomers by teaching them English and civics, usually through evening classes. As such instruction was to their benefit and did not infringe upon their ethnic life, it was generally welcomed by immigrant groups. The war turned the movement into a veritable "Americanization Crusade," dominated by chauvinist zealots who were determined to push forward even after the armistice in November 1918. The rising fear of Bolshevism and foreign subversion gave fresh impetus to the crusade, which continued unabated into the early 1920s, strongly backed by such groups as the American

Legion and the revived Ku Klux Klan. Several more states now passed legislation restricting the use of foreign languages, particularly in the teaching of common school subjects. Ultimately twenty-two states enacted laws of this type between 1918 and 1920, the year they were voided by the Supreme Court.

The efforts of the extreme Americanizers became increasingly offensive to America's immigrant population, allegedly contributing to the exceptionally heavy return migration, particularly to southern and eastern Europe, during the immediate postwar years. This gave rise to growing concern among industrial employers of labor. In 1919 an Interracial Council was established, including representatives of big business and of numerous immigrant nationalities, to oppose immigration restrictions and to encourage immigrants to remain in the United States. At a conference in April 1920 the council denounced nativist bigotry and urged a sympathetic attitude toward the foreign-born. By the following year both the red scare and the Americanization crusade had run their course. An exhibition in New York, "America's Making," in 1921, stressed the contributions of the nation's various ethnic communities, with substantial Swedish-American participation.[17]

The Americanization drive, with its growing xenophobia, created painful tensions within the Swedish-American community: Swedish Americans were long accustomed to considering themselves the "best Americanizers" among America's immigrant groups, needing no outside encouragement, but they also possessed a proud heritage of their own. They could both bay with the hounds and run with the hares. While some courageously stood up for their rights, it did not escape notice that, for instance, three state legislators of Swedish origin, including one born in Sweden, voted for the notorious Oregon language law in 1920.

Both restrictive American language legislation and what could appear to be Swedish-American acquiescence to such a policy aroused the towering indignation of the RFSBU in Sweden. Vilhelm Lundström filled the pages of its biweekly *Allsvensk samling* with alarming reports of a veritable Reign of Terror in the United States. These were largely based on information received from concerned Swedish Americans, yet they in turn provoked angry rejoinders from others, as will be seen.[18]

The outburst of antiforeign sentiment triggered by war and revolution had long been brewing in response to an unrestrained immigration of what seemed truly alarming proportions. There had long been much public outcry against the rising threat to America's traditional values and way of life.

A literacy test for prospective immigrants, first proposed in Congress in 1897, was finally passed over President Wilson's veto in 1917. Discussion of the immigration question meanwhile assumed an increasingly racial focus, based on the assumption of the superiority of the Northern European peoples. This viewpoint received its most influential expression in Madison Grant's widely read book, *The Passing of the Great Race* in 1916. In its assumption of race as the inner dynamic of history, of the superiority of the Nordic peoples ("the Great Race") in intelligence, enterprise, and daring, and in its concern for their decimation through war, excessively hot climates, and miscegenation with inferior breeds, it shows a remarkable similarity to the ideas of the Swede Gustaf Thyreen in 1911. According to Grant, the American nation had forfeited its "birthright" of Nordic racial purity by opening its doors to unrestricted immigration to gain cheap labor. His purpose was to warn his countrymen against holding to a misguided, sentimental liberalism that gravely imperiled America's continued greatness. He meanwhile regarded the Scandinavians as splendid human material and recognized Sweden as the home of the purest Nordic type. In 1922, Kenneth Roberts spoke out in the *Saturday Evening Post* against a laissez-faire policy of immigration and racial crossbreeding; the "mixture of Nordic with Alpine and Mediterranean stocks," he declared, "would produce only a worthless race of hybrids." The Ku Klux Klan, revived in 1915, agitated not only for "white" but for "Nordic" supremacy. In New England, and most likely elsewhere as well, the Klan had considerable Swedish-American support.[19]

When the literacy test of 1917 failed to reduce immigration significantly, such pressures, magnified by an economic slump during the immediate postwar years, induced Congress to pass America's first quota law in 1921, which permitted the annual immigration of 3 percent of each nationality (excluding Orientals) in the United States in 1910, with exceptions allowed for close relatives. Reactions in the Swedish-American press were mixed. Already in discussing the literacy test in 1917, *Svenska Amerikanaren* of Chicago had declared: "If restrictions are made on the immigration laws, they can only be of benefit to the whole country. The present restrictions are sparing us from the ignorant, superstitious hordes from Southern Europe who live under the sway of the Pope." It favored the Quota Law of 1921 from the start. Others, such as *Svenska Kuriren,* also in Chicago, were at first hesitant but were soon won over.[20]

The quota of 1921 proved no obstacle to the sudden heavy immigration from Sweden in 1923, which came to 24,948 persons, as compared with only 8,445 the year before and 7,036 the year after. This final spurt doubtless represented the release of an accumulated demand: persons who had previously planned to emigrate but had been held up by the war and economic hard times on both sides of the Atlantic since its end. Many, moreover, were surely anxious to get to the United States before quotas were reduced even further—as they were already the following year.[21]

Following the Quota Law of 1921 there was renewed agitation to reduce immigration even further, with racial arguments playing an increasingly prominent part. In 1924 Congress enacted a new law reflecting a clear North-European bias: annual immigration was restricted to 2 percent of each nationality in the census of 1890, which was dominated by the "Old Immigration." Again, this was generally accepted by the Swedish-American press. After some hesitation, *Svenska Kuriren* endorsed the new quota as advantageous to those immigrants actually desired in America, while condemning Polish and Italian protests as both unjustified and "considerably presumptuous." That the Swedish-American press reaction to immigration restriction was still so lukewarm O. Fritiof Ander would also later attribute to the apprehensions of older Swedish Americans regarding the politically radical and irreligious attitudes of many recent immigrants from the homeland.[22]

The 1924 law, however, included the Reed Amendment, which allowed for further adjustment of immigration quotas. This led to the National Origins Act of 1927, which set total annual immigration at 150,000, apportioned between nationalities according to their share of the "foreign stock" shown in the 1920 census. This meant a drastic reduction in the quotas for Germany, the Irish Free State, and the Scandinavian countries, together with a large increase for Great Britain, as well as increases for certain Southern and Eastern European countries. For Sweden, the quota shrank from 9,561 under the 1924 law, to 3,314, under the National Origins Act, which went into effect in 1929.[23]

Predictably, there was an indignant outcry in the Swedish-American press. *Svenska Kuriren,* on 10 June 1926, urged its readers to write their congressmen to preserve the 1924 Quota Law, "unless they seriously believe that the Swedes, whose family of settlers and nation-builders had worked side by side with Norwegian, Danish, and German pioneers in setting star after star in the American flag, were less worthy and less desirable . . . than the Russians, Italians, and English." *Svea* in Worcester, Massachusetts, on 26 October 1927, denounced the new restrictions as "idiotic and unjust." Carl J. Bengston asked indignantly in *The Lutheran Companion* on 26 October 1929: "Can anyone calculate wherein the United States will be benefitted by the immigration of more Italians, Poles and Irish [*sic*], Belgians and Dutch, and by reducing the quota of Germans and Scandinavians?"[24]

Beneath the implied humiliation of those long accustomed to regarding themselves as America's best immigrants there lay deeper fears. If the 1924 quota were not retained, *Augustana* warned on 17 June 1926, "all our socially constructive Swedish-American institutions, including the press, societies, fraternal orders, churches, old people's homes and orphanages— in a word, all that the Swedish Americans from the earliest times down to the present have with such great sacrifices built up, will slowly but surely wither and die." *Nordstjernan* in New York predicted, on 28 May 1929, the end of Swedish America.[25] The handwriting, it seemed, was on the wall. Just as the Swedish-American press reacted strongly against the new quota of 1927, it likewise protested against the National Society Against Emigration and its activities in Sweden, which similarly strove to cut off its life blood.[26]

Ultimately, however, the decline in Swedish emigration resulted neither from American legislation nor from the Swedish anti-emigration campaign. Except in 1926, Swedish immigration to the United States remained well under quota to the end of the decade. The real reasons lay in Sweden's growing economy, rising standard of living, and social welfare policies throughout these years. For those who still felt the urge to emigrate, Canada now offered an increasingly attractive alternative to the United States. Throughout the 1920s and 1930s, moreover, numbers of Swedish and other Scandinavian Americans, most by now American citizens, migrated north to make new homes in Western Canada.

With the end of World War I there was a recovery of nerve in Swedish America. The Americanization campaign so zealously promoted by Edwin Bjorkman and others gradually faded away. Meanwhile the press was free once again to speak out. Swedish-American newspapers condemned "100% Americanism" and demands for immediate Americanization as insulting to the country's foreign-born who had fought for their new homeland and deserved full recognition for their part in the victory. *Svenska Kuriren* in January 1920 blamed the war for having awakened "all the slumbering passions of class hate, bigotry, and desire to suppress others." *Augustana* consistently opposed restrictive language legislation, while the *Lutheran Companion*'s Swedish-born editor, Carl J. Bengston, an outspoken supporter of English in the church, repeatedly attacked the excesses of the Americanization campaign, once the war was over. "In the United States, in the twentieth century," Bengston wrote in November 1919, "there are those who consider it disloyal to speak any other tongue than English. Surely we will be outstripped in the race for supremacy along every line of human activity when we put a premium on ignorance."[27]

Organizational Swedish America on the whole weathered the storm well. This was particularly true of the churches, which had been growing in membership during the prewar years and—except for the Swedish Methodists—did so even after the onset of the Depression in 1930. Membership in the Augustana Lutheran Synod went from 179,204 in 1906, to 204,417 in 1916, to 311,425 in 1926. The Mission Covenant increased its fold from an estimated 29,147 in 1915, to 44,352 in 1932. This growth was furthered by an increased use of English in religious services. At the same time, the Swedish denominations strove to preserve their specifically Swedish-American character. In 1918, the Augustana Synod declared its independence from the Lutheran General Council, to which it had belonged since 1867, in order better to preserve its ethnic identity. When in

1930 Archbishop Nathan Söderblom, Sweden's primate, presented the synod with a bishop's cross as a gift from Sweden's bishops, there was strong opposition to accepting it to avoid any appearance of hierarchy or subordination.[28]

The secular societies likewise continued to thrive throughout the 1920s. The three large, federated mutual benefits societies, the Vikings, Svithiod, and especially the Vasa Order, assumed an ever more dominant role. The latter organization reached its peak in 1930, with over 72,000 members in 17 districts and 438 local lodges. Meanwhile, a wide proliferation of special-interest societies, for temperance, singing, folk dancing, sports, and other activities flourished throughout the 1920s.[29]

In one important area, meanwhile, cultural Swedish America failed to regain its full vitality from the prewar period: the Swedish-language press. In 1915 Swedish-American journalism was at its all-time high, with 72 newspapers and a total reported circulation of 651,430. Popular suspicion against anything foreign during America's involvement in the war cut badly into circulation, causing many publications to merge or go under. By 1919 there remained 63 newspapers with a circulation of 470,693, and the figures continued to decline, to 43 papers and 363,185 subscribers in 1930. With the onset of the Depression the attrition would become more precipitous.[30]

The decline was qualitative as well. By November 1918, when the monthly *Ungdomsvännen* ceased publication, having been preceded by the monthly *Valkyrian* in 1909 and the yearbook *Prärieblomman* in 1912, Swedish America no longer possessed the kind of high-quality literary and general interest periodical that had played so prominent a cultural role since the 1890s. Interested Swedish Americans were now dependent on English-language American publications for intellectual fare. There was similarly a steady decline in Swedish book publishing in America.[31]

By the 1920s Swedish America's cultural leadership was at last compelled to confront squarely the perplexing question of how to preserve the Swedish heritage in America—as well as which aspects of it—beyond the passing of the immigrant generation. Not surprisingly, opinion could be both ambivalent and sharply divided in both respects.

For most, language remained the crux of the matter. But here the U.S. censuses gives their inexorable evidence: those reporting Swedish as their mother tongue declined from 683,218 in 1910, to 643,203 in 1920, to 615,465 in 1930. In the latter year, moreover, only 1.5 percent of the Swedish-born over ten years of age could not speak English.[32] How widespread varying degrees of bilingualism may have remained throughout these decades the censuses do not reveal.

This development created a particularly difficult quandary for the churches. Traditionally they had championed the retention of Swedish as their language of worship and, as much as possible, as a living tongue within the Swedish-American community. Yet they had long been uncomfortably aware that they could, and did, lose younger members if they held too obdurately to the old language. If they were to weather the generational shift, concessions were unavoidable.

As noted, some congregations adopted varying forms of bilingualism during the prewar years, and in 1908 an Association of English Churches had been formed within the Augustana Synod. It became ever clearer that the faith must take precedence over language. As Pastor A. T. Seashore put it at the association's first meeting, "It is not that we love Swedish less, but that we love souls more."[33] Language was the medium, not the message.

The war increased tensions within the churches. "Shall we go on and dream of preserving a Swedish church in America until other churches have taken all our children?" asked Reverend Samuel M. Miller in the *Lutheran Companion* in December 1917. "Some of us who were born and brought up in this country do not at all feel that it is our duty to preserve Swedish culture and the Swedish language in America, but rather to inject all the inherited good things into the stream of American life by means of the language that America speaks and understands. . . . Oh! my dear Augustana Synod, is the future worth nothing to thee? Wilt thou insist on being blind to *the inevitable*"? Already in March that year Daniel Gottfrid took a more belligerent stance in the same church periodical. "Is it not a fact," he asked, "that provincialism is engendered and perpetuated in this country by keeping up the traditions and customs, particularly the languages, of the different European countries? This makes it difficult to unite in national thought and national movements. . . . I believe that those who are not willing to be loyal American citizens and drop the 'hyphen' ought to go back to the country from which they came. We can be loyal to only one country."

At its convocation of 1921, the Augustana Synod was greatly concerned with the problem of Swedish descendants who did not understand Swedish. Its Illinois Conference, meeting the following year, declared that its older members were aware of the demands of the times and realized that "the Lord can speak to their hearts even in English." Henceforward the Synod was ever more sensitive to the needs of its younger, as opposed to its older, membership. Generational change occurred within the ministry as well as the laity. Whereas up to 1914 most of the pastors ordained by the Augustana Synod had been Swedish-born, thereafter an ever-growing majority were American-born.[34]

Language policy nonetheless remained the bone of heated contention within the synod and beyond. Deep concern was expressed, not so much over the use of English where needed as over what many saw as an overly hasty abandonment of Swedish. This view was, for instance, eloquently expressed and widely disseminated by the Swedish-American press in a series of ten articles by leading representatives of various denominations and secular organizations between January and August 1922. The growing impatience of the all-out Americanizers within the Augustana Synod was meanwhile given forceful expression in the *Lutheran Companion* by Pastor J. E. Chester, who declared in April 1924, "If we mistake not, [the Church's] mission is the propagation of Christianity, and not the preservation of the national identity of a few Swedes." Because of their obduracy over language, he claimed, many congregations were now "stunted and dwarfed," thus "the sooner some of these 'liability' congregations fire the Swedish language and the national identity idea to the scrap heap the better for all concerned."[35]

The transition naturally took time, and living memory supplements an often scanty documentation to confirm that debate was frequently most intense at the grassroots level, in individual congregations directly confronted with the issues involved. In some cases the problem dragged out over many years, as in the Augustana Lutheran congregation in DeKalb, Illinois, where it remained a bone of contention from 1914 to 1940. By 1924 the passions aroused prompted Emeroy Johnson to observe in the *Lutheran Companion* that "this narrow-mindedness among people on both sides of the language problem constitutes a greater problem for our synod than the language problem itself."[36]

The 1920s saw the crucial crossover in the language usage of the Swedish-American denominations. Around 1930 subscriptions to the English-language *Lutheran Companion* for the first time surpassed those of the Swedish-language *Augustana,* both published by the Augustana Book Concern. In 1931 the Augustana Synod dissolved its Association of English Churches on the grounds that it was no longer needed.[37]

Still, some qualifications are necessary. In 1930, of 1,250 Augustana Lutheran congregations, only 150 used English exclusively, even though practically none remained entirely Swedish in language. Indeed, an editorial in *Augustana* in April 1924 opposed the idea of purely Swedish-speaking congregations since the segregation of older from younger generations would more quickly lead to the demise of Swedish in the church. In a number of cities Swedish-language radio ministries began to fill new needs for older worshipers. On the East Coast, particularly within the New England Conference of the Augustana Synod, where Swedish immigration was more recent and the Swedish-born element both proportionately more numerous and younger than in the Middle West, the language shift lagged by at least a decade. Among the Swedish Baptists and Methodists, whose survival as separate entities within larger American denominations was essentially dependent upon language, as well as within the Mission Covenant, resistance was more determined and change proceeded more slowly.[38]

The churches' retreat in the language issue was a hard blow to Vilhelm Lundström and the Society for the Preservation of Swedish Culture in Foreign Lands, accustomed as they were to regarding the Augustana Synod in particular as the bastion of the Swedish heritage in America. The society's journal, *Allsvensk samling,* had sternly criticized the Swedish Americans for what it considered their craven acceptance of America's wartime language restrictions, and Vilhelm Lundström soon thereafter rejoined the fray by accusing the Augustana Synod of abandoning the Swedish cause at the very time when Sweden and its culture were rising in international esteem. These attacks could not fail to arouse intense resentment among the Swedish-American clergy.

There were meanwhile those in Swedish America who felt, on the contrary, that *svenskhet*—Swedish language and culture—was being suffocated by the too close embrace of the churches, especially of the Augustana Synod. This was naturally a sensitive issue, but in 1909 G. N. Malm of Lindsborg, Kansas, had raised it in his novel *Charli Johnson,* with its depiction of a narrow-minded Nebraska pastor. In later correspondence with G. N. Swan in Iowa, Malm squarely condemned a pietistic puritanism which regarded any form of cultural activity outside its own immediate purview as sinful. "Herein lies the greatest obstacle to the preservation of the Swedish heritage," he wrote in 1921.

> One may point this out with the greatest respect for religion and for church activity in general. . . . Religion is one thing, the Swedish heritage something quite different. It denotes tradition, history, a particular culture, a particular folklore, and much besides which has not the least to do with religion. These concepts ought not be confused, but we are not likely to make any progress in Lindsborg precisely because these ideas are mixed together to the extent that the Swedish heritage means nothing more nor less than pure and unadulterated Lutheran doctrine and faith. Anything beyond this is EVIL.[39]

Among the secular organizations, the situation was more complex. Various of the older ones came increasingly to conceive their purpose as the cultivation of the Swedish heritage, to fill the widening gap left by the churches. And various new societies appeared specifically for this purpose. Yet here, too, the larger regional and national organizations could disregard generational change only at their peril. The Grand Lodge of the Vasa Order first discussed the language question in 1917 but held fast to Swedish. By 1923 it permitted its local lodges to use English if need be. Similar changes occurred, generally after much debate, in the Viking and Svithiod Orders.[40] In smaller, local, special-interest groups, especially in the East, it would seem most likely that change occurred more slowly.

Eloquent appeals were heard in Swedish America for the preservation of the Swedish language. Of these, the most passionate was surely a forty-four-page pamphlet published in 1923 by Professor J. S. Carlson of Gustavus Adolphus College, who in 1908 had written in pathetic tones of the passing of "America's Last Swede." All nationalities, he declared, contributed to the making of America and should thus claim for themselves, while allowing to others, the right to preserve what was best in their own heritages. He bitterly attacked the "Know-Nothingism" of the recent war years and the "Prussianism" of banning foreign languages at the very time when America was fighting against Germany. The new chauvinism reflected "the old English short-sightedness and narrow-mindedness, which has become in-grown even here," Carlson maintained. "But to hold to such stupidity is un-American."

A people's language expressed its culture and values, even in the case of dead languages such as Latin.

> One thing is certain: the spirit that dwells within the *Swedish* language, which is moreover a *living* language in body and soul, a beautiful and glorious language—*that* spirit stands in full harmony with the spirit that has prevailed, prevails, and should prevail in this, our new homeland. Sweden is freedom's *birthplace* on earth and America is freedom's great, new *homeland* on earth, and it was the Swedes who brought freedom from its *birthplace* to its *homeland.*

The Swedish Americans, Carlson declared, were "in heart and soul Americans before we came here, otherwise we would not have come. ... The Swede does not need to be Americanized in his political views and ways of thinking, nor in patriotism either, for in these respects he is American when he arrives: he comes *from* a free country *to* a free country. ... No one need therefore remind us that we *are,* much less urge us to *become,* Americans—we were Americans long before the prophets of the newborn Americanism existed."

The Swedes learned English willingly and well as the necessary common language of the land, but this should not mean abandoning Swedish. They were not "guests and outsiders" in America since they possessed "original rights" in the land where their tongue was no more foreign than English. To abandon one's attachment to one's own heritage meant "spiritual death." The mother tongue was the "language of the heart."[41] The United States now led the way toward an even larger world community. How well this noble experiment might succeed, Carlson held, would ultimately depend upon how well America managed to form its own cosmopolitan community and culture at home.[42]

Among the more dedicated defenders of Swedish language and culture in America, the physician Johannes Hoving and his wife Helga in New York played a particularly noteworthy role—all the more noteworthy, indeed, since neither came originally from Sweden. Dr. Hoving was born in Finland, in the traditionally cosmopolitan city of Viborg (Viipuri), near St. Petersburg. His wife, Helga (née Adamsen), was born in Copenhagen of partly Swedish but mainly Danish descent, although she enjoyed a successful career on the Swedish stage before marrying her Finland-Swedish husband. In 1903 the couple was forced to flee Finland due to Dr. Hoving's clandestine activities against the Russification campaign. When a brief stay in Sweden did not bring to light any promising prospects, they reluctantly emigrated the same year to New York.

They remained there until 1934 and soon became passionately involved in Swedish-related activities. These were so all-encompassing that the visiting Swedish journalist Erland Richter doubted in 1923 that they had ever yet dreamed a dream in English. "If so," he added, "they plead for absolution." At the beginning of World War I, before America's entry, Johannes Hoving was outspoken in his support of the German cause and American neutrality; this in time brought unpleasant social consequences. Meanwhile, in 1916, the Hovings joined Vasa Order of America in New York.[43] The St. Erik Lodge, to which they belonged, became the chosen forum for their crusade in defence of *svenskhet* in America, reinforced by an elite inner circle, S:t Eriks Förbundet (the Saint Erik Society). Their activities, Johannes Hoving proudly recalled, were not regarded kindly by many Swedish Americans, who prematurely considered their cause a lost one.[44]

Dr. Hoving became a frequent, featured speaker at Vasa Order and other Swedish-American functions in the Northeast, as well as a contributor to both Swedish and Swedish-American newspapers. He was convinced that following the wartime hysteria, Swedish-American pride and self-assertiveness were once again on the rise. He was thus strongly critical of the Swedish-American churches, especially of the Augustana Synod, for their weak-willed concessions in the language question; in his view, their historic mission was at least as much cultural as spiritual. He therefore placed his greatest hopes in the secular societies, above all the Vasa Order, which he wished might ultimately unify the whole Swedish-American community, while serving as the new bulwark of Swedish language and culture.[45]

In 1921, Helga Hoving established the Vasa Order's first children's group within the St. Erik Lodge. This was followed shortly by another in Brooklyn. Through the 1920s and 1930s the Hovings became increasingly convinced that Swedish language and culture could only be perpetuated by inculcating them at an early age. In this regard, parents had a moral obligation, as Johannes Hoving declared in a speech in New York shortly after the end of the war.

By keeping to Swedish as their conversational language with their children, parents are also able to maintain a certain authority over them, for the children will only later, if they make the effort, gain as great, or greater, proficiency in Swedish than their parents have. If, meanwhile, we speak English with them, they most often gain a certain ascendancy over us and feel themselves superior, if, for instance, we do not speak the proper American English they learn in school. And in this way can the first unwitting step be taken in the wrong direction ... through false reasoning they may then get the distorted idea that Sweden and everything Swedish are inferior to everything American in other respects as well.[46]

Swedish children's clubs would provide a powerful support to parental authority. Writing in *Nordstjernan* (New York) of the first public performance by Helga's little group in January 1921, Hoving explained: "In this manner, through Swedish children's songs, through the recitation of the works of Swedish poets and authors, and through the performance of Swedish folk dances and dance-games, it will be possible to awaken the minds and hearts of the children to the glories of the ancient Swedish culture—and the children will not be lost to the Swedish heritage."[47]

For the Hovings, the preservation of Swedish language and culture was a self-evident end in itself. Beyond that, Johannes Hoving's thinking is somewhat unclear. Like many at the time, he was strongly influenced by theories of Nordic racial superiority, and in 1922 he enthusiastically hailed "the world's first institute for racial biology" in Uppsala, under Professor Herman Lundborg, the prophet of a movement present-day Swedes would just as soon forget. Swedish Americans, he declared in a speech in Worcester, Massachusetts, in July 1922, should change their thinking about their own race, "so that we do not regard ourselves, for instance, as closer to Americans of other racial origins than to those of our own blood." He meanwhile expressed increasingly anti-Semitic views. For the Swedish element to contribute most greatly to making America a "stronger and nobler nation," he declared in 1922, Swedish Americans must keep their ancestral culture vital and their blood strains pure.[48]

For all their dedicated vision, the Hovings ultimately had only limited impact upon Swedish America. Throughout, their attitude was essentially "overseas-Swedish," in keeping with the viewpoint of the Society for the Preservation of Swedish Culture in Foreign Lands, rather than Swedish-American. As Dr. Hoving expressed it in January 1923: "Common descent has united all who have the same language, the same cultural development, and the same historic memories. He need not be regarded as a worse Swede, who by Fate's decree has been born in a land or part of the world other than Sweden, so long as he or she is of Swedish blood and has Swedish interests." To add point to this assertion, he spoke of the unshakable loyalty of the ancient Swedish element in Finland and Estonia, which likewise so greatly inspired the RFSBU and its "All-Swedish" ideal. Indeed, he was a unique example of an aspiring leader of America's Swedish community imbued with the fortress mentality of self-conscious historic ethnic minorities in the Eastern European borderlands.[49]

The Hovings' social ambitions were meanwhile as great as their cultural commitment. They moved in elite, cultivated Swedish circles in the greater New York area, beyond which they seldom strayed; it seems questionable whether they ever once ventured into the Midwestern Swedish-American heartland. They were avid for recognition, acclaim, and honor in the land where neither of them had been born, but which for both ever remained the home of their dreams and aspirations. Their contacts with Swedish America as a whole remained remote and in large degree mutually uncomprehending.

The distance was great—literally and figuratively—from the Hovings in Manhattan to G. N. Malm, the author of *Charli Johnson* in 1909, on the Kansas prairie. In 1919 Malm published a play, *Härute* (Out Here), for production in Lindsborg. His title unmistakably alluded to that of the Swedish writer Henning Berger's Chicago stories, *Därute* (Out There) from 1901; in contrast to Berger's sinister urban environment and European distaste for American values, Malm offered a healthful rural setting and a Swedish-American revindication of American ideals. The melodramatic plot concerns the frustration of a large oil company's attempt to exploit a small Kansas community.

The play meanwhile dwells at length upon the immigrant condition in America and the language question, expressing a resigned yet hopeful realism that stands in striking contrast to the intransigence of the cultural conservatives, such as J. S. Carlson and the Hovings. A revealing dialogue discusses the immigrant's situation:

INGRID: . . . And so during this time we have grown apart from them back home, for the more we become accustomed to conditions here, the more time they have, back home, to grow away from us, and with each day that passes the gap becomes wider and the distance longer. We have to remember that we change, we are no longer the same as we were. . . . Emigration, when it is real and for good, is a tragedy. One does violence to the noblest thing one has, love for home place and homeland. One pulls oneself up by the roots and throws oneself recklessly out into the world's tumult. One loses the sustenance of one's place on earth.

BORG: That is a beautiful thought . . . but we must not look at it that way. We must not let ourselves be frightened and we must not be too sensitive, for then we will get nowhere. We have come here to do good, each one in his own way, each with his pound. There at home we received our deep impressions, all of which have their great significance. . . . Why should not we be the bearers of culture, as well as other nations? How should the American race, if it is eventually to become a special race or nation of its own, be formed or cast if we Swedes do not contribute what we have that is beautiful and valuable? . . . If we rightly understand our task, we can do just as much here as back home, if we are true to our calling.[50]

The local pastor (seemingly modeled on Alfred Bergin) meanwhile represents a narrow, old-fashioned ecclesiastic conservatism in cultural matters which Borg, the leading character, considers to have done more harm than good. "You pastors keep harping all the time on preserving the language. . . . If you seek to uphold high Swedish here among our people, you are building on air. How can one demand that someone preserve what he has never possessed? The emigrant has as little to do with high Swedish as he does with Strindberg's books and Lindblad's songs."

When the pastor protests that the clergy have done what they could to preserve Swedish, Borg disagrees. "Not all you were able to do, but all you considered compatible with your interests. That you have done. You have kept within the framework of what was purely ecclesiastical and religious, and have forced upon the young people a catechism Swedish that is as boring and incomprehensible now as it was in my childhood. . . . That kind of thing arouses neither interest in nor love for the language." The good Swedish-American literary periodicals, such as *Prärieblomman* and *Ungdomsvännen*, need not have gone under if the clergy had given them their wholehearted support. Nor did the clergy support the Swedish-American newspapers unless they held orthodox religious views.[51] Borg then puts his hopes in the academic study of Swedish "as a beautiful and useful language, here and in every land," as well as in the American-Scandinavian Foundation's promotion of the translation of Sweden's literary treasures into English. In effect, Malm could envision the inevitable passing of the old immigrant ethnicity, based upon direct experience of the life of common people in the Old Country, and its replacement by a new understanding of and appreciation for Sweden's higher culture, both among Swedish descendants and within American society as a whole.[52] The contrast between the cultural optimism of Malm's *Charli Johnson* in 1909 and the wistful resignation of his *Härute* in 1919 is a measure of the divide separating prewar from postwar Swedish America.

If World War I had revealed to many old immigrants that God also understood English, it also perhaps made it easier to think the unthinkable regarding the marriage of language and heritage. President David Nyvall of North Park College represented much the same view as Malm in a letter to *Augustana* in 1921.

> By the preservation of the Swedish heritage we mean a cultural responsibility which we have inherited and hold from the land of our fathers, and which we cannot in conscience abandon because we have moved here. We do not so much mean the use of Swedish in daily conversation as its application in the widest sense as our contribution to the great, total sum of American idealism. We mean the translation in word and deed of Swedish thought, Swedish will, Swedish dreams, which we have brought here with us as our true riches. We mean the planting in American soil of seed which we have not only brought with us, but are.[53]

Since the 1890s a number of thoughtful and sensitive works had been written by Swedish Americans, and in some cases by Swedes, seeking to analyze and define Swedish America and the Swedish Americans. With due allowance for G. N. Malm's play, *Härute,* in 1919, such efforts were far fewer and markedly less original after the abrupt end of Swedish America's golden age in 1917.

The most ambitious example of this genre the 1920s could show in America was a twenty-nine-page booklet by Vilhelm Berger, published in Brooklyn in 1924. This brief, aphoristic essay reiterated what, over the past three decades, had become the well-established and conventional Swedish self-image, in both its positive and negative features, as well as its adaptation to American conditions. As elsewhere in his writings, Berger was concerned over the general monotony and superficiality of his countrymen's social and cultural activities in America.[54]

If the 1920s showed little original thought regarding the contemporary Swedish-American scene, they reveal a growing concern over preserving the cultural heritage of the past. The Society for the Preservation of Swedish Culture in America, following a slow start after its founding in 1910 and the suspension of its activity during America's involvement in World War I, achieved a modest development during the 1920s, with chapters in several towns and cities devoted to the study of Swedish literary and artistic culture. *Landskapsföreningar,* or provincial societies, flourished as never before during these years, culminating with the establishment in Chicago of a national federation of such groups, *Svensk-Amerikanska Hembygdsförbundet,* in 1929. Rising enrollments in Swedish language courses at Swedish-American colleges and state universities are noted throughout the decade.[55]

The Swedish heritage was bolstered meanwhile by the increasing commercialization of ethnic entertainment. The only Swedish-American roadshow to support itself entirely through its box-office receipts over a period of years, led by the legendary rustic comedian Hjalmar Peterson, alias "Olle i Skratthult," performed in Swedish-American communities, large and small, throughout the decade. A number of visiting artists from Sweden toured the United States. Gramophone records of Swedish folk and popular songs became widely available, while Swedish films, particularly rural folk comedies, could be seen in movie theaters in larger Swedish-American urban centers. Swedish radio programs went on the air. Certain Swedish publications, including handsomely illustrated Christmas yearbooks (*julkalendrar*) and popular periodicals featuring inspirational and light fictional fare for a largely rural readership were familiar in America by the 1920s, doubtless largely as gifts from relatives back home.[56]

An independent historical compilation from these years meanwhile deserves particular mention. In 1930, the year of his death, the veteran journalist Ernst Skarstedt, building upon an earlier work from 1897, brought out in Sweden his *Pennfäktare,* that indispensable work of reference on the lives and works of Swedish America's remarkable profusion of poets, authors, and journalists. Without these labors of love, our picture of Swedish-American cultural life would be immeasurably the poorer.[57]

The years between 1917 and 1930 were the great divide in the history of the Swedes in America. In 1917 Swedish America still represented a natural, inherent ethnicity, based primarily upon the living experience, customs, values, and language of Swedish-born immigrants, constantly reinforced by fresh blood from the homeland. By 1930 the Swedish-born were significantly fewer, older, and generally more assimilated into the American mainstream. As Ingrid said in G. N. Malm's *Härute,* "During this time we have grown away from them back home ... we are no longer what we were." Swedish ethnicity in America was by then well on its way to becoming a matter of personal sentiment, family tradition, and vague nostalgia, no longer strictly tied to ancestral customs or language, an attachment that varied, not only from one person to another, but even with changing times and circumstances within the lifetime of an individual.[58]

SEVENTEEN

A Changing Sweden and the Swedish Americans

If the fortunes of the National Society Against Emigration may be taken as a basic indicator, the anti-emigration movement in Sweden peaked by 1917. Membership in the society had climbed steeply since its foundation in 1907 and now totaled nearly 16,000. Thereafter it fell off just as precipitously. In 1920 there were some 12,500 members; by 1925 there were less than 3,000 when the organization, still under Adrian Molin's leadership, changed its name to *Sällskapet Hem i Sverige,* the Society for Homes in Sweden, and devoted itself entirely to land transactions and homebuilding. By 1941, at the end of its existence, only 337 life members remained.[1]

It may seem curious that the National Society gained its greatest support three years after the beginning of World War I had drastically reduced emigration from Sweden. It was, however, almost universally believed that the end of the war would signal the resumption of emigration on a massive scale.[2] Surely, too, Sweden's precarious neutrality in wartime demonstrated the potential dangers of a future shortage of manpower, while creating a heightened sense of patriotism and self-sacrifice.

The rapid decline of the National Society reflects the fact that such fears were not realized. The excitement of the crisis years passed. Although times were difficult in Sweden during the immediate postwar years, they were also hard in the United States. Swedish emigration remained at low levels through 1922, largely counterbalanced by high return migration. Thus, while total Swedish emigration to the United States came to 24,353 persons between 1919 and 1922, the net emigration amounted to no more than 8,110.[3] In the meantime, the first American quota law was passed in 1921. The final spurt in 1923, when 24,948 Swedes emigrated to America, was clearly motivated in large part by panicky concerns to get in before a new, reduced quota took effect. The 1924 restrictions were further tightened in 1927.

There was manifestly no further need for concerted efforts to discourage emigration. On the contrary, anxieties of a very different kind soon arose, which further undermined the society's support. Severe unemployment in the early postwar period, together with the prospect that large cohorts of children born around 1910 would soon join the labor market, gave rise to serious apprehensions over the closing off of emigration outlets abroad. As the official review of the society's accomplishments put it in 1932:

> The emigration question has, meanwhile, not lost its significance, but it has changed its character to the extent that it may be seen as an important national need that the country's younger generations may also train and acquire experience in foreign lands, that outposts may be established and maintained out there for Swedish trade and export, and so that our old colonies do not pine away and lose contact with the motherland due to a complete lack of new Swedish blood.[4]

In 1922 a conference was held, with representation from the National Society itself, to consider continued possibilities for some degree of emigration in the future. In 1923 the Social Democrat, Carl Lindhagen, moved in the Riksdag that the government investigate "suitable places of settlement" in "colonial lands." It may be recalled that his father, Albert Lindhagen, had made a similar motion in the Riksdag in 1869 for directed emigration to North America.

Much attention was given to seeking out opportunities abroad for Sweden's excess of engineers and other qualified experts. Throughout the 1920s numerous private schemes for agricultural colonies in such places as Canada, Australia, South Africa, and Argentina were bruited about. "We have now gradually come to realize in Sweden," Fredrik Lindskog wrote in the RFSBU's yearbook for 1925, "that stopping our emigration is neither possible nor, under existing conditions, is it even desirable."[5] Although no organized colonial enterprises resulted, emigration to such destinations did take place. Canada, at least temporarily, attracted many who might otherwise have gone to the United States.

It is nonetheless the measure of Sweden's dynamic economic development and expanding social services that during the course of the decade it was able to provide not only employment but a rising standard of living for its large and growing labor force, a process in which the emigration safety valve played only a very marginal role.[6]

The situation around 1920 is thus replete with ironies. In the United States, just as a long campaign to restrict immigration was nearing its goal, the Inter-Racial Council was organized in response to fears of a mass exodus of immigrants back to their homelands. And in Sweden, following a dedicated drive to curtail emigration, the imminence of American restrictions caused serious alarm, even within the declining National Society, over the closing of channels of migration.

If the National Society against Emigration was on the wane, the Society for the Preservation of Swedish Culture in Foreign Lands (RFSBU) was entering its most active phase, as thinking about emigration in Sweden shifted from how to prevent it to how to derive the greatest benefits from the existing overseas Swedish population. The Gothenburg society was, following the war, greatly concerned with providing moral and cultural support to the ethnic Swedish element in Finland and Estonia, who gained their independence in 1918, as well as in remote Gammalsvenskby in southern Russia, most of whose population—some nine hundred in all—were evacuated to Sweden in 1929. But the far larger Swedish and Swedish-descended population in North America naturally loomed large on the society's horizon.

In truth, the East Baltic Swedes, together with the small Swedish colonies in larger European cities, offered a considerably more gratifying field of endeavor for the RFSBU than did the Swedes across the Atlantic. The latter, with certain notable exceptions, showed not only a disconcerting indifference to but all too often a touchy resentment against any attempts to orchestrate their cultural activity from the homeland.

Beginning in May 1918, the RFSBU's biweekly *Allsvensk samling* resounded to a rising crescendo of alarm over wartime language restrictions in the supposedly free United States, in comparison with which the oppression of national minorities in imperial Russia, Germany, and Austro-Hungary was depicted as mere child's play. Articles appeared under such headings as "Language Persecution" or "Shall the Swedish Language Be Murdered?" No less indignation was vented against what appeared to be the Swedish Americans' all too supine acceptance of the loss of their language and heritage. At the news that an Augustana Lutheran congregation in Iowa had gone over entirely to English, *Allsvensk samling* editorialized—here as elsewhere doubtless in the voice of Vilhelm Lundström—in May 1918: "In truth, one is wordless at such a display of cowardice and toadying to the Americans! But if the Fort Dodge Swedes hope they can win the Americans' respect by so deeply debasing themselves, their nation, and their language, they are certainly mistaken."

It was to be expected, the paper stated, the oppression would separate the wheat from the chaff: the faint of heart and the opportunistic would fall by the wayside, whereas countless others would be aroused to defend their heritage. "Perhaps the language persecution of 1918 in the United States was needed to remind the Swedes what a boundless and invaluable treasure the otherwise so often neglected mother-tongue is," *Allsvensk samling* wrote in August 1918. "The death-knell has still not sounded," it stated in December that year. "It must never come. All is not lost. But woe to those of Swedish blood and bone who through indifference or open denial help to destroy the Swedes' sacred cultural birthright: possession of the proudest of Germanic tongues." Meanwhile, as the paper declared in May 1919, "One faithful soul, who works and strives, means more than ten renegades." As always, the example of the steadfast East Baltic Swedes was repeatedly evoked.

The RFSBU's alarm became, if anything, greater yet during the first half of 1919, as the Americanization crusade continued unabated. What at first might have seemed an outburst of wartime hysteria now appeared as the far greater menace of a "strong, deliberate, and ... ruthless nationalism," and "anticultural, despotic agitation for the unbridled tyranny of a dominant language."

Under the circumstances, *Allsvensk samling* welcomed the testimony of outraged Swedish Americans. Commenting upon a particularly bitter article in *Missionsvännen* in Chicago, it declared that it would itself have hesitated to speak in such forceful terms, "since certain organs in the Swedish language in America always see fit to take offense as soon as any criticism whatsoever—even the most tactful and well-meaning—of developments and actions among the Swedes in America is heard here at home."[7]

Hard-pressed between 100% Americanism and the stern rebukes of the RFSBU and others in Sweden, Swedish America's spokesmen struggled to preserve dignity and self-respect. *Augustana,* the Synod's Swedish-language weekly, declined, in August 1918, to attempt to correct false statements in *Allsvensk samling,* "in part because that paper has very few readers here and in part because its editors presumably do not read what we write in *Augustana.*" When *Svensk kyrkotidning* depicted the Swedish Americans as cowed and fearful during the war, *Augustana* responded indignantly, "Instead of 'anxiously loyal behavior,' *Kyrkotidning* should have said: a manly, loyal behavior, in keeping with the traditions of our people."

"The Lutheran Church in America must be a thoroughly American institution," the Synod's *Lutheran Companion* declared in April 1918, while condemning as "not only false, but vicious" any ideas that "we as Lutherans of Swedish extraction should keep ourselves separate from other citizens and not participate with them in the effort to realize the highest ideals of our country." In June 1918, it complained that "some Swedish papers and ... the Swedes generally in Sweden" failed to appreciate the difficulties faced by citizens of foreign birth or extraction in the United States. In response to criticism in *Allsvensk samling* it maintained that America in time of peril could not allow itself to be weakened as a nation. "And the sooner our friends over in Sweden learn this the better. If we cannot have relation with them on any other basis than that we retain and perpetuate every racial distinction as to language, mode of thought, and point of view and love of heart, then we are better off without retaining any relation with them at all."

In November 1918, soon after the armistice, G. N. Swan, president of the RFSBU's Swedish-American sister organization, wrote privately to

Vilhelm Lundström from Iowa, maintaining that Governor Harding's wartime language decree had not only been moderately applied but had been both legal and justified, since he "could not in any other way stop the subversive propaganda . . . that was being carried on not only by German, but even by Swedish clergymen."

Meanwhile, *Augustana* had, in December 1917, reaffirmed not only the right but the duty of Swedish parents to teach their children Swedish in America, and it thereafter steadfastly spoke out against language restrictions, both during and after the war. Once the conflict was over, the *Lutheran Companion,* too, protested stoutly against the excesses of the Americanization campaign.[8]

A growing awareness of Swedish-American sensibilities seems to have had effect, for after May 1919 the attacks in *Allsvensk samling* tapered off. The paper now began to note encouraging signs of a revival of spirit in Swedish America. By fall it carried two articles by Vilhelm Berger in New York that calmly discounted the seriousness of the existing situation and sought to explain objectively both the wartime language restrictions and the painful quandaries recently faced by Swedish Americans. By October 1919, *Allsvensk samling* was prepared to print a letter from Milwaukee categorically denying that anything rightly described as "language persecution" had indeed taken place in America, much less that wartime restrictions had anything to do with postwar European return migration. In an accompanying commentary, the editor sought to justify the paper's viewpoint by claiming that it had been based primarily upon material from the Swedish-American press.[9]

Still, the damage was done, even among Swedish Americans who had once placed high hopes in the RFSBU and its All-Swedish program. "I just wonder," G. N. Malm wrote to G. N. Swan in December 1920, "whether Vilhelm Lundström understands how hard-pressed we are with regard to Swedish in this country." "It often seems," he continued, "as though he believes we do not concern ourselves at all with these things. And sometimes it appears to me as though they back home have not fully grasped the fact that we are emigrants and not tourists, that we have left Sweden for all time to come."[10]

After only a brief respite, *Allsvensk samling* began, by early 1921, to reveal a new source of apprehension: that the Augustana Synod was abandoning its post as the foremost defender of the Swedish language in America. Letters from apprehensive Swedish Americans and articles from the Swedish-American press thereafter appeared in *Allsvensk samling,* which exaggerated the seriousness of their actual content through anonymous, indignant editorial comments. Although *Allsvensk samling* was officially edited by his wife, there could be no doubt that the guiding spirit—and pen—was Vilhelm Lundström's. Already in June 1921 it directly alleged that the decline of Swedish in the Augustana Synod was due to deliberate

policy rather than negligence, despite mounting protest within its membership. The same charge thereafter appeared repeatedly and with increasing
asperity.[11]

In an exchange of correspondence with A. G. Witting, one of the pillars
of the Swedish Cultural Society in America, printed in *Allsvensk samling*
in December 1922, Vilhelm Lundström publicly reiterated his "All-Swedish"
ideal. He denied that his movement sought to promote the return of
overseas Swedes to the homeland—"we are certainly not that ignorant
and sanguine"—even though this was apparently widely believed in
America, and sometimes even in Sweden. Its ideal was rather that the
Swedish language should be understood by as many people as possible
around the world, who were familiar with Sweden and spread knowledge
about it. It became ever clearer that "the significance and importance of
every people depends in the last analysis upon how far it can extend the
area of influence of its language and its culture—material and intellectual—
beyond its own frontiers," which was as much in the individual's as in the
fatherland's interest. Overseas Swedes should be loyal citizens of the lands
where they lived, while proving that "if one honors one's father and mother
and follows the voice of one's blood, one is simply a better citizen than
one otherwise would be." Lundström again evoked the example of the
Finland-Swedes, their country's "most loyal citizens," leaders in its "hard
struggle for freedom," and "bearers of order and culture," fitted for their
historic role by the determined preservation of their heritage.

Lundström now turned to the Swedes in the West. "Why does this
Americanization in a negative sense, that is, the elimination of Swedish
language, Swedish cultural activity, and the desire for Swedish solidarity,
succeed so often and to such a great extent?" Witting and others were right
about the influence of the American schools, and Lundström again took
the opportunity to attack America's antiforeign chauvinism during the recent war. But above all he condemned the Swedes' "frightful lack of a truly
national upbringing here at home."

Most of the emigrants of the 1870s through the 1890s had received
their schooling, minimal as it might be, during "the most 'Small-Swedish'
[*småsvensk*] period, when any naturally blossoming expression of Swedish
national pride was literally smothered under the weight of ridicule and
contempt. The Swedes, both at home and throughout the world, have
been on the verge of going under, thanks to this wholly perverse self-
destruction." At home, they had now begun to regain self-confidence, but
those who had left Sweden for other parts of the world still had little
Swedish national sentiment or will to uphold their heritage. Many of the
best minds in Swedish America, Lundström declared, accepted as a matter
of course that "the Swedish language and Swedish culture are going to
disappear and that the only thing that can be done is possibly to seek to
postpone the inevitable hour." The Swedish-American churches in particu-

lar were altogether too fatalistic in this regard. "There is no talk of preserving Swedish at any cost; no, there is concern only for making the transition
to English as smooth as possible!"[12]

Drumfire against the Augustana Synod continued unabated in *Allsvensk
samling,* under such headings as "How the Swedes Are Seeking to Kill the
Swedish Language in America" or "How Swedish Is Being Eradicated." The
Augustana clergy long bore this cross with remarkable forbearance. Many
of its leading figures were in sympathy with the "All-Swedish" ideal and
faithful members of the Society for the Preservation of Swedish Culture
in America. But while confronting the outright Americanizers within their
church, it was galling at the same time to have to face the shrill accusations
in *Allsvensk samling.* On 1 April 1922 the latter leveled a particularly bitter
attack against the synod for allegedly working "systematically" to eliminate
Swedish entirely within the church, a policy that must leave "every Swede
who still possesses the slightest spark of Swedish spirit dumfounded."[13]

The synod's spokesmen could not but respond. In April 1924 Pastor
Conrad Bergendoff protested in *Allsvensk samling* that "the person who
speaks Swedish because he is unable to use English is Swedish-minded
of necessity and not out of love," that Augustana's primary concern must
be the propagation of the faith, and that the synod lacked the resources
to teach Swedish to children if their parents would not do so. "The church,"
he wrote, "prefers to work where it is welcome and the more recent
immigrants from Sweden have not shown themselves to be concerned
with the service of the church. The Augustana Synod is as Swedish as its
membership is Swedish . . . it is not gratefully received by those who prefer
the Swedish language." He went on to warn that those who sought to
denigrate America's culture and spirit would never win friends for their
cause among Swedish Americans. Bergendoff's article was immediately
followed—without editorial comment—by an emotional appeal from Pastor Emil Lund in Minneapolis against the "*mindless* attack against all that is
Swedish" within the synod, which effectively reiterated *Allsvensk samling*'s
uncompromising position.[14]

Augustana, the Synod's Swedish-language organ, understandably was
especially sensitive to criticism from Sweden. In May 1924 its editors (L.
G. Abrahamson and Carl Kraft) accused *Allsvensk samling* of repeatedly
presenting a distorted picture in Sweden of the Augustana Synod and its
cultural activity, while complaining of its ignorance of actual conditions
in Swedish America. The synod did all it could—far more than any other
organization and at great sacrifice—to maintain Swedish language and
culture in America, but its essential purpose was and must be to preserve the
greatest treasure from the fatherland, the Swedish Lutheran faith. Besides, as
Augustana pointed out in July 1924, if the church did not use English
among those who no longer knew Swedish, "then, along with our congregations, our colleges and our cultural work will also go under."[15]

In April 1925 Vilhelm Lundström vented his mounting frustration in a lengthy blast printed in several Swedish newspapers. At a time of growing interest in Sweden for the Swedes in North America, one conference after the other within the synod went over to English, and numerous congregations removed the word "Swedish" from their names. Many of the younger clergy were indifferent if not downright hostile toward Swedish, with the approval of the synod's leadership.

It was repeatedly argued that the church's role was religious, not "Swedish-national." But Lundström wrote:

> Once the will to remain Swedish has died out within the Augustana Synod, it will have betrayed its historic mission, and it will—as its highest leadership has indeed long wished—then be swallowed up by a common Anglo-American Lutheranism, in which every trace of Swedish tradition will soon be swept away. . . . Sweden's church is indissolubly bound up with Swedish language and Swedish culture, and with their preservation and cultivation in the world. . . . If Augustana breaks with *that* tradition, it breaks with the church of our fathers. . . . [and] with its own proud past.

Once again, everything depended upon the will to remain steadfast, so strikingly demonstrated by Finland's Swedish element.[16]

In this article, Lundström wondered if the defense of *svenskhet* in America ought not better be entrusted to one of the large secular societies there. By this he doubtless sought to needle the Augustana Synod, whose antipathy toward such organizations was by no means dead. But Lundström was also serious, as would be evidenced by an article in his *Allsvenska linjer,* dated 1927, concerning the Vasa Order of America. The growing success of this organization Lundström attributed above all to its work to preserve the Swedish heritage. It was, he wrote, "unwaveringly *Swedish*."[17]

Lundström's attack in April 1925 provoked strong defensive responses from America. Already in May, Alfred Bergin, writing more in sorrow than in anger, regretted in *Augustana* that Lundström could not be enticed to visit America, in which case "there is no doubt that he would get other ideas about us and surely not speak such dreadfully mournful and disconsolate words about our future fate in this land." It should be understood, he wrote, that Swedish-American pastors possessed no more authority than their congregations allowed them; "In any event, the patriarchal era is over." Bergin pointed to the irony that after a half century of indifference, the homeland now interested itself in the Swedish Americans at the very time they were becoming fully integrated into American society, which even Vilhelm Lundström must recognize was in their best interests. It was, furthermore, not so certain that even if the Swedes in America lost their ancestral tongue they would lose their Swedish faith and identity, while this was indeed true of some who remained in the homeland. In September

Plate 20. The drill team of Thor Lodge No. 9, Independent Order of Vikings, Moline, Illinois, 1915. The ideal of Swedish immigrants as worthy descendants of the Vikings of yore loomed large in their self-image, rhetoric, and ceremonial by the beginning of the twentieth century. (Courtesy of Swenson Swedish Immigration Research Center, Augustana College, Rock Island, Illinois.)

Plate 21. "A visiting Swedish American." The returned emigrant, as he most conspicuously appeared at home: prosperous, nonchalantly self-confident, and boastful in his barbarous American Swedish about the "Greatest Land on Earth." (From Gunnar Cederschiöld, *Inföytingarna på Manhattan,* Stockholm, 1916.)

Skollärare Bengtzén: — Ska du ingen tidning ha i år, Per Mattson?
Per Mattson: — Va sulle ja me nor tidning i år, när sön min börte i Kalifolien skekar mek en packe tidningar frå Amerika vereveli måne?!!

Plate 22. Cartoon by Albert Engström. "*Schoolmaster Bengtzén:* Aren't you going to subscribe to a newspaper this year, Per Mattson? *Per Mattson* [in broad dialect]: Why should I take a paper this year when my son out in California sends me a bundle of papers every single month?" Swedish-American newspapers, sent back by relatives, were in fact the only regular reading in many poorer Swedish homes, as the novelist Vilhelm Moberg recalled from his own childhood. (From Albert Engström, *Gubbar, tokar, kloka och som folk är mest,* Stockholm, 1924.)

Plate 23. "On the landing stand Father and Mother and Brother, perhaps for the last time they give me their hands." The pathos of emigration as perceived by its critics in the homeland by the turn of the century. (By Hilding Nyman in *Strix,* Christmas number, 1900.)

Plate 24. Professor Rudolf Kjellén's certificate of membership in the National Society Against Emigration, 1911. An idealized vision of rural tranquility and contentment, surrounded by an intertwined Viking Age border pattern, as an emotional appeal to remain in, or return to, the old homeland. (The Uppsala University Library, Uppsala.)

Plate 25. The Engberg-Holmberg Publishing Company and its staff at 119 East Chicago Avenue in Chicago. One of the best known and longest-lived firms in the lively world of Swedish-language publishing when Swedish America was at its height. (Undated, but evidently from the later nineteenth century. Courtesy of Swedish Emigrant Institute, Växjö.)

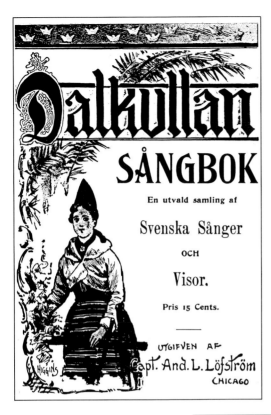

Plate 26. The ever-popular *Dalkullan* songbook was published annually during the first decades of this century by Anders Löfström, an old sailor on the Great Lakes, whose establishment on Chicago's Clark Street also dealt in snuff and other necessities.

Plate 27. *Prärieblomman 1902* title page. This yearbook, published in 1900 and from 1902 to 1913 by the Augustana Book Concern in Rock Island, Illinois, was the most prominent of several Swedish-American literary periodicals. It counted among its contributors most of Swedish America's cultural elite.

Plate 28. Two chapter vignettes from G. N. Malm's novel, *Charli Johnson, svensk-amerikan* (Chicago, 1909). The sturdy descendants of the Vikings and their new homes on the prairie idealized from a Swedish-American perspective.

"Jaså, herrarne tyckte det var bara humbug!"

Plate 29. Charli Johnson confronts the snobs from Sweden. In the climax of Malm's novel, Charli, having come to recognize his full conversion as a Swedish American, denounces the arrogance of the Swedish critics. The one on the right may well have been intended to represent P. P. Waldenström. (From G. N. Malm, *Charli Johnson, svensk-amerikan,* Chicago, 1909.)

Plate 30. Crown Prince Gustav Adolf (later Gustav VI Adolf) lays the cornerstone for the American-Swedish Historical Museum in Philadelphia, 1926. More than anything before, this ceremonial event, the highlight of the first official Swedish royal visit to the United States, symbolized the homeland's belated appreciation for the Swedish Americans and their accomplishments, following the end of the Great Migration. (From Albin Widén, *Svenskar som erövrat Amerika,* Stockholm, 1937.)

Plate 31. Johannes and Helga Hoving with Vasa Order children in "Father's and Mother's Land" in 1924, here at the John Ericsson Mausoleum in Filipstad, a traditional shrine for the celebration of Swedish-American friendship. The Hovings' visiting groups of members of the Vasa Order of America's children's clubs in 1924, 1929, and 1933 were widely feted and aroused immense enthusiasm in Sweden. Dr. Hoving in his patriarchal beard stands in the middle, with Helga in folk dress to his left. (From Gunnar Wickman, *Till fars och mors land*, Göteborg, 1924.)

Plate 32. Latter-day Vikings afloat. It is not known where or when this picture was taken, but it is most probably from the 1930s and from the East Coast, where younger immigrants raised in the National Romantic tradition of the homeland were then most numerous. Although the oarsmanship leaves something to be desired, this manifestation combines pride in Viking ancestors and traditional folk culture, by now the firmly established symbols of the ethnic heritage. (From Albin Widén, *Svenskar som erövrat Amerika*, Stockholm, 1937.)

that year Bergin expressed appreciation for Lundström's All-Swedish ideal but held that the situation of the Swedes in Finland, Estonia, and Gammalsvenskby offered no valid parallel to the present crisis in Swedish America.

Far stronger was an editorial in *Augustana* in December 1925, expressing bitterness that Vilhelm Lundström and *Allsvensk samling* had "for years" ignored or denigrated the synod's impressive cultural accomplishments, while printing letters from "irresponsible" persons in America. It might indeed be suspected that *Allsvensk samling* sought to undermine the synod. *Augustana*'s editors were deeply offended by Lundström's sanguine endorsement of the Vasa Order and other secular societies as the last best hope for the Swedish heritage in America. Compared with the Swedish-language activity of the Augustana Synod, the editors proudly maintained, that of the secular societies paled into insignificance. Leading figures in the Swedish state church, such as Bishop von Schéele and most recently Archbishop Nathan Söderblom, both of whom—in contrast to Lundström— had actually visited America, meanwhile expressed sympathy and understanding for the Augustana Synod's linguistic dilemma. Thereafter the controversy gradually died down in the pages of *Allsvensk samling* and *Augustana*.[18]

Charles A. Lindbergh, Jr.'s solo flight across the Atlantic in May 1927 created a greater sensation worldwide than any other single feat by an American of Swedish descent, either before or after. Swedish newspapers were jubilant over "the Swede, Lindbergh," but this was quickly countered in the press by critics who claimed Sweden could claim no credit, since it had driven its emigrants across the sea to America, where they had been able to accomplish things they could never have done at home. Such an attitude was, of course, directly opposed to the All-Swedish ideal, and Vilhelm Lundström did not fail to rise to the bait. Citizenship was one thing, he asserted, but "descent and race" another. If Swedes in the homeland celebrated the deeds of their kin abroad, overseas Swedes would be that much the prouder of their Swedish origins.[19]

Lundström found much to arouse his sacred indignation, but not all of it lay in America. In an undated essay in his *Allsvenska linjer* he called attention to Swedish America's literature, now dying out thanks largely to Swedish condescension and indifference. "There would perhaps not be many," he wrote, "who would have enough understanding to lament over this, but for us who believe in the value of unique and characteristic Swedish culture in the Swedish language it is cause for boundless sorrow."[20]

Lundström was doubtless right: few Swedes surely knew or cared enough about cultural Swedish America to feel very strongly about its passing. The final stage of World War I and the postwar period meanwhile created a far greater interest in the United States as a great new economic, military, and diplomatic force in the world. Swedish thinking about America in effect shifted in emphasis from "The Land of the Emigrants"—to use the title of E. H. von Koch's influential book from 1910—to the new world power.

In this role the United States aroused great hopes in Sweden, as elsewhere in Europe. Liberals hailed America's fight to "make the world safe for democracy" and President Wilson's Fourteen Points for a fair and honorable peace, although they came to experience much disillusionment over the actual peace settlement of 1919 and America's withdrawal into self-satisfied isolation. Conservatives, including many former Germanophiles, gained increased respect for America as the capitalist bulwark against Bolshevism. Among more progressive entrepreneurs the automation of American mass production exercised a growing fascination.[21] "America has become all the fashion now," the socialist Ture Nerman wrote in 1929: "The old cultured Europe has ruined itself in a great war and the United States has become its creditor. This inspires respect. . . . Bourgeois and Social Democrats lie prostrate in adoration. . . . Poor Europe gapes in wonderment at Rich Uncle across the ditch. . . . And quite naturally ruined Europe seeks to imitate America. Consciously and unconsciously, Europe becomes more Americanized with every day that passes."[22] The sharp satirical edge is unmistakable, and Nerman went on to a Marxian critique of American capitalism.

His criticisms were not new, but they are highly characteristic for their time and political milieu. Detailed studies of the attitudes of the Swedish socialist and labor movements toward America and the emigration are still strangely lacking, in contrast to the plentiful material illustrating the views of the political Right on the subject. It is evident nonetheless that they long remained ambivalent. From its beginnings in the mid-1880s, the socialist press in Sweden had regularly reported on working conditions and labor relations in the United States, in generally somber tones. Yet if conditions were hard for workers in America, they frequently seemed worse in Sweden. Emigration could weaken the forces of socialism and organized labor at home, yet it also provided welcome asylum for blackballed union activists or organizers harassed by the police, who could carry on the worldwide struggle against international capitalism beyond the sea. Most important, the constant menace of a mass decampment of Sweden's work force for the further shore remained a powerful political weapon. When various proposals were put forward by government and military authorities to restrict the right to emigrate during the early years of World War I, these were resolutely opposed by the socialist press and members of the Riksdag.[23]

Lars-Göran Tedebrand, who has studied the Swedish labor press between 1913 and 1927, has identified 1917 as the crucial turning point in its attitude toward America. In that year the Social Democratic party was first included in a governing coalition, opening prospects for its future political dominance; 1917 also witnessed the Communist revolution in Russia. Henceforward, the political Left in Sweden became set in its hostility toward capitalist America, reinforced by the red scare in America and the improvement of Sweden's living standards and welfare provisions throughout the 1920s. The trial of Nicola Sacco and Bartolomeo Vanzetti in Boston in 1920–21 and their execution in 1927, following the trial and execution of the Swedish-born IWW leader Joe Hill in 1915, catalyzed the rising anti-Americanism of the political Left throughout Europe. "American capitalism," Arthur Engberg wrote in *Socialdemokraten* in 1925, "is, in our eyes, one of the most ruthless that exists anywhere in the world . . . and the situation of the American proletarian is nothing less than frightful."[24] Others described America in yet more lurid terms. A good example is provided in 1923 by *Skräckväldet i Amerika* (The Reign of Terror in America)—whose paper cover, appropriately illustrated, also bears the title *Wallstreets blodiga välde* (Wall Street's Bloody Regime). Its author, John Andersson, a former syndicalist member of the IWW, was among the embittered radicals driven back to the homeland by postwar persecution in the United States.[25]

To return again to Ture Nerman: he was an intellectual socialist and his critique of America was as much cultural as socioeconomic. Whether radical or conservative, Swedish and other European intellectuals were alarmed at the threat posed by the rapid spread of American ideas and fashions to the Old World during the postwar years, most obtrusively in the form of jazz, popular dances, and the movies. Buoyant American materialism and optimism contrasted painfully with tired European *mondanité* and with the pall of Spenglerian pessimism that hung over postwar Europe. The reaction is perhaps best reflected in the literature of the 1920s, which significantly includes no noteworthy expressions of pro-Americanism.

A good example of literary skepticism toward America is provided by Gustaf Hellström (1882-1942), who as a correspondent in the United States for the liberal *Dagens nyheter* (Stockholm) in 1918 had been enthusiastic over the country's promising new role in the world. Disillusion soon followed, however, for by 1920, Hellström described an America sharply divided between an Anglo-Saxon ruling class and a mass of "immigrant cattle" and oppressed Negroes, possessing a crassly materialistic, superficial, hypocritical culture.[26]

Hellström's most significant novel, *Snörmakaren Lekholm får en idé* (Cordbraider Lekholm Gets an Idea) of 1927 offers meanwhile a finely shaded view of the impact of "Americanization" in Sweden. The greatest interest in this regard derives not from the main character, a Swedish American home on a visit to his family, but rather, by his younger brother, who, though he had never been to America, went about with his head filled with feverish, American-inspired ideas for Sweden's regeneration, thereby embodying the disquieting encroachment of an alien new mentality in an old cultural community.[27]

The Swedish film industry was already well developed by the early 1920s, when Hollywood became the American movie capital and began drawing liberally upon talent from Europe. Several Swedes made their mark there early on, most notably the actress Greta Garbo and the directors Mauritz Stiller and Victor Sjöström (Seastrom). In 1924 Sjöström persuaded one of the brightest stars of the Swedish literary firmament, Hjalmar Bergman, to accompany him as a scriptwriter. The latter soon had enough and returned to Sweden after a few months, but not before gathering ideas and atmosphere for perhaps his greatest novel, *Clownen Jac* (Jac the Clown), which appeared in 1930.[28]

The story deals with the life destiny of a world-famous Swedish-born comedian and millionaire, placed against an almost surreal Southern Californian backdrop of palm trees, pseudo-Spanish mansions, and ukulele-strumming "flappers" in bathing suits. Ultimately it reveals Bergman's own inner struggle to reconcile life with art. On another level, meanwhile, Bergman's Hollywood stands as a metaphor for all he saw as most bizarre, artificial, hollow, and banal in American life, in telling contrast to scenes in Jac's native Västmanland, where life remained close to the soil and to real values.[29]

Clownen Jac tells nothing about emigration or Swedes in America as such, but in his stage comedy, *Dollar,* from 1926, Bergman expressed himself on the impact of America upon the children of Swedish immigrants. The underlying motif is the by now well familiar theme of decadent but humane European refinement versus rational but soulless American effectivity, as they confront each other in a Lapland resort hotel. "Now the barbarian stands at our gate," one of the Swedish characters exclaims, "the barbarian who understands nothing and forgives nothing."[30]

The 1920s were meanwhile a period of growing interest in American literature in Sweden, although its acceptance was selective. It is symptomatic that Sinclair Lewis was the first American to be awarded the Nobel Prize in literature in 1930. His satire of the pretentiousness, hypocrisy, and banality of American life could be seen as a reassuring confirmation of what European social critics had long proclaimed. For this very reason the award caused very mixed feelings in the United States.[31] It is worth noting that Lewis's treatment of Swedes and other Scandinavians in his masterwork *Main Street* from 1920 was warmly sympathetic: they there represent a more genuine and truly dignified human type than the superficial Anglo-American society of Gopher Prairie.

"Some of us here in Europe look with aversion upon certain sides of the American mentality," Carl G. Laurin wrote in 1927, "and we do so with concern, for we see in the USA our own future."[32] He well captured the mood of the Swedish cultural establishment, for which America had come to symbolize the unwelcome forces of change throughout the world.

At the very time that America as a new power in the world assumed a mythic guise deeply disquieting to the intellectual elite, the Swedish emigration was undergoing a striking transformation from disturbing current problem to heroic legend. By the mid-1920s the Great Migration could at last be regarded as a past episode. Now, when it no longer represented a living threat, it could be laid to rest with suitable rites of commemoration, amid the conciliation of kinsmen from near and far.

This was accomplished with due solemnity in 1925–26 by the publication in Stockholm of a handsome collaborative work in two volumes, *Svenskarna i Amerika* (The Swedes in America), described in its subtitle as a "popular historic account in word and picture of the Swedes' life and marvelous destiny in the United States and Canada," edited by the historian and conservative Riksdag member Karl Hildebrand in Stockholm and the one-time Swedish-American journalist Axel Fredenholm in Gothenburg. Intended for wide distribution on both sides of the Atlantic, it was printed in large format, on high-quality paper, and lavishly illustrated; the luxury edition featured full leather binding and gilt-edged pages. But more than an eye-catching adornment to coffee table or bookshelf, it was a work of commemoration and celebration, as well as the first joint effort by Swedes and Swedish Americans to present the story of the emigration and of the Swedes in America.

These volumes were the work of many hands. Significantly, it would seem, few of the Swedish contributors were recognizable from the lively public debate over America and the emigration of the immediately preceding decades. Of the latter, some were now gone, such as Gustav Sundbärg, who had died in 1914; some, evidently including G. H. von Koch, had moved on to new concerns. Yet the omission of certain others from this enterprise may well have been more than fortuitous: Adrian Molin and Vilhelm Lundström, for instance, had often riled Swedish-American sensibilities, while P. G. Norberg had perhaps gone rather too far in praising the Swedish Americans to belabor his own countrymen in the eyes of some at home. The one notable exception was Pastor Per Pehrsson of Gothenburg, whose credentials appear sound on both sides: while he had been active in the Swedish anti-emigration movement, he had also shown real sympathy and warm appreciation for the Swedes in America. Otherwise, the Swedish contributors were—in this area at least—all relatively new faces and hence safely noncontroversial. The Swedish-American contingent, consisted meanwhile of prominent and long-established leaders within their own community, mainly clergymen, journalists, and educators.

The tone of the work was both conciliatory and self-congratulatory. The work, the editors hoped, would "serve the double purpose of increasing interest here at home for those kinsmen who live so far away, while at the same time deepening the latters' love for the Old Country."[33]

The first volume began with a lengthy account of Sweden's glorious past by Carl Hildebrand, culminating with a description of the country's recent economic, social, and cultural achievements. This was followed by chapters on the Swedes in North America, beginning with the Norse discovery, presented with moving pageantry. The stage was thus set for the epic of the great emigration beginning in the nineteenth century, which the Swedish writer Rütger Essén compared with the Viking expeditions a thousand years earlier. "The sacrifice this may have meant from the Swedish national point of view has meanwhile most certainly not been made in vain—all the less so as the old Swedish homeland has always had cause to regard with pride what its sons and daughters have accomplished in the overall life and development of the American people."[34]

Thereafter followed a sober and well-grounded presentation of Swedish settlement in America, stressing the pioneer period, by the veteran Ernst Skarstedt, who himself had experienced much of what he described. The saga he related was that of the settlers' "tough persistence, their unrelenting toil, determination, self-denial, and Nordic strength, which made it possible for them to overcome all obstacles and reach the goals they had set themselves." Ernst W. Olson contrasted the Swedes' "peaceful conquest" of America's prairie West with the plunder and exploitation that had characterized so much of the American Westward movement. They came, he wrote, to make, through their own toil, homes for themselves and their descendants through uncounted generations. This broad historical panorama in the Old Land and the New was supplemented by numerous specialized chapters on various aspects of Swedish-American life.[35]

Yet at this feast of concord, signs are not lacking of a certain amount of scuffling under the table. Swedish and Swedish-American writers obviously relished this unaccustomed opportunity to speak directly to each others' publics.

Among the Swedish contributors, Sven Hedin, that living symbol of Swedish national patriotism, sternly recalled to all that strong as personal ties across the ocean might be, "stronger than all bonds of kinship is still attachment to Fatherland."[36] Greetings from the various Swedish provinces meanwhile played heavily upon the presumed nostalgia of the emigrants, if not indeed at times upon an assumed, underlying sense of remorse, while some pointedly stressed values that distinguished local inhabitants from their relatives in America. For instance: "The people of Södermanland can surely never get the Swedish Americans' rush and bustle in their blood. They avail themselves of this century's advances, they are aware through the newspapers and radio of the events of the times, but the whole atmosphere in which they live is the tradition-bound echo of all those who before them have stubbornly and steadily tilled the soil and made history."

And from Bohuslän: "Welcome home, whenever you will. But come with a humble heart. 'God's Country' is good, to be sure, but Bohuslän is better. The people of Bohuslän know this, and they tolerate no superior airs."[37]

Axel Palmgren made bold to assert that P. P. Waldenström's widely read description from 1890, had been "on the whole, right" and surely "salutary, for from that time forward another, more understanding attitude toward the old fatherland began to become apparent." Knowledgeable Swedish-American readers must meanwhile have stared in disbelief at Palmgren's claim that Gustaf Gullberg's culturally snobbish *Boken om Chicago* from 1893 "gives an excellent snapshot of life out there in America"![38]

As a group, however, the Swedish-American contributors appear to have been even more defensive and eager to revindicate their community. This is hardly surprising. They were, on the average, older than their Swedish counterparts and had throughout their careers been deeply concerned with the relationship of emigrants to the old homeland. Moreover, while they followed with close attention what the Swedish press had to say about America and its Swedish inhabitants, they suffered the frustration of knowing that, with few exceptions, they and what they wrote were practically unknown in Sweden. *Svenskarna i Amerika* thus offered its Swedish-American contributors a chance, not to be missed, to say some things to the Old Country that had long needed to be said. In the balance, their chapters are the most substantive and interesting, in the light of their background.

In his introductory salutation in the second volume, Pastor G. A. Brandelle, president of the Augustana Synod, restated the matter of national sentiment from a Swedish-American perspective, in contrast to Sven Hedin's assertion in Volume I: "Even if they love their homeland with as much warmth as the Swedish people love Sweden—and who should begrudge them that?—there is nevertheless no country which the Swedish Americans regard so highly, next to their own, as the land of their fathers."[39]

Ernst Skarstedt undertook to deflate some hoary myths in Sweden about its emigrated sons and daughters. He reminded his readers that most of the earlier emigrants had not been independent farmers at home and thus had been poorly prepared for that role in America, especially in unfamiliar environments, a disadvantage that only hard work and determination could overcome. In contrast to the Swede, Helge Nelson, in the same volume, Skarstedt stoutly denied that Swedes had thrived best in those parts of North America that most closely resembled their homeland, a shrewd thrust at the traditional emphasis in Sweden upon the homesickness of the emigrants. "The Swedish settler," he held, "does not appear inferior to the Americans in his ability and willingness to adapt to new conditions." Indeed he maintained that those who had settled on the open prairies had done far better than those who felled trees and grubbed stumps in forested areas.[40]

Skarstedt directly contradicted an oft-repeated argument of the Swedish opponents of emigration when he denied that the great opportunities of the pioneer period for economic independence and prosperity were a thing of the past. They remained, he declared, as great as ever in both town and countryside. In the cultural sphere, the Swedish Americans had accomplished wonders, in view of their generally humble origins.[41]

The Swedish-American press was represented by Oliver A. Linder, long-time editor of *Svenska Amerikanaren* in Chicago, then America's leading Swedish-language newspaper, who made the most of this opportunity to answer directly long-standing criticisms from Sweden. No immigrant nationality in America, he claimed, had been as well served as the Swedes by a press that faithfully fulfilled its obligations to both the old and new homelands. This dual responsibility was not as problematic as it might seem, however, for the obvious need to fit the Swedish immigrant for life in the new land "need in no way exclude the preservation of the splendid Swedish heritage he had brought with him." Indeed, the Swedish-American press had always sought to foster love and respect for it.

"The accusation that has sometimes been made that the press has at times been almost hostile toward Sweden," Linder continued, "is too ridiculous to dignify with an answer."

> But the press has at times, with clear intention, taken up the fight to get rid of certain flaws that are a part of the Swedish nature and that stand in the way of the greatest success of the Swedish nationality in the new land. This has been taken, from time to time, to imply opposition to the Swedish heritage, but it should rather be realized that the Swedish-American press would have betrayed its most sacred duty if it had, without protest, allowed things to occur which might directly or indirectly have harmed the nationality in some way. The press has as its vital task to protect the nationality's reputation. In this regard, the Swedish-American press has kept good watch and has no sins to regret.

It was natural that Swedish-American newspapers should differ significantly from their Swedish counterparts in bearing the imprint of "so vital, so high-pressured an environment as the American." This was true not only of layout and appearance but also of the "journalistic spirit, which is evident in viewpoints based upon premises learned from American experience. Even purely Swedish conditions are sometimes seen through American eyeglasses, suggesting easy answers deriving from this same American experience." These preliminary comments, Linder held, "have seemed necessary to correct a common misunderstanding," before he could launch into a historical survey of the Swedish-American press.[42]

If there was little direct communication eastward across the Atlantic at the editorial level and thus from Swedish-America's opinionmakers to the Swedish intellectual elite, Linder was able to point out that "of two Chicago newspapers 10,000 and 8,000 copies respectively are sent each week to subscribers in Sweden." Unquestionably sizable numbers of other Swedish-American publications went the same way, largely to returned Swedish Americans or through gift subscriptions from relatives or friends in America. These surely served to sustain the traditional interest in, and sympathy for, the great land to the West among Sweden's working classes, especially in small towns and the countryside.[43]

Linder authored the following chapter, as well, on Swedish-American literature, to which he himself had contributed both poetry and short fiction. Like other Swedish-American commentators before him, he pointed to the characteristic literary vitality of this "people in exodus," among whom there were proportionately more writers, especially poets, than in the land of their origin. Much of their prolific production could not stand up to "exacting academic criticism," he was prepared to admit, but he held that "much of it can well stand beside the best that Swedish poetry has to offer."[44]

Considering the storms of the past, such jockeying for position between Swedish and Swedish-American contributors to *Svenskarna i Amerika* nonetheless amounted to no more than mere ripples upon the shining surface of the good will and mutual appreciation that could now begin to emerge, once emigration no longer represented either a threat to Sweden's well-being or a weapon in its internal conflicts.

Following the end of World War I there were other signs as well that a new dispensation was evolving in Sweden's relationship to America and its Swedish element. In 1919 the *Sverige-Amerika Stiftelsen* (Sweden-America Foundation) was established in Stockholm by a group of prominent persons of liberal or progressive-conservative outlook. Its purpose was, and has remained, to provide scholarships and grants to Swedes for study or practical internships in the United States.[45]

Sweden's evidently poor standing in the United States at the end of the war was the cause for much concern and discussion, both in the government and in the newly founded Sweden-America Foundation. Upon the latter's initiative, a committee was formed in 1920, with Foreign Ministry representation, leading to the establishment of *Svensk-amerikanska ny-hetsbyrån,* the American-Swedish News Exchange, which commenced operations in New York in 1922. As a private institution it avoided any appearance of an official propaganda agency and throughout the 1920s and 1930s it provided the American press with a news coverage of Sweden practically unrivaled by other foreign information services. It was responsible in high degree for America's growing awareness of and admiration for Sweden and for the accomplishments of Swedes at home and abroad. It also provided the Swedish press with news coverage from America.[46]

A third important transatlantic link was forged in 1924, when the first

Swedish lodge of the Vasa Order of America was established in Gothenburg. In time it would be followed by some fifty others throughout Sweden. By the 1920s there also existed in Sweden a variety of other Swedish-American clubs and societies, some of which still exist today.[47]

Both the Sweden-America Foundation and the Swedish branch of the Vasa Order of America have enjoyed notable success down to the present, as have the American-Swedish News Exchange and its successor since 1964, the Swedish Information Service. In contrast, the Society for the Preservation of Swedish Culture in Foreign Lands (RFSBU), despite its ambitious aims, was able to show few positive accomplishments as far as America was concerned. This must above all be attributed to the uncompromising attitude of Vilhelm Lundström, for whom the old homeland was to serve as the sole guiding beacon for all Swedes throughout the world. His high moralistic tone and stern reproaches fell increasingly upon deaf ears across the Atlantic. Under this shadow, meanwhile, the small, related Society for the Preservation of Swedish Culture in America languished throughout the 1920s, to the discouragement of many of its erstwhile supporters. Around 1924 Ernst W. Olson declared in an undated manuscript—presumably for a speech, perhaps to the society itself—that it ought rather to be called the "Society for Complaining over the Loss of Swedish Culture in America." To underline its independence, it changed its name in 1925 to the Swedish Cultural Society in America, although to little avail.[48]

The newer Swedish organizations were founded upon the premise of a genuine exchange of equal value to both sides. As an import from America, the Vasa Order in Sweden was by its very nature sympathetic toward Swedish America and its American, as well as its Swedish, values. The American-Swedish News Exchange spread enlightenment in both directions. Meanwhile, through study and direct personal contacts in the United States, the Sweden-American Foundation made it possible, as Professor Martin Lamm expressed it on its tenth anniversary in 1929, for a growing number of Sweden's future leaders in all fields "to familiarize themselves with conditions in that foreign land in a completely different manner than other visitors."[49] The results are strikingly evident today.

EIGHTEEN

Travelers from Afar

*T*he postwar decade witnessed a remarkable upsurge of writing in Sweden, as throughout Europe, about the United States, including accounts by unprecedented numbers of visitors to the great republic. According to the literary historian Gunnar Eidevall, "almost anyone able to write who then visited the USA seems to have found possibilities to present his viewpoints and impressions in periodicals or books."[1]

By the middle-1920s emigration was no longer a national problem. Growing numbers of politically engaged Swedes, while respecting America's status as a great power, were no longer convinced that it had positive lessons to teach Sweden regarding economic and social development, while American mass culture aroused profound misgivings among the intellectual elite.

The Swedish Americans appeared in Swedish eyes increasingly as relics of the past, ever more out of touch with modern Sweden as the years went by. Of the Swedish visitors to the United States during the 1920s, only Johan Benzendal and Erland Richter focused their accounts specifically on the American Swedes. The others devoted only part of their attention to them, although in so doing they could view the Swedish Americans within the wider context of American life, often with considerable insight.

As a group, the Swedish observers of America during the 1920s differed in significant respects from their predecessors earlier in the century. The economic and social reformers, including leaders of the anti-emigration movement, were now notably absent. In contrast, the cultural commentators were much in evidence. The status and occupations of the visitors, moreover, varied far more widely than before, including high Swedish dignitaries such as had never previously come to America. In 1924 Archbishop Nathan Söderblom, primate of the Swedish state church, visited the United States. Two years later, Crown Prince Gustav Adolf (later King Gustav VI Adolf) and Crown Princess Louise made a highly acclaimed official tour through the land. The Crown Prince's brother, Prince Wilhelm, who had visited the United States in 1908, made a lecture tour in 1927. The warmth and enthusiasm with which they were received by Swedish Americans everywhere shows how deeply gratified the latter were by these striking manifestations of appreciation that they felt the Old Country had so long denied them.

For the period, 1903 through 1917, a high degree of consensus was evident in Swedish visitors' views of America and the Swedish Americans. Attitudes were more varied during the 1920s, reflecting changing circumstances on both sides of the ocean. Certain recurrent themes are nevertheless discernable among those whose interests encompassed the Swedish element. These included the accomplishments of the Swedish Americans and their economic and social standing; their attitudes toward, respectively, their new and old homelands; the state of Swedish-American culture and institutions; the nature of the Swedish identity in America in the post-migration era; and future ties between Swedish descendants in the United States and their ancestral land. Such questions were familiar enough from past Swedish accounts, even though the answers now differed in significant ways. What seems notably different from the prewar years is that the Swedish Americans were no longer held up as models for their kinsmen at home. Their ways and attitudes appeared ever less relevant to Swedish society—if not as living examples of what it should strive to avoid.

Among our Swedish visitors, only Johan Benzendal in 1923 was implacably hostile toward America and all it stood for. The others show a sincere desire to appreciate the positive sides of American life and at least to understand those aspects they could not accept. From their accounts one gains on the whole a soberer, more reserved view of America than formerly, since the new land no longer seemed to offer a valid model for Sweden.

Except for Archbishop Söderblom, whose mind was on higher things, the visitors were commonly repelled by the crass materialism, extremes of wealth and poverty, cynicism and corruption in business and politics, callous treatment of arriving immigrants, racial prejudice, lawlessness and crime, banality of mass culture, and mindless conformity they encountered, to say nothing of the overall appearance of things. On a train from New York to Pennsylvania, Anna Lenah Elgström reflected in 1923: "An ugliness like American ugliness is not to be found in Europe. I mean the almost horrifying ugliness of disorder and uncompletedness to which American carelessness (quite simply plain, ordinary carelessness) can condemn a landscape."[2]

On the whole, meanwhile, the visitors were strongly impressed by American energy, optimism, friendliness, and at least in some cases by that sense of romantic excitement that Elgström in Chicago felt as intimations of "the lawless mysteries and adventures of untamed spaces." It was she, too, who best summarized the difference in conditions and outlook which for the Swedish immigrant distinguished life in the New and Old Worlds: "In a word, if his life in America is both more arduous and less secure than in the Old Country, it is in return much more stimulating and interest-arousing, even in the manner in which it spurs the development of his individual courage, strength, and enterprise."[3]

While most of our travelers contented themselves with describing what they observed among their emigrated countrymen in America, two at least gave some thought to the significance of the emigration as such. Archbishop Söderblom was sobered by the presence of a thousand Swedish emigrants, "mostly good-looking lads and fresh, blossoming young girls," aboard the Swedish-America Line's *Drottningholm* on his way across the Atlantic in that final peak year, 1923. Yet Sweden, he wrote, should not regard those who had gone to America as "lost sons and daughters," but should accept God's divine providence. "Since the days of the Thirty Years' War, the Swedes have achieved nothing outside their borders comparable to what the emigration to the United States has already signified and what it will mean in the future for the body and soul of the American nation."[4]

In 1926 the visiting Social Democratic politician Carl Lindhagen recalled the unsuccessful Riksdag proposal made in 1869 by his father, Albert Lindhagen, for Swedish state assistance to the emigrants in America to maintain close ties with the homeland. This had been largely motivated, according to Carl Lindhagen, by the realization that the departure of part of the labor force would provide increased opportunities for the remainder. "From this standpoint," he wrote, "the emigration must appear not only as a departure from an old fatherland but also as the founding of a new one"—at home. This was a natural enough thought in the later 1860s, but Carl Lindhagen reveals that it was not altogether dead in Social Democratic circles even in the mid-1920s.[5]

Our visitors' reactions to the Swedish Americans they encountered depended in large measure upon the latters' attitudes toward Sweden and things Swedish, which in turn was closely linked to their experiences in and ideas concerning their new homeland. There could be no denying that they had generally done well in a material sense, although it might be asked whether the price had not been too high in nonmaterial values. But such success—however modest—all too often led to what seemed immoderate boastfulness about America and its blessings, coupled with a demonstrative disdain for the Old Country which Swedish observers found repugnant.

"One's indignation is aroused," Maj Hirdman wrote, "by this almost stupid admiration for all that is not Swedish." Immigrant Swedish work-ingmen told her they had little for which to thank Sweden, where they had gone unemployed for years: "Sweden didn't give a d——n for me, and now I don't give a d——n for Sweden!" She wondered how soon it might be before a serious economic crisis would show them that America "didn't give a d——n" for them either. They seemed a people stubbornly determined "to obliterate themselves from the face of the earth."[6]

The Swedish American was found to be very touchy in his pride for America and the possibilities it offered him. As Anna Lenah Elgström expressed it: "Even if the homeland Swede learns to understand *him* better as a person ... even if we, as I say, do justice to the *Swede* in him—the *American* [in him] we can never satisfy except with enthusiastic praise, such as American propaganda has taught him to regard as the only proper attitude." She realized, meanwhile, that a nation composed of many nationalities must seek in every way to create its own national feeling. None, however, felt so strong a "personal pride" in America's greatness as the successful Swedish American. "One immediately feels in the air an almost moving sensitivity in him over the slightest possible reservation. There is indeed something of the married man's sensitivity over unfavorable ideas about his wife. He has perhaps sacrificed so much to win her that he must always see her in an idealized light and say to himself that those who do not appreciate her simply do not know her well enough."[7]

The entertainer Lydia Hedberg ("Bergslagsmor"), who toured Swedish America from 1920 to 1923, singing folk songs and telling dialect stories in her native folk dress, was ever concerned with her audience reaction. She found

> repeated proof that my singing softened their American hearts, whose very fibers must be moved by verses about the poor countryside at home in order that their true Swedish feelings might emerge. That which I sought most often lay deeply buried. . . . I came to see that these so boastful Swedish Americans find it difficult to suppress ... a feeling of shame over the fact that their expectations of America have been disappointed and that they, to stamp out any possible suspicion that they might have done as well in Sweden, must live in an imaginary world based upon boasting over how well they have done in Dollar-Land.

Their bitterness toward the old homeland, Hedberg was convinced, lay in the fact that it could not give them what they found in America.[8]

Nathan Söderblom distinguished between three types of Swedish Americans: those who never really came to feel at home in America, even though they might not thereafter feel at home in Sweden either; those who eagerly sought to Americanize as quickly and completely as possible, usually because of cultural impoverishment in their old homes; and the great majority who "take their fatherland with them wherever they may go" in the form of its proud and ancient cultural heritage, to their own lasting enrichment, as well as to that of both their new and old homelands.[9]

Archbishop Söderblom meanwhile noted considerable variety within the Swedish-American community, for which Lydia Hedberg in particular had a perceptive eye. The Swedish element in the East Coast cities, to which Maj Hirdman's experience was limited and with which Lydia Hedberg had her first contacts, consisted largely of recently arrived, younger immigrants. "There is an enormous difference," Hedberg wrote, "between the [Swedish] workers who emigrated ten, fifteen years ago, and those who emigrate now." American employers considered the recent arrivals as lazy as American or any other workers, although the real difference was the "socialist demands our present-day Swedish workers make regarding pay and treatment." Johan Benzendal considered that the "American sickness" most strongly affected the most recent immigrants, especially in the East.[10]

In the Northeast, the younger and more recent immigrants largely set the tone of the local, mainly urban Swedish-American community, in contrast to the Middle West, where Swedes had been heavily concentrated for generations in a largely rural environment. Lydia Hedberg, who traveled most widely for over three years, found herself progressively more at home with her emigrated countrymen as she progressed from East to West. From Minneapolis she reported a revealing conversation in Swedish with a streetcar conductor:

"Are you from Sweden?" "Yes indeed," was my reply. He looked at me a moment. "Are you also from Sweden?" I then asked. "Sure." "What part?" "I was born here in Minneapolis," he answered, a bit surprised at my question. "So—in Minnesota?" I smiled. "Sure!" He drew out the word in a tone that revealed his surprise that I could imagine that he might not be born in Minnesota. . . . And from that conversation it dawned clearly upon me that for the Swedes in Minnesota that state was Sweden.[11]

Again, it was in the East that Hedberg noted in particular a markedly greater tendency among women immigrants to Americanize more rapidly and indiscriminately than their male counterparts. "I was most surprised," she wrote shortly after her arrival, "by the behavior of the Americanized Swedish women. Most of them behaved in a most unpleasant manner, especially the younger ones. Already during their first week [in America] they affect bobbed hair, horn-rimmed glasses, and a mish-mash slang, which makes you astonished at what you hear." She repeatedly commented on the immigrant women's "wild enthusiasm for Dollar-Land." Still, she came to admit, in America, "their personal value is greater, their work lighter, their clothes prettier, their person more appreciated, the men are their slaves, and life is a bit more festive, if you will. No wonder that they do not wish to go back home again." The men, she claimed, found it harder to adapt to the new land and suffered greater homesickness.[12]

Anna Lenah Elgström, whose view of America bore a strong literary coloration, saw the Swedish-American woman in more idealized terms as the immigrant frontier wife and mother epitomized in Willa Cather's *My Ántonia,* and perceived a certain old-fashioned domesticity, as compared with American women generally, among those she encountered.[13]

Understandably the visitors' observations regarding Swedish-American cultural life centered largely upon the question of language. This in turn focused a good deal of attention upon the churches. The journalist Erland Richter was especially perceptive in discussing the Augustana Synod's dilemma.

> Regarding the pastor, he truly stands between two fires and he can hardly avoid being burned now and then, or at least scorched. To begin with, most of the Swedish pastors find themselves embarrassed when it comes to preaching in the English language. They may be familiar enough with conversational English, but preaching in English is more demanding. . . . And the young, American-born pastor in the Swedish church has the same problem when he must preach in the Swedish language. In both cases the preacher using what for him is a foreign tongue must undergo a kind of examination each time he preaches, in which the congregation is the involuntary or voluntary examiner. And after the sermon is over, those going out talk less about the sermon's content and what it ought to have taught them than about the more or less faulty manner in which it was delivered.[14]

Archbishop Söderblom, for all his concern for the preservation of the Swedish heritage in America, showed an understanding tolerance for the Augustana Synod's increasing adoption of English. "The message of God and of Him Whom He has sent must be given to all in the language in which they are most at home," he wrote.[15] Others had greater reservations, including Pastor J. Thulin, who accompanied the archbishop and who was convinced that the synod's English-speaking congregations thrived less well than its Swedish-speaking ones. Swedish, he wrote, still had greater cohesive power among the Swedes, even though he recognized the need for concessions to "many of the younger generation."[16]

The visitors were meanwhile generally in agreement that the churches had served as bulwarks of the Swedish heritage in the New World, a point made most forcefully by Archbishop Söderblom and Anna Lenah Elgström, even where they recognized they had not always promoted all the desirable qualities of Swedish culture. Pastor Thulin noted, however, that the more recent Swedish immigrants in the East were "not such rewarding material for congregational life as the farmers and middle-class folk in the West."[17]

Regarding the Swedish cultural life of the secular organizations, Johan Benzendal declared that it amounted to nothing, thanks to "sluggishness and indifference on the part of the Swedes themselves." Their activity was grounded "not on the bedrock that is our Swedish culture, but upon the such loose ground as the Swedish Americans' cultural and national consciousness." As an illustration he satirically described a dreary Midsummer celebration in "Flappville," somewhere in the Midwest.

> The games around the maypole consisted of an old maid and a dozen small children who tramped around the decorated flagpole singing a song I believed I had heard before, but just then could not place. After the children and the old maid had trudged around for a while and the Swedes had gathered in a clump to look at the performance, like people gathering around an injured person and an ambulance, the Big Band Music was heard, this time from some distance away, where the young people hung out.

Naturally the latter did not dance Swedish folk dances, preferring instead the "African Negro dances" that were the current rage.[18]

At the other extreme was Anna Lenah Elgström, who gave the secular societies, in particular the Vasa Order of America, high marks for upholding a Swedish identity in America. Even if their cultural activities might often seem mediocre and dated, they were an effective force for holding the Swedish-American community together, not least by providing a social meeting ground leading to Swedish marriages and new Swedish homes, and by providing the organizational framework for future developments. Through their activities, moreover, many American-born young people who at home had rebelled against their parents' ways discovered the fascination of their Old Country heritage. Like Pastor Thulin, she also noted a more intensive Swedish-American secular organizational life in the East than elsewhere in the country, where the churches were stronger.[19]

The press and literary culture were the particular target of Johan Benzendal, who did not treat them gently. His fictionalized alter ego, "Gösta Bookstedt," comes to America in 1923 with the idea of contributing a cultural section to a leading Swedish-American newspaper. When no such opportunity presents itself in Chicago, he ends up in "Flappville," where he becomes acquainted with the editor of the local "*Svenska Bladet.*" The latter describes the kind of trivia with which he must fill his paper to satisfy the "sacred subscribers"—farmers and workingmen—upon which its existence depends. "In Europe," the editor explains, "we looked down on farmers and workers and up to the intellectuals. Here we look down on the intellectuals and up to the workers and farmers. For it is the farmer who feeds us and the manual laborer who earns the most money."

> This isn't any high-falutin', classical, privileged newspaper like the Swedish ones which don't give a damn what the subscribers want and force upon their readers only what the high-brow editors *think* their readers ought to know! A Swedish-American newspaper is a *people's* newspaper. A paper for individuals, not for groups of like-thinkers. You see, here it is a matter of satisfying the subscribers, of giving them just what they want.[20]

A conversation with the proprietor of a pitiful little Swedish bookstore in "Foolsville," reveals that Bookstedt's barbs are not aimed exclusively at Swedish America. "Swedish literature is altogether too heavy, too gloomy, too pessimistic for us out here to be able to read it with pleasure," the bookseller explains. Americans want to read about "strong, healthy people, happy people, enterprising people." Moreover, "The Swedes out here in the Middle West . . . prefer to buy books in English, because they are more cheerful, always have a happy ending, and usually cost no more than a dollar."[21]

While Archbishop Söderblom was generous in his praise of the Augustana Synod, its cultivated clergy, and its educational institutions, the travelers were generally agreed that the overall cultural level of Swedish America was modest, if not mediocre. Maj Hirdman was oppressed by the drab conformity of life among Swedish working people in and around New York and their lack of any interest either in the labor movement or in any cultural activity. Anna Lenah Elgström recognized that something like the contemporary Swedish workers' educational movement would stand little chance of success in America. "What have they accomplished in the cultural sphere?" Benzendal's Bookstedt writes to his brother. "Where are the culture-bearers: authors, poets, painters, sculptors, musicians, scientists? . . . Might one not love to imagine that all those Swedes ought to have been able to accomplish something more? Instead of availing themselves of many opportunities and achieving great things, have they not squandered their time on bagatelles, on nonsense?" In no group in America, he claimed, had he found so little ambition as among his own countrymen there.[22] This judgment was, needless to say, both exaggerated and unfair.

Nonetheless, if the Swedish Americans did not greatly impress in the cultural sphere, opinion was sharply divided over the reasons for this. To Benzendal the case was clear: the Swedish immigrant lost his innate refinement and was ground down to the lowest cultural common denominator by American materialism and banality. Maj Hirdman spoke of a process of "numbing Americanization." Lydia Hedberg said almost the same thing, although with greater sympathy. "It simply cannot be helped," she wrote, "that our emigrated Swedes have lagged behind considerably with respect to culture, which is a matter of time having passed them by. Their intellect has stood still during the dog-years they have had to endure before they could make use of the new language and the customs of the land."[23]

The opposite view was represented by Anna Lenah Elgström. While she, too, recognized that Swedish-American cultural life could be often dull and unimaginative, she did not basically attribute this to America and she envisioned the future evolution of more vital Swedish cultural manifestations in the New World. Swedish-American cultural life she saw as the natural outgrowth of what the immigrants were accustomed to at home.

I must always ask myself why should one expect that things should be better with respect to the Swedes' cultural interests and awareness in the Land of Dollars, with its predominantly materialistic culture and infectious contempt for ideas? But it is a fact that we always somehow unconsciously demand more from Swedish Americans. I believe it is quite simply because they are better dressed, have more possessions around them, more complex and sophisticated living arrangements . . . in a word, because in regard to all the external things they have risen a step higher than their relatives at home. That higher rung of material culture confuses us; we compare them, not with their corresponding class at home, but with a class that in cultural refinement also stands a rung higher.[24]

In coming from an older to a newer civilization, Elgström maintained, the Swedish immigrant moved both forwards and backwards: America lay fifty years ahead of Sweden in technology and material comfort, but fifty years behind in its concept of society's responsibility for the well-being of its members. The immigrant's tastes, brought over from the Swedish countryside of an earlier era, remained preserved, as though under a glass bell. Meanwhile experience in America developed the immigrants' practical abilities. "He founds charities and sick insurance funds, and his contributions to higher cultural activity consist more of donation than creation." Meanwhile:

Even if that world [Swedish America] sometimes offends us with its naivety, its Karl XII patriotism and ethnographic provincial feeling, oleographs of King Oscar and Queen Sofia, grand rhetoric about Gustav II Adolf and the Battle of Lützen, and so on—when one thinks back on all the trials and storms these people have withstood, one's heart is warmed and one would wish that Sweden might better understand how honorably and handsomely they have nonetheless built their Sweden in America, built it with their own hands, as well as they have known how, from memories, childhood impressions, vague feelings, and strong nostalgia—but still have built it, without any help to speak of from outside. For we have certainly not given them much help.[25]

Was there a distinctive Swedish-American type, or indeed a "Swedish America," and if so, what were they? "I ask myself," Benzendal's Bookstedt says, "how am I to recognize the Swede, as such, in America?" He concluded that the latter possessed no clear characteristics. In America, all the old, traditional nonmaterial values are replaced by monetary values, he maintained. The immigrant becomes "an egotist, or, as the Americans say, an individualist." In this way, he comes to be essentially indistinguishable from all others, his "genuine Swedish character dissolved and vanished," and can only really be understood as an American. Under such circumstances, Swedish America was, in Benzendal's view, no more than a joke in bad taste, a cultural no-man's-land.[26] Lydia Hedberg was inclined to agree, to a point. "One thus does not penetrate right away," she wrote, "to those remnants of the Swedish soul and Swedish character that may remain among Swedes who have come here and their descendants. Often one must long search for it."[27]

The opposite view was again represented by Nathan Söderblom, who stressed the role of religion in preserving Swedish values and a sense of identity, and Anna Lenah Elgström, who envisioned Swedish America in broader terms.

> Everywhere, throughout the length and breadth of America, [Elgström main-tained,] they have spread themselves, these Swedes, in the most varied conditions, regions, and climates. But no matter how widely spread they are, and fragmented as well . . . by different denominations, attitudes toward life, and degrees of education . . . whoever has learned to know Swedish America thinks, despite all, of the Swedish people out there as a kind of cultural unity, formed by a, to a degree, new type of Swedish identity. The old mentality—the Swedish peasant mentality—uprooted from its accus-tomed soil, transplanted into an environment with vast international ramifica-tions, has been modified, developed, indeed at times also become more complex and superficial, but has still remained a unity, something deeply and faithfully Swedish.

The preservation of this Swedish America was above all the work of the churches and societies. "Within the framework of both, the majority of the first generation of emigrants and a large part of the second generation live a Swedish life, as it were, deep within their American [lives]. Within this framework lies Sweden in America." As was said of Boston, this was "not so much a place as an atmosphere."[28]

But what might become of Swedish America, now that the Great Migra-tion was ending? Again, opinions varied. For Benzendal, there was nothing of any substance to save. Lindhagen considered it a matter of course that the language, and with it the cultural heritage, would in due time fade away for lack of fresh blood from the Old Country. Lydia Hedberg was disturbed by the "panicky anxiety" among the children of well-to-do immi-grants to conceal their Swedish origins and thereby avoid any identification with the raw greenhorns who still arrived from their parents' homeland.[29]

Anna Lenah Elgström was meanwhile impressed by the success of the churches and societies in arousing the interest of the American-born in the language and customs against which they often rebelled at home. But even if Swedish should not in the long run survive as an everyday, conversational language, she was able to envision a new type of Swedish identity in America, perhaps even more meaningful than the old. She reported a conversation with an unidentified Swedish-American journalist (one may at least suspect that he was Vilhelm Berger):

The third generation! It has often received a university education [he explained]. Its members have often traveled to Europe and there come to realize the value of having an ancient cultural tradition to build upon. . . . Usually the third-generation Swedish American no longer speaks Swedish or even understands the language. But his higher education better prepares him to comprehend and recognize Swedish cultural values than was possible for his more or less half educated Swedish-speaking parents—they who only wished to forget what their parents in turn had told them about Sweden: "herring and potatoes and red cottages"—more than that they were unlikely to remember. But for Swedish Americans of the second generation this was often *all* there was to Sweden. It will surely be in this [third] generation, and perhaps even more in its children, that Sweden, if it continues to deepen its contacts with Swedish America, will above all find its most faithful and understanding friends.[30]

The old ethnicity, Elgström came to realize, became ever more remote from Swedish reality and could not, in the long run, survive in its geographic and cultural isolation:

Indeed, for so it *must* be. They are not Swedes any longer. They are Americans, and to falter between the old and new land is ultimately neither healthy nor even possible. One senses this strongly at some of the manifestations of the preservation of the Swedish heritage, to which some of our countrymen out there devote themselves with almost professional zeal—at these well-meaning attempts to hold onto a Swedish peasant tradition through provincial clubs, folk dances, and speeches in local dialect. They succeed only in appearing ethnographic and exotic.[31]

It was essential, Elgström felt, that Sweden seek to gain the interest of the Americans as a whole, which in turn would stimulate the pride of Swedish Americans in their nationality and ancestral land. She thus admired in particular the work of the American-Scandinavian Foundation in New York for its promotion of cultural exchange and the John Morton Museum (later renamed the American-Swedish Historical Museum) in Philadelphia for its highlighting of Swedish contributions to America from colonial times to the present. "All of this makes one feel that we stand at the threshold of a new epoch in Swedish America's history."[32]

Archbishop Söderblom could likewise envision the passing of the old ethnicity, followed by a more promising new beginning. Swedish might come to live "a new life as a learned, highly valued foreign language." Those who learned it through proper study acquired moreover "a cultivated language, and not a threadbare and mixed language, such as quite naturally has become common in Swedish America."[33]

At a speech held at the banquet honoring the Swedish crown prince and princess at Chicago's Palmer House in 1926, the Swedish vice consul, G. Bernhard Anderson, raised the question, whether love and respect for

Sweden would die out among the descendants of Swedish immigrants. In Fritz Henriksson's paraphrase:

> He does not believe so, but on the contrary is of the view that the second and third generations should appreciate the land from which their fathers came even more than those who have come here from Sweden, and supports this contention by maintaining that the young men and women, eager to learn, thanks to their education, knowledge, and broader horizons, see old Sweden in a different light from their elders, who did not themselves know their land.[34]

Like others before them, several of the visitors of the 1920s deplored the lingering ignorance that in Sweden still obstructed a proper appreciation of the Swedish Americans and their accomplishments in the New World. "The saga of the Swedes out there," Nathan Söderblom declared, "has still not been written for Sweden, and it is high time that it be written, before the living tradition from the Great Migration has died out. Much material has been collected."[35] The appearance in Sweden of Hildebrand and Fredenholm's *Svenskarna i Amerika*—to which Söderblom contributed a brief greeting—already in 1925 represented an important Swedish attempt to build bridges.

Anna Lenah Elgström and Erland Richter in particular were impressed by initiatives from the Swedish-American side to create close ties with Sweden. They and others meanwhile agreed that a good deal more could and should be done from the Swedish side. "We have far too long neglected them out there," Elgström wrote. "Not that they cannot manage without us! It would be altogether wrong to assume a protective air toward Swedish America. No—for our own sake."[36]

For certain of our travelers, Swedish America's greatest significance lay in the portents it gave of a better world to come—or of one to be avoided at all costs. The latter view was most forcefully represented by Johan Benzendal, and indeed is the key to his *Amerikanska brev*. Bookstedt concludes that the Swedish Americans—ground down by high-pressure work, unrestrained consumerism and the worship of the Almighty Dollar, trivial and sensationalist entertainment, and deadening conformism—are simply the first victims of a new dark age threatening the whole civilized world. "A wave of democratic leveling has begun to engulf all of the Old World, threatening its cultural life with destruction, as it has swept away mighty civilized peoples in the past. . . . This devastating wave comes this time as well from the West, from the barbarians, who now, as before, using the tools of civilized peoples in their gorilla hands, smash the ancient temple walls to clear a freer field for their raw, untamed energy."

The moral was that Sweden, too, was imperiled, as it became ever more open to "all kinds of influences from abroad . . . the import of foreign trumpery has more and more suffocated the development of that which is truly our own." The security and contentment so characteristic of traditional peasant society in Sweden was threatened by the "industrialization of agriculture" and "the new spirit of the times of unrest, uncertainty, lust for money and pleasure," which drove peace from the soul and aroused "harmful instincts." All of this led toward the "new democracy," by which Benzendal meant nothing less than "the downward spiral, devolution." But it was still not too late: the isolation of the peasant class had not been broken, it had not been absorbed into the proletariat. "The modern gorilla has not yet made his entry"—although there were disquieting signs of his approach. Thus, "we must take up arms against the individualistic spirit of the times."[37]

Others looked to Swedish America with more hopeful eyes. Archbishop Söderblom revealed much of the neo-Gothicism of the RFSBU and its intellectual godfathers in his belief in the Swedes' ancient educative mission in the world. In the new America this assumed profound significance through the Swedish Americans' "world-historical calling in the building of the most universal among the nations of the world." Behind these words lie intimations that in a world shattered by war and nationalist passions, America—the "new Europe"—might ultimately point the way to a new world order based on peace, tolerance, and prosperity.[38]

For all of her clear-sighted reservations, Anna Lenah Elgström likewise accepted America as the new Rome. "Dear Countrymen! No one comes back to Sweden after being away for some time without being struck by how self-contentedly, indeed, how narrow-mindedly, we go about in our corner of the world, and how much that corner needs to be filled with fresher winds, winds from the open spaces of the world—including those that come from the land across the ocean where our kinsmen are helping to build the future."[39]

One Swedish visitor during the 1920s deserves individual attention: Helge Nelson, professor of geography at Lund University since 1916, whose career was from the beginning marked by his special interest in North America. As early as 1909 he contributed an analysis of emigration from Öland to the Emigration Inquest. His first research visit to North America in 1921 was followed the next year by a book on Canada, the new frontier. He crossed the Atlantic again for further research in 1925 and 1926, and in the latter year published his two-volume *Nordamerika, bygd och svensk-bygd* (North America: Settlement and Swedish Settlement), which combined an excellent survey of the continent's physical, economic, and human geography north of the Rio Grande with sections describing the specific areas of Swedish settlement, including their history and cultural characteristics.[40]

This work may be considered epoch-making in more than one sense. Helge Nelson was both the first academic scholar and the first homeland

Swede to undertake a methodical study of the specific, widely scattered, and highly varied settlements, both rural and urban, which together comprised Swedish America. This he did with thoroughness and objectivity, albeit with pride in the accomplishments of his people in North America. His physical descriptions of the Swedish rural settlements are not without a certain lyricism, while his careful chronicling of the retreat of the Swedish language in different areas reflects a wistful resignation.

For Professor Helge Nelson, this was only a beginning. He would visit North America again in 1933 and two years later bring out an enlarged and revised version of his 1926 study: *Nordamerika, natur och kulturbygd* (North America: Nature and Settlement). The final and fullest summation of his life work, concentrating upon his own emigrated countrymen, would be his two-volume study, *The Swedes and the Swedish Settlements in North America,* published in 1943, with its uniquely valuable statistical tables and distribution maps.[41] Until well past his retirement in 1947 he remained the lone pioneer in the study of the Swedes in North America within the Swedish academic establishment and his work remains of fundamental importance. Only gradually would others in Sweden follow in his footsteps.

By all evidence, a considerable number of Swedish Americans visited their old homeland during the prosperous 1920s. In view of the rapid changes taking place in Sweden in recent years, many if not most of them must have felt much as did Lars P. Nelson, who in an account appearing already in 1918 described his journey as a "voyage of discovery," for "so it surely is for one who has long been away. One does not recognize the country, it has changed so much."

Aside from this observation, Nelson has little of interest to relate, and the period from 1917 to 1930, reveals a surprising dearth, in both quantity and quality, of published Swedish-American accounts of individual travel to the Old Country, compared with the prewar decades and even, to a degree, with the leaner 1930s and later. Possibly the magnitude and pace of change in the homeland during the 1920s was so overwhelming for emigrants from a very different Sweden that they were perplexed as to how they should react. Perhaps Peter Södergren of Los Angeles spoke for many in 1925 when he wrote, "It was not Stockholm or other large cities that were the object of our trip, but rather it was the countryside, the country people, and country life that most interested us."[42]

The experience of coming back could still be a mixed one. Returning from the United States, the Swedish visitors Lydia Hedberg, Erland Richter, and Anna Lenah Elgström were indignant over the cold and arrogant manner in which they sometimes saw Swedish-American visitors treated.[43]

In 1923, as the last sizable wave of Swedes passed through Gothenburg on their way to America, that city celebrated its three-hundredth anniversary. In anticipation of a goodly Swedish-American attendance at the Gothenburg Exhibition of that year, the newspaper *Stockholms dagblad* set up a tourist bureau which issued a guidebook. This *Turistbok* is of particular interest for the indications it gives of what Swedish-American visitors were presumed not to know about the new Sweden and how they might be expected to behave, unless suitably warned in advance.

It often happens [its introduction stated], that an American Swede who after many years' absence from Sweden returns to visit his old homeland finds it difficult, if not impossible, to come to terms with conditions in Sweden. He encounters a good many misunderstandings, which deprive him of much of the pleasure he had rightly anticipated. This can surely not be ascribed to conditions in Sweden, but results from the fact that the visitor cannot immediately readjust to Swedish customs, with which during many years' stay in America he has usually lost touch. Not to mention the change in his personality which living in a young, immensely rich land, surging with energy and optimism, brings about. And the change Sweden has undergone since he left it.[44]

A second introduction by Herman Virde, formerly of the Swedish consulate in San Francisco, meanwhile sounded a cautionary note:

The Swedes at home are conscious of the love the Swedes in America feel for Sweden and rejoice at being able to hold out the warm hand of brotherhood and make their visit here as pleasant as possible. . . . You have surely not come here to tell us how much larger and richer in many respects America is than Sweden, but rather the purpose of your journey to old Sweden is certainly to be able to see relatives and friends again, to form new ties of friendship here, and to enjoy Sweden's varied and glorious nature. . . . Sweden is one of the world's oldest civilized countries, its customs have been crystallized from the experience of centuries and suited exactly to the Swedish character. It is therefore advisable to think carefully before throwing out a lot of new ideas and suggestions for improvement. To hear one's own voice has a certain fascination, but it is often most instructive to listen to what others have to say.[45]

The book meanwhile set forth in its first pages "some of the things an American Swede ought to observe and know during his visit to Sweden," by a "former American Swede." Most notably these included:

1) Avoid speaking English and be careful not to mix English phrases and words into the Swedish language. 2) When you come together with Swedes, do not talk about America and conditions there, unless you find a *real* interest in the subject. 3) In conversation, use the pronoun "you" [*Ni*] sparingly, employing instead the person's title and last name. If one wishes to show common courtesy, one does not use the title "herr" in conversation if another [more specific] title may be used. . . . 5) In Sweden, a gentleman normally

takes off his hat when he enters an office, a restaurant, or even often a shop. 6) If you wish to get information from a police constable, do not forget first to lift your hat, for his reply may otherwise be quite curt (simply a gesture with the hand appears impolite; in America it would seem ridiculous to lift one's hat to a policeman, but that is not how it is here).[46]

In contrast to this guarded reserve toward ordinary Swedish-Americans revisiting their homeland was the rapturous welcome given to the groups of young visitors from the Vasa Order of America's children's clubs brought to "Father's and Mother's Land" in 1924 and 1929 by Helga and Johannes Hoving, under the sponsorship of the RFSBU in Gothenburg. In particular, the first group of forty-five children from the original New York and Brooklyn clubs, accompanied by several mothers, created a sensation in 1924.[47]

The purpose of this tour was explained by G. Hilmer Lundbeck, head of the New York office of the Swedish-America Line, in a circular letter to the Vasa lodges: "This ought to be a campaign of conquest by the Vasa Order in old Sweden! Our children will take them by storm there at home. Not because they can accomplish so much or teach them back home anything they themselves cannot do much better, but because they will see, there at home, that we here in America keep up our traditions and wish to preserve our Swedish heritage in the second, third, and fourth generations."[48]

Dressed in their Swedish folk costumes, the youngsters sang Swedish songs and performed Swedish dances and dance-games to large and appreciative audiences in many localities in Sweden. Little Oscar Thorngren was a particular success when he recited in Swedish:

> I am but a little lad
> and little wisdom have I gained.
> But some day, when grown I am
> And more have learned from Father and from Mother,
> of the land where Viking sails have swelled
> and the cradles of Caroline heroes stood—
> of the land where steadfastness, honesty, and courage
> are changeless as the Giants' realm. . . .
> then will I—in tender tones and trumpet blast—
> tell of Sweden, land of saga in the North![49]

On such occasions, there were few dry eyes in the house.

The Vasa children were widely feted. In 1924 they were received both by Archbishop Söderblom and by King Gustav V. On numerous festive occasions, the children and their public were addressed by local notables who underlined the significance of their visit. *"Swedish children!,"* the burgomaster of Marstrand declared:

> Indeed, in the word *Swedish* lies all the deep meaning of our warm greeting. Certainly we do not forget that the proud Star-Spangled Banner is now your national symbol, but the blue-gold flag that here greets you still speaks a language that *must* captivate your young hearts to love. . . . May you then, in the depth of your souls remember that you are *Swedish children* and may you . . . feel that, as one of our great skalds sings, "Sweden, Sweden, Sweden, Fatherland" is also the "home of your yearning," your "home on earth."

Although their future life work presumably lay in America, the youngsters were admonished in Uddevalla that "this land feels about you and has the same demands upon you as if you still belonged to it entirely and undividedly." In Gothenburg, Vilhelm Lundström—at the time hotly engaged in his feud with the Augustana Synod—told the Vasa children that their visit overcame the weariness he often felt and gave him hope for the future of the Swedish race, "now that we have found each other again."[50]

The first Vasa children's tour aroused widespread enthusiasm in Swedish America, and especially within the Vasa Order, as witnessed by the establishment after 1924 of numerous new Vasa children's clubs throughout the United States. By 1929, when the Hovings led their second group to Sweden, there were already thirty-five such clubs throughout the country, and the participants came from several states.

The second tour followed, generally, in the footsteps of the first and enjoyed the same heartwarming success with the press and public. The young visitors were delighted with Sweden. "When I first set foot on my parents' ancestral soil," a girl from New York wrote afterwards, "it was if it were not a foreign country. I felt at home . . . . Sweden is so marvelously beautiful. My greatest astonishment is that its people can leave the country and that many remain away from such a beautiful land." Sweden, a boy from Detroit wrote, "was the land of my dreams and I wanted to go there. When I had seen it I didn't want to come back to America. I thought the time there was so short. And now I long only to return to Sweden again."[51]

In his numerous speeches during the tour, Johannes Hoving repeatedly expressed his conviction that the preservation of ancestral language and traditions by America's immigrant groups was essential for the maintenance of social order. "Americanization must take place in such a manner that family bonds are not broken. The immigrants' home languages should be preserved and the children encouraged to hold to their parents' languages, thereby serving as intermediaries between the cultures of their parents' old homelands and that culture which is evolving in America."[52]

The 1929 Vasa children's tour coincided with the arrival in Sweden of some nine hundred former inhabitants of the village of Gammalsvenskby in southern Russia. The presence in the homeland of representatives of the Swedish diaspora from both East and West naturally called forth editorial comment in the press. Johannes Hoving made a kind of pious pilgrimage to visit the newly arrived villagers from the steppe—these ultimate Swedes—in their camp in Jönköping. "Despite the oppression their forefathers have been subjected to through the centuries in Russia," he marvelled, "they have not lost their original nationality. Try to claim, then, that Swedish customs and language cannot survive for centuries, even under unbearable external and internal political circumstances!" When he told the refugees of efforts to uphold the Swedish heritage in America, they warmly approved. "This, they considered, ought to work for the Swedish Americans as well as they [themselves] had managed to succeed over the centuries." Here, surely, Hoving saw his most cherished dream for the future of *svenskhet* in America.[53]

"Does it, or does it not, have any significance whether our kinfolk abroad keep, develop, and defend their Swedish characteristics, and that they are proud of their Swedish origins?" *Köpings-Posten* asked, apropos of the children's tour. "Indeed it does! That such is the case is the most powerful proof of the vitality and inner strength of the old Swedish culture and a demonstration that this culture can well hold its place for generations in competition on foreign ground."[54]

These were cries from the heart at a time when the end of the Great Migration meant that for coming generations, "Father's and Mother's Land" would be—America.

During the period between 1917 and 1930, Sweden and the United States became both closer and more remote. Both societies became progressively more industrialized and urbanized—while yet looking back nostalgically to visions of a recent rural past. The gap in living standards and popular culture narrowed. In Sweden, where this transformation began late and moved rapidly during these years, the changes taking place often seemed to bear the imprint of America and were judged accordingly, as welcome innovations or as threats to traditional values.

Yet between Sweden and Swedish America the distance widened. Net Swedish emigration to the United States declined to low levels, beginning already in 1914. By the 1920s, the immigrant community was both aging and shrinking. Badly shaken by the trauma of World War I and largely deprived of fresh blood—except to a degree in the Northeast—Swedish America, while gaining in prosperity and organization, lost much of its prewar spirit and creative vitality, becoming increasingly mainline American in outlook and preoccupations. The contrast with only a decade earlier is striking and sobering.

It was this suddenly graying Swedish America with which Swedish visitors during the 1920s came in contact. Arriving from a rejuvenated home-land, where the conservative national awakening from the turn of the century and the socialist struggle for a better way of life for all were giving rise to a new consensus and confidence, these travelers received an often dreary impression of life among their countrymen in America, who, from a Swedish point of view, dreamed—if it was conceded that they dreamed at all—of a Sweden that had ceased to exist or was rapidly disappearing.

Yet most of the Swedish visitors felt, or came to feel, a genuine sympathy for the Swedish Americans, and even for the time-worn rituals of their first-generation immigrant ethnicity. Some still harbored hopes that with encouragement from home, the old forms might somehow be preserved for the future. Others, meanwhile—like certain of Swedish America's own more clear-sighted spokesmen—could envision the passing, with dignity, of the old integral ethnicity, from whose ashes a new ethnicity, inspired by Sweden's national cultural heritage, would arise, phoenix-like, among the American-born descendants of those who had sought new homes in the New World.

NINETEEN

The Afterglow

*I*n 1929 the new restrictive American immigration quotas under the National Origins Act went into effect; henceforward Sweden's allotment would be 3,314 persons annually. In October of that year the New York stock market crashed, setting off the worldwide Great Depression. For the United States, this would become the severest and longest economic crisis the nation had ever faced. Although likewise badly shaken, Sweden would prove better able to weather the storm.

Looking back, these two events in 1929 would seem the final landmarks of the great European migration to America. At the time, however, this did not appear so evident. There was much movement across the Atlantic, albeit largely—and only temporarily, it was imagined—back to the Old World. Until World War II once again closed the sea lanes, there were still those who believed that the return of better times in America would bring down the immigration barriers to replenish the nation's labor supply.[1]

There remained in America a large element of Swedish immigrants, many still in their most active years, and of their descendants. For them, the Great Migration was of recent memory, and relations with the land of their origin remained a matter of vital concern, both to their former countrymen and to themselves. Thus the afterglow of the 1930s has its place in any consideration of the migration era, and particularly of the relationship between those who left and those who stayed in the old homeland.

During the Depression years Swedish transatlantic migration by no means ceased, but the direction of flow was reversed. In 1930, for the first time since 1875, when the Swedish government began recording returns— and surely for the first time ever—remigrants from America outnumbered Swedish immigrants to the United States, and by a substantial margin. This trend continued unbroken throughout the decade. Between 1930 and 1939, only 9,133 Swedes immigrated to the United States, while 30,639 moved back to Sweden, a ratio of over three to one. In 1932, the peak year, Swedish return migrants outnumbered immigrants by 5,654 to 474.[2] While many remigrants may have expected to return to America when times improved, it seems evident that only relatively few ultimately did so.

This backflow had its impact upon Swedish America's demographic profile. In 1930 the United States census shows the Swedish stock at its peak of 1,562,685 persons. But the first, Swedish-born generation had declined to 595,250, as compared with the second, American-born generation of 967,453. By 1940 the Swedish element had decreased to 1,301,390, including 445,070 Swedish- and 856,320 American-born. Naturally, the total number of Swedish descendants in the United States was constantly increasing, but the census did not record ethnic origin past the second generation. The Swedes were by now among the older immigrant groups in America. Both the first and second generations were aging and contracting, but whereas in 1930 the Swedish-born amounted to 38.1 percent of the enumerated Swedish stock, by 1940 they came to 34.2 percent. During the same period, the median age of the Swedish-born rose from 52 to 58 years, becoming the highest among major immigrant groups in America. In 1920 their median age had been only 44.6 years.[3]

The return migration of the 1930s undoubtedly had overall consequences for Swedish America out of proportion to its numbers. Research has shown that the incidence of remigration was highest within the first few years after arrival and among younger immigrants who had not yet married, started families, obtained settled employment, or acquired property.[4] This would indicate that a high proportion of the returnees had been among the most recent immigrants of the 1920s, those whose contacts with the Old Country remained the closest and who had tended to concentrate in urban centers with an active Swedish ethnic life. Their departure left behind a Swedish-American population on the whole not only older but also of longer residence in the United States, hence more assimilated, more American in its ways and attitudes. Hard times meanwhile reduced the numbers who could afford to visit the Old Country. Direct contacts with Sweden became sparse, until they were largely suspended during World War II. At this time of increasing world renown for Sweden, Swedish Americans found their old homeland becoming ever more remote from the world of their own experience.[5]

The Great Depression and demographic change affected the nature and scope of Swedish-American institutional and cultural life. The economic crisis bore heavily upon the foreign-born, especially upon younger, unskilled workers. In many states those lacking American citizenship were ineligible for unemployment relief, while aliens found to be public charges could be subject to deportation. The situation aroused the established Swedish-American community to impressive efforts to assist countrymen in need by filling the gaps left by an inadequate public welfare system. Sture Lindmark, who recounted this voluntary relief work in some detail, characterized it as "a final desperate but vigorous attempt to hold together the Swedish population in America."[6] It was, however, an effort that could not be sustained indefinitely. Fortuitously, when its support began to fail, the new Democratic administration under Franklin D. Roosevelt came to power in 1933 and commenced its national program of public relief.

The Depression meanwhile undermined Swedish America's institutional base. For want of economic support, numerous Swedish ethnic organizations, publications, and businesses went under. Among the secular societies, the large national or regional organizations had the greatest powers of survival, but they too were hard pressed; the Vasa Order of America, for instance, declined from its peak membership of over 72,000 in 1930 to under 57,000 by 1934. Not surprisingly, only the Swedish-American churches continued to grow in membership throughout the troubled decade of the 1930s. Sture Lindmark is surely right in concluding that the Depression was a major milestone in the Americanization of the Swedish ethnic group.[7]

Demographic change led to the progressive Americanization of what remained of organized Swedish ethnic life. Its outward signs of ethnicity became increasingly symbolic, rather than substantive. Old family traditions meanwhile seemed ever more remote to the children and grandchildren of immigrants long established in America.

Language usage is, as always, a basic guide to ethnic maintenance, and here, perhaps especially, both the Depression and demographic change made deep inroads. In 1930 there were still forty-nine Swedish-language periodicals of all types; by 1940 their number was halved, to twenty-five. The publication of books in Swedish now became a rarity; only fourteen literary works are noted to have appeared in that language between 1931 and 1940. The use of Swedish in church services continued to decline. In Illinois, for example, half the Augustana Lutheran congregations had gone over entirely to English by 1935 and 76 percent of them by 1940, by which date half of the Mission Covenant congregations in the state had done the same.[8]

Although the secular societies had come to see themselves as the foremost guardians of Swedish language and traditions during the 1920s, they too faced the problem of survival after the end of the Great Migration. Indeed, their cultural stance left them less secure than the churches in the face of changing language usage, as Vilhelm Berger had observed in 1916. By 1923 the language barrier was breached, at least in principle, in the Vasa Order of America, although change occurred slowly.[9] The language dilemma was especially painful for the Swedish Cultural Society in America, that small but steadfast offshoot of the RFSBU in Sweden, for which preservation of the mother tongue was the heart of its program. Ivar Ericson agonized over whether the society should on occasion make use of English. In the society's commemorative volume in 1938, he wrote:

> Our Swedish sentiments rebel against this, but our common sense tells us that we must preserve our Swedish heritage abroad, even if this requires using foreign means. Sweden and its progress are known throughout the world today, not because of isolation and withdrawal, but because we have described our history and our work in a language comprehensible to the listener. Let us maintain the Swedish language at our meetings, speak it among ourselves as often and as much as we can, sing and lecture in it, a lovelier and more sonorous language does not exist on earth. But let us teach those who do not understand this wonderful language to understand what Swedish culture has given to the world.[10]

There was, however, one hopeful sign the champions of Swedish language and culture did not fail to recognize. Throughout the 1930s, while Swedish as a vernacular language was on the wane in America, enrollment in Swedish language and literature courses, both at Swedish-American colleges and at those state universities that offered them, was steadily rising.[11] To those capable of grasping it, this could be seen as the portent of a new ethnicity.

The 1930s witnessed the last great debate over the preservation of the Swedish language in America, between Johannes Hoving and Vilhelm Berger in New York. Dr. Hoving naturally represented the traditional ideal of ethnic maintenance in America. In a speech given in New York in 1930, printed in several Swedish-American newspapers, he sternly took his compatriots in America to task for failing, in their complacency, to rally in a great common effort to uphold their language and heritage. He berated the churches for their refusal to cooperate in this regard. He meanwhile categorically opposed the establishment of English-speaking Vasa lodges to attract the younger generations.

> For as soon as we have created such English-speaking lodges in some numbers interests will creep in which differ from those we have set up as our ideals. But if we establish Swedish-speaking lodges among the second generation the proper Swedish spirit will remain and the Swedish heritage will not be lost. To claim that a sense of Swedishness could be preserved if the Swedish language disappears is pure nonsense. That would mean the end of a Swedish identity within two generations, for the second generation lacks resistance and the third has forgotten its origins and the Swedish cultural accomplishments which their forefathers have carried out here in America or in the homeland.

"The better we succeed in upholding our language," Hoving proclaimed in 1931, "the more secure we may be in our wish to bring culture in its various forms over to America."[12]

In 1933 Hoving brought out an impassioned article in *Nordstjernan* (New York) accusing its editor, his "good friend" Vilhelm Berger, of claiming that the Swedish heritage could survive in America even without the language, and that efforts to maintain the latter were worse than useless. This led him to a declaration of his fundamentally pluralist credo for America. "I do not believe in the future triumph of cosmopolitanism, but rather of nationalism. Nor do I believe in the improvement of the races of humanity through an unrestrained and uncontrolled mixing in the so-called melting pot, but instead in true progress if the national groups here are preserved and intermix as little as possible, which need not prevent them from being good friends, helpful neighbors, and the like."[13]

Johannes Hoving's attack hardly did justice to Vilhelm Berger, who had stated his views on the language question in a series of articles in his newspaper in 1933, published in book form the same year. There were idealists, Berger held, who believed the Swedish tongue could be maintained in perpetuity in America and who considered language the alpha and omega of the Swedish heritage. He admitted he had felt so himself twenty-five or thirty years earlier, but the observations of the past ten or fifteen years had brought him to different conclusions. No valid comparison could be made between the East Baltic Swedes and the Swedish Americans. The RFSBU in Sweden and the Swedish Cultural Society in America still dreamed, he wrote, of creating "an intellectual [New Sweden], with the Swedish language as its talisman, a kind of freemasonry, which to be sure would be English-speaking on weekdays up to 6:00 o'clock, but thereafter Swedish-speaking at home and in the societies in the evenings, as well as in church on Sundays." But, Berger continued, "Why not let the language question solve itself in a natural way? That of which the heart is full, the mouth will speak. Let each one speak the language in which he or she is best able to express his or her thoughts."[14]

Berger thus dismissed the usual opinion of the Swedish-American press, that "the Swedish heritage and Swedish language are like a pair of Siamese twins who must remain joined together in order to live." All kinds of artificial efforts to keep the language alive had produced no more than a "varnish, sometimes thick, sometimes thin," that hardly reached down to the bedrock of true Swedish culture. Moreover, Berger attacked the blithe assumption of the innate superiority of *svenskhet* to Americanism, for "love of freedom, respect for the law, a sense of justice, industriousness, conscientiousness, and similar virtues" were no less traditionally American than Swedish qualities.[15]

In place of a faded and shopworn ethnographic display of "certain disconnected manifestations of Swedish culture," Berger looked forward to the emergence of a new ethnicity, freed from the albatross of a dying language, based upon a broader knowledge of the history, culture, and accomplishments of the Swedes in the Old World and the New. To this end he put his faith in the Augustana Lutheran Church, the new John Morton Museum in Philadelphia, and similar institutions, which could prepare the way for a new "sense of nationality, which can bring together Swedish descendants here more naturally and more strongly than Swedish culture and language have ever been able to do. ... This will be the transplanting of the Swedish heritage in America, a development that need not be fed a mass of sentimentality to be kept alive." A few would meanwhile always learn Swedish out of genuine interest. The important thing was for the Swedish descendants to continue the "Nordic historical mission, which in all times and wherever [Nordic peoples] have settled, consists of contributing freely, and without requiring compensation, their rich cultural treasures and good qualities of character."[16]

As with Johannes Hoving, Vilhelm Berger's thoughts regarding language derived from his overall view of his countrymen in America, set forth in innumerable newspaper articles and short stories since the turn of the century and presented in book form in 1924. He elaborated his views further in his books from 1934 and 1937, the year before his death. In truth his attitudes toward his fellow Swedish Americans were complex, even seemingly paradoxical. Throughout his career he was their dedicated antiquarian, the careful compiler of information concerning their mixed Swedish-American dialect, their congregations (especially Augustana-Lutheran), their organizations, their newspapers, and the place-names they had left on the map of America.[17] He was proud to identify with his compatriots in America, yet he remained the clear-eyed realist who had seen the New World from the bottom up during his hard "dog-years," and he refused to idealize or sentimentalize over them.

To judge the Swedish Americans rightly, he now held, it should be remembered that they consisted of those who, despite their best efforts, had been unable to better their lot in Sweden. They "may in many ways be taken to represent reaction against the old social injustices in Sweden." They thus tended to be "people for whom tradition, family relationships, and security over the centuries mean nothing." Their ideal became the self-made man through hard work. In more recent decades, Swedish immigrants had come from more varied backgrounds, but it was these first arrivals who laid the groundwork for Swedish America and still largely set its tone. As a community it was "immensely tradition-bound and conveys something of the 1870s and 1880s." Its archaic traits remained noteworthy.[18]

This was no less true of religious than of secular life. Berger was a loyal Augustana Lutheran and had always emphasized the Augustana Synod in particular as the stronghold of Swedish cultural values in the New World. But this did not keep him from accusing its clergy of failing to keep up with the times and for an all too frequent narrow and authoritarian dogmatism. "The pastors," he allowed himself to say in 1937, "the Swedish Americans must have gotten for the sake of their sins." The non-Lutheran denominations he nonetheless felt unsuited to the Swedish character.[19]

The social and cultural life resting on these foundations drew Berger's sharpest strictures. That it was superficial, banal, and derivative he had repeatedly declared in the past, but by the 1930s this criticism became ever more central to his view of Swedish America. He granted that there was a vital musical life, but he considered his countrymen's theatrical tastes deplorable. Literary creativity languished in the face of discouraging indifference. He regretted the total lack in the societies of "evening entertainments with programs of an educational nature," such as were now so successful in working-class circles in Sweden, and which could have familiarized participants with present-day developments in the old homeland. Instead the Swedish Americans distracted themselves with mindless, commercial mass entertainments or with empty pomp and ceremony within their clubs and lodges. All of this created the idea that social activity must be pursued outside the home, which impoverished family life, more intimate social contacts, and the observance of old household customs. "Does this search for entertainment satisfy our countrymen?" Berger asked. "Most certainly not, for one so often hears the complaint that one cannot really enjoy oneself as much here as in Sweden." The reason was their uncritical acceptance of American popular culture. They were generally markedly indifferent to anything requiring intellectual effort. "Swedish America," he wrote wearily in 1937, "is the promised land of mediocrities."[20]

In the clubs and lodges, Swedish Americans cultivated their love of pomp and circumstance to the full. Their rituals were performed with a solemnity reminiscent of a Swedish high mass or the installation of an American president. Their members delighted in celebrating the visits of cultural celebrities from Sweden, although "their messages and accomplishments easily become incidental; for [the members] the banquet is the main thing."

> Speeches are then made which may give the Swedish guests of honor to believe that the speakers are ready to move home to Sweden the following day. "*Du gamla, du fria*" is sung in unison and "I will live, I will die in the North" is rendered with such feeling that the banquet hall reverberates, even though not a single one of the participants would wish to return to Sweden to stay. The whole thing is merely emotional intoxication, but when the Swedish visitor returns home to Sweden he there bears witness to the strong love and homesickness for Sweden which he has had the opportunity to observe among his expatriate countrymen.[21]

What, then, of Swedish America's future, as Berger saw it in the 1930s, near the end of his long years in its service?

There can surely be no talk of a purely Swedish-American culture, which like that of Hellas has grown out of the soil. To develop such takes centuries and we have not been here for much more than a couple of generations. But one thing is certain, which is that there are expressions of culture among Svea's descendants in America, something they are not really quite prepared to accept in Sweden. These cultural developments quite naturally have their roots in Sweden's culture and have encountered certain influences from America's. They will scarcely evolve into an independent Swedish-American culture . . . but future researchers will perhaps be able to trace some influence or another within the American culture of the future. That will be the treasure we brought with us from the Land of the Midnight Sun as our own inheritance, that will be the fruit of our often fumbling cultural strivings, that will become, sometime far in the future, the sum total of Swedish America's history.[22]

By the 1930s, Berger was quite prepared to let go of the Swedish America he knew—and toward which he had felt both love and exasperation. He had already long since set his hopes upon a truer and deeper appreciation of Sweden's higher cultural heritage among the educated and cosmopolitan descendants of those who had once left the stony hillsides of the old homeland in search of a better future across the sea.[23]

While he freely borrowed ideas where he found them, Vilhelm Berger had become with time Swedish America's foremost interpreter during the last stages of the migration era. It should, however, be remembered that his Swedish America had long been primarily that of the urban and industrial Northeast and that the horizon could look somewhat different from the perspectives of Chicago or Seattle, Mora, Minnesota, or Swedesburg, Iowa.

As the Great Migration receded into the past, the preservation and commemoration of that past became an ever more urgent concern within the Swedish-American community. This would seem belied by the demise of the Swedish Historical Society of America; its last *Bulletin* appeared in June 1932, and its final meeting was held in 1934. Like many other Swedish-American organizations it fell victim to the economic strains of the Depression, after being weakened by personal conflicts within its leadership.[24] Yet these factors may have been as much symptoms as causes. The society had never exceeded five hundred members and seems to have languished as early as the later 1920s. At that time, Professor George M. Stephenson of the University of Minnesota emerged as its leading figure and editor of its publications. Meanwhile, a competing movement arose, inspired and led by Dr. Amandus Johnson in Philadelphia.

Stephenson, the first American academic historian of Swedish origins to devote himself to the history of his ethnic group in the United States, was a staunch apostle of the New History, with its ideal of strict scholarly objectivity. In 1926 he demonstrated this approach in *A History of American Immigration, 1820–1924,* a groundbreaking work in its field. Through the 1920s he brought out articles and edited documents on Swedish-

American history, in the publications of the Swedish Historical Society in America and elsewhere, and in 1927 he published a monograph on the origins of the Augustana Synod.[25] As the society's editor, Stephenson strove to establish the new standards of scholarship and encouraged contributions by younger academics and graduate students.

This new direction, however, quite evidently cost the society much needed support. Those within the Swedish-American community interested in its history were, on the whole, accustomed to sturdy filiopietism in the spirit of J. A. Enander and his disciples, for whom the essential purpose of history was to glorify and commemorate. This traditional viewpoint was most conspicuously represented by Dr. Amandus Johnson, author of *The Swedish Settlements on the Delaware* in 1911 and former member of the department of Germanic languages at the University of Pennsylvania, who wrote a brief survey, *Swedish Contributions to American National Life, 1638–1921* in connection with the New York exhibition "America's Making" in 1921. This describes in glowing terms the heroic qualities and achievements of the Swedes in the New World since Viking times. A comparison with the even shorter, calm and even-handed account *Den svenska folkstammen i Amerika* (The Swedish Race in America), brought out in Stockholm in 1928 by the visiting Andrew A. Stomberg, the American-born professor of Scandinavian at the University of Minnesota and a leading figure in the Swedish Historical Society in America, reveals the widening gap between two opposed concepts of history.

In 1924 Amandus Johnson launched ambitious plans for the building of a national Swedish-American museum in Philadelphia, the cradle of American liberty on what had once been Swedish territory, in conjunction with the sesquicentennial celebration there of American independence in 1926 and with an eye to the upcoming three-hundredth anniversary of the founding of the New Sweden colony in 1938. Although he at first encountered much skepticism over the idea of raising a half million dollars and building a museum far removed from the Midwestern Swedish-American heartland, Johnson crusaded with tireless zeal.

By the end of 1925 sizable donations began coming in. Here was a cause with real appeal to wealthy and socially prominent Swedish Americans: an imposing monument in brick and mortar, dedicated to the splendid past and remarkable contributions of their people to the building of America. Its attractiveness may have been enhanced by another consideration, which Johnson later recalled. In Minnesota in 1924 he was deeply troubled by the following the new Farmer-Labor party was gaining among Swedish Americans; the museum, he hoped, "would help to make the Swedish Americans more patriotic and counteract radicalism." Those disappointed by earlier attempts to rally a factious Swedish America welcomed a common cause that ought to transcend all internal cleavages.[26]

A new organization, the American Sons and Daughters of Sweden, was established to raise funds. The campaign was so successful that in June 1926, the visiting Swedish Crown Prince Gustav Adolf, as one of the high points of his American visit during that sesquicentennial year, laid the cornerstone for the John Morton Memorial Museum on land provided by the city of Philadelphia. Construction proceeded apace, and in 1929 the stately building was opened to the public.

Johnson and the museum faced lean times during the Depression years, but support somehow continued and increased with the approach of the 1938 New Sweden Jubilee, for which it was to play the role Johnson had long envisioned for it. When finally completed by that time, its grand entrance hall was adorned with murals depicting heroic scenes from the history of colonial New Sweden, and its various theme rooms, named after such prominent figures as John Hanson, John Ericsson, Fredrika Bremer, and Jenny Lind, contained exhibits concerning those areas of activity associated with them. The emphasis was—and still remains—upon great names and personal achievements; only relatively modest attention was given to ordinary immigrants during the great migration and their descendants.[27]

The small Swedish Historical Society in America could hardly stand up against such competition, nor was the austere scholar, George Stephenson, a match for the colorful Amandus Johnson when it came to arousing enthusiasm and support among Swedish Americans. Swedish-American historical interest was split between the enthusiasts of a new filiopietism, led by Johnson, and that small group, primarily of academic scholars, who looked to Stephenson as their model.[28] Still, the latter element did not disappear, and with time its work would have increasing impact. In 1930 the Augustana Historical Society was established in Rock Island, Illinois. Its focus was, and remains, largely the history of the Augustana Lutheran Synod, its leading figures, and educational institutions, although it soon likewise showed an interest in broader questions affecting American immigration and ethnic life in general. It has seldom had more than a hundred dues-paying members, yet it still exists today and has published over thirty books.[29]

That the decline of the Swedish Historical Society left a void at the very time when it seemed more vital than ever to chronicle a rapidly vanishing Swedish America is reflected in the publication in Chicago of an ambitious collaborative work in three volumes in 1931, *The Swedish Element in America*, edited by Erik G. Westman and E. Gustav Johnson, and intended as a grand, retrospective survey. Significantly for its time, it was the first such work to be offered in English. As an overview it falls well short of the mark. Its subtitle suggests its lack of guiding themes or clear-cut organization: "A Comprehensive History of Swedish-American Achievements from 1638 to the Present Day, Including a Biographical History of Outstanding Swedish Men and Women Who Occupy Prominent Places in All Walks of Life in the United States Today." It provides no background to the emigration from Sweden nor any connected narrative of Swedish settlement in the United States but consists instead of a rather haphazard potpourri of articles, long and short, on various aspects of Swedish-American life and achievement, together with biographical sketches of a host of better- or lesser-known persons. There are, moreover, important gaps in its coverage. In 1934 an additional tome, labeled confusingly both as volume 4 and as a second edition of the work, appeared, containing further material and announcing that other "editions" (i.e., volumes) would be forthcoming, although none appeared thereafter.

For all its shortcomings, however, *The Swedish Element in America* fulfilled a useful purpose. The Swedes, its introduction stated, had by now "arrived" in American life and society. The immigration was a closed chapter that would not recur and for lack of fresh blood the days of the old Swedish America were now numbered. It was thus essential that as much of its past as possible be saved and recorded before it was too late, for the inspiration of future generations. Its numerous contributors consisted mainly of graying veterans from the heyday of Swedish America before World War I— principally clergymen, journalists, and educators—who in their time had written historical and cultural essays for such publications as *Valkyrian, Prärieblomman,* or *Ungdomsvännen,* and later, in some cases, for Karl Hildebrand and Axel Fredenholm's *Svenskarna i Amerika,* published in Stockholm, in 1925–26. Thus, *The Swedish Element in America* drew upon an impressive and irrecoverable pool of personal experience and knowledge. It remains a veritable mine of information, much of it unique, which regrettably has been largely forgotten or overlooked by more recent research.[30]

In the meantime, the early 1930s saw the definitive breakthrough of the academically trained professional historians of Swedish America. Before 1930, George Stephenson was virtually alone in his discipline—other academics active in the field, such as Amandus Johnson or Andrew A. Stomberg, having been trained in other fields. In 1932 he came out with his *magnum opus* in the field, *The Religious Aspects of Swedish Immigration,* a work far broader in scope than its title would suggest. In the meantime, a number of younger historians, including Florence E. Janson, John S. Lindberg, and O. Fritiof Ander, made their debuts.[31]

An institution that would play a major role up to the present in maintaining a Swedish heritage in America came into existence at the turn of the decade: the American Institute of Swedish Arts, Literature and Science (later renamed the American-Swedish Institute) in Minneapolis at the end of 1929. It has engaged in a wide variety of social and cultural activities, supported by a large membership in the Twin Cities and beyond.[32]

It may seem paradoxical that three important institutions should appear on the scene at the beginning of the Great Depression and should survive the hard years that followed, when numerous older Swedish-American organizations failed. It may not have escaped notice, however, that the museum in Philadelphia and the institute in Minneapolis came to be designated as "American-Swedish"—rather than "Swedish-American." Neither they nor the Augustana Historical Society in Rock Island were committed to the preservation of the Swedish language, per se. All three were oriented primarily toward the descendants of immigrants, rather than the immigrants themselves, and moreover toward a certain level of prosperity, education, and social standing. Already during the 1930s the new ethnicity, divorced—amicably or otherwise—from the old language, was beginning to manifest itself.

In Sweden, interest in America, including its Swedish element, appear to have cooled between the mid-1920s and the mid-1930s, since attention was ever more focused upon developments in the homeland, even though the RFSBU continued to maintain its concern for Swedish America.[33] The contrast between the values of the Old versus the New World likewise continued as a theme in Swedish writing, while pulp literature featuring adventure in American settings continued to flourish.

The newer American literature made its real breakthrough in Sweden following Sinclair Lewis's Nobel Prize in 1930, largely thanks to the efforts of such enthusiasts as Anna Lenah Elgström. Its new popularity, however, particularly in leftist intellectual circles, derived largely from the social and cultural criticism of American conditions conveyed by such authors as John Dos Passos, Theodore Dreiser, or John Steinbeck. The return, during the Depression, of many disillusioned emigrants from America added substance to this generally dark picture.[34]

Swedish Americans who sought to return permanently to their old homeland meanwhile often felt they were inhospitably received. The eminent artist of the American Southwest, Carl Oscar Borg, returning to his old homeland in 1938, was filled with foreboding, as he envisioned a Mother Svea who gathered to her ample bosom those children she had "borne in her prosperity," while cruelly repulsing those from across the sea whom she "bore in her days of poverty and misery, and for that reason hates."[35]

Traveling to the United States in 1939, the journalist Carl Mangård wrote of an older Swedish-American couple on their way back. Their old home community in Västergötland had taxed them heavily, draining their American savings, but no employment was to be found. "Sweden wanted only their money but did not ask for their labor. It was rather similar to when they had left their native place for the first time and garlanded with flowers followed the Swedish bloodstream toward the West. Their bitterness toward the place to which, during their long and drudgerous years in America, they had longed to return, was simply so much the greater." In response to such problems, *Utlandssvenskarnas förening* (The Overseas-

Swedish Society)—presently *Föreningen svenskar i världen* (Society for Swedes in the World)—was established in Stockholm in 1938, to promote the practical interests of Swedes abroad, including those who returned home.[36]

By the mid-1930s Swedish interest in America began to revive. The United States, under Franklin D. Roosevelt's new Democratic administration, showed signs of recovering from the depths of the Depression. In 1933, Anna Lenah Elgström again visited the United States. To her, the New Deal amounted to nothing less than a benevolent "revolution." Roosevelt, in her eyes, strove to restore America's classic Jeffersonian balance between "the right to the free development of personality and the right to property," when the latter, represented by rapacious giant corporations, threatened to overwhelm the former. The new America gave fresh hope for the future of justice, democracy, and humanity in a troubled world.[37]

Interestingly, Elgström, a committed Swedish Social Democrat, chose not to make direct comparisons between Roosevelt's New Deal and the Social Democratic regime under Premier Per Albin Hansson which had come to power in Sweden only a few weeks before Roosevelt's election; indeed, she scarcely mentions Sweden in her book. But the parallels are implicit. By the early 1930s Swedish Social Democracy could well begin to have more benign second thoughts about the United States, while growing admiration there for Sweden's own impressive recent accomplishments was gratifying.

There was meanwhile another factor that received mounting publicity in Sweden: the imminent celebration in 1938 of the three-hundredth anniversary of the colonizing of New Sweden on the Delaware, for which preparations began on both sides of the Atlantic by 1934. The timing was thus opportune for the appearance in 1935 of the Lund geographer Professor Helge Nelson's second edition of his book on North America, following his third visit there in 1933, in which he "sought to indicate the continuous assimilation of the old Swedish settlements into the American cultural milieu."[38]

In 1935 Albin Widén, a novelist and ethnologist, took leave from the Nordic Museum in Stockholm to carry on historical-ethnographic research among the Swedes in America. He later claimed that in Sweden it was then easier to obtain research support to study native cultures in Africa than to study Swedish America. He nonetheless received a grant from the Sweden-America Foundation to pursue this novel interest.

His academic background in ethnology, a discipline highly developed with respect to traditional folkways in Sweden, set Widén apart from the great majority of Swedish visitors to America who were journalists of various kinds. Widén's *Svenskar som erövrat Amerika* (Swedes Who Conquered America), which came out in 1937, contains much sensitively observed ethnographic detail from Swedish America together with a survey of its history. The book, meanwhile, reveals the novelist as much as the ethnologist. Widén was clearly aware of need for a popularly written survey of Swedish-American life and culture, of reasonable length and price, capable of reaching a much wider public in Sweden than Hildebrand and Fredenholm's luxurious two-volume *Svenskarna i Amerika* and in time for the New Sweden Jubilee. The panorama Widén here presented was a heroic one, in the neo-Gothicist tradition of such stalwarts as J. A. Enander, Carl Sundbeck, Vilhelm Lundström, and Amandus Johnson, the last of whom he particularly admired. He saw the great migration as an irresistible, elemental force of nature, more psychological than economic.[39]

For Widén "the Swedish pioneers in the West were the last of the Vikings." Their history in the New World thus constituted one of the greatest epics in the Swedish people's common past, but one which remained all too little known in the homeland. If, from time to time, the Swedes held out a "brother's hand" across the Atlantic, it had all too often been "in hopes that their countrymen on the other side would put money into it," Widén could not but observe.[40]

Very much in the same heroic tone and in response to growing Swedish interest in the approaching New Sweden Jubilee was Nils Jacobsson's well-researched and popularly written history of the colony in 1938, the fullest treatment of the subject to come out in Sweden, as well as the first to include its post-Swedish period. Jacobsson stated as his purpose "to strengthen the ties that link us with our countrymen across the Atlantic and with the people of the United States."[41]

In recent years it has been widely accepted that the citizens of Sweden enjoy probably the world's highest standard of living and quality of life. Yet at the beginning of this century, Sweden still remained notably backward in development. Conditions there have been transformed much more rapidly and suddenly, even within living memory, than in the United States. In no period was this more evident than during the interwar years, once Sweden economically recovered from the postwar recession of 1920 through 1922. It was then that Sweden entered what has been called its "Second Age of Greatness," one no less impressive than that of its seventeenth-century Baltic empire.[42]

The period saw the evolution of an ever more comprehensive system of social welfare, supplemented by a highly successful cooperative movement initiated in 1910, largely by G. H. von Koch, which held the costs of essential consumers' goods down to reasonable levels. Labor disputes were progressively diminished through negotiation. Quality of life kept pace with rising wages and material standards. Although buffeted by the Great Depression, Sweden proved remarkably successful in meeting the crisis at a time when the United States was still struggling to stay afloat.

To the outside world, Sweden by the 1930s seemed an almost miraculous island of prosperity, enlightenment, and democracy in a world filled with dark forebodings over the future of reason, peace, and freedom. Nowhere did this arouse greater admiration than in the United States. Sweden had gotten good press in America throughout the 1920s, thanks in large part to the dedicated efforts of the American-Swedish News Exchange in New York. But the vogue for Sweden and things Swedish might be said to have begun with the visit of fourteen American journalists to the Stockholm Exposition of 1930, resulting in a plethora of articles in American periodicals. A series by R. H. Markham in the *Christian Science Monitor,* beginning in February 1932, entitled "Halfway to Utopia: In Sweden," launched the theme of Sweden as a model society, quickly taken up by numerous newspapers and magazines. In 1934 Agnes Rothery came out with her *Sweden: The Land and the People,* the first book in English to give an overall presentation of modern Swedish life and society.[43]

Although it did not start the trend, no work had as great an impact in establishing the almost uniquely favorable image of Sweden in America in the 1930s as *Sweden: The Middle Way* by Marquis Childs, the Washington correspondent for the *St. Louis Post-Dispatch,* which came out in 1936. What Childs admired above all in the Swedes was their imperturbable common sense, their concentration upon the "immediate, practical problem" and refusal to seek "short-cuts to Utopia." With calm deliberation they had proceeded to rectify that which was ailing in their society. To those who feared for the future of democracy and free enterprise in the world, Sweden offered fresh hope. The Swedes strove to "check the very tendencies by which capitalism tends to destroy itself." They were, he claimed, the "ultimate pragmatists."[44] Two years earlier, in 1934, the Swedish Social Democrat Anna Lenah Elgström had lauded the Americans for essentially the same qualities and aspirations.

Marquis Childs' *Sweden: The Middle Way* created a sensation among educated and influential circles in America.[45] Appearing in the year of Franklin D. Roosevelt's reelection to the American presidency, it contained ideas that were caught up in American political debate: the new Swedish "People's Home" became associated with the Democratic New Deal in the minds both of Roosevelt's supporters and his opponents. Already in September 1934 the influential *Literary Digest,* had declared that "Sweden today offers perhaps the best example of . . . those ideals which the Roosevelt Administration is striving to attain." The same year, F.D.R. was proud to proclaim publicly that he was the "only president to have Swedish blood in his veins," having fortuitously discovered a Swedish settler in New Amsterdam among his forebears.

It was a strange reversal of roles. Since American independence, the United States had served as the prime model for Sweden: for both what it should strive to become or seek to avoid. By the 1930s Sweden had become the model for America, in both senses. To liberals in America,

Sweden provided the conclusive argument for the soundness of their vision of progress. By the same token, for American conservatives, it became essential, already by the mid-1930s, to prove that the Swedish model was flawed, overvalued, or in any event irrelevant to American circumstances. This basic controversy has continued to the present.[46]

Meanwhile other factors played their part in drawing America's attention to Sweden and the Swedes. No Swede probably ever enjoyed such celebrity in the United States and beyond as the "divine" Greta Garbo in Hollywood, where she was joined in 1939 by the young Ingrid Bergman. The operatic tenor Jussi Björling was widely known, as were the sculptor Carl Milles and the explorer Sven Hedin. And in New York, chic new Swedish restaurants were beginning to initiate the fashionable world in the delights of the *smörgåsbord.*[47]

How did all of this affect the Swedish-American community? *Nordstjernan* in New York wrote in November 1934: "Has not Sweden today in a more peaceful manner won a name for itself which in some degree can compete with that won on the field of battle in the age of the Gustavs and Karls? Was, for that matter, Sweden's name better known then than it is now? In America they seem to vie with one another in singing the praises of Sweden and the Swedes. It has even gone so far that it is hard work to keep up with all the praise that is being written." In Minneapolis, *Svenska Amerikanska Posten* claimed that "Sweden enjoys a better press than any other country. . . . It is therefore perhaps not so strange that the Swedish Americans have been aroused and begun to hold to their Swedish origins."[48]

Some observers were meanwhile not so sure that most Swedish Americans really understood or appreciated the recent developments in the old homeland. Those manifestly most affected by the new image of Sweden were Americans, in particular intellectuals, of non-Swedish origins, without or preconceptions about the country. Allan Kastrup, who visited the United States in late 1936, later recalled, "The Swedish Americans I met maintained, to be sure, that 'it was much more fun than before to be a Swede in America,' but they more often mentioned the crown prince's visit in 1926 and Charles Lindbergh than they did the 'Middle Way.'" "When a Swedish American declares that he is proud of his Swedish origins," Vilhelm Berger wrote in 1937, "he always has in mind Sweden's so-called Age of Greatness, the era of the Thirty Years' War and even of Karl XII's wars. . . . That Sweden is now experiencing a true age of greatness, the Swedish American is neither able nor willing to grasp, even though he hears it daily from the Americans."[49]

A number of Swedish visitors left accounts of America during the 1930s, although they were surely fewer than during the preceding decade when, even then, America's Swedish element had become ever more peripheral to their main concerns. Those who had something to say about Swedish

America during the 1930s are too few to seek out any broader lines of consensus, and so will be dealt with individually.

Hjalmar Rangman, a "free-church" preacher whose *Det stora landet i väster* (The Great Land to the West) appeared in 1931, is worth mentioning only because his ideas seem so stereotypical, above all in his depiction of the juggernaut of "King Dollar" before which the inhabitants of the land prostrate themselves in the dust.[50]

A far more significant and readable account is given in 1933 by Oscar Rydqvist, a well-known columnist for the liberal *Dagens nyheter,* whose attitude toward America is sympathetic, often enthusiastic. Rydqvist was altogether captivated by the sheer exuberance of the Swedish-American social life of the societies and lodges. He left an unforgettable account of a birthday celebration at the imposing Swedish Club of Chicago in the midst of the Depression that recalls the old Viking spirit of jestful defiance of impending disaster.

> A festive evening, the most festive during these weeks in America. . . . The whole hall is filled with sturdy Swedes. . . . They pound each other on the back and laugh uproariously. Most of those present are building contractors who have been ruined by the crisis. But no one who did not know this in advance would be able to guess it. Here all cares are banned. . . . I have never seen a more joyful group of Swedes. Yes, joyful—that is the right word, for otherwise joyfulness is hardly something that comes naturally to us. Here Sweden and America have been joined together in a very happy union. Now they march into the banquet room, which is festively adorned with garlands, flowers, flags. Amid a tumult of voices, they take their places, slapping each other on the knee.

The *smörgåsbord* was such that Rydqvist had never seen the like. And when the men's chorus burst forth with "Mandom, mod och morska män" and "Ja, må han leva!" guests, waiters, and waitresses joined in lustily. "I have never heard such singing as in that Swedish bastion," Rydqvist wrote. . . . I never believed I would meet such uninhibited Swedes."[51]

Soon thereafter, he attended an evening entertainment at the Viking Temple on Sheffield Avenue, "one of the folksier Swedish gathering places in Chicago." Spirits were high. A fiddler played tunes from Norrland, which were warmly applauded.

> Then three comedians appear, with guitar, accordion, and banjo. They wobble about on unsteady legs and crack jokes. It is like being at the Hundred and Twenty-Five Man Club in Sundsvall when the century was young. The only difference is that these youths make their jokes in English—it is for that matter interesting to observe that most of the program is given in English. It is the Americanization that gathers speed with each passing year—now even a Swedish evening in Chicago is only a third in Swedish. . . . The

audience laughed with abandon. If I never heard Swedes sing as they did in the Swedish Club, I never heard a Swedish public laugh as they did in the Viking Temple.

When the comics "Tripp, Trapp, and Trull" made their entrance singing a dialect ditty about the delights of summer, "the whole drab locale dissolved into a sea of bliss."[52]

Five years later, in May 1936, the immigration historian Marcus Lee Hansen, who was of Danish-Norwegian ancestry, gave his address, "The Problem of the Third Generation Immigrant," before the Augustana Historical Society in Rock Island. His thesis, the "principle of third generation interest" would, especially from the 1950s on, be particularly influential in American ethnic studies.[53]

Apropos of another historical theory, Hansen declared in his speech that "it was bound to come and to appear in the very decade" when it was presented, and that it had in fact been anticipated in earlier writings. Hansen's own idea of "third generation interest" is indeed similarly fore-shadowed in Swedish America—if not elsewhere as well. Already in 1917 Ernst Skarstedt had noted a rising interest in Sweden and its language among the third and fourth generations. Strong intimations of this idea were given by Anna Lenah Elgström in 1927. Nowhere, however, does it emerge more clearly, prior to Hansen's speech, than in Rydqvist's book in 1933.[54]

Olof Lamm, the Swedish consul-general in New York, expressed to Rydqvist his growing respect for the Swedish Americans.

> One has to remember that we are in America. That is what they so easily forget in Sweden when they concern themselves with the Swedish Americans. The American nation is in a state of rapid development and the Swedish Americans must become part of that nation. Up to now they have not fully appreciated this in Sweden. They have concentrated one-sidedly upon trying to preserve the Swedish language in America in the belief that this is the only way to maintain the Swedish heritage. Oh, I can assure you that often out here I have encountered the strongest sense of Swedish identity among Swedish Americans who only with great difficulty can make themselves understood in the language of their fathers.

Oliver A. Linder, the editor of *Svenska Amerikanaren* in Chicago put the matter more succinctly. "The third generation is nowadays proud to be of Swedish origin. . . . That is something that can have its psychological significance in the future, even if the third generation of today is not Swedish-speaking."[55]

Lewi Pethrus, leader of the growing Pentecostal movement in Sweden, traveled during 1937 in America, where a visit twelve years earlier gave him a useful perspective. His main concern was American religious life, the flourishing state of which, especially among the more evangelistic sects, inclined him toward a generally favorable view of the country. His account meanwhile reflects the effects of the large exodus back to the homeland. At religious meetings this had resulted in a marked decline of the numbers of those able to understand Swedish, hastening the shift to English, which opened their doors to persons of other origins, causing them to lose their ethnic character.[56]

At the same time, Pethrus was very much aware of the new respect Sweden now commanded in the United States and how this aroused the ethnic pride of the Swedish Americans, many of whom—including his own uncles—had harbored understandable bitterness toward the old land where they had known only poverty and social inferiority. He bought and read Marquis Childs' *Sweden: The Middle Way* and noted the identification in America of Roosevelt's New Deal with the new Sweden.[57]

A visitor with a very different perspective that same year, 1937, was Albert Viksten, a novelist of proletarian background from Norrland and a committed socialist, whose account was largely concerned with the Swedish Americans. Viksten was deeply affected by what he saw as the inescapable fate of the immigrant. "There is not one," he wrote, "who does not bear within him a longing and who does not feel something of the tragedy of exile in his life."[58]

In particular, Viksten's sympathy lay with those stalwarts of the labor movement who had been forced to emigrate from Sweden following the General Strike of 1909, including some of his own former comrades. He recalled how it had been "precisely the alert and intelligent, the idealisti-cally inclined" who departed, "unschooled folk with an almost religious belief in freedom and right," leaving organizational life in their old home communities "anemic." For most, social idealism was broken by hard American realities, and by middle age formerly "fiery red" radicals became the core of the many Swedish-American ethnic societies.[59]

Awareness of more recent developments in Sweden could meanwhile arouse bittersweet feelings among those who still held to the ideals of their youth. "Here in this country," Viksten quoted from a letter to *Svenska Amerikanen-Tribunen* in Chicago, "there [are] champions of the labor movement and cooperative movement who were driven out of Sweden because they helped to make Sweden what it now is. . . . We were quickly forgotten, but we still exist here, even if they now have no interest in us. But we have not complained. We cleared the way for those who have now become big at home, helped them to get the well-paid jobs they now have." Viksten shared the view of these veterans that the Good Cause in Sweden was now falling into the hands of well-fed careerists. Speaking of an old comrade in arms in Chicago, Viksten described him as an "individual-ist, a strong soul, and a Swede through and through, of the type which, unfortunately, is becoming more and more rare, even in the homeland."[60]

Like other Swedish leftist observers, Viksten warmed notably toward America and the Swedish Americans upon actual contact. This becomes increasingly evident through the course of his account and he concluded by admitting he had "traveled out there as a skeptic and returned filled with enthusiasm."[61] The strong love for and interest in Sweden he found among its emigrants in America meanwhile led him to condemn indignantly the homeland's indifference toward a Swedish culture on American soil which without help, he was convinced, could not survive much longer.[62]

For our purposes, certainly the most interesting of the Swedish visitors during this period was Vilhelm Lundström, who as a member of the official Swedish delegation to the New Sweden Tricentennial at last visited the United States for the first and only time in 1938. Recalling his stern rebukes to the Swedish Americans during the war and early postwar years, it comes as something of a surprise that he now, two years before his death, expressed warm sympathy and appreciation for them. Not that any of his basic views had changed, but Lundström now encountered the Swedish Americans first-hand, in their own habitat, at a time when enthusiasm for Sweden and Swedish contributions to the building of America was at its height. He was taken well in hand by his friends, especially in the Swedish Cultural Society in America. It was, he now claimed, one of the sorrows of his life that he had not had more opportunity to explore Swedish America. The Swedish emigrants, he felt moved to recall, had been among the "strongest, most capable, and enterprising, a choice selection among our people ... whom it is a pleasure to call one's countrymen." He was deeply moved by the landmarks of the Swedes' peaceful conquest of the great continent. Visits to Chicago and the Twin Cities brought Lundström into direct contact with a natural, sincere but unforced *svenskhet* that despite the passing of time and generations lived on with a tenacity he seems hardly to have anticipated.[63]

Lundström was now prepared to recognize that the beginnings of a "conscious movement for the preservation of Swedish culture abroad" must be attributed to the Swedish Americans themselves, through their churches and newspapers. These were the work of simple people with little schooling from their homeland, but arose, in any case, "from good, old Swedish peasant stock, like all our Swedish culture." Still, the time had surely come—if only it had come earlier!—for the Swedes of the homeland to bend every effort toward supporting the durable and resurgent Swedish presence in the New World. There were, to be sure, successful Swedish descendants who showed little interest in their background and even belittled efforts to save their heritage, and with such persons visiting Swedes often came in contact. But in Lundström's sanguine view they gave little indication of "what is actually going on within the deeper strata of Swedish America, and it is just within these layers that the new *svenskhet* is in so many places coming to the surface."[64]

Carl Mangård was among the Swedish journalists who covered the New Sweden Tricentennial celebration in 1938, after which he toured the United States from east to west. Most of his account consists of sketches of individual Swedish Americans. Like Oscar Rydqvist, he offers few general reflections but some arresting vignettes. Of a Swedish Good Templar lodge meeting in Los Angeles he wrote, for instance:

> Concerning the discussion it was amusing to note how hard it was for some of the speakers at the meeting to stick to Swedish. As soon as they had a hard time finding some word or expression they went over to English and continued talking in that language. This took place altogether automatically and without the person in question noticing it. I thought, meanwhile, that most of them spoke their mother-tongue quite well despite 30 or 40 years abroad. And to hear about Sweden—I was called upon to tell something about conditions in the Old Country—was for them a rare pleasure; that I could clearly see.

A woman in that lodge gave Mangård new insight into what it meant to put down roots on a distant shore. On her last visit home, her aunt had asked if she expected to die in California. "Yes," she had replied. "If I died in Sweden, no one would come to my funeral without an invitation. If I die in California, I know all my friends will come . . . without being asked."[65]

Like other Swedish visitors at this time, Mangård was impressed with Sweden's high standing in American opinion by the Tricentennial year and the boost this gave to Swedish-American pride. Persons unsuspected of any Swedish background, he wrote, willingly turned out to take part on the committees preparing for the commemoration and in some cases proved to speak "perfect Swedish." "Nowadays it is fashionable to be Swedish," an old immigrant told Mangård in Illinois.[66]

There were understandably few travel accounts by Swedish-American visitors to the Old Country during the Depression years. Travel to Sweden that did take place was poorly documented, with one exception: the third group pilgrimage of Vasa children led by Johannes and Helga Hoving in 1933.

For economic reasons, only twenty-five children, all from the New York and Brooklyn Vasa children's clubs, took part, although some seventy clubs had now been established throughout the United States. All but four within the group were girls, some of whom had participated in earlier tours. Some were now in their teens. The tour covered much the same itinerary as the previous two and was received with the same enthusiasm by the press and public.[67] Throughout the tour the Hovings were very much in the public eye, and their frequent speeches and statements to the press show the idealized picture of Swedish America—more aspiration than reality—they were eager to convey in "Father's and Mother's Land." The doctor was, as before, at pains to stress a new blossoming of ethnic life and appreciation for the benefits of cultural pluralism in the United States, while presenting a highly sanguine view of the importance to America of its Swedish element.[68]

Dr. Hoving emphasized growing interest in Sweden and its heritage among the younger, American-born generations, to which both the present tour and the rapid spread of Vasa children's clubs throughout America bore witness. *Dagens nyheter* in Stockholm reported that the Vasa children's clubs included "most of the young people of Swedish descent between the ages of five and twenty-five."[69] Swedish readers no doubt responded warmly when Johannes Hoving declared in Växjö that children in the group kept asking, "Why should we live in America when we have such a wonderful country as Sweden?" Or when Helga told *Dagens nyheter* in Stockholm that "the children feel more at home here than in their actual homeland on the other side of the Atlantic." When interviewed by the press, some of the young travelers made similarly enthusiastic statements. The two million Swedes in America, Dr. Hoving proclaimed in Nyköping, longed "in their souls" to return to Sweden.[70]

In *Smålands allehanda* (Jönköping), Carl Atterling sounded a venerable note when he wrote:

> The Vasa children were a group of Sweden enthusiasts. How much do they not have to teach us here at home! Sometimes we find proof of our tragic lack of enthusiasm and that we are wanting in a sense of history is made manifest. Therefore the appearance of these children is like a bright banner of youth and a life-giving leaven to minds wearied by the unrest of our times in this blessed land of peace. Perhaps they do not themselves suspect what they give us of inspiration and fresh promise. We have, in our awkwardness, usually not been able to give them more than a recognizing glance when blue eyes have met across the ocean, and a heart that must flow over. They are, indeed, our own![71]

Shortly after accompanying the Vasa children back to America, the Hovings moved permanently back to Sweden in 1934.[72] One might imagine the day on which Johannes Hoving, for the first time, became a Swedish subject as the proudest of his life.

An immediate concern for him was the writing of his *Läsebok och uppslagsbok för Vasabarnen i Amerika,* a reader and reference book for members of the Vasa children's clubs published in Stockholm in 1935. It described Sweden's geography, nature, population, history, economy, and culture, and contained sections on the Swedes in the United States and Canada. The lengthy historical sections were written in the National-Romantic spirit so characteristic of the author, while those dealing with more recent times stressed Sweden's impressive progress in all areas, as well as the great contributions of Swedes to American life. As ever, Hoving prophesied the sturdy survival of the Swedish language and heritage in America and admonished his young readers against ever marrying persons of other race or nationality.[73]

In America Johannes Hoving had often taken his Swedish-American compatriots sternly to task for their lack of zeal for the good cause. During his later years in Sweden, however, he tended increasingly to idealize, justify, and defend them in speech and writing. In 1944 he declared that "a love of the homeland such as is found among the Swedes in America you would surely seek in vain here at home." He continued to lecture, periodically, on "great Swedish deeds in America" almost up to his death in 1954.[74]

When Johannes Hoving took the third Vasa children's group back to New York in 1933 he had with him several scrapbooks filled with hundreds of newspaper clippings concerning its tour.[75] In comparison the recorded experiences of individual Swedish Americans who visited the Old Country during the 1930s are sparse indeed and create an often prosaic impression. Perhaps Nels S. Lidney and Augusta Hägerman may be taken as characteristic examples. Lidney, from California, was in Sweden from 1932 to 1933, mainly in his home area in rural Västergötland. Typically among the modest accounts of old emigrants home on a visit, he is moved at the first sight of the rock-bound coast of his native land and upon his immediate return to the humble home of his childhood. Much of his account is concerned with reunions with relatives and old friends, as well as with former Swedish-American acquaintances and the families of people he knew in California.[76]

Augusta Hägerman, who lived on a farm in Washington State after thirty years in New York, was a considerably better stylist, having long contributed tales and reminiscences of Swedish rural life to Swedish-American newspapers. In 1936 she revisited the homeland she had last seen in 1889 at the age of fifteen. Aboard the Swedish-America Line's *Gripsholm* Hägerman was seized by apprehensions which surely many in her situation must have felt.

> All who had been close to me were gone, and 47 years is a long time, and the sands of time cover all the traces my fathers have left upon the shore. What was there for me to do on this trip? There was no longer a single door which I could open and say, "Here is my home, here I shall stay." And where were the path, the well, the flower beds, the barn? No acquaintance sat by the fireside and welcomed me. Why should I travel to the land of the cuckoo and the lark? Even they lived on in new generations. The thrush that lived on the cottage roof under the tiles lived there no more. Perhaps the roof was gone, the cottage torn down.

Indeed, the latter fear proved all too true, for where her childhood home once stood there was now a field of waving oats. There remained only the fallen-in remains of the old earth cellar and the thorny wild rose bush, "which had grown large and luxuriant from the rotting roof thatch."[77] The prevailing tone of Hägerman's account is one of sweet melancholy and incredulity over change and the passing of time. She was nonetheless gratified to see signs of a more abundant life in her old neighborhood. Houses and barns were newer and larger, livestock more numerous and of improved breeds, oxen had been entirely replaced by horses, while women, freed from thralldom in the barn, were able to devote themselves to creating "model homes." Meanwhile, the farmworkers' humble dwellings were giving way to well-to-do townsmens' summer cottages. These were "artistic" and picturesque, but their owners had no real feeling for old local traditions.[78] The latters' town-bred Arcadianism was surely similar to the diffuse nostalgia for a rural Sweden, unconnected with specific locality, so lovingly cultivated by institutional Swedish America.

Augusta Hägerman meanwhile greatly enjoyed her stay. She discovered many who remembered her. The titles to some of her chapters provide a good summary of her activities: "From House to House among Relatives and Childhood Friends and Coffee Parties and Dinners," "Visit to Grandmother's Grave in Gösslunda," "More Relatives and More Coffee," "Parting Visits," "I Receive Gifts of Various Kinds." On one day alone, she attended no less than six coffee parties, which prevented her from accepting a dinner invitation that evening. Four such parties in one day, she sighed, would surely be the maximum for a healthy young person, but if an old lady went to six, "it would be just as well to begin negotiating with an undertaker." Although her trip included Gothenburg and Stockholm, she had almost nothing to say about Swedish urban life, other than that "big cities have never especially interested me"—despite her long years in New York—and to describe Stockholm, in passing, as a "Babylon."[79]

Like other twentieth-century Swedish-American visitors to the home country, both before and since, Lidney and Hägerman recognized that life, in a material sense, had improved in Sweden since they had left for America. Still, this revelation hardly inspired in them the bright-eyed enthusiasm of an Agnes Rothery or a Marquis Childs. The old emigrants did not come home to discover the new Sweden, but rather to rediscover what might still remain of the distant world of their childhood and youth. Modernity, with all its constant, restless change, was the everyday reality of their life in America; consciously or subconsciously they could well resent its encroachment into the land they cherished in idyllic memory. In Sweden they yearned to recover, however fleetingly, the old, reassuring certainties of childhood. To them, Gösslunda parish meant immeasurably more than Stockholm, the nation's capital and showplace. Modern Sweden could, moreover, stir disquieting suspicions that their emigration, with all the sacrifice and deprivation it had entailed over the years, had not really been necessary after all, that maybe—just maybe—it had been a mistake that could not now be undone.

Returning to Los Angeles, Nels Lidney concluded, "We had now moved from the land of mystique and tradition, Sweden, to the more materialistic America." One senses, nonetheless, relief as well as nostalgia upon his return to his familiar world of present work, friends, and surroundings.[80]

An example of how elderly Swedish-American visitors appeared to a younger generation in their old homeland is meanwhile provided by a later reminiscence of my wife's aunt in Stockholm, from her youth in rural Uppland.

> You asked in a letter about our relationship to some emigrant. Yes, there was a cousin of our mother, we don't remember the name. They, her husband was along, came to Ledinge, and they were older retired people then. She was a spectacle for us. She had all kinds of necklaces and bracelets, the fanciest clothes, she swished and jangled around, high bust, great high hairdo, pretty teeth, with *gold* in them. But when evening, or rather morning, came, then all the finery had disappeared. She looked so little and worn. No bust, no hair, and the mouth—well, it just wasn't there! Her husband looked the same both night and day. He was bent, ached in his joints, but good and kind. But she was always on the go.[81]

The grand finale of the great Swedish vogue in America during the 1930s—and, it may be said, of a century of interaction between the Swedes of the homeland and their emigrated kinsmen in the United States—was the celebration of the New Sweden Tricentennial during the summer of 1938. The observances had long been under preparation on both sides of the Atlantic and were accompanied by a traveling exhibition of Swedish art, a historical exhibit mainly devoted to Sweden's seventeenth-century Age of Greatness at the American-Swedish Historical Museum (formerly the John Morton Memorial Museum) in Philadelphia, lecture series in various parts of America by Swedish notables, the issue of special Tricentennial stamps, coins, and medals, and the promotion of letter-writing between American and Swedish schoolchildren. A Swedish-American exhibition was held in Gothenburg's Maritime Museum, cosponsored by the RFSBU.

In Sweden several books were published in English for distribution in the United States dealing with modern Swedish society and life. In America, Adolph B. Benson, professor of German and Scandinavian at Yale University, and Naboth Hedin, head of the American-Swedish News Exchange in New York, both Swedish-born but American-educated, brought out a stout volume under the auspices of the Swedish American Tercentenary Association, *Swedes in America, 1638-1938,* with chapters by a host of contributors—among them Vilhelm Berger, Oliver A. Linder, and Ernst W. Olson, well known from similar collaborative efforts in the past—on Swedish contributions to the building of America in virtually all areas of achievement. Its tone, naturally, is warmly self-congratulatory.[82]

In June the official Swedish delegation, some fifty strong, headed by

Crown Prince Gustav Adolf, representing his eighty-year-old father, Gustav V, crossed the Atlantic on the Swedish-America Line's *Kungsholm,* together with a nine-man Finnish delegation. Sadly, the opening ceremonies on 27 June met with double misfortune: torrential rain and a sudden illness that prevented the popular crown prince—well remembered from 1926—from taking part. Carl Milles's sculpture of the ship *Fågel Grip,* the Swedish "Mayflower" of 1638, was nonetheless dedicated in Wilmington, Delaware. President Roosevelt headed the official American delegates, spoke proudly of his own Swedish colonial ancestry, and expressed "grateful acknowledgement of the outstanding contribution made to our national life by men and women of Swedish blood."[83]

Ceremonies were held the following day at the American-Swedish Historical Museum in Philadelphia, thus realizing Amandus Johnson's long-cherished dream. Thousands of Swedish Americans from around the country had meanwhile assembled in Wilmington and Philadelphia. Regrettably, arrangements did not allow much chance for direct contact with the official Swedish delegation, causing some disappointment, as Sten Dehlgren of Stockholm's *Dagens nyheter* noted. "To be sure, [Swedish Americans] were allowed to be present as spectators of the motor cavalcade and for a few brief minutes they had the opportunity of showing their lusty skill in folk dancing and singing," he wrote, "but that was about all."[84]

The Swedish delegation, soon joined by the crown prince, moved on to New York, Chicago, and Minneapolis, with members of the group visiting Swedish-American centers from coast to coast. A culminating high point of this tour was the gathering of some seventy-five thousand Swedish Americans at Chicago's Soldiers Field on 16 July for an elaborate program including, according to the official account, "hundreds of children in colorful native costumes [who] performed folk dances, pageants, and flower dances."[85]

All in all, the Tricentennial was judged to have been a great success. Writing in *Göteborgs Handels- och sjöfartstidning,* Naboth Hedin declared:

> If the historical horizon of the two states [Delaware and Pennsylvania] has been moved back half a century [to 1638], then that of the Swedish Americans has been moved back two and a half centuries. From now on it will never be necessary for Americans of Swedish descent to point out to American citizens of different origins that their people were among the first in America. Everyone knows this now, and the only way to let them know it was through such a celebration.

"America has learned to recognize and to acknowledge, openly and honestly, what a noble folk element it has received upon its soil from the Swedish race," the Augustana pastor S. G. Öhman wrote, "It is not England alone that is America's motherland. Sweden, too, has her share in its maternity."[86]

The following year Sweden celebrated yet another triumph through its highly publicized participation in the New York World's Fair held during the summer of 1939. The Swedish Pavilion, combining modern with traditional elements, was greatly admired, as were its impressive displays of Swedish industrial products and applied arts. This was no less true of the lavish *smörgåsbord* featured by its restaurant, which more than anything quickly naturalized the word itself into the American venacular. "The Swedish exhibits," the *New York Post* declared, "are the work of a nation which even now appears on the eve of that better world of tomorrow that the Fair heralds." That same summer, Sweden also took part, on a more modest scale, in the Golden Gate International Exposition in San Francisco.[87]

The two World's Fairs had hardly closed their gates before German forces invaded Poland on 1 September 1939. Two months later, on 30 November, the Soviet Union attacked Finland. And on 9 April 1940, the Germans began their conquest of Denmark and Norway. In a world engulfed in war, the Indian summer of Swedish America faded into the irretrievable past.

TWENTY

Epilogue

*I*mmigration from Sweden, albeit on a very limited scale and of a different character, has continued down to the present, and a Swedish America, much modified with time, still exists. But the great European migration has receded ever farther into the past.

The second World War, while it did not subject Swedish Americans to the same traumas as the first, prolonged the period of dwindling personal contacts at the grassroots level that had begun with the end of large-scale immigration in the 1920s and the heavy return migration of the 1930s. Only after the end of the war have closer contacts once more developed, although by now between kinfolk ever more separated by time, experience, and values. The gap between Sweden and America both narrowed and widened: material standards and ways of life became closer, while sociopolitical ideals grew farther apart.

At the human level living links were broken as old immigrants with close personal associations in Sweden died, as well as those who could remember them in the homeland. Statistics give their irrefutable evidence: the Swedish-born declined in the United States from 324,944 in 1950 to 77,157 in 1980, while the total Swedish stock in the first and second generations went during the same period from 1,189,639 down to 806,138. By 1950, moreover, the median age of the Swedish-born was 63.6 years, the highest among major American ethnic groups by that time.

The 1980 U.S. census made a significant departure from previous practice when it replaced the classification "foreign stock" with the new optional category of "single ancestry group," with which individuals could identify themselves, regardless of other, mixed ancestry and number of generations in the United States. That year 1,288,341 Americans chose to identify themselves as "Swedish." The same census also revealed that 100,063 persons over the age of five—of whom close to a quarter were obviously American-born—claimed knowledge of Swedish.[1] These figures tell much about the state of Swedish ethnicity in America today.

After World War II Americans generally turned away from the collective ideals of Roosevelt's New Deal toward a reawakened spirit of individual enterprise, long reinforced by Cold War fears, while the Swedes, under Social Democratic leadership, launched ambitious programs of comprehensive social welfare. America and Sweden thus came to represent opposing ideals within the non-Communist world, giving rise to criticism from both sides.

Swedish Americans have not always found it easy either to understand or to appreciate the new Sweden that has evolved since the Great Migration ended a half century ago. From the beginning they have tended to be staunchly individualistic and generally conservative politically. Most of them take their religion seriously and are faithful churchgoers. They are often skeptical toward too much social welfare, protection, regulation, and taxation, while they may be appalled by low church attendance, assertive secularism, and the new morality—or immorality—in sexual matters. Periodic waves of vocal anti-Americanism, particularly in younger radical circles, arouse their indignation. At the same time, Swedish Americans have frequently regretted the apparent loss of the Swedes' unique cultural characteristics in an increasingly cosmopolitan and seemingly "Americanized" world.[2]

Homeland Swedes, especially on the intellectual Left, have meanwhile tended to suspect the sincerity of American conventional religion and morality, while attacking what they often have seen as a superficial and commercialized culture. They have frequently condemned any manifestations of American imperialism—military, economic, or cultural—throughout the world. To the extent that they have taken notice specifically of their own kinsmen in America, they have shown incredulity and often regret that the latter should hold to traditional American, rather than contemporary Swedish, viewpoints.

Meanwhile, never have such large numbers of visitors crossed the Atlantic in both directions since overseas travel has become a mass phenomenon. Swedish visitors and their published accounts of America have only relatively seldom been concerned more than fleetingly with the Swedish Americans. Where they appear, the Swedish commentators have shown either happy surprise over the amount of the old ethnicity they have come across, mainly in the rural Midwest, or bemused, often wistful incredulity over the contrast between the old emigrants and their late twentieth-century American progeny.[3]

The culture shock meanwhile awaiting aging Swedish-born Americans upon returning to the land of their birth after long decades of absence has never been greater. Indeed, some have deliberately avoided facing it, like the old immigrant in rural Minnesota who informed a visiting Swede:

"There are some things I don't want to see!"[4] Still, seeing once again the scenes of childhood and relatives and friends grown gray like themselves has been deeply moving for most who have experienced it, and many have returned repeatedly in later years. For younger Americans of Swedish descent, the encounter with the ancestral homeland has often meant the fulfillment of long-cherished dreams, although the Sweden they have found has often stood in striking contrast to that preserved in family tradition.[5]

The passing of the immigrant generation and, increasingly, of its children, has meanwhile by no means meant a decline in interest in the Swedish-American heritage. In America the establishment in 1948 of the Swedish Pioneer Historical Society (since 1983 the Swedish-American Historical Society) and of the Swenson Swedish Immigration Research Center at Rock Island, Illinois, in 1981 have both reflected and maintained a steady interest in history and genealogy. In both Sweden and America, the immensely popular immigrant novels of the Swedish author Vilhelm Moberg, published between 1949 and 1959, established as nothing had before the heroic image of Swedish immigrants in the new land. Building largely upon the wave of enthusiasm they created, institutions—most notably the Emigrant Register in Karlstad since 1960 and the Swedish Emigrant Institute in Växjö since 1965—together with a growing series of annual commemorative events, have maintained an unflagging interest in Sweden. Around 1960 Swedish academic scholarship at last addressed itself seriously to the emigration, which has resulted in research of high quality. Few ethnic groups have been as well favored in this regard.[6]

The older institutional Swedish America has by now largely vanished. In 1962 the Augustana Synod became part of the new Lutheran Church in America, now merged into the Evangelical Lutheran Church of America, while the Swedish branches of other American denominations have likewise ceased to exist. Many venerable clubs and societies have quietly disappeared, while only four Swedish-American newspapers are still published, now largely in English. The Swedish language is presently seldom heard in church services or club meetings, and then mainly for sentimental reasons before a largely uncomprehending public. Swedish immigrants from the post-World War II period have generally been educated professionals, settled largely in urban centers outside of traditional Swedish America. They generally regard themselves as "overseas Swedes," rather than as "Swedish Americans," and feel little in common with the older immigrants and their descendants.

Still, paradoxical as it might seem, the older Swedish America has been steadily replaced by a multitude of new Swedish-interest organizations in the United States. The umbrella association, the Swedish Council of America, founded in 1972, has expanded from its original three participating organizations to presently well over a hundred. Many of them have enthusiastically sought out and introduced Swedish customs and traditions unknown to the great majority of the old immigrants, thereby nurturing group identity and ties with the ancestral land. Their members are generally better acquainted with contemporary Sweden than most Swedish Americans in the past could ever be. It has been as the Swedish-American minister, John P. Miller, foretold in 1945. Although its older institutions might die out, "This does not mean that Swedish America will lose its significance as a bridge between America and Sweden. On the contrary, Swedish descendants who are fully integrated into American society have greater potential to serve here as connecting links than the first generation, who had to work hard for their bread in a foreign land."[7]

Nothing, of course, compels native-born Americans to take any interest in their origins. Yet a large and, by all appearances, growing proportion do. To maintain ties with one or more branches of one's family tree in America is today above all a matter of individual choice and personality. It is an essentially elective ethnicity.[8] Thus having weathered the transition from the older, integral ethnicity of the immigrants, there seems no good reason to imagine that the new Swedish America need ever disappear, at least within the foreseeable future.

In Sweden, Gustav Sundbärg declared in 1906, "there is scarcely any question, be it political, social, or economic that is not directly or indirectly affected by the emigration."[9] The weighty proceedings of the Emigration Inquest he directed between 1907 and 1913 amply bore out this diagnosis. He might have added that the emigration affected or was affected by virtually everything that took place in the United States as well. The conclusions to this study could run in many possible directions. We shall, however, concentrate upon certain fundamental questions.

The Swedes became a folk divided through emigration and, as time passed, by questions affecting the common or differing identity of those who left and those who stayed. By the turn of the century, National Romanticism in Sweden encouraged an intensive search for an authentic national character and culture, as a result of which the place of emigration and of the emigrant in the Swedish national community became ever more problematic.

By that time the Swedes in America—most of whom had left Sweden before the National Romantic breakthrough—were evolving their own patterns of thought and behavior, as much in reaction to conditions and opinion in the old homeland as in the new. The Swedish Americans, facing a greater diversity of geographic and occupational conditions over a lengthier period than most immigrant groups in America, meanwhile never developed a single, uniform identity despite their constant appeals for unity. Within their community significant variants may be observed, perhaps most characteristically with reference to matters affecting religion and ideas of freedom.

The dominant ethnic ideology was unquestionably that which emerged under the aegis of the Augustana Synod, in part because the Swedes were traditionally Lutheran, and the synod was always by far the largest Swedish-American denomination; in part, too, because, thanks to J. A. Enander and his followers, its viewpoint was most fully and consistently worked out and propagated through the pulpit, press, and classroom. Augustana Swedish-Americanism stressed ethnic solidarity and respect for tradition and authority, both ecclesiastical and civil. It cherished the vision of Sweden as "freedom's homeland on earth" but conceived of freedom as essentially independence from foreign (including papal) domination. Thus J. S. Carlson could declare in 1923 that the Swedish immigrant "comes *from* a free country *to* a free country" and that "no one need therefore remind us that we *are,* much less urge us to *become,* Americans."[10] Such a standpoint nonetheless left its protagonists in a logically somewhat ambivalent position: if the Swedish Americans were so Swedish, why had they left Sweden, aside from purely material considerations? If they were American, why did they continue to adhere to a religious and cultural institution so intimately associated with the historic Swedish state and society?

A second, albeit largely overlapping identity was that of the Swedish-American evangelistic free churches: Methodists, Baptists, Adventists, Mormons, and other Anglo-American denominations, as well as Eric-Janssonism and the Mission Covenant, which broke away from Swedish Lutheranism. Due, surely, to its smaller numbers and denominational diversity, this group never clearly articulated its viewpoint, although the Swedish sociologist E. H. Thörnberg offered some keen insights. In effect, the free church people, whether converted before or after emigration, made a cleaner break with the old country, not only geographically but ideologically. Indeed, emigration and conversion, based on free, individual choice, represented parallel processes of alienation from the past. In their view, Swedes did indeed have to come to America to find true freedom, from bureaucratic and ecclesiastical constraints. Many felt, in Thörnberg's words, that "the farther they had come from Sweden, the closer they had come to God." Their values tended to be as individualistic in secular as in religious matters. It was natural for them to identify as their proudest Swedish quality a fierce love of freedom as it had long ago existed in Sweden but could now be found, by those with true Swedish spirit, only in America.[11]

The search for liberty of conscience shaded over into a freethinking or outright secular attitude within parts of the Swedish-American community, for which it meant freedom from organized religion or indeed from any religion at all. This element was best represented by secular newspapers and organizations in Chicago and other large cities, which long engaged in heated feuds with the "church folk." The freethinkers, too, were generally enthusiastic believers in American free enterprise, although by the 1890s, some of its Swedish-American apostles, like Hans Mattson or especially

C. F. Peterson, came to realize that if unrestrained it became self-destructive through monopoly capitalism. In such a situation, Peterson envisioned his Swedish-American countrymen as a valiant vanguard in the coming struggle to preserve America's Jeffersonian ideals, as they had once been in the war to free the slaves.[12]

Augustana-Lutheran, free-church, and freethinking Swedish Americans were united in loyalty to America's civic values and to their somewhat differing visions of their nationality's proud part in realizing and defending them in their new homeland. The freethinking viewpoint meanwhile shaded into the socialistic, which in principle rejected not only monopoly capitalism but the American bourgeois regime as a whole as oppressors of the working class. Swedish socialists and union members emigrated in large numbers to the United States from the 1890s on, but it was a source of constant chagrin to the little group of the righteous, as well as to radicals in Sweden, that most soon abandoned class solidarity for individual gain, as well as the idealistic cultural ambitions of their movement at home. Their view of the Swedish Americans tended thus to be a negative rather than a positive one. The Swedes, as they saw it, might have come to America hoping to find freedom from class oppression but instead found—and accepted—a mindless wage slavery.

Homeland Swedes of differing social classes, cultural backgrounds, and political philosophies thought of their emigrated countrymen, positively or negatively, largely on the basis of which Swedish America they had in mind. The original Augustana version naturally appealed in particular to conservative traditionalists and romantic nationalists, while it repelled political and labor radicals. The former in turn rejoiced at the failure of socialism in America, especially among its Swedish element. Free-church and free-thinking individualism held, it would seem, particular appeal for much of the peasant and middle classes but was suspect both to conservatives and to radicals, who cherished ideals of national or class solidarity. The variations would seem as many as the shades of difference within Swedish America itself.

Questions must be raised regarding the extent to which writers on both sides of the Atlantic expressed their own actual views and how representative these views were of Swedish and Swedish-American thinking in general about America, emigration, and emigrants.

Elbert Hubbard once opined: "Writers seldom write the things they think. They simply write the things they think other folks think they think."[13] If his meaning eludes exact interpretation, it at least points up the complexity of the problem of accurately conveying attitudes through words. (I regularly remind my students that I cannot grade them on what they know or think, only upon what they say.) It must nonetheless be our working hypothesis that the writers we have dealt with said, on the whole, what they believed, even if ulterior motives may at times be apparent or at least suspected. We seem on firmer ground by virtue of the sheer numbers of those who took up the pen in this discussion, both Swedes and Swedish Americans. Concerning the latter, G. N. Swan was of the view in 1930 that his Swedish-American countrymen seemed somehow more afflicted by the "writer's itch" than Americans of other background.[14] The ideas expressed during different periods also generally fall into easily recognizable categories. But it must still be asked how accurately the articulate elite reflected the thinking of the broader masses in both Sweden and Swedish America. Such is indeed the perennial problem of any study of public opinion.

It is not difficult to perceive certain built-in biases. The immigrants who succeeded in America were naturally more communicative than those who encountered adversity, a point often made by opponents of emigration in Sweden, who in turn overplayed the theme of those who "went under."

In studying a culture there is moreover an understandable tendency to concentrate upon its institutional forms. "There is no doubt," Albin Widén wrote in 1937, "that the history of Swedish culture in America is above all that of the Swedish-American organizations. A Swedish American is a person who belongs to a Swedish association—often he belongs to many."[15] We cannot accept so simple a formulation today. Ethnicity for much of the immigrant community, especially among more recent arrivals who had not yet established themselves, was always primarily a natural but unstructured way of life, based upon informal and shifting networks of relatives, old friends, and new acquaintances in the boardinghouse, bunkhouse, or tenement, at the workplace, saloon, or grocery store, or simply over the back fence. This was the "little world" upon which institutional Swedish America only occasionally and fleetingly impinged, and which, by its very nature, has left relatively little direct documentation, aside from the preserved letters and reminiscences of individual Swedish Americans.

Settled immigrants with steady incomes and families were more likely to become regular members of congregations and societies, largely for the social conviviality they offered, as well as to subscribe to Swedish-American periodicals. Using the example of metropolitan Chicago, Anita R. Olson has recently shown how the creation of the institutional ethnic cultural community served to compensate for the loss of the old ethnic core neighborhoods through progressive geographic dispersion. But even for the ethnically organized, what Ulf Beijbom has called the ideological "superstructure," conceived by Swedish America's small intelligentsia of clergymen, educators, and journalists, surely seemed largely irrelevant, at least to their everyday concerns.[16] Meanwhile, there were always many Swedes who settled far from others of their own nationality and who quietly adapted to life in purely American—or in any event non-Swedish—surroundings.

Those who wielded the pen, both in Sweden and in Swedish America, often reflected the double alienation they experienced in the American environment amid an overwhelmingly working-class immigrant population, which tended to regard them as outsiders. The theme is a recurrent one, not least in the realm of fiction. Persons of cultivated background seem often to have had unrealistically high hopes as to the kind of Swedish national culture their countrymen ought to sustain on American soil and to have felt correspondingly exaggerated disappointment over the latters' failure to fulfill such expectations. In 1904 Carl Sundbeck believed that meeting the Swedish Americans on solemn and festive occasions—as he frequently did—revealed their true nature and most cherished ideals.[17] Many others, especially visitors from Sweden, have been inclined to believe the same, thus widening the gap between dream and reality.

Nonetheless, giving due consideration to the predilections of the articulate few, we remain convinced—on the basis of the widest accessible expression of views—of the fundamental proposition that those who wrote for the public both reflected and formed mass public opinion, directly or indirectly, on both sides of the Atlantic.

If there was a dialogue between Sweden and Swedish America during the migration era, it was strangely unbalanced, indeed in some respects a "dialogue of the deaf," at least on the intellectual level. While Swedish-American opinionmakers closely followed the expression of views in Sweden regarding America and their group, communication eastward at this level was scanty at best. When a group of Swedish-American newspapermen queried a number of prominent Swedes regarding the reputation of the Swedish-American press, P. P. Waldenström, recently returned from his first visit to America, replied in 1892 that it was so little known in Sweden that one could scarcely speak about any reputation whatsoever. Communication in this direction was primarily at the grassroots level, through the letters of ordinary emigrants to their relatives and friends, their visits to Sweden, and the money and gift subscriptions to Swedish-American periodicals they sent home. The average Swede, "L.F.L." wrote to the Emigration Inquiry from Minnesota in 1907, knew "just as much about American conditions as authors and journalists" in Sweden. P. G. Norberg was convinced in 1910 that he knew more. And, significantly, he drew different conclusions.[18]

Finally it must be asked how representative the relationship between homeland Swedes and Swedish Americans may be of the relations within other nationalities divided by migration. To be sure, the Swedes differed from various other European peoples in significant ways. Unlike the Irish and various Central and Eastern European nationalities, they were not, and had never really been, victims of any foreign oppression upon which they could blame their emigration. In this they differed somewhat even from their neighbors, the Finns and Norwegians, whose lands were joined since 1809 and 1814 in increasingly unpopular dynastic unions under the Russian and Swedish crowns, respectively. If Swedes claimed oppression in their homeland, they could only attribute it to persons no less Swedish than themselves. This could seem all the more intolerable since Sweden gloried in its ancient traditions of law-bound liberty and constitutional, parliamentary rule.

Largely because of such traditions, as well as their North European, Germanic, and Protestant background, Swedish immigrants were on the whole welcomed by the Anglo-Americans. Compared with other groups they were less affected by native prejudice in America, although as a proud and sensitive people they greatly resented whatever they encountered of it. Their kindred background made it relatively easy for them to learn English and generally to adapt to American ways—if not always entirely to American values. It was soon possible for them to identify more closely with the older Americans than with more recent immigrants from other parts of Europe, especially as they proudly counted themselves among North America's first European colonizers. All of these factors complicated their efforts to assert the Swedish side of their identity in terms acceptable to their old homeland.

Yet these reservations aside, the relationship between Swedes and Swedish Americans is surely similar in its essentials to that of other nationalities divided by migration, both to North America and to other parts of the world. "Those people who cross the ocean and their descendants," Andrew Greely has written of the Irish, "add one set of experiences to the ancient heritage while those who stay behind add another set of experiences." This recalls Oscar Handlin's view that those who came to America from traditional European peasant societies tended to remain conservative in religion and outlook to compensate the loss of the old sense of wholeness at home, whereas those who stayed but were uprooted from the old rural way of life by the forces of change tended to become more radical and progressive, since they did not have to compensate for leaving the old homelands. This observation would seem as valid for the Swedes, generally speaking, as for those groups with which Handlin was most familiar.[19] Swedish visitors to America have repeatedly been impressed by how much of the "Old Sweden" they have found preserved there.

As with other nationalities, both homeland Swedes and Swedish Americans have—in different times and contexts—sought to emphasize either their differences or their similarities. In 1931 O. Fritiof Ander spoke of a Swedish Americanism that revealed a sense of superiority over "Swedes in Sweden" thanks to migration and over "ordinary Americans" due to Swedish origins.

Conversely, the Irish in Ireland, Andrew Greeley relates, often wonder what right the Irish Americans have to consider themselves Irish, when they ought to be "Yanks," to which the latter protest, "What the hell do you mean, Yanks?" "To paraphrase Bernard Shaw slightly," he goes on, "Old Ireland and Great Ireland . . . are two people divided by a common heritage." I have heard Swedes living in America express similar irritation over Swedish descendants playing at being Swedes. Jan Olof Olsson described the Swedish Americans' dilemma in 1958. "Before, they were not well regarded in Sweden because, among other things, they did not seem to approve of the Sweden they had left; now they are taken to task for a confused and sentimental affection for the Sweden their grandparents or great-grandparents left and for wearing blue and gold socks and neckties when they come to visit. They are never as they ought to be."[20] Yet in the background we hear the long chorus from both sides of the ocean invoking the ties of blood and heritage.

Lars Ljungmark has recently shown that the attitudes of Swedish Canadians toward the far larger Swedish population in the United States has in significant ways been analogous to the latters' attitudes toward the Swedes in the homeland. Doubtless feelings have been similarly ambivalent among other emigrants and their compatriots at home.[21]

For those who remained in their homelands there could meanwhile be no escaping the forces of change, as emigrants returning after long years abroad were often painfully reminded. Surely many a Swedish-American farm family in, say, Minnesota or Washington State lived a life closer to what they or their forebears had left than did their relatives in Stockholm or Norrköping.

In America, too, Oscar Handlin has written, "those who stubbornly stayed in the place of their birth often found themselves made aliens by changes in the world around them. Many a Brahmin, grown old on Beacon Hill, looked across the [Boston] Common in the 1890's and found himself almost as much a stranger to his city as the newcomers who had transformed it. His reactions and theirs were linked; only theirs were more visible."

The reminiscences of Sara Bixby Smith, growing up on a California cattle ranch in the 1870s and dreaming of her grandmother's home amid the pine forests of Maine, strikingly recall Anna Olson's "prairie child" in Kansas during those same years, imagining her grandmother's home in the Värmland forests. And Americans could react to those who left their midst in the same ways as Europeans. "I well remember in my native town of Albany, Vermont," a man in Wyoming declared in 1948, "that a person who emigrated West was looked upon much in the light of a deserter to the flag. I recall hearing my elders speak in a most contemptuous tone of a former resident: 'Oh, he went out West, somewheres.' That properly disposed of him."[22]

Europeans, as well as Americans, reacted to migration above all in terms of what they believed its impact to be upon their own countries and regions. In part they responded to directly observable effects. But beyond that, Europeans either welcomed or condemned what they perceived as an overall process of "Americanization" at home and were concerned over ways in which their own emigrants might aid in its advance. "Such a state,"

P. A. Wallmark wrote of America in *Allmänna Journalen* already in 1824, "must always arouse apprehensions in Europe as a living criticism of its social institutions."[23]

To be sure, it was often more convenient to attribute changes, welcome or unwelcome, to America, rather than to natural internal developments; for instance, population movement within Sweden was always much greater than emigration in both magnitude and impact, but it naturally attracted less attention. To the extent that actual American-inspired changes did take place in the old homelands, it is evident that new ideas and values were largely transmitted through their emigrant groups, even though the emigrants themselves characteristically cultivated nostalgia for the homeland as they had left it, for what Marion J. Nelson has described as a "lost Atlantis." To distinguish between emigrant—as opposed to general American—influences in the former homelands meanwhile raises particularly complex questions, as the Swedish example shows.[24]

To what extent the homelands underwent "Americanization," as opposed to universal processes of adaptation to changing conditions in the world, has been much discussed and debated, not least with regard to Sweden.[25] Surely many opponents to change have, in essence, agreed with Samuel Johnson's comment to Boswell in 1778, "I am willing to love all mankind, *except an American.*" Yet perceptive Europeans have looked deeper. In the foreword to a reprint of his satirical novel *Pandoras ask* (Pandora's Box) from 1957, Bo Setterlind wrote in 1960 that he sought to describe "a way of life that has gone furthest in America but which people may be drawn into, wherever they may find themselves in the world. . . . an America which we, almost all of us, bear within ourselves, but which for most remains undiscovered."[26]

In its widest perspective, the relationship between Swedes and Swedish Americans—as between other divided peoples—is a reflection of a general crisis confronting the world over the past two centuries or more. America, with its immigrant populations, has served as the touchstone in the emotion-laden, yet often ambivalent struggle between unrelenting modernization and nostalgic antimodernism, between past and future.

Appendixes
Notes
An Essay on Sources
Index

APPENDIX ONE

Annual Emigration from and Remigration to Sweden, 1851–1940

Year	Emigration	Remigration
1851	931	—
1852	3,026	—
1853	2,620	—
1854	3,980	—
1855	586	—
1856	969	—
1857	1,762	—
1858	512	—
1859	208	—
1860	266	—
1861	758	—
1862	947	—
1863	1,216	—
1864	2,593	—
1865	3,906	—
1866	4,466	—
1867	5,893	—
1868	21,472	—
1869	32,053	—
1870	15,430	—
1871	12,985	—
1872	11,838	—
1873	9,486	—
1874	3,380	—
1875	3,591	927
1876	3,702	819
1877	2,921	715
1878	4,242	481
1879	12,761	350

Year	Emigration	Remigration
1880	36,273	399
1881	40,620	553
1882	44,359	798
1883	25,678	1,334
1884	17,664	1,923
1885	18,222	2,391
1886	27,913	1,875
1887	46,252	1,767
1888	45,561	2,221
1889	28,529	2,736
1890	29,487	3,168
1891	36,134	3,546
1892	40,990	3,714
1893	37,321	4,827
1894	9,529	7,343
1895	14,982	5,392
1896	14,874	4,441
1897	10,109	4,849
1898	8,534	4,645
1899	11,842	4,357
1900	16,209	4,024
1901	20,306	3,621
1902	33,151	3,297
1903	35,439	3,537
1904	18,533	4,505
1905	20,520	4,110
1906	21,242	4,511
1907	19,325	4,677
1908	8,873	6,308
1909	18,331	4,854
1910	23,529	4,609
1911	15,571	4,411
1912	13,896	4,681
1913	16,329	4,684
1914	9,589	4,647
1915	4,538	3,055
1916	7,268	2,989
1917	2,462	2,344
1918	1,416	1,565
1919	3,777	3,436
1920	6,691	5,341
1921	5,430	4,387
1922	8,455	3,079
1923	24,948	2,258
1924	7,036	2,320
1925	8,637	2,000

Year	Emigration	Remigration
1926	9,693	2,070
1927	8,735	2,442
1928	9,179	2,578
1929	6,951	2,405
1930	2,868	3,935
1931	919	4,810
1932	474	5,654
1933	682	4,308
1934	710	2,919
1935	560	2,457
1936	664	1,895
1937	876	1,471
1938	634	1,690
1939	746	1,500
1940	619	544

Source: Lars Ljungmark, *Den stora utvandringen* (Stockholm, 1965), 179–80.

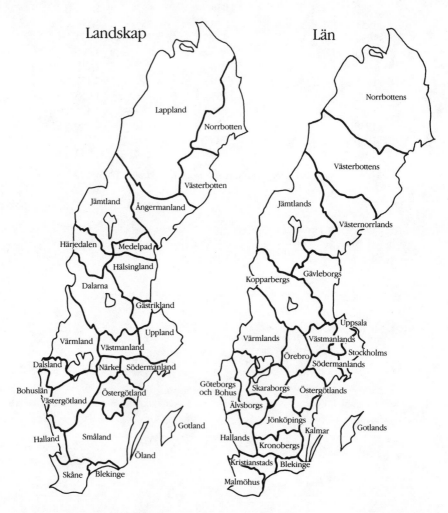

Maps of the Swedish provinces (*landskap*) and the districts (*län*). (Adapted from Nils William Olsson, *Tracing Your Swedish Ancestry*, Stockholm, Royal Swedish Ministry of Foreign Affairs, 1965. Courtesy of the author.)

APPENDIX TWO

A Note on Swedish Regions and Their Inhabitants

*A*s the maps (*left*) will show, Sweden is composed of twenty-five historic provinces or *landskap* (the word is the same in singular and plural). Since the seventeenth century, however, the country has been divided for administrative purposes into twenty-four districts or *län* (also singular and plural). Some of these districts have the same names and boundaries as old provinces, like Östergötland or Värmland. Others have the same names but different boundaries, like Södermanland or Jämtland. Yet others have altogether different names and boundaries, like Malmöhus or Kronobergs *län*.

This is complicated, but two considerations help to avoid confusion. First, when an administrative district is referred to, the word *län* invariably follows its name. When a Swede simply speaks of Västerbotten, for instance, he means the province or *landskap* rather than the much larger Västerbottens *län*, which must always be specifically identified in this way.

Second, although the old *landskap* no longer have any administrative significance, Swedes traditionally identify with them, rather than with the *län*, except in official connections. The inhabitant of a *landskap* is designated by a name deriving from that of his or her province, usually with the ending -ing for a man or -ska for a woman. Thus a *Värmlänning* or *Värmländska* is from *Värmland*, and *Ölänning* from Öland, and so on. The name Norrland applies collectively to the whole of northern Sweden—about two-thirds of the country—and its inhabitants may be referred to as *Norrlänningar* as well as by their provincial names.

APPENDIX THREE

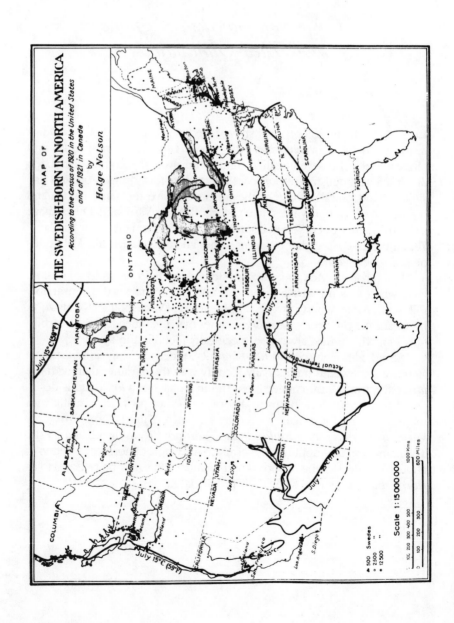

MAP OF

THE SWEDISH-BORN IN NORTH AMERICA

According to the Census of 1920 in the United States
and of 1921 in Canada

by

Helge Nelson

▲ 500 Swedes
● 2500 „
■ 12500 „

Scale 1:15 000 000

Notes

SBL   *Svenskt biografiskt lexikon* (Stockholm, 1907–)
SMoK   *Svenska män och kvinnor* (Stockholm, 1942–)
SSIRC   Swenson Swedish Immigration Research Center, Augustana
      College, Rock Island, Illinois
Sw. Pioneer Hist. Q.   *Swedish Pioneer Historical Quarterly* (1950–81)
Sw.-Am. Hist. Q.   *Swedish-American Historical Quarterly* (1982–).
      (Follows *Swedish Pioneer Historical Quarterly,* above.)

ONE
Prologue: Before the Great Migration

1. On New Sweden, see Amandus Johnson, *The Swedish Settlements on the Delaware,* 2 vols. (New York, 1911); Nils Ahnlund, *Nya Sverige* (Stockholm, 1938); Alf Åberg, *The People of New Sweden* (Stockholm, 1987).

2. On Swedish interest in America during the early eighteenth century, see my "Clio and Swedish America: Historians, Organizations, Publications," in Nils Hasselmo, ed., *Perspectives on Swedish Immigration* (Chicago, 1978), 4.

3. Pehr Kalm, *En resa til Norra America,* 3 vols. (Stockholm, 1753–61); Israel Acrelius, *Beskrifning om de Swenska församlingars forna och närwarande tillstånd, uti det så kallade Nya Sverige . . . uti Norra Amerika* (Stockholm, 1759). Cf. Peter Kalm, *Travels into North America,* trans. John Reinhold Foster, 3 vols. (Warrington, 1770; London, 1771), and Adolph B. Benson, ed., *Peter Kalm's Travels in North America,* 2 vols. (New York, 1937); Israel Acrelius, *A History of New Sweden,* trans. William M. Reynolds (Philadelphia, 1874; reprint, n.p., 1966). For early Swedish accounts, see Esther Elisabeth Larson, *Swedish Commentators on America, 1638–1865: An Annotated List of Selected Manuscripts and Printed Materials* (New York, 1963).

4. Harald Elovson, *Amerika i svensk litteratur 1750–1820. En studie i komparativ litteraturhistoria* (Lund, 1930), 227. This work is basic for the period it covers. For European and Swedish interest in America in the longer perspective, see also Sigmund Skard, "Amerika i Europas liv," in Lars Åhnebrink, ed., *Amerika och Norden* (Stockholm, Göteborg, & Uppsala,

1964), 12–28, and Harald Elovson, "Den liberala Amerikabilden i Sverige," in the same volume, 75–109.

5. Elovson, *Amerika i svensk litteratur,* 9–39, esp. 10–11.

6. A. C. Fraser, ed., *The Works of George Berkeley,* 4 vols. (Oxford, 1901), IV, 365–66; Elovson, *Amerika i svensk litteratur,* 14, 21.

7. Elovson, *Amerika i svensk litteratur,* 42, 47–48.

8. *Ibid.,* 35.

9. My *Scandinavia in the Revolutionary Era, 1760–1815* (Minneapolis, 1986), 123. For Swedish reactions to the American Revolution, see ch. 5 of this work; also my "Sweden and the War of American Independence," *William & Mary Quarterly,* 3d. ser., 23 (1966): 403–30; Elovson, *Amerika i svensk litteratur,* chs. 2–4. Adolph B. Benson, *Sweden and the American Revolution* (New Haven, 1926) and Amandus Johnson, *Swedish Contributions to American Freedom, 1776–1783,* 2 vols. (Philadelphia, 1953–57) remain of value.

10. My *Scandinavia in the Revolutionary Era,* 123.

11. Elovson, *Amerika i svensk litteratur,* 172–73. For Swedish thought regarding the French Revolution, see *ibid.,* chs. 3–4.

12. Cf. my *Scandinavia in the Revolutionary Era.*

13. Nils Runeby, *Den nya världen och den gamla. Amerikabild och emigrationsuppfattning i Sverige 1820–1860* (Uppsala, 1969), 77. This, too, is an essential work for the period it deals with.

14. *Ibid.,* 32.

15. Elovson, *Amerika i svensk litteratur,* 252.

16. Runeby, *Den nya världen,* 30; Elovson, *Amerika i svensk littteratur,* 280–81, 295. Cf. Esaias Tegnér, *Samlade skrifter,* ed. Ewert Wrangel & Fredrik Böök, 10 vols. (Stockholm, 1919–25), III, 164.

17. Elovson, *Amerika i svensk litteratur,* 6.

18. On the impact of these and other foreign commentators on America, down to 1860, see esp. *ibid.* and Runeby, *Den nya världen.*

19. Cf. my "Sweden and the War of American Independence," 416–18; my *Count Hans Axel von Fersen: Aristocrat in an Age of Revolution* (Boston, 1975), 29–36.

20. Elovson, *Amerika i svensk litteratur,* 69–70, 222–26. Cf. Nils Collin, *Dagbok från New Jersey 1770–86,* ed. Robert Murray (Stockholm, 1988).

21. Cf. Runeby, *Den nya världen,* 25.

22. A. L. Klinckowström, *Bref om de Förenta Staterna, författade under en resa till Amerika åren 1818, 1819, 1820,* 2 vols. (Stockholm, 1824), in English translation by Franklin D. Scott, *Baron Klinckowström's America* (Evanston, Ill., 1952); C. G. Gosselman, *Resa i Norra Amerika* (Nyköping, 1835); C. D. Arfwedson, *The United States and Canada in 1832, 1833, and 1834,* 2 vols. (London, 1834), *Förenta Staterna och Canada åren 1832, 1833 och 1834,* 2 vols. (Stockholm, 1835). Carl Ulrik von Hauswolff, *Teckningar utur Sällskapslifvet i Nord Amerikas Förenta Stater,* 2 vols. (Norrköping, 1835). Regarding this literature, see esp. Runeby, *Den vya världen.*

23. Runeby, *Den nya världen,* 110.

24. *Ibid.,* 67–69, 140–41, 146, 149. On Wijk, cf. Per Clemensson, *Två göteborgare på resa i Nya och Gamla Werlden* (Göteborg, 1978).

25. See Nils William Olsson, *Swedish Passenger Arrivals in New York, 1820–1850* (Chicago, 1967) and *Swedish Passenger Arrivals in U.S. Ports, 1820–1850 (except New York)* (Stockholm & St. Paul, 1979); Axel Friman, "Swedish Emigration to North America, 1820–1850," *Sw. Pioneer Hist. Q.* 27 (1976): 153–77.

26. See W. E. Svedelius, *Studier i Sveriges statskunskap,* I (Uppsala, 1875; no vol. II), 352–56; Franklin D. Scott, "Sweden's Constructive Opposition to Emigration," *Journal of Modern History* 37 (1965): 307. The eighteenth-century debate still awaits fuller treatment.

27. Petrus Læstadius, *Tankar om fattigdomen och fattigvården i Sverige* (Stockholm,

1840), 33, 39. Cf. Runeby, *Den nya världen,* 117.

28. Elovson, *Amerika i svensk litteratur,* 168, 228, 246; Runeby, *Den nya världen,* 102.

29. Runeby, *Den nya världen,* 35.

TWO

The Flow Begins, 1840–1865

1. Gustaf Unonius, *Minnen från en sjuttonårig vistelse i Nordvästra Amerika,* 2 vols. (Uppsala, 1861–62); English translation, *A Pioneer in Northwest America,* trans. J. Oscar Backlund, ed. Nils William Olsson, 2 vols. (Minneapolis, 1950, 1960).

2. Stephenson, trans. and ed., *Letters Relating to Gustaf Unonius,* 50–51, 68–76.

3. Runeby, *Den nya världen,* 165. For the overall history of the Swedish emigration and Swedes in America, the following works are recommended. Lars Ljungmark, *Swedish Exodus* (Carbondale, Ill., 1979); Nils Hasselmo, *Swedish America* (New York, 1976), Ulf Beijbom, *Amerika, Amerika* (Stockholm, 1977); and my *Letters from the Promised Land: Swedes in America, 1840–1914* (Minneapolis, 1975) provide useful introductions. For fuller treatment, see Florence E. Janson, *The Background of Swedish Immigration, 1840–1930* (Chicago, 1931); John S. Lindberg, *The Background of Swedish Emigration to the United States* (Minneapolis, 1930), and Harald Runblom and Hans Norman, eds., *From Sweden to America* (Uppsala & Minneapolis, 1976). For a working guide to the very extensive bibliography in the field, see my *Letters* (2d paperback edition, 1990), 325–28.

4. George M. Stephenson, trans. and ed., "Documents Relating to Peter Cassel and the Settlement at New Sweden," *Swedish American Historical Bulletin* 2:1 (1929): 55–62 (Swedish and English texts). Cf. my *Letters,* 28–33. On the Cassel party and New Sweden, see my book, *The Search for Ancestors: A Swedish-American Family Saga* (Carbondale, Ill., 1979), chs. 3–4, as well as the special number of the *Sw. Pioneer Hist. Q.* 32 (April 1981).

5. [Peter Cassel,] *Beskrifning öfwer Norra Amerikas Förenta Stater* (Westerwik, 1846). This work is given, in the original Swedish and English translation, in Stephenson, ed., "Documents Relating to Peter Cassel."

6. My *Letters,* 39–41. On Erik Jansson and Bishop Hill, see Olov Isaksson and Sören Hallgren, *Bishop Hill: A Utopia on the Prairie* (Stockholm, 1969); Paul Elmen, *Wheat Flour Messiah* (Carbondale, Ill., 1976); my "The Eric-Janssonists and the Shifting Contours of Community," *Western Illinois Regional Studies* 12 (1989): 17–35. An excerpt from Erik Jansson's "Parting Speech" (*Avskedstal*) is given in Albin Widén, *Amerikaemigrationen i dokument* (Stockholm, 1966), 12. For general background, see George M. Stephenson's important study, *The Religious Aspects of Swedish Immigration* (Minneapolis, 1932).

7. Carlo Cipolla in *Literacy and Development in the West* (Harmondsworth, 1966), 115, estimates that by 1850 adult literacy in Sweden was as high as 90 percent, the highest of all the European countries he has surveyed.

8. Stephenson, "Documents Relating to Peter Cassel," 58; George M. Stephenson, "Typical America Letters," *Yearbook of the Swedish Historical Society of America* 7 (1921–22): 54–55. Cf. my *Letters,* 30, 86–87. Note also the early immigrant letters given in George M. Stephenson, "When America Was the Land of Canaan," *Minnesota History,* 10 (1929): 237–60. "The Swarming of the Swedes" is a chapter title from Stephenson's *Religious Aspects of Swedish Immigration.* On the overall significance of America-letters, see my *Letters,* esp. 16–17, 112–13, 207. Cf. the Norwegian historian, Ingrid Semmingsen's "Utvandring og kontakt med Amerika," in Lars Åhnebrink, ed., *Amerika och Norden* (Stockholm, 1964), 65–74. A case study of a particular chain migration in Sweden and America is provided by my *Search for Ancestors.* See also Robert C. Ostergren, *A Community Transplanted* (Madison, Wisc., 1988).

9. Märtha Ångström, "Swedish Emigrant Guide Books of the Early 1850's," *Yearbook of the American Swedish Historical Foundation, 1947* (Philadelphia, 1947), 22–48, esp. 47; Cf. Roy W. Swanson, "Some Swedish Emigrant Guide Books of the Second Half of the Nineteenth

Century," *Yearbook of the Swedish Historical Society of America* 11 (St. Paul, 1926): 103–24; Johan Bolin, *Beskrifning öfwer Nord-Amerikas Förenta Stater* (Wexjö, 1853).

10. Carl E. Swalander, *Tillförlitliga underrättelser om Nord-Amerikas Förenta Stater* (Göteborg, 1853), 16. Cf. Ångström, "Swedish Emigrant Guide Books," 33.

11. See Curt von Wachenfeldt, "Background to Peter Cassel's Emigration," *Sw. Pioneer Hist. Q.* 32 (1981): 95–105.

12. Cf. the example of Carl Johan Chilberg (Kilberg) and Knäred parish, Halland, in 1853, given in my *Search for Ancestors,* 42.

13. A. A. Stomberg, "Letters of an Early Emigrant Agent in the Scandinavian Countries," *Swedish-American Historical Bulletin* 3 (1930): 7–52; Paul W. Gates, "The Campaign of the Illinois Central Railroad for Norwegian and Swedish Immigrants," *Norwegian-American Studies and Records* 6 (Northfield, Minn., 1931), 66–87.

14. See C. R. Lyle, II, "America Discovers Vinland: Scholarly Controversy in the Period, 1830–1950," *Sw. Pioneer Hist. Q.* 19 (1968): 174–93; Lloyd Hustvedt, *Rasmus Bjørn Anderson* (Northfield, Minn., 1966), 311–16; my "Clio and Swedish America," 6; Frederick Hale, "Nordic Immigration: The New Puritans?" *Sw. Pioneer Hist. Q.* 28 (1977): 27–44; Charles Loring Brace, *The Norse-Folk; or, a Visit to the Homes of Norway and Sweden* (New York, 1857), iii, also 133.

15. Stephenson, "Documents Regarding Peter Cassel," esp. 38, 47–49. Cf. Runeby, *Den nya världen,* 203, 207–8.

16. Stephenson, "Documents Regarding Peter Cassel," 75–76. (Printed in *Östgötha Correspondenten,* 7, 14 July 1849.)

17. Charles J. Hoflund, *Getting Ahead: A Swedish Immigrant's Reminiscences, 1834–1887,* ed. H. Arnold Barton (Carbondale, Ill., 1989), 23; Vilhelm Moberg, *The Emigrants,* trans. Gustaf Lannestock (New York, 1951), 127–28; Eric Norelius, *Early Life of Eric Norelius 1833–1862: A Lutheran Pioneer,* trans. Emeroy Johnson (Rock Island, Ill., 1934), 76.

18. Widén, *Amerikaemigrationen i dokument,* 14–15. Cf. my *Letters,* 44.

19. D. A. Peterson, "From Östergötland to Iowa," *Sw. Pioneer Hist. Q.* 22 (1971): 139–40. Cf. my *Letters,* 54–55.

20. Runeby, *Den nya världen,* 191, 438.

21. *Ibid.,* 294.

22. *Ibid.,* 277, 295–96, 371, 441.

23. *Ibid.,* 389.

24. *Ibid.,* 213, 304, 432.

25. *Ibid.,* 241, 338, 342.

26. *Ibid.,* 215, 241, 368–69.

27. *Ibid.,* 297. In a lengthy anti-emigration tract in 1792–93 that was never published, Nils Collin had warned of the exaggerated praise of America in letters from European immigrants. (Elovson, *Amerika i svensk litteratur,* 224–45.)

28. My *Letters,* 91. Cf. Runeby, *Den nya världen,* 412–20; poem, *ibid.,* 417.

29. Runeby, *Den nya världen,* 388, 404, 433, 442–43, 445.

30. *Ibid.,* 236.

31. *Ibid.,* 216, 254–55. For general background, cf. Stephenson, *Religious Aspects.*

32. Runeby, *Den nya världen,* 312, 315, 325. Cf. Stephenson, *Religious Aspects;* Henry C. Whyman, *The Hedstroms and the Bethel Ship Saga: Methodist Influence on Swedish Religious Life* (Carbondale, Ill., 1992).

33. Runeby, *Den nya världen,* 232, 367, 376, 411–12.

34. *Ibid.,* 221, 233, 440.

35. *Ibid.,* 229.

36. *Ibid.,* 215, 222, 230, 232, 244.

37. *Ibid.,* 233, 404, 440.

38. *Ibid.,* 439; my *Letters,* 90.

39. Per Adam Siljeström, *Resa i Förenta Staterna,* 2 vols. (Stockholm, 1852–54); Runeby, *Den nya världen,* 381.

40. Fredrika Bremer, *Hemmen i den Nya Verlden,* 2 vols. (Stockholm, 1853–54), in translation, *The Homes of the New World,* 3 vols. (London, 1853); Gunnar Eidevall, *Amerika i svensk 1900-talslitteratur* (Stockholm, 1983), 19. Cf. Elovson, "Den liberala amerikabilden," 85; Runeby, *Den nya världen,* 384–87.

41. John Norton, ed. and trans., "Anders Wiberg's Account of a Trip to the United States in 1852–1853," *Sw. Pioneer Hist. Q.* 29 (1978): 89–116, 162–79, esp. 93–95, 99, 102, 107–10, 178.

42. Runeby, *Den nya världen,* 198, 239, 394, 400.

43. Carl David Arfwedson, *Några få ord till dem, som nästa år ämna från Sverige och Norrige utflytta till Förenta Staterna, af en opartisk Landsman* (Stockholm, 1842), esp. 1, 2.

44. C. A. von Nolcken, "Några ord om Svenska Allmogens utflyttning till andra werldsdelar," *Läsning för Allmogen* (Lund, 1855), 37–48, esp. 38–39, 47–48. Cf. J. H. F. Mahn, *Kalifornien i Sverige eller Guldgrufworna för wårt Jordbruk* (Stockholm, 1864), esp. 77–78; Runeby, *Den nya världen,* 406.

45. Runeby, *Den nya världen,* 407. Concerning Riehl and his influence in Sweden, cf. Bo Grandien, *Rönndruvans glöd* (Stockholm, 1987), 89–91, 219–21.

46. Ph. v. T., "Varningsord till Utvandrare," *Läsning för Folket,* vol. 25, no. 3 (Stockholm, 1859), 286–88.

47. Anonymous, "Warning för Utwandrare," *Läsning för Folket,* vol. 29, no. 1 (1863), 60–72, esp. 61, 68–71; Runeby, *Den nya världen,* 354. Cf. Nils Runeby, "Gustaf Unonius and Propaganda Against Emigration," *Sw. Pioneer Hist. Q.* 24 (1973): 94–107.

48. See Robert L. Wright, *Swedish Emigrant Ballads* (Lincoln, Nebr., 1965); Knut Brodin, *Emigrantvisor och andra visor* (Stockholm, 1938). Cf. Rochelle Wright and Robert L. Wright, *Danish Emigrant Ballads and Songs* (Carbondale, Ill., 1983); Elovson, "Den liberala amerikabilden," 86–87.

49. Runeby, *Den nya världen,* 241–45, 422–23, 427–30.

50. *Ibid.,* 351–52.

51. S. W. Olson, ed. och trans., "Early Letters to Erland Carlsson," Augustana Historical Society, *Publications,* 5 (Rock Island, Ill., 1935), 113–17. Cf. my *Letters,* 69–73. In the original Swedish in my *Brev från löftets land. Svenskar berättar om Amerika 1840–1914* (Stockholm, 1979)—the Swedish edition of my *Letters*—83–86.

52. Kjell Bondestad, "The American Civil War and Swedish Public Opinion," *Sw. Pioneer Hist. Q.* 19 (1968): 95–115; Elovson, "Den liberala amerikabilden," 90. For European reactions to the American Civil War, cf. Halvdan Koht, *The American Spirit in Europe* (Philadelphia, 1949), ch. 8.

53. On the Swedish Americans and the Civil War, see Nels Hokanson, *Swedish Immigrants in Lincoln's Time* (New York, 1942).

54. Måns Hultin, *Resa till Amerika 1864,* ed. Erik Gamby (Helsingfors, 1958), 58–59. Cf. my *Letters,* 101–2.

55. See my article, "The Life and Times of Swedish-America," *Sw.-Am. Hist. Q.* 35 (1984): 282–96, esp. 284–86; Dag Blanck, "'A Language Does Die Easily. . . .': Swedish at Augustana College, 1860–1900," *Sw.-Am. Hist. Q.* 33 (1982): 288–305, esp. 291–92; O. Fritiof Ander, *T. N. Hasselquist* (Rock Island, Ill., 1931), 229.

56. See my "Måns Jakob's Grindstone, or Documentary Sources and the Transferance of Swedish Material Culture to America," *Sw.-Am. Hist. Q.* 38 (1987): 29–40.

57. See my *Search for Ancestors,* 59–60. Cf. Runeby, *Den nya världen,* 382.

58. See esp. Stephenson, *Religious Aspects.*

59. Olson, "Early Letters to Erland Carlsson," 111. Cf. my *Letters,* 68–69.

60. See Runeby, *Den nya världen,* 15–17, 156.

61. Cf. *ibid.,* 246, 453, 460–62.

THREE

A New Sweden Across the Sea

1. The first, introductory section of this chapter is based largely on my *Letters*, 107–11. For fuller background, see esp. Janson, *Background of Swedish Immigration*, and Norman and Runblom, eds., *From Sweden to America*.

2. Sweden kept regular statistics on emigration, beginning in 1851, and on remigration from 1875. See Appendix 1.

3. *History of Warren County, Pennsylvania* (n.p., 1877), 168, quoted in Inga Holmberg, "En lång historia—140 år med svenska invandrare i Jamestown" (unpublished seminar paper, Dept. of History, Uppsala University, 1991), 6. Cf. Richmond Mayo Smith, *Emigration and Immigration* (New York, 1890), 144, 146.

4. M. W. Montgomery, *A Wind from the Holy Spirit in Sweden and Norway* (New York, 1885), 6–8; cf. "An American Evaluation of the Scandinavians Here in 1884," *Sw. Pioneer Hist. Q.* 7 (1956): 144–47; also, Albert Shaw, "The Scandinavians in the United States," *The Chautauquan* (Dec. 1887), 169–72. Cf. F. H. B. McDowell, "The Newer Scandinavia," *Scandinavia* 3 (1886), 147–80, 203–14, esp. 147–48. Cf. Frederick Hale, "Nordic Immigrants: The New Puritans?" *Sw. Pioneer Hist. Q.* 28 (1977): 24–44.

5. See my "Scandinavian Immigrant Women's Encounter with America," *Sw. Pioneer Hist. Q.* 15 (1974): 37–42; Ann-Sofie Kälvemark, "Utvandring och självständighet. Några synpunkter på den kvinnliga emigrationen från Sverige," *Historisk tidskrift* (1983), 140–74; Ulf Beijbom, "Pigornas förlovade land," in his *Svenskamerikanskt. Människor och förhållanden i Svensk-Amerika* (Växjö, 1990), 99–136; Joy K. Lintelman, "'On My Own': Single, Swedish, and Female in Turn-of-the-Century Chicago," in Philip J. Anderson and Dag Blanck, eds. *Swedish-American Life in Chicago* (Urbana, 1992), 89–99.

6. See my "Life and Times of Swedish-America."

FOUR

A Group Portait for Those at Home

1. [P. J.Bladh,] *Bland bättre folk och pack i "det förlofvade landet"* (Stockholm, 1871), 1–2.

2. Cf. my *Scandinavia in the Revolutionary Era*, 345.

3. Cf. Alrik Gustafson, *A History of Swedish Literature* (Minneapolis, 1961); E. N. Tigerstedt, *Svensk litteraturhistoria* (4th ed., Stockholm, 1971).

4. J. Stadling, *Genom den stora Vestern. Reseskildringar* (Stockholm, 1883), 316–18.

5. August Strindberg, *Tjänstekvinnans son,* 2 vols. (Stockholm, 1887), II, in *Samlade skrifter,* 55 vols. (Stockholm, 1912–20), XIX, 108–9; Elovson, "Den liberala amerikabilden," 99–104. Harald Elovson, "August Strindberg and Emigration to America until ca. 1890," *Americana Norvegica* 3 (1971): 129–52, and "August Strindberg and Emigration to the United States, 1890–1912," *Americana Norvegica* 4 (1973): 47–67. On Kjellberg, cf. Olof Lagercrantz, *August Strindberg* (MånPocket ed., Stockholm, 1979), 113.

6. Mauritz Rubenson, *Skildringar från Amerika och England i bref under hösten 1867* (Stockholm, 1868), 9. Cf. Rubenson's emigrant guide, *Den nya Amerika-Boken för svenska utvandrare* (Stockholm, 1869).

7. Ernst Beckman, *Amerikanska studier,* 2 vols. (Stockholm, 1883), I: *Våra landsmän i Amerika,* 11, 15.

8. Axel Lindvall, *Minnen från en färd genom Amerika* (Karlskrona, 1890), 100.

9. Rubenson, *Skildringar,* 14.

10. Ernst Beckman, *Från Nya Verlden. Reseskildringar från Amerikas Förenta Stater* (Stockholm, 1877), 112, 168; Bladh, *Bland bättre folk och pack,* 87; C.E.H. Gestrin, *I Amerika. Intryck och erfarenheter under ett tolfårigt vistande i Förenta Staterna af en f. d. Stockholmsno-*

tarie, 2 parts in 1 (Stockholm, 1881), I, 5. See also my "Swedish Travelers' Accounts of Chicago," in Anderson and Blanck, eds., *Swedish-American Life in Chicago*, 103–11.

11. Beckman, *Amerikanska studier*, I, 106.

12. Rubenson, *Skildringar*, 51; Beckman, *Amerikanska studier*, I, 54–55, 72.

13. Lindvall, *Minnen från en färd*, 43–44, 55, 72.

14. Hugo Nisbet, *Två år i Amerika. Reseskildringar* (Stockholm, 1874), 61–66.

15. Ernst Beckman, *Amerikanska studier*, I, 44, 51–52, 80, 88, 98, 103.

16. *Ibid.*, 152–53.

17. *Ibid.*, 42, 49.

18. Nisbeth, *Två år i Amerika*, 42–43, 58–59, 147.

19. Beckman, *Från Nya Verlden*, 89–91, 95–96.

20. Beckman, *Amerikanska studier*, I, 59–61, 86.

21. C. J. Nyvall, *Reseminnen från Amerika af C. J. N.* (Kristinehamn, 1876), 77; cf. my *Letters*, 171.

22. Stadling, *Genom den stora Vestern*, 59, 319–20; Isador Kjellberg, *Föredrag om Amerika, hållet i Stockholm den 18 febr. 1883* (Stockholm, 1883), 10–12, 25–29.

23. Beckman, *Från Nya Verlden*, 180.

24. Nisbeth, *Två år i Amerika*, 39–40. Regarding the disappearance of folk dress in a Minnesota settlement, see Alfred Bergin, "I Amerikas Dalarna, eller svenskarne i och omkring Cambridge, Minn.," *Prärieblomman 1903*, 125–26.

25. Beckman, *Amerikanska studier*, I, 11, and *Från Nya Verlden*, 88.

26. Gestrin, *I Amerika*, I, 22–24.

27. August Andrén, "Som emigrant i USA på 1860- och 1870-talen," *Halland och hallänningar, Årsbok* 3 (Halmstad, 1956), 49–50. Cf. my *Letters*, 130–31.

28. Cf. Beckman, *Från Nya Verlden*, 198–210; Gestrin, *I Amerika*, I, 176–90. For a more general discussion of Swedish and European views on the American woman, see Lars Wendelius, *Bilden av Amerika i svensk prosafiktion 1890–1914* (Uppsala, 1982), ch. 3.

29. Beckman, *Amerikanska studier*, I, 52–53.

30. *Ibid.*, 49; Beckman, *Från Nya Verlden*, 193–98.

31. Beckman, *Amerikanska studier*, I, 139–42, 150.

32. Stadling, *Genom den stora Vestern*, 26, 48; Beckman, *Amerikanska studier*, I, 122–23.

33. Cf. Beckman, *Från Nya Verlden*, 107–8.

34. Rubenson, *Skildringar*, 54–55. Cf. Nisbeth, *Två år i Amerika*, 74.

35. Rubenson, *Skildringar*, 56–57; Nisbeth, *Två år i Amerika*, 74–75.

36. Rubenson, *Skildringar*, 56; Cf. Nyvall, *Reseminnen*, 45, 49, 105, 108–9, 111, 112; Stadling, *Genom den stora Vestern*, 275.

37. Beckman, *Amerikanska studier*, I, 134–38.

38. Kjellberg, *Föredrag*, 39–40, 42.

39. Rubenson, *Skildringar*, 56; Nisbeth, *Två år i Amerika*, 41; Nyvall, *Reseminnen*, 35–56; Beckman, *Från Nya Verlden*, 86–87; Kjellberg, *Föredrag*, 39.

40. Nyvall, *Reseminnen*, 77. Cf. my *Letters*, 171.

41. Gunnar Westin, *Emigranterna och kyrkan. Brev från och till svenskar i Amerika 1849–1892* (Stockholm, 1932), 135–37. Cf. my *Letters*, 159–60.

42. Rubenson, *Skildringar*, 57–58.

43. Beckman, *Amerikanska studier*, I, 111–12.

44. *Ibid.*, 112–13. Cf. Anna Williams, *Skribent i Svensk-Amerika. Jakob Bonggren, journalist och poet* (Uppsala, 1991), 97–98.

45. Andrén, "Som emigrant i USA på 1860- och 1870-talen," 48–49; Albin Widén, *När Svensk-Amerika grundades* (n.p., 1961), 133–34; cf. my *Letters*, 131–32, 169; Rubenson, *Skildringar*, 58. Cf. Lindvall, *Minnen från en färd*, 160.

46. Beckman, *Amerikanska studier*, I, 147.

47. Nisbeth, *Två år i Amerika*, 129–31.

48. *Ibid.*, 131; Beckman, *Från Nya Verlden*, 110, and *Amerikanska studier*, I, 85, 175–77;

George M. Stephenson, ed., "*Hemlandet* Letters," *Yearbook of the Swedish Historical Society of America, 1922–1923,* 139; cf. my *Letters,* 134.

49. Nisbeth, *Två år i Amerika,* 131; Beckman, *Från Nya Verlden,* 110, and *Amerikanska studier,* I, 176; Kjellberg, *Föredrag,* 44–45.

50. Elovson, "Den liberala amerikabilden," 93.

FIVE

The Creation of a Swedish-American Identity

1. Albin Widén, *När Svensk-Amerika grundades* (n.p., 1961), 124, 125, 130, 139; Kjellberg, *Föredrag,* 44.

2. Hans Mattson, *Reminiscences: The Story of an Emigrant* (St. Paul, 1891) and *Minnen af Öfverste H. Mattson* (Lund, 1891). On Mattson, see also Lars Ljungmark, *For Sale: Minnesota* (Göteborg, 1971) and "Hans Mattson's Minnen: A Swedish-American Monument," *Sw. Pioneer Hist. Q.* 29 (1978): 57–68; Victor Greene, *American Immigrant Leaders, 1800–1910* (Baltimore, 1987), 80–83. On his visits to Sweden, see also Tell G. Dahllöf, "Three Americans Look at Sweden," *Sw. Pioneer Hist. Q.* 17 (1966): 180–83.

3. Mattson, *Reminiscences,* 109.

4. *Ibid.,* 95, 109, 111.

5. *Ibid.,* 104–5.

6. *Ibid.,* 105–6, 112–13.

7. *Ibid.,* 113–14, 124–25, 127, 129.

8. *Ibid.,* 110–12.

9. Ernst Skarstedt, *Vagabond och redaktör. Lefnadsöden och tidsbilder* (Seattle, 1914). On Skarstedt, see his *Våra pennfäktare* (San Francisco, 1897), 154–57, and *Pennfäktare* (Stockholm, 1930), 169–71; Emory Lindquist, *An Immigrant's American Odysses: A Biography of Ernst Skarstedt* (Rock Island, Ill., 1974). See also Dahllöf, "Three Americans Look at Sweden," 183–84.

10. Skarstedt, *Vagabond och redaktör,* 361–62, 286.

11. *Ibid.,* 274–75, 278.

12. *Ibid.,* 287, 291.

13. *Ibid.,* 287–88, 290.

14. *Ibid.,* 289, 295.

15. On Enander, see Skarstedt, *Våra pennfäktare,* 51–53, and *Pennfäktare,* 54–55; Anders Schön, "Dr. Joh. A. Enander. En minnesruna," *Prärieblomman 1911,* 16–45; Conrad Bergendoff, "A Significant Enander Document," *Sw. Pioneer Hist. Q.* 21 (1970): 5–25; Greene, *American Immigrant Leaders,* 78–80.

16. For the cultural and literary background to Enander's ideas, see Alrik Gustafson, *A History of Swedish Literature* (Minneapolis, 1961); E. N. Tigerstedt, *Svensk litteraturhistoria* (4th. ed., Stockholm, 1971); Bo Grandien, *Rönndruvans glöd. Nygöticistiskt i tanke, konst och miljö under 1800-talet* (Stockholm, 1987), esp. 140.

17. Joh. A. Enander, *Förenta Staternas Historia, utarbetad för den svenska befolkningen i Amerika,* 2d ed., 4 parts in 2 vols. (Chicago, 1882), I:1, iii.

18. Joh. A. Enander, *Valda skrifter af Joh. A. Enander,* I (Chicago, 1892). No subsequent volumes appeared. J. A. Enander, "Sveriges roll i världshistorien," unpubl., undated manuscript in Göteborgs landsarkiv. I am indebted to Dag Blanck, Uppsala, for a copy of this manuscript. Cf. also Dag Blanck, "Constructing an Ethnic Identity: The Case of the Swedish-Americans and Johan Alfred Enander" (unpublished seminar paper, Dept. of History, Uppsala Univ., 1986).

19. Enander, *Förenta Staternas Historia,* I:1, 50–51, 186, and *Valda skrifter,* I, 13–22.

20. Enander, *Förenta Staternas Historia,* I:1, 50–51.

21. Enander, *Valda skrifter,* I, 59, 259–61.

22. Enander, *Förenta Staternas Historia,* I:1, 55; II:1, 26–27.

23. *Ibid.,* II:1, 27, 65–67.

24. Enander, *Valda skrifter,* I, 23, 27–28, 73–74, 268, 271, 273–74, 278.

25. Enander, *Förenta Staternas Historia,* II:1, 27–31.

26. Enander, *Valda skrifter,* dedication (n.p.), 64.

27. Mattson, *Reminiscences,* 291–92, 313–14.

28. T. N. Hasselquist, "En amerikanares omdöme om kyrkliga förhållanden i Sverige," *Teologisk Tidskrift* (1871), 185–86; Nisbeth, *Två år i Amerika,* 41; Beckman, *Amerikanska studier,* I, 50, 55.

29. See Hans Mattson, ed., *250th Anniversary of the First Swedish Settlement in America, September 14th 1888* (Minneapolis, 1888). Cf. Mattson, *Reminiscences,* 292–95.

30. Mattson, *250th Anniversary,* 43.

31. *Ibid.,* 5–17, esp. 8, 11.

32. *Ibid.,* 18–29, esp. 27–28. Enander's speech is also given in somewhat revised form in his *Valda skrifter,* I, 29–43.

33. Statement of Incorporation, undated [1889], Swedish Historical Society of America Collection, Carton 1, Minnesota Historical Society, St. Paul; Eric Johnson and C. F. Peterson, *Svenskarne i Illinois* (Chicago, 1880). Cf. my "Clio in Swedish America"; Ulf Beijbom, "The Historiography of Swedish America," *Sw. Pioneer Hist. Q.* 31 (1980): 257–85.

SIX

What Was Sweden to Do?

1. Beckman, *Amerikanska studier,* I, 178.

2. A. A., "Per Swensson hemma och Per Swensson hinsidan oceanen (Berättelse ur werkligheten)," *Läsning för folket* 35 (1869), 113–19.

3. *Ibid.,* 122–28.

4. Beckman, *Amerikanska studier,* I, 23; Kjellberg, *Föredrag,* 50–52.

5. Albert Lindhagen, *Yttrande i Riksdagens Andra Kammare angående emigrationen af A.L.* (Stockholm, 1869) esp. 3–4, 9–10, 12–13, 16. Cf. Carl Lindhagen, *På vikingafärd i Västerled* (Stockholm, 1926), 187–89; Stephenson, *Religious Aspects,* 434–36; Ann-Sofie Kälvemark, *Reaktionen mot utvandringen. Emigrationsfrågan i svensk debatt och politik 1901–1904* (Uppsala, 1972), 35, 56–58.

6. Franklin D. Scott, "Sweden's Constructive Opposition," *Journal of Modern History* 37 (1965): 311.

7. Cf. Johan Andersson, *Amerika eller Sverige? Några ord om emigrationen, dess orsaker och verkningar* (Kalmar, 1870), 310. Cf. Scott, "Sweden's Constructive Opposition," 310.

8. Alex. Nilsson, *Amerika sådant det är!* (Stockholm, 1871), esp. 49, 154, and *Beskrifning öfver Amerika* (Göteborg, 1872), esp. 79, 83, 94–95.

9. C. F. Bergstedt, "Röster från Amerika om utvandringen," *Samtiden,* 38 (20 Sept. 1873): 593–99, and 40 (3 Oct. 1874): 625–32.

10. Nisbeth, *Två år i Amerika,* 9, 13–16, 128–29; Beckman, *Från Nya Verlden,* 113; Stadling, *Genom den stora Vestern,* 49; Kjellberg, *Föredrag,* 21.

11. W. E. Svedelius, *Studier i Sveriges statskunskap,* I (Uppsala, 1875), esp. 381, 385–86, 388–90.

12. Beckman, *Från Nya Verlden,* 112–13. Cf. J. A. Leffler, "Om utvandringen," *Nationalekonomiska förhandlingar 1889* (Stockholm, 1892), 45–58, esp. 58.

13. Knut Wicksell, *Om utvandring. Dess betydelse och orsaker* (Stockholm, 1882), esp. 23–24, 27–29, 32, 55–56, 61, 68, 76.

14. O. Bergström, *Tankar öfver emigrationen samt råd till utvandrare* (Stockholm, 1882), esp. 1–14, 56. Cf. *Genesis,* 9:1.

15. Gustav Sundbarg, *Bidrag till utvandringensfrågan från befolkningsstatistisk synpunkt,*

Uppsala universitets årsskrift: Filosofi, 1884, 1885 (Uppsala, 1885, 1885–86). Quotation, II, 138.

16. Kälvemark, *Reaktionen mot utvandringen*, 43–56. Cf. Hans Norman and Harald Runblom, *Amerikaemigrationen i källornas belysning* (Gävle, 1980), 68–70.

17. Axel Lindberg, *Några betraktelser rörande främjandet af landets jordbruk och hämmandet af emigrationen* (Uppsala, 1882), esp. 31. Cf. C. A. Sjöcrona, *Om utwandringen. Utlåtande afgifvet på nådig befallning* (Mariestad, 1882), esp. 7–8, 13–19.

18. Lindberg, *Några betraktelser,* 29; J. A. Leffler, "Våra jordbruksarbetare med särskildt afseende på den amerikanska konkurrensen," *Nationalekonomiska Föreningens förhandlingar 1887* (Stockholm, 1888), 49–58, esp. 55–57.

19. Rubenson, *Skildringar,* 52; Allan Kastrup, *The Swedish Heritage in America* (Minneapolis, 1975), 603. Lindberg, in *Några betraktelser,* 29, in 1882 and Beckman, *Amerikanska studier,* I, 182, in 1883, also urge "bringing America to Sweden."

20. "Fjalar's" verse cited in Beckman, *Amerikanska studier,* I, 179; Carl Snoilsky, *Dikter af Carl Snoilsky. Tredje samlingen* (Stockholm, 1883), 244–53, esp. 247, 251–53.

21. Sidney W. Cooper, *Rambles in Sweden: A Series of Letters from Sweden to a Newspaper in America* (Gothenburg, 1884), esp. 29–30, 187–88, 198–203. The American newspaper mentioned in the title is not identified. Cf. Charles A. Sumner, *Notes on Travel in Sweden* (New York, 1895), which tells of meeting many Swedes in 1885 who longed to emigrate, see esp. 112, 137, 185–86, 251, 266, 279.

SEVEN

Changing Signals

1. Cf. John Higham, *Strangers in the Land: Patterns of American Nativism, 1860–1925* (2d ed., New York, 1981), chs. 4–5; Edward George Hartmann, *The Movement to Americanize the Immigrant* (New York, 1948), ch. 1. For rising apprehension in America over unrestricted immigration in this period, cf. Richmond Mayo-Smith's *Emigration and Immigration: A Study in Social Science* (New York, 1890), the first purportedly scholarly study of the subject.

2. Cf. Kälvemark, *Reaktionen mot utvandringen,* 63.

3. G. Svensson, *Amerika-Boken. Ny och tillförlitlig rådgifvare för emigranter* (Stockholm, 1892); P. W. Wilander, ed., *Emigrantens vän, eller svenskarne på västra halfklotet. Hvad de göra och säga* (Östersund, 1902), esp. 65–75. Cf. Anonymous, *Hänforelsens makt och betydelse. Af en återkommen svensk-amerikan* Svenska folkets öresskrifter, utgifna på Folkupplysningsföretagets förlag, No. 9 (Stockholm, 1897).

4. On Sweden's National Awakening during the 1890s, see esp. Alrik Gustafson, *History of Swedish Literature* (Minneapolis, 1961), ch. 9; E. N. Tigerstedt, *Svensk litteraturhistoria* (4th. ed., Stockholm, 1971), ch. 9; Andreas Lindblom, *Sveriges konsthistoria* (Stockholm, 1947); *Svenska turistföreningen 100 år* (Stockholm, 1986), esp. 12. For a rich evocation of the general cultural ambiance, Staffan Björck, *Heidenstam och sekelskiftets Sverige* (Stockholm, 1946) and the essays in *Fataburen 1991: 90-tal. Visioner och vägval* (Stockholm, 1991).

5. See Gunnar Eidevall, *Amerika i svensk 1900-talslitteratur. Från Gustaf Hellström till Lars Gustafsson* (Stockholm, 1983); Wendelius, *Bilden av Amerika;* Carl L. Anderson, *The Swedish Acceptance of American Literature* (Philadelphia, 1957), esp. ch. 1; Knut Hamsun, *Fra det moderne Amerikas Aandsliv* (Copenhagen, 1889), in Eng. trans. by Barbara Gordon Morgridge, *The Cultural Life of Modern America* (Cambridge, Mass., 1969); Dag Blanck, *Sverige-Amerika stiftelsen* (Stockholm, 1989), 6. Cf. Harald Næss, *Knut Hamsun og Amerika* (Oslo, 1969); Elovson, "Den liberala amerika-bilden"; Skard, "Amerika i Europas liv."

6. "C. J. U." [C. J. Malmquist,] *Hvilket lands folk är månne det lyckligaste?* (3d ed., Örebro, 1894), esp. 7–8, 51–68. Cf. Vilhälm Nordin, *Ur en emigrants anteckningsbok. Några sanningar om Amerika* (Stockholm, 1902).

7. C. J. U., *Hvilket lands folk,* 53; Wilander, *Emigrantens vän,* 67.

8. Cf. Emeroy Johnson, "Swedish Academies in Minnesota," *Sw. Pioneer Hist. Q.* 32 (1981): 20–40, and "Swedish Elementary Schools in Minnesota Lutheran Congregations," *Sw.-Am. Pioneer Q.* 30 (1979): 172–82.

9. See Ulf Beijbom, "Swedish-American Organizational Life," in Harald Runblom and Dag Blanck, eds., *Scandinavia Overseas* (Uppsala, 1986), 52–81, and Beijbom, "Svenskamerikanismen," in his *Svenskamerikanskt,* 137–60; Timothy J. Johnson, "The Independent Order of Svithiod: A Swedish-American Lodge in Chicago," in Anderson and Blanck, eds., *Swedish-American Life in Chicago,* 348–63.

10. See Hjalmar Nilsson, "Svensk sång i Amerika. En kort återblick," *Prärieblomman 1902,* 150–61; O. P. Ohlson, "Den svenska sången i Amerika," *Prärieblomman 1906,* 57–79; Helmer Örtengren, "Swedish Chorus Singing in America—A Feat of Culture," *Sw. Pioneer Hist. Q.* 22 (1971): 3–20. Cf. J. R. Christianson, "The Urbanization of Immigrant Peasants: Can Music Help?" in Odd S. Lovoll, ed., *Scandinavians and Other Immigrants in Urban America* (Northfield, Minn., 1985), 171–88; Dag Blanck, "Swedish Americans and the 1893 Columbian Exposition," in Anderson and Blanck, eds., *Swedish-American Life in Chicago,* 267–82.

11. Nilsson, "Svensk sång," 154–58.

12. Carl A. Swensson, *Åter i Sverige. Bilder och minnen från mina fäders land* (Chicago, 1897), 111–12, 123. Cf. English version, *Again in Sweden* (Chicago, 1898), 109–24.

13. Carl A. Swensson, *I Sverige. Minnen och bilder från mina fäders land* (Stockholm, 1891), 17, 19–20, 23–26.

14. See Dag Blanck, "An Invented Tradition: The Creation of a Swedish-American Consciousness at Augustana College, 1860–1900," in Runblom and Blanck, eds., *Scandinavia Overseas,* 98–115, esp. 109–11. Cf. Joshua Fishman and Vladimir Nahirny, "American Immigrant Groups: Ethnic Identification and the Problem of Generations," *Sociological Review* 13 (1965): 311–26; Werner Sollors, "Introduction," in Werner Sollors, ed., *The Invention of Ethnicity* (New York, 1989), ix–xx.

15. Nils Hasselmo, *Swedish America* (New York, 1976), 31–32; Dahllöf, "Three Americans Look at Sweden," 185. Cf. Dorothy Burton Skårdal, *The Divided Heart: Scandinavian Immigrant Experience Through Literary Sources* (Oslo and Lincoln, Nebr., 1974).

16. Mattson, *250th Anniversary,* 35; Swensson, *I Sverige,* 218. Cf. Skarstedt, *Vagabond och redaktör,* Hugo Hammar, *Som emigrant i U.S.A.* (Stockholm, 1938); Sten Carlsson, "Swedish Engineers in Chicago," in Anderson and Blanck, eds., *Swedish-American Life in Chicago,* 181–92; Byron J. Nordstrom, "*Trasdockan:* The Yearbook of the Swedish Engineers' Society of Chicago," in Anderson and Blanck, eds., *Swedish-American Life in Chicago,* 193–212.

17. O. Fritiof Ander, "The Swedish-American Press and the American Protective Association," *Church History,* 6 (1937), 165–79; Barton, *Search for Ancestors,* 130–31. For examples of American attitudes toward Scandinavians, cf. Kendric C. Babcock, "Scandinavians in the Northwest," *Forum* 14 (1892), 103–9, and Julian Ralph, "Our Swedish Fellow Citizens," *Harper's Weekly* 40 (25 April 1896), 419, 422.

EIGHT

Visitations and Counter-Visitations

1. Cf. Skard, "Amerika i Europas liv," 21.

2. P. Waldenström, *Genom Norra Amerikas Förenta Stater. Reseskildringar* (Chicago, 1890), 10–11. Cf. Karl A. Olsson, "Paul Peter Waldenström and Augustana," in J. Iverne Dowie and Ernest M. Espelie, eds., *The Swedish Immigrant Community in Transition* (Rock Island, Ill., 1963), 116; Ulf Beijbom, "Fyra forskningsresande," in his *Svenskamerikanskt,* 210–16.

3. Waldenström, *Genom Norra Amerikas Förenta Stater,* 10.

4. *Ibid.,* 44, 160.

5. *Ibid.,* 166, 194–95, 375.

6. *Ibid.,,* 11, 128, 167–68, 244, 276–81, 284–92.

7. *Ibid.,* 340–41.

8. *Ibid.,* iii, 240–41, 261–83 *passim.,* esp. 268–71, 274.

9. *Ibid.,* 257, 271.

10. *Ibid.,* 398–99.

11. Andrew A. Stomberg, *Den svenska folkstammen i Amerika* (Stockholm, 1928), 39–40.

12. Isador Kjellberg, *Amerika-bok. Anteckningar—från författarens besök i Nya Verlden år 1890—om huru våra dervarande vänner och anförvanter, bröder och systrar, ha det* (Linköping, 1892).

13. *Ibid.,* 3–4.

14. *Ibid., passim,* esp. 22–23, 27–28, 30, 57.

15. *Ibid.,* 19, 35–36, 45–46.

16. *Ibid.,* 51, 60–61.

17. See Olof Lagercrantz, *August Strindberg* (MånPocket ed., Stockholm, 1979), 133–34; Eric Hobsbawm, *The Age of Capital, 1848–1875* (New York: Mentor paperback, 1979), 337–38.

18. Hjalmar Cassel, *Bland svenskar och yankees* (Stockholm, 1894). On Cassel, see Hans Leander, ed., *Publicistklubbens porträttmatrikel vid femtioårsjubileet 1924* (Stockholm, 1924), 79; *SBL,* VII, 646.

19. Cassel, *Bland svenskar och yankees,* 41–42, 175–76.

20. *Ibid.,* 62–64.

21. *Ibid.,* 151–52.

22. *Ibid.,* 87–88, 91–92, 181–83.

23. *Ibid.,* 65–69.

24. *Ibid.,* 70–72.

25. K. J. Bohlin, *Genom den stora Västern* (Stockholm, n.d. [1893]), esp. 8–9, 25, 28–29, 207–8, 210–16; Gustaf Gullberg, *Boken om Chicago* (Stockholm, 1893), esp. 64, 76–75, 115, 182–83, 185–86, 193–94.

26. K. H. Gez. von Schéele, *Hemlandstoner. En hälsning från modern Svea till dotterkyrkan i Amerika,* 2 vols. (Stockholm, 1894–95), esp. 1–8, 9, 149, 309–10. Cf. E. A. Zetterstrand, "Kyrkoherde Per Pehrsson," *Prärieblomman 1911,* 186.

27. August Palm, *Ögonblicksbilder från en tripp till Amerika* (Stockholm, 1901), 71–72. Ulf Beijbom, "Fyra forskningsresande," in his *Svenskamerikanskt,* 216–21, 231–37.

28. Palm, Ögonblicksbilder, 62, 115, 154, 177–80.

29. *Ibid.,* 61.

30. *Ibid.,* 79–80, 138, 143–54 *passim.*

31. *Ibid.,* 209–10.

32. *Ibid.,* 98–99, 118, 210–11.

33. *Ibid.,* 243.

34. For general background, cf. R. Laurence Moore, *European Socialists and the American Promised Land* (New York, 1970); for coverage and opinion on America in the Swedish socialist press, see Fred Nilsson, *Emigrationen från Stockholm till Nordamerika 1880–1893* (Stockholm, 1970), chs. 6 and 7, and Lars-Göran Tedebrand, "America in the Swedish Labor Press, 1880s to 1920s," in Marianne Debouzy, ed., *In the Shadow of the Statue of Liberty* (Saint-Denis, 1988), 57–73.

35. Waldenström, *Genom Norra Amerikas Förenta Stater,* 615.

36. P. Waldenström, *Nya färder i Amerikas Förenta Stater* (Stockholm, 1902), 47; cf. 240.

37. *Ibid.,* 238–39.

38. *Ibid.,* 118, 163, 267–68, 273–74, 276, 406–7. Cf. Olsson, "Paul Peter Waldenström and Augustana."

39. Waldenström, *Nya färder,* 47, 49, 118, 129, 218, 250, 279–80, 389, 411.

40. *Ibid.,* 220–21, 258–59.

41. *Ibid.,* 94–95.

42. *Ibid.,* 47–48, 159, 240–43, 419, 507–8.

43. Cf. Skard, "Amerika i Europas liv," 19–20.

44. Ninian Wærner, "Modern," in *Mina hundår i Amerika* (Stockholm, 1900), 82–83. Cf. Wendelius, *Bilden av Amerika*, 158.

45. Gabriel Carlson [Frithjof Colling], *Mister Colesons Sverigeresa. Svensk-amerikansk humoresk* (Minneapolis, 1896). On Colling, see Skarstedt, *Våra pennfäktare*, 38–39, and *Pennfäktare*, 47.

46. Swensson, *I Sverige*, 41.

47. *Ibid.*, 3–16, esp. 16.

48. *Ibid.*, 504–5.

49. *Ibid.*, 35.

50. *Ibid.*, 9, 11, cf. 33, 35.

51. See Ernst Skarstedt, "Läroverkspresidenten Carl Swensson," *Prärieblomman 1905*, 77–93. Also Daniel M. Pearson, *The Americanization of Carl Aaron Swensson* (Rock Island, Ill., 1977).

52. Swensson, *I Sverige*.

53. *Ibid.*, 192–93, cf. 259.

54. *Ibid.*, 237.

55. *Ibid.*, 412.

56. *Ibid.*, 100–101, 198. Cf. 374.

57. *Ibid.*, 134, 242.

58. *Ibid.*, 139–40, 186–89, 218. In 1714, Pastor Eric Björck deplored the profanity he found at home, upon returning from his years on the Delaware. See Jesper Swedberg, *America Illuminata*, ed. Robert Murray (Stockholm, 1985), 121.

59. Swensson, *I Sverige*, 309–12.

60. *Ibid.*, 161, 283, 319, 352, 529–30.

61. *Ibid.*, 178–80.

62. *Ibid.*, 494–95.

63. *Ibid.*, 527. For Swedish-American indignation over Swedish chauvinism at this time, cf. Peter Södergren's reminiscences of incidents during a visit to Sweden in 1900, in his *Levnadsöden och reseskildringar* (Los Angeles, 1932), 56, 58.

64. Swensson, *I Sverige*, 268–69. Cf. 478.

65. *Ibid.*, 239.

66. *Ibid.*, 335–36, 457, 459.

67. *Ibid.*, 120–21, 207, 283.

68. *Ibid.*, 427–28.

69. *Ibid.*, 487–95.

70. *Ibid.*, 528.

71. Swensson, *Åter i Sverige* and *Again in Sweden, Sketches and Reminiscences from the Land of Our Forefathers* (Chicago, 1898). Cf. Dahllöf, "Three Americans Look at Sweden," 184–90.

72. Swensson, *Again in Sweden*, 107, 125–65 *passim*, 297, 604–7.

73. *Ibid.*, 125, 130–31.

74. *Ibid.*, 566, 570.

75. *Ibid.*, 383.

76. *Ibid.*, 563.

77. *Ibid.*, 125, 638.

78. Frans Albin Lindstrand ("Onkel Ola"), *I öster-och västerled* (Chicago, 1899), 336–87, esp. 340, 372, 376–78, 381–82.

79. Oscar W. Anderson, "A Summer in Småland" trans. M. Margaret Anderson (unpublished manuscript at Swenson Swedish Immigration Research Center, Rock Island, Ill.). On Anderson, see Skarstedt, *Våra pennfäktare*, 14–15, and *Pennfäktare*, 22.

80. *Vårt land* (Jamestown, N.Y.), 8 June, 8 Sept. 1898. Here and following in M. Margaret Anderson's translation.

81. *Ibid.*, 14 July 1898.
82. *Ibid.*, 14 July 1898.
83. *Ibid.*, 21 July, 11, 25 Aug., 1, 15 Sept. 1898.
84. *Ibid.*, 2, 9 June 1898.
85. *Ibid.*, 9 June, 25 Aug. 1898.
86. *Ibid.*, 9 June 1898.
87. *Ibid.*, 30 June, 4 Aug. 1898.
88. *Ibid.*, 1, 8 Sept. 1898.

NINE

Swedish America Self-Appraised

1. Gustaf Sjöström, *Jan Olsons äfventyr, eller en vermländsk emigrants resor och lefnadsöden i det Norra Amerika* (Chicago, 1892), 67, 269–70. On Sjöström, see Skarstedt, *Våra
pennfäktare*, 152–54, and *Pennfäktare*, 168.
2. Sjöström, *Jan Olsons äfventyr*, 52–54.
3. *Ibid.*, 77, 110, 172.
4. *Ibid.*, 296–97.
5. Joh. A. Enander, *Nordmännen i Amerika eller Amerikas upptäckt* (Rock Island, Ill.,
1893); *Valda skrifter*, I, 69–89; Anders Schön, "Dr. Joh. A. Enander. En minnesruna," *Prärieblomman 1911*, 31, 45.
6. O. N. Nelson, *History of the Scandinavians and Successful Scandinavians in the United
States*, 2 vols. (Minneapolis, 1893–97; rev. ed. 1904); Eric Norelius, *De svenska luterska
församlingarnas och svenskarnes historia i Amerika*, 2 vols. (Rock Island, Ill., 1890, 1916).
Cf. my "Clio in Swedish America;" Beijbom, "The Historiography of Swedish America."
7. Victor Nilsson, *Sweden* (New York, 1899), esp. 9–10, 30, 263–65, 405, 432–33.
8. Lars P. Nelson, *What Has Sweden Done for the United States?* (Rock Island, Ill., 1903),
esp. 25–26, 28, 31.
9. W. W. Thomas, Jr., *Sweden and the Swedes* (2d printing, Chicago, 1892), esp. 1–3, 13–
17, 28, 162, 731–32; Swedish version, *Från slott till koja. Minnen från en flerårig vistelse i
Sverige* (Stockholm, 1891).
10. Ernst W. Olson, Anders Schön, and Martin J. Engberg, *History of the Swedes of Illinois*,
2 vols. (Chicago, 1908), I, 147–64; Dag Blanck, "Pomp and Circumstance in Swedish-America:
The Role of Ceremonial for an Ethnic Group" (unpublished seminar paper, Department of
History, Uppsala University, 1988); Swensson, *Åter i Sverige*, 663–64.
11. Mattson, *Reminiscences*, 298–300.
12. Swensson, *Again in Sweden*, 131, 143–44, 630. In his Swedish version of this work,
Åter i Sverige, 172, Swensson expressed himself more cautiously in comparing Swedish
Americans with homeland Swedes: "They are no worse, they are in many respects much
better than their brothers back home in the far North." There are other, interesting differences
between the two versions.
13. David Nyvall, *Svenskhet i Amerika* (Minneapolis, n.d. [1892]), 4, 7–8. On Nyvall, see
G. N. S. [G. N. Swan,] "David Nyvall," *Ungdomsvännen* (1907), 145–46; Skarstedt, *Pennfäktare*,
141; Philip J. Anderson, "David Nyvall and Swedish-American Education," in Anderson and
Blanck, *Swedish-American Life in Chicago*, 327–42.
14. Nyvall, *Svenskhet i Amerika*, 12–24.
15. *Ibid.*, 24–25. Much the same ideas of dual loyalty and pluralism are expressed in O.
Olsson's "Något om en sann svensk-amerikansk patriotism," a speech evidently from the mid-
1890s, in *Samlade skrifter af O. Olsson* (Rock Island, Ill., 1912), 341–50.
16. C. F. Peterson, *Sverige i Amerika. Kulturhistoriska och biografiska teckningar* (Chicago,
1898). On Peterson, see Skarstedt, *Våra pennfäktare*, 142–45 and *Pennfäktare*, 151–52.

17. Peterson, *Sverige i Amerika*, 3.

18. *Ibid.*, 4-7.

19. *Ibid.*, 42, 68-72, 76, 84.

20. *Ibid.*, 71-73, 178-82.

21. *Ibid.*, 95-96, 146-48.

22. *Ibid.*, 147-52.

23. *Ibid.*, 6, 203-10.

24. *Ibid.*, 267-72, 276.

25. *Ibid.*, 355-62, 410.

26. *Ibid.*, 115, 409-14.

27. *Ibid.*, 458-59.

28. *Ibid.*, 295-97, 302, 319, 325.

29. *Ibid.*, 289-93. Cf. Hamsun, *Cultural Life of Modern America*, 10; Waldenström, *Nya färder*, 50.

30. Peterson, *Sverige i Amerika*, 448, 456.

31. *Ibid.*, 6-7, 100, 456-57, 468.

32. *Ibid.*, 216-17, 238, 469-71.

33. *Ibid.*, 324, 326-27.

34. *Ibid.*, 305, 327, 466-68.

35. Sjöström, *Jan Olsons äfventyr*, 110; [Ludvig,] "Svensk-amerikansk hälsning till Sverige," *Ungdomsvännen* (1902), 293.

36. Lawrence Carlson, "If Russia Decided to Annex Sweden, How Should We Swedish-Americans Then Conduct Ourselves?" *Sw. Pioneer Hist. Q.* 8 (1957): 3-18.

TEN

The Homeland Faces Its Emigration Crisis

1. Pontus Fahlbeck, "Emigrationen. Dess orsaker och medlen att stäfja den," *Statsvetenskaplig tidskrift för politik-statistik-ekonomi* (Oct. 1903), 6.

2. *Ibid.*, 8-10.

3. *Ibid.*, 7, 12-13.

4. See ch. 6, above.

5. Cf. Olle Gellerman, *Staten och jordbruket 1867-1918* (Uppsala, 1958), 55-56; Elisabet Stavenow-Hidemark, "Småbruksrörelsen—idé och verklighet," *Fataburen 1967* (Stockholm, 1967), 65-80.

6. Fahlbeck, "Emigrationen," 3-4.

7. Sundbärg, *Bidrag till utvandringsfrågan*, 138. See also Kälvemark, *Reaktionen mot utvandringen*, 64, 178, 202-3.

8. Kälvemark, *Reaktionen mot utvandringen*, 73-77, 108-9, 112-17, 119-21, 135-37, 140-41.

9. Gustav Sundbärg, "Emigrationen," *Föreningen Heimdals föreläsningar läsåret 1905-1906*, No. 8 (Uppsala, 1906), 3.

10. *Ibid.*, 4-6. Cf. Fahlbeck, "Emigrationen," 3.

11. Sundbärg, "Emigrationen," 6, 9-11.

12. *Ibid.*, 11-12.

13. *Ibid.*, 14-20. Cf. Sundbärg's earlier *Sveriges land och folk. Historisk-statistisk handbok* (Stockholm, 1901), 126-31, in which he speculated, in a more positive tone, over the Swedish character.

14. Sundbärg, "Emigrationen," 22.

15. Gustav Sundbärg, "Emigrationen II," *Heimdals politiska småskrifter*, 2:1 (Uppsala, 1907), 32.

16. *Ibid.*, 11.

17. *Ibid.*, 32–33.

18. F. A. Wingborg, *Emigrationen. Några erinringar* (Stockholm, 1903), 1, 16; Beijbom, *Svenskamerikanskt,* 116.

19. Wingborg, *Emigrationen,* 12–14.

20. *Några råd till dem som ämna utvandra till Amerika* (Göteborg, 1903), 3–6. Cf. Scott, "Sweden's Constructive Opposition," 312.

21. *Några råd,* 8–9, 12.

22. *Ibid.,* 15–16.

23. Adrian Molin, *Svenska spörsmål och kraf* (2d ed., Stockholm, 1906), 135–41. The first, anonymous edition came out in Stockholm, in 1905.

24. See L. G. Abrahamson, "Licenciat C. L. Sundbeck och betydelsen af hans resa i Förenta Staterna," *Prärieblomman 1903,* 102–6. Also *SMoK,* VII:316; Ulf Beijbom, "Fyra forskningsresande," in his *Svenskamerikanskt,* 221–30.

25. Carl Sundbeck, *Svensk-amerikanerna. Deras materiella och andliga sträfvanden* (Rock Island, Ill., 1904), esp. 118–19, 350.

26. Cf. Viktor Rydberg, *Undersökningar i germansk mytologi,* 2 vols. (Stockholm, 1886–89), partial English trans. by R. B. Anderson, *Teutonic Mythology,* 3 vols. (London, 1889), and *Fädernas gudasaga* (Stockholm, 1887).

27. Carl Sundbeck, *Svenskarne i Amerika* (Stockholm, 1900), xii.

28. *Ibid.,* esp. xii, 5, 91–92.

29. *Ibid.,* 107.

30. Abrahamson, "Licenciat C. L. Sundbeck"; Sundbeck, *Svensk-amerikanerna,* 475.

31. Carl Sundbeck, *Svensk-Amerika lefve! Några tal hållna i Amerika* (Stockholm, 1904; also Rock Island, Ill., 1905).

32. Sundbeck, *Svensk-amerikanerna,* 18; *Svensk-Amerika lefve!,* 26.

33. Sundbeck, *Svensk-amerikanerna,* 59–62, 301–2; *Svensk-Amerika lefve!,* 26–30.

34. Sundbeck, *Svensk-amerikanerna,* 79, 90, 92, 108–9, 112, 119–20; *Svensk-Amerika lefve!,* 8–9.

35. Sundbeck, *Svensk-amerikanerna,* 18, 92, 164, 382.

36. *Ibid.,* 112, 474–75; *Svensk-Amerika lefve!,* 17, 28–29, 50. On the theme, widely shared in conservative, patriotic circles by the turn of the century, that Sweden had gone through a period of national degradation since Karl XII's death in 1718, see Herbert Tingsten, *Gud och fosterlandet. Studier i hundra års skolpropaganda* (Stockholm, 1969), 155–64.

37. Sundbeck, *Svensk-amerikanerna,* 99, 161–62, 200–201, 217–18, 385–86, 389; *Svensk-Amerika lefve!,* 18–19.

38. Sundbeck, *Svensk-amerikanerna,* 34; cf. *Svensk-Amerika lefve!,* 49.

39. *Svensk-Amerika lefve!,* 78.

40. Sundbeck, *Svensk-amerikanerna,* 217, 301–2; *Svensk-Amerika lefve!,* 23–25.

41. Sundbeck, *Svensk-amerikanerna,* 17–19, 25, 109–10, 201, 342; *Svensk-Amerika lefve!,* 25, 47–49.

42. Sundbeck, *Svensk-amerikanerna,* 141–42, 145, 153, 160–62, 224–25, 293, 327–28; *Svensk-Amerika lefve!,* 16–18, 54–55.

43. Sundbeck, *Svensk-amerikanerna,* 260–62, 398, 400. Cf. Erica Simon, *Reveil national et culture populaire en Scandinavie. La genèse de la højskole nordique 1844–1878* (Stockholm, 1960) and Enok Mortensen, *Schools for Life: A Danish-American Experiment in Adult Education* (Solvang, Cal., 1977).

44. Sundbeck, *Svensk-amerikanerna,* 475; *Svensk-Amerika lefve!,* 65. Cf. Kälvemark, *Reaktionen mot utvandringen,* 113n.

45. Sundbeck, *Svensk-amerikanerna,* 118–19, 201, 288–89, 294; *Svensk-Amerika lefve!,* 25.

46. Beijbom, *Svenskamerikanskt,* 12.

47. Sundbeck, *Svensk-amerikanerna,* 195, 476; *Svensk-Amerika lefve!,* 43.

ELEVEN
The Search for Answers

1. *Skandinavia* (Worcester, Mass.), 11 July 1900.
2. Sweden, *Emigrationsutredningen,* 21 vols. (Stockholm, 1908–13) (henceforth EU), *Betänkande* (1913), 1–6. Cf. Kälvemark *Reaktionen mot utvandringen,* 145–56. Sweden did make a notable effort to put its best foot forward at the St. Louis World's Fair in 1904. Cf. "Svenskarnas dag i St. Louis," *Ungdomsvännen 1904,* 220–21.
3. Beckman, *Från Nya Verlden* (1877) and *Amerikanska studier* (1883).
4. EU, *Betänkande,* 6–12. Cf. Kälvemark, *Reaktionen mot utvandringen,* 157–70.
5. EU, *Betänkande,* 12–39. Cf. Kälvemark, *Reaktionen mot utvandringe,* 193.
6. EU, *Betänkande,* 39–41; Sundbärg, "Emigrationen," 3.
7. On the Emigration Inquest and the full titles of its volumes, see Emory Lindquist, "Sweden's Search for Answers: *The Emigration Survey,* Then and Now," *Sw.-Am. Hist. Q.* 37 (1986): 159–73; Kälvemark, *Reaktionen mot utvandringen,* esp. 202; Scott, "Sweden's Constructive Opposition," 314–16.
8. EU, *Betänkande,* 316, 326, 348.
9. *Ibid.,* 381, 397–98, 411, 442.
10. *Ibid.,* 287–88, 380–81, 476.
11. *Ibid.,* 357, 383.
12. *Ibid.,* 307, 335, 422, 445, 489, 523.
13. *Ibid.,* 307, 335, 410, 422.
14. *Ibid.,* 383. Cf. *Ibid.,* 307, 381
15. *Ibid.,* 288, 381, 492.
16. EU, *Bilaga* VII: *Utvandrarnas egna uppgifter* (1908), 7–30.
17. *Ibid.,* 31–128.
18. "Bref fran svenskar i Amerika," EU, *Bilaga* VII, 129–263. Cf. Emory Lindquist, "Appraisal of Sweden and America by Swedish Emigrants: The Testimony of Letters in *Emigrationsutredningen* (1907)," *Sw. Pioneer Hist. Q.* 17 (1966): 78–95.
19. See, for example, EU, *Bilaga* VII:186–88, 252. Cf. my *Letters,* 281–84, 290.
20. EU, *Bilaga* VII:205–6, 255–56; also 158, 160, 233. Cf. my *Letters,* 276–77, 279, 284–85, 289, 290–92.
21. EU, *Bilaga* VII:165, 233. Cf. my *Letters,* 281, 289.
22. EU, *Bilaga* VII:144, 160, 195, 233. Cf. my *Letters,* 13, 279, 289.
23. EU, *Bilaga* VII:218–20. Cf. my *Letters,* 287–88.
24. EU, *Bilaga* VII:218–19. Cf. my *Letters,* 286–87.
25. EU, *Bilaga* VII:165. Cf. my *Letters,* 281. Italicized passage in English.
26. EU, *Bilaga* VIII: *Bygdeundersökningar* (1908), 82–84. Cf. my *Letters,* 292–93.
27. Molin, *Svenska spörsmål och kraf,* 142, 144–46. See also Molin's "Huru befordra en återinvandring af svensk-amerikaner till Sverige," *Svenska dagbladet* (18 Aug. 1907), 3.
28. EU, *Betänkande,* 4–6, 9; EU, *Bilaga* XX: *Svenskarna i utlandet* (1911), 11; E. J. Ljungberg, "Några synpunkter på emigrationefrågan," *Det nya Sverige* (1910), 50–58.
29. Nils Runeby, "Amerika i Sverige. Herman Lagercrantz, emigrationen och den nationella väckelsen," *Arkivvetenskapliga studier,* 3 (1962): esp. 164, 174–75; Herman Lagercrantz, *I skilda vägar* (3d ed. Stockholm, 1945), esp. 260–67, 269–98; Vilhelm Berger, "Prins Wilhelms besök i Förenta Staterna," *Prärieblomman 1908,* 13–32; E. A. Z. [E. A. Zetterstrand,] "Är en återinflyttning till Sverige af svensk-amerikaner önskvärd?" *Ungdomsvännen* (1908), 18–19. Cf. Scott, "Sweden's Constructive Opposition," 313–14.
30. EU, *Bilaga* XX:20–22.
31. *Ibid.,* 35–39, 41–50.
32. Runeby, "Amerika i Sverige," 168–69, 178–82, 184.

33. EU, *Betänkande,* 661, 692–93.

34. *Ibid.,* 661, 755, 764–65.

35. *Ibid.,* 818, 830–36, 862–66.

36. *Ibid.,* 871, 877, 882.

37. *Ibid.,* 882–84.

38. *Ibid.,* 886–87.

39. *Ibid.,* 888–90.

40. *Ibid.,* 890.

41. EU, *Bilaga* XVI: *Det svenska folklynnet* (1911). The following citations are to the commercially published edition, *Det svenska folklynnet* (Stockholm, 1911). *Ibid.,* 7.

42. Gustav Sundbärg, *Tankar i utvandringsfrågan* (Stockholm, 1913). Concerning Swedish concepts of their national character, see Carl G. Laurin, *Svensk självpröfning* (Stockholm, 1912), which shows the often remote antecedents of Sundbärg's principal ideas, and Tingsten, *Gud och fosterlandet,* 194–200. Also Staffan Björck, *Heidenstam och sekelskiftets Sverige* (Stockholm, 1946), esp. ch. 6: Åke Daun & Ingrid Forsman, "Gustav Sundbärg och det svenska folklynnet," *Kungl. Vitterhets, Historie och Antikvitets Akademiens Konferenser,* 13 (1985): 33–45.

43. Cf. Kälvemark, *Reaktionen mot utvandringen,* 203; Daun & Forsman, "Gustav Sundbärg och det svenska folklynnet," 33; Gustav Sundbärg, *Sveriges land och folk. Historisk-statistisk handbok* (Stockholm, 1901), 126–31; G. S. "Det svenska folklynnet," *Ungdomsvännen* (1900), 28–29, 50–51.

44. Sundbärg, *Det svenska folklynnet,* 6, 37, 116.

45. *Ibid.,* 8.

46. Cf. Daun & Forsman, "Gustav Sundbärg och det svenska folklynnet," 38.

47. Sundbärg, *Det svenska folklynnet,* 4, 18, 26, 80–82, 86–87.

48. *Ibid.,* 16–17, 117–20.

49. *Ibid.,* 27–33.

50. *Ibid.,* 22, 35, 45–46, 49–50, 53, 56–57, 61–68, 121.

51. *Ibid.,* 10, 12–13, 18, 26, 37, 73–74, 77–78, 86–87, 92, 94, 96–97, 101, 103, 111, 135–37. Cf. Kristian Kvidt, "Scandinavian Discord on Emigration," *Sw. Pioneer Hist. Q.* 25 (1974): 254–63.

52. Sundbärg, *Det svenska folklynnet,* 117, 121–34.

53. *Ibid.,* 140, 142.

54. P. G. Norberg, "Svenskarnas Amerika och Amerikas svenskar," EU, *Bilaga,* XX; P. Norden (P. G. Norberg), *En brygga öfver hafvet. En bok om svenskar och svensk-amerikaner* (Stockholm, 1910), see esp. 128.

55. EU, *Bilaga* XX:127.

56. *Ibid.,* 124, 126, 127.

57. G. H. von Koch, "Svenskarna i Förenta staterna," EU, *Bilaga* XX:129–71; cf. G. H. von Koch, *Emigranternas land. Studier i amerikanskt samhällslif* (Stockholm, 1910). On von Koch, see Agnes Wirén, *G. H. von Koch. Banbrytare i svensk socialvård* (Stockholm, 1980).

58. EU, *Bilaga* XX, esp. 170–71.

59. *Ibid.,* 138–39.

60. *Ibid.,* 138.

61. E. H. Thörnberg, "Emigrationen från Sverige till Amerika," in his *Amerikanska samhällsproblem* (Stockholm, 1912), 1–32, esp. 7, 31–32. Cf. Brinley Thomas, *Migration and Economic Growth* (Cambridge, 1954); Harald Runblom & Hans Norman, eds., *From Sweden to America: A History of the Migration* (Uppsala & Minneapolis, 1976).

62. E. H. Thörnberg, "Svensk-amerikanerne och Sverige," *Svensk tidskrift* (1913), 325–34.

63. Sundbärg, "Emigrationen," 11–12, and "Emigrationen II," 6; EU, *Bilaga,* VII:220; my *Letters,* 288.

64. Kälvemark, *Reaktionen mot utvandringen,* 157–66, 182.

65. Scott, "Sweden's Constructive Opposition," 316.
66. EU, *Betänkande,* 9; *SMoK.,* I:193.

TWELVE

The Anti-Emigration Movement

1. On the organization of *Nationalföreningen* and its leadership, including Adrian Molin, see Gustaf Berg, *Nationalföreningen mot emigrationen 1907–1912* (Stockholm, 1912), 3–7; Scott, "Sweden's Constructive Opposition," 316–18; Kälvemark, *Reaktionen mot utvandringen,* 130–34; Michael Shephard, "Adrian Molin: Study of a Swedish Right-Wing Radical," (unpublished Ph.D. dissertation, Northwestern University, 1969) and "The Romantic, Rural Orientation of the National Society Against Emigration," *Sw. Pioneer Hist. Q.* 21 (1970): 70–74. On the "Young Right" and its ideology, cf. Shepard, "Adrian Molin," ch. 2; Nils Elvander, *Harald Hjärne och konservatismen* (Stockholm, 1961), esp. 293–308.
2. Adrian Molin, *Vanhäfd. Inlägg i emigrationsfrågan* (2d ed., Stockholm, 1911), 24. (The first edition came out in Stockholm the same year.) Molin's views on emigration in this book are largely previewed in his pamphlet, *Emigrationen. Några synpunkter,* Föreningen Heimdals politiska skrifter, vol. 3, no. 1 (Uppsala, 1910).
3. Molin, *Vanhäfd,* 22–23, 109.
4. *Ibid.,* iii–v, 21 23, 87, 115, 116–17.
5. *Ibid.,* see esp. 3, 13, 15, 19. Cf. Shephard, "Rural, Romantic Orientation," 74.
6. Molin, *Vanhäfd,* 5–6, 8–9.
7. *Ibid.,* 19–22, 58–59, 109. On conservative hopes for rural landholding as the antedote to socialism, see Olle Gellerman, *Staten och jordbruket 1867–1918* (Stockholm, 1958), 55–66.
8. Molin, *Vanhäfd,* 144, 146.
9. *Ibid.,* 119, 124, 127–36, 147–48.
10. See esp. Shephard, "Rural, Romantic Orientation," 73–81, and "Adrian Molin," *passim.*
11. *Nationalföreningen mot emigration. Hvad den vill och hvad den gör* (Stockholm, 1915), 1; Scott, "Sweden's Constructive Opposition," 318–19.
12. Scott, "Sweden's Constructive Opposition," 327–32; Berg, *Nationalföreningen mot emigrationen,* 11–14; *Nationalföreningen . . . Hvad den vill,* 7–8; *Svensk emigrations- och egnahemspolitik åren 1907–1932* (Stockholm, 1932); Gellerman, *Staten och jordbruket,* 109–87; Stavenow-Hidemark, "Småbruksrörelsen."
13. Scott, "Sweden's Constructive Opposition," 324–27.
14. *Ibid.,* 320; Berg, *Nationalföreningen mot emigrationen,* 7–8, *Nationalföreningen . . . Hvad den vill,* 4–6.
15. *Res icke till Amerika!* This one-page appeal was published on the back pages of the society's pamphlets. See also Scott, "Sweden's Constructive Opposition," 320–21; *Nationalföreningen . . . Hvad den vill,* 4.
16. T. W. Schönberg, *Sanningen om Amerika* (Stockholm, 1909), esp. 3, 7–8. See also Henry von Kræmer, *Ett ord till amerikafararen* (Stockholm, 1909).
17. W. Swanston Howard, *När Maja Lisa kom hem från Amerika* (Stockholm, 1908), esp. 3, 6–7, 9–11. Cf. Scott, "Sweden's Constructive Opposition," 321–22.
18. E. Lindblom, *Per Jansons Amerika-resa* (Stockholm, 1909), esp. 11. Cf. Scott, "Sweden's Constructive Opposition," 322. On Lindblom, see Skarstedt, *Pennfäktare,* 108–9.
19. Gustaf Carlsson, ed., *Svenska allmogehem* (Stockholm, 1909), 7, 11, 13–16. On Molin's belief in smallholding, cf. his *Svenska spörsmål och kraf,* 47–52.
20. Carlsson, *Svenska allmogehem,* 16.
21. *Ibid.,* preface (n.p.). Cf. Scott, "Sweden's Constructive Opposition," 323; Shephard, "Rural, Romantic Orientation," 80. On the architectural aspects of the Own-Home movement, cf. Stavenow-Hidemark, "Småbruksrörelsen," 68–77.

22. *Svensk emigrations- och egnahemspolitik,* 132–33, 138–41. Scott, "Sweden's Constructive Opposition," 329–31; Shephard, "Rural, Romantic Orientation," 82–83; Stavenow-Hidemark, "Småbruksrörelsen," 77–79.

23. M. V. Wester, *Småbruksrörelse för eller mot emigrationen* (Stockholm, 1913), esp. 22–26. Regarding other contemporary criticisms of the Own-Home movement, see *Svensk emigrations-och egnahemspolitik,* 123–26.

24. Cecilia Milow, *Älskar du ditt fosterland?* (Stockholm, 1904), esp. 17, 18. See also "Emigrantminnen av N.," *Läsning för folket* (1904): 101–29, which warns, "you know what you have, but not what you will get" (129).

25. *Hvad Anders lärde i Amerika. Hans egen berättelse upptecknad af M.* (Stockholm, 1907), 4–9.

26. *Ibid.,* 24–25, 27–28, 37–38.

27. *Ibid.,* 40–44.

28. *Ibid.,* esp. 5–9, 34, 41–44.

29. Herbert Tingsten, *Gud och fosterlandet. Studier i hundra års skolpropaganda* (Stockholm, 1969), 131, 172–73; Sonja Svensson, *Läsning för folkets barn. Folkskolans Barntidning och dess förlag 1892–1914* (Stockholm, 1983), 204–6.

30. C. Thorborg, *Emigrationsfrågan studerad hemma och i Amerika* (Karlstad, 1906), 3–5.

31. *Ibid.,* 5–6, 39–41.

32. G. Thyreen, *Skall jag resa till Amerika? Kortfattad skildring af Förenta Staterna vid 20:de århundradets början* (Stockholm, 1911), 9–153 *passim.* Cf. *ibid.,* 150–51 on Thyreen in America.

33. *Ibid.,* 5–6, 156–59, 161–64, 170.

34. *Ibid.,* 4, 85–86, 147–48, 154–56, 164, 171–72, 234.

35. On "Germanist" racial thought in Sweden in this period, see Matti Klinge, "De svenskspråkigas 1910-tal: germanism och konservatism," in his *Från lojalism till rysshat* (Ekenäs, 1988), 220–34; Gunnar Broberg, "Statens institut för rasbiologi—tillkomståren," in Gunnar Broberg, et al., eds., *Kunskapens trädgård* (Stockholm, 1988), 178–221.

36. Thyreen, *Skall jag resa till Amerika?,* 49, 158–60, 234.

37. *Ibid.,* 29–31, 48–50, 98, 145. On the persistence since the eighteenth century of theories of the degeneration of Europeans in the New World environment, see Edward P. Hutchinson, "A Forgotten Theory of Immigration," in O. Fritiof Ander, ed., *In the Trek of the Immigrants* (Rock Island, Ill., 1964), 49–57.

38. Thyreen, *Skall jag resa till Amerika?,* 51, 168–69.

39. *Ibid.,* 85–86, 171–72, 174–82, 201–10, 221–29.

40. *Ibid.,* 173, 197–201.

41. *Ibid.,* 229–37.

42. Carl Bruhn, *Stanna hemma! Amerikanska penndrag* (Stockholm, 1916), 5, 9, 12, 34. On Bruhn's adventurous life in the U.S.A. and Central America, see Skarstedt, *Pennfäktare,* 39–40.

43. Bruhn, *Stanna hemma!,* 20–21, 36–37, 50–51, 59.

44. *Ibid.,* 48, 50–60.

45. *Ibid.,* 7–8, 50–51, 58, 60, 61.

THIRTEEN

Transatlantic Visions and Images

1. "'Riksföreningens' förhistoria," Riksföreningen för svenskhetens bevarande i utlandet [hereafter RFSBU], *Årsbok 1909* (Göteborg, 1909), 1–9.

2. Vilh. Lundström, "Kring svenskar, svenskhet och svensk-minnen i U.S.A.," in *Till Trettonårsdagen 1908 3/XII 1938* (Göteborg, 1938), 8; RFSU, *Årsbok 1909,* 10. On Lundström, cf.

H. S. Nyberg, et al., *Svenskt bortom gränserna. Sju kapitel om Vilhelm Lundström* (Göteborg, 1971), esp. 7–18, 67–72, 73–86; Bengt Bogärde, *Vilhelm Lundström och svenskheten* (Göteborg, 1992) and my review of this book in *Sw.-Am. Hist. Q.* 44 (1993): 166–68. Also an excellent unpublished term paper in intellectual history at Gothenburg University, Mårten Frankby's "Vilh. Lundström—Konservativ idéspridare och allsvensk eldsjäl" (1990, 36 pp.), for a copy of which I am indebted to Dr. Lennart Limberg of Riksföreningen Sverigekontakt, Gothenburg.

3. Lundström, "Kring svenskar," 5–7.

4. *Ibid.*, 8.

5. Vilh. Lundström, *Allsvenska linjer* (Göteborg, 1930), 1–2; cf. 17, 57–62.

6. *Ibid.*, 2–3; cf. 15–16.

7. *Ibid.*, 16–17.

8. *SMok*, VII:316.

9. "'Riksföreningens' förhistoria," 3–5; RFSBU, *Årsbok 1909–17*, cf. esp. 1909, "Förord," n.p.

10. Lundström, *Allsvenska linjer*, 4–13, 15–16. Cf. Ragnar Pomoell, "Vilhelm Lundström och Finlands svenskar," in Nyberg, et al., *Svenskt bortom gränserna*, 73–86.

11. Per Pehrsson, "Svenskheten i Amerika. Några reseintryck," RFSBU, *Årsbok 1910*, 1–40, esp. photograph of the proclamation, facing p. 1. This article was also published as a separate booklet under the title, *Svenskarne i Amerika* (Göteborg, 1910).

12. Stephenson, *Religious Aspects of Swedish Immigration*, 450–51.

13. Per Pehrsson, *Råd och anvisningar för utvandrare till Amerika* (Gävle, 1912), esp. 3–6.

14. Verner von Heidenstam, *Endymion* (Stockholm, 1889). Cf. Elovson, "Den liberala amerikabilden," 105; Harald Elovson, "Heidenstam och Amerika," *Edda* (1933): 93–107. For Swedish literature and America in this period, see esp. Wendelius, *Bilden av Amerika* and Gunnar Eidevall, *Amerika i svensk 1900-talslitteratur. Fran Gustaf Hellström till Lars Gustafsson* (Stockholm, 1983).

15. Gustaf Fröding, *Gitarr och dragharmonika* (Stockholm, 1891), in *Skrifter av Gustaf Fröding. Ungdomsdikter, Gitarr och dragharmonika* (Stockholm, 1935), 195.

16. Per Hallström, *Vilsna fåglar* (Stockholm, 1894).

17. Hilma Angered-Strandberg, *Den nya världen* (Stockholm, 1898), *På prärien* (Stockholm, 1898), and *Från det nya och gamla landet* (Stockholm, 1899). Her later novel, *Hemma* (Stockholm, 1912), deals with a returned Swedish American in Sweden. Cf. *SBL*, 1 (1918), 787–90; *SMoK*, 1 (1942), 108–9. Hjalmar Cassel's *Bland svenskar och yankees* (Stockholm, 1894) must be considered essentially a lightly fictionalized travel account. (See ch. 8, above.)

18. Angered-Strandberg, *Den nya världen*, esp. 45–46, 156–59, 232, 234; *På prärien*, 31–32, 36, 44–46, 48, 126–27, 170–71. Cf. "Ur tvännes lif," in *Från det nya och gamla landet*, 43–84.

19. Henning Berger, *Där ute. Skisser* (Stockholm, 1901), in *Skrifter i urval av Henning Berger* (Stockholm, 1923), 10, 12, 14; Sven Lagerstedt, *Drömmaren från Norrlandsgatan. En studie i Henning Bergers liv och författarskap* (Stockholm, 1963), ch. 2; Wendelius, *Bilden av Amerika*, 56. On Berger's other American novels, see also Ernst Ekman, "A Swedish View of Chicago in the 1890s: Henning Berger," *Sw. Pioneer Hist. Q.* 25 (1974): 230–40.

20. Berger, *Därute*, 82; Henning Berger, *Bendel & Co.* (Stockholm, 1910), 89.

21. Henry von Kræmer, *Ur frihetslandets järnkäftar. En svensk emigrants erfarenheter i U.S.A.* (Stockholm, 1914) and *Mexiko-Amerika. Resebrev* (Stockholm, 1914).

22. Selma Lagerlöf, *Nils Holgerssons underbara resa genom Sverige*, 2 vols. (Stockholm, 1906–7), ch. 16, "Den gamla bondkvinnan," II:222–27. Cf. Herbert Tingsten, *Gud och fosterlandet* (Stockholm, 1969), 239–44.

23. K. G. Ossian-Nilsson, *Samlade dikter 1900–1905*, 2 vols. (Stockholm, 1907), I: 1, 16–17. "Sverge," translated by Roger McKnight in Vilhelm Moberg, *The Unknown Swedes*, ed. and trans. Roger McKnight (Carbondale, Ill., 1988), 33; Ossian-Nilsson, *Samlade dikter*, II:12, esp. "Amerikaner," 6–8.

24. This literature is treated in Wendelius, *Bilden av Amerika, passim.*
25. Per Hallström, *Erotikon* (Stockholm, 1908). Cf. for example Ernst Didering, *Arvtagarne* (Stockholm, 1914); Alfred Ebenhard, *När Smed-Erik och Pligg-Jan fick Amerikafrämmande* (Vimmerby, 1932); Kurt Göransson, *Karlsson får Amerika-arv* (Borlänge, 1932) and *Miss Persson från USA* (Sköllersta, 1934). I am indebted to Anne-Charlotte Harvey for help concerning the Swedish popular stage. Swedish films, from 1897, are catalogued and summarized in *Svensk filmografi,* 6 vols. to date (Stockholm, 1977–   ).
26. Cf. Carl L. Anderson, *The Swedish Acceptance of American Literature* (Philadelphia, 1957).

FOURTEEN

Visitors to Alien Shores

1. Cf. ch. 8, above.
2. P. Norden (P. G. Norberg), *En brygga öfver hafvet. En bok om svenskar och svensk-amerikaner* (Göteborg, 1910); Norberg, "Svenskarnas Amerika." See also *Publicistklubbens porträttmatrikel 1936,* ed. Waldemar von Sydow (Stockholm, 1936), 425; *Vem är det 1916* (Stockholm, 1916), 265.
3. G. H. von Koch, "En lifsfråga för Sveriges folk," *Social tidskrift* (1903): 281–83; *Emigranternas land. Studier i amerikanskt samhällslif* (Stockholm, 1910); von Koch, "Svenskarna i Förenta staterna." Cf. Kälvemark, *Reaktionen mot utvandringen,* 59–61. Also Agnes Wirén, *G. H. von Koch. Banbrytare i svensk socialvård* (Stockholm, 1980), esp. 147–62.
4. Adrian Molin, "Svenskarne i Amerika," in his *Vanhäfd,* 27–87.
5. Pehrsson, "Svenskheten i Amerika."
6. Ida Gawell-Blumenthal, *Stintans amerikafärd* (Stockholm, 1908). On Swedish entertainers in America during this period, see also Ingemar Liman, "The Skansen Dancers' Tour of America, 1906–1907," *Sw.-Am. Hist. Q.* 34 (1983): 224–34.
7. O. Olofsson, *Minnen och intryck från en Amerikaresa* (Kristinehamn, 1912).
8. C. P. Carlsson, *I palmernas skugga. En hälsning från stjärnbanérets land* (Karlstad, 1913).
9. John Wahlborg, *Stjärnbanér i blågult. Svensk-amerikansk berättelse* (Gefle, 1915).
10. Von Kræmer, *Mexiko-Amerika,* esp. 107, 118–19, and *Ur frihetslandets järnkäftar,* esp. 1–4, 46–47. Cf. *Ett ord till Amerikafararen* (Stockholm, 1909). On socialist attitudes toward America in this period, see R. Laurence Moore, *European Socialists and the American Promised Land* (New York, 1970); Lars-Göran Tedebrand, "America in the Swedish Labor Press, 1880s to 1920s," in Marianne Debouzy, ed., *In the Shadow of the Statue of Liberty* (St. Denis, 1988).
11. Ture Nerman, *I Vilda Västern. En Amerika-tripp i världskrigstid* (Stockholm, 1935). An excerpt, under the title "Amerikaniseringen och arbetarna," came out in *Folkets dagblad* in 1929. Cf. Eidevall, *Amerika i svensk 1900-talslitteratur,* 49.
12. Gunnar Cederschiöld, *Infödingarna på Manhattan* (Stockholm, 1916).
13. Knut Barr, *På studentsångfärd till Amerika* (Stockholm, 1905); Rudolf Kjellén, *Sångare- och turistfärder* (Stockholm, 1908); Inge Lund, *En piga i USA. En pennskafts äventyr* (Stockholm, 1917).
14. Norden, *Brygga,* 137–39; von Koch, *Emigranternas land,* 323–24. Cf. Wahlborg, *Stjärnbanér,* 10.
15. Molin, *Vanhäfd,* 31–37; von Koch, *Emigranternas land,* 318–19; Nerman, *I Vilda Västern,* 88, 96–97, 151–56.
16. Norden, *Brygga,* 66; von Koch, *Emigranternas land,* 341–42; Carlsson, *I palmernas skugga,* 114; von Kræmer, *Mexiko-Amerika,* 129–37; Nerman, *I Vilda Västern,* 92; Wahlborg, *Stjärnbanér,* 51–53; Molin, *Vanhäfd,* 38–39, 52, 72.
17. Norden, *Brygga,* 91; von Koch, *Emigranternas land,* 333–34; Molin, *Vanhäfd,* 54–59.
18. Von Koch, *Emigranternas land,* 333–34; Molin, *Vanhäfd,* 33; von Kræmer, *Ur frihetslandets järnkäftar,* 62; Cf. Olofsson, *Minnen och intryck,* 68.

19. Molin, *Vanhäfd*, 36–37; von Kræmer, *Ur frihetslandets järnkäftar*, 37; von Koch, *Emigranternas land*, 342. Cf. von Koch, "Svenskarna i Förenta staterna," 170.

20. Wahlborg, *Stjärnbanér*, 24–25, 66–67; von Koch, *Emigranternas land*, 323–24; von Kræmer, *Ur frihetslandets järnkäftar*, 61, 94–98. Cf. von Kræmer, *Mexiko-Amerika*, 118–46; von Koch, "Svenskarna i Förenta staterna," 338–39.

21. Pehrsson, "Svenskheten in Amerika," 24; Molin, *Vanhäfd*, 33–35, 74–75, 84–86; von Koch, *Emigranternas land*, 199, 335–38; G. H. von Koch, "'Sveriges framtid hotad?'" *Valkyrian* 13 (1909), 518. Cf. Olofsson, *Minnen och intryck*, 59; Cederschiöld, *Infödingarna*, 228–32, 239–40; Nerman, *I Vilda Västern*, 73, 96–97.

22. Norden, *Brygga*, 16–17, 30–31, 78, 82, 153; von Koch, *Emigranternas land*, 324 and "Sveriges framtid hotad?" 518–19. Cf. Olofsson, *Minnen och intryck*, 38; Pehrsson, "Svenskheten i Amerika," 4; Wahlborg, *Stjärnbanér*, 151.

23. Molin, *Vanhäfd*, 60–71; von Koch, *Emigranternas land*, 320; Norden, *Brygga*, 29.

24. Von Koch, *Emigranternas land*, 333 and "Sveriges framtid hotad?" 517–18; Norden, *Brygga*, 57.

25. Molin, *Vanhäfd*, 74.

26. Norden, *Brygga*, 57.

27. *Ibid.*, 57; Norberg, "Svenskarnas Amerika," 27; Pehrsson, "Svenskheten i Amerika," 3, 8; von Koch, *Emigranternas land*, 363–64, 370, 378–80; Carlsson, *I palmernas skugga*, 174–75; Cederschiöld, *Infödingarna*, 226.

28. Norden, *Brygga*, 64–66. Cf. Norberg, "Svenskarnas Amerika," 126.

29. Norden, *Brygga*, 15–20, 37, 40.

30. Von Kræmer, *Ur frihetslandets järnkäftar*, 6–7, 11–13, 17, 33, 47–49, 60, and *Mexiko-Amerika*, 113.

31. Norden, *Brygga*, 57–59; Carlsson, *I palmernas skugga*, 7, 52, 75–76, 211–12; Gawell-Blumenthal, *Stintans amerikafärd*, 186; Pehrsson, "Svenskheten i Amerika," 25.

32. Cederschiöld, *Infödingarna*, 216–19.

33. Von Koch, *Emigranternas land*, 321–22.

34. Pehrsson, "Svenskheten i Amerika," 18–19; Norden, *Brygga*, 37–38, 40; Gawell-Blumenthal, *Stintans amerikafärd*, 110–11. Cf. Cederschiöld, *Infödingarna*, 225–26; Olofsson, *Minnen och intryck*, 60–61; Wahlborg, *Stjärnbanér*, 65–66, 90.

35. Molin, *Vanhäfd*, 82–83, 124; Cederschiöld, *Infödingarna*, 220, 226–27, 234–39; Pehrsson, "Svenskheten i Amerika," 18–19; von Koch, *Emigranternas land*, 320.

36. Von Koch, *Emigranternas land*, 326–27, 333, 338; Molin, *Vanhäfd*, 76; Rudolf Kjellén, *Nationell samling* (Stockholm, 1906), 199–206; von Kræmer, *Mexiko-Amerika*, 98–100, 108, 113, 119, 123–24, and *Ur frihetslandets järnkäftar*, 45–46, 48–49, 60.

37. Pehrsson, "Svenskheten i Amerika," 3, 12–18.

38. Norden, *Brygga*, 37–40, 54, 93–95.

39. Von Koch, *Emigranternas land*, 320, 326–27, 350–51, 353–57.

40. Molin, *Vanhäfd*, 76.

41. Pehrsson, "Svenskheten i Amerika," 2–3, 9, 11–12, 15; Olofsson, *Minnen och intryck*, 31, 43, 60; Carlsson, *I palmernas skugga*, 209, 223–24; Wahlborg, *Stjärnbanér*, 132–40.

42. Von Koch, "Sveriges framtid hotad?" 518; Norden, *Brygga*, 115–16; Molin, *Vanhäfd*, 81–82.

43. Norden, *Brygga*, 103, 106–7. Cf. Molin, *Vanhäfd*, 76; Pehrsson, "Svenskheten i Amerika," 12–14.

44. Molin, *Vanhäfd*, 76–81; Norden, *Brygga*, 102; Pehrsson, "Svenskheten i Amerika," 15–18. Regarding reactions in the Swedish-American press to Molin's criticisms, see Anna Williams, *Skribent i Svensk-Amerika. Jakob Bonggren, journalist och poet* (Uppsala, 1991), 51–52.

45. Pehrsson, "Svenskheten i Amerika," 20–22; Nerman, *I Vilda Västern*, 90–91; von Koch, *Emigranternas land*, 378. Cf. Gawell-Blumenthal, *Stintans amerikafärd*, 92.

46. Wahlborg, *Stjärnbanér*, 62–63; von Koch, *Emigranternas land*, 354, 378; Olofsson, *Minnen och intryck*, 38–39, 77; Pehrsson, "Svenskheten i Amerika," 21–22.

47. Molin, *Vanhäfd*, 81–82.

48. *Ibid.*, 380; Von Koch, *Emigranternas land*, 356–57, 376–77.

49. Pehrsson, "Svenskheten i Amerika," 10–11. Cf. Olofsson, *Minnen och intryck*, 60–61.

50. Norden, *Brygga*, 9, 32–34, 126–27.

51. *Ibid.*, 83.

52. *Ibid.*, 134–35. Cf. Harald Elovson, "Heidenstam och Amerika," *Edda* (1933), 97–98; Cederschiöld, *Infödingarna*, 216–17; Pehrsson, "Svenskheten i Amerika," 25–26; Wahlborg, *Stjärnbanér*, 70–71.

53. Pehrsson, "Svenskheten i Amerika," 26; Cederschiöld, *Infödingarna*, 20–22; Olofsson, *Minnen och intryck*, 67; Molin, *Vanhäfd*, 77–79.

54. Von Koch, "Sveriges framtid hotad," 517; Norden, *Brygga*, 57–59. Cf. Wahlborg, *Stjärnbanér*, 151.

55. Von Koch, *Emigranternas land*, 381; Pehrsson, "Svenskheten i Amerika," 5.

56. Von Koch, *Emigranternas land*, 380–83; Norden, *Brygga*, 148–49; Pehrsson, "Svenskheten i Amerika," 5, 10.

57. Molin, *Vanhäfd*, 82–83.

58. Von Koch, *Emigranternas land*, 383. Cf. Pehrsson, "Svenskheten i Amerika," 25; Norden, *Brygga*, 146.

59. Molin, *Vanhäfd*, 80.

60. Cederschiöld, *Infödingarna*, 225–26; Lewi Pethrus, *Västerut* (Stockholm, 1937), 57–58.

61. Lund, *Som piga i U.S.A.*, 205–6, 217–22.

62. Cederschiöld, *Infödingarna*, 226; John P. Miller, *Vart togo de vägen?* (Chicago, 1945), 217–18.

63. Albin Widén, *Amandus Johnson, svenskamerikan. En levnadsteckning* (Stockholm, 1970), 54–55. Cf. my *Letters*, 258–59.

64. See ch. 9, above.

65. Joh. A. Enander, "Svensk-Amerikas dag i Norrköping," *Prärieblomman 1907*, esp. 69–78; Hj. A. L——th, "Svensk-Amerikanernas dag i Norrköping," *Ungdomsvännen* (1906), 240–41.

66. Victor Nilsson, *Sångarfarden till Sverige 1910. Illustrerade resebrefsskildringar* (Chicago, n.d./c. 1910), 7–8.

67. *Ibid.*, 10–11.

68. *Ibid.*, 56, 68, 172–73, 177, 196, 208.

69. Alex. Olsson, *På turistfärd genom Amerika och Europa. Kortfattade skildringar från en resa sommaren 1908* (San Francisco, 1909), 51, 88–89.

70. *Ibid.*, foreword (n.p.), 52, 70, 80, 83.

71. *Ibid.*, 56–60.

72. *Ibid.*, foreword (n.p.), 62, 68–69, 102–3, 125–26.

73. Alfred Bergin, *Under furor och palmer. Reseintryck från Europa vid Världskrigets början* (n.p., 1916), 11–12, 99–100, 107–8.

74. *Ibid.*, 84–85, 95, 105, 120, 144–48, 150, 157, 170.

75. *Ibid.*, 127–30, 146, 148–50, 163.

76. *Ibid.*, 126, 164–78, 188, 193.

77. Wahlborg, *Stjärnbanér*, 89–90.

78. Norden, *Brygga*, 148.

FIFTEEN

The Heyday of Swedish America

1. Sture Lindmark, *Swedish America, 1914–1932: Studies in Ethnicity with Emphasis on Illinois and Minnesota* (Uppsala, 1971), 11–12, 27–28; Ljungmark, *Den stora utvandringen*, 198.

2. Nelson, *Swedes and Swedish Settlements;* Ljungmark, *Den stora utvandringen,* 190–98.

3. Ljungmark, *Den stora utvandringen,* 132, 135; Ulf Beijbom, *Swedes in Chicago: A Demographic and Social Study of the 1846–1880 Immigration* (Uppsala, 1971), 11.

4. See my "Stage Migration and Ethnic Maintenance," *Sw. Pioneer Hist. Q.* 30 (1979): 231–33.

5. For evidence in the Swedish-American press of the rallying of Swedish America from the turn of the century, see Anna Williams, *Skribent i Svensk-Amerika. Jakob Bonggren, journalist och poet* (Uppsala, 1991), esp. 118, 167, 170.

6. See my "Old Swedish Traditions," *Sw.-Am. Hist. Q.,* 33 (1982): 236–40, and "Old Swedish Customs: An Interim Report," *Sw.-Am. Hist. Q.* 34 (1983): 175–77. Also my "Cultural Interplay between Sweden and Swedish America," *Sw.-Am. Hist. Q.* 43 (1992): 5–18; Ulf Beijbom, *Svenskamerikanskt,* 138–39. Cf. Eric Hobsbawn, "Introduction," in Eric Hobsbawn and Terrence Ranger, *The Invention of Tradition* (Cambridge, 1983), 1–14. For in-depth studies of representative rural and urban Swedish-American communities during this time, see esp. Phebe Fjellström, *Swedish-American Colonization in the San Joaquin Valley in California* (Uppsala, 1970) and Lars Wendelius, *Kulturliv i ett svenskamerikanskt lokalsamhälle: Rockford, Illinois* (Uppsala, 1990).

7. *Minnesskrift med anledning af Augustana-synodens femtioåriga tillvaro* (Rock Island, Ill., 1910); E. A. Zetterstrand, "Kyrkoherde Per Pehrsson," *Prärieblomman 1911,* 186, 191–94; Ulf Beijbom, "Swedish-American Organizational Life," in Harald Runblom and Dag Blanck, eds., *Scandinavia Overseas* (Uppsala, 1986), 52–81; Anne-Charlotte Hanes Harvey, "Swedish-American Theatre," in Maxine Seller, ed., *Ethnic Theatre in the United States* (Westport, Conn., 1984), 491–524; Henriette C. K. Naeseth, *The Swedish Theatre of Chicago, 1868–1950* (Rock Island, Ill., 1951); Lars Furuland, "From *Vermländingarne* to *Slavarna på Molokstorp:* Swedish-American Theater in Chicago," in Anderson and Blanck, eds., *Swedish-American Life in Chicago,* 133–49; E. Einar Andersson, ed., *Hembygden. Historik av Chicagos svenska hembygdsföreningar. A Century of Progress* (Chicago, 1933); Einar Anderson, "Våra hembygdsföreningar," *Svenska Kulturförbundets Minnesskrift* (Chicago, 1938), 42–45.

8. Nils Hasselmo, *Amerikasvenska. En bok om språkutvecklingen i Svensk-Amerika* (Lund, 1974), 63–65; 68–72, and *Swedish America: An Introduction* (New York, 1976), 41–44; Lindmark, *Swedish America,* 206–9, 223, 226; Williams, *Skribent i Svensk-Amerika,* 31, 100; Raymond Jarvi, "The Rise and Fall of the House of Engberg-Holmberg," in Anderson and Blanck, eds., *Swedish-American Life in Chicago,* 255–63; also Pehrsson, "Svenskheten i Amerika," 15–18; E. Walfred Erickson, *Swedish-American Periodicals: A Descriptive Bibliography* (New York, 1979); G. N. Swan, *Swedish-American Literary Periodicals* (Rock Island, Ill., 1936); Birgitta Svensson, "*Prärieblomman* (1900–1913): A Swedish-American Cultural Manifestation," *Sw.-Am. Hist. Q.,* 43 (1992): 156–69.

9. For Swedish-American accomplishments in American life during this period, see esp. Ernst Skarstedt, *Svensk-amerikanska folket i helg och söcken* (Stockholm, 1917).

10. *Svensk varu- och bokkatalog utgifven af Carl Dahlen, 629 Third Avenue, New York, N.Y.* (New York, 1913), esp. 3.

11. Little has yet been written on Swedish-American radicalism. See, however, Henry Bengston, *Skandinaver på vänsterflygeln i USA* (Stockholm, 1955), of which an English translation is forthcoming; Tedebrand, "America in the Swedish Labor Press," esp. 59–63; Franklin D. Scott, "Literature in Periodicals of Protest of Swedish America," *Sw. Pioneer Hist. Q.* 16 (1965): 193–215; Michael Brook, "Radical Literature in Swedish America: A Narrative Survey," *Sw. Pioneer Hist. Q.* 20 (1969): 111–32. Cf. my *Letters from the Promised Land,* 217–22, 226–29, 294–96.

12. Gustav Andreen, "Grundläggarnes dag vid Augustana College," *Prärieblomman 1903,* 293–98, esp. 297.

13. David Nyvall, "Den svenska nationalkaraktären och dess amerikanisering," *Prärieblomman 1903,* 282–92, esp. 286–87, 291–92.

14. L. G. Abrahamson, "Licentiat C. L. Sundbeck och betydelsen af hans resa i Förenta Staterna," *Prärieblomman 1903,* 100–114, esp. 101–2, 106–12, 114.

15. See ch. 9, above.

16. Joh. A. Enander, "Svensk-Amerikas dag i Norrköping," *Prärieblomman* (1907), 69–90, esp. 78, 81–83, 85–86.

17. Theodore A. Hessell, *Farbror Slokums memoarer. Skildringar ur värkligheten,* 2 vols. (Chicago, 1909–10), I:13, 191–92, 201, 204, 209; II:30, 33, 37, 155–57. On Hessel, see Skarstedt, *Pennfäktare,* 77–78.

18. See Fjellström, *Swedish-American Colonization in the San Joaquin Valley;* Gary Brain, "'The Ship Sailed On': Swedish-American Migration to Rural California," *Sw.-Am. Hist. Q.* 51 (1990): 220–33; Karin Schill, "I kamp for det svenska. Svenskamerikansk press 1869–1923" (unpublished seminar paper, Department of History, Stockholm University, 1989). I am indebted to Professor Herman Schück for a copy of the latter work. Cf. Daniel M. Pearson, *The Americanization of Carl Aaron Swensson* (Rock Island, Ill., 1977), 142–44.

19. David Nyvall, "Kulturlif och byalag," *Prärieblomman 1907,* 163–74, esp. 169, 172.

20. *Referat öfver organisationsmötet af Augustana-synodens Kolonisationsförening i Chicago, Illinois, den 11 och 12 juli 1913* (n.p., 1913), esp. 6.

21. Alfred Bergin, "Behåll fädernehemmet!" *Ungdomsvännen* (1915), 218–19.

22. Gustav Andreen, *Det svenska språket i Amerika,* Studentföreningen Verdandis småskrifter, Vol. 11, No. 87 (Stockholm, 1900); E. A. Zetterstrand, "Några skäl hvarfor svenskarne i Amerika böra bevara det svenska språket," *Ungdoms-Vännen* (1899), 124–26, "Engelskans inflytande på det svenska språket i Amerika," *Ungdomsvännen* (1904), 179–80, 204, 206–7, 243–44, and "Svenskan i Amerika bedömd af en svensk vetenskapsman," *Ungdomsvännen* (1904), 348–50; Ruben G:son Berg, "Svenskan i Amerika," *Språk och stil* 4 (1904), 1–21; Felix Vivo [Vilhelm Berger,] "Några ord i vår språkfraga," *Valkyrian* 13 (1904), 132–36; Amandus Johnson, "Bör svensk-amerikanen bevara fädrens språk?" *Ungdomsvännen* (1904), 312–13, 332–33; E——n, "Den svensk-amerikanska litteraturens framtid," *Ungdomsvännen* (1905), 88–90; Medikus, "Den svensk-amerikanska litteraturens framtid," *Ungdomsvännen* (1905), 240–41; R. D. H., "Ärans och hjältarnes språk," *Ungdomsvännen* (1911), 168–69; A. A. Stomberg, "Svenskhetens bevarande i Amerika," *Ungdomsvännen* (1911), 46–47; Alfred Bergin, "Svenskhetens lifstecken i Amerika," *Ungdomsvännen* (1911), 81; Lindmark, *Swedish America,* 197. Cf. Enander, "Svenska språket," in *Valda skrifter,* 355.

23. Lindmark, *Swedish America,* 192–93, 197, 203–4, 206–10, 260–64, 276–77; cf. Hasselmo, *Amerikasvenska,* 55–57.

24. C. A. Lindvall, "Svenska språket i Amerika," *Yearbook of the Swedish Historical Society of America, 1914–15* (Chicago, 1915), 13–21, esp. 16, 18, 21. Also printed with slight variations as "Har det svenska språket någon framtid i Amerika?" in *Ungdomsvännen* (July 1916), 209–11. Cf. Hasselmo, *Amerikasvenska,* 45.

25. C. A. Lindvall, "Vårt stora kulturarv," *Yearbook of the Swedish Historical Society of America, 1916–17* (Chicago, 1917), 11–20, esp. 13–14, 17–18.

26. S. M. Hill, "Ledarskapet i Svensk-Amerika," *Yearbook of the Swedish Historical Society of America, 1914–15* (Chicago, 1915), 31–37.

27. For details on Person, see Skarstedt, *Pennfäktare,* 149–50; Ulf Jonas Björk, "Nothing but a Hired Hand: Johan Person and the Swedish-American Press," *Sw.-Am. Hist. Q.* 42 (1991): 5–23.

28. Johan Person, *Svensk-amerikanska studier* (Rock Island, Ill., 1912), 9–10.

29. *Ibid.,* 10–11, 13–14.

30. *Ibid.,* 10–12, 37–40, 41, 45. Cf. Person's short story, "Nykomlingen," in his *I Svensk Amerika,* 2d ed. (Worcester, Mass., 1900), 13–18.

31. Person, *Svensk-amerikanska studier,* 42–45, 63, 77–78.

32. *Ibid.,* 55–56.

33. *Ibid.,* 114–17.

34. *Ibid.,* 117.

35. *Ibid.,* 140–44.

36. *Ibid.,* 145–50.

37. *Ibid.,* 73–76.

38. *Ibid.,* 48–50, 92–97, 107–13.

39. *Ibid.,* 22–23, 29–30, 57–62, 66.

40. *Ibid.,* 22–23, 61, 81–85, 124, 144, 151–72.

41. Vilhelm Berger, *Svensk-amerikanska meditationer* (Rock Island, Ill., 1916), 7–16; cf. "Några tankar i emigrationsfrågan," in *Ungdomsvännen* (March 1908), 94–96, and *Valkyrian* (Feb. 1909), 89–93. On Berger, see Skarstedt, *Pennfäktare,* 30–31; Emory Lindquist, "Vilhelm Berger: Swedish-American Journalist and Author," *Sw. Pioneer Hist. Q.* 32 (1981): 248–64; Ulf Beijbom, "Vilhelm Berger, en skildrare av emigranternas hundår," *Personhistorisk tidskrift* 77 (1981): 64–81. Cf. Hildebrand and Fredenholm, eds., *Svenskarna i Amerika,* II: 208.

42. Berger, *Svensk-amerikanska meditioner,* 128–34.

43. *Ibid.,* 128–34; Vilhelm Berger, "The American-Scandinavian Society," *Valkyrian* (1909), 117–19; Erik J. Friis, *The American-Scandinavian Foundation, 1910–1960: A Brief History* (New York, 1961).

44. A. A. Stomberg, "Beaktansvärda sträfvanden för den nordiska kulturens bevarande i Amerika," *Prärieblomman 1912,* 29–37, esp. 331–32.

45. G. N. Swan, "En återblick," Swedish Historical Society of America, *Yearbook, 1914–15* (Chicago, 1915), 38–54; Roy Swanson, "Our Predecessors," *Sw. Pioneer Hist. Q.* I (1950): 12–20; my "Clio and Swedish America," 9–10. Cf. E. Gustav Johnson, "Articles Published by the Swedish Historical Society of America, 1905–1934," *Sw. Pioneer Hist. Q.* 14 (1963): 127–35.

46. Amandus Johnson, *The Swedish Settlements on the Delaware,* 2 vols. (Philadelphia, 1911), esp. I: xvii–xi. On Johnson, see Widén, *Amandus Johnson.*

47. Eric Norelius, *De svenska lutherska församlingarnas och svenskarnes historia i Amerika,* II (Rock Island, Ill., 1916).

48. Skarstedt, *Svensk-amerikanska folket,* esp. 9–11, 22–23, 305. Cf. Emory Lindquist, *An Immigrant's American Odyssey: A Biography of Ernst Skarstedt* (Rock Island, Ill., 1974), 169, 210–11; also Hasselmo, *Amerikasvenska,* 48.

49. Kendric Charles Babcock, *The Scandinavian Element in the United States* (Urbana, Ill., 1914), 9–11. Babcock's "The Scandinavians in the Northwest," *Forum* 14 (1892): 103–7, "The Scandinavian Contingent," *Atlantic* 77 (1896): 660–70, and "The Scandinavian Element in the American Population," *American Historical Review* 16 (1911): 300–310.

50. Babcock, *The Scandinavian Element,* 17, 109, 114, 171, 179, 181–82. For general background on the "theory of Teutonic Origins" in America and the resultant Philoscandinavianism, see E. N. Saveth, *American Historians and European Immigrants, 1875–1925* (New York, 1948).

51. For background on Swedish-American literature, see Dorothy Burton Skårdal, *The Divided Heart: Scandinavian Immigrant Experience Through Literary Sources* (Oslo and Lincoln, Nebr., 1974); Hasselmo, *Amerikasvenska,* 29–35, and *Swedish America,* 30–35; Göran Stockenström, "Sociological Aspects of Swedish-American Literature," in Nils Hasselmo, ed., *Perspectives on Swedish Immigration* (Chicago, 1978), 256–78.

52. Johan Person, "Från fosterland till fosterlandskärlek," *Prärieblomman 1903,* 181–94. See also Vilhelm Berger, "Egna-hems-frågan. Svensk-amerikansk skiss," *Prärieblomman 1905,* 67–76. Also reprinted in Berger's *Hundår och lyckodagar* (New York, 1905).

53. C. W. Andeer, "I vetenskapens intresse," *Ungdomsvännen* (1903), 265–68, esp. 268, "Svensk-amerikanen," *Ungdomsvännen* (1904), 73–75, and "Den nya tiden," *Ungdomsvännen* (1915), 169–73, 207–9. On Andeer, see Skarstedt, *Pennfäktare,* 18.

54. Vandringsman [Fritiof Colling], *I Sverige och Amerika. Hvarjehanda småbitar af vandringsman* (Tidaholm, 1906), 83–90.

55. *Ibid.,* 115–24.

56. Axel Lundeberg, *John Johnsons hemkomst från Amerika* (Chicago, 1907), esp. 21–29.

On Lundeberg, see Skarstedt, *Pennfäktare,* 39; Don Heinrich Tolzmann, "Dr. Axel Lundeberg: Swedish-American Scholar in the Midwest," *Sw. Pioneer Hist. Q.* 24 (1973): 33–42.

57. *"Amerikas siste svensk." Tal hållet af Fil d:r J. S. Carlson* (Minneapolis, 1908), 16 pp. On Carlson, see Skarstedt, *Pennfäktare,* 44.

58. Carl Atterling, "Om det blefve allvar. Framtida situationsbilder," *Prärieblomman 1912,* 11–28, esp. 13–15, 23. On Atterling, cf. Lars Wendelius, "Literary Milieus and Profiles in a Swedish-American Community," in Dag Blanck and Harald Runblom, eds., *Swedish Life in American Cities* (Uppsala, 1991), 119–20.

59. Anna Olsson, *En prärieunges funderingar* (Rock Island, Ill., 1917), esp. 108–9. The author also brought out her own English version of this book, *"I'm Scairt": Childhood Days on the Prairie* (Rock Island, Ill., 1927). On Olsson, see Skarstedt, *Pennfäktare,* 145. Cf. my "Through Children's Eyes," *Sw.-Am. Hist. Q.* 41 (1990): 131–32.

60. G. N. Malm, *Charli Johnson, svensk-amerikan. Verklighetsbilder ur folklifvet bland svenskarne i Vestern på 1890-talet* (Chicago, 1909). Cf. Dorothy Burton Skårdal, "The Literary Achievement of G. N. Malm," in Emory Lindquist, et al., *G. N. Malm: A Swedish Immigrant's Varied Career* (Lindsborg, Kan., 1989), 59–120, esp. 60–80; Nils Hasselmo, "Language and the Swedish Immigrant Writer: From a Case Study of G. N. Malm," in *ibid.,* 121–32.

61. Malm, *Charli Johnson,* esp. 125, 127, 130, 148, 162, 171, 193–204, 215, 225–26. Cf. Ernst Skarstedt, "Intryck och minnen från en sommarresa till Östern," *Prärieblomman 1911,* 51–77.

62. Malm, *Charli Johnson,* 226–35, 254.

63. O. Fritiof Ander, "An Immigrant Community During the Progressive Era," in J. Iverne Dowie and Ernest M. Espelie, eds., *The Swedish Immigrant Community in Transition: Essays in Honor of Dr. Conrad Bergendoff* (Rock Island, Ill., 1963), 165.

SIXTEEN

Swedish America at the Divide

1. Lindmark, *Swedish-America,* 71–72; Salomon Henschen, "Den europeiska konflikten. Från svensk synpunkt," *Ungdomsvännen* (1914), 337–38; Annie Åkerhielm, "Hvilken kultur skall segra?" *Ungdomsvännen* (1915), 197–98; Signe Ankarfelt, "Den germanska rasen och den individuella friheten," *Ungdomsvännen* (1916), 54–55. Ch. 6 (64–136) of Lindmark's *Swedish-America* provides the fullest treatment of Swedish America during World War I. See also Finis Herbert Capps, *From Isolationism to Involvement: The Swedish Immigrant Press in America, 1914–1945* (Chicago, 1966), ch. 3. Cf. Carl H. Chrislock, *Ethnicity Challenged: The Upper Midwest Norwegian-American Experience in World War I* (Northfield, Minn., 1981).

2. Lindmark, *Swedish-America,* 72–75; Capps, *From Isolation to Involvement,* 37–49.

3. Lindmark, *Swedish-America,* 77.

4. Johannes Hoving, *I svenskhetens tjänst,* 5 vols. (Stockholm, 1944–53), I:274, 298.

5. Lindmark, *Swedish-America,* 91–96. Cf. Bruce L. Larson, *Lindbergh of Minnesota: A Political Biography* (New York, 1973), chs. 8, 9.

6. Carl J. Bengston, "Varen amerikanske," *Ungdomsvännen* (Oct. 1918), 238–39.

7. Lindmark, *Swedish-America,* 65–67, 104, 215. Cf. Chrislock, *Ethnicity Challenged,* 81–83.

8. Lindmark, *Swedish-America,* 194–97. Cf. Nels J. A. Larson, "Life in Saskatchewan, 1918–1925: A Story of a Pioneer Missionary Family," *Sw.-Am. Hist. Q.* 36 (1985): 39–55, which recounts the story of a Swedish-American pastor hounded out of his Minnesota parish for alleged pro-German sentiments.

9. Lindmark, *Swedish-America,* 98–100, 109–14; "Metropolitan Council, The John Ericsson League of Patriotic Service," *Ungdomsvännen* (1918), 119. Cf. Chrislock, *Ethnicity Challenged,* 71, 111–12.

10. Lindmark, *Swedish-America*, 79–88; C. A. Lönnquist, "Den femte juni" (poem), *Ungdomsvännen* (1917), 168; Ernst W. Olson, "A Word to Patriots in All Camps," *Ungdomsvännen* (1917), 191–92. Cf. Capps, *From Isolationism to Involvement*, 52–53.

11. Lindmark, *Swedish-America*, 100–103. Cf. Franklin D. Scott, *Sweden: The Nation's History* (rev. ed., Carbondale, Ill., 1988), 468–75; Mats Kihlberg, "Aktivismens huvudorgan Svensk Lösen," in Mats Kihlberg and Donald Söderlind, *Två studier i svensk konservatism 1916–1922* (Uppsala, 1961), 9–89; Shepard, "Adrian Molin," ch. 3. On the deterioration of Swedish-American relations after America's entry into the war, cf. the memoirs of Herman Lagercrantz, who again served as Swedish minister to Washington, *I skilda vägar*, 360–61.

12. Lindmark, *Swedish-America*, 114–28.

13. *Ibid.*, 79, 96–97; Chrislock, *Ethnicity Challenged*, 99, 104–5. Cf. George M. Stephenson, "The Attitude of Swedish Americans Toward the World War," *Proceedings of the Mississippi Valley Historical Association* 10 (1918–19): 79–94.

14. Lindmark, *Swedish-America*, 128–29; Capps, *From Isolationism to Involvement*, 57–58, 59.

15. Lindmark, *Swedish-America*, 140; Lars-Göran Tedebrand, "America in the Swedish Labor Press, 1880s to 1920s," in Marianne Debouzy, ed., *In the Shadow of the Statue of Liberty* (St. Denis, l988), 72; Henry Bengston, *Skandinaver på vänsterflygeln* (Stockholm, 1955).

16. Sophia I. Wakkure [pseud. for Carlson,] *En emigrantflickas öden* (Chicago, n.d.). The protagonists in Wakkure's other anticapitalist novel, *Samhällets nomander* (Chicago, n.d.), published by the same organization around the same time, are Finland-Swedish immigrants. I am indebted, for details about the author, to Michael Brook of Nottingham, England, via Tell G. Dahllöf, Stockholm.

17. See Edward G. Hartmann, *The Movement to Americanize the Immigrant* (New York, 1948); George M. Stephenson, *A History of American Immigration, 1820–1924* (New York, 1926), 170–71, 174–75, 228–29; Higham, *Strangers in the Land*, 232, 257–58, 261–62, 303; Theodore Saloutos, "Exodus U.S.A.," in O. Fritiof Ander, ed., *In the Trek of the Immigrants* (Rock Island, Ill., 1964), 197–215; Amandus Johnson, *Swedish Contributions to American National Life, 1638–1921* (New York, 1921), 61–64. On growing American interest in immigrant cultures during the 1920s and 1930s, see Oscar Handlin, "Immigration in American Life: A Reappraisal," in Henry Steele Commager, ed., *Immigration and American History* (Minneapolis, 1961), 22–23.

18. See ch. 17, below.

19. Higham, *Strangers in the Land*, 155–57, chs. 10, 11; Madison Grant, *The Passing of the Great Race* (4th ed., New York, 1922); esp. 10–12, 18, 69, 90, 124, 168–69, 177, 193, 206–11, 228, 236; Stephenson, *History of American Immigration*, 170–92; Lindmark, *Swedish-America*, 137–40. I am indebted to Prof. Kevin Hickey of Assumption College, Worcester, Mass., for information on Swedish Americans and the Klan in that area.

20. Lindmark, *Swedish-America*, 147, 149–53; Capps, *From Isolationism to Involvement*, 111.

21. Ljungmark, *Den stora utvandringen*, 179.

22. Lindmark, *Swedish-America*, 138, 154–55; Capps, *From Isolationism to Involvement*, 111–12; O. Fritiof Ander, "The Effects of the Immigration Law of 1925 upon a Minority Immigrant Group," *Annual Report of the American Historical Association for the Year 1942*, III (Washington, 1942), 343–52, esp. 350–51.

23. For quotas under the National Origins Act, see Samuel Eliot Morison and Henry Steele Commager, *The Growth of the American Republic*, 2 vols. (4th ed., New York, 1950), II:909.

24. Lindmark, *Swedish-America*, 155–57; Capps, *From Isolationism to Involvement*, 112–13.

25. *Augustana* (17 Jun. 1926), 379; Lindmark, *Swedish-America*, 158.

26. Lindmark, *Swedish-America*, 159–60.

27. *Ibid.*, 69, 111, 129–32; *Lutheran Companion* (1 Feb. 1919), 54; (15 Feb. 1919), 77–

78; (16 Aug. 1919), 427; (1 Nov. 1919), 574; (29 Nov. 1919), 622; *Augustana* (5 Dec. 1918), 788–89; (29 Jan. 1920), 72; (5 Feb. 1920), 88.

28. Lindmark, *Swedish-America*, 238–39, 248–53, 255–59.

29. *Ibid.*, 304–20; Beijbom, "Svenskamerikanismen," in his *Svenskamerikanskt*, 143–44.

30. Lindmark, *Swedish-America*, 206–9, 223–28; cf. Hasselmo, *Amerikasvenska*. 68–70.

31. Cf. "Ett ord till Ungdomsvännens prenumeranter," *Ungdomsvännen* (Nov.–Dec. 1918), 268.

32. Lindmark, *Swedish-America*, 192.

33. *Ibid.*, 262–64.

34. *Ibid.*, 239, 242, 265, 301; *Lutheran Companion* (31 Mar. 1917), 151; (22 Dec. 1917), 639–40. Cf. Gustav Andreen, "Augustanasynoden och dess verksamhet," in Karl Hildebrand and Axel Fredenholm, eds., *Svenskarna i Amerika*, 2 vols. (Stockholm, 1925–26), II:104–5; Conrad Bergendoff, *The Augustana Ministerium, 1850–1962* (Rock Island, Ill., 1980).

35. *Augustana* (19 Jan. 1922), 41; (2 Feb. 1922), 73, 76; (9 Feb. 1922), 90; (16 Feb. 1922), 107; (23 Feb. 1922), 122–23; (23 Mar. 1922), 187; (27 Apr. 1922), 263; (4 May 1922), 279; (1 Jun. 1922), 232; (24 Aug. 1922), 532–33; (31 Aug. 1922), 555; *Lutheran Companion* (19 Apr. 1924), 247.

36. Lindmark, *Swedish-America*, 266–67, 273; *Lutheran Companion* (31 Mar. 1917), 151; (22 Dec. 1917), 639–40; (2 Feb. 1924), 76.

37. Hasselmo, *Amerikasvenska*, 66–68, and *Swedish America*, 43–44; Lindmark, *Swedish-America*, 210, 281.

38. Lindmark, *Swedish-America*, 281–86; *Augustana* (10 Apr. 1924), 232. Cf. Helge Nelson, *Nordamerika. Natur, bygd och svenskbygd*, 2 vols. (Stockholm, 1926), II:294.

39. G. N. Malm to G. N. Swan, Lindsborg, Kan., 2 June 1921. G. N. Swan Papers, SSIRC. I am indebted to Dag Blanck for this and other materials from that collection.

40. Lindmark, *Swedish-America*, 307–12.

41. J. S. Carlson, *Varför böra vi behålla och bevara, vårda och bruka svenska språket i Amerika* (Hastings, Minn., 1923), 3, 5–6, 9–18, 20–22, 26, 30.

42. *Ibid.*, 31, 34–36, 40–44. On Carlson, cf. Hasselmo, *Amerikasvenska*, 40, 42–44, 50–54.

43. Hoving, *I svenskhetens tjänst*, I:274, 278, 281, 289; II:13; Erling Richter, *Kära släkten i U.S.A.* (Stockholm, 1923), 131.

44. Hoving, *I svenskhetens tjänst*, I:281.

45. *Ibid.*, I:302; II:16, 146, 179, 184; III:19–20, 33–34, 41, 56–57.

46. *Ibid.*, II:16.

47. *Ibid.*, II:153–54, 227, 241; III:19–20.

48. Hoving, *I svenskhetens tjänst*, II:42, 157–58, 183. Cf. Gunnar Broberg, "Lundborg, Herman," in *SBL*, 24 (1982–84), 234–39, and "Statens institut för rasbiologi—tillkomståren," in Gunnar Broberg, et al., eds., *Kunskapens trädgårdar* (Stockholm, 1988), 178–221; Tomas Hammar, *Sverige åt svenskarna. Invandringspolitik, utlänningskontroll och asylrätt 1900–1932* (Stockholm, 1964), 363–70.

49. Hoving, *I svenskhetens tjänst*, II:158, 184–85.

50. G. N. Malm, *Härute. Verklighetsbilder ur svensk-amerikanernas hvardagslif i fyra akter* (Lindsborg, Kan., 1919), 14–16, 40–42.

51. *Ibid.*, 29–32, 107–8. Cf. G. N. Malm to G. N. Swan, Lindsborg, Kan., 26 Dec. 1920, SSIRC.

52. Malm, *Härute*, 32–33, 38. Cf. Dorothy Burton Skårdal's discussion of *Härute* in Emory Lindquist, et al., *G. N. Malm: A Swedish Immigrant's Varied Career* (Lindsborg, Kan., 1989), 105–15. See also G. N. Malm, "En sommardag på Jan Swansons farm," in Karl Hildebrand and Axel Fredenholm, eds., *Svenskarna i Amerika*, 2 vols. (Stockholm, 1926), II:28–37. Cf. Skårdal in Lindquist, et al., *G. N. Malm*, 80–105, 117–20. The story is translated by Bertil Van Boer in Lindquist, et al., *G. N. Malm*, 215–21.

53. David Nyvall "Svenskhetens bevarande," *Augustana* (22 Dec. 1921).

54. Vilhelm Berger, *Svenska folklynnet i förskingring* (Brooklyn, 1924), esp. 25–26. This essay was based upon a lecture he had given ten years earlier at Upsala College.

55. Andersson, "Våra hembygdsföreningar" and *Hembygden*; Lindmark, *Swedish-America*, 307, 313–17.

56. No study of this commercialization has been made. See, however, Harvey, "Swedish-American Theatre," in Maxine Seller, ed., *Ethnic Theatre in the United States* (Westport, Conn., 1984), 491–524; Anne-Charlotte Harvey and Richard Hulan, "'Teater, visafton och bal': The Swedish-American Road Show in Its Heyday," *Sw.-Am. Hist. Q.* 37 (1986): 126–41.

57. Ernst Skarstedt, *Våra pennfäktare* (San Francisco, 1897) and *Pennfäktare* (Stockholm, 1930). Cf. Joseph Alexis' *La littérature suédoise d'Amérique* (Paris, 1930), a superficial survey of the work of 22 Swedish-American writers offered as a doctoral dissertation at the University of Paris by a later professor of Germanic languages at the University of Nebraska. On Alexis, see Adolph B. Benson and Naboth Hedin, eds., *Swedes in America, 1638–1938* (New Haven, 1938), 61, 64, 284.

58. Cf. my "Who Is a Swedish American?" *Sw. Pioneer Hist. Q.* 31 (1980): 83–85, and "Marcus Lee Hansen and the Swedish Americans," in Peter Kivisto and Dag Blanck, eds., *American Immigrants and Their Generations* (Urbana, Ill., 1990), 113–25.

SEVENTEEN

A Changing Sweden and the Swedish Americans

1. *Nationalföreningen ... Hvad den vill;* Paul Bergholm, *Nationalföreningen mot emigrationen 1907–1917* (Stockholm, 1917); *Svensk emigrations- och egnahemspolitik,* 79–80; Scott, "Sweden's Constructive Opposition," 319, 327, 331–32.

2. *Svensk emigrations- och egnahemspolitik,* 31, 64–66; Gellerman, *Staten och jordbruket,* 66.

3. Ljungmark, *Den stora utvandringen,* 179.

4. *Svensk emigrations- och egnahemspolitik,* 71–111, esp. 75–76. Cf. Michael Shepard, "Adrian Molin, Study of a Right-Wing Radical" (unpublished doctoral dissertation, Northwestern University, 1969), 234–35. There is no real study of Swedish reactions to American immigration restrictions.

5. *Svensk emigrations- och egnahemspolitik,* 98–102; Fredrik Lindskog, "Några synpunkter i fråga om den svenska emigrationens organisation," *Årsbok utgiven av Riksföreningen för svenskhetens bevarande i utlandet* (1925), 73–89, esp. 75.

6. *Svensk emigrations- och egnahemspolitik,* 77–79, 99–100.

7. *Allsvensk samling* (1 May 1918), 3, (1 Aug. 1918), 1–3; (2 Sept. 1918), 1–2; (2 Dec. 1918), 5; (2 Jan. 1919); 1–2; (1 Mar. 1919), 3–4; (15 Mar. 1919), 1–2; (1 May 1919), 2–3.

8. *Augustana* (6 Dec. 1917), 800; (1 Aug. 1918), 496; (5 Dec. 1918), 788–89; *Lutheran Companion* (27 Apr. 1918), 201; (20 July 1918), 361–62, 368; G. N. Swan to V. Lundström, Sioux City, Iowa, 20 Nov. 1918, Swan Papers, SSIRC.

9. *Allsvensk samling* (1 Sept. 1919); 1–4, (15 Sept. 1919), 7; (1 Oct. 1919), 4; Vilhelm Berger, "Språkförföljelsen och dess orsaker," *Allsvensk samling* (15 Sept. 1919), 8–9 and "De svenskes villighet att ge efter," *Allsvensk samling* (15 Nov. 1919), 4; Jennie M. Ericson, "Amerikabref," *Allsvensk samling* (15 Oct. 1919), 3.

10. G. N. Malm to G. N. Swan, Lindsborg, Kan., 16 Mar. 1920, Swan Papers, SSIRC.

11. *Allsvensk samling,* esp. (15 Jan. 1921), 4; (1 June 1921), 3; (15 Aug. 1921), 3; (15 Feb. 1922), 3.

12. "En brevväxling om svenskheten i Amerika," *Allsvensk samling* (1 Dec. 1922), 5–6; Lundström's reply to Witting is reprinted in his *Allsvenska linjer,* 80–87. Regarding Lundström's vision of Swedish as a world language, cf. Nyberg, "Emigrationen och Riksföreningens bakground," in Nyberg, et al., *Svenskt bortom gränserna,* 14.

13. *Allsvensk samling*, esp. (15 Feb. 1923), 4; (16 Apr. 1923), 5; (3 May 1923), 3; (15 June 1923), 2; (1 Mar. 1923), 1; (15 Mar. 1924), 3; (1 Apr. 1924), 2; (15 May 1924), 4–5, 6.

14. *Allsvensk samling* (14 Apr. 1924), 3. Cf. Stephenson, *Religious Aspects*, 454–55. Letter from Emil Lund, *Allsvensk samling* (14 Apr. 1924), 3. On the more recent immigrants' lack of interest in the Augustana Lutheran church, see Vilhelm Berger in *Allsvensk samling* (15 Nov. 1919), 4, and *Augustana* (25 Mar. 1920), 200.

15. *Augustana* (1 May 1924), 280–81; (3 July 1924), 224–25.

16. "Augustana-Synoden och svenskheten," *Allsvensk samling* (16 Apr. 1925), 4. Cf. Stephenson, *Religious Aspects*, 453–54.

17. "Den svenske veteranen," in Lundström, *Allsvenska linjer*, 97–100.

18. *Augustana* (14 May 1925), 310–11; (3 Sept. 1925), 570; (8 Oct. 1925), 648; (10 Dec. 1925), 792–93; (25 Mar. 1926), 184–85; (24 July 1930), 488–89. Cf. S. G. Öhman in *Allsvensk samling* (15 Apr. 1926), 1–2.

19. "Av svensk stam," in Lundström, *Allsvenska linjer*, 130–33.

20. "En förbisedd och döende litteratur," in Lundström, *Allsvenska linjer*, 134–40.

21. Cf. Skard, "Amerika i Europas liv," 21–22.

22. Nerman, *I Vilda Västern*, 138–39. This passage first appeared in *Folkets dagblad* (Stockholm) in 1929. Cf. Eidevall, *Amerika i svensk 1900-tals litteratur*, 49.

23. Nerman, *I Vilda Västern*, 151–56. Lars-Göran Tedebrand, "America in the Swedish Labor Press, 1880s to 1920s," in Marianne Debouzy, ed., *In the Shadow of the Statue of Liberty* (St. Denis, 1988), esp. 70.

24. Tedebrand, "America in the Swedish Labor Press," 70–73.

25. John Andersson, *Wallstreets blodiga välde (Skräckväldet i Amerika)* (Stockholm, 1923), 7, 122.

26. Nerman, *I Vilda Västern*, 140; Gustaf Hellström, *Förenta Staterna och världsfreden* (Stockholm, 1918) and *Ett rekommendationsbrev* (Stockholm, 1920). Cf. Eidevall, *Amerika i svensk 1900-tals litteratur*, 132–34, 139.

27. Gustaf Hellström, *Snörmakare Lekholm får en idé* (Stockholm, 1927).

28. Cf. my "The Swedes and Tinsel Town," *Sw.-Am. Hist. Q.* 35 (1984): 95–97.

29. Hjalmar Bergman, *Clownen Jac* (Stockholm, 1930).

30. Hjalmar Bergman, *Dollar. Komedi i tre akter* (Stockholm, 1926), esp. 31, 77, 93, 153–54.

31. Cf. Carl L. Anderson, *The Swedish Acceptance of American Literature* (Philadelphia, 1957); Allan Kastrup, *Med Sverige i Amerika. Opinioner, stämningar och upplysingsarbete* (Malmö, 1985), 48–49; *Les prix Nobel, an 1930* (Stockholm, 1931), 49–53, 57–58, 104.

32. Cf. Eidevall, *Amerika i svensk 1900-tals litteratur*, 61–64, 75, 77–78.

33. Karl Hildebrand and Axel Fredenholm, eds., *Svenskarna i Amerika*, 2 vols. (Stockholm, 1925–26), I, foreword, n.p.

34. *Ibid.*, I:200, 226.

35. *Ibid.*, I:319; II:316.

36. *Ibid.*, I:14.

37. *Ibid.*, I:88, 230, 268.

38. *Ibid.*, II:321–22.

39. *Ibid.*, II:7.

40. *Ibid.*, I:327. Cf. *ibid.*, I:359–60.

41. *Ibid.*, I:326, 331–32.

42. *Ibid.*, II:180–81.

43. *Ibid.*, II:185.

44. *Ibid.*, II:193–94. Cf. Oliver A. Linder, *I Västerland. Stycken på vers och prosa* (Rock Island, Ill., 1914).

45. Dag Blanck, *Sverige-Amerika stiftensen. De första sjuttio åren* (Stockholm, 1989), 6–7.

46. Kastrup, *Med Sverige i Amerika*, 31–32, 33–41.

47. See *Turistbok. Tips för amerikasvenskar på besök i Sverige* (Stockholm, 1923). 16.
48. G. N. Malm to G. N. Swan, Lindsborg, Kan., 2 June 1921, Swan Papers, SSIRC; Ernst W. Olson, "Våra Kulturbevare. Några ord med tydlig adress" (manuscript), Ernst W. Olson Papers, SSIRC; Alfred Bergin in *Augustana* (3 Sept. 1925), 570.
49. Blanck, *Sverige-Amerika stiftelsen,* 7.

EIGHTEEN
Travelers from Afar

1. Eidevall, *Amerika i svensk 1900-tals litteratur,* 50–51. For an interesting comparison during this period, cf. Earl R. Beck, *Germany Rediscovers America* (Tallahassee, Fla., 1968).
2. Anna Lenah Elgström and Gustaf Collijn, *U.S.A. Liv och teater* (Stockholm, 1927), 392. Cf. Eidevall, *Amerika i svensk 1900-tals litteratur,* 59–62.
3. Elgström, *U.S.A.,* 304, 377.
4. Nathan Söderblom, *Från Uppsala till Rock Island. En predikofärd i Nya Världen* (Stockholm, 1924), 302, 306, 308, 345, 363. For Söderblom's restatement of this same idea in 1928, see A. A. Stomberg, *Den svenska folkstammen i Amerika* (Stockholm, 1928), 6. Cf. Söderblom's wife's account of their journey, *En Amerikabok* (Stockholm, 1925).
5. Carl Lindhagen, *På vikingafärd i Västerled* (Stockholm, 1926), 187–90.
6. Maj Hirdman, *Resa till Amerika* (Stockholm, 1926), 72–74; Bergslagsmor (Lydia Hedberg), *Reseminnen från U.S.A.* (Skövde, 1925), 29. Cf. Johan Benzendal, *Amerikanska brev* (Uppsala, 1925), 79.
7. Elgström, *U.S.A.,* 380, 382.
8. Bergslagsmor, *Reseminnen,* 74, 78, 174. Cf. *ibid.,* 34.
9. Söderblom, *Från Uppsala till Rock Island,* 309–17.
10. Bergslagsmor, *Reseminnen,* 150–51; Benzendal, *Amerikanska brev,* 167–68.
11. Bergslagsmor, *Reseminnen,* 48, 105–7, 126. Cf. Ester Blenda Nordström's affectionate portrayal of an old Swedish-American farm couple in Minnesota, in her *Amerikanskt* (Stockholm, 1923), which otherwise has little to say about Swedish immigrants.
12. Bergslagsmor, *Reseminnen,* 29, 33, 171, 174.
13. Elgström, *U.S.A.,* 409–12.
14. Erland Richter, *Kära släkten i U.S.A* (Stockholm, 1923), 104–5.
15. N. Söderblom, *Från Uppsala till Rock Island,* 328–29.
16. J. Thulin, *De våra i Västern* (Uppsala, 1924), 45. Cf. Richter, *Kära släkten,* 105–6; Benzendal, *Amerikanska brev,* 131–47.
17. Söderblom, *Från Uppsala till Rock Island,* 332–48 *passim.*; Elgström, *U.S.A.,* 391, 406–7; Thulin, *De våra i Västern,* 17; Bergslagsmor, *Reseminnen,* 93, 97.
18. Benzendal, *Amerikanska brev,* 78–79, 241–42.
19. Elgström, *U.S.A.,* 406–7, 421–23, 388–90, 414–16, 423–24; Thulin, *De våra i Västern,* 17.
20. Benzendal, *Amerikanska brev,* 82, 84–85, 89.
21. *Ibid.,* 200–202.
22. N. Söderblom, *Från Uppsala till Rock Island,* 332–39, 343–48; Benzendal, *Amerikanska brev,* 112, 130, 207–8; Hirdman, *Resa till Amerika,* 70–71; Elgström, *U.S.A.,* 378–79.
23. Benzendal, *Amerikanska brev,* 240; Hirdman, *Resa till Amerika,* 71 Bergslagsmor, *Reseminnen,* 44.
24. Elgström, *U.S.A.,* 378, 422–24.
25. *Ibid.,* 379, 426–27.
26. Benzendal, *Amerikanska brev,* 45, 166, 170–71, 229–35.
27. Bergslagsmor, *Reseminnen,* 83.
28. Söderblom, *Från Uppsala till Rock Island,* 217, 317–25, 332–39, 343–48; Elgström, *U.S.A.,* 83, 374, 384–85.

29. Lindhagen, *På vikingafärd,* 189–90; Bergslagsmor, *Reseminnen,* 81.

30. Elgström, *U.S.A.,* 432. Cf. my "Marcus Lee Hansen and the Swedish Americans," in Peter Kivisto and Dag Blanck, eds., *American Immigrants and their Generations: Studies and Commentaries on the Hansen Thesis after Fifty Years* (Urbana, Ill., 1990), 113–25.

31. *Ibid.,* 425.

32. *Ibid.,* 432–39. Cf. Thulin, *De våra i Västern,* 197.

33. N. Söderblom, *Från Uppsala till Rock Island,* 332.

34. Fritz Henriksson, *Med Sveriges kronprinspar genom Amerika* (Stockholm, 1926), 197.

35. N. Söderblom, *Från Uppsala till Rock Island,* 218–22, 278–80; Elgström, *U.S.A.,* 376, 378, 439–40; Richter, *Kära släkten,* 142–43.

36. Elgström, *U.S.A.,* 389–90, 414–21, 428–30, 434–36, 437–39; Richter, *Kära släkten,* 128, 131, 138–39. Cf. Söderblom, *Från Uppsala till Rock Island,* 218.

37. Benzendal, *Amerikanska brev,* 225–28, 245–54. Note the enthusiastic review of this book in *Allsvensk samling* (15 Mar. 1926), 6.

38. Söderblom, *Från Uppsala till Rock Island,* 215–22, 308, 325.

39. Elgström, *U.S.A.,* 304, 310, 331–46, 439–41. Cf. Eidevall, *Amerika i svensk 1900-tals litteratur,* 61–62.

40. Helge Nelson, "Öland," EU, *Bilaga* VIII:6 (1909), *Canada. Nybyggarlandet* (Stockholm, 1922), and *Nordamerika. Natur, bygd och svenskbygd,* 2 vols. (Stockholm, 1926).

41. Helge Nelson, *Nordamerika. Natur och kulturbygd* (Stockholm, 1935) and *The Swedes and the Swedish Settlements in North America,* 2 vols. (Lund, 1943).

42. Lars P. Nelson, *En upptäcktsresa genom Sverige* (Stockholm, 1918), Foreword, n.p.; Peter Södergren, *Levnadsöden och reseskildringar* (Los Angeles, 1932), 93.

43. Bergslagsmor, *Reseminnen,* 190–93; Richter, *Kära släkten,* 142–48; Elgström, *U.S.A.,* 378.

44. *Turistbok. Tips för amerikasvenskar på besök i Sverige* (Stockholm, 1923), 5–6.

45. *Ibid.,* 7–8.

46. *Ibid.,* 9.

47. Johannes Hoving, *Vasabarnens från Amerika trenne resor i fars och mors land 1924, 1929, 1933. Minnen och intryck* (Stockholm, 1935); Gunnar Wickman, *Till fars och mors land. Vasaordens barnklubbars Sverigeresa 1924* (Göteborg, 1924).

48. Hoving, *Vasabarnen,* 13.

49. *Ibid.,* 32.

50. *Ibid.,* 21–22, 23–24, 29, 37, 62, 77–80.

51. *Ibid.,* 95–113, 217–18, 243.

52. *Ibid.,* 204, 242–43.

53. *Ibid.,* 120, 236–37.

54. *Ibid.,* 161.

NINETEEN

The Afterglow

1. Oscar Rydqvist, *En handfull amerikanskt. Journalistiska strövtåg* (Stockholm, 1933), 199–200; Hoving, *I svenskhetens tjänst,* III: 165–66.

2. Ljungmark, *Den stora utvandringen,* 180. No study of Swedish migration specifically for the period 1930–40 has been made.

3. Lindmark, *Swedish America,* 28, 34; E. P. Hutchinson, *Immigrants and Their Children, 1850–1950* (New York, 1956), 17.

4. Lars-Göran Tedebrand, "Remigration from America to Sweden," in Harald Runblom and Hans Norman, eds., *From Sweden to America: A History of the Migration* (Minneapolis, 1976), 201–27.

5. Cf. my "The Summer of '46," *Sw.-Am. Hist. Q.* 35 (1984): 3–5.

6. Lindmark, *Swedish America*, 162–90, esp. 190. For a valuable description of widespread unemployment and need among Swedish immigrants in Chicago during these years, see John P. Miller, *Vart togo de vägen?* (Chicago, 1945).

7. Lindmark, *Swedish America*, 180, 237–48, 304–6, 310–12, 317, 319.

8. Hasselmo, *Amerikasvenska*, 63–72.

9. Lindmark, *Swedish America*, 308–9; Berger, *Svensk-amerikanska meditationer*, 96–97. Cf. Beijbom, "Svenskamerikanismen," in his *Svenskamerikanskt*, 148–49.

10. *Svenska kulturförbundets minnesskrift* (Chicago, 1938), 35.

11. *Ibid.*, 27; Lindmark, *Swedish America*, 213–15.

12. Hoving, *I svenskhetens tjänst*, III:32–35, 53, 72.

13. *Ibid.*, III:125–27.

14. Vilhelm Berger, *Svensk-Amerika i målbrottet* (New York, 1933), 3–4, 12–13, 17, 19–25. Cf. Felix Vivo's [i.e., Berger's] earlier "Några ord i vår språkfråga," *Valkyrian* 13 (1904): 132–36.

15. *Svensk-Amerika i Målbrottet*, 13–14, 17.

16. *Ibid.*, 15, 17, 19–25.

17. Cf. Vilhelm Berger, *Vår kyrka* (Brooklyn, 1912), *Svenska tidningar i New York, N.Y.* (New York, 1929), *Svensk-amerikanska språket* (New York, 1934), and "Svenska namn på Amerikas karta," *Namn och Bygd*, 26 (1938): 61–102.

18. Vilhelm Berger, *En hjärnarbetares funderingar* (New York, 1934), 7, 13, 14.

19. *Ibid.*, 13, 33–36, 56–57; Vilhelm Berger, *En näve svensk-amerikanskt. Aforismer* (New York, n.d. [1937]), 10.

20. Berger, *Hjärnarbetares funderingar*, 17, 19, 20–21, 23, 29, 45; *En näve*, 8, 14, 17.

21. Berger, *En näve*, 17, 19, 25.

22. Berger, *Hjärnarbetares funderingar*, 24–25.

23. Cf. ch. 15, above.

24. Roy Swanson, "Our Predecessors," *Sw. Pioneer Hist. Q.* 1 (1950): 12–20; Oral information from Dr. Albin Widén, Bromma, Sweden.

25. George M. Stephenson, *A History of American Immigration, 1820–1924* (New York 1926) and *The Founding of the Augustana Synod, 1850–1860* (Rock Island, Ill., 1927). Cf. Ander, "Four Historians."

26. Amandus Johnson, *Swedish Contributions to American National Life, 1638–1921* (New York, 1921); A. A. Stomberg, *Den svenska folkstammen i Amerika* (Stockholm, 1928); *Augustana* (3 Sept. 1925), 570; (9 Sept. 1926), 568–69; Beijbom, "The Historiography of Swedish America," 274–79; Albin Widén, *Amandus Johnson, svenskamerikan. En levnadsteckning* (Stockholm, 1970), 133–48, esp. 142 (quotation). Cf. my "The Swedish-American Historical Society: A Milestone Reached," in *Archives and History: Minutes and Reports of the 18th Conference on Archives and History* (St. Louis: Concordia Historical Institute, 1985), 117–23.

27. Widén, *Amandus Johnson*, 149–67, and *Svenskar som erövrat Amerika*, 56–70.

28. Conrad Peterson, "Twenty-Five Years of the Swedish Historical Society of America," *Swedish-American Historical Bulletin* (March, 1930), esp. 5–6, 16, 18; Carlton C. Qualey, "The Minnesota School of Ethnic Historians," unpublished paper, courtesy of the author; my "Historians of the Scandinavians in North America," in J. R. Christianson, ed., *Scandinavians in America: Literary Life* (Decorah, Iowa, 1985), 48–49.

29. Conrad Bergendoff, "On the Fiftieth Anniversary of the Augustana Historical Society," *Sw. Pioneer Hist. Q.* 22 (1971): 202–11.

30. Erik G. Westman and E. Gustav Johnson, eds., *The Swedish Element in America*, 4 vols. (Chicago, 1931–34), see esp. I:1–3.

31. John S. Lindberg, *The Background of Swedish Emigration to the United States* (Minneapolis, 1930); Florence E. Janson, *The Background of Swedish Immigration, 1840–1930* (Chicago, 1931). O. Fritiof Ander, *T. N. Hasselquist: The Career and Influence of a Swedish-*

American Clergyman, Journalist and Educator (Rock Island, Ill., 1931); Stephenson, *Religious Aspects.* Cf. my "Clio and Swedish America," 12–14.

32. Sherry Butcher-Younghans, *The American-Swedish Institute: A Living Heritage* (Minneapolis, 1989).

33. Cf. Vilhelm Lundström's introduction to *Svenska kulturförbundets minnesskrift,* 7–8.

34. Cf. Erik Asklund, *Lilla land* (Stockholm, 1933); Per Nilsson-Tannér, *Det nya Eden. Ett svenskt emigrationsäventyr* (Stockholm, 1934); Skard, "Amerika i Europas liv," 21–22; Eidevall, *Amerika i svensk 1900-tals litteratur,* 86; Carl L. Anderson, *The Swedish Acceptance of American Literature* (Philadelphia, 1957); Alrik Gustafson, *A History of Swedish Literature* (Minneapolis, 1961), 470–71; Lars-Göran Tedebrand "America in the Swedish Labor Press, 1880s to 1920s," in Marianne Debouzy, ed., *In the Shadow of the Statue of Liberty* (St. Denis, 1988), 73.

35. Albin Widén, *Carl Oscar Borg. Ett konstnärsöde* (Stockholm, 1953), 147–48. Cf. Hoving, *I svenskhetens tjänst,* IV:132.

36. Carl Mangård, *Svenska öden i Amerika. En resa från Atlanten till Stilla havet* (Uppsala, 1939), 259; Hoving, *I svenskhetens tjänst,* IV:132.

37. Anna Lenah Elgström, *U.S.A. i örnens tecken* (Stockholm, 1934), 7, 10, 16, 17, 20–23, 30, 243, 245, 248, 251.

38. Helge Nelson, *Nordamerika. Natur och kulturbygd,* 2 vols. (Stockholm, 1935), I:10.

39. Widén, *Svenskar som erövrat Amerika,* esp. 175–85; conversations with Albin Widén; obituary for Albin Widén, *Sw.-Am. Hist. Q.* 35 (1984): 179–80. See Widén's biography, *Amandus Johnson* (1970).

40. Widén, *Svenskar som erövrat Amerika,* 10, 34–35, 37, 89–91, 100, 129.

41. Nils Jacobsson, *Svenska öden vid Delaware 1638–1831* (Stockholm, 1938). Cf. Jacobsson's earlier *Svenskar och indianer* (Stockholm, 1922).

42. Ingvar Andersson, *A History of Sweden* (London, 1955), 431.

43. Kastrup, *Med Sverige i Amerika,* 43, 45–48, 50–51. Agnes Rothery, *Sweden: The Land and the People* (New York, 1934), 4–5. Kastrup, *Med Sverige i Amerika,* 48, 50; Marquis Childs, "Sweden: Where Capitalism Is Controlled," *Harper's Magazine* 167 (November 1933): 758.

44. Marquis Childs, *Sweden: The Middle Way* (rev. ed., New Haven, 1966), 4, 13, 50, 116, 160–61.

45. Kastrup, *Med Sverige i Amerika,* 55–58, 61–66.

46. *Ibid.,* 51, 52, 57. Cf. Widén, *Svenskar som erövrat Amerika,* 159, 172. Also Merle Curti, "Sweden in the American Social Mind of the 1930s," in J. Iverne Dowie and J. Thomas Treadway, eds., *The Immigration of Ideas* (Rock Island, Ill., 1968), 159–84.

47. Kastrup, *Med Sverige i Amerika,* 54, 69–71; Widén, *Svenskar som erövrat Amerika,* 172. For an American appreciation of the Swedish and other Scandinavian elements from this period, see William Seabrook, *These Foreigners* (New York, 1938), ch. 2.

48. Kastrup, *Med Sverige i Amerika,* 53–54. Cf. Widén, *Svenskar som erövrat Amerika,* 172.

49. Kastrup, *Med Sverige i Amerika,* 59; Berger, *En näve,* 25.

50. Hjalmar Rangman, *Det stora landet i Väster. Glimtar från natur och folkliv* (Uppsala, 1931), 162, 211–24.

51. Rydqvist, *En handfull amerikanskt,* 145–47.

52. *Ibid.,* 147–48.

53. Marcus Lee Hansen, *The Problem of the Third Generation Immigrant* (reprint ed., Rock Island, Ill., 1987), esp. 15. For discussion, see Kivisto and Blanck, eds., *American Immigrants and Their Generations.*

54. Hansen, *Third Generation Immigrant,* 25. Skarstedt, *Svensk-amerikanska folket,* 21–22. Cf. my "Marcus Lee Hansen and the Swedish Americans," in Kivisto and Blanck, eds., *American Immigrants and Their Generations,* 120–22.

55. Rydqvist, *En handfull amerikanskt*, 193–97, 199–200. Cf. Rangman, *Det stora landet i Väster*, 223.

56. Lewi Pethrus, *Västerut. En resenärs erfarenheter* (Stockholm, 1937), 31, 35–36.

57. *Ibid.*, 41, 132, 137.

58. Albert Viksten, *Guds eget land* (Stockholm, 1938), 75–76, 209.

59. *Ibid.*, 90–92.

60. *Ibid.*, 77–79, 93, 201, 209.

61. *Ibid.*, 214.

62. *Ibid.*, 80, 88–90, 100–101, 103–4, 109–19, 207–8, 211–14.

63. Fritz Henriksson, et al., *Sweden's Participation in the U.S. Celebration of the New Sweden Tercentenniary* (Stockholm, 1939), 21–22; Lundström, "Om svenskar," 11–14, 19, 22.

64. Lundström, "Om svenskar," 18–22.

65. Mangård, *Svenska öden i Amerika*, 79–80, 81.

66. *Ibid.*, 40, 42.

67. Hoving, *Vasabarnen*, 260–61, 290, 397.

68. *Ibid.*, 280, 318, 365, 367, 381–82, 385.

69. *Ibid.*, 280, 290, 318, 373.

70. *Ibid.*, 313, 324, 329, 366, 373.

71. *Ibid.*, 341.

72. Hoving, *I svenskhetens tjänst*, III:30.

73. Johannes Hoving, *Läsebok och uppslagsbok för Vasabarnen i Amerika* (Stockholm, 1935), esp. 133–34. Its similarity in patriotic tone to Swedish schoolbooks of the time is shown by Herbert Tingsten, *Gud och fosterlandet* (Stockholm, 1969).

74. Hoving, *I svenskhetens tjänst*, IV:82, 132, 195, 225, 226, 228, 232, 300, 304; V:51–54, 129–36, 143, 144–47, 199–201; Johannes Hoving, *Den svenska kolonisationen i Amerika under 300 år och dess betydelse för Amerika och Sverige* (Stockholm, 1940).

75. Hoving, *Vasabarnen*, 7, 389.

76. Nels S. Lidney, *Reseminnen och skildringar från Sverige 1932–33* (n.d., n.p. [evidently Los Angeles, c. 1934]).

77. Augusta Hägerman, *Gökens och lärkans land* (Seattle, 1944), 19, 37–40.

78. *Ibid.*, 45, 64–65.

79. *Ibid.*, 97, 122, 161, 212, 227.

80. Lidney, *Reseminnen*, 176–77.

81. Letter from Iris Andersson to Aina Barton, in my *Letters*, 299–300.

82. See Henriksson, et al., *Sweden's Participation;* Benson and Hedin, eds., *Swedes in America.* The latter book was reissued in somewhat revised form as *Americans from Sweden* (Philadelphia and New York, 1950), which provided the basis for Axel Boëthius, et al., eds., *Vår svenska stam på utländsk mark. I Västerled* (Stockholm, 1952), sponsored by the RFSBU. For the 1938 Tricentennial, cf. also the Swedish radio reportage, *Svenska emigrantöden i USA. Sven Jerrings reportageresa 1937 och Delawarefirandet 1938,* 2 tape cassettes, ed. Göran Elgemyr and Hans Sjöström (Stockholm, 1988), as well as *Svenska-amerikanska utställningen 1938* (Göteborg, 1938).

83. For the celebrations, see Henriksson, et al., *Sweden's Participation,* esp. 169, 176–77. Also Mangård, *Svenska öden i Amerika,* 22–53; Widén, *Amandus Johnson,* 168–78; the Elgemyr and Sjöström cassette tapes.

84. Henriksson, et al., *Sweden's Participation,* 105, 149–50.

85. *Ibid.*, 119.

86. *Ibid.*, 155; Widén, *Amandus Johnson,* 172.

87. Kastrup, *Med Sverige i Amerika,* 67–69.

TWENTY
Epilogue

1. Emory Lindquist, "The Swedish Population in the the United States, 1900–1950," *Sw. Pioneer Hist. Q.* 5 (1954): 20–23, "The Swedish Stock in the United States, 1900–1950," *Sw. Pioneer Hist. Q.* 6 (1955): 66–70, and "The Swedish-Born Population and the Swedish Stock: The United States Census of 1960 and Comparative Data with Some Concluding Observations," *Sw. Pioneer Hist. Q.* 16 (1965): 76–90; Gunnar Lonaeus, "Stand Up and Be Counted," *Sw. Pioneer Hist. Q.* 24 (1973): 223–30; David O'Connor, "The Swedish Element in America: Confirming the Trends—The 1980 Census," *Sw.-Am. Hist. Q.* 37 (1986): 111–25; E. P. Hutchinson, *Immigrants and Their Children, 1850–1950* (New York, 1956), 17.

2. Cf. my *Letters,* 308; my "Swedish Americans and the Old Country"; Kastrup, *Med Sverige i Amerika.*

3. See, for ex., Vilhelm Moberg, *Den okända släkten. En bok om svenskarna i Amerika igår och idag* (2d ed., Stockholm, 1968), English translation, by Roger McKnight, *The Unknown Swedes A Book about Swedes and America, Past and Present* (Carbondale, Ill., 1988); Jan Olof Olsson, *Chicago* (Stockholm, 1958); Jan Olof Olsson and Margareta Sjögren, *Amerikafeber* (Stockholm, 1962); Lasse Holmqvist, *Mera på luffen i USA* (Stockholm, 1979); Folke Hedblom, *Svensk-Amerika berättar* (Stockholm, 1982); Tord and Eivor Wallström, *Potatiskorv & pionjärer* (Höganäs, 1988). Note also Anders Johansson, *Amerika—dröm eller mardröm?* (Stockholm, 1985), which depicts the America of the Swedish immigrants as a nightmare, in terms reminiscent of the early twentieth-century anti-emigration movement.

4. Tell G. Dahllöf, "Three Americans Look at Sweden," *Sw. Pioneer Hist. Q.* 17 (1966): 190.

5. Todd Engdahl, "The Third Generation Speaks," *Sw. Pioneer Hist. Q.* 22 (1971): 97–101; my "Swedish Americans and the Old Country."

6. Vilhelm Moberg, *Utvandrarna* (Stockholm, 1949), *Invandrarna* (1952), *Nybyggarna* (1956), and *Sista brevet till Sverige* 1959), in English translation by Gustaf Lannestock, *The Emigrants* (New York, 1951), *Unto a Good Land* (1954), and *The Last Letter Home* (1961). Also, my "Clio and Swedish America" and "Historians of the Scandinavians in North America"; Beijbom, "Historiography of Swedish America."

7. John P. Miller, *Vart togo de vägen?* (Chicago, 1945), 222. Cf. my "Cultural Interplay between Sweden and Swedish America," *Sw.-Am. Hist. Q.* 43 (1992): 5–18.

8. See my "Who Is a Swedish American?" *Sw. Pioneer Hist. Q.* 31 (1980): 83–85.

9. See ch. 10, above.

10. See ch. 16, above. Cf. Blanck, "An Invented Tradition."

11. E. H. Thörnberg, "Svenska folkrörelser och emigrationen," *Det nya Sverige* (1914), 228–43, and *Sverige i Amerika, Amerika i Sverige* (Stockholm, 1938), esp. 10, 14, 20–21, 79, 83, 99, 123, 128–32, 134–35.

12. See ch. 9, above.

13. Quoted in *Scandinavian-American Bulletin,* 35:8 (Aug. 1990), 10.

14. G. N. Swan, *Swedish-American Literary Periodicals* (Rock Island, Ill., 1936), 12.

15. Widén, *Svenskar som erövrat Amerika,* 103.

16. Beijbom, "Svenskamerikanismen," in his *Svenskamerikanskt,* esp. 153–60; Anita R. Olson, "The Community Created: Chicago Swedes, 1880–1920," in Anderson and Blanck, eds., *Swedish-American Life in Chicago,* 49–59; Lindmark, *Swedish America,* 18–19.

17. Sundbeck, *Svensk-amerikanerna,* 119–20.

18. Alfred Söderström, *Blixtar på tidningshorisonten* (Warroad, Minn.,1910), 117–20.

19. Andrew M. Greeley, *The Irish Americans* (New York, 1981), 17; Oscar Handlin, *The Upprooted* (New York, 1951), 112–13.

20. O. Fritiof Ander, *T. N. Hasselquist* (Rock Island, Ill., 1931), 229–30; Greeley, *The Irish Americans,* 17; Jan Olof Olsson, *Chicago* (Chicago, 1958), 79.

21. Lars Ljungmark, "Swedes in Winnipeg up to the 1940s: Inter-Ethnic Relations," in Blanck and Runblom, *Swedish Life in American Cities,* 60–61; Harald Runblom, "Emigranten och fosterlandet," *Kungl. Vitterhets, Historie och Antikvitets Akademiens Konferenser,* 13 (Stockholm, 1985), 131–47; Ingrid Semmingsen, "Immigration and the Image of America in Europe," in Henry Steele Commager, ed., *Immigration and American History* (Minneappolis, 1961), 26–54. Some particularly interesting parallels are provided by, among other works, Kerby A. Miller, *Emigrants and Exiles: Ireland and the Irish Exodus to North America* (New York, 1985) and Theodore A. Saloutos, *They Remember America* (Berkeley, 1956).

22. Oscar Handlin, "Immigration in American Life: A Reappraisal," in Commager, ed., *Immigration and American History,* 12; Sara Bixby Smith, *Adobe Days* (3d ed., Los Angeles, 1931); Stewart H. Holbrook, *The Yankee Exodus* (New York, 1950), 287.

23. Runeby, *Den nya världen,* 52. Cf. Elovson, *Amerika i svensk litteratur,* 10–11.

24. Erik J. Friis, ed., *The Scandinavian Presence* (New York, 1976), xx. Cf. Thörnberg, *Sverige i Amerika, Amerika i Sverige,* which seeks to trace specifically *Swedish-American* influences in Sweden, esp. regarding religion and general attitudes. See also Olsson, *Chicago,* 79–80.

25. See, for ex., Halvdan Koht, *The American Spirit in Europe* (Philadelphia, 1949); Franklin D. Scott, "American Influences in Norway and Sweden," *Journal of Modern History* 18 (1946): 37–47; Thorvald Höjer, "Swedish Emigration and the Americanization of Sweden: Some Reflections," *Sw. Pioneer Hist. Q.* 10 (1959): 43–51.

26. James Boswell, *The Life of Samuel Johnson,* 3 vols. (2d ed., London, 1793), III:75; Bo Setterlind, *Pandoras ask* (reprint ed., Stockholm, 1960), 5.

An Essay on Sources

$\mathcal{T}$n a study such as this, dealing largely with writers and their published work, most references may be readily located in the notes via the text and index. It ought therefore to suffice here to discuss available finding aids and the more important secondary works relevant to the topic as a whole.

As mentioned in the preface, there is no bibliography specifically for the subject of this study. The literature on Swedish emigration and the Swedes in America is, however, one of the largest and best for any ethnic group in America, and there are several good sources for materials useful to aspects of my work. A recent general bibliography, updated to 1989, is provided in my *Letters from the Promised Land: Swedes in America, 1840–1914* (3d ed., Minneapolis, 1990; rev. Swedish ed., *Brev från löftets land*, Stockholm, 1979). See also Harald Runblom and Hans Norman, *From Sweden to America: A History of the Migration* (Uppsala and Minneapolis, 1976), 325–68. The standard, although now badly outdated, compilation is O. Fritiof Ander, *The Cultural Heritage of the Swedish Immigrant: Selected References* (Rock Island, Ill., 1956), which still contains much of interest. (See also the general surveys cited in chapter 2, note 3, above.) In addition, E. Gustav Johnson, "Articles Published by the Swedish Historical Society of America, 1905–1934," *Swedish Pioneer Historical Quarterly*, 14 (1963): 127–35, and "Articles on Swedish-American Subjects in 'Prärieblomman,'" *Swedish Pioneer Historical Quarterly* 6 (1955): 102–21, are useful; see also Carl E. Mattson, "Register över uppsatser om Svensk-Amerika och Svensk-Amerikaner i *Prärieblomman* (1900–1913) och *Valkyrian* (1897–1909)," *Yearbook of the Swedish Historical Society of America*, VI: 1916–1917 (Chicago, 1917), 89–120. The *Swedish-American Historical Quarterly* 37:1, for January 1986 comprises the journal's "Bibliography of Articles Published, 1950–1985," which may be supplemented through its annual bibliographies.

Esther Elisabeth Larson surveys *Swedish Commentators on America, 1638–1865* (New York, 1963). Extensive bibliographies concerned specifically with Swedish attitudes toward America and the emigration and with Swedish-American culture are found in Harald Elovson, *Amerika i svensk litteratur 1750–1820* (Lund, 1930), Nils Runeby, *Den nya världen och den gamla. Amerikabild och emigrationsupp-*

fattning i Sverige 1820–1860 (Uppsala, 1969), and George M. Stephenson, *The Religious Aspects of Swedish Immigration* (Minneapolis, 1932). On the Tell G. Dahllöf Collection, which was of such central importance for my research, see Tell G. Dahllöf, "Sueco-Americana. Några randanmärkningar kring en boksamling," *Biblis* (1970), 55–90. After I had there pieced together my own working bibliography, Gunilla Larsson and Eva Tedenmyr brought out an invaluable catalogue of its Swedish-American imprints, *Svenskt tryck i Nordamerika. Katalog över Tell G. Dahllöfs samling* (Stockholm, 1988). Larsson and Tedenmyr, of Stockholm's Royal Library, continue work on a comprehensive bibliography of Swedish-American publications as part of the Swedish BIBLIS on-line data base; see also their article, "The Royal Library and Swedish-American Imprints," *Swedish-American Historical Quarterly* 43 (1992): 179–93. On the American side, a major resource is *Guide to Swedish-American Archival and Manuscript Sources in the United States,* compiled by Kermit B. and Kristine B. Westerberg (Chicago, 1983).

Concerning historical writing on Swedish emigration and Swedish America, see my "Clio and Swedish America: Historians, Organizations, Publications," in Nils Hasselmo, ed., *Perspectives on Swedish Immigration* (Chicago, 1978), 3–24, and "Historians of the Scandinavians in North America," in J. R. Christianson, ed., *Scandinavians in America: Literary Life* (Decorah, Ia., 1985), 42–58, together with Ulf Beijbom, "The Historiography of Swedish America," *Swedish Pioneer Historical Quarterly* 31 (1980): 257–85; also the introduction to Philip J. Anderson and Dag Blanck, eds., *Swedish-American Life in Chicago: Cultural and Urban Aspects of an Immigrant People, 1850–1930* (Urbana, Ill., 1992), 1–16, a volume containing much of interest to my study. Byron J. Nordstrom, "Swedish America: Changing Perspectives," in Odd S. Lovoll, ed., *Nordics in America: The Future of Their Past* (Northfield, Minn., 1993), 90–99, is also useful. See, too, Robert S. Salisbury, "Swedish-American Historiography and the Question of Americanization," *Swedish Pioneer Historical Quarterly* 29 (1978): 117–36.

A number of monographs deal with significant aspects of my topic in particular periods, especially the following: Elovson, *Amerika i svensk litteratur 1750–1820* and Runeby, *Den nya världen och den gamla* (1820–60), cited above; my "Sweden and the War of American Independence," *William & Mary Quarterly,* 3d ser., 23 (1966): 408–30; Kjell Bondestad, "The American Civil War and Swedish Public Opinion," *Swedish Pioneer Historical Quarterly* 19 (1968): 95–115; Lars Wendelius, *Bilden av Amerika i svensk prosafiktion 1890–1914* (Uppsala, 1982); Gunnar Eidevall, *Amerika i svensk 1900-talslitteratur. Från Gustaf Hellström till Lars Gustafsson* (Stockholm, 1983); Franklin D. Scott, "Sweden's Constructive Opposition to Emigration," *Journal of Modern History* 37 (1965): 307–35 (also in his *Trans-Atlantica,* New York, 1979); Ann-Sofie Kälvemark, *Reaktionen mot utvandringen. Emigrationsfrågan i svensk debatt och politik 1901–1904* (Uppsala, 1972), which spans a longer period than its title implies; and Sture Lindmark, *Swedish America, 1914–1932* (Uppsala, 1971). Except for the older work by Elovson, the Swedish publications above provide—as is the usual practice nowadays—extensive English summaries. On Sweden in American opinion since the 1920s, Allan Kastrup, *Med Sverige i Amerika. Opinioner, stämningar och upplysningsarbete* (Malmö, 1985) is highly useful.

It will be noted that the big gap in coverage is the period 1864–1890, which saw the heaviest Swedish emigration and which I hope the present work, among other things, may help to fill. In his thoughtful essay, "Emigranten och fosterlandet. Svensk-amerikanernas bild av Sverige," in *Att vara svensk*, Kungl. Vitterhets, Historie och Antikvitets Akademien, *Konferenser*, 13 (Stockholm, 1985), 131–47, Harald Runblom touches upon some basic concerns of my study, as he likewise does in a broader context in Hans Norman and Harald Runblom, *Transatlantic Connections: Nordic Migration to the New World after 1800* (Oslo, 1988).

On Swedish America's ethnic culture, George M. Stephenson, *The Religious Aspects of the Swedish Immigration,* cited above, remains of fundamental importance, covering far more than its title suggests. Helge Nelson's magisterial work, *The Swedes and the Swedish Settlements in North America,* 2 vols. (Lund, 1943) emphasizes Swedish America's regional, hence its cultural diversity. Several essays by Ulf Beijbom, included in his *Utvandrarna och Svensk-Amerika* (Stockholm, 1983) and *Svenskamerikanskt. Människor och förhållanden i Svensk-Amerika* (Växjö, 1990), offer valuable insights; see also his "Swedish-American Organizational Life," in Harald Runblom and Dag Blanck, eds., *Scandinavia Overseas* (Uppsala, 1986), 52–81. In "The Community Created: Chicago Swedes, 1880–1920," in Anderson and Blanck, eds., *Swedish-American Life in Chicago,* 49–59, Anita R. Olson shows how progressive geographical dispersion was successfully counteracted by the creation of the ethnic institutional community. Lars Furuland writes on "The Swedish-American Press as a Literary Institution of the Immigrants" in Anderson and Blanck, eds., *Swedish-American Life in Chicago,* 124–33, while J. Oscar Backlund briefly surveys the newspapers in *A Century of the Swedish-American Press* (Chicago, 1952). Dag Blanck's articles are important, particularly "'A Language Does Not Die Easily . . .': Swedish at Augustana College, 1860–1900," *Swedish-American Historical Quarterly* 33 (1982): 288–305, and "An Invented Tradition: The Creation of a Swedish-American Consciousness at Augustana College," in Runblom and Blanck, eds., *Scandinavia Overseas,* 98–115. Blanck's dissertation at Uppsala University, tentatively titled *A Tradition Invented,* on Swedish-American culture at Augustana, is expected to be published shortly and promises to be an important contribution.

Ernst Skarstedt, *Våra Pennfäktare* (San Francisco, 1897) and *Pennfäktare* (Stockholm, 1930) remain indispensable sources of information on Swedish-American writers. Göran Stockenström writes on "Sociological Aspects of Swedish-American Literature" in Hasselmo, ed., *Perspectives on Swedish Immigration,* 256–78, and Eric Johannesson analyzes the Swedish-American intellectual elite in "Scholars, Pastors and Journalists: The Literary Canon of Swedish America," in Dag Blanck and Harald Runblom, eds., *Swedish Life in American Cities* (Uppsala, 1991), 95–109. A thought-provoking study is Dorothy Burton Skårdal, *The Divided Heart: Scandinavian Immigrant Experience Through Literary Sources* (Oslo and Lincoln, Nebr., 1974); see, meanwhile, my reservations in "Two Versions of the Immigrant Experience," *Swedish Pioneer Historical Quarterly* 30 (1979): 159–61. Lars Wendelius provides a significant cultural study of a middle-sized but important Swedish-American community in *Kulturliv i ett svenskamerikanskt lokalsamhälle: Rockford, Illinois* (Uppsala, 1990), summarized in his "Literary Milieus and Profiles in a Swedish-American Community," in Blanck and Runblom, eds., *Swedish Life in American Cities,* 110–30. On the Swedish language in America, the fundamental work is Nils Hasselmo, *Amerikasvenska* (Uppsala, 1974).

My own writings, which in varying degree foreshadow this book, include—besides those cited above—in particular *The Search for Ancestors: A Swedish-*

American Family Saga (Carbondale, Ill., 1979; rev. Swedish ed., *Släkten*, Stockholm, 1979); "Scandinavian Immigrant Women's Encounter with America," *Swedish Pioneer Historical Quarterly* 25 (1974): 37–42; "Swedish Americans and the Old Country," Kungl. Humanistiska Vetenskaps-Samfundet i Uppsala, *Årsbok 1981–1982* (Uppsala, 1982), 5–10; "The Life and Times of Swedish America," *Swedish-American Historical Quarterly* 35 (1984): 282–96; "Måns Jakob's Grindstone, or Documentary Sources and the Transference of Swedish Material Culture to North America," *Swedish-American Historical Quarterly* 38 (1987): 29–40; "Cultural Interplay between Sweden and Swedish America," *Swedish-American Historical Quarterly* 43 (1992): 5–18; "As They Tell It Themselves: The Testimony of Immigrant Letters," in Odd S. Lovoll, ed., *Nordics in America: The Future of Their Past* (Northfield, Minn., 1993), 138–45; and "Swedish Reactions to the Emigration Question around the Turn of the Century, "*Swedish-American Historical Quarterly* 44 (1993): 84–101.

The basic viewpoints of Americanization versus parallel development in the old homeland are presented by Franklin D. Scott in "American Influences in Norway and Sweden," *Journal of Modern History* 18 (1946): 37–47 (also in his *Trans-Atlantica*) and Thorvald Höjer, "Swedish Emigration and the Americanization of Sweden: Some Reflections," *Swedish Pioneer Historical Quarterly* 10 (1959): 43–51. They are reconciled in broader perspective by Ingrid Semmingsen in her "Emigration and the Image of America in Europe," in Henry Steele Commager, ed., *Immigration and American History* (Minneapolis, 1961), 26–54. The countercurrent is discussed by Merle Curti in "Sweden in the American Social Mind of the 1930s," in J. Iverne Dowie and J. Thomas Tredway, eds., *The Immigration of Ideas* (Rock Island, Ill., 1968), 159–84.

The literature on American immigration is, of course, immense. A number of works not specifically or exclusively devoted to Swedish migration or Swedes in America provide important background and insights to my topic. The best overall survey of American immigration at present is, in my view, Thomas J. Archdeacon, *Becoming American: An Ethnic History* (New York, 1983), perhaps especially in its treatment of the interaction between older Americans and successive waves of immigrants, the subject of John Higham's classic *Strangers in the Land: Patterns of American Nativism, 1860–1925* (2d ed., New Brunswick, N.J., 1963). E. N. Saveth, *American Historians and European Immigrants, 1875–1925* (New York, 1948) gives useful background.

Oscar Handlin's celebrated work, *The Uprooted* (New York, 1951) offers sensitive psychological insight into to the difficulties of the immigrant experience, although it has been much criticized. It should be counterbalanced with John Bodnar's later rejoinder, *The Transplanted: A History of Immigrants in Urban America* (Bloomington, Ind., 1985), which stresses the immigrants' capacity to conserve the essential values of their native cultures, adapted to new circumstances. Milton M. Gordon's *Assimilation in American Life* (New York, 1964) is a basic work in its field; his distinctions between "acculturation" and functional "assimilation" are in part anticipated by his fellow sociologist Peter A. Munch's penetrating "Segregation and Assimilation of Norwegian Settlements in Wisconsin," *Norwegian-American Studies* 18 (1954): 102–40. Joshua Fishman, et al., *Language Loyalty in the United States* (The Hague, 1966) provides a comparative perspective on a central element of cultural preservation. Victor R. Greene, *American Immigrant Leaders, 1800–*

1910: Marginality and Identity (Baltimore, 1987), is an important study involving several major ethnic groups (including the Swedes). Three works that are particularly illuminating regarding aspects of immigrants' relations with other former homelands are Mack Walker, *Germany and the Emigration, 1816–1885* (Cambridge, Mass., 1964), Theodore Saloutos, *They Remember America: The Story of the Repatriated Greek-Americans* (Berkeley, 1956), and Kerby A. Miller, *Emigrants and Exiles: Ireland the Irish Exodus to North America* (New York, 1985).

Considerable attention, especially during the past decade, has been devoted to the genesis of ethnic identities. E. J. Hobsbawm and Terrence Ranger, eds., *The Invention of Tradition* (Cambridge, 1983), particularly Hobsbawm's introductory essay, offers much insight, as do Werner Sollors, *Beyond Ethnicity: Consent and Descent in American Culture* (New York, 1986) and Werner Sollors, ed., *The Invention of Ethnicity* (New York, 1989), especially Sollors's introduction. A fine recent survey of this whole discussion is Kathleen Neils Conzen, et al., "The Invention of Ethnicity: A Perspective from the U.S.A," *Journal of American Ethnic History* 12 (1992): 3–41, with commentary in the same volume, 42–63. John Robert Christianson's "Scandinavian-Americans," in John D. Buenker and Lorman A. Ratner, eds., *Multiculturalism in the United States: A Comparative Guide to Acculturation and Ethnicity* (Westport, Conn., 1992), notes the evolution of an increasingly "Scandinavian" identity among descendants of Nordic immigrants. Henry Steele Commager's essay, "The Search for a Usable Past," in his volume, *The Search for a Usable Past and Other Essays in Historiography* (New York, 1967), 3–27, deserves rereading in connection with the writing of Swedish-American history. John Bodnar has much of significance to relate, while also giving some specific attention to the Swedish Americans, in his *Remaking America: Public Memory, Commemoration, and Patriotism in the Twentieth Century* (Princeton, 1992).

A basic concern of my study is the relationship between ethnicity and generation. The classic essay on this theme is Marcus Lee Hansen, *The Problem of the Third Generation Immigrant* (Rock Island, Ill., 1937), which holds that what the children try to forget, the grandchildren seek to remember. For the debate over the Hansen thesis, see Peter Kivisto and Dag Blanck, eds., *American Immigrants and Their Generations* (Urbana, Ill., 1990), in which my own contribution deals with "Marcus Lee Hansen and the Swedish Americans" (113–25). Vladimir Nahirny and Joshua Fishman, in "American Immigrant Groups: Ethnic Identification and the Problem of Generations," *Sociological Review* 13 (1965): 311–26, discuss intergenerational shifts in the content of ethnicity.

Of enduring value concerning overall European-American cultural relations are two studies by Norwegian scholars: Halvdan Koht, *The American Spirit in Europe: A Survey of Transatlantic Influences* (Philadelphia, 1949) and Sigmund Skard, *The American Myth and the European Mind* (New York, 1961). Also important are the essays by Scandinavian and American scholars in Lars Åhnebrink, ed., *Amerika och Norden* (Uppsala, 1964), especially Sigmund Skard, "Amerika i Europas liv" (11–28), Ingrid Semmingsen, "Utvandring og kontakt med Amerika" (65–74), and Harald Elovson, "Den liberala amerikabilden i Sverige" (75–109). Interesting parallels to Swedish opinion are found in Earl R. Beck, *Germany Rediscovers America* (Tallahassee, Fl., 1968) and, for Norway, in Jørund Mannsåker, *Utvandringa til Nord-Amerika i norsk skjønlitteratur* (Oslo, 1971).

Index

H. ARNOLD BARTON is a professor of history at Southern Illinois University at Carbondale. Born in Los Angeles, he graduated from Pomona College and received his Ph.D. at Princeton University. He previously taught at the University of Alberta, Edmonton, Canada, and the University of California at Santa Barbara. He is the author of several books on Scandinavian history in the eighteenth and early nineteenth centuries and on Swedish-American history. He served as editor of the *Swedish-American Historical Quarterly* from 1974 to 1990. In 1989 he received an honorary doctorate from Uppsala University in Sweden.